Lecture Notes in Computer Science 12288

More information about this series at http://www.springer.com/series/7407

Nathalie Bertrand · Nils Jansen (Eds.)

Formal Modeling and Analysis of Timed Systems

18th International Conference, FORMATS 2020
Vienna, Austria, September 1–3, 2020
Proceedings

 Springer

Editors
Nathalie Bertrand 🆔
Inria
Université de Rennes
Rennes, France

Nils Jansen 🆔
Radboud University
Nijmegen, The Netherlands

ISSN 0302-9743   ISSN 1611-3349   (electronic)
Lecture Notes in Computer Science
ISBN 978-3-030-57627-1   ISBN 978-3-030-57628-8   (eBook)
https://doi.org/10.1007/978-3-030-57628-8

LNCS Sublibrary: SL1 – Theoretical Computer Science and General Issues

This Springer imprint is published by the registered company Springer Nature Switzerland AG
The registered company address is: Gewerbestrasse 11, 6330 Cham, Switzerland

Preface

In this current book, we present the proceedings of the 18th International Conference on Formal Modeling and Analysis of Timed Systems (FORMATS 2020). This edition of FORMATS was a special one. Amid a global crisis, we as a community strived to maintain a healthy and safe research environment. Early on, after many countries started shutting down most of public life as a reaction to the novel coronavirus, we decided that QONFEST 2020, and with it FORMATS, CONCUR, FMICS, and QEST, would not take place in Vienna but as a virtual event.

Despite the critical and difficult times, we are very happy to present a strong and interesting program for FORMATS 2020. In total, we received 36 submissions, and each one was reviewed by at least 3 Program Committee (PC) members. The committee, consisting of 28 members, decided to accept 16 very strong papers for which the decisions where mostly unanimous.

FORMATS 2020 targeted timing aspects of systems from the viewpoint of different communities within computer science and control theory. In particular, the aim of FORMATS 2020 was to promote the study of fundamental and practical aspects of timed systems, and be more inclusive to researchers from different disciplines that share interests in modeling and analysis of timed systems. As an example, FORMATS encouraged submissions related to foundations and semantics, methods and tools, as well as techniques, algorithms, data structures, and software tools for analyzing timed systems and resolving temporal constraints.

Moreover, we strongly encouraged contributions dedicated to applications. To further foster emerging topics, we organized two special sessions:

Data-Driven Methods for Timed Systems: This session concerned all kind of data-driven methods such as machine learning or automata learning that consider timing aspects. Examples are automata learning for timed automata or reinforcement learning with timing constraints. The session was chaired by Guillermo Alberto Perez.

Probabilistic and Timed Systems: Real-time systems often encompass probabilistic or random behavior. We are interested in all approaches to model or analyze such systems, for instance through probabilistic timed automata or stochastic timed Petri nets. This session was chaired by Arnd Hartmanns.

In addition to the regular talks for the accepted papers, FORMATS 2020 featured an excellent invited talk by Alessandro Abate, together with an overview paper that is part of these proceedings. Moreover, invited talks by Roderick Bloem and Annabelle McIver were organized jointly with the other conferences within QONFEST. Further details may be found at https://formats-2020.cs.ru.nl/index.html.

Finally, some acknowledgments are due. First, we want to thank Ezio Bartocci for the great organization of QONFEST 2020. Second, thanks to the Steering Committee of FORMATS 2020, and notably to Martin Fränzle, for their support, to all the PC members and additional reviewers for their work in ensuring the quality of the contributions to FORMATS 2020, and to all the authors and participants for contributing to this event. Finally, we thank Springer for hosting the FORMATS proceedings in its *Lecture Notes in Computer Science* series, and to EasyChair for providing a convenient platform for coordinating the paper submission and evaluation.

It was an honor for us to serve as PC chairs of FORMATS 2020, and we hope that this edition of the conference will inspire the research community to many further ideas and direction in the realm of timed systems.

July 2020   Nathalie Bertrand
                                                                                  Nils Jansen

Organization

Steering Committee

Rajeev Alur, USA
Eugene Asarin, France
Martin Fränzle (Chair), Germany
Thomas A. Henzinger, Austria
Joost-Pieter Katoen, Germany
Kim G. Larsen, Denmark
Oded Maler (Founding Chair, 1957–2018), France
Pavithra Prabhakar, USA
Mariëlle Stoelinga, The Netherlands
Wang Yi, Sweden

Program Committee

Mohamadreza Ahmadi	California Institute of Technology, USA
C. Aiswarya	Chennai Mathematical Institute, India
Nicolas Basset	Université Grenoble Alpes, France
Nathalie Bertrand (PC Co-chair)	Inria, France
Anne Bouillard	Huawei Technologies, France
Patricia Bouyer	CNRS, France
Milan Ceska	Brno University of Technology, Czech Republic
Rayna Dimitrova	The University of Sheffield, UK
Uli Fahrenberg	École Polytechnique, France
Gilles Geeraerts	Université libre de Bruxelles, Belgium
Arnd Hartmanns	University of Twente, The Netherlands
Frédéric Herbreteau	University of Bordeaux, France
Laura Humphrey	Air Force Research Laboratory, USA
Nils Jansen (PC Co-chair)	Radboud University, The Netherlands
Sebastian Junges	University of California, Berkeley, USA
Gethin Norman	University of Glasgow, UK
Marco Paolieri	University of Southern, California, USA
Guillermo Perez	University of Antwerp, Belgium
Hasan Poonawala	University of Kentucky, USA
Krishna S.	IIT Bombay, India
Ocan Sankur	CNRS, France
Ana Sokolova	University of Salzburg, Austria
Jiri Srba	Aalborg University, Denmark
B. Srivathsan	Chennai Mathematical Institute, India

Ufuk Topcu	The University of Texas at Austin, USA
Patrick Totzke	The University of Liverpool, UK
Jana Tumova	KTH Royal Institute of Technology, Sweden
Frits Vaandrager	Radboud University, The Netherlands
Masaki Waga	National Institute of Informatics, Japan
Lijun Zhang	Chinese Academy of Sciences, China

External Reviewers

Benoit Barbot	Florian Lorber
Frederik M. Bønneland	Nicolas Markey
Mingshuai Chen	Ritam Raha
Murat Cubuktepe	Pierre-Alain Reynier
Thao Dang	Adam Rogalewicz
Chen Fu	Morten Konggaard Schou
Shibashis Guha	Georg Schuppe
Nicolas Halbwachs	Pouria Tajvar
James Hamil	Bo Wu
Alexis Linard	Zhe Xu

Contents

Deep Reinforcement Learning
with Temporal Logics

Mohammadhosein Hasanbeig$^{(\boxtimes)}$, Daniel Kroening, and Alessandro Abate

Department of Computer Science, University of Oxford, Oxford, UK
{hosein.hasanbeig,daniel.kroening,alessandro.abate}@cs.ox.ac.uk

Abstract. The combination of data-driven learning methods with formal reasoning has seen a surge of interest, as either area has the potential to bolstering the other. For instance, formal methods promise to expand the use of state-of-the-art learning approaches in the direction of certification and sample efficiency. In this work, we propose a deep Reinforcement Learning (RL) method for policy synthesis in continuous-state/action unknown environments, under requirements expressed in Linear Temporal Logic (LTL). We show that this combination lifts the applicability of deep RL to complex temporal and memory-dependent policy synthesis goals. We express an LTL specification as a Limit Deterministic Büchi Automaton (LDBA) and synchronise it on-the-fly with the agent/environment. The LDBA in practice monitors the environment, acting as a modular reward machine for the agent: accordingly, a modular Deep Deterministic Policy Gradient (DDPG) architecture is proposed to generate a low-level control policy that maximises the probability of the given LTL formula. We evaluate our framework in a cart-pole example and in a Mars rover experiment, where we achieve near-perfect success rates, while baselines based on standard RL are shown to fail in practice.

Keywords: Model-free reinforcement learning · Deep learning · Linear temporal logic · Continuous-state and continuous-action Markov decision processes

1 Introduction

Deep Reinforcement Learning (RL) is an emerging paradigm for autonomous decision-making tasks in complex and unknown environments. Deep RL has achieved impressive results over the past few years, but often the learned solution is evaluated only by statistical testing and there is no systematic method to guarantee that the policy synthesised using RL meets the expectations of the designer of the algorithm. This particularly becomes a pressing issue when applying RL to safety-critical systems.

Furthermore, tasks featuring extremely sparse rewards are often difficult to solve by deep RL if exploration is limited to low-level primitive action selection. Despite its generality, deep RL is not a natural representation for how

© Springer Nature Switzerland AG 2020
N. Bertrand and N. Jansen (Eds.): FORMATS 2020, LNCS 12288, pp. 1–22, 2020.
https://doi.org/10.1007/978-3-030-57628-8_1

humans perceive sparse reward problems: humans already have prior knowledge and associations regarding elements and their corresponding function in a given environment, e.g. "keys open doors" in video games. Given useful domain knowledge and associations, a human expert can find solutions to problems involving sparse rewards, e.g. when the rewards are only received when a task is eventually fulfilled (e.g., finally unlocking a door). These assumed high-level associations can provide initial knowledge about the problem, whether in abstract video games or in numerous real world applications, to efficiently find the global optimal policies, while avoiding an exhaustive unnecessary exploration, particularly in early stages.

The idea of separating the learning process into two (or more) synchronised low- and high-level learning steps has led to hierarchical RL, which specifically targets sparse reward problems [49]. Practical approaches in hierarchical RL, e.g. options [43], depend on state representations and on the underlying problem simplicity and/or structure, such that suitable reward signals can be effectively engineered by hand. These methods often require detailed supervision in the form of explicitly specified high-level actions or intermediate supervisory signals [2,9,29,30,43,52]. Furthermore, most hierarchical RL approaches either only work in discrete domains, or require pre-trained low-level controllers. HAC [32], a state-of-the-art method in hierarchical RL for continuous-state/action Markov Decision Processes (MDPs), introduces the notion of Universal MDPs, which have an augmented state space that is obtained by a set of strictly sequential goals.

This contribution extends our earlier work [19,20,22,57] and proposes a one-shot[1] and online deep RL framework, where the learner is presented with a modular high-level mission task over a continuous-state/action MDP. Unlike hierarchical RL, the mission task is not limited to sequential tasks, and is instead specified as a Linear Temporal Logic (LTL) formula, namely a formal, un-grounded, and high-level representation of the task and of its components. Without requiring any supervision, each component of the LTL property systematically structures a complex mission task into partial task "modules". The LTL property essentially acts as a high-level exploration guide for the agent, where low-level planning is handled by a deep RL architecture. LTL is a temporal logic that allows to formally express tasks and constraints in interpretable form: there exists a substantial body of research on extraction of LTL properties from natural languages [16,38,55].

We synchronise the high-level LTL task with the agent/environment: we first convert the LTL property to an automaton, namely a finite-state machine accepting sequences of symbols [3]; we then construct on-the-fly[2] a synchronous product between the automaton and the agent/environment; we also define a reward function based on the structure of the automaton. With this automated reward-

---

[1] One-shot means that there is no need to master easy tasks first, then compose them together to accomplish a more complex tasks.

[2] On-the-fly means that the algorithm tracks (or executes) the state of an underlying structure (or a function) without explicitly constructing it.

shaping procedure, an RL agent learns to accomplish the LTL task with max probability, and with no supervisory assistance: this is in general hard, if at all possible, by conventional or handcrafted RL reward shaping methods [43,49,52]. Furthermore, as elaborated later, the structure of the product partitions the state space of the MDP, so that partitions are solely relevant to specific task modules. Thus, when dealing with sparse-reward problems, the agent's low-level exploration is efficiently guided by task modules, saving the agent from exhaustively searching through the whole state space.

Related Work. The closest lines of work comprise model-based [4,8,12–15,24, 25,42,44] and model-free [7,11,17,27,28,51] RL approaches, aiming to synthesise policies abiding by a given temporal logic property. In model-based RL, a model of the MDP is firstly inferred and later an optimal policy is generated over the learned model. This approach is known to hardly scale to large-dimensional problems, which are in practice studied with model-free RL. Additionally, in standard work on RL for LTL, formulae are translated to Deterministic Rabin Automata (DRA), which are known to be doubly exponential in the size of the original LTL formula. Conversely, in this work we use a specific Limit Deterministic Büchi Automaton (LDBA) [45], which we have employed in the context of RL in [18]: this is only an exponential-sized automaton for LTL\GU (a fragment of LTL), and has otherwise the same size as DRA for the rest of LTL. This can significantly enhance the convergence rate of RL. Other variants of LDBAs have been employed in cognate work [7,17,28,39].

Another closely-related line of work is the "curriculum learning" approach [2], in which the agent masters easier instruction-based sub-tasks first, to then compose them together in order to accomplish a more complex task. In this work, instead, the complex task is expressed as an LTL property, which guides learning and directly generates policies: it thus has no need to start from easier sub-tasks and to later compose corresponding policies together. In other words, the proposed method learns policies for the general complex task in a "one-shot" scenario.

To the best of authors' knowledge, no research has so far enabled model-free RL to generate policies for general LTL properties over continuous-state/action MDPs: relevant results are applicable to finite MDPs [8,11,12,17,21,44,51], or are focused on sub-fragments of LTL [10,23,26,31,33,42], such as finite-horizon formulae. Many practical problems require continuous, real-valued actions to be taken in over uncountable state variables: the simplest approach to solve such problems is to discretise state and action spaces of the MDP [1]. However, beyond requiring the knowledge of the MDP itself, discretisation schemes are expected to suffer from the trade off between accuracy and curse of dimensionality.

Contributions. To tackle the discussed issues and push the envelope of state of the art in RL, in this work and propose a modular Deep Deterministic Policy Gradient (DDPG) based on [34,47]. This modular DDPG is an actor-critic architecture that uses deep function approximators, which can learn policies in continuous state and action spaces, optimising over task-specific LTL satisfaction probabilities. The contributions of this work are as follows:

- We deal with continuous-state/action, unknown MDPs. The proposed model-free RL algorithm significantly increases the applicability of RL for LTL synthesis.
- The use of LTL (and associated LDBAs) with deep RL allows us to efficiently solve problems with sparse rewards, by exploiting relationships between sub-tasks. Rewards are automatically assigned on-the-fly with no supervision, allowing one to automatically modularise a global complex task into easy sub-tasks.
- The use of LDBA in DDPG introduces technical issues to the learning process, such as non-determinism, which are addressed in this work.

2   Problem Framework

The environment with which the agent interacts is assumed to be an unknown black-box. We describe the underlying agent/environment model as an MDP, however we emphasise that the MDP is unknown and the learning agent is unaware of the transition (i.e., the dynamics) and the spatial labels (environmental features grounded to tasks). This works assumes that the dynamics of the interaction are Markovian, namely memory-less.

Definition 1 (General MDP [5]**).** *The tuple* $\mathfrak{M} = (\mathcal{S}, \mathcal{A}, s_0, P, \mathcal{AP}, L)$ *is a general MDP over a set of continuous states* $\mathcal{S} = \mathbb{R}^n$, *where* $\mathcal{A} = \mathbb{R}^m$ *is a set of continuous actions, and* $s_0 \in \mathcal{S}$ *is the initial state.* $P : \mathcal{B}(\mathbb{R}^n) \times \mathcal{S} \times \mathcal{A} \to [0,1]$ *is a Borel-measurable conditional transition kernel which assigns to any pair of state* $s \in \mathcal{S}$ *and action* $a \in \mathcal{A}$ *a probability measure* $P(\cdot|s,a)$ *on the Borel space* $(\mathbb{R}^n, \mathcal{B}(\mathbb{R}^n))$, *where* $\mathcal{B}(\mathbb{R}^n)$ *is the set of all Borel sets on* $\mathbb{R}^n$. $\mathcal{AP}$ *is a finite set of atomic propositions and a labelling function* $L : \mathcal{S} \to 2^{\mathcal{AP}}$ *assigns to each state* $s \in \mathcal{S}$ *a set of atomic propositions* $L(s) \subseteq 2^{\mathcal{AP}}$.

Definition 2 (Path). *An infinite path* ρ *starting at* s_0 *is a sequence of states* $\rho = s_0 \xrightarrow{a_0} s_1 \xrightarrow{a_1} \dots$ *such that every transition* $s_i \xrightarrow{a_i} s_{i+1}$ *is allowed in* $\mathfrak{M}$, *i.e.* s_{i+1} *belongs to the smallest Borel set* B *such that* $P(B|s_i, a_i) = 1$.

At each state $s \in \mathcal{S}$, an agent behaviour is determined by a Markov policy π, which is a mapping from states to a probability distribution over the actions, i.e. $\pi : \mathcal{S} \to \mathcal{P}(\mathcal{A})$. If $\mathcal{P}(\mathcal{A})$ is a degenerate distribution then the policy π is said to be deterministic.

Definition 3 (Expected Discounted Return [49]**).** *For a policy* π *on an MDP* $\mathfrak{M}$, *the expected discounted return is defined as:*

$$U^{\pi}(s) = \mathbb{E}^{\pi}[\sum_{n=0}^{\infty} \gamma^n \ R(s_n, a_n)|s_0 = s],$$

where $\mathbb{E}^{\pi}[\cdot]$ denotes the expected value given that the agent follows policy π, $\gamma \in [0,1)$ ($\gamma \in [0,1]$ when episodic) is a discount factor, $R : \mathcal{S} \times \mathcal{A} \to \mathbb{R}$ is the reward, and $s_0, a_0, s_1, a_1, \ldots$ is the sequence of state-action pairs generated by policy π.

It has been shown that constant discount factors might yield sub-optimal policies [7,17]. In general the discount factor γ is a hyper-parameter that has to be tuned. There is standard work in RL on state-dependent discount factors [37,40,54,56], that is shown to preserve convergence and optimality guarantees. A possible tuning strategy to resolve the issues of constant discounting is as follows:

$$\gamma(s) = \begin{cases} \eta & \text{if } R(s,a) > 0, \\ 1 & \text{otherwise,} \end{cases} \tag{1}$$

where $0 < \eta < 1$ is a constant. Hence, Definition 3 is reduced to [37]:

$$U^{\pi}(s) = \mathbb{E}^{\pi}[\sum_{n=0}^{\infty} \gamma(s_n)^{N(s_n)} R(s_n, \pi(s_n)) | s_0 = s], \ 0 \leq \gamma \leq 1, \tag{2}$$

where $N(s_n)$ is the number of times a positive reward has been observed at s_n.

The function $U^{\pi}(s)$ is often referred to as value function (under the policy π). Another crucial notion in RL is action-value function $Q^{\pi}(s,a)$, which describes the expected discounted return after taking an action a in state s and thereafter following policy π:

$$Q^{\pi}(s,a) = \mathbb{E}^{\pi}[\sum_{n=1}^{\infty} \gamma^n R(s_n, a_n) | s_0 = s, a_0 = a].$$

Accordingly, the recursive form of the action-value function can be obtained as:

$$Q^{\pi}(s,a) = R(s,a) + \gamma Q^{\pi}(s_1, a_1), \tag{3}$$

where $a_1 = \pi(s_1)$. Q-learning (QL) [53] is the most extensively used model-free RL algorithm built upon (3), for MDPs with finite-state and finite-action spaces. For all state-action pairs QL initializes a Q-function $Q^{\beta}(s,a)$ with an arbitrary finite value, where β is an arbitrary stochastic policy.

$$Q^{\beta}(s,a) \leftarrow Q^{\beta}(s,a) + \mu[R(s,a) + \gamma \max_{a' \in \mathcal{A}}(Q^{\beta}(s',a')) - Q^{\beta}(s,a)]. \tag{4}$$

where $Q^{\beta}(s,a)$ is the Q-value corresponding to state-action (s,a), $0 < \mu \leq 1$ is called learning rate (or step size), $R(s,a)$ is the reward function, γ is the discount factor, and s' is the state reached after performing action a. The Q-function for the remaining of the state-action pairs is not changed in this operation. QL is an off-policy RL scheme, namely policy β has no effect on the convergence of the Q-function, as long as every state-action pair is visited infinitely many times. Thus, for the sake of simplicity, we may drop the policy index β from the action-value function. Under mild assumptions, QL converges to a unique limit, and a greedy policy π^* can be obtained as follows:

$$\pi^*(s) = \operatorname*{argmax}_{a \in \mathcal{A}} Q(s,a), \tag{5}$$

and π^* corresponds to the optimal policy that is generated by dynamic programming [6] to maximise the expected return, if the MDP was fully known:

$$\pi^*(s) = \arg\sup_{\pi \in \mathcal{D}} U^\pi(s), \tag{6}$$

where $\mathcal{D}$ is the set of stationary deterministic policies over the state space $\mathcal{S}$. The Deterministic Policy Gradient (DPG) algorithm [47] introduces a parameterised function $\mu(s|\theta^\mu)$ called actor to represent the current policy by deterministically mapping states to actions, where θ^μ is the function approximation parameters for the actor function. Further, an action-value function $Q(s,a|\theta^Q)$ is called critic and is learned as described next.

Assume that at time step t the agent is at state s_t, takes action a_t, and receives a scalar reward $R(s_t, a_t)$. In case when the agent policy is deterministic, the action-value function update can be approximated by parameterising Q using a parameter set θ^Q, i.e. $Q(s_t, a_t|\theta^Q)$, and by minimizing the following loss function:

$$L(\theta^Q) = \mathbb{E}^\pi_{s_t \sim \rho^\beta}[(Q(s_t, a_t|\theta^Q) - y_t)^2], \tag{7}$$

where ρ^β is the probability distribution of state visits over $\mathcal{S}$, under any given arbitrary stochastic policy β, and $y_t = R(s_t, a_t) + \gamma Q(s_{t+1}, a_{t+1}|\theta^Q)$ such that $a_{t+1} = \pi(s_{t+1})$.

The actor parameters are updated along the derivative of the expected return, which [47] has shown to be a policy gradient, as follows:

$$\begin{aligned}
\nabla_{\theta^\mu} U^\mu(s_t) &\approx \mathbb{E}_{s_t \sim p^\beta}[\nabla_{\theta^\mu} Q(s, a|\theta^Q)|_{s=s_t, a=\mu(s_t|\theta^\mu)}] \\
&= \mathbb{E}_{s_t \sim p^\beta}[\nabla_a Q(s, a|\theta^Q)|_{s=s_t, a=\mu(s_t)} \nabla_{\theta^\mu} \mu(s|\theta^\mu)|_{s=s_t}].
\end{aligned} \tag{8}$$

DDPG further extends DPG by employing a deep neural network as function approximator and updating the network parameters via a "soft update" method, which is explained later in the paper.

2.1 Linear Temporal Logic (LTL)

We employ LTL to encode the structure of the high-level mission task and to automatically shape the reward function. LTL formulae φ over a given set of atomic propositions $\mathcal{AP}$ are syntactically defined as [41]:

$$\varphi ::= true \mid \alpha \in \mathcal{AP} \mid \varphi \wedge \varphi \mid \neg\varphi \mid \bigcirc \varphi \mid \varphi \mathbin{U} \varphi, \tag{9}$$

where the operators $\bigcirc$ and U are called "next" and "until", respectively. For a given path ρ, we define the i-th state of ρ to be $\rho[i]$ where $\rho[i] = s_i$, and the i-th suffix of ρ to be $\rho[i..]$ where $\rho[i..] = s_i \xrightarrow{a_i} s_{i+1} \xrightarrow{a_{i+1}} s_{i+2} \cdots$

Definition 4 (LTL Semantics [41]**).** *For an LTL formula φ and for a path ρ, the satisfaction relation $\rho \models \varphi$ is defined as*

$$\rho \models \alpha \in \mathcal{AP} \iff \alpha \in L(\rho[0]),$$
$$\rho \models \varphi_1 \wedge \varphi_2 \iff \rho \models \varphi_1 \wedge \rho \models \varphi_2,$$
$$\rho \models \neg\varphi \iff \rho \not\models \varphi,$$
$$\rho \models \bigcirc\varphi \iff \rho[1..] \models \varphi,$$
$$\rho \models \varphi_1 U\varphi_2 \iff \exists j \geq 0 : \rho[j..] \models \varphi_2 \wedge \forall i, 0 \leq i < j, \rho[i..] \models \varphi_1.$$

The operator next $\bigcirc$ requires φ to be satisfied starting from the next-state suffix of ρ. The operator until U is satisfied over ρ if φ_1 continuously holds until φ_2 becomes true. Using the until operator U we can define two temporal modalities: (1) eventually, $\Diamond\varphi = true\ U\ \varphi$; and (2) always, $\Box\varphi = \neg\Diamond\neg\varphi$. LTL extends propositional logic using the temporal modalities until U, eventually $\Diamond$, and always $\Box$. For instance, constraints such as "eventually reach this point", "visit these points in a particular sequential order", or "always stay safe" are expressible by these modalities. Further, these modalities can be combined with logical connectives and nesting to provide more complex task specifications. Any LTL task specification φ over $\mathcal{AP}$ expresses the following set of words $Words(\varphi) = \{\sigma \in (2^{\mathcal{AP}})^\omega$ s.t. $\sigma \models \varphi\}$, where $(2^{\mathcal{AP}})^\omega$ is set of all infinite words over $2^{\mathcal{AP}}$. The set of associated words $Words(\varphi)$ is expressible using a finite-state machine [3]. Limit Deterministic Büchi Automata (LDBA) [45] are shown to be succinct finite-state machines for this purpose [46]. We first define a Generalized Büchi Automaton (GBA), then we formally introduce LDBA.

Definition 5 (Generalized Büchi Automaton). *A GBA $\mathfrak{A} = (\mathcal{Q}, q_0, \Sigma, \mathcal{F}, \Delta)$ is a state machine, where $\mathcal{Q}$ is a finite set of states, $q_0 \subseteq \mathcal{Q}$ is the set of initial states, $\Sigma = 2^{\mathcal{AP}}$ is a finite alphabet, $\mathcal{F} = \{F_1, ..., F_f\}$ is the set of accepting conditions where $F_j \subseteq \mathcal{Q}, 1 \leq j \leq f$, and $\Delta : \mathcal{Q} \times \Sigma \to 2^{\mathcal{Q}}$ is a transition relation.*

Let Σ^ω be the set of all infinite words over Σ. An infinite word $w \in \Sigma^\omega$ is accepted by a GBA $\mathfrak{A}$ if there exists an infinite run $\theta \in \mathcal{Q}^\omega$ starting from q_0 where $\theta[i+1] \in \Delta(\theta[i], w[i])$, $i \geq 0$ and, for each $F_j \in \mathcal{F}$, $inf(\theta) \cap F_j \neq \emptyset$, where $inf(\theta)$ is the set of states that are visited infinitely often in the sequence θ.

Definition 6 (LDBA [45]**).** *A GBA $\mathfrak{A} = (\mathcal{Q}, q_0, \Sigma, \mathcal{F}, \Delta)$ is limit-deterministic if $\mathcal{Q}$ is composed of two disjoint sets $\mathcal{Q} = \mathcal{Q}_N \cup \mathcal{Q}_D$, such that:*

- $\Delta(q, \alpha) \subset \mathcal{Q}_D$ *and* $|\Delta(q, \alpha)| = 1$ *for every state $q \in \mathcal{Q}_D$ and for every $\alpha \in \Sigma$,*
- *for every $F_j \in \mathcal{F}$, $F_j \subseteq \mathcal{Q}_D$,*
- $q_0 \in \mathcal{Q}_N$*, and all the transitions from $\mathcal{Q}_N$ to $\mathcal{Q}_D$ are non-deterministic ε-transitions. An ε-transition allows an automaton to change its state without reading any atomic proposition.*

Intuitively, the defined LDBA is a GBA that has two components, an initial ($\mathcal{Q}_N$) and an accepting one ($\mathcal{Q}_D$). The accepting component includes all the accepting states and has deterministic transitions. As it will be further elaborated below, ε-transitions between $\mathcal{Q}_N$ and $\mathcal{Q}_D$ can be interpreted as "guesses" on reaching $\mathcal{Q}_D$. We finally introduce the following notion.

Definition 7 (Non-accepting Sink Component). *A non-accepting sink component of the LDBA* $\mathfrak{A}$ *is a directed graph induced by a set of states* $Q \subseteq \mathcal{Q}$ *such that (1) the graph is strongly connected; (2) it does not include all of the accepting sets* F_k, $k = 1, ..., f$ *that are necessary to satisfy the associated LTL formula; and (3) there exist no other strongly connected set* $Q' \subseteq \mathcal{Q}$, $Q' \neq Q$ *such that* $Q \subseteq Q'$. *We denote the union of all non-accepting sink components of* $\mathfrak{A}$ *as* $\mathbb{N}$. *The set* $\mathbb{N}$ *includes those components in the automaton that are non-accepting and impossible to escape from. Thus, a trace reaching them is doomed to not satisfy the given LTL property.*

3   Modular DDPG

We consider an RL problem in which we exploit the structural information provided by the LTL specification, by constructing sub-policies for each state of the associated LDBA. The proposed approach learns a satisfying policy without requiring any information about the grounding of the LTL task to be specified explicitly. Namely, the labelling assignment (as in Definition 1) is a-priori unknown, and the algorithm solely relies on experience samples gathered online.

Given an LTL mission task and an unknown black-box continuous-state/action MDP, we aim to synthesise a policy that satisfies the LTL specification with max probability. For the sake of clarity and to explain the core ideas of the algorithm, for now we assume that the MDP graph and the transition kernel are known: later these assumptions are entirely removed, and we stress that the algorithm can be run model-free. We relate the MDP and the automaton by synchronising them, in order to create a new structure that is firstly compatible with deep RL and that secondly encompasses the given logical property.

Definition 8 (Product MDP). *Given an MDP* $\mathfrak{M} = (\mathcal{S}, \mathcal{A}, s_0, P, \mathcal{AP}, L)$ *and an LDBA* $\mathfrak{A} = (\mathcal{Q}, q_0, \Sigma, \mathcal{F}, \Delta)$ *with* $\Sigma = 2^{\mathcal{AP}}$, *the product MDP is defined as* $\mathfrak{M}_{\mathfrak{A}} = \mathfrak{M} \otimes \mathfrak{A} = (\mathcal{S}^{\otimes}, \mathcal{A}, s_0^{\otimes}, P^{\otimes}, \mathcal{AP}^{\otimes}, L^{\otimes}, \mathcal{F}^{\otimes})$, *where* $\mathcal{S}^{\otimes} = \mathcal{S} \times \mathcal{Q}$, $s_0^{\otimes} = (s_0, q_0)$, $\mathcal{AP}^{\otimes} = \mathcal{Q}$, $L^{\otimes} : \mathcal{S}^{\otimes} \rightarrow 2^{\mathcal{Q}}$ *such that* $L^{\otimes}(s, q) = q$ *and* $\mathcal{F}^{\otimes} \subseteq \mathcal{S}^{\otimes}$ *is the set of accepting states* $\mathcal{F}^{\otimes} = \{F_1^{\otimes}, ..., F_f^{\otimes}\}$, *where* $F_j^{\otimes} = \mathcal{S} \times F_j$. *The transition kernel* $P^{\otimes}$ *is such that given the current state* (s_i, q_i) *and action* a, *the new state* (s_j, q_j) *is obtained such that* $s_j \sim P(\cdot|s_i, a)$ *and* $q_j \in \Delta(q_i, L(s_j))$.

In order to handle ε-*transitions we make the following modifications to the above definition of product MDP:*

- *for every potential* ε-*transition to some state* $q \in \mathcal{Q}$ *we add a corresponding action* ε_q *in the product:*

$$\mathcal{A}^{\otimes} = \mathcal{A} \cup \{\varepsilon_q, q \in \mathcal{Q}\}.$$

- *The transition probabilities corresponding to* ε-*transitions are given by*

$$P^{\otimes}((s_i, q_i), \varepsilon_q, (s_j, q_j)) = \begin{cases} 1 & \text{if } s_i = s_j, \ q_i \xrightarrow{\varepsilon_q} q_j = q, \\ 0 & \text{otherwise.} \end{cases}$$

Remark 1. Recall that an ε-transition between $\mathcal{Q}_N$ and $\mathcal{Q}_D$ corresponds to a guess on reaching $\mathcal{Q}_D$ without reading a label and changing a state in the MDP $\mathfrak{M}$ (see the definition of $P^\otimes$ above). This entails that if, after an ε-transition, the associated label in the accepting set of the automaton cannot be read or no accepting state in $\mathcal{Q}_D$ is visited, then the guess was wrong, hence the automaton must have entered the non-accepting sink component $\mathbb{N}$ (Definition 7). These semantics are leveraged in the case studies, and are generally applicable when the constructed LDBA contains ε-transitions.   □

By constructing the product MDP, we synchronise the current state of the agent with that of the automaton. This allows to evaluate partial satisfaction of the corresponding LTL property, and consequently to modularise the high-level LTL task into sub-tasks. Hence, with a proper reward assignment based on the LTL property and its associated LDBA, the agent can break down a complex task into a set of easier sub-tasks. We elaborate further on task modularisation in the next subsection.

In the following we define an LTL-based reward function, emphasising that the agent does not need to know the model structure or the transition probabilities (or their product). Before introducing a reward assignment for the RL agent, we need to present the ensuing function:

Definition 9 (Accepting Frontier Function). *For an LDBA* $\mathfrak{A} = (\mathcal{Q}, q_0, \Sigma, \mathcal{F}, \Delta)$*, we define* $Acc : \mathcal{Q} \times 2^\mathcal{Q} \rightarrow 2^\mathcal{Q}$ *as the accepting frontier function, which executes the following operation over a given set* $\mathbb{F} \subset 2^\mathcal{Q}$ *for every* $F_j \in \mathcal{F}$*:*

$$Acc(q, \mathbb{F}) = \begin{cases} \mathbb{F}_{\setminus\{F_j\}} & (q \in F_j) \wedge (\mathbb{F} \neq F_j), \\ \{F_k\}_{k=1}^{f} {}_{\setminus\{F_j\}} & (q \in F_j) \wedge (\mathbb{F} = F_j), \\ \mathbb{F} & otherwise. \end{cases}$$

In words, once the state $q \in F_j$ and the set $\mathbb{F}$ are introduced to the function Acc, it outputs a set containing the elements of $\mathbb{F}$ minus F_j. However, if $\mathbb{F} = F_j$, then the output is the family set of all accepting sets of the LDBA, minus the set F_j. Finally, if the state q is not an accepting state then the output of Acc is $\mathbb{F}$. The accepting frontier function excludes from $\mathbb{F}$ the accepting set that is currently visited, unless it is the only remaining accepting set. Otherwise, the output of $Acc(q, \mathbb{F})$ is $\mathbb{F}$ itself. Owing to the automaton-based structure of the Acc function, we are able to shape a reward function (as detailed next) without any supervision and regardless of the dynamics of the MDP.

We propose a reward function that observes the current state $s^\otimes$, the current action a, and the subsequent state $s^{\otimes'}$, to provide the agent with a scalar value according to the current automaton state:

$$R(s^\otimes, a) = \begin{cases} r_p \ if \ q' \in \mathbb{A}, \ s^{\otimes'} = (s', q'), \\ r_n \ if \ q' \in \mathbb{N}, \ s^{\otimes'} = (s', q'), \\ 0, & otherwise. \end{cases} \qquad (10)$$

Here r_p is a positive reward and r_n is a negative reward. A positive reward r_p is assigned to the agent when it takes an action that leads to a state, the label of which is in $\mathbb{A}$, and a negative reward r_n is given upon reaching $\mathbb{N}$ (Definition 7). The set $\mathbb{A}$ is called the accepting frontier set, is initialised as the family set $\mathbb{A} = \{F_k\}_{k=1}^{f}$, and is updated by the following rule every time after the reward function is evaluated: $\mathbb{A} \leftarrow Acc(q', \mathbb{A})$. The set $\mathbb{N}$ is the set of non-accepting sink components of the automaton, as per Definition 7.

Remark 2. The intuition underlying (10) is that set $\mathbb{A}$ contains those accepting states that are visited at a given time. Thus, the agent is guided by the above reward assignment to visit these states and once all of the sets F_k, $k = 1, ..., f$, are visited, the accepting frontier $\mathbb{A}$ is reset. As such, the agent is guided to visit the accepting sets infinitely often, and consequently, to satisfy the given LTL property. We shall discuss issues of reward sparseness in Sect. 3.1.   □

Given the product MDP structure in Definition 8 and the automatic formal reward assignment in (10), any algorithm that synthesises a policy maximising the associated expected discounted return over the product MDP, maximises the probability of satisfying the property φ. Note that, unlike the case of finite MDPs [18], proving the aforementioned claim is not trivial as we cannot leverage notions that are specific to finite MDPs, such as that of Accepting Max End Component (AMEC). Thus, the probability of satisfaction cannot be equated to the probability of reaching a set of states in the product MDP (i.e., the AMEC) and we have to directly reason over the accepting condition of the LDBA.

Theorem 1. *Let φ be a given LTL formula and $\mathfrak{M}_{\mathfrak{A}}$ be the product MDP constructed by synchronising the MDP $\mathfrak{M}$ with the LDBA $\mathfrak{A}$ expressing φ. Then the optimal stationary Markov policy on $\mathfrak{M}_{\mathfrak{A}}$ that maximises the expected return, maximises the probability of satisfying φ and induces a finite-memory policy on the MDP $\mathfrak{M}$.*

Remark 3. Please see the Appendix for the proof. Note that the optimality of the policy generated by the DDPG scheme depends on a number of factors, such as its structure, number of hidden layers, and activation functions. The quantification of the sub-optimality of the policy generated by DDPG is out of the scope of this work.   □

3.1   Task Modularisation

In this section we explain how a complex task can be broken down into simple composable sub-tasks or modules. Each state of the automaton in the product MDP is a "task divider" and each transition between these states is a "sub-task". For example consider a sequential task of visit a and then b and finally c, i.e. $\Diamond(a \wedge \Diamond(b \wedge \Diamond c))$. The corresponding automaton for this LTL task is given in Fig. 1. The entire task is modularised into three sub-tasks, i.e. reaching a, b, and then c, and each automaton state acts as a divider. By synchronising the MDP $\mathfrak{M}$ and the LDBA $\mathfrak{A}$, each automaton state divides those parts of the state space $\mathcal{S}$, whose boundaries are sub-tasks, namely automaton transitions. Furthermore, the LDBA specifies the relations between subs-tasks, e.g. ordering and repetition.

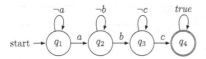

Fig. 1. LDBA for a sequential task expressed by $\lozenge(a \wedge \lozenge(b \wedge \lozenge c))$.

By exploiting the relationship between sub-tasks, and also limiting the agent exploration to the relevant regions of the state space for each sub-task, it can efficiently guide the learning to solve problems with sparse rewards.

Given an LTL task and its LDBA $\mathfrak{A} = (\mathcal{Q}, q_0, \Sigma, \mathcal{F}, \Delta)$, we propose a modular architecture of $n = |\mathcal{Q}|$ separate actor and critic neural networks, along with their own replay buffer. A replay buffer is a finite-sized cache in which transitions sampled from exploring the environment are stored. The replay buffer is then used to train the actor and critic networks. The set of neural nets acts as a global modular actor-critic deep RL architecture, which allows the agent to jump from one sub-task to another by just switching between the set of neural nets. For each automaton state q_i an actor function $\mu_{q_i}(s|\theta^{\mu_{q_i}})$ represents the current policy by deterministically mapping states to actions, where $\theta^{\mu_{q_i}}$ is the vector of parameters of the function approximation for the actor. The critic $Q_{q_i}(s, a|\theta^{Q_{q_i}})$ is learned based on (7).

The modular DDPG algorithm is detailed in Algorithm 1. Each actor-critic network set in this algorithm is associated with its own replay buffer $\mathcal{R}_{q_i}$, where $q_i \in \mathcal{Q}$ (line 4, 12). Experience samples are stored in $\mathcal{R}_{q_i}$ in the form of

$$(s_i^\otimes, a_i, R_i, s_{i+1}^\otimes) = ((s_i, q_i), a_i, R_i, (s_{i+1}, q_{i+1})).$$

When the replay buffer reaches its maximum capacity, the samples are discarded based on a first-in/first-out policy. At each time-step, actor and critic are updated by sampling a mini-batch of size $\mathcal{M}$ uniformly from $\mathcal{R}_{q_i}$. Therefore, in the algorithm the actor-critic network set corresponding to the current automaton state q_t, is trained based on experience samples in $\mathcal{R}_{q_t}$ (line 12–17).

Further, directly implementing the update of the critic parameters as in (7) is shown to be potentially unstable, and as a result the Q-update (line 14) is prone to divergence [36]. Hence, instead of directly updating the networks weights, the standard DDPG [34] introduces two "target networks", μ' and Q', which are time-delayed copies of the original actor and critic networks μ and Q, respectively. DDPG uses "soft" target updates to improve learning stability, which means that μ' and Q' slowly track the learned networks, μ and Q. These target actor and critic networks are used within the algorithm to gather evidence (line 13) and subsequently to update the actor and critic networks. In our algorithm, for each automaton state q_i we make a copy of the actor and the critic network: $\mu'_{q_i}(s|\theta^{\mu'_{q_i}})$ and $Q'_{q_i}(s, a|\theta^{Q'_{q_i}})$ respectively. The weights of both target networks are then updated as $\theta' = \tau\theta + (1 - \tau)\theta'$ with a rate of $\tau < 1$ (line 18). Summarising, to increase stability and robustness in learning, for each automaton state q_i

---

Algorithm 1: Modular DDPG

---

    input : LTL task φ, a black-box agent/environment
    output: trained actor and critic networks

1 convert the LTL property φ to LDBA $\mathfrak{A} = (\mathfrak{Q}, q_0, \Sigma, \mathcal{F}, \Delta)$
2 randomly initialise $|\mathfrak{Q}|$ actors $\mu_i(s|\theta^{\mu_i})$ and critic $Q_i(s, a|\theta^{Q_i})$ networks with
    weights θ^{μ_i} and θ^{Q_i}, for each $q_i \in \mathfrak{Q}$, and all state-action pairs (s, a)
3 initialize $|\mathfrak{Q}|$ target networks μ'_i and Q'_i with weights $\theta^{\mu'_i} = \theta^{\mu_i}$, $\theta^{Q'_i} = \theta^{Q_i}$
4 initialise $|\mathfrak{Q}|$ replay buffers $\mathcal{R}_i$
5 **repeat**
6   initialise $|\mathfrak{Q}|$ random processes $\mathfrak{N}_i$
7   initialise state $s_1^{\otimes} = (s_0, q_0)$
8   **for** $t = 1$ **to** *max_iteration_number* **do**
9   choose action $a_t = \mu_{q_t}(s_t|\theta^{\mu_{q_t}}) + \mathfrak{N}_{q_t}$
10   observe reward r_t and the new state (s_{t+1}, q_{t+1})
11   store $((s_t, q_t), a_t, R_t, (s_{t+1}, q_{t+1}))$ in $\mathcal{R}_{q_t}$
12   sample a random mini-batch of $\mathcal{M}$ transitions
             $((s_i, q_i), a_i, R_i, (s_{i+1}, q_{i+1}))$ from $\mathcal{R}_{q_t}$
13   set $y_i = R_i + \gamma Q'_{q_{i+1}}(s_{i+1}, \mu'_{q_{i+1}}(s_{i+1}|\theta^{\mu'_{q_{i+1}}})|\theta^{Q'_{q_{i+1}}})$
14   update critic Q_{q_t} and $\theta^{Q_{q_t}}$ by minimizing the loss:
             $L = 1/|\mathcal{M}| \sum_i (y_i - Q_{q_t}(s_i, a_i|\theta^{Q_{q_t}}))^2$
15   update the actor policy μ_{q_t} and $\theta^{\mu_{q_t}}$ by maximizing the sampled policy
         gradient:
16          $\nabla_{\theta^{\mu_{q_t}}} U^{\mu_{q_t}} \approx 1/|\mathcal{M}| \sum_i [\nabla_a Q_{q_t}(s, a|\theta^{Q_{q_t}})|_{s=s_i, a=\mu_{q_t}(s_i|\theta^{\mu_{q_t}})}$
17          $\nabla_{\theta^{\mu_{q_t}}} \mu_{q_t}(s|\theta^{\mu_{q_t}})|_{s=s_i}]$
18   update the target networks: $\theta^{Q'_{q_t}} \leftarrow \tau\theta^{Q_{q_t}} + (1 - \tau)\theta^{Q'_{q_t}}$
         $\theta^{\mu'_{q_t}} \leftarrow \tau\theta^{\mu_{q_t}} + (1 - \tau)\theta^{\mu'_{q_t}}$
19   **end**
20 **until** *end of trial*

---

we have a pair of actor and critic networks, namely $\mu_{q_i}(s|\theta^{\mu_{q_i}})$, $\mu'_{q_i}(s|\theta^{\mu'_{q_i}})$ and $Q'_{q_i}(s, a|\theta^{Q'_{q_i}})$, $Q_{q_i}(s, a|\theta^{Q_{q_i}})$ respectively.

4 Experiments

In this section we showcase the simulation results of Modular DDPG in two case studies: a cart-pole setup and in a mission planning problem for a Mars rover.

In the cart-pole example (Fig. 2) a pendulum is attached to a cart, which moves horizontally along a friction-less track [50]. The agent applies a horizontal force to the cart. The pendulum starts upright, and the goal is (1) to prevent the pendulum from falling over, and (2) to move the cart between the yellow and green regions while avoiding the red (unsafe) parts of the track.

The second case study deals with a Mars rover, exploring areas around the Melas Chasma [35] and the Victoria crater [48]. The Melas Chasma area displays

Fig. 2. Cart-pole case study (a.k.a. inverted pendulum on a cart) [50].

a number of signs of potential presence of water, with possible river valleys and lakes (Fig. 3 (a)). The blue dots, provided by NASA, indicate Recurring Slope Lineae (RSL) on the surface of Mars [35], which are possible locations of liquid water. The agent task is to first visit low-risk RSL (on the right of the area) and then to visit high-risk RSL (on the left), while avoiding unsafe red regions. The Victoria crater (Fig. 3 (b)) is an impact crater located near the equator of Mars. Layered sedimentary rocks are exposed along the wall of the crater, providing information about the ancient surface condition of Mars [48]. A NASA Mars rover has been operating around the crater and its mission path is given in Fig. 3 (b). The scenario of interest in this work is to train an RL agent that can autonomously control the rover to accomplish the safety-critical complex task.

In each experiment, we convert tasks expressed as LTL properties into corresponding LDBAs, and use them to monitor the modular DDPG algorithm, thus implicitly forming a product automaton. For each actor/critic structure, we have used a feed-forward neural net with 2 fully connected hidden layers and 400 ReLu units in each layer.

MDP Structure. In the cart-pole experiment the pendulum starts upright with an initial angle between −0.05 and 0.05 rads. The mass of the cart is 1 kg and that of the pole is 100 g. The length of the pole is 1 m. The force applied by the agent to the cart ranges from −10 to 10 N. A learning episode terminates if the pendulum deviates more than 0.21 rad from the vertical position, or if the cart enters any of the red regions at any time. The yellow region ranges from −2.15 to −1.85 m, and symmetrically the green region is from 1.85 to 2.15 m. The unsafe red region lies at the left of −4 m and at the right of 4 m.

In the Mars rover experiments, let the area of each image be the state space S of the MDP, where the rover location is a state $s \in S$. At each state s the rover has a continuous range of actions $A = [0, 2\pi)$: when the rover takes an action it moves to another state (e.g., s') towards the direction of the action and within a range that is randomly drawn within the interval $(0, D]$, unless the rover hits the boundary of the image, which restarts the learning episode.

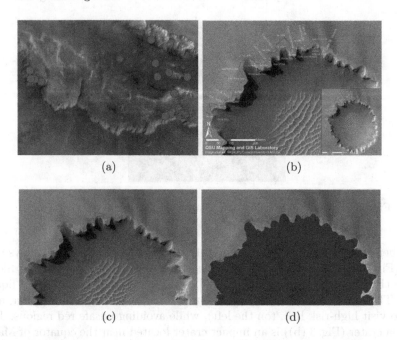

(a)   (b)

(c)   (d)

Fig. 3. (a) Melas Chasma in the Coprates quadrangle, map color spectrum represents elevation, where red is high (unsafe) and blue is low. (b) Victoria crater and opportunity rover mission traverse map [48], (c) replicated points of interest, and (d) unsafe area (red). Image courtesy of NASA, JPL, Cornell, and Arizona University. (Color figure online)

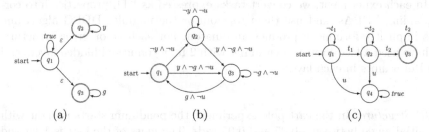

(a)   (b)   (c)

Fig. 4. LDBAs expressing formula (11) in (a), (12) in (b), and (13) in (c).

In the actual Melas Chasma exploration mission (Fig. 3 (a)), the rover is deployed on a landing location that is not precisely known. We therefore encompass randomness over the initial state s_0. Conversely, in the second experiment (Fig. 3 (b)) the rover is supposed to have already landed and it starts its mission from a known state.

The dimension of the area of interest in Fig. 3 (a) is 456.98 × 322.58 km, whereas in Fig. 3 (b) is 746.98 × 530.12 m. Other parameters in this numerical example have been set as $D = 2$ km for Melas Chasma, $D = 10$ m for the Victoria crater. We have used the satellite image with additive noise as the

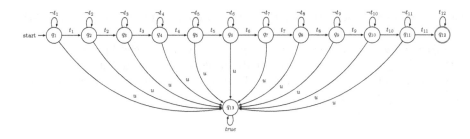

Fig. 5. LDBA expressing the LTL formula in (14).

black-box MDP for the experiment. Note that the rover only needs its current state (coordinates in this case), the state label (without seeing the entire map), and the LTL task (Algorithm 1, line 11). The given maps in the paper are for illustration purposes and to elucidate the performance of the output policy.

Specifications. In the cart-pole setup the properties of interest are expressed by the following two LTL formulae:

$$\lozenge\square y \vee \lozenge\square g, \tag{11}$$

$$\square\lozenge y \wedge \square\lozenge g \wedge \square\neg u, \tag{12}$$

where y is the label of the yellow region, g denotes the green region, and u is the label denoting when either the pendulum falls or when the cart enters the red regions on the track. We call the experiment with (11) *Cart-pole-1* and that with (12) *Cart-pole-2*. Note that the task in Cart-pole-2 is a surveillance finite-memory specification: such tasks can be easily expressed in LTL and achieved by the modular DDPG architecture, but are impossible to solve with conventional RL.

In the first of the Mars rover case studies, over the Melas Chasma area (Fig. 3 (a)) the control objective is expressed by the following LTL formula:

$$\lozenge(t_1 \wedge \lozenge t_2) \wedge \square(\neg u), \tag{13}$$

where t_1 stands for "target 1", t_2 stands for "target 2" and u stands for "unsafe" (the red region in Fig. 3 (d)). Target 1 corresponds to the RSL (blue dots) on the right with a lower risk of the rover going to unsafe region, whereas the "target 2" label goes on the left RSL that are a bit riskier to explore. Conforming to (13), the rover has to visit any of the right dots at least once and then proceed to the any of the left dots, while avoiding unsafe areas. From (13) we build the associated LDBA as in Fig. 4.

The mission task for the Victoria crater is taken from a NASA rover mission [48] and is expressed by the following LTL formula:

$$\lozenge(t_1 \wedge \lozenge(t_2 \wedge \lozenge(t_3 \wedge \lozenge(t_4 \wedge \lozenge(... \wedge \lozenge(t_{12})))))) \wedge \square(\neg u), \tag{14}$$

where t_i represents the "i-th target", and u represents "unsafe" regions. The i-th target in Fig. 3 (c) is the i-th red circle from the bottom left along the crater rim. According to (14) the rover is required to visit the checkpoints from the bottom left to the top right sequentially, while avoiding a fall into the crater, which mimicks the actual path in Fig. 3 (b). From (14), we build the associated LDBA as shown in Fig. 5.

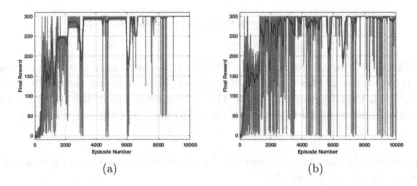

(a)   (b)

Fig. 6. Learning curves (dark blue) obtained averaging over 10 randomly initialised experiments in the cart-pole setup with the task specified in (11) for (a) and in (12) for (b). Shaded areas (light blue) represent the envelopes of the 10 generated learning curves. (Color figure online)

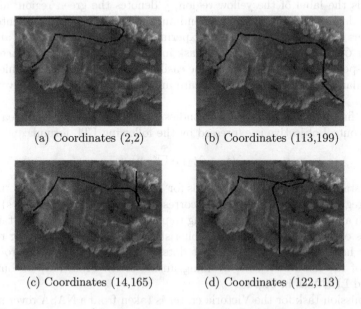

(a) Coordinates (2,2)   (b) Coordinates (113,199)

(c) Coordinates (14,165)   (d) Coordinates (122,113)

Fig. 7. Paths generated by the learnt policy in the Melas Chasma experiment.

Experimental Outcomes. In each cart-pole experiment we have employed three actor-critic neural network pairs and ran simulations for 10,000 episodes. We have then tested the trained network across 200 runs. Modular DDPG has achieved a success rate of 100% (Table 1) and Fig. 6 shows the learning progress. The learning run time has been 57 min.

In the Melas Chasma experiment we have employed 4 actor-critic neural network pairs and ran simulations for 10,000 episodes. We have then tested the trained network for all safe starting position. Our algorithm has achieved a success rate of 98.8% across 18,202 landing positions, as reported Table 1. Figure 7 gives the example paths generated by our algorithm. The learning run time has been 5 h.

In the Victoria crater experiment we have used 13 actor-critic neural network pairs. We have ran simulations for a total of 17,000 episodes, at which point it had already converged. The learning run time was 2 days. We have then tested the trained network across 200 runs. Our algorithm has achieved a success rate of 100% across all runs starting from t_1 (Table 1). Figure 8 shows a generated path that bends away from the crater, due to the back-propagation of the negative reward in (10) associated with violating the safety constraint.

Discussion. In all the experiments, the modular DDPG algorithm has been able to automatically modularise the given LTL task and to synthesise a successful policy. We have employed stand-alone DDPG as a baseline for comparison. In the cart-pole example, without synchronising the LDBA with the actor/environment, stand-alone DDPG cannot learn a policy for the non-Markovian task in (12). Hierarchical RL methods, e.g. [32], are able to generate goal-oriented policies, but only when the mission task is sequential and not particularly complex: as such, they would not be useful for (12). Furthermore, in state-of-the-art hierarchical RL there are a number of extra hyper-parameters to tune, such as the sub-goal horizons and the number of hierarchical levels, which conversely the one-shot modular DDPG does not have. The task in (11)

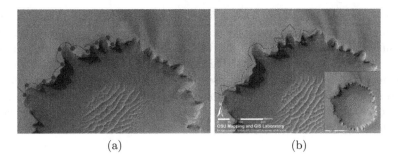

(a)   (b)

Fig. 8. (a) Path generated by the policy learnt via modular DDPG around the Victoria crater, vs (b) the actual Mars rover traverse map [48].

Table 1. Success rates: statistics are taken over at least 200 trials

Case study	Algorithm	Success rate
Cart-pole-1	Stand-alone DDPG	100%
	Modular DDPG	100%
Cart-pole-2	Stand-alone DDPG	0%
	Modular DDPG	100%
Melas Chasma*	Stand-alone DDPG	21.4%
	Modular DDPG	98.8%
Victoria Crater	Stand-alone DDPG	0%
	Modular DDPG	100%

*The statistics for the M. Chasma study are taken over different initial positions

is chosen to elucidate how the modular DDPG algorithm can handle cases in which the generated LDBA has non-deterministic ε-transitions.

In the Mars rover examples, the reward function for the stand-alone DDPG is r_p if the agent visits all the checkpoints in proper order, and r_n if the agent enters regions with unsafe labels. However, the performance of stand-alone DDPG has been quite poor, due to inefficient navigation. In relatively simple tasks, e.g. the Melas Chasma experiment, stand-alone DDPG has achieved a positive success rate, however at the cost of very high sample complexity in comparison to Modular DDPG. Specifically, due to its modular structure, the proposed architecture requires fewer samples to achieve the same success rate. Each module encompasses a pair of local actor-critic networks, which are trained towards their own objective and, as discussed before, only samples relevant to the sub-task are fed to the networks. On the other hand, in standard DDPG the whole sample set is fed into a large-scale pair of actor-critic networks, which reduces sample efficiency.

5 Conclusions

We have discussed a deep RL scheme for continuous-state/action decision making problems under LTL specifications. The synchronisation of the automaton expressing the LTL formula with deep RL automatically modularises a global complex task into easier sub-tasks. This setup assists the agent to find an optimal policy with a one-shot learning scheme. The high-level relations between sub-tasks become crucial when dealing with sparse reward problems, as the agent exploration is efficiently guided by the task modules, saving the agent from exhaustively exploring the whole state space, and thus improving sample efficiency.

Acknowledgements. The authors would like to thank Lim Zun Yuan for valuable discussions and technical support, and to anonymous reviewers for feedback on previous drafts of this manuscript.

Appendix: Proof of Theorem 1

Theorem 1. *Let φ be a given LTL formula and $\mathfrak{M}_\mathfrak{A}$ be the product MDP constructed by synchronising the MDP $\mathfrak{M}$ with the LDBA $\mathfrak{A}$ associated with φ. Then the optimal stationary Markov policy on $\mathfrak{M}_\mathfrak{A}$ that maximises the expected return, maximises the probability of satisfying φ and induces a finite-memory policy on the MDP $\mathfrak{M}$.*

Proof. Assume that the optimal Markov policy on $\mathfrak{M}_\mathfrak{A}$ is $\pi^{\otimes*}$, namely at each state $s^\otimes$ in $\mathfrak{M}_\mathfrak{A}$ we have

$$\pi^{\otimes*}(s^\otimes) = \operatorname*{argsup}_{\pi^\otimes \in \mathcal{D}^\otimes} U^{\pi^\otimes}(s^\otimes) = \operatorname*{argsup}_{\pi^\otimes \in \mathcal{D}^\otimes} \mathbb{E}^{\pi^\otimes}[\sum_{n=0}^{\infty} \gamma^n R(s_n^\otimes, a_n)|s_0^\otimes = s^\otimes], \quad (15)$$

where $\mathcal{D}^\otimes$ is the set of stationary deterministic policies over the state space $S^\otimes$, $\mathbb{E}^{\pi^\otimes}[\cdot]$ denotes the expectation given that the agent follows policy $\pi^\otimes$, and $s_0^\otimes, a_0, s_1^\otimes, a_1, \ldots$ is a generic path generated by the product MDP under policy $\pi^\otimes$.

Recall that an infinite word $w \in \Sigma^\omega$, $\Sigma = 2^{AP}$ is accepted by the LDBA $\mathfrak{A} = (\mathcal{Q}, q_0, \Sigma, \mathcal{F}, \Delta)$ if there exists an infinite run $\theta \in \mathcal{Q}^\omega$ starting from q_0 where $\theta[i+1] \in \Delta(\theta[i], w[i])$, $i \geq 0$ and, for each $F_j \in \mathcal{F}$, $inf(\theta) \cap F_j \neq \emptyset$, where $inf(\theta)$ is the set of states that are visited infinitely often in the sequence θ. From Definition 8, the associated run θ of an infinite path in the product MDP $\rho = s_0^\otimes \xrightarrow{a_0} s_1^\otimes \xrightarrow{a_1} \ldots$ is $\theta = L^\otimes(s_0^\otimes)L^\otimes(s_1^\otimes)\ldots$. From Definition 9 and (10), and since for an accepting run $inf(\theta) \cap F_j \neq \emptyset$, $\forall F_j \in \mathcal{F}$, all accepting paths starting from $s_0^\otimes$, accumulate infinite number of positive rewards r_p (see Remark 2).

In the following, by contradiction, we show that any optimal policy $\pi^{\otimes*}$ satisfies the property with maximum possible probability. Let us assume that there exists a stationary deterministic Markov policy $\pi^{\otimes+} \neq \pi^{\otimes*}$ over the state space $S^\otimes$ such that probability of satisfying φ under $\pi^{\otimes+}$ is maximum.

This essentially means in the product MDP $\mathfrak{M}_\mathfrak{A}$ by following $\pi^{\otimes+}$ the expectation of reaching the point where $inf(\theta) \cap F_j \neq \emptyset$, $\forall F_j \in \mathcal{F}$ and positive reward is received ever after is higher than any other policy, including $\pi^{\otimes*}$. With a tuned discount factor γ, e.g. (1),

$$\mathbb{E}^{\pi^{\otimes+}}[\sum_{n=0}^{\infty} \gamma^n R(s_n^\otimes, a_n)|s_0^\otimes = s^\otimes] > \mathbb{E}^{\pi^{\otimes*}}[\sum_{n=0}^{\infty} \gamma^n R(s_n^\otimes, a_n)|s_0^\otimes = s^\otimes] \quad (16)$$

This is in contrast with optimality of $\pi^{\otimes*}$ (15) and concludes $\pi^{\otimes*} = \pi^{\otimes+}$. Namely, an optimal policy that maximises the expected return also maximises the probability of satisfying LTL property φ. It is easy to see that the projection of policy $\pi^{\otimes*}$ on MDP $\mathfrak{M}$ is a finite-memory policy π^*. $\qquad\square$

References

1. Abate, A., Katoen, J.P., Lygeros, J., Prandini, M.: Approximate model checking of stochastic hybrid systems. Eur. J. Control **16**(6), 624–641 (2010)
2. Andreas, J., Klein, D., Levine, S.: Modular multitask reinforcement learning with policy sketches. In: ICML, pp. 166–175 (2017)
3. Baier, C., Katoen, J.P.: Principles of Model Checking. MIT Press, Cambridge (2008)
4. Belzner, L., Wirsing, M.: Synthesizing safe policies under probabilistic constraints with reinforcement learning and Bayesian model checking. arXiv preprint arXiv:2005.03898 (2020)
5. Bertsekas, D.P., Shreve, S.: Stochastic Optimal Control: The Discrete-Time Case. Athena Scientific, USA (2004)
6. Bertsekas, D.P., Tsitsiklis, J.N.: Neuro-Dynamic Programming, vol. 1. Athena Scientific, USA (1996)
7. Bozkurt, A.K., Wang, Y., Zavlanos, M.M., Pajic, M.: Control synthesis from linear temporal logic specifications using model-free reinforcement learning. arXiv preprint arXiv:1909.07299 (2019)
8. Brázdil, T., et al.: Verification of Markov decision processes using learning algorithms. In: Cassez, F., Raskin, J.-F. (eds.) ATVA 2014. LNCS, vol. 8837, pp. 98–114. Springer, Cham (2014). https://doi.org/10.1007/978-3-319-11936-6_8
9. Daniel, C., Neumann, G., Peters, J.: Hierarchical relative entropy policy search. In: Artificial Intelligence and Statistics, pp. 273–281 (2012)
10. De Giacomo, G., Favorito, M., Iocchi, L., Patrizi, F.: Imitation learning over heterogeneous agents with restraining bolts. In: Proceedings of the International Conference on Automated Planning and Scheduling, vol. 30, pp. 517–521 (2020)
11. De Giacomo, G., Iocchi, L., Favorito, M., Patrizi, F.: Foundations for restraining bolts: reinforcement learning with LTLf/LDLf restraining specifications. In: ICAPS, vol. 29, pp. 128–136 (2019)
12. Fu, J., Topcu, U.: Probably approximately correct MDP learning and control with temporal logic constraints. In: Robotics: Science and Systems (2014)
13. Fulton, N.: Verifiably safe autonomy for cyber-physical systems. Ph.D. thesis, Carnegie Mellon University Pittsburgh, PA (2018)
14. Fulton, N., Platzer, A.: Safe reinforcement learning via formal methods: toward safe control through proof and learning. In: Proceedings of the AAAI Conference on Artificial Intelligence (2018)
15. Fulton, N., Platzer, A.: Verifiably safe off-model reinforcement learning. In: Vojnar, T., Zhang, L. (eds.) TACAS 2019. LNCS, vol. 11427, pp. 413–430. Springer, Cham (2019). https://doi.org/10.1007/978-3-030-17462-0_28
16. Gunter, E.: From natural language to linear temporal logic: aspects of specifying embedded systems in LTL. In: Monterey Workshop on Software Engineering for Embedded Systems: From Requirements to Implementation (2003)
17. Hahn, E.M., Perez, M., Schewe, S., Somenzi, F., Trivedi, A., Wojtczak, D.: Omega-regular objectives in model-free reinforcement learning. In: Vojnar, T., Zhang, L. (eds.) TACAS 2019. LNCS, vol. 11427, pp. 395–412. Springer, Cham (2019). https://doi.org/10.1007/978-3-030-17462-0_27
18. Hasanbeig, M., Abate, A., Kroening, D.: Logically-constrained reinforcement learning. arXiv preprint arXiv:1801.08099 (2018)
19. Hasanbeig, M., Abate, A., Kroening, D.: Certified reinforcement learning with logic guidance. arXiv preprint arXiv:1902.00778 (2019)
20. Hasanbeig, M., Abate, A., Kroening, D.: Logically-constrained neural fitted Q-iteration. In: AAMAS, pp. 2012–2014 (2019)

21. Hasanbeig, M., Abate, A., Kroening, D.: Cautious reinforcement learning with logical constraints. In: Proceedings of the 19th International Conference on Autonomous Agents and MultiAgent Systems, pp. 483–491. International Foundation for Autonomous Agents and Multiagent Systems (2020)

22. Hasanbeig, M., Kantaros, Y., Abate, A., Kroening, D., Pappas, G.J., Lee, I.: Reinforcement learning for temporal logic control synthesis with probabilistic satisfaction guarantees. In: Proceedings of the 58th Conference on Decision and Control, pp. 5338–5343. IEEE (2019)

23. Hasanbeig, M., Yogananda Jeppu, N., Abate, A., Melham, T., Kroening, D.: Deepsynth: program synthesis for automatic task segmentation in deep reinforcement learning. arXiv preprint arXiv:1911.10244 (2019)

24. Huang, C., Xu, S., Wang, Z., Lan, S., Li, W., Zhu, Q.: Opportunistic intermittent control with safety guarantees for autonomous systems. arXiv preprint arXiv:2005.03726 (2020)

25. Hunt, N., Fulton, N., Magliacane, S., Hoang, N., Das, S., Solar-Lezama, A.: Verifiably safe exploration for end-to-end reinforcement learning. arXiv preprint arXiv:2007.01223 (2020)

26. Jansen, N., Könighofer, B., Junges, S., Bloem, R.: Shielded decision-making in MDPs. arXiv preprint arXiv:1807.06096 (2018)

27. Junges, S., Jansen, N., Dehnert, C., Topcu, U., Katoen, J.-P.: Safety-constrained reinforcement learning for MDPs. In: Chechik, M., Raskin, J.-F. (eds.) TACAS 2016. LNCS, vol. 9636, pp. 130–146. Springer, Heidelberg (2016). https://doi.org/10.1007/978-3-662-49674-9_8

28. Kazemi, M., Soudjani, S.: Formal policy synthesis for continuous-space systems via reinforcement learning. arXiv preprint arXiv:2005.01319 (2020)

29. Kearns, M., Singh, S.: Near-optimal reinforcement learning in polynomial time. Mach. Learn. **49**(2–3), 209–232 (2002)

30. Kulkarni, T.D., Narasimhan, K., Saeedi, A., Tenenbaum, J.: Hierarchical deep reinforcement learning: integrating temporal abstraction and intrinsic motivation. In: NIPS, pp. 3675–3683 (2016)

31. Lavaei, A., Somenzi, F., Soudjani, S., Trivedi, A., Zamani, M.: Formal controller synthesis for continuous-space MDPs via model-free reinforcement learning. In: 2020 ACM/IEEE 11th International Conference on Cyber-Physical Systems (ICCPS), pp. 98–107. IEEE (2020)

32. Levy, A., Konidaris, G., Platt, R., Saenko, K.: Learning multi-level hierarchies with hindsight. In: International Conference on Learning Representations (ICLR) (2019)

33. Li, X., Ma, Y., Belta, C.: A policy search method for temporal logic specified reinforcement learning tasks. In: ACC, pp. 240–245 (2018)

34. Lillicrap, T.P., et al.: Continuous control with deep reinforcement learning. arXiv:1509.02971 (2015)

35. McEwen, A.S., et al.: Recurring slope lineae in equatorial regions of Mars. Nat. Geosci. **7**(1), 53–58 (2014)

36. Mnih, V., et al.: Playing atari with deep reinforcement learning. arXiv preprint arXiv:1312.5602 (2013)

37. Newell, R.G., Pizer, W.A.: Discounting the distant future: how much do uncertain rates increase valuations? J. Environ. Econ. Manag. **46**(1), 52–71 (2003)

38. Nikora, A.P., Balcom, G.: Automated identification of LTL patterns in natural language requirements. In: ISSRE, pp. 185–194 (2009)

39. Oura, R., Sakakibara, A., Ushio, T.: Reinforcement learning of control policy for linear temporal logic specifications using limit-deterministic generalized Büchi automata. IEEE Control Syst. Lett. **4**(3), 761–766 (2020)
40. Pitis, S.: Rethinking the discount factor in reinforcement learning: a decision theoretic approach. arXiv preprint arXiv:1902.02893 (2019)
41. Pnueli, A.: The temporal logic of programs. In: Foundations of Computer Science, pp. 46–57 (1977)
42. Polymenakos, K., Abate, A., Roberts, S.: Safe policy search using Gaussian process models. In: Proceedings of AAMAS, pp. 1565–1573 (2019)
43. Precup, D.: Temporal abstraction in reinforcement learning. Ph.D. thesis, University of Massachusetts Amherst (2001)
44. Sadigh, D., Kim, E.S., Coogan, S., Sastry, S.S., Seshia, S.A.: A learning based approach to control synthesis of Markov decision processes for linear temporal logic specifications. In: CDC, pp. 1091–1096 (2014)
45. Sickert, S., Esparza, J., Jaax, S., Křetínský, J.: Limit-deterministic Büchi automata for linear temporal logic. In: Chaudhuri, S., Farzan, A. (eds.) CAV 2016. LNCS, vol. 9780, pp. 312–332. Springer, Cham (2016). https://doi.org/10.1007/978-3-319-41540-6_17
46. Sickert, S., Křetínský, J.: MoChiBA: probabilistic LTL model checking using limit-deterministic Büchi automata. In: Artho, C., Legay, A., Peled, D. (eds.) ATVA 2016. LNCS, vol. 9938, pp. 130–137. Springer, Cham (2016). https://doi.org/10.1007/978-3-319-46520-3_9
47. Silver, D., Lever, G., Heess, N., Thomas Degris, D.W., Riedmiller, M.: Deterministic policy gradient algorithms. In: ICML (2014)
48. Squyres, S.W.: Exploration of Victoria crater by the Mars rover opportunity. Science **324**(5930), 1058–1061 (2009)
49. Sutton, R.S., Barto, A.G.: Reinforcement Learning: An Introduction, vol. 1. MIT Press, Cambridge (1998)
50. Tassa, Y., et al.: Deepmind control suite. arXiv preprint arXiv:1801.00690 (2018)
51. Toro Icarte, R., Klassen, T.Q., Valenzano, R., McIlraith, S.A.: Teaching multiple tasks to an RL agent using LTL. In: AAMA, pp. 452–461 (2018)
52. Vezhnevets, A., Mnih, V., Osindero, S., Graves, A., Vinyals, O., Agapiou, J., et al.: Strategic attentive writer for learning macro-actions. In: NIPS, pp. 3486–3494 (2016)
53. Watkins, C.J., Dayan, P.: Q-learning. Mach. Learn. **8**(3–4), 279–292 (1992)
54. Wei, Q., Guo, X.: Markov decision processes with state-dependent discount factors and unbounded rewards/costs. Oper. Res. Lett. **39**(5), 369–374 (2011)
55. Yan, R., Cheng, C.H., Chai, Y.: Formal consistency checking over specifications in natural languages. In: DATE, pp. 1677–1682 (2015)
56. Yoshida, N., Uchibe, E., Doya, K.: Reinforcement learning with state-dependent discount factor. In: 2013 IEEE 3rd Joint International Conference on Development and Learning and Epigenetic Robotics (ICDL), pp. 1–6. IEEE (2013)
57. Yuan, L.Z., Hasanbeig, M., Abate, A., Kroening, D.: Modular deep reinforcement learning with temporal logic specifications. arXiv preprint arXiv:1909.11591 (2019)

On the Semantics of Polychronous Polytimed Specifications

Hai Nguyen Van[1](✉)(iD), Thibaut Balabonski[1], Frédéric Boulanger[1,2](iD),
Chantal Keller[1](iD), Benoît Valiron[1,2], and Burkhart Wolff[1]

[1] Université Paris-Saclay, CNRS, LRI, Orsay, France
[2] CentraleSupélec, Gif-sur-Yvette, France

Abstract. In this paper, we study the semantics of a specification language for the coordination of concurrent systems, which supports time at different levels: various time domains, polychrony, and mixed metric/-logical time constraints. The language itself is defined by a denotational semantics. In order to be able to construct the possible timelines for verification purposes, we also define a symbolic operational semantics, which is the reference for an efficient implementation of a tool for runtime-testing of heterogeneous systems. This study presents a novel way to link these two semantics by taking advantage of a coinductive unfolding principle of these timelines. Furthermore, these semantics and their equivalence have been formalized in the Isabelle/HOL proof assistant, together with proofs for soundness, completeness and progress.

Keywords: Concurrency · Coordination · Semantics · Timed behaviors

1 Introduction

The design of complex systems involves different formalisms for modeling their different parts or aspects. The global model of a system may therefore consist of a coordination of concurrent sub-models that use differential equations, state machines, synchronous data-flow networks, discrete event models and so on. This raises the interest in *architectural composition languages* that allow for "bolting the respective sub-models together", along their various interfaces, and specifying the various ways of collaboration and coordination.

We are interested in languages for specifying the timed coordination of subsystems by addressing the following conceptual issues:

- events may occur in different subsystems at unrelated times, leading to *polychronous* systems [6], not necessarily under a common base clock,
- the behavior of the subsystems is observed only at a series of discrete instants,
- the instants at which a system is observed may be arbitrary and should not change its behavior (stutter-invariance),
- the coordination between subsystems involves *causality*, so the occurrence of an event may cause the occurrence of other events, possibly after a delay,

© Springer Nature Switzerland AG 2020
N. Bertrand and N. Jansen (Eds.): FORMATS 2020, LNCS 12288, pp. 23–40, 2020.
https://doi.org/10.1007/978-3-030-57628-8_2

- the domain of time (discrete, rational, continuous, ...) may be different in the subsystems, leading to *polytimed* systems,
- the time frames of different subsystems may be related (for instance, time in a GPS satellite and in a GPS receiver on Earth are different but related).

Figure 1 presents a heterogeneous model with subsystems modeled with a timed finite state machine, discrete events, and synchronous dataflows. To model the full system, some architectural glue is needed to coordinate these subsystems.

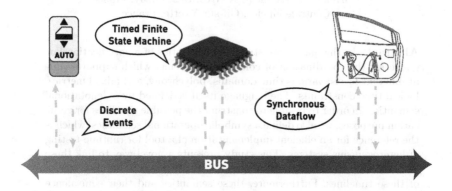

Fig. 1. The power window: a heterogeneous timed system model

In order to tackle the heterogeneous nature of the subsystems, we abstract their behavior as clocks. Each clock models an event – something that can occur or not at a given time. This time is measured in a time frame associated with each clock, and the nature of time (integer, rational, real or any type with a linear order) is specific to each clock. When the event associated with a clock occurs, the clock *ticks*. In order to support any kind of behavior for the subsystems, we are only interested in specifying what we can *observe* at a series of discrete instants. There are two constraints on observations: a clock may tick only at an observation instant, and the time on any clock cannot decrease from an instant to the next one. Also, it is always possible to add arbitrary observation instants, which allows for stuttering and modular composition of systems. Finally, a *run* is defined by a sequence of these observation instants. We can now consider the concept of *timed specification language*, which is a set of formulae that constrains the space of possible runs. This correspondence from specifications to run space is precisely a *denotational semantics*, and specifications are composed by intersecting the denoted run sets of constraint formulae.

For monitoring and online testing of heterogeneous systems, an *operational semantics* was defined in [23] to calculate concrete prefixes of runs. However, the rules of this semantics are somewhat arbitrary and not suitable for reasoning about complete runs. Our study presents a minimal specification language named TESL$^-$ (a side-effect-free subset of TESL [4]) for which our main results are:

– a denotational and an operational semantics for TESL⁻,
– a formal validation of the operational semantics w.r.t. the denotational semantics by means of proofs for soundness, completeness and progress.

This constitutes also the outline of our paper. Compared to [23], which relied on an ad hoc operational semantics of TESL[1] implemented in Standard ML, the present work relies on properly defined and mechanized semantics. Moreover, the logical structure used for linking both semantics allows for easily-defined extensions of the language.

All definitions and theorems have been formalized into the Isabelle/HOL proof assistant [24, 25] and have been accepted in the Archive of Formal Proofs, giving us a high level of confidence in our results. The latest version of the mechanized theory is available online at github.com/heron-solver/TESL-Theory. However, this paper is self-contained: all the key intermediate lemmas are stated using mathematical notations and their proofs are sketched.

2   TESL⁻

We present here the TESL⁻ minimal specification language in two parts: a basic causal one and a temporal one.

2.1   The Causality Part

Here is a grammar for the purely causal part of the language:

$$\Psi \qquad ::= \qquad \langle atom \rangle \wedge \ldots \wedge \langle atom \rangle$$
$$\langle atom \rangle \qquad ::= \qquad \langle clock \rangle \ \texttt{sporadic} \ \langle timestamp \rangle \ \texttt{on} \ \langle clock \rangle$$
$$| \qquad \langle clock \rangle \ \texttt{implies} \ \langle clock \rangle$$

where $\langle clock \rangle \in \mathbb{K}$ (set of clocks), and $\langle timestamp \rangle \in \mathbb{T}$ (domain of timestamps). The meaning of a specification Ψ and of the atomic formulae are as follows:

– the composition of specifications is their conjunction $\wedge$,
– a **sporadic on** requires a tick on the first clock, at an instant where the time has the specified value in the time frame of the second clock[2],
– an **implies** atom models instantaneous causality. It specifies that in every instant, if the first clock ticks, the second ticks too.

In order to define the semantics of the above syntax, we formally define the idea of runs and instants as previously introduced. The set of *runs* is defined by a clock-indexed Kripke model: $\mathsf{Runs} = \mathbb{N} \to \mathbb{K} \to (\mathbb{B} \times \mathbb{T})$, where $\mathbb{K}$ is an

---

[1] wdi.centralesupelec.fr/software/TESL/.
[2] The two clocks in **sporadic on** may be identical, which means that this clock must tick at the given time stamp.

enumerable set of *clocks*, $\mathbb{B}$ is the set of booleans – used to indicate that a clock *ticks* at a given instant – and $\mathbb{T}$ is a universal metric time space with some linear ordering $\leq_{\mathbb{T}}$. Also, we constrain this run space to prevent time from flowing backwards, in other words a run $\rho \in$ Runs must be *monotonic*[3]:

$$\forall n \in \mathbb{N}.\ \forall C \in \mathbb{K}.\quad \pi_2(\rho\ n\ C)\ \leq_{\mathbb{T}}\ \pi_2(\rho\ (n+1)\ C)$$

A run is simply a infinite-sequence of *instants*. From a position n and a run ρ, we can extract the instant $\rho_n \in \mathbb{K} \to (\mathbb{B} \times \mathbb{T})$. Instants describe the status of each clock at a given observation. We define two projections to get the status of a clock C at an instant ρ_n:

- ticks($\rho_n(C)$) indicates whether C ticks
- time($\rho_n(C)$) is the timestamp of C at that instant.

The denotation $[\![\Psi]\!]_{\mathsf{TESL}}$ of a TESL$^-$ formula Ψ is defined inductively as follows:

$$[\![\psi_0 \wedge \ldots \wedge \psi_k]\!]_{\mathsf{TESL}}$$
$$\stackrel{\text{def}}{=}\ [\![\psi_0]\!]_{\mathsf{TESL}}\ \cap\ \ldots\ \cap\ [\![\psi_k]\!]_{\mathsf{TESL}}$$
$$[\![C_1\ \texttt{sporadic}\ \tau\ \texttt{on}\ C_2]\!]_{\mathsf{TESL}}$$
$$\stackrel{\text{def}}{=}\ \{\rho \in \mathsf{Runs}\ |\ \exists n \in \mathbb{N}.\ \mathsf{ticks}(\rho_n(C_1)) \wedge \mathsf{time}(\rho_n(C_2)) = \tau\}$$
$$[\![C_{\mathsf{master}}\ \texttt{implies}\ C_{\mathsf{slave}}]\!]_{\mathsf{TESL}}$$
$$\stackrel{\text{def}}{=}\ \{\rho \in \mathsf{Runs}\ |\ \forall n \in \mathbb{N}.\ \mathsf{ticks}(\rho_n(C_{\mathsf{master}})) \implies \mathsf{ticks}(\rho_n(C_{\mathsf{slave}}))\}$$

2.2   The Temporal Part

We introduce here some operators concerning time and duration.

$$\langle atom \rangle\quad ::=\quad \ldots$$
$$|\quad \texttt{time relation}\ (\langle clock \rangle,\ \langle clock \rangle)\ \in \langle relation \rangle$$
$$|\quad \langle clock \rangle\ \texttt{time delayed by}\ \langle duration \rangle\ \texttt{on}\ \langle clock \rangle\ \texttt{implies}\ \langle clock \rangle$$

where $\langle relation \rangle \subseteq \mathbb{T} \times \mathbb{T}$ and $\langle duration \rangle \in \mathbb{T}$. The meaning of these operators is:

- a **time relation** atom gives a relation between the time frames of two clocks. The time stamps of the clocks must be in the relation at every instant,
- a **time delayed** atom represents delayed causality. When the first (master) clock ticks, the duration is added to the current time on the second (measuring) clock to obtain the date at which the third (slave) clock has to tick.

---

[3] π_2 being the second projection, with $\pi_2(x,y) = y$.

The denotation of these operators is as follows:

$[\![\texttt{time relation } (C_1,\ C_2)\ \in R]\!]_{\mathsf{TESL}}$

$\stackrel{\text{def}}{=} \{\rho \in \mathsf{Runs} \mid \forall n \in \mathbb{N}.\ \big(\mathsf{time}(\rho_n(C_1)), \mathsf{time}(\rho_n(C_2))\big) \in R\}$

$[\![C_{\mathsf{master}} \texttt{ time delayed by } \delta\tau \texttt{ on } C_{\mathsf{meas}} \texttt{ implies } C_{\mathsf{slave}}]\!]_{\mathsf{TESL}}$

$\stackrel{\text{def}}{=} \{\rho \in \mathsf{Runs} \mid \forall n \in \mathbb{N}.\ \mathsf{ticks}(\rho_n(C_{\mathsf{master}}))$

$$\implies \forall m \geq n.\ \mathsf{time}(\rho_m(C_{\mathsf{meas}})) = \mathsf{time}(\rho_n(C_{\mathsf{meas}})) + \delta\tau$$

$$\implies \mathsf{ticks}(\rho_m(C_{\mathsf{slave}}))\}$$

A time relation makes it possible to specify, for example, that time on one clock flows 2.5 times as fast as on another clock. Using the floor function $\lfloor \_ \rfloor$, it is also possible to establish a relation between continuous and discrete time frames.

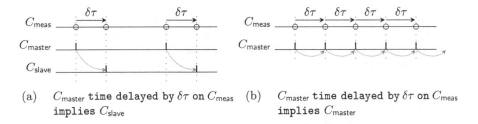

(a) C_{master} **time delayed by** $\delta\tau$ **on** C_{meas}
        implies C_{slave}

(b) C_{master} **time delayed by** $\delta\tau$ **on** C_{meas}
        implies C_{master}

Fig. 2. Time delays and periodicity

The **time delayed** construct introduces *durations* in causal relationships. Figure 2a shows the causal relation between C_{master} and C_{slave}, and the duration measured in the time frame of clock C_{meas}. Figure 2b shows how to specify a periodic clock using this construct. Notice that there are no ticks on clock C_{meas} in this example, it is only used as a time frame to measure durations.

2.3   An Application Example: The Car Power Window

The car power window [3], illustrated in Fig. 1, is an example of timed coordination of four subsystems: a control button, a timed finite state machine, a synchronous data flow (SDF) model of the electro-mechanical parts, and a discrete events (DE) model of the CAN bus, which interconnects the other subsystems.

For the sake of brevity, we consider only the raising of the window. Therefore, the button can only be pulled up and released, what we model by the `btn_up` and `btn_neutral` events. Similarly, we consider the `up` and `stop` input events for the timed finite state machine, as well as its `power` output event, which denotes the sending of a power command to the electromechanical subsystem (the value of this command is ignored in our temporal coordination model).

The model of the electromechanical subsystem has an `update_power` input, which corresponds to an update of the power to deliver to the motor. However, according to the SDF nature of this subsystem, this information is only taken into account when it reacts to compute its next state, which occurs every 50 ms and is modeled by a `react` input event. This periodic activation is part of the design of this subsystem, and it must be enforced for the regulation of the current in the motor to work properly. Here is a TESL specification for the power window:

```
 1   unit-clock btn_up      // the button is pulled up
 2   unit-clock btn_neutral // the button is released
 3   unit-clock up          // the TFSM receives an up event
 4   unit-clock stop        // the TFSM receives a stop event
 5   unit-clock power       // the TFSM produces a power event
 6   unit-clock update_power // the SDF model gets a new power command
 7   unit-clock react       // the SDF model reacts to its inputs
 8   rational-clock realtime // real-time in seconds
 9   rational-clock bus     // time scale of the CAN bus
10
11   time relation realtime = 0.002 * bus
12   btn_up time delayed by 1.0 on bus implies up
13   btn_neutral time delayed by 1.0 on bus implies stop
14
15   // Inputs of the TFSM trigger an instantaneous update of its output
16   up implies power
17   stop implies power
18
19   // The transmission delay on the CAN bus is 2 ms
20   power time delayed by 1.0 on bus implies update_power
21
22   // The window must react every 50 ms (periodic clock)
23   react time delayed by 0.05 on realtime implies react
```

This specification ignores the values that are sent over the bus, it specifies only when things happen since its goal is to coordinate the behaviors of the subsystems. Lines 1 to 7 declare the clocks that compose the interface of the subsystems for the architectural glue, as explained on Fig. 1. The `unit-clock` keyword simply sets the domain of timestamps of these clocks to a single value. Lines 8 and 9 declare chronometric clocks used to measure elapsed time on the CAN bus and in the real world. Their time domain is the rationals. Line 11 is an example of a relation between two time frames. It specifies that when 1 unit of time elapses on the bus clock, 0.002 s elapses on the real time clock, which means that time is measured in units of 2 ms on the bus clock. Lines 12 and 13 specify that when the button is pulled up or released, the timed finite state machine receives its `up` or `stop` input event 1 unit of time later, measured in the time frame of the bus clock (2 ms in real time). Lines 16 and 17 specify that the state machine reacts instantaneously to its inputs by producing its `power` output event. Line 20 specifies the transmission delay on the bus between the state machine and the SDF subsystem. Last, line 23 specifies that the reaction of the SDF subsystem is periodic, because it implies itself with a delay of 50 ms.

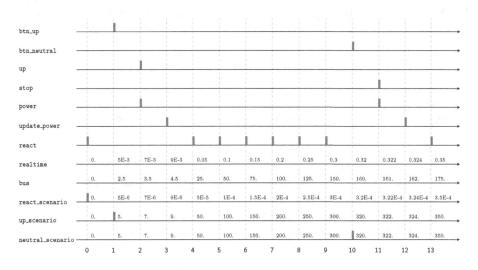

Fig. 3. A satisfying run for the example of the power window specification

Figure 3 depicts a satisfying run. The user pulls the button up (clock `btn_up`) at 5 ms (on the time scale of the `realtime` clock). The controller receives this information (clock `up`) at 7 ms due to the transmission delay on the CAN bus, and immediately sets the power for the window motor (clock `power`). Then, the mechanical part receives the command at 9 ms (clock `update_power`). The next tick of the periodic `react` clock occurs at 50 ms, which is the time at which the new value of the power is taken into account and the window starts moving up. At 320 ms, the user releases the button, which switches back to neutral (clock `btn_neutral`). The new value of the power is updated at 324 ms because of the transmission delays between the button and the controller, and between the controller and the mechanical parts. The next reaction of the window (clock `react`) occurs at 350 ms, which is the time at which the window stops moving up.

The additional clocks `react_scenario`, `up_scenario` and `neutral_scenario` are used to describe the user interface simulation scenario.

2.4 Properties of the Semantics

An important property that we derive directly from the denotational semantics is invariance by stuttering. When we combine two specifications Ψ_1 and Ψ_2, clocks in Ψ_2 may tick at instants where no clock in Ψ_1 ticks. Therefore, runs that satisfy S_1 should still satisfy it when these stuttering instants are added. Other specification languages, such as LTL [16,17], seek stutter-invariance to avoid the exponential explosion of the search space when checking properties [7,12,15,21]. In TESL, this idea is fully explored in the mechanized theory as previously mentioned.

3 Operational Semantics

We define an operational semantics to be able to constructively derive all possible satisfying runs for a given specification. This operational semantics works on configurations, which are composed of three parts informally called the *past*, the *present* and the *future*. The semantic rules unfold the constraints of the future into the present, and the non-deterministic choices that are made in the present are then stored into the past. The decisions on the past are expressed using *primitive constraints* defined in Subsect. 3.1. The combination of the past, the present and the future is called a *configuration*, as presented in Subsect. 3.2. The reduction rules on configurations are presented in Subsect. 3.3.

3.1 Primitives

The *primitives* in Definition 2 describe prefixes of satisfying runs. Note that compared to TESL⁻ atomic formulae, they deal with fixed instant indexes.

Definition 1 (Time Variables). *The set of time variables* $\mathbb{V}$ *contains symbols* tvar_n^C *with* $n \in \mathbb{N}$ *and* $C \in \mathbb{K}$. *Note that* tvar_n^C *stands for the symbolic value of time on clock* C *at instant* n.

Definition 2 (Run Primitives). A run primitive $\gamma \in \Gamma$ is one of:

- $C \Uparrow_n$ constrains clock C to tick at instant index n;
- $C \not\Uparrow_n$ constrains clock C not to tick (to be idle) at instant index n;
- $C \Downarrow_n x$ constrains clock C to have timestamp x at instant index n, where x can be a variable in $\mathbb{V}$, or a constant in $\mathbb{T}$;
- $(\mathrm{tvar}_{n_1}^{C_1}, \mathrm{tvar}_{n_2}^{C_2}) \in R$ constrains values $\mathrm{tvar}_{n_1}^{C_1}$ and $\mathrm{tvar}_{n_2}^{C_2}$ to be in relation R.

The semantics of these primitives is given by $[\![\_]\!]_{\text{prim}}$ as:

$$[\![\{\gamma_0 \; ; \; \ldots \; ; \; \gamma_k\}]\!]_{\text{prim}} \stackrel{\text{def}}{=} [\![\gamma_0]\!]_{\text{prim}} \cap \ldots \cap [\![\gamma_k]\!]_{\text{prim}}$$

$$[\![C \Uparrow_n]\!]_{\text{prim}} \stackrel{\text{def}}{=} \{\rho \in \text{Runs} \mid \text{ticks}(\rho_n(C)) \text{ is true}\}$$

$$[\![C \nUparrow_n]\!]_{\text{prim}} \stackrel{\text{def}}{=} \{\rho \in \text{Runs} \mid \text{ticks}(\rho_n(C)) \text{ is false}\}$$

$$[\![C \Downarrow_n x]\!]_{\text{prim}} \stackrel{\text{def}}{=} \{\rho \in \text{Runs} \mid \text{time}(\rho_n(C)) = x\} \text{ with } x \text{ in } \mathbb{T} \text{ or } \mathbb{V}$$

$$[\![(\text{tvar}_{n_1}^{C_1}, \text{tvar}_{n_2}^{C_2}) \in R]\!]_{\text{prim}}$$
$$\stackrel{\text{def}}{=} \{\rho \in \text{Runs} \mid \text{time}(\rho_{n_1}(C_1)) \text{ and } \text{time}(\rho_{n_2}(C_2)) \text{ are in } R\}$$

3.2 Configurations

The operational semantics transforms *configurations*, which represent the "current" state of the construction of a symbolic run and have three parts:

- the past Γ is a collection of primitive constraints that represents what has been decided in previous instants (the prefix of the run);
- the present Ψ contains the constraints on the instant under scrutiny (what can or cannot be added to the prefix);
- the future Φ contains the constraints on the future behavior of the run.

Definition 3 (Configuration). A *configuration* is a tuple $\Gamma \models_n \Psi \triangleright \Phi$, where n is the index of the current instant, Γ the context, which contains primitives describing the "past", Ψ the TESL$^-$-formula to be considered in the "present", and Φ the TESL$^-$-formula to satisfy in the "future" of the run.

3.3 Reduction Rules

The semantics consists in rules that transform configurations in two ways:

1. Moving constraints from the future to the present (introduction), which amounts to turning the "next" instant into the current instant;
2. Consuming constraints in the present to produce primitive constraints in the past (elimination).

The introduction rule initializes a new instant by incrementing the index counter and moving the constraints from the future into the present.

Definition 4 (Introduction Rule $\rightarrow_i$). The relation $\rightarrow_i$ is the smallest relation satisfying:

$$\Gamma \models_n \varnothing \triangleright \Phi \quad \rightarrow_i \quad \Gamma \models_{n+1} \Phi \triangleright \varnothing \qquad (\text{instant}_i)$$

The elimination rules consume constraints on the present and produce primitive constraints on the past as well as constraints on the future, which correspond to consequences of the choices made for the current instant. The application of these rules adds constraints to Γ and makes the run more defined.

Definition 5 (Elimination Rules $\rightarrow_e$). The relation $\rightarrow_e$ is the smallest relation satisfying the rules given in Table 1.

Table 1. Elimination Rules for TESL^- formulae

$$\Gamma \models_n \Psi \wedge (C_1 \text{ sporadic } \tau \text{ on } C_2) \triangleright \Phi \qquad\qquad (\text{sporadic} - \text{on}_{e1})$$
$$\rightarrow_e \Gamma \models_n \Psi \triangleright \Phi \wedge (C_1 \text{ sporadic } \tau \text{ on } C_2)$$

$$\Gamma \models_n \Psi \wedge (C_1 \text{ sporadic } \tau \text{ on } C_2) \triangleright \Phi \qquad\qquad (\text{sporadic} - \text{on}_{e2})$$
$$\rightarrow_e \Gamma \cup \left\{ C_1 \Uparrow_n, \ C_2 \Downarrow_n \tau \right\} \models_n \Psi \triangleright \Phi$$

$$\Gamma \models_n \Psi \wedge (C_\text{master} \text{ implies } C_\text{slave}) \triangleright \Phi \qquad\qquad (\text{implies}_{e1})$$
$$\rightarrow_e \Gamma \cup \left\{ C_\text{master} \not{\Uparrow}_n \right\} \models_n \Psi \triangleright \Phi \wedge (C_\text{master} \text{ implies } C_\text{slave})$$

$$\Gamma \models_n \Psi \wedge (C_\text{master} \text{ implies } C_\text{slave}) \triangleright \Phi \qquad\qquad (\text{implies}_{e2})$$
$$\rightarrow_e \Gamma \cup \left\{ C_\text{master} \Uparrow_n, \ C_\text{slave} \Uparrow_n \right\} \models_n \Psi \triangleright \Phi \wedge (C_\text{master} \text{ implies } C_\text{slave})$$

$$\Gamma \models_n \Psi \wedge (\text{time relation } (C_1, \ C_2) \ \in R) \triangleright \Phi \qquad\qquad (\text{time} - \text{relation}_e)$$
$$\rightarrow_e \Gamma \cup \left\{ (\text{tvar}_n^{C_1}, \ \text{tvar}_n^{C_2}) \in R \right\} \models_n \Psi \triangleright \Phi \wedge (\text{time relation } (C_1, \ C_2) \ \in R)$$

$$\Gamma \models_n \Psi \wedge (C_\text{master} \text{ time delayed by } \delta t \text{ on } C_\text{meas} \text{ implies } C_\text{slave}) \triangleright \Phi \qquad (\text{time} - \text{delayed}_{e1})$$
$$\rightarrow_e \Gamma \cup \left\{ C_\text{master} \not{\Uparrow}_n \right\} \models_n \Psi \triangleright \Phi \wedge (C_\text{master} \text{ time delayed by } \delta t \text{ on } C_\text{meas} \text{ implies } C_\text{slave})$$

$$\Gamma \models_n \Psi \wedge (C_\text{master} \text{ time delayed by } \delta t \text{ on } C_\text{meas} \text{ implies } C_\text{slave}) \triangleright \Phi \qquad (\text{time} - \text{delayed}_{e2})$$
$$\rightarrow_e \Gamma \cup \left\{ C_\text{master} \Uparrow_n \right\} \models_n \Psi \wedge (C_\text{slave} \text{ sporadic } (\text{tvar}_n^{C_\text{meas}} + \delta t) \text{ on } C_\text{meas})$$
$$\triangleright \ \Phi \wedge (C_\text{master} \text{ time delayed by } \delta t \text{ on } C_\text{meas} \text{ implies } C_\text{slave})$$

It is necessary to apply elimination rules until the present of the configuration is empty and the introduction rule can be applied to progress to the next instant. Here are different possibilities to eliminate constraints from the present:

- C_1 sporadic τ on C_2: this formula can be postponed to a later instant (Rule sporadic $-$ on$_{e1}$), or satisfied in the current instant by adding ticking and timestamp primitives to the context (Rule sporadic $-$ on$_{e2}$),
- C_master implies C_slave: either clock C_master does not tick (Rule implies$_{e1}$), or both C_master and C_slave tick in the current instant (Rule implies$_{e2}$). In both cases, the formula is copied into the future to be satisfied at every instant,
- time relation $(C_1, \ C_2) \ \in R$: the corresponding primitive is added to constrain the timestamps on clocks C_1 and C_2 at the current instant, and the formula is put into the future since it has to be satisfied at every instant,
- C_master time delayed by δt on C_meas implies C_slave: either clock C_master does not tick and we only copy the formula into the future (Rule time $-$ delayed$_{e1}$); or it ticks and we need to force a tick on C_slave when the time on C_meas reaches $\text{tvar}_n^{C_\text{meas}} + \delta t$, which is the current timestamp on measuring clock C_meas delayed by duration δt. The formula is copied into the future (Rule time $-$ delayed$_{e2}$).

3.4   Local Termination

Proposition 1 (Termination of Elimination Rules).
The relation $\rightarrow_e$ is well-founded.

Proof. All of the elimination rules strictly decrease the number of formulae in the "present" of the configuration, and a configuration with an empty "present" is in normal form with respect to $\rightarrow_e$.

Definition 6 (Reduction $\rightarrow$). We define $\rightarrow \overset{\text{def}}{=} \rightarrow_i \cup \rightarrow_e$.
A reduction step is either an introduction or an elimination.

4   Relating Operational and Denotational Semantics

In this section, we give key properties of the operational semantics. We are interested in establishing soundness (Theorem 1), completeness (Theorem 2), and progress (Theorem 3) with respect to the denotational semantics defined in Sect. 2.

4.1   Stepwise Denotational Semantics

In Subsect. 2.1 and Subsect. 2.2, we have defined a denotational semantics to characterize the runs that satisfy a specification. Definition 7 gives a stepwise version of this definition, which constrains the behavior only from a given instant.

Definition 7 (Stepwise Interpretation of TESL$^-$ formulae).
The *stepwise interpretation* of a TESL$^-$ formula Ψ, noted $[\![\Psi]\!]^{\geq i}_{\mathrm{TESL}}$, is defined as in Table 2.

Table 2. Stepwise interpretation of TESL$^-$ formulae

$$[\![\psi_0 \wedge \ldots \wedge \psi_k]\!]^{\geq i}_{\mathrm{TESL}} \overset{\text{def}}{=} [\![\psi_0]\!]^{\geq i}_{\mathrm{TESL}} \cap \ldots \cap [\![\psi_k]\!]^{\geq i}_{\mathrm{TESL}}$$

$$[\![C_1 \text{ sporadic } \tau \text{ on } C_2]\!]^{\geq i}_{\mathrm{TESL}}$$
$$\overset{\text{def}}{=} \{\rho \in \mathsf{Runs} \mid \exists n \geq i.\ \mathsf{ticks}(\rho_n(C_1)) \wedge \mathsf{time}(\rho_n(C_2)) = \tau\}$$

$$[\![C_{\mathsf{master}} \text{ implies } C_{\mathsf{slave}}]\!]^{\geq i}_{\mathrm{TESL}}$$
$$\overset{\text{def}}{=} \{\rho \in \mathsf{Runs} \mid \forall n \geq i.\ \mathsf{ticks}(\rho_n(C_{\mathsf{master}})) \implies \mathsf{ticks}(\rho_n(C_{\mathsf{slave}}))\}$$

$$[\![\text{time relation } (C_1,\ C_2) \in R]\!]^{\geq i}_{\mathrm{TESL}}$$
$$\overset{\text{def}}{=} \{\rho \in \mathsf{Runs} \mid \forall n \geq i.\ (\mathsf{time}(\rho_n(C_1)), \mathsf{time}(\rho_n(C_2))) \in R\}$$

$$[\![C_{\mathsf{master}} \text{ time delayed by } \delta\tau \text{ on } C_{\mathsf{meas}} \text{ implies } C_{\mathsf{slave}}]\!]^{\geq i}_{\mathrm{TESL}}$$
$$\overset{\text{def}}{=} \{\rho \in \mathsf{Runs} \mid \forall n \geq i.\ \mathsf{ticks}(\rho_n(C_{\mathsf{master}})) \implies$$
$$\forall m \geq n.\ \mathsf{time}(\rho_m(C_{\mathsf{meas}})) = \mathsf{time}(\rho_n(C_{\mathsf{meas}})) + \delta\tau \implies \mathsf{ticks}(\rho_m(C_{\mathsf{slave}}))\}$$

This stepwise interpretation from instant 0 matches the denotational interpretation:

Lemma 1 (Start Step). *For any TESL$^-$ formula Ψ, $[\![\Psi]\!]_{\text{TESL}} = [\![\Psi]\!]_{\text{TESL}}^{\geq 0}$.*

Proof. From the definitions of $[\![\Psi]\!]_{\text{TESL}}^{\geq 0}$ and $[\![\Psi]\!]_{\text{TESL}}$ and from $n \in \mathbb{N} \iff n \geq 0$.

The next proposition links the operational and denotational semantics. The structure of the right hand term in the equations in Table 3 matches the reduction rules of the operational semantics. Therefore, the coinductive unfolding of the denotational semantics is similar to the derivation of a reduction step in the operational semantics. The past-present-future pattern is also visible here: the past is described by $[\![\_]\!]_{\text{prim}}$ (denotation of fixed primitives), the present by $[\![\_]\!]_{\text{TESL}}^{\geq i}$, which denotes runs that are valid from the current instant, and the future by $[\![\_]\!]_{\text{TESL}}^{\geq i+1}$, which denotes runs that are valid from the next instant.

Proposition 2 (Coinductive Unfolding). *The stepwise interpretation can be coinductively unfolded as presented in Table 3.*

Table 3. Coinductive unfolding of stepwise interpretation

$$[\![C_1 \text{ sporadic } \tau \text{ on } C_2]\!]_{\text{TESL}}^{\geq i}$$
$$= \left([\![C_1 \Uparrow_i]\!]_{\text{prim}} \cap [\![C_2 \Downarrow_i \tau]\!]_{\text{prim}}\right) \cup [\![C_1 \text{ sporadic } \tau \text{ on } C_2]\!]_{\text{TESL}}^{\geq i+1}$$

$$[\![C_{\text{master}} \text{ implies } C_{\text{slave}}]\!]_{\text{TESL}}^{\geq i}$$
$$= \left([\![C_{\text{master}} \not\Uparrow_i]\!]_{\text{prim}} \cup \left([\![C_{\text{master}} \Uparrow_i]\!]_{\text{prim}} \cap [\![C_{\text{slave}} \Uparrow_i]\!]_{\text{prim}}\right)\right)$$
$$\cap [\![C_{\text{master}} \text{ implies } C_{\text{slave}}]\!]_{\text{TESL}}^{\geq i+1}$$

$$[\![\text{time relation } (C_1, C_2) \in R]\!]_{\text{TESL}}^{\geq i}$$
$$= [\![(\text{tvar}_{C_1}^i, \text{tvar}_{C_2}^i) \in R]\!]_{\text{prim}} \cap [\![\text{time relation } (C_1, C_2) \in R]\!]_{\text{TESL}}^{\geq i+1}$$

$$[\![C_{\text{master}} \text{ time delayed by } \delta\tau \text{ on } C_{\text{meas}} \text{ implies } C_{\text{slave}}]\!]_{\text{TESL}}^{\geq i}$$
$$= [\![C_{\text{master}} \not\Uparrow_i]\!]_{\text{prim}} \cap [\![C_{\text{master}} \text{ time delayed by } \delta\tau \text{ on } C_{\text{meas}} \text{ implies } C_{\text{slave}}]\!]_{\text{TESL}}^{\geq i+1}$$
$$\cup [\![C_{\text{master}} \Uparrow_i]\!]_{\text{prim}} \cap [\![C_{\text{slave}} \text{ sporadic } \text{tvar}_{C_{\text{meas}}}^i + \delta\tau \text{ on } C_{\text{meas}}]\!]_{\text{TESL}}^{\geq i}$$
$$\cap [\![C_{\text{master}} \text{ time delayed by } \delta\tau \text{ on } C_{\text{meas}} \text{ implies } C_{\text{slave}}]\!]_{\text{TESL}}^{\geq i+1}$$

Proof. By unfolding the quantifiers and substituting parts with Definition 2 and Definition 7. The rules of Table 3 state that $[\![\Psi]\!]_{\text{TESL}}^{\geq i}$ can be decomposed into what happens at index i and what happens starting from index $i + 1$.

This *coinductive* pattern explains the behavior of the operational semantics at a denotational level and bridges the gap between those semantics.

4.2   Soundness

To establish *soundness*, we define the meaning of a configuration.

Definition 8 (Interpretation of Configurations).
The interpretation of a configuration $\Gamma \models_n \Psi \triangleright \Phi$ *is:*

$$\llbracket \Gamma \models_n \Psi \triangleright \Phi \rrbracket_{\text{config}} \overset{\text{def}}{=} \llbracket \Gamma \rrbracket_{\text{prim}} \cap \llbracket \Psi \rrbracket_{\text{TESL}}^{\geq n} \cap \llbracket \Phi \rrbracket_{\text{TESL}}^{\geq n+1}$$

It is trivial to show that the interpretation of a TESL$^-$ formula Ψ is the same as the interpretation of the initial configuration starting at Ψ.

Lemma 2 (Start Configuration). *For any TESL$^-$ formula Ψ, we have*

$$\llbracket \Psi \rrbracket_{\text{TESL}} = \llbracket \varnothing \models_0 \Psi \triangleright \varnothing \rrbracket_{\text{config}}$$

Proof. The proof is done by unfolding Definition 8: $\llbracket \varnothing \rrbracket_{\text{prim}}$ and $\llbracket \varnothing \rrbracket_{\text{TESL}}^{\geq n+1}$ are the whole set of runs, since $\varnothing$ is not constraining anything, and $\llbracket \Psi \rrbracket_{\text{TESL}}^{\geq 0}$ is $\llbracket \Psi \rrbracket_{\text{TESL}}$ by Lemma 1.

We now show that each reduction step is sound, in the sense that if a run satisfies a derived configuration, it also satisfies the original configuration.

Lemma 3 (Sound Reduction). *For any reduction $(\Gamma \models_n \Psi \triangleright \Phi) \to (\Gamma' \models_{n'} \Psi' \triangleright \Phi')$, we have $\llbracket \Gamma \models_n \Psi \triangleright \Phi \rrbracket_{\text{config}} \supseteq \llbracket \Gamma' \models_{n'} \Psi' \triangleright \Phi' \rrbracket_{\text{config}}$.*

Proof. By Definitions 6 and 8, and case analysis on $\to$. In the $\to_i$ case, the reduction is of the form $\Gamma \models_n \Psi \triangleright \varnothing \to \Gamma \models_{n+1} \varnothing \triangleright \Psi$: the semantics of both sides are the same. In $\to_e$ case, $n' = n+1$ and we use Proposition 2 to decompose the semantics at instant n using the semantics at instant $n + 1$.

Finally, we show soundness by generalizing Lemma 2 and Lemma 3 to an arbitrary number of reductions from the initial configuration.

Theorem 1 (Soundness). *Let Ψ be a TESL$^-$ formula. For all k and all configurations $\Gamma' \models_{n'} \Psi' \triangleright \Phi'$ such that $\varnothing \models_0 \Psi \triangleright \varnothing \to^k \Gamma' \models_{n'} \Psi' \triangleright \Phi'$, we have*

$$\llbracket \Psi \rrbracket_{\text{TESL}} \supseteq \llbracket \Gamma' \models_{n'} \Psi' \triangleright \Phi' \rrbracket_{\text{config}}$$

Proof. By induction on k. For the base case, when $k = 0$ we have $\Gamma' = \Psi' = \varnothing$. Lemma 2 then tells us that $\llbracket \Psi \rrbracket_{\text{TESL}} = \llbracket \Gamma' \models_{n'} \Psi' \triangleright \Phi' \rrbracket_{\text{config}}$. For the inductive case, we suppose that the result is true for k and we consider $k + 1$ reductions:

$$\varnothing \models_0 \Psi \triangleright \varnothing \to^k \Gamma' \models_{n'} \Psi' \triangleright \Phi' \to \Gamma'' \models_{n''} \Psi'' \triangleright \Phi''.$$

The induction hypothesis tells us that $\llbracket \Psi \rrbracket_{\text{TESL}} \supseteq \llbracket \Gamma' \models_{n'} \Psi' \triangleright \Phi' \rrbracket_{\text{config}}$, and we can conclude using Lemma 3 and the transitivity of $\supseteq$.

4.3   Completeness

Completeness consists in showing that if a run ρ belongs to the denotation of a configuration, it is always possible to derive a new configuration whose denotation also contains ρ. For this, we first define the direct successors of a configuration.

Definition 9 (Direct Successors). For any configuration $\Gamma \models_n \Psi \triangleright \Phi$,

$$\mathcal{C}_{\mathrm{next}}(\Gamma \models_n \Psi \triangleright \Phi) \overset{\mathrm{def}}{=} \{\Gamma' \models_{n'} \Psi' \triangleright \Phi' \mid (\Gamma \models_n \Psi \triangleright \Phi) \rightarrow (\Gamma' \models_{n'} \Psi' \triangleright \Phi')\}$$

Then we show that any denoted run belongs to some successor configuration.

Lemma 4 (Complete Direct Successors). *For any configuration* $\Gamma \models_n \Psi \triangleright \Phi$,

$$\llbracket \Gamma \models_n \Psi \triangleright \Phi \rrbracket_{\mathrm{config}} \subseteq \bigcup_{X \in \mathcal{C}_{next}(\Gamma \models_n \Psi \triangleright \Phi)} \llbracket X \rrbracket_{\mathrm{config}}$$

Proof. Similarly to the proof of Lemma 3, we proceed by induction on the number of formulae in Ψ. If Ψ is empty, the only possible reduction is $\rightarrow_i$: the reduction is of the form $\Gamma \models_n \Psi \triangleright \varnothing \rightarrow \Gamma \models_{n+1} \varnothing \triangleright \Psi$ and there is only one possible X, whose semantics is $\llbracket \Gamma \models_n \Psi \triangleright \Phi \rrbracket_{\mathrm{config}}$. If Ψ is not empty, the reduction is a $\rightarrow_e$-reduction. The case is solved using Proposition 2 to decompose the semantics at instant n using the semantics of the possible reductions at instant $n+1$.

Hence, completeness holds for an arbitrary number of reductions starting from the initial configuration.

Theorem 2 (Completeness). *Let* Ψ *be a TESL$^-$ formula and* ρ *a satisfying run, i.e.* $\rho \in \llbracket \Psi \rrbracket_{\mathrm{TESL}}$. *For all* k, *there is a configuration* $\Gamma' \models_{n'} \Psi' \triangleright \Phi'$ *such that* $\varnothing \models_0 \Psi \triangleright \varnothing \rightarrow^k \Gamma' \models_{n'} \Psi' \triangleright \Phi'$ *and* $\rho \in \llbracket \Gamma' \models_{n'} \Psi' \triangleright \Phi' \rrbracket_{\mathrm{config}}$

Proof. By induction on k. For $k = 0$, we conclude using Lemma 2. For the inductive case, we assume that the result is true for k and consider the $k+1$ case. From the induction hypothesis we find a configuration $\Gamma' \models_{n'} \Psi' \triangleright \Phi'$ such that $\varnothing \models_0 \Psi \triangleright \varnothing \rightarrow^k \Gamma' \models_{n'} \Psi' \triangleright \Phi'$ and $\rho \in \llbracket \Gamma' \models_{n'} \Psi' \triangleright \Phi' \rrbracket_{\mathrm{config}}$. From Lemma 4, we deduce that there is some $X \in \mathcal{C}_{\mathrm{next}}(\Gamma \models_n \Psi \triangleright \Phi)$ such that $\rho \in \llbracket X \rrbracket_{\mathrm{config}}$. This X is the configuration we are looking for to close the inductive case.

4.4   Progress

Progress ensures the increase of the length of the run in construction. We establish that for any instant index, a configuration can be "executed" to produce a run prefix whose length is incremented by 1 (Lemma 5). Then in Theorem 3 we show that for any instant index, a specification can be "executed" to produce a run prefix of such length from the initial configuration.

Lemma 5 (Instant Index Increase). *Let $\Gamma \models_n \Psi \rhd \Phi$ be a configuration and ρ a satisfying run, i.e. $\rho \in [\![\Gamma \models_n \Psi \rhd \Phi]\!]_{\text{config}}$. There is Γ', Ψ', Φ' and a number of reductions k such that $\Gamma \models_n \Psi \rhd \Phi \to^k \Gamma' \models_{n+1} \Psi' \rhd \Phi'$ and $\rho \in [\![\Gamma' \models_{n+1} \Psi' \rhd \Phi']\!]_{\text{config}}$.*

Proof. By induction on the size of Ψ. When Ψ is empty, we can just pick $k = 1$ as the reduction will be a $\to_i$-reduction, and both sides of the reduction will have the same semantics. Now, supposing that the result is true for any Ψ containing i formulae, let's assume that Ψ contains $i + 1$ formulae. Lemma 4 tells us that there exists a configuration X such that $\Gamma \models_n \Psi \rhd \Phi \to X$ and $\rho \in [\![X]\!]_{\text{config}}$. Since Ψ is not empty, the reduction is a $\to_e$-reduction and the "present" part of X is now of size i: we can apply the induction hypothesis and close the case.

Theorem 3 (Progress). *Let Ψ be a TESL$^-$ formula and ρ a satisfying run, i.e. $\rho \in [\![\Psi]\!]_{\text{TESL}}$. For all n, there is Γ', Ψ', Φ' and a number of reductions k such that $\varnothing \models_0 \Psi \rhd \varnothing \to^k \Gamma' \models_n \Psi' \rhd \Phi'$ and $\rho \in [\![\Gamma' \models_n \Psi' \rhd \Phi']\!]_{\text{config}}$.*

Proof. The proof is by induction on n. For the base case, $n = 0$ we can pick $k = 0$, and both sides of the reduction are equal. For the induction step, from the induction hypothesis we have Γ', Ψ', Φ' and a number k such that $\varnothing \models_0 \Psi \rhd \varnothing \to^k \Gamma' \models_n \Psi' \rhd \Phi'$ and $\rho \in [\![\Gamma' \models_n \Psi' \rhd \Phi']\!]_{\text{config}}$. With Lemma 5 we obtain the required configuration at instant $n + 1$.

5   Runtime Monitoring and Testing

Our theories allow for straightforward tactic execution of the operational rules of TESL$^-$ via the Isabelle proof engine. This turned out to be too inefficient for even runs with a few simulation steps due to the internal mechanism of the proof assistant. Nevertheless, the separate implementation of the operational semantics, named Heron, which we use for monitoring and testing [23], can be regarded with greater confidence. Indeed, its operational rules directly correspond to the operational semantics of the Isabelle/HOL implementation, which has been proved equivalent to the denotational semantics.

6   Related Work

TESL is a polychronous and polytimed language. Polymorphic time exists in the family of synchronous languages that were designed in the 1980's, such as Lustre [13], Esterel [2] and Signal [18]. In these languages, time is purely logical (there are no dates nor chronometric durations), and can be used for modeling occurrences of any kind of events, hence the polymorphic nature of time. Thereafter, Prelude [26] and Zélus [5] extended the Lustre programming language with the addition of support for metric time.

As opposed to the latter synchronous models which derive all clocks from a common root clock (defining the instants where the system reacts), polychronous models [28] do not constrain all clocks to derive from a single reaction clock, allowing a more relaxed and concurrent execution of systems. Polychrony is supported by the Signal language and in Polychronous automata [19].

Another source of inspiration in our work is CCSL [10,20], the Clock Constraints Specification Language, which supports asynchronous constraints on the occurrence of events. It has an executable semantics [30] and a denotational semantics [9,22]. However, all these approaches do not support chronometric clocks, with dates and durations. They measure time in numbers of ticks on a clock, not in elapsed durations on a time scale. In opposition, TESL supports chronometric time, and allows different clocks to live in different time frames.

Timed automata [1] support both discrete events and measuring durations on a time scale, with several mechanization approaches of their semantics [11,14,27]. However, this time scale is global and uniform: all clocks in a timed automaton progress at the same rate. Our model considers a larger scope of time with polychronous clocks flowing independently from each other.

The GEMOC initiative [8] has been targeting the development of frameworks to facilitate the integration of heterogeneous modeling languages. In particular, the BCOoL language [29] is specifically targeted at coordination patterns for Domain Specific Events (interface of a domain specific modeling language).

7   Future Work

A few directions of extension for our work are worth mentioning:

– it might be worthwhile to look for even more fundamental operators on clock-indexed models and derive a kind of core language-theory that is even more compact albeit more expressive,
– we are interested in general architectural operators allowing to combine subsystem specifications to larger ones (*e.g.*, with hidden or local clocks),
– we plan to explore the code generation features of Isabelle/HOL to produce certified solvers from the derived operational rules of our timed languages.

8   Conclusion

This study investigates the semantics of timed languages using clock-indexed Kripke models. Illustrated by a minimalist language that supports event- and timed-based constraints over polychronous clocks, we show a novel way to relate from one side, a denotational semantics, whose advantages are to be logically consistent by construction, compositional and trace-based, with an operational semantics that constructs symbolic runs and is thus suited for verification purposes. This technique is based on the observation that time, decomposed in an intuitive past-present-future pattern, can be reflected in both semantics through an operational unfolding principle. Yet, the time model we chose to study exhibits several challenging properties: time constraints can be both logical and metric, clocks are polychronous (no global clock) and polymorphic (various domain types) and clock constraints can be synchronous or asynchronous.

The unfolding principle of time in both denotational and operational semantics allows us to establish crucial properties such as stutter-invariance at the denotational level, as well as the equivalence results given by correctness and completeness. Finally, local termination and progress properties bridge the gap towards trustworthy verification tools.

References

1. Alur, R., Dill, D.L.: A theory of timed automata. Theor. Comput. Sci. **126**, 183–235 (1994)
2. Berry, G.: The foundations of Esterel. In: Plotkin, G., Stirling, C., Tofte, M. (eds.) Proof, Language, and Interaction, pp. 425–454. MIT Press, Cambridge (2000)
3. Boulanger, F., Hardebolle, C., Jacquet, C., Marcadet, D.: Semantic adaptation for models of computation. In: 2011 11th International Conference on Application of Concurrency to System Design, pp. 153–162 (June 2011). https://doi.org/10.1109/ACSD.2011.17
4. Boulanger, F., Jacquet, C., Hardebolle, C., Prodan, I.: TESL: a language for reconciling heterogeneous execution traces. In: 12th ACM/IEEE International Conference on Formal Methods and Models for Codesign (MEMOCODE 2014), Lausanne, Switzerland, pp. 114–123 (October 2014)
5. Bourke, T., Pouzet, M.: Zélus: a synchronous language with ODEs. In: Proceedings of the 16th International Conference on Hybrid Systems: Computation and Control, HSCC 2013, pp. 113–118. Association for Computing Machinery, New York (2013). https://doi.org/10.1145/2461328.2461348
6. Brunette, C., Talpin, J.P., Gamatié, A., Gautier, T.: A metamodel for the design of polychronous systems. J. Logic Algebr. Program. **78**(4), 233–259 (2009). https://doi.org/10.1016/j.jlap.2008.11.005. , iFIP WG1.8 Workshop on Applying Concurrency Research in Industry
7. Clarkson, M.R., Finkbeiner, B., Koleini, M., Micinski, K.K., Rabe, M.N., Sánchez, C.: Temporal logics for hyperproperties. In: Abadi, M., Kremer, S. (eds.) POST 2014. LNCS, vol. 8414, pp. 265–284. Springer, Heidelberg (2014). https://doi.org/10.1007/978-3-642-54792-8_15
8. Cheng, B.H.C., Combemale, B., France, R.B., Jézéquel, J.-M., Rumpe, B. (eds.): Globalizing Domain-Specific Languages. LNCS, vol. 9400. Springer, Cham (2015). https://doi.org/10.1007/978-3-319-26172-0
9. Deantoni, J., André, C., Gascon, R.: CCSL denotational semantics. Research report RR-8628, Inria (November 2014)
10. Garcés, K., Deantoni, J., Mallet, F.: A model-based approach for reconciliation of polychronous execution traces. In: SEAA 2011–37th EUROMICRO Conference on Software Engineering and Advanced Applications. IEEE, Oulu (August 2011)
11. Garnacho, M., Bodeveix, J.-P., Filali-Amine, M.: A mechanized semantic framework for real-time systems. In: Braberman, V., Fribourg, L. (eds.) FORMATS 2013. LNCS, vol. 8053, pp. 106–120. Springer, Heidelberg (2013). https://doi.org/10.1007/978-3-642-40229-6_8
12. Groote, J.F., Vaandrager, F.: An efficient algorithm for branching bisimulation and stuttering equivalence. In: Paterson, M.S. (ed.) ICALP 1990. LNCS, vol. 443, pp. 626–638. Springer, Heidelberg (1990). https://doi.org/10.1007/BFb0032063
13. Halbwachs, N., Caspi, P., Raymond, P., Pilaud, D.: The synchronous dataflow programming language LUSTRE. Proc. IEEE **79**(9), 1305–1320 (1991)

14. Hale, R., Cardell-Oliver, R., Herbert, J.: An embedding of timed transition systems in HOL. Form. Methods Syst. Des. **3**(1), 151–174 (1993)
15. Klein, J.: Compositional synthesis and most general controller. Ph.D. thesis, Technische Universität Dresden (2013)
16. Kučera, A., Strejček, J.: The stuttering principle revisited. Acta Inf. **41**(7–8), 415–434 (2005). https://doi.org/10.1007/s00236-005-0164-4
17. Lamport, L.: What good is temporal logic? In: Mason, R.E.A. (ed.) IFIP Congress on Information Processing, pp. 657–668 (1983)
18. Le Guernic, P., Benveniste, A., Bournai, P., Gautier, T.: Synchronous data flow programming with the language SIGNAL. In: IFAC Proceedings 2nd IFAC Workshop on Adaptive Systems in Control and Signal Processing 1986, Lund, Sweden, 30 June–2 July 1986, vol. 20, no. 2, pp. 359–364 (1987)
19. Le Guernic, P., Gautier, T., Talpin, J.P., Besnard, L.: Polychronous automata. In: 9th International Symposium on Theoretical Aspects of Software Engineering, TASE 2015, Nanjing, China, pp. 95–102. IEEE Computer Society (September 2015)
20. Mallet, F., Deantoni, J., André, C., De Simone, R.: The clock constraint specification language for building timed causality models. Innov. Syst. Softw. Eng. **6**(1–2), 99–106 (2010)
21. Michaud, T., Duret-Lutz, A.: Practical stutter-invariance checks for ω-regular languages. In: Fischer, B., Geldenhuys, J. (eds.) SPIN 2015. LNCS, vol. 9232, pp. 84–101. Springer, Cham (2015). https://doi.org/10.1007/978-3-319-23404-5_7
22. Montin, M., Pantel, M.: Mechanizing the denotational semantics of the clock constraint specification language. In: Abdelwahed, E.H., Bellatreche, L., Golfarelli, M., Méry, D., Ordonez, C. (eds.) MEDI 2018. LNCS, vol. 11163, pp. 385–400. Springer, Cham (2018). https://doi.org/10.1007/978-3-030-00856-7_26
23. Nguyen Van, H., Balabonski, T., Boulanger, F., Keller, C., Valiron, B., Wolff, B.: A symbolic operational semantics for TESL. In: Abate, A., Geeraerts, G. (eds.) FORMATS 2017. LNCS, vol. 10419, pp. 318–334. Springer, Cham (2017). https://doi.org/10.1007/978-3-319-65765-3_18
24. Nipkow, T., Klein, G.: Concrete Semantics: With Isabelle/HOL. Springer, Switzerland (2014). https://doi.org/10.1007/978-3-319-10542-0
25. Nipkow, T., Wenzel, M., Paulson, L.C.: Isabelle/HOL: A Proof Assistant for Higher-Order Logic. Springer, Heidelberg (2002). https://doi.org/10.1007/3-540-45949-9
26. Pagetti, C., Forget, J., Boniol, F., Cordovilla, M., Lesens, D.: Multi-task implementation of multi-periodic synchronous programs. Discret. Event Dyn. Syst. **21**(3), 307–338 (2011). https://hal.inria.fr/inria-00638936
27. Paulin-Mohring, C.: Modelisation of timed automata in Coq. In: Kobayashi, N., Pierce, B.C. (eds.) TACS 2001. LNCS, vol. 2215, pp. 298–315. Springer, Heidelberg (2001). https://doi.org/10.1007/3-540-45500-0_15
28. Talpin, J.-P., Brandt, J., Gemünde, M., Schneider, K., Shukla, S.: Constructive polychronous systems. In: Artemov, S., Nerode, A. (eds.) LFCS 2013. LNCS, vol. 7734, pp. 335–349. Springer, Heidelberg (2013). https://doi.org/10.1007/978-3-642-35722-0_24
29. Larsen, M.E.V,, Deantoni, J., Combemale, B., Mallet, F.: A behavioral coordination operator language (BCOoL). In: 18th International Conference on Model Driven Engineering Languages and Systems (MODELS 2015) (August 2015)
30. Zhang, M., Mallet, F.: An executable semantics of clock constraint specification language and its applications. In: Artho, C., Ölveczky, P.C. (eds.) FTSCS 2015. CCIS, vol. 596, pp. 37–51. Springer, Cham (2016). https://doi.org/10.1007/978-3-319-29510-7_2

Backward Symbolic Optimal Reachability in Weighted Timed Automata

Rémi Parrot$^{(\boxtimes)}$ and Didier Lime

École Centrale de Nantes, LS2N, UMR CNRS 6004, Nantes, France
`remi.parrot@ec-nantes.fr`

Abstract. We address the problem of computing the infimum accumulated weight for the reachability of some goal location in weighted timed automata. While there already exist efficient techniques to solve this problem, we propose here a *backwards* symbolic algorithm computing the accumulated weight to the goal, instead of the accumulated weight from the initial state. Going backwards has in itself a few advantages: most notably it does not require any extrapolation operation to ensure termination. Also it may be more efficient than going forward if the set of co-reachable states is smaller than the set of reachable states. Backwards algorithms are also instrumental in several problems beyond reachability, like control problems for instance. We obtain our backward algorithm by proposing extensions of the classical action and time predecessor operations on zones to account for weights. We have implemented the approach and report on its performance.

1 Introduction

The design of timed systems, including for instance critical real-time embedded systems, is a challenging issue, with high stakes. Safety is of course of particular interest but given the limited resources (e.g., memory or energy) such systems usually have, so is optimisation.

This has lead to the development of dedicated formalisms, like timed automata [1] and extensions of those, namely *weighted* (or priced) time automata [2,3], to account for resource consumption.

The success of those formalisms relies on the availability of efficient algorithms and data structures (in particular *Difference Bound Matrices*, DBM) for their analysis, and of state-of-the-art tools, like Uppaal [19], implementing them. Those successful techniques have been extended to the setting of weighted timed automata [17] and then further refined [11,22,23], retaining much of their efficiency, and are available in tools like Uppaal-CORA[1] and TiAMo[2].

Much of the efficiency of those tools for solving infimum weight reachability in weighted timed automata comes from the extension of zones, representing in a symbolic manner the values of the clocks, to weighted zones including an expression of the weight from the initial state. This extension of course

---

[1] http://people.cs.aau.dk/~adavid/cora/index.html.
[2] https://git.lsv.fr/colange/tiamo.

© Springer Nature Switzerland AG 2020
N. Bertrand and N. Jansen (Eds.): FORMATS 2020, LNCS 12288, pp. 41–57, 2020.
https://doi.org/10.1007/978-3-030-57628-8_3

comes with extensions of the algorithms to efficiently handle zones represented as DBMs. Based on that data structure the exploration of the state-space classically proceeds in a forward manner, by iteratively computing successors, rather than backwards, by computing predecessors. This is mostly due to the fact that state-of-the-art tools extend timed automata with finite-range integer variables for modelling convenience, and that there are many predecessors by a transition with an integer variable assignment like $i \leftarrow 2$.

The backwards approach has some advantages of its own however: most notably it does not require any extrapolation operation to ensure termination [12,16], while its treatment in the weighted case is not trivial [11] (and arguably it is already the case for plain timed automata [9]). Also it may be more efficient than going forward if the set of co-reachable states is smaller than the set of reachable states. Backwards algorithms are also instrumental in several problems beyond reachability, like control problems for instance [13,21]. A hybrid forward/backward approach like that of [13], generalised in [14], also allows to circumvent the "predecessor of assignment" problem mentioned above.

We therefore propose here an extension of the classical time and action predecessors for timed automata, lifting them to the weighted case in the spirit of [17], by encoding in zones the accumulated weight to the goal, instead of the accumulated weight from the start. This allows us to easily adapt the classical exploration algorithm of [23] so that it works in a backward manner. We have implemented this algorithm and report on its performances.

Backwards algorithms for weighted timed automata have already been studied in more general contexts: for probabilistic timed automata in [6,7], where the property studied is cost-bounded reachability with only non-negative weights, and for optimal timed control in [10] with an additional assumption on weight cycles. The main difference with our work is that in both cases, they are not interested in the efficient representation and computation of the symbolic states, which is the crux of this article.

The paper is organized as follows: Sect. 2 recalls the basics of weighted timed automata, Sect. 3 introduces the operators needed to perform backward infimum weight reachability and the corresponding algorithm. We proceed with a small experimental evaluation in Sect. 4 and, finally, we conclude in Sect. 5.

2   Weighted Timed Automata

We denote by $\mathbb{R}$ the set of real numbers, by $\mathbb{Q}$ the set of rational numbers, by $\mathbb{Z}$ the set of integers, and by $\mathbb{N}$ the set of natural numbers (including 0). The subset of non-negative real numbers is denoted by $\mathbb{R}_{\geq 0}$.

For any sets A and B we denote by B^A the set of mappings from A to B.

A *clock constraint* on finite set X is a *conjunction* of expressions of the form $x \sim k$, with $x \in X$, $k \in \mathbb{N}$, and $\sim \in \{<, \leq, =, \geq, >\}$. We denote by $\mathcal{C}(X)$ the set of clock constraints, and by $\mathcal{C}'(X)$ its subset where $\sim \in \{<, \leq\}$.

Definition 1 (Weighted Timed Automaton). *A weighted timed automaton (WTA) is a tuple* $\mathcal{A} = (L, l_0, X, E, \mathsf{Inv}, \mathsf{weight})$ *where:*

- L *is a finite set of* locations;
- $l_0 \in L$ *is an initial* location;
- X *is a finite set of* clocks;
- $E \subseteq L \times \mathcal{C}(X) \times 2^X \times L$ *is a finite set of* edges. *Let* $(l, g, R, l') \in E$. *This corresponds to an edge in the automaton with source location* l, *guard* g, *set of clocks to reset to zero* R, *and target location* l';
- $\mathsf{Inv} \in (\mathcal{C}'(X))^L$ *is a mapping giving for each location an* invariant;
- $\mathsf{weight} : \mathbb{Z}^{L \cup E}$ *is a weight mapping giving for each edge a discrete weight and for each location a weight rate.*

A *clock valuation* is a mapping from X to $\mathbb{R}_{\geq 0}$. We denote by $\mathbf{0}$ the null valuation such that $\forall x, \mathbf{0}(x) = 0$. Given a clock x and $d \in \mathbb{R}_{\geq 0}$, $v + d$ is the valuation such that $\forall x, (v + d)(x) = v(x) + d$. Valuation $v - d$ is defined similarly. Given a set of clocks to reset to zero, R, $v[R]$ is the valuation such that $v[R](x) = 0$ if $x \in R$ and $v(x)$ otherwise.

Given a clock constraint g, we say that valuation v satisfies g, denoted by $v \models g$ if substituting each clock x with $v(x)$ in g gives a boolean expression that evaluates to true. In the sequel, we often slightly abuse the notations and denote also by g the set of valuations that satisfy g.

A state of a WTA is a tuple $(l, v, w) \in L \times \mathbb{R}_{\geq 0}^X \times \mathbb{R}$. The semantics of a WTA is a timed transition system [18]:

Definition 2 (Semantics of a WTA). *The semantics of WTA* $\mathcal{A} = (L, l_0, X, E, \mathsf{Inv}, \mathsf{weight})$ *is the timed transition system* $(\mathcal{Q}, q_0, \rightarrow)$ *where:*

- $\mathcal{Q}$ *is the subset of* $L \times \mathbb{R}_{\geq 0}^X \times \mathbb{R}$ *such that for all* $(l, v) \in \mathcal{Q}, v \models \mathsf{Inv}(l)$;
- $q_0 = (l_0, \mathbf{0}, 0)$;
- $\rightarrow$ *is a subset of* $\mathcal{Q} \times (E \cup \mathbb{R}_{\geq 0}) \times \mathcal{Q}$. *We write* $q \xrightarrow{\alpha} q'$ *to denote that* $(q, \alpha, q') \in \rightarrow$. *Relation* $\rightarrow$ *is decomposed as:*
  - *Discrete transitions: for* $e \in E$, $(l, v, w) \xrightarrow{e} (l', v', w')$ *iff* $e = (l, g, R, l') \in E$, *with* $v \models g$, $v' = v[R]$, *and* $w' = w + \mathsf{weight}(e)$;
  - *Time elapsing: for* $d \in \mathbb{R}_{\geq 0}$, $(l, v, w) \xrightarrow{d} (l, v', w')$ *iff* $v' = v + d$, *and* $w' = w + \mathsf{weight}(l) \cdot d$.

A *run* in a WTA is a possibly infinite sequence $\rho = q_1 \alpha_1 q_2 \alpha_2 \cdots$ such that for all i, $q_i \xrightarrow{\alpha_i} q_{i+1}$. We denote by $\mathsf{init}(\rho)$ the first state of run ρ. Similarly, $\mathsf{last}(\rho)$ denotes the last state of finite run ρ. We denote by $\mathsf{Runs}(q, \mathcal{A})$ the set of runs starting in state q and by $\mathsf{Runs}(\mathcal{A})$ the set $\mathsf{Runs}(q_0, \mathcal{A})$.

A state q is *reachable* if there exists a finite run ρ such that $\mathsf{init}(\rho) = q_0$ and $\mathsf{last}(\rho) = q$. A location l is reachable if (l, v, w) is reachable for some v and some w.

The weight of a finite run ρ is $\mathsf{weight}(\rho) = w' - w$ where (l, v, w) is the first state of ρ for some value of l and v, and (l', v', w') is the last state of ρ for some value of l' and v'.

Let $\mathsf{lastl}(\rho)$ denote the *location* of the last state in finite run ρ. The infimum weight to reach some location l is defined as $\mathsf{infweight}(l) = +\infty$ if l is not reachable, and $\mathsf{infweight}(l) = \inf_{\substack{\rho \in \mathsf{Runs}(\mathcal{A}) \\ \mathsf{lastl}(\rho)=l}} \mathsf{weight}(\rho)$ otherwise.

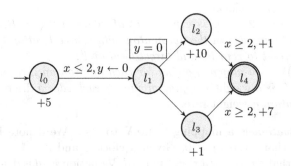

Fig. 1. A weighted timed automaton.

Example 1. Figure 1 presents a classical example of weighted timed automaton from [10]. Actually, it is a weighted timed game in that article but we treat it here as a WTA. It has two clocks x and y, constrained by the guards written on transitions (e.g. $x \leq 2$ from l_0 to l_1) and invariants (e.g. $\boxed{y = 0}$ on l_1), and possibly reset to zero (e.g. $y \leftarrow 0$ from l_0 to l_1). The initial location is l_0. Weight is updated discretely on transitions (on both transitions to l_4, $+1$ and $+7$) and with time with a derivative written below the location (e.g. $+5$ for l_0). When no such indication is present, we assume the weight is not updated. The minimum weight to reach l_4 by going through l_2 (and leaving it as soon as possible) is $5t + 10(2 - t) + 1 = 21 - 5t$, with $0 \leq t \leq 2$ the time spent in l_0. When going through l_3, it is $5t + (2 - t) + 7 = 9 + 4t$. Hence the minimum weight to reach l_4 is 9, obtained for $t = 0$ and by going through l_3.

In Sect. 3, we propose a backwards symbolic zone-based algorithm to compute $\mathsf{infweight}(l)$. Given a set of goal locations Goal, we assume that the weight of all runs to a location in Goal is uniformly lower-bounded: there exists a constant M such that $\forall l \in \mathsf{Goal}, \mathsf{infweight}(l) \geq M$. This condition in particular prevents negative weight cycles, the detection of which would make the algorithm more complex. For further informations see [11].

3   Weighted Symbolic Predecessor

There is in general an infinite number of states in a WTA. In order to provide an algorithm to compute infimum weights we group them into a finite number of *symbolic states*. Such a symbolic state consists of all the states that can be reached by taking a given sequence of edges (whatever the delays in between).

They are therefore defined by the common location l of all those states and the union $\mathcal{D}$ of all their valuations.

Assuming an arbitrary order on clocks, clock valuations can be seen as vectors of $\mathbb{R}_{\geq 0}^{|X|}$, where $|X|$ is the (finite) number of clocks. Set $\mathcal{D}$ is a convex polyhedron of $\mathbb{R}_{\geq 0}^{|X|}$ [10]. Its projection on clocks is defined as a conjunction of constraints of the form $x_i \sim k_{i0}$, $-x_i \sim k_{0i}$, or $x_i - x_j \sim k_{ij}$, with for all i, j, $x_i, x_j \in X, k_{ij} \in \mathbb{Z}$ and $\sim \in \{<, \leq\}$ [18]. Such a polyhedron is called a *zone*.

In [23], the authors prove that inequalities relating weight and clock variables can be computed and handled separately from the projection of Z on clock variables, and that polyhedron $\mathcal{D}$ can be represented by a finite union of *weighted zones*.

Definition 3 (Weighted Zone). *A weighted zone is a tuple $\mathcal{Z} = (Z, w, r)$ where:*

- *Z is a zone;*
- *w is the weight of the point in Z with infimum coordinates, called the offset, and noted Δ_Z (it exists and is unique due to the forms of the constraints shaping Z);*
- *$r \in \mathbb{Z}^X$ gives for each clock its contribution to the evolution of the weight for points in Z.*

Then for a given valuation $v \in \mathbb{R}_{\geq 0}^X$, the weight of the valuation in the weighted zone $\mathcal{Z}$ is:

$$\mathsf{Weight}(v, \mathcal{Z}) = w + \sum_{x \in X} r(x)(v(x) - \Delta_Z(x))$$

Now weighted symbolic states are represented by pairs of the form $(l, \mathcal{Z})$, and are subsets of the set of states $\mathcal{Q}$.

In the backward computation context, the weight of weighted zones will represent the (opposite of the) infimum remaining weight from a given valuation, to reach the goal. Thus, the weight of the null valuation in the weighted zone obtained in the initial location is exactly the opposite of the infimum weight to reach the goal from the initial state.

Definition 4. *Let $\mathcal{A} = (L, l_0, X, E, \mathsf{Inv}, \mathsf{weight})$ be a WTA. Let $e = (l, g, R, l')$ be an edge, and let $\mathcal{D}$ be a set of states of (the semantics of) $\mathcal{A}$. Then:*

$$\mathsf{Pred}_e(\mathcal{D}) = \{(l, v, w) \mid \exists (l', v', w') \in \mathcal{D} \text{ s. t. } (l, v, w) \xrightarrow{e} (l', v', w')\}$$

$$\mathsf{Pred}_\delta(\mathcal{D}) = \{(l, v, w) \mid \exists d \geq 0, (l', v', w') \in \mathcal{D}, \text{ s. t. } (l, v, w) \xrightarrow{d} (l', v', w')$$
$$\text{and } w = \sup\{w' - t \cdot \mathsf{weight}(l) \mid t \geq 0, (l, v + t, w') \in \mathcal{D}\}\}$$

Given a set of states D of an (unweighted) timed automaton, any point in the past of D is in general the time predecessor of an infinity of points in D (corresponding to infinitely many delays), Pred_δ computes one with an optimal weight among all of them.

Let $\mathsf{cl}(Z)$ denote the topological closure of zone Z. Note that if $\mathcal{D}$ is actually defined by a weighted zone $\mathcal{Z} = (Z, w, r)$, we can equivalently write the sup in Pred_δ as $\max\{\mathsf{Weight}(v + t, \mathcal{Z}) - t \cdot \mathsf{weight}(l) \mid t \geq 0, (l, v + t) \in \mathsf{cl}(Z)\}$. Moreover, if $\mathcal{Z}$ is unbounded then the supremum might not be finite and then the result of Pred_δ is empty.

In the following we will sometimes need to shrink a weighted zone by intersecting it with a non-weighted zone. This implies a change of offset.

Definition 5. *Let* $\mathcal{Z} = (Z, w, r)$ *be a weighted zone, and let* Z' *be a zone. Then* $\mathcal{Z} \cap Z'$ *is the weighted zone* (Z'', w'', r), *where* $Z'' = Z \cap Z'$, *and* $w'' = \mathsf{Weight}(\Delta_{Z''}, \mathcal{Z})$. *In particular, for a guard* g *we have* $\mathcal{Z} \cap g = (Z'', w'', r)$, *where* $Z'' = Z \wedge g$, *and* $w'' = \mathsf{Weight}(\Delta_{Z''}, \mathcal{Z})$.

Definition 6 (Facet). *The facets of the zone* Z *are the derived zones* $\mathsf{cl}(Z) \wedge (x = n)$, *for each constraint* $x \sim n$ *defining the zone. The facets can be grouped as follows:*

- *The facets defined by* lower *bounds on* individual *clocks,* $x \geq n$, *are called* lower facets, *and we denote* $\mathsf{LF}(Z)$ *the set of lower facets of* Z;
- *Similarly, the facets defined by* upper *bounds on* individual *clocks,* $x \leq n$, *are called* upper facets, *and we denote* $\mathsf{UF}(Z)$ *the set of upper facets of* Z.

In the following, for a weighted zone $\mathcal{Z} = (Z, w, r)$ *we denote by* $\mathsf{UF}(\mathcal{Z})$ *and* $\mathsf{LF}(\mathcal{Z})$ *the set of weighted zones defined naturally by* $\mathcal{F} \in \mathsf{UF}(\mathcal{Z})$ *(resp.* $\mathsf{LF}(\mathcal{Z})$) *iff there exists* $F \in \mathsf{UF}(Z)$ *(resp.* $\mathsf{LF}(Z)$) *s.t.* $\mathcal{F} = (F, w_F, r)$, *with* $w_F = \mathsf{Weight}(\Delta_F, \mathcal{Z})$.

In [17], the authors also define *relative* facets, corresponding to diagonal constraints, but we will not need them here.

Some more operations on weighted zones are required to compute the predecessors of weighted symbolic states.

First we need a relaxation operator to account for all clock valuations that might be predecessors of some valuations by an edge with a reset. This leads to an "inverse reset" operator.

Definition 7. *Let* $\mathcal{Z} = (Z, w, r)$ *be a weighted zone, and* $R \subseteq X$ *a subset of the clock set.*

We denote by $\mathsf{relax}_R(Z)$ *the zone* Z *from which all constraints (except non-negativity) on every clock in* R *are removed. That is:* $\mathsf{relax}_R(v) = \{v' \in \mathbb{R}_{\geq 0}^X | \forall x \notin R, \ v'(x) = v(x)\}$ *and* $\mathsf{relax}_R(Z) = \bigcup_{v \in Z} \mathsf{relax}_R(v)$.

Then the zone obtained by taking backward a reset of the clocks in R *is* $Z[R]^{-1} = \mathsf{relax}_R(Z \wedge (R = 0))$, *where* $R = 0$ *is a shorthand for* $\bigwedge_{y \in R}(y = 0)$.

We further define $\mathcal{Z}[R]^{-1} = (Z', w', r')$ *such that:* $Z' = Z[R]^{-1}$, $w' = w$, *and* $r'(x) = 0$ *if* $x \in R$ *and* $r(x)$ *otherwise.*

Second, we need to account for the past of clock valuations, that is valuations from which we can reach a given valuation (or a set of them) by some delay.

Definition 8. *Let* $\mathcal{Z} = (Z, w, r)$ *be a weighted zone, where* F *is a lower or upper facet of* Z, *derived from a constraint* $y \sim n$, *and* $\mathcal{F} = \mathcal{Z} \cap (y \sim n) = (F, w_F, r)$ *the related weighted zone. Let* $p \in \mathbb{Z}$ *be a weight-rate.*

Then, the past of Z is $Z^{\downarrow} = \{v \mid \exists d \in \mathbb{R}_{\geq 0}, \ v + d \in Z\}$.

And similarly, we define the past of $\mathcal{F}$ with rate p as $\mathcal{F}^{\downarrow p} = (Z', w', r')$ such that $Z' = F^{\downarrow}$, $r'(y) = -(\sum_{x \neq y} r(x) - p)$, $r'(x) = r(x)$ for every $x \neq y$, and $w' = w_F + \sum_{x \in X} r'(x) \cdot (\Delta_{Z'}(x) - \Delta_F(x))$.

The intuition behind w' is that we compute the weight of the new offset $\Delta_{Z'}$ relatively to the offset of the facet. Notice that in the case where F is a lower facet, we have $\Delta_F = \Delta_Z$ and $w_F = w$.

Finally, we define a notation for the subtraction of weight, on weighted zones.

Definition 9. *Let $\mathcal{Z} = (Z, w, r)$ be a weighted zone, and let $n \in \mathbb{Z}$. Then $\mathcal{Z} - n$ is the weighted zone $(Z, w - n, r)$.*

We now have all the tools to compute the Pred-operations on weighted symbolic states. We start with the action predecessor, i.e., predecessor by an edge.

Theorem 1 (Action Predecessor). *Let $\mathcal{A} = (L, l_0, X, E, \mathsf{Inv}, \mathsf{weight})$ be a WTA. Let $e = (l, g, R, l') \in E$, and let $\mathcal{Z}' = (Z', w', r')$ be a weighted zone. Then:*
$$\mathsf{Pred}_e((l', \mathcal{Z}')) = (l, (\mathcal{Z}'[R]^{-1} - \mathsf{weight}(e)) \cap g \cap \mathsf{Inv}(l))$$

Proof. If we forget about the weights, it is a classical result that symbolic states are closed under action predecessor operator. We assume that it is also the case for weighted symbolic states, and we prove that it is sufficient to have only one weighted symbolic state to describe the action predecessor of one weighted symbolic state (unlike for action Post-operator [17]).

We note $\mathsf{Pred}_e((l', \mathcal{Z}')) = (l, \mathcal{Z}_1)$ with $\mathcal{Z}_1 = (Z_1, w_1, r_1)$ and $(\mathcal{Z}'[R]^{-1} - \mathsf{weight}(e)) \cap g \cap \mathsf{Inv}(l) = \mathcal{Z}_2$ with $\mathcal{Z}_2 = (Z_2, w_2, r_2)$.

We want to prove that $\mathcal{Z}_1 = \mathcal{Z}_2$, which is equivalent to $Z_1 = Z_2$ and for every $v \in Z_1$, $\mathsf{Weight}(v, \mathcal{Z}_1) = \mathsf{Weight}(v, \mathcal{Z}_2)$. Equality $Z_1 = Z_2$ directly follows from the literature on timed automata (see, e.g., [12]), so we focus on weights. Note that with respect to that, the invariant plays no role since it cannot modify the zone offset due to its particular form.

Equality of Weight Offsets. We now prove that $w_1 = w_2$. Let $q = \mathsf{weight}(e)$.

Let us define Δ'_{Z_1} such that $(l, \Delta_{Z_1}) \xrightarrow{e} (l', \Delta'_{Z_1})$. By definition of Pred_e, we have: $w_1 = \mathsf{Weight}(\Delta_{Z_1}, \mathcal{Z}_1) = \mathsf{Weight}(\Delta'_{Z_1}, \mathcal{Z}') - q$. Thus, $w_1 = w' + \sum_{x \in X} r'(x)(\Delta'_{Z_1}(x) - \Delta_{Z'}(x)) - q$. But, $\Delta'_{Z_1} = \Delta_{Z_1}[R]$, so $\Delta'_{Z_1}(x) = 0$ if $x \in R$ and $\Delta_{Z_1}(x)$ if $x \notin R$. And $Z' \wedge (R = 0) \neq \emptyset$ (otherwise the transition e would not have been taken), therefore $\forall x \in R$, $\Delta_{Z'}(x) = 0$. So we obtain: $w_1 = w' + \sum_{x \notin R} r'(x)(\Delta_{Z_1}(x) - \Delta_{Z'}(x)) - q$.

Besides, we have, by definition of the operations $\mathcal{Z} \cap g$, and $\mathcal{Z} - q$, $w_2 = \mathsf{Weight}(\Delta_{Z_2}, \mathcal{Z}'[R]^{-1}) - q$. We note $\mathcal{Z}_3 = \mathcal{Z}'[R]^{-1} = (Z_3, w_3, r_3)$. We have, by definition of the operation $[R]^{-1}$: $Z_3 = Z'[R]^{-1}$ (thus $\Delta_{Z_3} = \Delta_{Z'}$), and $w_3 = w'$, and $r_3(x) = 0$ if $x \in R$ and $r'(x)$ if $x \notin R$. So, it gives $\forall v \in Z_3$, $\mathsf{Weight}(v, \mathcal{Z}_3) = w' + \sum_{x \notin R} r'(x)(v(x) - \Delta_{Z'}(x))$. Finally, we obtain:
$$w_2 = w' + \sum_{x \notin R} r'(x)(\Delta_{Z_2}(x) - \Delta_{Z'}(x)) - q$$
As $Z_1 = Z_2$, we have $\Delta_{Z_1} = \Delta_{Z_2}$, so we can conclude that $w_1 = w_2$.

Equality of Weight. We finally prove that for any $v \in Z_1$, $\mathsf{Weight}(v, \mathcal{Z}_1) = \mathsf{Weight}(v, \mathcal{Z}_2)$.

Let $v \in Z_1$, then $\exists v' \in Z'$ such that $(l, v) \xrightarrow{e} (l', v')$ and $\mathsf{Weight}(v, \mathcal{Z}_1) = \mathsf{Weight}(v', \mathcal{Z}') - q$. Thus we have: $w_1 + \sum_{x \in X} r_1(x)(v(x) - \Delta_{Z_1}(x)) = w' + \sum_{x \in X} r'(x)(v'(x) - \Delta_{Z'}(x)) - q$. Yet $w_1 = w' + \sum_{x \notin R} r'(x)(\Delta_{Z_1}(x) - \Delta_{Z'}(x)) - q$, so by injecting the value of w_1 we obtain: $\sum_{x \in X} r_1(x)(v(x) - \Delta_{Z_1}(x)) = \sum_{x \in R} r'(x)(v'(x) - \Delta_{Z'}(x)) + \sum_{x \notin R} r'(x) (v'(x) - \Delta_{Z'}(x) - (\Delta_{Z_1}(x) - \Delta_{Z'}(x)))$. Moreover, $\forall x \in R, v'(x) = \Delta_{Z'}(x) = 0$ and $\forall x \notin R, v'(x) = v(x)$, therefore we get: $\sum_{x \in X} r_1(x)(v(x) - \Delta_{Z_1}(x)) = \sum_{x \notin R} r'(x)(v(x) - \Delta_{Z_1}(x))$ and, by adding w_1 to both sides, this gives: $\mathsf{Weight}(v, \mathcal{Z}_1) = w_1 + \sum_{x \notin R} r'(x)(v(x) - \Delta_{Z_1}(x))$.

Moreover, $r_2(x) = 0$ if $x \in R$ and $r'(x)$ otherwise, by definition of $\mathcal{Z}_2$. Thus, the weight in $\mathcal{Z}_2$ is: $\mathsf{Weight}(v, \mathcal{Z}_2) = w_2 + \sum_{x \notin R} r'(x)(v(x) - \Delta_{Z_2}(x))$. Since $w_1 = w_2$ and $\Delta_{Z_1} = \Delta_{Z_2}$, this finally gives $\mathsf{Weight}(v, \mathcal{Z}_1) = \mathsf{Weight}(v, \mathcal{Z}_2)$.   □

As for the time Post-operator [17], weighted symbolic states are not directly closed under Pred_δ operator: a split of the weighted zone is needed. For example, let us consider the weighted zone (Z, w, r) depicted in Fig. 2, with $w = -3$, $r(x) = 2$ and $r(y) = -1$. If we want to compute the time predecessor of this weighted zone in l_1 with a weight rate of 3, we will have to split $Z^\downarrow$ in three subzones: Z, $F_1^\downarrow = (Z^\downarrow \setminus Z) \wedge (x - y \leq 1)$ and $F_2^\downarrow = (Z^\downarrow \setminus Z) \wedge (x - y \geq 1)$.

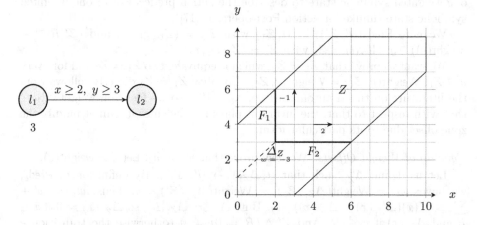

Fig. 2. Example of time predecessor of a weighted zone

The following theorem formalizes this intuition and gives an expression to compute the Pred_δ operator.

Theorem 2 (Time Predecessor). *Let* $\mathcal{A} = (L, l_0, X, E, \mathsf{Inv}, \mathsf{weight})$ *be a WTA. Let* $l \in L$, *with* $\mathsf{weight}(l) = p$, $\mathsf{Inv}(l) = J$, *and let* $\mathcal{Z}' = (Z', w', r')$ *be a weighted zone. Then:*

$$\mathsf{Pred}_\delta((l, Z')) = \begin{cases} (l, Z') \cup \bigcup_{\mathcal{F} \in \mathsf{LF}(Z')}(l, \mathcal{F}^{\downarrow p} \cap J), & \text{if } p \geq \sum_{x \in X} r'(x) \\ \bigcup_{\mathcal{F} \in \mathsf{UF}(Z')}(l, \mathcal{F}^{\downarrow p} \cap J), & \text{if } p < \sum_{x \in X} r'(x) \end{cases}$$

To prove Theorem 2, we need three technical lemmas.

Lemma 1. *Let Z be a zone. Then the following holds:*

1. *if $\mathsf{UF}(Z) \neq \emptyset$, then $Z^\downarrow \subseteq \bigcup_{F \in \mathsf{UF}(Z)} F^\downarrow$*
2. *$Z^\downarrow \subseteq Z \cup \bigcup_{F \in \mathsf{LF}(Z)} F^\downarrow$*

Proof. 1. Assume $\mathsf{UF}(Z) \neq \emptyset$. So there exists some facets $F_i = (x_i = n_i) \wedge Z$ for $x_i \in X$, $n_i \in \mathbb{N}$, and $x_i \leq n_i$ the upper constraints of Z.

Consider $v \in Z^\downarrow$. Then there exists $d \geq 0$ such that $v + d \in Z$. In particular, the latter satisfies the constraint of the upper bound constraints. For the corresponding to F_i: $(v + d)(x_i) \leq n_i$. Let $d_m = \min_i(n_i - v(x_i))$. By construction $d_m \geq d \geq 0$. We prove that $v + d_m$ belongs to some upper facet. By definition of d_m, there exists x_j such that $v(x_j) + d_m = n_j$ and $\forall x_i \neq x_j$, $v(x_i) + d_m \leq n_i$, so $v + d_m$ satisfies the upper bound constraints of $\mathsf{cl}(Z)$.

Moreover, for every $x_i \in X$, and every lower bound constraint $(x_i \geq m_i)$ of $\mathsf{cl}(Z)$, $v + d \models (x_i \geq m_i)$, and since $d_m \geq d$, $v(x_i) + d_m \geq m_i$. Finally, diagonal constraints are trivially verified since $(v + d_m)(x_j) - (v + d_m)(x_k) = v(x_j) - v(x_k) = (v + d)(x_j) - (v + d)(x_k)$.

We conclude that $v + d_m \in \mathsf{cl}(Z)$ and $v + d_m \models (x_j = n_j)$, which means $v + d_m \in F_j$ and therefore $v \in F_j^\downarrow$. And, finally, $Z^\downarrow \subseteq \bigcup_{F \in \mathsf{UF}(Z)} F^\downarrow$.

2. In the sequel, we write $\prec$ for an element of $\{<, \leq\}$ and $\succ$ for an element of $\{>, \geq\}$. Let $v \in Z^\downarrow$, then $\exists d \in \mathbb{R}_{\geq 0}$ such that $v + d \in Z$. Then for every $x_i \in X$, if $(x_i \succ m_i)$ is the corresponding lower bound constraint of Z, then $v + d \models (x_i \succ m_i)$. Let $d_M = \max_{x_i \in X}(m_i - v(x_i))$.

If $d_M \leq 0$ then $\forall x_i$, $m_i - v(x_i) \leq d_M \leq 0$ so $v(x_i) \geq m_i$. Yet $\forall x_i$, if $(x_i \prec m_i)$ is the corresponding upper bound constraint of Z, then $v + d \models (x_i \prec n_i)$ and then $v(x_i) \prec n_i$. Similarly any diagonal constraint $(x_i - x_j \prec p_{ij})$ of Z is also satisfied by $v + d$, and thus by v since $v(x_i) + d - (v(x_j) + d) = v(x_i) - v(x_j)$. So $v \in Z$.

Otherwise, $d_M > 0$. By definition of d_m, there exists x_j such that $v(x_j) + d_M = m_j$ and $\forall x_i \neq x_j$, $v(x_i) + d_M \geq m_i$. Yet $\forall x_i \in X$, $d \geq m_i - v(x_i)$, in particular $d \geq m_j - v(x_j) = d_M$. So for every x_i, $v(x_i) + d_M \leq v(x_i) + d \leq n_i$. As before, $v + d_M$ also trivially satisfies the diagonal constraints of $\mathsf{cl}(Z)$ and therefore, $v + d_M \in \mathsf{cl}(Z)$ and $v + d_M \models (x_j = m_j)$. So $v + d_M \in F_j$ with $F_j = \mathsf{cl}(Z) \wedge (x_j = m_j) \in \mathsf{LF}(Z)$. Therefore $v \in F_j^\downarrow$, and finally $v \in \bigcup_{F \in \mathsf{LF}(Z)} F^\downarrow$. $\square$

Lemma 2. *Let Z be a zone, and F be a facet of Z derived from a constraint on a single clock $x \sim n$. Let $v \in F^\downarrow$. Then there exists d_F such that $v + d_F \in F$. And the following holds:*

1. if $F \in \mathsf{LF}(Z)$, then $d_F = \min_{\substack{d \geq 0 \\ v+d \in \mathsf{cl}(Z)}}$ (d)

2. if $F \in \mathsf{UF}(Z)$, then $d_F = \max_{\substack{d \geq 0 \\ v+d \in \mathsf{cl}(Z)}}$ (d)

Proof. The facet is defined by $F = \mathsf{cl}(Z) \wedge (x = n)$. Thus, $v + d_F \in F$ gives $v(x) + d_F = n$.

1. $F \in \mathsf{LF}(Z)$: Assume there exists $d \in \mathbb{R}_{\geq 0}$ such that $v + d \in \mathsf{cl}(Z)$ and $d < d_F$. We have in particular $v(x) + d < v(x) + d_F = n$, therefore $v + d$ does not satisfy the guard ($x \geq n$), hence $v + d \notin \mathsf{cl}(Z)$. This is a contradiction, and the result follows.

2. $F \in \mathsf{UF}(Z)$: Assume there exists $d \in \mathbb{R}_{\geq 0}$ such that $v + d \in \mathsf{cl}(Z)$ and $d > d_F$. We have in particular $v(x) + d > v(x) + d_F = n$, therefore $v + d$ does not satisfy the guard ($x \leq n$), hence $v + d \notin \mathsf{cl}(Z)$. This is a contradiction, and the result follows. □

Lemma 3. *Let $\mathcal{Z} = (Z, w, r)$ be a weighted zone, F be a lower or upper facet of Z, derived from a constraint $y \sim n$, with $\sim \in \{<, \leq, \geq, >\}$, and $\mathcal{F} = (F, w, r)$ be the corresponding weighted zone. Let $p \in \mathbb{N}$ be a weight-rate.*
Then, $\mathsf{Weight}(v, \mathcal{F}^{\downarrow p}) = \mathsf{Weight}(v + d_F, \mathcal{Z}) - d_F \cdot p$, with $d_F = n - v(y)$.

Proof. Writing $m = \sum_{x \in X} r(x) - p$, we have:

$$
\begin{aligned}
\mathsf{Weight}(v + d_F, \mathcal{Z}) - d_F \cdot p &= w + \sum_{x \in X} r(x)(v(x) + d_F - \Delta_Z(x)) - d_F \cdot p \\
&= w + \sum_{x \in X} r(x)(v(x) - \Delta_Z(x)) + d_F \cdot m \\
&= w + \sum_{x \in X} r(x)(v(x) - \Delta_Z(x)) - m \cdot (v(y) - n)
\end{aligned}
$$

Moreover, F is derived from the constraint $y \sim n$, we have $\Delta_F(y) = n$. Then, $\mathsf{Weight}(v + d_F, \mathcal{Z}) - d_F \cdot p$ can be rewritten as:

$$
\begin{aligned}
\mathsf{Weight}(v + d_F, \mathcal{Z}) - d_F \cdot p &= w + \sum_{x \in X} r(x)(v(x) - \Delta_Z(x)) - m \cdot (v(y) - \Delta_F(y)) \\
&= w + \sum_{x \in X} r(x)(\Delta_F(x) - \Delta_Z(x)) + \sum_{x \in X} r(x)(v(x) - \Delta_F(x)) - m \cdot (v(y) - \Delta_F(y)) \\
&= w_F + \sum_{x \neq y} r(x)(v(x) - \Delta_F(x)) - (\sum_{x \neq y} r(x) - p) \cdot (v(y) - \Delta_F(y))
\end{aligned}
$$

Let us denote by (Z', w', r') the weighted zone $\mathcal{F}^{\downarrow p}$. Then by definition $r'(y) = -(\sum_{x \neq y} r(x) - p)$ and $\forall x \neq y$, $r'(x) = r(x)$:

$$
\mathsf{Weight}(v + d_F, \mathcal{Z}) - d_F \cdot p = w_F + \sum_{x \in X} r'(x)(v(x) - \Delta_F(x))
$$

Recall that the weight w' of the offset $\Delta_{Z'}$ of $\mathcal{F}^{\downarrow p}$ is defined as:

$$w' = w_F + \sum_{x \in X} r'(x)(\Delta_{Z'}(x) - \Delta_F(x))$$

So finally:

$$\mathsf{Weight}(v + d_F, \mathcal{Z}) - d_F \cdot p = w' + \sum_{x \in X} r'(x)(v(x) - \Delta_{Z'}(x)) = \mathsf{Weight}(v, \mathcal{F}^{\downarrow p})$$

$\square$

Proof (Theorem 2). In order to prove this theorem we proceed by double inclusion.

$\subseteq$ Let $(l, v, w) \in \mathsf{Pred}_\delta((l, \mathcal{Z}'))$. Then there exists $d \in \mathbb{R}_{\geq 0}$ such that $v + d \in Z'$, by definition of Pred_δ, and therefore $v \in Z'^{\downarrow}$. Also, by definition of Pred_δ, we have:

$$w = \max\{\mathsf{Weight}(v + t, \mathcal{Z}') - t \cdot \mathsf{weight}(l) \mid t \geq 0, v + t \in \mathsf{cl}(Z')\}$$

For every $t \in \mathbb{R}_{\geq 0}$, writing $m = \sum_{x \in X} r'(x) - p$, we have:

$$
\begin{aligned}
\mathsf{Weight}(v + t, \mathcal{Z}') - t \cdot \mathsf{weight}(l) &= w' + \sum_{x \in X} r'(x)(v(x) + t - \Delta_{Z'}(x)) - t \cdot p \\
&= w' + \sum_{x \in X} r'(x)(v(x) - \Delta_{Z'}(x)) + t \cdot m \\
&= \mathsf{Weight}(v, \mathcal{Z}') + t \cdot m
\end{aligned}
$$

In order to maximize this, we consider the derivative $m = \sum_{x \in X} r'(x) - p$.

- If $p \geq \sum_{x \in X} r'(x)$: Then we need to minimize t. Lemma 1 gives $v \in Z' \cup \bigcup_{F \in \mathsf{LF}(Z')} F^{\downarrow}$.
  - **If** $v \in Z'$: Then, we can take $t = 0$ to minimize the weight, and we obtain $w = \mathsf{Weight}(v, \mathcal{Z}')$. Thus $(l, v, w) \in (l, \mathcal{Z}')$.
  - **Else** $v \in \bigcup_{F \in \mathsf{LF}(Z')} F^{\downarrow}$: Then, there exists $F \in \mathsf{LF}(Z')$ such that $v \in F^{\downarrow}$. Facet F is defined by $F = \mathsf{cl}(Z') \wedge (y = n)$, with $y \in X$ and $n \in \mathbb{N}$. Then, $v \in F^{\downarrow}$ gives that there exists $d_F \in \mathbb{R}_{\geq 0}$ s.t. $v + d_F \in F$. Thus, $v(y) + d_F = n$. Lemma 2 gives that d_F is the minimal value of d such that $d \geq 0$ and $v + d \in \mathsf{cl}(Z')$.
    Then, if we note $\mathcal{F} = (F, w', r')$, we have $v \in F^{\downarrow}$. Moreover $w = \mathsf{Weight}(v + d_F, \mathcal{Z}') - d_F \cdot p$, thus Lemma 3 gives $w = \mathsf{Weight}(v, \mathcal{F}^{\downarrow p})$. Finally, $v \models J$ by definition of the time predecessor, thus $(l, v, w) \in (l, \mathcal{F}^{\downarrow p} \cap J)$.
- **Else** $p < \sum_{x \in X} r'(x)$: Then we need to maximize t.
  Let us suppose that $\mathsf{UF}(Z') = \emptyset$. Then $\bigcup_{\mathcal{F} \in \mathsf{UF}(Z')}(l, \mathcal{F}^{\downarrow p} \cap J) = \emptyset$. Let t_M the value of t that maximizes the weight, that is to say $w = \mathsf{Weight}(v + t_M, \mathcal{Z}') - t_M \cdot \mathsf{weight}(l)$ and $v + t_M \in \mathsf{cl}(Z')$. Let $\epsilon > 0$, then $v + t_M + \epsilon \in \mathsf{cl}(Z')$ because Z' has no upper facet. Moreover, because $t_M + \epsilon > t_M$ and

because $\sum_{x \in X} r'(x) - p > 0$, we have $\mathsf{Weight}(v + t_M + \epsilon, \mathcal{Z}') - (t_M + \epsilon) \cdot \mathsf{weight}(l) > \mathsf{Weight}(v + t_M, \mathcal{Z}') - t_M \cdot \mathsf{weight}(l)$. Which means that t_M does not maximize the weight: $\mathsf{Weight}(v, \mathcal{Z}) < \mathsf{Weight}(v + t_M, \mathcal{Z}') + t_M \cdot \mathsf{weight}(l)$. So the supremum in the expression of Pred_δ is infinite and $\mathsf{Pred}_\delta((l, \mathcal{Z}')) = \emptyset$ also (and we actually could not take a point from it).

Assume now that $\mathsf{UF}(Z') \neq \emptyset$. Lemma 1 gives $v \in \bigcup_{F \in \mathsf{UF}(Z')} F^\downarrow$. Then, there exists $F \in \mathsf{UF}(Z')$ such that $v \in F^\downarrow$. Facet F is defined by $F = \mathsf{cl}(Z') \wedge (y = n)$, with $y \in X$ and $n \in \mathbb{N}$. Then, $v \in F^\downarrow$ gives that there exists $d_F \in \mathbb{R}_{\geq 0}$ s.t. $v + d_F \in F = \mathsf{cl}(Z') \wedge (y = n)$. Thus, $v(y) + d_F = n$. Lemma 2 gives that d_F is the maximal value of d such that $d \geq 0$ and $v + d \in \mathsf{cl}(Z')$.

Thus, if we note $\mathcal{F} = (F, w', r')$, we have $w = \mathsf{Weight}(v + d_F, \mathcal{Z}') + d_F \cdot p$, thus Lemma 3 gives $w = \mathsf{Weight}(v, \mathcal{F}^{\downarrow p})$ and $(v, w) \in \mathcal{F}^{\downarrow p}$. Moreover, $v \models J$ by definition of the time predecessor, thus $v \in \mathcal{F}^{\downarrow p} \cap J$. Therefore, $(l, v, w) \in (l, \mathcal{F}^{\downarrow p} \cap J)$.

This concludes the proof for the left-to-right inclusion.

$\boxed{\supseteq}$ Consider now the right-to-left inclusion:

- **If** $p \geq \sum_{x \in X} r'(x)$: Let $(l, v, w) \in (l, \mathcal{Z}' \cap J) \cup \bigcup_{\mathcal{F} \in \mathsf{LF}(\mathcal{Z}')} (l, \mathcal{F}^{\downarrow p} \cap J)$. We still have $\mathsf{Weight}(v + t, \mathcal{Z}') - t \cdot \mathsf{weight}(l) = \mathsf{Weight}(v, \mathcal{Z}') + t \cdot (\sum_{x \in X} r'(x) - p)$, for every $t \in \mathbb{R}_{\geq 0}$.
  - **If** $(l, v, w) \in (l, \mathcal{Z}')$: Then, we have $v \in \mathcal{Z}'$, so there exists $d \in \mathbb{R}_{\geq 0}$ s.t. $v + d \in \mathcal{Z}'$ ($d = 0$). Also, since $\sum_{x \in X} r'(x) - p \leq 0$, the maximum of $\mathsf{Weight}(v, \mathcal{Z}') + t \cdot (\sum_{x \in X} r'(x) - p)$ is obtained for $t = 0$, thus $w = \mathsf{Weight}(v, \mathcal{Z}')$. We thus have $(l, v, w) \in \mathsf{Pred}_\delta((l, \mathcal{Z}'))$.
  - **Else** $\exists \mathcal{F} \in \mathsf{LF}(\mathcal{Z}')$ s.t. $(l, v, w) \in (l, \mathcal{F}^{\downarrow p} \cap J)$: We note $\mathcal{F} = (F, w', r')$, with $F = \mathsf{cl}(Z') \wedge (y = n)$. Then $v \in F^\downarrow$, thus $\exists d \in \mathbb{R}_{\geq 0}$ s.t. $v + d \in F \subseteq \mathsf{cl}(Z')$. Moreover, $v \models J$ because $v \in F^\downarrow \wedge J$. Then, Lemma 3 gives $w = \mathsf{Weight}(v, \mathcal{F}^{\downarrow p}) = \mathsf{Weight}(v + d_F, \mathcal{Z}) - d_F \cdot p$, with $d_F = n - v(y)$. Also, we have $v + d_F \in F \subseteq \mathsf{cl}(Z')$ (because $v(y) + d_F = n$). Furthermore d_F is the minimal $d \geq 0$ such that $v + d \in \mathsf{cl}(Z')$ according to lemma 2. Then $w = \max\{\mathsf{Weight}(v + t, \mathcal{Z}') - t \cdot \mathsf{weight}(l) \mid t \geq 0, v + t \in \mathsf{cl}(Z')\}$, and finally $(l, v, w) \in \mathsf{Pred}_\delta((l, \mathcal{Z}'))$
- **Else** $p < \sum_{x \in X} r'(x)$: Then $\exists \mathcal{F} \in \mathsf{UF}(\mathcal{Z}')$ s.t. $(l, v, w) \in (l, \mathcal{F}^{\downarrow p} \cap J)$, we note $\mathcal{F} = (F, w', r')$, with $F = \mathsf{cl}(Z') \wedge (y = n)$. We still have $\mathsf{Weight}(v + t, \mathcal{Z}') - t \cdot \mathsf{weight}(l) = \mathsf{Weight}(v, \mathcal{Z}') + t \cdot (\sum_{x \in X} r'(x) - p)$, for every $t \in \mathbb{R}_{\geq 0}$. First $v \in F^\downarrow$, thus $\exists d \in \mathbb{R}_{\geq 0}$ s.t. $v + d \in F \subseteq \mathsf{cl}(Z')$. Second, $v \models J$ because $v \in F^\downarrow \wedge J$. Then, Lemma 3 gives $w = \mathsf{Weight}(v, \mathcal{F}^{\downarrow p}) = \mathsf{Weight}(v + d_F, \mathcal{Z}) - d_F \cdot p$, with $d_F = n - v(y)$. Also, we have $v + d_F \in F \subseteq \mathsf{cl}(Z')$ (because $v(y) + d_F = n$). Furthermore d_F is the maximal $d \geq 0$ such that $v + d \in \mathcal{Z}'$ according to Lemma 2. Then as $\sum_{x \in X} r'(x) - p > 0$, we indeed have $w = \max\{\mathsf{Weight}(v + t, \mathcal{Z}') - t \cdot \mathsf{weight}(l) \mid t \geq 0, v + t \in \mathsf{cl}(Z')\}$, and finally $(l, v, w) \in \mathsf{Pred}_\delta((l, \mathcal{Z}'))$. □

Using the Pred_δ and Pred_e operators, we can straightforwardly adapt the algorithm of [23] to work backwards, which gives Algorithm 1.

Starting from a set of goal locations Goal, we build initial set of symbolic states by combining with each of these locations the universal zone $\mathbb{R}_{\geq 0}^X$ (defined by all clocks should be non-negative) on set of clocks X, with a weight uniformly equal to 0.

The algorithm works as usual with a passed list PASSED and a waiting list WAITING. At each iteration, we pick a waiting symbolic state and if it contains the initial state of the automaton, which is then necessarily the offset of the zone, we check if the corresponding weight (the opposite of the weight of the offset since we start from 0 at the goal and subtract the weights as we go backwards) is better than the current value of WEIGHT. If so we update WEIGHT.

Then we add all predecessors of the current symbolic state to the waiting list, unless some bigger and cheaper symbolic state has already been visited.

To capture this last notion of bigger and cheaper we use the classical subsumption operator $\preccurlyeq$ defined as:

Definition 10. *Let* $(l, \mathcal{Z})$, *with* $\mathcal{Z} = (Z, w, r)$, *and* $(l', \mathcal{Z}')$, *with* $\mathcal{Z}' = (Z', w', r')$ *be two symbolic states. We say that* $(l, \mathcal{Z})$ *is subsumed by* $(l', \mathcal{Z}')$, *and we write* $(l, \mathcal{Z}) \preccurlyeq (l', \mathcal{Z}')$, *if: (1)* $l = l'$, *(2)* $Z \subseteq Z'$ *and (3) for all* $v \in Z$, $\mathsf{Weight}(v, \mathcal{Z}) \leq \mathsf{Weight}(v, \mathcal{Z}')$.

In the usual definition the weight in $\mathcal{Z}$ would be higher than in $\mathcal{Z}'$ but remember that our weight is the *opposite* of the remaining weight to the goal.

Algorithm 1. Symbolic algorithm for optimal weight

1: WEIGHT $\leftarrow +\infty$
2: PASSED $\leftarrow \emptyset$
3: WAITING $\leftarrow \{(l, (\mathbb{R}_{\geq 0}^X, 0, \mathbf{0})) \mid l \in \mathsf{Goal}\}$
4: **while** WAITING $\neq \emptyset$ **do**
5:     select and remove $S = (l, (Z, w, r))$ from WAITING
6:     **if** $l = l_0$ **and** $\mathbf{0} \in Z$ **and** $-w <$ WEIGHT **then**
7:         WEIGHT $\leftarrow -w$
8:     **end if**
9:     **if** for all $S' \in$ PASSED, $S \not\preccurlyeq S'$ **then**
10:         add S to PASSED
11:         for all $e = (l, g, R, l') \in E$, for all $S' \in \mathsf{Pred}_\delta(\mathsf{Pred}_e(S))$, add S' to WAITING
12:     **end if**
13: **end while**
14: **return** WEIGHT

Algorithm 1 has the classical advantage of exploring only co-reachable states (but may of course explore non-reachable states). Also in contrast to the discrete successor operator for weighted symbolic states, the Pred_e operator never splits zones. Finally, zone abstraction/normalization is not necessary to ensure termination when computing backwards [12,16], while it should be handled carefully when working forward [11].

4 Implementation and Experiments

We have implemented the technique in Roméo [20]. The implementation and all
the benchmarks presented here are freely available[3]. Note that Roméo is a tool
designed for time Petri nets, a model close to timed automata, but with some
expressiveness differences [5]. The zone graph techniques are however perfectly
usable for time Petri nets [15]. The forward technique of [17] is not implemented
in Roméo, so we instead compare with the similar forward technique presented
in [8]. Also, since Roméo deals with Petri nets, where markings can be seen as
the values of a finite set of integer variables, a purely backward method would be
impractical as explained in the introduction, so we have implemented a mixed
forward backward approach in which we first precompute the reachable state-
space and then compute backward on this. Therefore, for the comparison to be
fair, we look at examples with negative costs (but no negative cycles), for which
the whole state-space would have to be explored anyway.

First we look at the aircraft landing problem described in [4]. The modelling
with a Petri-net like model (even using also additional integer variables) is fairly
different from the original one: in particular we cannot test a global clock without
resetting it with time Petri nets. In accordance with the above comments, we
have also made it so that planes that land early actually get some bonus (negative
cost). For all these reasons, we had to limit to a small subset of the planes in
the original model to get some reasonable performances.

Second we look at the scheduling example of [8], in which we need to execute
some periodic task set, on two processors, possibly using renewable energy (which
counts as a negative cost), the availability of which depends on meteorological
conditions. We add an additional constraints that instances of tasks should not
overlap, which reduces the state-space quite a bit.

Both approaches give the same results on all examples, which is a good point.
The results are presented in Table 1.

Table 1. Results on an Intel Core i7-7700 CPU @ 3.60 GHz with 32 GB of RAM.

Aircrafts/tasks		Landing				Scheduling			
		3	4	5	6	2	3	4	5
Forward	Time (s)	1	4	14	50	1	17	196	1044
	Mem. (MB)	8	48	205	756	17	177	1501	5826
Backward	Time (s)	<1	6	46	322	<1	6	50	251
	Mem. (MB)	17	112	504	1804	13	61	209	504

We see that for the aircraft landing problem, the forward approach performs
clearly better, though both techniques scale exponentially with the number of
aircrafts (and hence of clocks, as expected). In the scheduling problem, for the

---

[3] http://romeo.rts-software.org/releases/FORMATS2020.tgz.

original problem of [8], with 4 tasks, we get 60 s (785 MB) forward and 52 s (402 MB) backward. If we increase the execution time of task 2 from 4 to 16 (reaching a utilization factor of 1 for processor 1 if it were alone), we get the numbers in Table 1, where the backward approach is now clearly better.

We conjecture the performance is heavily impacted by the size of the co-reachable state-space. For the aircraft problem, using internal statistics, we estimate the number of co-reachable states to represent more than 80% of the reachable state-space, while we estimate it to less than 50% in the scheduling problem. It is even less (around 35%) for the original version but most of the time (around 65%) is used for the state-space precomputation, which is much bigger than with the modified task 2 (where the precomputation only takes 15% of the total time).

5   Conclusion

We have proposed extensions of the classical backwards operators for timed automata so that they can compute the remaining weight to some goal location in a weighted setting. This allows us to devise a backwards optimal cost reachability algorithm.

On the practical side, we have implemented the algorithm in the tool Roméo, and we have reported on its performance on two (slightly modified) case-studies from the literature. This experimental evaluation shows that the algorithm may outperform the classical forward approach, in particular, as could be expected, when the set of co-reachable states is significantly smaller than the set reachable states.

While this algorithm has advantages on its own, it is also a step towards symbolic and efficient verification and optimization for more expressive properties and we now want to investigate timed computation tree logic and controllability.

References

1. Alur, R., Dill, D.: A theory of timed automata. Theor. Comput. Sci. **126**(2), 183–235 (1994)
2. Alur, R., La Torre, S., Pappas, G.J.: Optimal paths in weighted timed automata. In: Di Benedetto, M.D., Sangiovanni-Vincentelli, A. (eds.) HSCC 2001. LNCS, vol. 2034, pp. 49–62. Springer, Heidelberg (2001). https://doi.org/10.1007/3-540-45351-2_8
3. Behrmann, G., et al.: Minimum-cost reachability for priced time automata. In: Di Benedetto, M.D., Sangiovanni-Vincentelli, A. (eds.) HSCC 2001. LNCS, vol. 2034, pp. 147–161. Springer, Heidelberg (2001). https://doi.org/10.1007/3-540-45351-2_15
4. Behrmann, G., Larsen, K.G., Rasmussen, J.I.: Optimal scheduling using priced timed automata. SIGMETRICS Perform. Eval. Rev. **32**(4), 34–40 (2005)
5. Bérard, B., Cassez, F., Haddad, S., Lime, D., Roux, O.H.: The expressive power of time Petri nets. Theor. Comput. Sci. **474**, 1–20 (2013)

6. Berendsen, J., Jansen, D.N., Katoen, J.: Probably on time and within budget: on reachability in priced probabilistic timed automata. In: 3rd International Conference on the Quantitative Evaluation of Systems (QEST 2006), pp. 311–322. IEEE Computer Society, Riverside (September 2006)

7. Berendsen, J., Jansen, D.N., Vaandrager, F.W.: Fortuna: model checking priced probabilistic timed automata. In: 7th International Conference on the Quantitative Evaluation of Systems (QEST 2010), pp. 273–281. IEEE Computer Society, Williamsburg (September 2010)

8. Boucheneb, H., Lime, D., Parquier, B., Roux, O.H., Seidner, C.: Optimal reachability in cost time Petri nets. In: Abate, A., Geeraerts, G. (eds.) FORMATS 2017. LNCS, vol. 10419, pp. 58–73. Springer, Cham (2017). https://doi.org/10.1007/978-3-319-65765-3_4

9. Bouyer, P.: Untameable timed automata!. In: Alt, H., Habib, M. (eds.) STACS 2003. LNCS, vol. 2607, pp. 620–631. Springer, Heidelberg (2003). https://doi.org/10.1007/3-540-36494-3_54

10. Bouyer, P., Cassez, F., Fleury, E., Larsen, K.G.: Optimal strategies in priced timed game automata. In: Lodaya, K., Mahajan, M. (eds.) FSTTCS 2004. LNCS, vol. 3328, pp. 148–160. Springer, Heidelberg (2004). https://doi.org/10.1007/978-3-540-30538-5_13

11. Bouyer, P., Colange, M., Markey, N.: Symbolic optimal reachability in weighted timed automata. In: Chaudhuri, S., Farzan, A. (eds.) CAV 2016. LNCS, vol. 9779, pp. 513–530. Springer, Cham (2016). https://doi.org/10.1007/978-3-319-41528-4_28

12. Bouyer, P., Laroussinie, F.: Model checking timed automata. In: Modeling and Verification of Real-time Systems, pp. 111–140. ISTE - Wiley (2008)

13. Cassez, F., David, A., Fleury, E., Larsen, K.G., Lime, D.: Efficient on-the-fly algorithms for the analysis of timed games. In: Abadi, M., de Alfaro, L. (eds.) CONCUR 2005. LNCS, vol. 3653, pp. 66–80. Springer, Heidelberg (2005). https://doi.org/10.1007/11539452_9

14. Enevoldsen, S., Guldstrand Larsen, K., Srba, J.: Abstract dependency graphs and their application to model checking. In: Vojnar, T., Zhang, L. (eds.) TACAS 2019. LNCS, vol. 11427, pp. 316–333. Springer, Cham (2019). https://doi.org/10.1007/978-3-030-17462-0_18

15. Gardey, G., Roux, O.H., Roux, O.F.: State space computation and analysis of time Petri nets. Theory Pract. Logic Program. (TPLP) **6**(3), 301–320 (2006). Special Issue on Specification Analysis and Verification of Reactive Systems

16. Herbreteau, F., Srivathsan, B., Walukiewicz, I.: Better abstractions for timed automata. Inf. Comput. **251**, 67–90 (2016)

17. Larsen, K., et al.: As cheap as possible: effcient cost-optimal reachability for priced timed automata. In: Berry, G., Comon, H., Finkel, A. (eds.) CAV 2001. LNCS, vol. 2102, pp. 493–505. Springer, Heidelberg (2001). https://doi.org/10.1007/3-540-44585-4_47

18. Larsen, K.G., Pettersson, P., Yi, W.: Model-checking for real-time systems. In: Reichel, H. (ed.) FCT 1995. LNCS, vol. 965, pp. 62–88. Springer, Heidelberg (1995). https://doi.org/10.1007/3-540-60249-6_41

19. Larsen, K.G., Pettersson, P., Yi, W.: Uppaal in a nutshell. J. Softw. Tools Technol. Transf. (STTT) **1**(1–2), 134–152 (1997)

20. Lime, D., Roux, O.H., Seidner, C., Traonouez, L.-M.: Romeo: a parametric model-checker for Petri nets with stopwatches. In: Kowalewski, S., Philippou, A. (eds.) TACAS 2009. LNCS, vol. 5505, pp. 54–57. Springer, Heidelberg (2009). https://doi.org/10.1007/978-3-642-00768-2_6

21. Maler, O., Pnueli, A., Sifakis, J.: On the synthesis of discrete controllers for timed systems. In: Mayr, E.W., Puech, C. (eds.) STACS 1995. LNCS, vol. 900, pp. 229–242. Springer, Heidelberg (1995). https://doi.org/10.1007/3-540-59042-0_76

22. Rasmussen, J.I., Larsen, K.G., Subramani, K.: Resource-optimal scheduling using priced timed automata. In: Jensen, K., Podelski, A. (eds.) TACAS 2004. LNCS, vol. 2988, pp. 220–235. Springer, Heidelberg (2004). https://doi.org/10.1007/978-3-540-24730-2_19

23. Rasmussen, J.I., Larsen, K.G., Subramani, K.: On using priced timed automata to achieve optimal scheduling. Form. Methods Syst. Des. **29**(1), 97–114 (2006)

Certifying Emptiness of Timed Büchi Automata

Simon Wimmer[1]([✉]) [iD], Frédéric Herbreteau[2] [iD], and Jaco van de Pol[3] [iD]

[1] Fakultät für Informatik, Technische Universität München, Munich, Germany
wimmers@in.tum.de
[2] Univ. Bordeaux, CNRS, Bordeaux INP, LaBRI, UMR 5800, 33400 Talence, France
[3] Department of Computer Science, Aarhus University, Aarhus, Denmark

Abstract. Model checkers for timed automata are widely used to verify safety-critical, real-time systems. State-of-the-art tools achieve scalability by intricate abstractions. We aim at further increasing the trust in their verification results, in particular for checking liveness properties. To this end, we develop an approach for extracting certificates for the emptiness of timed Büchi automata from model checking runs. These certificates can be double checked by a certifier that we formally verify in Isabelle/HOL. We study liveness certificates in an abstract setting and show that our approach is sound and complete. To also demonstrate its feasibility, we extract certificates for several models checked by TChecker and Imitator, and validate them with our verified certifier.

Keywords: Timed automata · Certification · Model checking

1 Introduction

Real-time systems are notoriously hard to analyze due to intricate timing constraints. A number of model checkers for timed automata (TA) [1] have been implemented and successfully applied to the verification of safety-critical timed systems. Checking liveness properties of timed automata has revealed to be particularly important, as emphasized by a bug in the standard model of the CSMA/CD protocol that has been discovered only recently [16]. Several algorithms have been implemented to scale the verification of liveness specifications to larger systems [16,22,26,32,33]. Users of timed automata model checkers put a high amount of trust in their verification results. However, as verification algorithms get more complex, it becomes highly desirable to justify the users' confidence in their correctness.

There are two main approaches to ensure high degrees of trustworthiness of automated tools: verification and certification. In the first approach, correctness of the verification tool (its implementation and its theory) is proved using another semi-automated method. This technique has been applied to model checkers [13,34] and SAT solvers [7]. In the second approach, the automated

© Springer Nature Switzerland AG 2020
N. Bertrand and N. Jansen (Eds.): FORMATS 2020, LNCS 12288, pp. 58–75, 2020.
https://doi.org/10.1007/978-3-030-57628-8_4

tool produces a certificate, i.e. a proof for its verification result. Then an independent tool, the certifier, checks that the proof is indeed valid. In the best case, the certifier itself is formally verified. Examples include SAT certificate checking [20,23] and unreachability checking of TA [37].

The certification approach promises many advantages over verification, since certificate checking is much simpler than producing the certificate. This drastically reduces the burden of semi-automated verification, which is a laborious task. While proving correctness of a competitive verification tool might be prohibitively complicated, it may be feasible to construct an efficient verified certifier instead (in the case of SAT [23], the verified certifier was even faster than the original SAT solvers). Finally, there is a wide variety of model checking algorithms and high-performance implementations, which are suited for different situations. Instead of verifying them one by one, these tools could produce certificates in a common format, so they can be checked by a single verified certifier.

1.1 Related Work

Model checking LTL properties for timed automata [1,16,22,26,32,33] consists of three conceptual steps: the LTL formula is transformed into a Büchi automaton, the semantics of the TA is computed as a (finite) zone graph, and the cross-product of these objects is checked for accepting cycles. The two main alternative algorithms for detecting accepting cycles are Nested Depth-First Search (NDFS) and the inspection of the Strongly Connected Components (SCC). The NDFS algorithm was generalized to TA in LTSmin [21,22] and extended to parametric TA in Imitator [2,28]. The SCC-based algorithm has also been generalized to TA in TChecker [16,19]. Both algorithms support *abstraction and subsumption between states* to reduce the state space.

Verified Model Checking. An early approach targeted the verification of a μ-calculus model checker in Coq [27]. The NDFS algorithm was checked in the program verifier Dafny [25,31], while a multi-core version of it was checked in the program verifier Vercors [8,30]. A complete, *executable* LTL model checker was verified in the interactive theorem prover Isabelle/HOL [13] and later extended with partial-order reduction [9]. A verified model checker for TA, Munta [34], has also been constructed in Isabelle/HOL [29,36].

Certification. A certifier for reachability properties in TA has been proposed very recently [37]. A certification approach for LTL model checking was proposed in [15]. It uses k-liveness to reduce the problem to IC3-like invariant checking.

Contributions. In this paper, we extend certificates for unreachability of TA [37] to certificates for liveness properties, i.e. emptiness of timed Büchi automata (TBA). We propose a common certification approach for tools using different algorithms and various abstractions [16,22]. These certificates can be much smaller than the original state space, due to the use of subsumption and abstraction. The difficulty here is that a careless application of subsumption can introduce spurious accepting cycles. Our new contributions are[1]:

---

[1] An artifact containing our code and benchmarks is available on figshare [35].

- We introduce an abstract theory for certificates of Büchi emptiness, which can be instantiated for zone graphs of TBA with subsumptions.
- We developed a fully, mechanically verified certifier in Isabelle/HOL. In particular, our certifier retains the ability to check certificates in parallel.
- We show that the previous certifier for reachability and our extension to Büchi emptiness are compatible with implicit abstraction techniques for TA.
- We demonstrate feasibility by generating and checking certificates for two external model checkers, representing the NDFS and the SCC approach.

Note that checking counter-examples is easy in practice, but checking "true" model checking results is much harder. This is exactly what we address with certifying emptiness of TBA. The main application would be to increase the confidence in safety-critical real-time applications, which have been verified with an existing model checker. Another possible application of the certifier would be to facilitate a new model checking contest for liveness properties of TA.

2   Timed Automata and Model Checking

In this section, we set the stage for the rest of the paper by recapitulating the basic notions of TA and summarizing the essential concepts of TBA verification.

2.1   Verification Problems for Timed Automata

A TA $A = (Q, q_0, F, I, T, X)$ is a finite automaton extended with a finite set of *clocks* X. Q is a finite set of states with initial state $q_0 \in Q$ and accepting states $F \subseteq Q$. I associates an *invariant* constraint to every state and T associates a *guard* constraint g and *clock reset* $R \subseteq X$ to each transition. Here *(clock) constraints* are conjunctions of formulas $x \# c$, where x is a clock, $c \in \mathbb{N}$ and $\# \in \{<, \leq, =, \geq, >\}$. Observe that we exclude diagonal constraints of the form $x - y \# c$. An example of a timed automaton is depicted in Fig. 1.

A clock valuation $v : X \rightarrow \mathbb{R}_{\geq 0}$ associates a non-negative real value to each clock $x \in X$. A configuration is a pair (q, v) where q is a state and v is a clock valuation. The initial configuration is $(q_0, \mathbf{0})$. Without loss of generality, we assume that the initial clock valuation $\mathbf{0}$ satisfies the invariant $I(q_0)$. There are two kind of steps from a configuration (q, v):

delay $(q, v) \rightarrow_\delta (q, v')$ for a delay $\delta \in \mathbb{R}_{\geq 0}$ if for every clock $x \in X$, $v'(x) = v(x) + \delta$, and v' satisfies the invariant $I(q)$;

transition $(q, v) \rightarrow_t (q', v')$ for transition $t = (q, g, R, q') \in T$ if v satisfies the guard g, $v'(x) = 0$ if $x \in R$ and $v'(x) = v(x)$ otherwise, and v' satisfies $I(q')$.

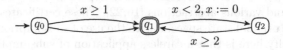

Fig. 1. Timed (Büchi) automaton with initial state q_0 and accepting state q_1.

We write $(q, v) \to_{\delta,t} (q', v')$ if there exists a configuration (q, v'') such that $(q, v) \to_{\delta} (q, v'') \to_t (q', v')$. A run of a timed automaton is an (infinite) sequence of transitions of the form: $(q_0, \mathbf{0}) \to_{\delta_0, t_0} (q_1, v_1) \to_{\delta_1, t_1} \cdots$. A run is *non-Zeno* if the sum of its delays is unbounded.

The *reachability problem* asks, given a timed automaton A, if there exists a finite run from the initial configuration $(q_0, \mathbf{0})$ to an accepting configuration (q_n, v_n) such that $q_n \in F$.

In timed Büchi automata (TBA), F is interpreted as a Büchi acceptance condition. The *liveness problem* then asks, whether a given TBA A is non-empty, i.e. if there is an infinite non-Zeno run from the initial configuration $(q_0, \mathbf{0})$ that visits infinitely many accepting configurations (q_i, v_i) with $q_i \in F$. In this paper, we work under the common assumption that TA only admit non-Zeno runs (see [33] for a construction to enforce this on every TA).

Both problems are known to be PSPACE-complete [1]. Due to density of time, these two verification problems cannot be solved directly from the transition system induced by configurations and steps. A well-known solution to this problem is the region graph construction of Alur and Dill [1]. Yet, it is not used in practice, as the region graph is enormous even for rather simple automata.

2.2   Zone Graph and Abstractions

The practical solution that is implemented in state-of-the-art tools like UPPAAL [24], TChecker [19] and the Imitator tool [2] is based on zones. Let us fix a set of clocks X. A zone Z is a set of valuations represented as a conjunction of constraints of the form $x \# c$ or $x - y \# c$ for $x, y \in X$, $\# \in \{<, \leq, =, \geq, >\}$ and $c \in \mathbb{Z}$. Zones can be efficiently represented using Difference Bound Matrices (DBMs) [12]. Moreover, zones admit a canonical representation, hence equality and inclusion of two zones can be checked efficiently [6].

We now define the symbolic semantics [11] of a TA A. Let q, q' be two states of A, and let $W, W' \subseteq \mathbb{R}^X_{\geq 0}$ be two non-empty sets of clock valuations. We have $(q, W) \Rightarrow^t (q', W')$ for some transition $t \in T$, if W' is the set of all clock valuations v' for which there exists a valuation $v \in W$ and a delay $\delta \in \mathbb{R}_{\geq 0}$ such that $(q, v) \to_{\delta,t} (q', v')$. In other words, W' is the strongest postcondition of W along transition t. The symbolic semantics of A, denoted by $\Rightarrow$, is the union of all $\Rightarrow^t$ over $t \in T$. The symbolic semantics is a sound and complete representation of the finite and infinite runs of A. Indeed, A admits a finite (resp. infinite) run $(q_0, v_0) \to_{\delta_0, t_0} (q_1, v_1) \to_{\delta_1, t_1} \ldots (q_n, v_n) \to_{\delta_n, t_n} \ldots$ if and only if there exists a finite (resp. infinite) path $(q_0, W_0) \Rightarrow^{t_0} (q_1, W_1) \Rightarrow^{t_1} \ldots (q_n, W_n) \Rightarrow^{t_n} \ldots$ such that $v_i \in W_i$ for all $i \geq 0$ and $W_0 = \{\mathbf{0}\}$ [11]. It is well-known that if Z is a zone, and $(q, Z) \Rightarrow (q', W')$ then W' is a zone as well [6]. Since $\{\mathbf{0}\}$ is a zone, all the reachable nodes in $\Rightarrow$ are zones as well. The reachable part of $\Rightarrow$ is called the *zone graph* of A. The nodes of the zone graph are denoted as (q, Z) in the sequel and the zone graph is simply denoted by its transition relation $\Rightarrow$. Figure 2a depicts the zone graph of the automaton in Fig. 1.

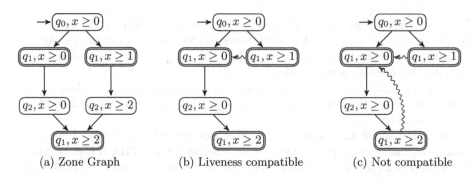

Fig. 2. Three subsumption graphs for the automaton in Fig. 1.

Still, the zone graph of a timed automaton may be infinite. As a remedy, finite abstractions have been introduced in the literature [4,5,11].

An *abstraction* α transforms a zone Z into a zone $\alpha(Z)$ such that $Z \subseteq \alpha(Z)$, $\alpha(\alpha(Z)) = \alpha(Z)$, and every run that is feasible from a valuation $v' \in \alpha(Z)$ is simulated by a run from a valuation $v \in Z$. Such abstractions are called extrapolations in the literature [5]. An abstraction is finite when the set of abstracted zones $\{\alpha(Z) \mid Z$ is a zone$\}$ is finite. Given an abstraction α, the *abstracted zone graph* has initial node $(q, \alpha(\{\mathbf{0}\}))$ and transitions of the form $(q, Z) \Rightarrow_\alpha^t (q', \alpha(Z'))$ for each transition $(q, Z) \Rightarrow^t (q', Z')$. Let $\Rightarrow_\alpha$ denote the union of all $\Rightarrow_\alpha^t$ over $t \in T$. The abstracted zone graph is sound and complete: there is a run $(q_0, v_0) \to_{\delta_0, t_0} (q_1, v_1) \to_{\delta_1, t_1} \cdots (q_n, v_n) (\to_{\delta_n, t_n} \ldots)$ in A if and only if there is an infinite path $(q_0, Z_0) \Rightarrow_\alpha^{t_0} (q_1, Z_1) \Rightarrow_\alpha^{t_1} \cdots (q_n, Z_n) (\Rightarrow_\alpha^{t_n} \ldots)$ with $v_i \in Z_i$ for all $i \geq 0$. Hence, when α is a finite abstraction, the verification problems for a TA A can be algorithmically solved from its abstracted zone graph. The abstraction Extra_{LU}^+ [5] is implemented by state-of-the-art verification tools UPPAAL [24] and TChecker [19]. Our results hold for any finite, sound and complete abstraction. The abstracted zone graph is denoted $\Rightarrow_\alpha$ in the sequel.

2.3 Subsumption

Consider the TA in Fig. 1 and its zone graph in Fig. 2a. Observe that every run that is feasible from node $(q_1, x \geq 1)$ is also feasible from $(q_1, x \geq 0)$ since the zone $x \geq 1$ is included in the zone $x \geq 0$ (recall that zones are sets of clock valuations). We say that $(q_1, x \geq 1)$ is *subsumed* by the node $(q_1, x \geq 0)$. As a result, if an accepting node is (repeatedly) reachable from $(q_1, x \geq 1)$, then an accepting node is also (repeatedly) reachable from $(q_1, x \geq 0)$.

This leads to a crucial optimization for the verification of TA: reachability and liveness verification problems can be solved without exploring subsumed nodes. This optimization is called inclusion abstraction in [11]. Figure 2b shows the graph obtained when the exploration is stopped at node $(q_1, x \geq 1)$. All the runs that are feasible from $(q_1, x \geq 1)$ are still represented in this graph, as they can be obtained by first taking the subsumption edge from $(q_1, x \geq 1)$

to $(q_1, x \geq 0)$ (depicted as a blue squiggly arrow), and then any sequence of (actual or subsumption) edges from $(q_1, x \geq 0)$. Such graphs with both actual and subsumption edges are called *subsumption graphs* in the sequel.

It is tempting to use subsumption as much as possible, and only explore maximal nodes (w.r.t. zone inclusion). While this is correct for the verification of reachability properties, subsumption must be used with care for liveness verification. The bottom node $(q_1, x \geq 2)$ in Fig. 2b is also subsumed by the node $(q_1, x \geq 0)$. A subsumption edge can thus be added between these two nodes as depicted in Fig. 2c. However, due to this new subsumption edge, the graph has a Büchi accepting path (of actual and subsumption edges) that does not correspond to any run of the timed automaton in Fig. 1. Indeed, subsumption leads to an overapproximation of the runs of the automaton. While all the runs from node $(q_1, x \geq 2)$ are feasible from node $(q_1, x \geq 0)$, the converse is not true: the transition $q_1 \xrightarrow{x<2, x:=0} q_2$ is not feasible from $(q_1, x \geq 2)$.

The subsumption graphs in Fig. 2b and 2c can be seen as certificates issued by verification algorithms. The graph in Fig. 2b is a valid certificate for liveness verification as 1) it contains no accepting paths, and 2) every run of the automaton is represented in the graph. In constrast, the graph in Fig. 2c is not a valid certificate for liveness verification as it has an accepting path that does not correspond to any run of the automaton. In the next sections, we introduce an algorithm to check the validity of certificates produced by liveness verification algorithms, as well as a proven implementation of the algorithm.

3   Certificates for Büchi Emptiness

In this section, we study certificates for Büchi emptiness in the setting of a slight variation of well-structured transition systems [14]. First, we present reachability invariants, which certify that every run in the original system can be simulated on the states given in the invariant. Next, we show that the absence of certain cycles in the invariant is sufficient to prove that the original transition system does not contain accepting runs. Then, we add a proof of absence of these cycles to the certificate. Finally, we instantiate this framework for the case of TA.

3.1   Self-simulating Transition Systems

A *transition system* $(S, \rightarrow)$ consists of a set of states S and a transition relation $\rightarrow \subseteq S \times S$. If S is clear from the context, we simply write $\rightarrow$. We say that $s_1 \rightarrow s_2 \rightarrow \ldots \rightarrow s_n$ is a path or that $s_1 \rightarrow s_2 \rightarrow \ldots$ is an (infinite) run in $\rightarrow$ if $s_i \rightarrow s_{i+1}$ for all i. Given an initial state s_0 and a predicate for accepting states ϕ, the path $s_0 \rightarrow s_1 \rightarrow \ldots \rightarrow s_n$ is accepting if $\phi(s_n)$. A run $s_0 \rightarrow s_1 \rightarrow \ldots$ is an (accepting) Büchi run if $\phi(s_i)$ for infinitely many i.

A transition system $\rightarrow$ is simulated by the transition system $\rightarrow'$ if there exists a simulation relation $\sqsubseteq$ such that:

$$\forall s, s', t.\ s \sqsubseteq s' \wedge s \rightarrow t \longrightarrow \exists t'.\ s' \rightarrow' t' \wedge t \sqsubseteq t'$$

This *simulation property* can be lifted to paths and runs:

Proposition 1. *If* $s_1 \rightarrow s_2 \rightarrow \ldots \rightarrow s_n\ (\rightarrow \ldots)$ *is a path (run) and* $s_1 \sqsubseteq t_1$, *then there is a path (run)* $t_1 \rightarrow' t_2 \rightarrow' \ldots \rightarrow' t_n\ (\rightarrow \ldots)$ *with* $s_i \sqsubseteq t_i$ *for all* i.

Definition 1. *A* self-simulating transition system *(SSTS)* $(S, \rightarrow, \preceq)$ *consists of a transition system* $(S, \rightarrow)$ *and a quasi-order (a reflexive and transitive relation)* $\preceq\, \subseteq S \times S$ *on states such that* $\rightarrow$ *is simulated by* $\rightarrow$ *itself for* $\preceq$.

In comparison to well-structured transition systems [14], our definition is slightly more relaxed, as we only demand that $\preceq$ is a quasi order, not a well-quasi order. Intuitively, transitivity of $\preceq$ is needed to allow for correct simulation by arbitrary "bigger" nodes. In TA, $\preceq$ corresponds to subsumption $\subseteq$, and $\rightarrow$ corresponds to $\Rightarrow$.

3.2 Reachability Invariants on Abstract Transition Systems

In this section, we introduce the concept of *reachability invariants* for SSTS.

Definition 2. *A set* $I \subseteq S$ *is a* reachability invariant *of an SSTS* $(S, \rightarrow, \preceq)$ *iff for all* $s \in I$ *and* t *with* $s \rightarrow t$, *there exists a* $t' \in I$ *such that* $t \preceq t'$.

A useful invariant is also fulfilled by some inital state. Such states will show up in theorems below. In the remainder, unless noted otherwise, $(S, \rightarrow, \preceq)$ is an SSTS and I is a reachability invariant of it. Figures 2a to 2c all form a reachability invariant for the zone graph from Fig. 2a.

As was observed by Wimmer and von Mutius [37], reachability invariants can directly be applied as certificates for *unreachability*.

Definition 3. *A predicate* ϕ *(for accepting states) is* compatible *with an SSTS* $(S, \rightarrow, \preceq)$ *iff for all* $s, s' \in S$, *if* $\phi(s)$ *and* $s \preceq s'$, *then also* $\phi(s')$.

An invariant I can now certify that no accepting state s with $\phi(s)$ is reachable:

Theorem 1. *If* $\forall s \in I.\ \neg\phi(s)$, *for some compatible* ϕ, $s_0 \in S$ *and* $s_0' \in I$ *with* $s_0 \preceq s_0'$, *then there is no accepting path* $s_0 \rightarrow s_1 \rightarrow \ldots \rightarrow s_n$ *with* $\phi(s_n)$.

Note that this approach to certifying unreachability is also complete: if no accepting state is reachable from s_0 in $(S, \rightarrow, \preceq)$, we can simply set $I := S$. However, this is not practical for infinite transition systems, of course. Thus we will revisit the question of completeness for TA below.

Finally, we observe that the invariant can be limited to a restriction of $\preceq$.

Definition 4. *A pair $(I, \trianglelefteq)$ of a set $I \subseteq S$ and a binary relation $\trianglelefteq$ is a* restricted reachability invariant *of an SSTS $(S, \rightarrow, \preceq)$ iff:*

1. *For all $s \in I$ and t with $s \rightarrow t$, there exists a $t' \in I$ such that $t \trianglelefteq t'$.*
2. *For all s, t, if $s \trianglelefteq t$, then also $s \preceq t$.*

In Figure 2, the $\rightsquigarrow$-arrows would play the role of $\trianglelefteq$. In Figure 2b, $(q_1, x \geq 0)$ is subsumed by both $(q_1, x \geq 1)$ and $(q_1, x \geq 2)$, but as we have seen in Figure 2c, it is crucial to disregard these subsumptions. Therefore we need to consider restricted reachability invariants.

For any restricted reachability invariant, we can define a simulating transition system $\rightarrow_\trianglelefteq$:

Definition 5. *The transition system $(S, \rightarrow_\trianglelefteq)$ is defined such that $s \rightarrow_\trianglelefteq t'$ iff there exists a t such that $s \rightarrow t$ and $t \trianglelefteq t'$.*

This simulation theorem is the key property of restricted reachability invariants[2]:

Theorem 2. *Given $s_1 \trianglelefteq t_1$ with $t_1 \in I$, if $s_1 \rightarrow s_2 \rightarrow \ldots \rightarrow s_n (\rightarrow \ldots)$ is a path (run), then there is a path (run) $t_1 \rightarrow_\trianglelefteq t_2 \rightarrow_\trianglelefteq \ldots \rightarrow_\trianglelefteq t_n (\rightarrow \ldots)$ such that $s_i \trianglelefteq t_i$ and $t_i \in I$ for all i.*

Analogously to $\rightarrow_\trianglelefteq$, the transition system $\rightarrow_\preceq$ can be defined, and Theorem 2 can be proved for $\rightarrow_\preceq$. This is used for the proof of Theorem 1 (see [37]).

3.3   Büchi Emptiness on Abstract Transition Systems

In this section, we first give a general means of certifying that a transition system does not contain a cycle, and then combine the idea with reachability invariants to certify the absence of Büchi runs on SSTS.

Definition 6. *Given a transition system $\rightarrow$ and an accepting state predicate ϕ, a* topological numbering *of $\rightarrow$ is a function f with an integer range such that:*

1. *For all s, t, if $s \rightarrow t$, then $f(s) \geq f(t)$.*
2. *For all s, t, if $s \rightarrow t$ and $\phi(s)$, then $f(s) > f(t)$.*

Proposition 2. *Let f be a topological numbering of $\rightarrow$ and ϕ. If there exists a path of the form $s \rightarrow s_1 \rightarrow s_2 \rightarrow \ldots \rightarrow s$, then $\neg\phi(s)$.*

These certificates are also complete:

Proposition 3. *If there is no path $s \rightarrow s_1 \rightarrow s_2 \rightarrow \ldots \rightarrow s$ with $\phi(s)$ in $\rightarrow$, then the following are topological numberings for $\rightarrow$.*

1. *The number of accepting states that are reachable from a node: $f(s) :=$ $|\{x \mid s \rightarrow^* x \wedge \phi(x)\}|$ (assuming $\{x \mid s \rightarrow^* x \wedge \phi(x)\}$ is finite for any s).*

---

[2] All proofs are omitted for brevity and can be found in the appendix of the online version of this paper on arXiv: https://arxiv.org/abs/2007.04150.

2. If h is a topological numbering (in the classical sense) of the strongly connected components (SCCs) of $\rightarrow$, then set $g(s) := h(C)$ if $s \in C$.

We now lift this idea to the case of (restricted) reachability invariants.

Definition 7. *Given an SSTS* $(S, \rightarrow, \preceq)$, *an accepting state predicate* ϕ, *and a corresponding restricted reachability invariant* $(I, \trianglelefteq)$, *a restricted topological numbering of* $(S, \rightarrow, \preceq)$ *is a function* f *with an integer range such that:*

1. *For all* $s, t' \in I$ *and* $t \in S$, *if* $s \rightarrow t$, *and* $t \trianglelefteq t'$, *then* $f(s) \geq f(t')$.
2. *For all* $s, t' \in I$ *and* $t \in S$, *if* $s \rightarrow t$, $t \trianglelefteq t'$, *and* $\phi(s)$, *then* $f(s) > f(t')$.

Moreover, let $\leadsto_{\trianglelefteq}$ *be the restriction of* $\rightarrow_{\trianglelefteq}$ *to* I, *i.e. the transition system such that* $s \leadsto_{\trianglelefteq} t'$ *iff* $s, t' \in I$ *and there exists a* t *such that* $s \rightarrow t$ *and* $t \trianglelefteq t'$.

Now, f is clearly a topological numbering for $\leadsto_{\trianglelefteq}$. Thus $\leadsto_{\trianglelefteq}$ is free of accepting cycles. Additionally, the transition system $\leadsto_{\trianglelefteq}$ trivially simulates $\rightarrow_{\trianglelefteq}$ with $s \sqsubseteq s'$ iff $s' = s$ and $s \in I$. Therefore, any accepting cycle $s \rightarrow_{\trianglelefteq}^{+} s$ in $\rightarrow_{\trianglelefteq}$ with $s \in I$ and $\phi(s)$ yields an accepting cycle $s \leadsto_{\trianglelefteq}^{+} s$. Hence $\rightarrow_{\trianglelefteq}$ is free of accepting cycles.

From this, we conclude our main theorem that allows one to certify absence of Büchi runs in a transition system $\rightarrow$.

Theorem 3. *Let* f *be a restricted topological numbering of* $(S, \rightarrow, \preceq)$ *for a compatible predicate* ϕ *and a finite restricted reachability invariant* $(I, \trianglelefteq)$. *Then, for any initial state* $s_0 \in S$ *with* $s_0 \trianglelefteq t_0$ *for* $t_0 \in I$, *there is no Büchi run from* s_0.

In practice, a certificate can now be given as a finite restricted reachability invariant I as described above, and a corresponding restricted topological numbering f. Both properties can be checked locally for each individual state in I.

3.4   Instantiation for Timed Automata

We now want to instantiate this abstract certification framework for the concrete case of TBA. Our goal is to certify that the zone graph $\Rightarrow$ does not contain any Büchi runs. As the zone graph is complete, this implies that the underlying TBA is empty. Thus we set $\rightarrow := \Rightarrow$. Subsumptions in the zone graph shall correspond to the self-simulation relation of the SSTS. Hence we define $\preceq$ such that $(q, Z) \preceq (q', Z')$ iff $q' = q$ and $Z \subseteq Z'$.

To certify unreachability, it is sufficient to consider arbitrary subsumptions in the zone graph, i.e. $\trianglelefteq := \preceq$ [37]. In other words it is sufficient to check that the given certificate I is a reachability invariant for $(S, \rightarrow, \preceq)$. We have not yet given the set of states S. Abstractly, S is simply the set of non-empty states, i.e. $S := \{(q, Z) \mid Z \neq \emptyset\}$. If it was allowed to reach empty zones, then soundness of the zone graph would not be given. In practice, the certifier needs to be able to compute $\Rightarrow$ effectively, typically using the DBM representation of zones. To this end one wants to add the assumption on states that all DBMs are in canonical form. One needs to ensure that states are split according to ϕ, i.e. $\forall (q, Z) \in S. Z \subseteq \Phi(q) \lor Z \cap \Phi(q) = \emptyset$ where $\Phi(q) = \{v \mid \phi(q, v)\}$. This is trivial for commonly used properties that concern only the finite state part.

Following these considerations, we propose the following certifier for the emptiness of TBA. A certificate C is a set of triplets (q, Z, i) where q is a discrete state, Z is a corresponding zone, and i is the topological number for (q, Z). The certifier runs Algorithm 1 on this certificate. The algorithm extends the one by Wimmer and Mutius [37] with the topological numbers for liveness checking.

Theorem 4. *If* BÜCHI-EMPTINESS(ϕ, C, q_0) *accepts the certificate, then* $\Rightarrow_{DBM}$ *has no Büchi run for* ϕ. *Consequently, the underlying TBA is empty.*

The proof constructs a suitable $\trianglelefteq$ such that $(q, Z) \trianglelefteq (q, Z')$ if $Z \subseteq Z'$ and $(q, Z', k) \in C$, where k is selected to be minimal. Setting $I := \{(q, Z) \mid \exists i.\, (q, Z, i) \in C)\}$ and $f(q, Z) := \min\{i \mid (q, Z, i) \in C\}$, Theorem 3 can be applied.

Algorithm 1. Certifier for the emptiness of TBA

1: **procedure** BÜCHI-EMPTINESS(ϕ, C, q_0)
2:     **for all** $(q, Z, i) \in C$ **do**   ▷ All DBMs are well-formed
3:         **if** $Z = \emptyset \vee Z$ is not canonical
4:             **then reject certificate**
5:     **if** $\nexists(q_0, Z_0, i) \in C.\, \{\mathbf{0}\} \subseteq Z_0$ ▷ The initial state is covered
6:         **then reject certificate**
7:     **for all** $(q, Z, i) \in C$ **do**   ▷ The certificate is:
8:         **for all** (q_1, Z_1) s.t. $(q, Z) \Rightarrow (q_1, Z_1)$ **do**
9:             **if** $(\nexists(q_1, Z_1', j) \in C.\, Z_1 \subseteq Z_1'$ ▷ an invariant,
                     $\wedge (\phi(q) \longrightarrow i > j) \wedge i \geq j)$ ▷ and a topological numbering
10:             **then reject certificate**
11:     **accept certificate**

The algorithm inherits several beneficial properties from [37]. First, it can easily be parallelized. Most importantly however, the certifier does not need to compute an abstraction operation α. Suppose the model checker starts with a state $(q_0, \{\mathbf{0}\})$ and explores the transition $(q_0, \{\mathbf{0}\}) \Rightarrow (q_1, Z_1)$. The model checker could then abstract zone Z_1 to $\alpha(Z_1)$, and explore more edges from $(q_1, \alpha(Z_1))$, e.g. $(q_1, \alpha(Z_1)) \Rightarrow (q_2, Z_2)$. The certificate just needs to include $(q_0, \{\mathbf{0}\})$, $(q_1, \alpha(Z_1))$, and $(q_2, \alpha(Z_2))$, and the certificate checker just needs to check the following inclusions: $\{\mathbf{0}\} \subseteq \{\mathbf{0}\}$, $Z_1 \subseteq \alpha(Z_1)$, and $Z_2 \subseteq \alpha(Z_2)$. The checker does not need to compute α as $\alpha(Z_1)$ and $\alpha(Z_2)$ are part of the certificate.

It is rather easy to see that these certificates are also complete for timed automata. For any finite abstraction α, the abstracted zone graph $\Rightarrow_\alpha$ is finite and complete. Thus, for a starting state $(q_0, \{\mathbf{0}\})$ the set

$$I := \{(q, Z) \mid (q_0, \{\mathbf{0}\}) \Rightarrow_\alpha^* (q, Z)\}$$

is a trivial finite reachability invariant that can be computed effectively for common abstractions α. Moreover, if the underlying TBA is empty, then $\Rightarrow_\alpha$ cannot contain a Büchi run either, since the abstract zone graph is complete. Because $\Rightarrow_\alpha$ is finite, this means it cannot contain a cycle through ϕ. Hence a forward numbering of I can be given by computing the strongly connected components of I. However, this type of certificate is not of practical interest as subsumptions are not considered. How certificates can be obtained for model checking algorithms that make use of subsumption is the topic of Sect. 5.1.

4 Incorporating Advanced Abstraction Techniques

We have already discussed that the techniques that were presented above are in principle agnostic to the concrete abstraction α used. This, however, is only true for standard verification algorithms for T(B)A that use zone inclusion $Z \subseteq Z'$ as a simulation relation on the abstract zone graph. There is also the noteworthy abstraction $\alpha_{\preceq LU}$ [5], which is the coarsest zone abstraction that can be defined from clock bounds L, U [18]. Herbreteau et al. have shown that even though $\alpha_{\preceq LU}(Z)$ is usually not a zone, it can be checked whether $Z \subseteq \alpha_{\preceq LU}(Z')$ directly from the DBM representation of Z and Z', without computing $\alpha_{\preceq LU}(Z')$ [18]. Hence, one can use $\alpha_{\preceq LU}$-subsumption over zones, $Z \subseteq \alpha_{\preceq LU}(Z')$, instead of standard inclusion $Z \subseteq Z'$ to explore fewer symbolic states. This technique can also be integrated with our certification approach. This time, we will need more knowledge about the concrete abstraction α, however.

We first describe the concept of time-abstract simulations, on which the definition of $\alpha_{\preceq LU}$ is based.

Definition 8. *A time-abstract simulation between clock valuations is a quasi-order $\preceq$ such that if $v \preceq v'$ and $(q, v) \to_{\delta,t} (q_1, v_1)$ then there exist δ' and v_1' such that $(q, v') \to_{\delta',t} (q_1, v_1') \wedge v_1 \preceq v_1'$.*

Behrmann et al. defined the simulation $\preceq_{LU}$ based on the clock bounds L and U, and showed that it is a time-abstract simulation [5] (in fact one can show that $\preceq_{LU}$ is even a simulation, i.e. $\delta' = \delta$). For any $\preceq$, one can define the corresponding abstraction $\alpha_{\preceq}(Z) = \{v \mid \exists v' \in Z. v \preceq v'\}$. This yields a sound and complete abstraction for any time-abstract simulation $\preceq$ [5]. Observe that $\alpha_{\preceq}(Z)$ is the set of all valuations that are simulated by a valuation in Z w.r.t. $\preceq$. As a result, every sequence of transitions feasible from $\alpha_{\preceq}(Z)$ is also feasible from Z (although with different delays).

The implicit abstraction technique based on the subsumption check $Z \subseteq \alpha_{\preceq}(Z')$ is compatible with our certification approach for any $\alpha_{\preceq}$ for which $\preceq$ is a time-abstract simulation, and in particular $\alpha_{\preceq LU}$. Actually, we are still able to use algorithm BÜCHI-EMPTINESS with the only modification that the condition $Z_1 \subseteq Z_1'$ is replaced with $Z_1 \subseteq \alpha_{\preceq}(Z_1')$. We will justify this by showing that if the algorithm accepts the certificate, then it represents a restricted reachability invariant with a suitable topological numbering for $\Rightarrow_{\alpha_{\preceq}}$. This means that $\Rightarrow_{\alpha_{\preceq}}$ does not have a Büchi run (Theorem 3), which, as $\alpha_{\preceq}$ is a complete abstraction, implies that the underlying TBA does not have a Büchi run either.

We first prove the following monotonicity property (which can be seen as a generalization of Lemma 4 in the work of Herbreteau et al. [18]).

Proposition 4. *Let $\preceq$ be a time-abstract simulation. If $\alpha_\preceq(W) \subseteq \alpha_\preceq(W')$, $(q, W) \Rightarrow^t (q_1, W_1)$, and $(q, W') \Rightarrow^t (q_1, W_1')$, then $\alpha_\preceq(W_1) \subseteq \alpha_\preceq(W_1')$.*

Reminding ourselves that $\alpha_\preceq$ is idempotent, if follows that if $(q, W) \Rightarrow^t (q_1, W_1)$ and $(q, \alpha_\preceq(W)) \Rightarrow^t (q_1, W_1')$ for some states q, q_1, and sets of valuations W, W_1, and W_1', then $\alpha_\preceq(W_1) = \alpha_\preceq(W_1')$. In other words, $\Rightarrow$ simulates $\Rightarrow_{\alpha_\preceq}$ for $\sqsupseteq$ defined as $(q, W) \sqsupseteq (q, Z) \longleftrightarrow W = \alpha_\preceq(Z)$.

Now, we show that the conditions of Definitions 4 and 7 can be transferred along this simulation.

Theorem 5. *Assume that the following conditions hold:*

1. *For all states q, and zones Z, Z', Z'', if $(q, Z) \trianglelefteq (q, Z')$, then $Z \subseteq \alpha_\preceq(Z')$. Moreover, if $\alpha_\preceq(Z) = \alpha_\preceq(Z')$ and $(q, Z) \trianglelefteq (q, Z'')$, then $(q, Z') \trianglelefteq (q, Z'')$.*
2. *For all q, Z, if $\phi((q, \alpha_\preceq(Z)))$, then $\phi((q, Z))$.*
3. *$(I, \trianglelefteq)$ satisfies condition (1) of Definition 4 for $\Rightarrow$.*
4. *f is a restricted topological numbering for $\Rightarrow$, $(I, \trianglelefteq)$, and ϕ.*

Let $(q, W) \trianglelefteq' (q, W') \longleftrightarrow \exists Z, Z'. W = \alpha_\preceq(Z) \wedge W' = \alpha_\preceq(Z') \wedge (q, Z) \trianglelefteq (q, Z')$, $I' := \{s' \mid \exists s \in I. s \sqsubseteq s'\}$ and $f'(s') := Min\{f(s) \mid s \in I \wedge s \sqsubseteq s'\}$. Then

1. *$(I', \trianglelefteq')$ is a restricted reachability invariant for $(\Rightarrow_{\alpha_\preceq}, \subseteq)$.*
2. *f' is a restricted topological numbering for $\Rightarrow_{\alpha_\preceq}$, $(I', \trianglelefteq')$, and ϕ.*

Algorithm BÜCHI-EMPTINESS ensures that there exist an invariant $(I, \trianglelefteq)$ and a numbering f that fulfill the conditions of Theorem 5 for $\Rightarrow$ (as indicated after Theorem 4). Thus, if the algorithm accepts the certificate, there is a restricted reachability invariant $(I', \trianglelefteq')$ with a corresponding topological numbering f' for $\Rightarrow_{\alpha_\preceq}$. Hence $\Rightarrow_{\alpha_\preceq}$ does not have a Büchi run.

5   Evaluation

In this section, we first give a brief description of the model checking algorithms we consider and describe how certificates can be extracted from them. Then, we outline the general architecture of our certification tool chain, and finally we present some experiments on standard TA models.

5.1   Extracting Certificates from Model Checkers

We consider the two state-of-the-art algorithms for checking Büchi emptiness for TA: the NDFS-based algorithm by Laarman et al. [22] and the iterative SCC-based algorithm by Herbreteau et al. [16]. Both algorithms can be applied to any abstracted zone graph $\Rightarrow_\alpha$ for a finite, sound and complete abstraction α. As was noted by Herbreteau et al. [16], they also have in common that their correctness can be justified on the basis that they both compute subsumption graphs that are *liveness compatible*, in the sense that they do not contain any cycle with an accepting node and a subsumption edge.

Considering NDFS for TA from [22] more closely, it prunes the search space by using subsumption in certain safe places. In particular, the outer (blue) search is pruned when it reaches a state s that is subsumed by a state on which the inner (red) search has been called, i.e. $s \sqsubseteq t$ and t is red. In order to generate a liveness-compatible subsumption graph, the blue search exports all the states which are not subsumed along with their $\rightarrow$-successors. Moreover, the algorithm exports $\rightsquigarrow$-edges as soon as the pruning by subsumption is applied.

The iterative algorithm from [16] interleaves reachability analysis and SCC decompositions. The reachability analysis computes a subsumption graph with maximal subsumption: a subsumption edge $s \rightsquigarrow t'$ is added whenever a new state t is visited from s, and t is subsumed by some visited state t'. The resulting graph $\rightarrow \cup \rightsquigarrow$ is a subsumption graph that preserves state reachability, but that may not be liveness compatible. Therefore, an SCC decomposition is run, and all subsumption edges from SCCs that contain both an accepting node and a subsumption edge are removed. States which are not subsumed anymore are re-explored in the next iteration of the main loop. Upon termination, the subsumption graph $\rightarrow \cup \rightsquigarrow$ is liveness compatible.

Both algorithms compute liveness compatible subsumption graphs. In order to obtain a certificate we run one extra SCC decomposition of the graph with $\rightarrow \cup \rightsquigarrow$-edges from which we compute a topological ordering.

5.2   General Architecture

Our certifier is implemented as an extension of the tool Munta [34], which has been fully verified in Isabelle/HOL [36,37]. Figure 3 depicts the architecture of our tool chain to certify the emptiness of a given TBA. The model (a TBA) and the acceptance property are given in the input format of Munta. For the model checker in the middle, we used Imitator and TChecker. In a first step, the Munta model is translated to an input model for the model checker. The model checker decides whether the given TBA is empty. If not, then either the model checker's answer is correct or it has found a spurious counterexample; in both cases no certificate can be extracted. Otherwise, the model checker emits a certificate consisting of a number of symbolic states and the set of edges in the subsumption graph. The latter can either include proper transitions ($\rightarrow$) and subsumptions ($\rightsquigarrow$) (this is done for Imitator with NDFS and subsumption), or the edges that merge these two types ($\rightsquigarrow'$) (which is done for TChecker and for Imitator with state merging enabled, see Sect. 5.3). In either case, in the next step where the certificate is translated to Munta's binary input format for certificates, the SCC numbers (c.f. Proposition 3) are re-computed blindly from these edges. This step additionally makes use of a renaming dictionary to map from human readable labels for states, actions, etc., to natural numbers.

Finally, the TBA model, the translated certificate, and the renaming are given to Munta. If it accepts the certificate, then there is an Isabelle/HOL theorem that guarantees that the given TBA is indeed empty. If the certificate is rejected, any of the steps in the tool chain could have failed. Note that the basis of trust is minimal. One just needs to ensure that the model represents what one has

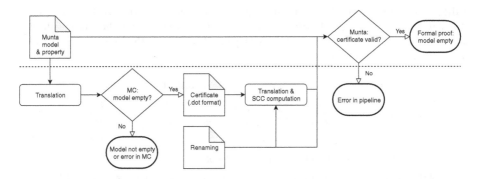

Fig. 3. Workflow of the certifier pipeline. The dashed line is the trust boundary. If the correct model is given, then the answer on the right can be trusted.

in mind, and to trust the correctness of Munta. To trust Munta, one essentially needs to trust its TBA semantics, which is less than 200 lines long, some core parts of Isabelle/HOL, and an SML compiler (MLton in our case). For details, we refer the interested reader to previous publications on Munta [34, 37].

5.3 Experiments

We have evaluated our approach on the TBA models that were also used by Herbreteau et al. [16]. These are inspired by standard TA benchmarks, and all consist of the product of a TA model and an additional Büchi automaton that encodes the complement of the language of a given LTL formula that one wants to check. Details are given by Herbreteau et al. [16].

For Imitator we tried two methods: NDFS with subsumption and reachability analyis with merging [3]. Imitator does not apply abstractions (since it was designed for parametric TA), so the full zone graph is often infinite and most NDFS runs fail. The one that succeeds generates a valid certificate. *Merging* tries to reduce the number of zones, by computing the exact convex hull of zones. This creates new zones that could subsume several existing ones, and often yields a finite zone graph. The certificate produced by merging is always a reachability invariant but not necessarily a subsumption graph. Merging may introduce spurious cycles, in which case the certificate is not liveness compatible; these cases are caught by the Munta certifier. If there are no (spurious) accepting cycles, we obtain a valid and quite small certificate. Note that the generalization from subsumption graphs to our certificates is crucial to allow for merging.

Table 1 summarizes our experimental results. TChecker was run with the algorithm from [16] and [22] and Imitator with the algorithm from [22], and with a reachability procedure with full merging. The *** entries indicate cases where Imitator did not terminate within 30 s. The results show that the certifier accepts those certificates that we expect it to accept, but also rejects those that stem from subsumption graphs that are not liveness compatible. Moreover, the certifier was fully verified in Isabelle/HOL and still yields reasonable performance, certifying models with more than a 100 k symbolic states in under 230 s.

Table 1. Benchmark results on a 2017 MacBook Pro with 16 GB RAM and a Quad-Core Intel Core i7 CPU at 3.1 GHz. For each algorithm, we show whether the certificate was accepted, the number of DBMs in the certificate, and the time for certificate checking on a single core in seconds.

Model	TChecker						Imitator					
	Iterative SCC			NDFS			Merge			NDFS		
CC1	✓	57	0.01	✓	3281	0.06	✓	58	0.01		***	
CC4	✓	195858	221.56	✓	32575	7.75		***			***	
CC5	✓	65639	30.63	✓	143057	218.98		***			***	
FD1	✓	214	0.02	✓	677	0.03	✗	294	0.02	✓	1518	0.11
FI1	✓	65	0.01	✓	71	0.00	✓	136	0.00		***	
FI2	✓	314	0.01	✓	344	0.01	✓	589	0.01		***	
FI4	✓	204	0.00	✓	224	0.01	✓	793	0.01		***	
FI5	✓	3091	0.13	✓	2392	0.09	✗	863	0.03		***	

6 Conclusion

Starting from an abstract theory on self-simulating transition systems, we have presented an approach to extract certificates from state-of-the-art model checking algorithms (including state-of-the-art abstraction techniques) that decide emptiness of timed Büchi automata. The certificates prove that a given model is indeed Büchi empty. We have verified the theory and a checker for these certificates in Isabelle/HOL, using the tool Munta as a basis. We demonstrated that our approach is feasible by extracting certificates for some standard benchmark models from the tools TChecker and Imitator. We hope that our work can help to increase confidence in safety-critical systems that have been verified with timed automata model checkers. Furthermore, we envision that our tool could help in the organization of future competitions for such model checkers.

To close, we want to illuminate some potential future directions of research. First, one is usually not only interested in the emptiness of TBA per se, but more generally in the question if a TA model satisfies some LTL requirements. Thus, our tool would ideally be combined with a verified translation from LTL formulas to Büchi automata or with a certifier for such a construction. The former has been realized by the CAVA project [13], while an avenue towards the latter is opened by the recent work of Seidl et al. [10].

Second, Herbreteau et al. have developed a technique of computing abstractions for TA on the fly, starting from very coarse abstractions and refining them as needed [17]. It seems that our approach is in principle compatible with this technique when augmenting certificates with additional information on the computed abstractions, whose validity would have to be checked by the certifier.

Third, one could attempt to reduce the size of the certificates. In one approach, reachability certificates have been compressed after model checking (c.f. [37]). On the other hand, model checking algorithms could speculate that the given TBA is empty, and use this fact to use additional subsumptions to reduce the search space, while risking to miss accepting runs. However, given the certification step afterwards, this is of no concern. For instance, one could remove the red search from the NDFS algorithm, and use subsumption on blue nodes instead of red nodes, as a quick pre-check. If the result passes the certifier, we are done.

Finally, as our theory is not specific to timed automata per se, it could be interesting to find other application domains for this approach to certification. In light of the large body of existing work on well-structured transition systems, this looks particularly promising as any such system is also self-simulating.

References

1. Alur, R., Dill, D.L.: A theory of timed automata. Theoretical Comput. Sci. **126**(2), 183–235 (1994). https://doi.org/10.1016/0304-3975(94)90010-8
2. André, É., Fribourg, L., Kühne, U., Soulat, R.: IMITATOR 2.5: a tool for analyzing robustness in scheduling problems. In: Giannakopoulou, D., Méry, D. (eds.) FM 2012. LNCS, vol. 7436, pp. 33–36. Springer, Heidelberg (2012). https://doi.org/10.1007/978-3-642-32759-9_6
3. André, É., Soulat, R.: Synthesis of timing parameters satisfying safety properties. In: Delzanno, G., Potapov, I. (eds.) RP 2011. LNCS, vol. 6945, pp. 31–44. Springer, Heidelberg (2011). https://doi.org/10.1007/978-3-642-24288-5_5
4. Behrmann, G., Bouyer, P., Fleury, E., Larsen, K.G.: Static guard analysis in timed automata verification. In: Garavel, H., Hatcliff, J. (eds.) TACAS 2003. LNCS, vol. 2619, pp. 254–270. Springer, Heidelberg (2003). https://doi.org/10.1007/3-540-36577-X_18
5. Behrmann, G., Bouyer, P., Larsen, K.G., Pelanek, R.: Lower and upper bounds in zone-based abstractions of timed automata. Int. J. Softw. Tools Technol. Transfer (STTT) **8**(3), 204–215 (2006)
6. Bengtsson, J., Yi, W.: Timed automata: semantics, algorithms and tools. In: Lectures on Concurrency and Petri Nets: Advances in Petri Nets. LNCS, vol. 3908, pp. 87–124. Springer, Heidelberg (2004). https://doi.org/10.1007/978-3-540-27755-2_3
7. Blanchette, J.C., Fleury, M., Lammich, P., Weidenbach, C.: A verified SAT solver framework with learn, forget, restart, and incrementality. J. Autom. Reasoning **61**(1-4), 333–365 (2018). https://doi.org/10.1007/s10817-018-9455-7
8. Blom, S., Darabi, S., Huisman, M., Oortwijn, W.: The VerCors tool set: verification of parallel and concurrent software. In: Polikarpova, N., Schneider, S. (eds.) IFM 2017. LNCS, vol. 10510, pp. 102–110. Springer, Cham (2017). https://doi.org/10.1007/978-3-319-66845-1_7
9. Brunner, J., Lammich, P.: Formal verification of an executable LTL model checker with partial order reduction. J. Autom. Reason. **60**(1), 3–21 (2018)
10. Brunner, J., Seidl, B., Sickert, S.: A verified and compositional translation of LTL to deterministic Rabin automata. In: Harrison, J., O'Leary, J., Tolmach, A. (eds.) ITP 2019, September 9–12, 2019, Portland, OR, USA. LIPIcs, vol. 141, pp. 11:1–11:19. Schloss Dagstuhl - Leibniz-Zentrum für Informatik (2019). https://doi.org/10.4230/LIPIcs.ITP.2019.11

11. Daws, C., Tripakis, S.: Model checking of real-time reachability properties using abstractions. In: Steffen, B. (ed.) TACAS 1998. LNCS, vol. 1384, pp. 313–329. Springer, Heidelberg (1998). https://doi.org/10.1007/BFb0054180

12. Dill, D.L.: Timing assumptions and verification of finite-state concurrent systems. In: Sifakis, J. (ed.) CAV 1989. LNCS, vol. 407, pp. 197–212. Springer, Heidelberg (1990). https://doi.org/10.1007/3-540-52148-8_17

13. Esparza, J., Lammich, P., Neumann, R., Nipkow, T., Schimpf, A., Smaus, J.-G.: A fully verified executable LTL model checker. In: Sharygina, N., Veith, H. (eds.) CAV 2013. LNCS, vol. 8044, pp. 463–478. Springer, Heidelberg (2013). https://doi.org/10.1007/978-3-642-39799-8_31

14. Finkel, A., Schnoebelen, P.: Well-structured transition systems everywhere! Theoret. Comput. Sci. **256**(1), 63 – 92 (2001). https://doi.org/10.1016/S0304-3975(00)00102-X, iSS

15. Griggio, A., Roveri, M., Tonetta, S.: Certifying proofs for LTL model checking. In: 2018 Formal Methods in Computer Aided Design (FMCAD) pp. 1–9 (2018)

16. Herbreteau, F., Srivathsan, B., Tran, T.T., Walukiewicz, I.: Why liveness for timed automata is hard, and what we can do about it. In: Lal, A., Akshay, S., Saurabh, S., Sen, S. (eds.) FSTTCS. LIPIcs, vol. 65, pp. 48:1–48:14. Schloss Dagstuhl (2016)

17. Herbreteau, F., Srivathsan, B., Walukiewicz, I.: Lazy abstractions for timed automata. In: Sharygina, N., Veith, H. (eds.) Computer Aided Verification, pp. 990–1005. Springer, Heidelberg (2013). https://doi.org/10.1007/978-3-642-39799-8_71

18. Herbreteau, F., Srivathsan, B., Walukiewicz, I.: Better abstractions for timed automata. Inf. Comput. **251**, 67–90 (2016)

19. Herbreteau, F., Point, G.: TChecker (2019). https://github.com/fredher/tchecker

20. Heule, M., Hunt, W., Kaufmann, M., Wetzler, N.: Efficient, verified checking of propositional proofs. In: Ayala-Rincón, M., Muñoz, C.A. (eds.) Interactive Theorem Proving, pp. 269–284. Springer, Cham (2017). https://doi.org/10.1007/978-3-319-66107-0_18

21. Kant, G., Laarman, A., Meijer, J., van de Pol, J., Blom, S., van Dijk, T.: LTSmin: high-performance language-independent model checking. In: Baier, C., Tinelli, C. (eds.) TACAS 2015. LNCS, vol. 9035, pp. 692–707. Springer, Heidelberg (2015). https://doi.org/10.1007/978-3-662-46681-0_61

22. Laarman, A., Olesen, M.C., Dalsgaard, A.E., Larsen, K.G., van de Pol, J.: Multi-core emptiness checking of timed Büchi automata using inclusion abstraction. In: Sharygina, N., Veith, H. (eds.) CAV, pp. 968–983. Springer, Heidelberg (2013). https://doi.org/10.1007/978-3-642-39799-8_69

23. Lammich, P.: Efficient verified (UN)SAT certificate checking. In: de Moura, L. (ed.) Automated Deduction - CADE 26, pp. 237–254. Springer, Cham (2017). https://doi.org/10.1007/978-3-319-63046-5_15

24. Larsen, G.K., Pettersson, P., Yi, W.: Uppaal in a nutshell. Software Tools for Technology Transfer **1**(1), 134–152 (1997)

25. Leino, K.R.M.: Developing verified programs with Dafny. In: ICSE, pp. 1488–1490. IEEE Computer Society (2013)

26. Li, G.: Checking timed büchi automata emptiness using LU-abstractions. In: Ouaknine, J., Vaandrager, F.W. (eds.) FORMATS 2009. LNCS, vol. 5813, pp. 228–242. Springer, Heidelberg (2009). https://doi.org/10.1007/978-3-642-04368-0_18

27. Namjoshi, K.S.: Certifying model checkers. In: Berry, G., Comon, H., Finkel, A. (eds.) CAV 2001. LNCS, vol. 2102, pp. 2–13. Springer, Heidelberg (2001). https://doi.org/10.1007/3-540-44585-4_2

28. Nguyen, H.G., Petrucci, L., van de Pol, J.: Layered and collecting NDFS with subsumption for parametric timed automata. In: ICECCS, pp. 1–9. IEEE Computer Society (2018)

29. Nipkow, T., Lawrence C. Paulson, Wenzel, M.: Isabelle/HOL - A Proof Assistant for Higher-Order Logic, LNCS, vol. 2283. Springer, Cham (2002). https://doi.org/10.1007/3-540-45949-9

30. Oortwijn, W., Huisman, M., Joosten, S.J.C., van de Pol, J.: Automated verification of parallel nested DFS. In: Biere, A., Parker, D. (eds.) TACAS 2020, Proceedings, Part I. Lecture Notes in Computer Science, vol. 12078, pp. 247–265. Springer, Heidelberg (2020). https://doi.org/10.1007/978-3-030-45190-5_14

31. Pol, J.C.: Automated verification of nested DFS. In: Núñez, M., Güdemann, M. (eds.) FMICS 2015. LNCS, vol. 9128, pp. 181–197. Springer, Cham (2015). https://doi.org/10.1007/978-3-319-19458-5_12

32. Tripakis, S.: Checking timed Büchi emptiness on simulation graphs. ACM Trans. Comput. Logic 10(3) (2009)

33. Tripakis, S., Yovine, S., Bouajjani, A.: Checking timed Büchi automata emptiness efficiently. Formal Methods Syst. Des. **26**(3), 267–292 (2005)

34. Wimmer, S.: Munta: a verified model checker for timed automata. In: André, É., Stoelinga, M. (eds.) FORMATS 2019, Proceedings. Lecture Notes in Computer Science, vol. 11750, pp. 236–243. Springer, Heidelberg (2019). https://doi.org/10.1007/978-3-030-29662-9_14

35. Wimmer, S., Herbreteau, F., van de Pol, J.: Certifying emptiness of timed büchi automata: Artifact (2020). https://doi.org/10.6084/m9.figshare.12620582.v1

36. Wimmer, S., Lammich, P.: Verified model checking of timed automata. In: Beyer, D., Huisman, M. (eds.) TACAS 2018, pp. 61–78. Springer, Cham (2018). https://doi.org/10.1007/978-3-319-89960-2_4

37. Wimmer, S., von Mutius, J.: Verified certification of reachability checking for timed automata. In: Biere, A., Parker, D. (eds.) TACAS 2020, Proceedings, Part I. Lecture Notes in Computer Science, vol. 12078, pp. 425–443. Springer, Cham (2020). https://doi.org/10.1007/978-3-030-45190-5_24

Learning Specifications for Labelled Patterns

Nicolas Basset[1], Thao Dang[1], Akshay Mambakam[1(✉)],
and José Ignacio Requeno Jarabo[2]

[1] VERIMAG/CNRS, University Grenoble Alpes, Grenoble, France
{nicolas.basset1,thao.dang,Akshay.Mambakam}@univ-grenoble-alpes.fr
[2] Department of Computing, Mathematics, and Physics, Western Norway University
of Applied Sciences (HVL), Bergen, Norway
jirj@hvl.no

Abstract. In this work, we introduce a supervised learning framework
for inferring temporal logic specifications from labelled patterns in signals, so that the formulae can then be used to correctly detect the same
patterns in unlabelled samples. The input patterns that are fed to the
training process are labelled by a Boolean signal that captures their
occurrences. To express the patterns with quantitative features, we use
parametric specifications that are increasing, which we call Increasing
Parametric Pattern Predictor (IPPP). This means that augmenting the
value of the parameters makes the predicted pattern true on a larger set.
A particular class of parametric specification formalisms that we use is
Parametric Signal Temporal Logic (PSTL). One of the main contributions of this paper is the definition of a new measure, called ϵ-count, to
assess the quality of the learned formula. This measure enables us to compare two Boolean signals and, hence, quantifies how much the labelling
signal induced by the formula differs from the true labelling signal (e.g.
given by an expert). Therefore, the ϵ-count can measure the number of
mismatches (either false positives or false negatives) up to some error
tolerance ϵ. Our supervised learning framework can be expressed by a
multicriteria optimization problem with two objective functions: the min-
imization of false positives and false negatives given by the parametric
formula on a signal. We provide an algorithm to solve this multi-criteria
optimization problem. Our approach is demonstrated on two case studies
involving characterization and classification of labeled ECG (electrocardiogram) data.

Keywords: Signal pattern matching · Monotonic specification
learning · Pareto multi-criteria optimization · Signal Temporal Logic

1 Introduction

Complex systems consist of various inter-connected components for which rigorous modelling is difficult. Due to technological advances a large amount of data

This work has been partially supported by the ANR Project ANR-15-IDEX-02.

N. Bertrand and N. Jansen (Eds.): FORMATS 2020, LNCS 12288, pp. 76–93, 2020.
https://doi.org/10.1007/978-3-030-57628-8_5

from such systems is available. However, to ensure that systems behave correctly, formal specifications defining the intended behaviour are needed. Data-driven modelling involves the process of learning models and specifications of systems from the traces they generate. Once learnt they can be used for analysing and monitoring these systems. This is particularly useful when rigorous mathematical models based on first principles are difficult to obtain.

In this context, supervised learning involves designing a specification from a given set of labelled signals, so that the specification is later used to label signals via monitoring. One approach is to start from nothing but a sample of labelled signals and learn a logical specification, essentially by enumerating formulae of increasing size (using suitable heuristics) to come up with one that is good enough w.r.t. the sample. A more suitable approach is to exploit prior knowledge made available in the form of a parametric specification. For instance, an engineer observing the behaviours of a concrete collection of cars would ask for the parameter valuations p_1 and p_2 for the following emergency brake pattern: "the car can pass from speed 30 m/s to p_1 m/s within less than p_2 seconds."

Our work is of the second kind, following the trend initiated by [7] with parametric specifications written in Parametric Signal Temporal Logic (PSTL). We are inspired by several works on PSTL [7,11] whose aim was to compute the validity domain of a parametric formula, i.e., the set of parameter valuations that makes the formula true on a (or a set of) signal. Though in our experiments we use PSTL with the extended semantics of [8], our framework is not specific to it and can be applied to other specification formalisms. To provide a generic approach which is not tied to a specific specification formalism, we introduce the notion of parametric pattern predictors (PPP). A PPP is a parametric operator Ψ_p that transforms unlabelled signal s to a labelling Boolean signal $\Psi_p(s)$ that is true on time points where the pattern is predicted. We focus our attention on PPPs that are increasing: when the value of p increases for any given signal s, the set of time points where $\Psi_p(s)$ is true expands.

In our framework, we allow the learned specification Ψ_p to produce some false positives and false negatives on parts of the training signals, i.e., there are time points where Ψ_p predicts a pattern while there is none, or misses it. We are interested in computing several sets of parameter valuations (called *solution sets*) which ensure that the "quantities" of false positive and/or false negatives are lower than given bounds. To define such quantities, we can use neither counts of time points or of intervals nor the Lebesgue measure since, as we will see later, these measures are not suitable. Instead we adapt the notion of ϵ-separated set from information theory [18] to propose a new measure, called ϵ-count, with suitable properties (Proposition 1). Our method for computing solution sets is similar to the method for approximating monotonic validity domains, proposed in [7]. The main difference is that the constraints on false positives and false negatives involve two sets monotonic in opposite directions. To this end, we develop an algorithm that computes the intersection of an upset and a downset in $\mathbb{R}^n$.

The main contributions of the paper can be summarized as follows:

- A generic framework of learning parameter valuations for increasing parametric pattern predictors with quantitative constraints on false positives and false negatives.
- A measure called ϵ-count for expressing "how often" a Boolean signal is true and its application to extend the quantitative notions of false positives and false negatives to Boolean labelling signals.
- An algorithm to compute the intersection of an upset and a downset that are queried from a membership oracle.

Section 2 presents our specification learning framework. Section 3 describes the algorithm that computes the intersection of an upset and a downset in $\mathbb{R}^n$. Section 4 demonstrates our approach on two case studies involving ECG signals. More details and proofs can be found in the technical report [4].

Related Work on PSTL. Parameters in PSTL can be used to express constraints both on values and time bounds. They are called space and timing parameters respectively in [11]. In [7] two different methods for computing validity domains for PSTL formulae are presented. The first method demonstrates how exact validity domains can be computed using quantifier elimination, in principle. Though complete and exact, the main drawback of this approach is the exponential worst case complexity in nested depth of formulae. The second method computes approximations of monotonic validity domains using query functions. This method forms the foundation of our contributions regarding monotonic validity domains. Another method which computes validity domains recursively is proposed in [11]. This method deals only with space parameters and leaves handling timing parameters for future work.

Other works which utilize PSTL for the tasks of clustering and classification are as follows. They concentrate on extracting features and computing a single solution rather than complete validity domains. In [28], template PSTL formulae are used to extract features. These features are then used in an unsupervised learning context to cluster traces. In [29], Hausdorff distance based on monotonic validity domains boundaries [22] is used as a distance metric for traces. Clustering was used to generate labelling and then construct specifications from monotonic PSTL templates. In [24], monotonic PSTL formulae are enumerated using formula signatures. Computation of validity domain boundaries [22] is combined with checks for misclassification rate for parameter estimation. The resulting algorithm is used to search for an STL formula to classify traces. Another enumeration based method for classifying traces using robustness value based decision trees is proposed in [23]. Grid sampling is used to estimate timing parameters. Both the aforementioned enumeration based methods deal with learning classifiers from example labelling (i.e. supervised learning). In [17], parameter estimation for PSTL is formulated as multi-objective optimization with respect to robustness. For inferring the structure of STL formulae in the absence of templates, they propose an incremental construction approach.

It is to be noted that we explicitly capture certain features using the quantitative semantics of extended STL [8]. This simplifies the task by avoiding their encoding as unknown parameters.

Other Related Work. Temporal logic and timed automata provide a framework to describe and reason about occurrence of events and their correlations in time. Unsupervised learning of hybrid timed automata from real-valued signals was investigated in [30]. In [14] and [21] Timed Regular Expressions (TRE) and LTL specifications respectively are mined from system traces using formula templates and event binding. Quantitative Regular Expressions (QRE) have been used to express specifications for arrhythmia-detection algorithms [5]. Recently, shape expressions have been proposed for learning specifications and features from signals [27]. The problem of learning Linear Temporal Logic (LTL) formulae without any requirements of a priori information in the form of formula templates has been recently explored in [26]. Learning STL specifications using different restrictions on the syntax has been studied in a series of papers by others. A sub-class of STL called reactive STL is investigated in [19]. The formulae in this sub-class are enumerated by defining a partial order and simulate annealing is used for parameter estimation. Another sub-class named inference PSTL is proposed in [20] for learning formulae that detect anomalies. A decision tree approach combined with a restricted set of PSTL primitives using impurity measures is proposed in [12].

2   Specification Learning Framework

Before introducing our specification learning framework we need few preliminaries on signals and partial order on $\mathbb{R}^n$.

Signals. A *signal* s is a function from $\mathbb{R}$ to $\mathbb{R}$. A *Boolean signal* w is a signal that takes its values in $\mathbb{B} = \{0,1\}$, with the common interpretation of 1 and 0 as true and false. The *support* of a signal w denoted by $\mathbf{supp}(w)$ is the smallest closed set that contains the set $\{t \mid w(t) \neq 0\}$. We consider only signals with bounded support (aka. compact support[1]). The signal $t \mapsto 0$ which is always false is denoted by $\mathbf{0}$.

Partial Order on $\mathbb{R}^n$. Given two vectors $p, q \in \mathbb{R}^n$, we say that p is lower than q, denoted by $p \leq q$, if $\forall i, p_i \leq q_i$. A set $\overline{X}$ is an *upset* if for all $p, q \in \mathbb{R}^n$ such that $p \leq q$ if $p \in \overline{X}$ then $q \in \overline{X}$. A set $\underline{X}$ is a *downset* if for all $p, q \in \mathbb{R}^n$ such that $q \leq p$ if $p \in \underline{X}$ then $q \in \underline{X}$. The boundary consisting of all the minimal elements of an upset (or all the maximal elements of a downset) is called a *Pareto front* in the field of multi-criteria optimization. The *box* between two vectors $\underline{x}$ and $\overline{x}$ with $\underline{x} \leq \overline{x}$ is $\lfloor \underline{x}, \overline{x} \rceil = \{y \mid \underline{x} \leq y \leq \overline{x}\}$.

---

[1] A subset of $\mathbb{R}$ is compact if and only if it is closed and bounded.

2.1   Parametric Pattern Predictor

The labels of patterns in our problem are modelled using Boolean signals that we call *labelling signals*. A labelling signal λ_s for a signal s being 1 or 0 at a time point indicates respectively the occurrence or absence of a pattern in s at this time point. Particular cases of labelling signals are those whose support is a list of time points where patterns occur. In these cases, a pattern is a discrete event, and several labelling signals can be merged together to form what is called a timed word in timed automata theory [6]. We prefer using Boolean signals in continuous time for two main reasons. We want to allow patterns to have duration, that is their occurrence lasts continuously throughout a time interval (composed thus of uncountable number of points). They can be considered both as input or output signals for monitoring tools for temporal properties in dense time, such as StlEval [8] which we will use for our experiments.

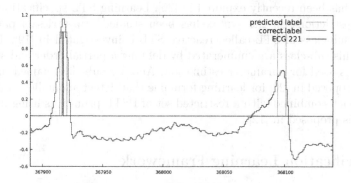

Fig. 1. Showing the single false positive of $\Psi^{ch}_{(8.20,0.64,-0.44)}$ for ECG 221

Example 1. *Consider electro-cardiograms (ECG) from the MIT-BIH Arrhythmia Database of Physionet [16, 25]. They are provided with annotations of timestamps where normal or abnormal peaks occur. The annotations for the normal peaks can be modelled into a labelling signal that is 1 when a normal peak occurs and 0 everywhere else. A portion of ECG 221 is depicted as in Fig. 1 where the blue labelling signal comes from the database.*

Our aim is to develop a pattern predictor, a tool that generates a labelling signal for a given signal. For ECG signals, it is used to annotate them with normal peaks, such as in Fig. 1 the red signal is predicted by our tool.

Definition 1 ((Increasing) Parametric Pattern Predictor (IPPP)). *A parametric pattern predictor (PPP) is a function that maps a vector p of reals to an operator Ψ_p that maps real-valued signals to Boolean-valued signals. Ψ is said increasing if for all $p \leq p'$, for all signal s, $\forall t \in [0, l)$ with l the length of s, $\Psi_p(s)(t) \leq \Psi_{p'}(s)(t)$.*

Example 2. *Formula (1) specified in the extended STL² [8] gives a simple and rough characterization of a normal ECG peak.* $\Psi^{ch}_{(p_1,p_2,p_3)}(s)(t) = 1$ *if the maximum of s on $[t - p_1, t + p_1]$ is above $-p_3$, and its variation is within the bound p_2 on $[t - c, t - p_1]$ and on $[t + p_1, t + c]$. The parameter domains are $p_1 \in [0, 70]$, $p_2 \in [0, 1]$ and $p_3 \in [-1, 0]$. Here, $c = 70$ is a constant representing an upper limit on p_1. Note that if one increases (p_1, p_2, p_3), the property is easier to achieve.*

$$\Psi^{ch}_{(p_1,p_2,p_3)} := ((\text{Max}_{[-c,-p_1]} s - \text{Min}_{[-c,-p_1]} s) \leq p_2) \wedge$$
$$((\text{Max}_{[-p_1,p_1]} s) \geq -p_3) \wedge ((\text{Max}_{[p_1,c]} s - \text{Min}_{[p_1,c]} s) \leq p_2) \quad (1)$$

We remark again that although our work uses the extended STL [8], our framework can be applied to other specification formalisms. Indeed, many matching problems can be cast into an IPPP, for instance matching as closely as possible a signal for the longest time possible. More formally, we can define an IPPP Ψ^π such that $\Psi^\pi_{(p_1,p_2)}(s)$ is 1 at time t if the signal s restricted on the interval $[t, t + T - p_1]$ is point-wise p_2-close to a given signal π (representing a shape of interest), that is, $\forall t' \in [0, T - p_1], |s(t + t') - \pi(t')| \leq p_2$. The idea of matching such predefined shapes is inspired by the work on shape expression [27].

2.2   Quantifying Mismatches via ϵ-count

A labelled signal (s, λ_s) is a pair of signal s and labelling signal λ_s. We aim at learning parameters p for an IPPP Ψ_p so that for every given labelled signal (s, λ_s), the labelling signals $\Psi_p(s)$ and λ_s should match together as much as possible. We measure two kind of mismatches by measuring "how often" the two following signals are true. The *false positive signal* $\neg\lambda_s \wedge \Psi_p(s)$ indicates when the predictor predicts an occurrence when there is none. The *false negative signal* $\lambda_s \wedge \neg\Psi_p(s)$ indicates when the predictor misses an actual occurrence.

The phrase "how often" may make one think of counting events like occurrences of a peak. However we cannot count the points where a Boolean formula is true since they are in general uncountable. Counting the intervals where a Boolean signal is true is also problematic since it is not always increasing with the support of the signal. For example, a Boolean signal defined as $b(t) := s(t) < p$ has support that increases with p, but such interval counting is not monotonically increasing with p. Also there can be infinitely many intervals. Last but not least, the most standard measure of subsets of $\mathbb{R}$ is the Lebesgue's measure. This is not convenient for our purpose because a signal whose support is the disjoint union of many intervals of almost-null measure which are quite far apart will entails a small measure while for such a signal we want instead a big "count" because it can represent the number of mismatches. In this work we introduce the notion of ϵ-count, inspired by the notions of ϵ-separated sets and ϵ-capacity proposed in [18].

---

² Here and in the rest of the paper we slightly simplified the syntax of [8] by replacing $(\text{On}_{[a,b]} \text{Max} s)$ by $(\text{Max}_{[a,b]} s)$ whose value in t is $\max_{t' \in [t+a,t+b]} s(t')$.

Definition 2 (ϵ-separated set and ϵ-count). *Given a boolean signal w, a set S of reals is ϵ-separated w.r.t. w if $S \subseteq supp(w)$ and for every $t, t' \in S$ with $t \neq t'$, it holds that $|t - t'| \geq \epsilon$. The ϵ-count of a signal w is $c_\epsilon(w) = \max\{|S| \mid S \text{ is } \epsilon\text{-separated w.r.t. } w\}$.*

Proposition 1. *The ϵ-count of a signal w is determined in a greedy manner with the following recursive equations: $c_\epsilon(\mathbf{0}) = 0$ and $c_\epsilon(w) = 1 + c_\epsilon(w')$ where $w'(t) = 0$ if $t < \epsilon + \min(supp(w))$ and $w'(t) = w(t)$ otherwise.*

Proposition 2. *1. The ϵ-count is null iff it is applied to the constant signal $\mathbf{0}$.*
2. The ϵ-count is increasing: if $w \leq w'$ then $c_\epsilon(w) \leq c_\epsilon(w')$.
3. The ϵ-count satisfies a triangular inequality: $c_\epsilon(w \vee w') \leq c_\epsilon(w) + c_\epsilon(w')$.

2.3   Parameter Identification Problems

Given bounds $\mathbf{f}_+, \mathbf{f}_-$ on the allowed ϵ-count of false-positives and false-negatives, we are interested in the following three sets:

$$\mathtt{Dom+}(\Psi, \mathcal{S}, \mathbf{f}_+) = \{p \mid \forall(s, \lambda_s) \in \mathcal{S}, c_\epsilon(\Psi_p(s) \wedge \neg\lambda_s) \leq \mathbf{f}_+\}, \tag{2}$$

$$\mathtt{Dom-}(\Psi, \mathcal{S}, \mathbf{f}_-) = \{p \mid \forall(s, \lambda_s) \in \mathcal{S}, c_\epsilon(\neg\Psi_p(s) \wedge \lambda_s) \leq \mathbf{f}_-\}, \tag{3}$$

$$\mathtt{DomInter}(\Psi, \mathcal{S}, \mathbf{f}_+, \mathbf{f}_-) = \mathtt{Dom+}(\Psi, \mathcal{S}, \mathbf{f}_+) \cap \mathtt{Dom-}(\Psi, \mathcal{S}, \mathbf{f}_-). \tag{4}$$

For convenience, we call them respectively the *positive, negative* and *intersection* solution sets. It is also of great interest to compute the set of couples $(\mathbf{f}_+, \mathbf{f}_-)$, called *set of feasible error bounds*, for which a solution exists:

$$\mathcal{P}(\Psi, \mathcal{S}) = \{(\mathbf{f}_+, \mathbf{f}_-) \mid \mathtt{DomInter}(\Psi, \mathcal{S}, \mathbf{f}_+, \mathbf{f}_-) \neq \emptyset\}. \tag{5}$$

In addition, we are interested in a relaxed version of the identification problem for false positive bounding, by tolerating a difference of σ time units in matching the labels. This can be done by replacing λ_s with the signal[3] $F_{[-\sigma,\sigma]} \lambda_s$ in (2). More concretely, the solution set of the corresponding σ-relaxed problem is:

$$\mathtt{Dom+}^\sigma(\Psi, \mathcal{S}, \mathbf{f}_+) = \{p \mid \forall(s, \lambda_s) \in \mathcal{S}, c_\epsilon(\Psi_p(s) \wedge \neg F_{[-\sigma,\sigma]} \lambda_s) \leq \mathbf{f}_+\}.$$

Hence, the corresponding relaxed version of the intersection solution set (4) is

$$\mathtt{DomInter}^\sigma(\Psi, \mathcal{S}, \mathbf{f}_+, \mathbf{f}_-) = \mathtt{Dom+}^\sigma(\Psi, \mathcal{S}, \mathbf{f}_+) \cap \mathtt{Dom-}(\Psi, \mathcal{S}, \mathbf{f}_-). \tag{6}$$

Note that $\mathtt{Dom+}(\Psi, \mathcal{S}, \mathbf{f}_+)$ is a downset and $\mathtt{Dom-}(\Psi, \mathcal{S}, \mathbf{f}_-)$ is an upset (see the beginning of Sect. 2) because Ψ is increasing. Sets of this kind can be learned from membership queries as proposed in [9,22]. The set $\mathtt{DomInter}(\Psi, \mathcal{S}, \mathbf{f}_+, \mathbf{f}_-)$ is the intersection of an upset and a downset, we thus face a new problem that we address in Sect. 3. The set $\mathcal{P}(\Psi, \mathcal{S})$ is an upset and its minimal elements form a Pareto front. We compute it via membership-queries for couples $(\mathbf{f}_+, \mathbf{f}_-)$. They are done via non-emptiness checking of $\mathtt{DomInter}(\Psi, \mathcal{S}, \mathbf{f}_+, \mathbf{f}_-)$ which is an easier problem than computing the whole set.

---

[3] where $(F_{[-\sigma,\sigma]} \lambda_s)(t) = 1$ iff $\exists t' \in [t - \delta, t + \delta], s(t') = 1$.

3   Intersecting an Upset and a Downset in $\mathbb{R}^n$

In this section, we describe our algorithm for estimating the intersection of an upset and a downset in $\mathbb{R}^n$ which is required to compute $\texttt{DomInter}(\Psi, \mathcal{S}, \texttt{f}_+, \texttt{f}_-)$. The upset and downset are accessed via membership oracles, that is, two Boolean-valued functions $\rho_+ : \mathbb{R}^n \to \mathbb{B}$ and $\rho_- : \mathbb{R}^n \to \mathbb{B}$ which are respectively monotonically increasing and decreasing with respect to the input.

A point where ρ_+ and ρ_- are both 1 (resp. 0) is called a positive (resp. negative) intersection point. Our approach involves intersection search on the diagonal of a hyper-rectangular parameter space.

Algorithm 1 builds on linear intersection search to compute the positive intersection of an upset and a downset for the multi-dimensional case. An alternative approach is to compute separately the two sets and then their intersection. Computing directly the intersection has the advantage of quickly eliminating the regions that surely do not contain a solution to focus on examining the rest. We can also modify Algorithm 1 to make queries about emptiness of the intersection without computing it exhaustively.

Intersection on a Line and Expansion. The procedure *boundary* finds the Pareto boundary of a monotonically increasing function on a given line using the classical idea of binary search. The procedure *intersect* finds the intersection of two monotonic Boolean functions ρ_+ (increasing) and ρ_- (decreasing) on a line $\langle \underline{x}, \overline{x} \rangle$. Before starting intersection search on a line, by simple queries on the endpoints we can sometimes altogether discard (o_c=*discard*) or fully accept (o_c=*accept*) the bounding hyper-rectangle. This happens when the hyper-rectangle is wholly contained in a negative or a positive intersection. When this is not the case, we query for the values of ρ_+ and ρ_- at the midpoint. If a point in the intersection is found we return with the result on whether it is positive (o_c=*splitpos*) or negative (o_c=*splitneg*). Otherwise, we continue the search recursively by discarding the half segment not containing an intersection. This is possible because ρ_+ and ρ_- are monotonically increasing and decreasing respectively. In this way we end up either finding an intersection or returning a line segment of length equal to an error bound ε containing the intersection (o_c=*notfound*). On a line (p_0, p_1), we can have three outcomes of the search. The first two outcomes are when a point p_c in the positive intersection (Fig. 2b) or the negative intersection (Fig. 2a) is found. For these cases, we can divide the line into two segments (p_0, p_c) and (p_c, p_1). On these segments we can apply the classical binary search to find the Pareto fronts corresponding to the monotonically decreasing and monotonically increasing functions. We call this operation an *expansion*. In Fig. 2a,2b, the points p_+, p_- represent the points where the Pareto fronts for the monotonically increasing and decreasing functions respectively intersect with the line (p_0, p_1). The third and last case is when no intersection has been found.

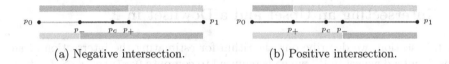

(a) Negative intersection.   (b) Positive intersection.

Fig. 2. Intersection on a line.

Decomposing the Box and Continuing the Search. Algorithm 1 uses the result of the binary intersection search on the diagonal of a box to deduce which regions (inside the box) do or do not contain a solution and which are undecided. Then, it decomposes the undecided region into sub-boxes and recursively processes the resulting sub-boxes (see Fig. 3) There are three cases:

- *No intersection* has been found (see Fig. 3c). As a result of monotonicity, we know that the sub-boxes R_1 and R_2 do not contain a solution, and proceed with the remaining region which is decomposed into two overlapping sub-boxes U_1 and U_2. This decomposition is formulated in Sect. 3.1.
- A *negative intersection* has been found (see Fig. 3a). We can identify a line segment on the diagonal where a solution can not exist and deduce that the regions R_1 and R_2 do not contain a solution. The decomposition of the undecided region leads to two sub-boxes U_1 and U_2 (see Sect. 3.2).
- A *positive intersection* has been found (see Fig. 3b). We obtain the sub-boxes U_1 and U_2 as in the previous cases but use the procedure in Sect. 3.1 twice to obtain overlapping sub-boxes U_3, U_4, U_5 and U_6.

The decompositions into non-overlapping and overlapping sub-boxes are denoted by I_{nov} and I_{ov} in Algorithm 1 and explained in detail in Sects. 3.1 and 3.2.

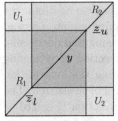   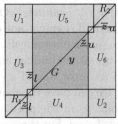   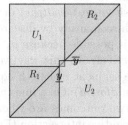

(a) Negative intersection   (b) Positive intersection   (c) No intersection found

Fig. 3. Illustration of sub-boxes.

Before continuing, we need a formal definition of sub-boxes resulting from subdivision based on points $\underline{y} < \overline{y}$ on the diagonal of a box $\lfloor \underline{x}, \overline{x} \rfloor$. These sub-boxes are products of sub-intervals I_{α_i} where for each dimension, their bounds are taken among the following sequence of coordinates $\underline{x}_i < \underline{y}_i < \overline{y}_i < \overline{x}_i$.

Algorithm 1. Pareto front intersection algorithm

1: **Input**: A box $X = \lfloor 0, 1 \rceil$; ρ_+ and ρ_- are respectively monotonically increasing and decreasing Boolean-valued functions; error bounds δ and ε.

2: **Output**: A set of boxes S containing the positive intersection of ρ_+ and ρ_- and a set L representing the undecided region such that $|L| \leq \delta$. All sets are represented by unions of boxes.

3: $L = \{X\}$; $S = \emptyset$ ▷ initialization

4: **repeat**

5:      **pop** first $\lfloor \underline{x}, \overline{x} \rceil \in L$ ▷ take the largest box

6:      $\{\langle \underline{y}, \overline{y} \rangle, o_c\} = intersect(\langle \underline{x}, \overline{x} \rangle, \rho_+, \rho_-, \varepsilon)$ ▷ intersect search on the diagonal

7:      **if** $o_c == splitpos$ **then**   ▷ found a positive intersection.

8:          $\langle \underline{z}_l, \overline{z}_l \rangle = boundary(\langle \underline{x}, \underline{y} \rangle, \rho_+, \varepsilon)$

9:          $\langle \underline{z}_u, \overline{z}_u \rangle = boundary(\langle \overline{y}, \overline{x} \rangle, \neg \rho_-, \varepsilon)$

10:          $S = S \cup \lfloor \overline{z}_l, \underline{z}_u \rceil$

11:          $L = L \cup I_{nov}(\underline{x}, \overline{x}, \overline{z}_l, \underline{z}_u) \cup I_{ov}(\underline{x}, \underline{z}_u, \underline{z}_l, \overline{z}_l) \cup I_{ov}(\overline{z}_l, \overline{x}, \underline{z}_u, \overline{z}_u)$ ▷ see Fig. 3b

12:      **else if** $o_c == splitneg$ **then**   ▷ found a negative intersection.

13:          $\langle \underline{z}_l, \overline{z}_l \rangle = boundary(\langle \underline{x}, \underline{y} \rangle, \neg \rho_-, \varepsilon)$

14:          $\langle \underline{z}_u, \overline{z}_u \rangle = boundary(\langle \overline{y}, \overline{x} \rangle, \rho_+, \varepsilon)$

15:          $L = L \cup I_{nov}(\underline{x}, \overline{x}, \underline{z}_l, \underline{z}_u)$ ▷ see Fig. 3a

16:      **else if** $o_c == accept$ **then**

17:          $S = S \cup \lfloor \underline{x}, \overline{x} \rceil$

18:      **else if** $o_c \neq discard$ **then**   ▷ no intersection found

19:          $L = L \cup I_{ov}(\underline{x}, \overline{x}, \underline{y}, \overline{y})$ ▷ see Fig. 3c.

20:      $\mathtt{Vol}(L) = \mathtt{Vol}(X) - \mathtt{Vol}(Z)$

21: **until** $\mathtt{Vol}(L) \leq \delta$

22: **return** S, L

Definition 3 (Sub-interval encoding). *A sub-interval $I_{\alpha_i} \subseteq \lfloor \underline{x}, \overline{x} \rceil$ is encoded by its subscript $\alpha_i \in \{l, m, u, \mathrm{U}, \mathrm{L}, \mathrm{T}\}$ which is a letter such that $\alpha_i = l$ for the lower interval $[\underline{x}_i, \underline{y}_i]$; $\alpha_i = \mathrm{U}$ for its complement $[\underline{y}_i, \overline{x}_i]$; $\alpha_i = u$ for the upper interval $[\overline{y}_i, \overline{x}_i]$; $\alpha_i = \mathrm{L}$ for its complement $[\underline{x}_i, \overline{y}_i]$; $\alpha_i = m$ for the middle interval $[\underline{y}_i, \overline{x}_i]$; and $\alpha_i = \mathrm{T}$ for the whole interval $[\underline{x}_i, \overline{x}_i]$.*

Definition 4 (Sub-boxes). *Given $\alpha = (\alpha_1, \ldots, \alpha_n) \in \{l, m, u, \mathrm{U}, \mathrm{L}, \mathrm{T}\}^n$ and four n-dimensional points $\underline{x} = (\underline{x}_1, \ldots, \underline{x}_n)$, $\overline{x} = (\overline{x}_1, \ldots, \overline{x}_n)$, $\underline{y} = (\underline{y}_1, \ldots, \underline{y}_n)$, $\overline{y} = (\overline{y}_1, \ldots, \overline{y}_n)$ such that $\underline{x} \leq \underline{y} \leq \overline{y} \leq \overline{x}$, the sub-box of $\lfloor \underline{x}, \overline{x} \rceil$ induced by α and $\lfloor \underline{y}, \overline{y} \rceil$ is $B_\alpha = \prod_{i=1}^{n} I_{\alpha_i}$ with I_{α_i} defined in Definition 3.*

3.1 Decomposition into Overlapping Sub-boxes

This decomposition, proposed in [9], is useful when we have to remove from a box $\lfloor \underline{x}, \overline{x} \rceil$ the downward closure of $\underline{y}$ (i.e. $B_{(l, \ldots, l)} = \lfloor \underline{x}, \overline{y} \rceil$) and the upward-closure of $\overline{y}$ (i.e. $B_{(u, \ldots, u)} = \lfloor \underline{y}, \overline{x} \rceil$). The resulting sub-boxes can overlap but this decomposition is only used with points that are ε-close. At least in one dimension i the overlap is restricted to the middle interval $[\underline{y}_i, \overline{y}_i]$ whose length is at most ε leading to a negligible volume when ε is small compared to the length of $[\underline{x}_i, \overline{y}_i]$ and $[\underline{y}_i, \overline{x}_i]$.

Definition 5 (Overlapping sub-boxes). *Let $\underline{x}, \underline{y}, \overline{y}, \overline{x}$ be 4 n-dimensional points with $\underline{x} < \underline{y} < \overline{y} < \overline{x}$. We define*

$$I_{ov}(\underline{x}, \overline{x}, \underline{y}, \overline{y}) = \{B_\alpha \mid \alpha \in \mathbb{D}_n\}$$

where $(\mathbb{D}_n)_{n \in \mathbb{N}}$ is a sequence of set of words defined inductively as follows:

$\mathbb{D}_2 = \{\text{LU}, \text{UL}\}, \mathbb{D}_3 = \{\text{LUT}, \text{TLU}, \text{UTL}\}$, *and for* $n \geq 4$ $\mathbb{D}_{n+1} = \text{T}\mathbb{D}_n \cup \text{LU}^n \cup \text{UL}^n$.

As an example $\mathbb{D}_4 = \{\text{TLUT}, \text{TTLU}, \text{TUTL}, \text{LUUU}, \text{ULLL}\}$

Proposition 3. *The set $I_{nov}(\underline{x}, \overline{x}, \underline{y}, \overline{y})$ contains $(2n - 3)$ boxes whose union is the complement in $\lfloor \underline{x}, \overline{x} \rceil$ of $B_{(l,...,l)} \cup B_{(u,...,u)}$.*

3.2   Decomposition into Non-overlapping Sub-boxes

In case a negative intersection has been found the set of points in the upward-closure of $\underline{y}$ should be removed. This is the sub-box $B_{(\text{U},...,\text{U})} = \lfloor \underline{y}, \overline{x} \rceil$. The same reasoning holds for the downward-closure of $\overline{y}$ which is $B_{(\text{L},...,\text{L})} = \lfloor \underline{x}, \overline{y} \rceil$.

Definition 6 (Non-overlapping sub-boxes). *We define $\mathbb{A}_n$, $\mathbb{C}_n$, $\mathbb{E}_n$ recursively as follows*

$$\mathbb{E}_0 = \mathbb{A}_0 = \mathbb{C}_0 = \emptyset \text{ and for } n \geq 1$$

$$\mathbb{E}_{n+1} = m\mathbb{E}_n \cup u\mathbb{A}_n \cup l\mathbb{C}_n, \quad \mathbb{A}_{n+1} = l\text{T}^n \cup \text{U}\mathbb{A}_n, \quad \mathbb{C}_{n+1} = u\text{T}^n \cup \text{L}\mathbb{C}_n.$$

Let $\underline{x}, \underline{y}, \overline{y}, \overline{x}$ be 4 n-dimensional points with $\underline{x} < \underline{y} < \overline{y} < \overline{x}$. We define

$$I_{nov}(\underline{x}, \overline{x}, \underline{y}, \overline{y}) = \{B_\alpha \mid \alpha \in \mathbb{E}_n\}.$$

Proposition 4. *The set $I_{nov}(\underline{x}, \overline{x}, \underline{y}, \overline{y})$ contains $(n^2 - n)$ boxes whose union is the complement in $\lfloor \underline{x}, \overline{x} \rceil$ of $B_{(\text{U},...,\text{U})} \cup B_{(\text{L},...,\text{L})}$.*

As an illustration we give $\mathbb{A}_n, \mathbb{C}_n, \mathbb{E}_n$ for the dimensions 1, 2 and 3:

n	1	2	3
$\mathbb{A}_n$	l	$l\text{T} \cup u l$	$l\text{TT} \cup u l\text{T} \cup u u l$
$\mathbb{C}_n$	u	$u\text{T} \cup \text{L}u$	$u\text{TT} \cup \text{L}u\text{T} \cup \text{LL}u$
$\mathbb{E}_n$	$\emptyset$	$lu \cup ul$	$mlu \cup mul \cup ul\text{T} \cup uul \cup lu\text{T} \cup l\text{L}u$

4   Experiments

We have implemented the algorithms proposed in this work and incorporated them as additions to ParetoLib [2,10] (a Python library for Pareto-Front learning) and the tool StlEval [3,8]. Implementations in the ParetoLib library only deal with upsets (or downsets). To satisfy this, one can easily replace some of the parameters with their opposite.

We now present some experimental results obtained by using our supervised learning framework to analyse labelled electrocardiogram (ECG). ECG signals capture information about electrical activity of the heart and can help detect anomalies in its functioning. We characterize several features (e.g. peaks and ditches) as parametric specification, and provide the intersection solution set for the involved parameters with the best possible trade-off between false positives and false negatives.

4.1   Learning STL Specifications for Labelled ECGs

We present our results on three ECGs (100, 123, 221) each containing between 1500 to 2500 labelled pulses taken from the MIT-BIH Arrhythmia Database of Physionet [16,25]. We use the formula (1) from Sect. 2 to characterize a parameter predictor Ψ^{ch} for a normal heart pulse. Given a set $\mathcal{S}$ of labelled ECG signals, the upper bounds $\mathtt{f_-}$ and $\mathtt{f_+}$ on the numbers of false negatives and positives respectively and a matching tolerance value σ, we use the intersection algorithm to find the relaxed intersection solution set $\mathtt{DomInter}^\sigma(\Psi^{ch}, \mathcal{S}, \mathtt{f_+}, \mathtt{f_-})$ as defined in (6) (that is the set of parameter values p such that the predictor Ψ^{ch}_p can predict normal heart pulses on the labelled signal set $\mathcal{S}$ with the numbers of false positives and false negatives bounded by $\mathtt{f_+}$ and $\mathtt{f_-}$).

Trade Off Between False Negatives and False Positives. Using a modification of Algorithm 1, we query about emptiness of $\mathtt{DomInter}^\sigma(\Psi^{ch}, \mathcal{S}, \mathtt{f_+}, \mathtt{f_-})$ and compute the set $\mathcal{P}(\Psi^{ch}, \mathcal{S})$ of feasible error bounds as defined in (5). We recall that Algorithm 1 explores the parameter space up to a given bound δ on volume. In our experiments we search until we have reduced the volume of the undecided region to V_δ percentage of the total volume of the parameter space. The Pareto front that we obtain asymptotically becomes exact as the value of V_δ tends to zero. In Fig. 4 we show two Pareto front approximations for ECG-100; the front separating the brown and the green regions corresponds to $V_\delta = 1\%$. The Pareto front separating the red and the brown regions corresponds to $V_\delta = 0.1\%$ and is more accurate owing to better exploration.

Looking at Fig. 4, it is pertinent to ask why the predictor (1) cannot match the labelling with better accuracy for ECG-100. Actually, our formula only takes the shape of the heart pulses into account but not their time period. Some heart pulses in ECG-100 are not labelled as normal because they violate the natural rhythm of the heart and arrive too soon or too late. It is thus not possible to distinguish them by considering only the shape. For ECG-221, the predictor (1) can match the labelling with no false negatives and only a single false positive (shown in Fig. 1). For ECG-123, it can match with a single false negative and no false positives.

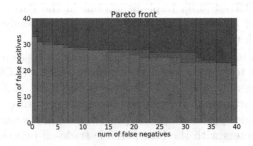

Fig. 4. ECG 100, $V_\delta = 1\%$ vs $V_\delta = 0.1\%$

3D Intersections. Once we have computed $\mathcal{P}(\Psi^{ch}, \mathcal{S})$ with adequate accuracy, we can use Algorithm 1 to further explore the parameter space for different values of V_δ, f_- and f_+. Some exploration results are depicted in Fig. 5 and the associated computation time in Table 1.

Table 1. Computation time for 3D intersection solution sets.

ECG n^0	f_-	f_+	$V_\delta = 1\%$	$V_\delta = 0.1\%$	$V_\delta = 0.01\%$	τ^a
221	0	1	62 s	262 s	1279 s	19 s
123	1	0	103 s	592 s	3189 s	36 s
100	0	33	758 s	5273 s	18670 s	12 s

[a] τ represents the time taken to find the first point in the solution set.

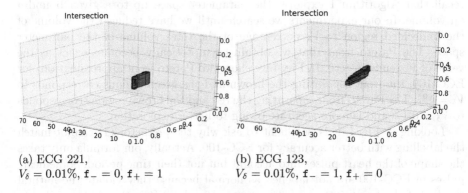

(a) ECG 221,
$V_\delta = 0.01\%$, $f_- = 0$, $f_+ = 1$

(b) ECG 123,
$V_\delta = 0.01\%$, $f_- = 1$, $f_+ = 0$

Fig. 5. Case study 1: intersection solution sets in 3D

4.2   Classification of ECGs

We now demonstrate the application of our approach to binary classification of signals, using the ECGFiveDays dataset from the UCR Time Series Classification Archive [15]. More concretely, we consider two classes of ECGs taken 5 days apart from the same person and want to find a classifier that can correctly predict given an ECG, on which day it was observed (day_1 or day_5). In [23], an enumerative method over STL is applied to solve this problem in the absence of a priori information. By defining expressive and meaningful features, we show how more informative formulae can be obtained with less training data (23 traces as compared to 300 in [23]). The features are based on the well known theoretical modelling of ECG signal as P and T waves combined with a QRS complex (see e.g. [13]). For each ECG in the dataset, we observe two prominent peaks with a ditch in between. We define STL formulae to quantify some features of the signal around the ditch and the peaks as shown in Table 2. The range of feature values (D_1,D_5) for day_1 and day_5 observed in the ECGs are shown in the last two columns of Table 2. They can be computed using a slight modification of classical binary search.

Enumeration of Formulae and Finding a Classifier. We rank the features using the measure[4] $m = |D_1 \triangle D_5|/|D_1 \cup D_5|$. We then enumerate all the distinct pairs (φ_i, φ_j) of features using lexicographical ordering over rank. For each pair we use the intersection algorithm to learn the parameters which make the disjunction formula ($\Psi := \varphi_i \vee \varphi_j$) classify correctly the ECGs given in the training data. Let S_1 and S_2 be the labelled signals corresponding to the classes day_1 and day_5 of ECGs respectively. We compute the intersection of $Dom-(\Psi, S_1, f_-)$ and $Dom+(\Psi, S_2, f_+)$.

Table 2. Features and formulae.

Feature	Formula	D_1 for day_1	D_5 for day_5
Def. of peak	$(s \geq (Max_{[-10,10]}\ s)) \wedge s \geq 1$	NA	NA
Def. of ditch	$(s \leq (Min_{[-10,10]}\ s)) \wedge s \leq -1$	NA	NA
Depth of the ditch	$(Min_{[0,136]}\ s) \leq p\ \{or \geq p\}$	$(-6.12, -4.767)$	$(-6.51, -5.71)$
Location of the ditch	$F_{[\theta_1,\theta_2]}$ ditch	$(51.00, 58.99)$	$(51.00, 59.99)$
Height of peak 1	$(Max\ s\ U\ ditch) \leq p\ \{or \geq p\}$	$(1.01, 5.42)$	$(0.77, 3.81)$
Location of peak 1	$F_{[\theta_1,\theta_2]}$ peak	$(48.00, 56.99)$	$(0.00, 55.99)$
Height of peak 2	ditch $\wedge ((Max_{[0,60]}\ s) \leq p)\ \{or \geq p\}$	$(1.25, 3.296)$	$(1.43, 2.58)$
Location of peak 2	ditch $\wedge F_{[\theta_1,\theta_2]}$ peak	$(25.00, 30.99)$	$(23.00, 26.99)$

Results for ECG5days Classify. Table 3 summarizes our results for five different training and testing configurations. For the first configuration, we use the original 23 training traces and 861 testing traces from [1] without any changes.

---

[4] $\triangle$ is the symmetric difference of two sets.

For the other configurations we split the training set of size 861 and use one portion for training and the other for testing. The number of traces used for training and testing are mentioned within brackets in the first column of Table 3. For example, in the second row we indicate that for configuration 2 we use 100 traces for training and the remaining 761 for testing. Note that for configuration 4 we use all the 861 traces for training and have no traces for testing. For this configuration, the reason we did not find a solution could be because we required 100% training accuracy. For configuration 5, when we keep the same data split but allow $f_-, f_+ = 2$, we succeed in finding a formula. The 0/0 in the column for testing error is because the test set is empty. Note that, for a PSTL formula each parameter valuation in the solution set produces a classifier. Two such classifiers we found, $\Psi^{cl_1}_{(28.3,11.0,4.0)}$ and $\Psi^{cl_2}_{(27.5,1.0,-1.3)}$ have error values 2/861 and 17/861 respectively on the original testing set.

$$\Psi^{cl_1}_{(p_1,p_2,p_3)} := (\texttt{ditch} \wedge F_{[p_1,c_2-p_2]}\,\texttt{peak}) \vee (\,(\text{Max } s\ U\ \texttt{ditch}) \geq p_3)$$

$$\Psi^{cl_2}_{(p_1,p_2,p_3)} := (\texttt{ditch} \wedge F_{[p_1,c_2-p_2]}\,\texttt{peak}) \vee (\texttt{ditch} \wedge (\text{Max}_{[0,c_2]}\ s) \leq -p_3) \quad (7)$$

Table 3. Results for learning (case study 2). See Formula (7) for Ψ^{cl_1}, Ψ^{cl_2}

Configuration	time (s)			Testing error		Training error	
	$\delta = 10^{-1}$	$\delta = 10^{-2}$	$\delta = 5.10^{-3}$	Ψ^{cl_1}	Ψ^{cl_2}	Ψ^{cl_1}	Ψ^{cl_2}
Confg. 1 (23, 861)	2	184	787	2/861	17/861	0/23	0/23
Confg. 2 (100, 761)	1.5	6	10	2/761	17/761	0/100	0/100
Confg. 3 (300, 561)	2	3	5	2/561	NA[a]	0/300	NA
Confg. 4 (861, 0)	13	79	153	NA	NA	NA	NA
Confg. 5 (861, 0)	5	8.5	12	0/0	NA	2/861	NA

[a] NA: Not Applicable. Parameter search is unsuccessful.

5 Conclusion and Future Work

In this paper, we presented a new method for extracting knowledge from labelled signals based on monotonic parametric specifications. To this end, we introduced the ϵ-count, to measure the amount of mismatch between two Boolean signals (e.g., the Boolean signal induced by the labelled input sample, and the one defined by our learned specification). We then formulated the learning process as a multi-criteria optimization problem with constraints on the ϵ-counts of false positives and false negatives. Finally, we proposed an algorithm to solve this problem based on the intersection of an upset and a downset, and then applied it in particular for learning monotonic PSTL specifications. We demonstrated the performance of our approach on two case studies involving ECG signals.

As future work, we will investigate the computation of the exact or approximate solution sets for non-monotonic parametric specification. To partially solve this, we can find the minimal set of parameters according to heuristic multi-criteria optimization. However there exist trade-offs among parameters and also between tightness and robustness. Finding tightest parameters for the given training examples might not generalize well. Methods that intelligently explore the parameter space uncovering these trade-offs are needed. Second, we would like to investigate efficient representations for solution sets. We found the need for this when dealing with timing parameters. The formula $F_{[\tau_1,\tau_2]}\,\varphi$ is monotonic with respect to τ_1 and τ_2, but τ_1 and τ_2 are related by an implicit constraint, $\tau_1 \leq \tau_2$. Replacing multiple occurrences of a parameter with distinct symbols as suggested in [28] might not be straightforward for timing parameters. Consequently, it becomes more difficult to use boxes to represent the solution set. The problem of selecting optimal parameter assignments from the solution set in order to maximize average classification accuracy can also be studied.

References

1. ECGFiveDays data set. http://www.timeseriesclassification.com/description.php?Dataset=ECGFiveDays
2. Implementation of Pareto front intersection algorithm. https://gricad-gitlab.univ-grenoble-alpes.fr/verimag/tempo/multidimensional_search/-/tree/intersectionAkshay
3. Implementation of the StlEval ϵ-count operator. https://gricad-gitlab.univ-grenoble-alpes.fr/verimag/tempo/StlEval/-/tree/akshayTest
4. Learning specifications for labelled patterns (technical report). http://www-verimag.imag.fr/TR/TR-2020-1.pdf
5. Abbas, H., Rodionova, A., Mamouras, K., Bartocci, E., Smolka, S.A., Grosu, R.: Quantitative regular expressions for arrhythmia detection. IEEE/ACM Trans. Comput. Biol. Bioinform. **16**(5), 1586–1597 (2019)
6. Alur, R., Dill, D.L.: A theory of timed automata. Theoret. Comput. Sci. **126**(2), 183–235 (1994)
7. Asarin, E., Donzé, A., Maler, O., Nickovic, D.: Parametric identification of temporal properties. In: Khurshid, S., Sen, K. (eds.) RV 2011. LNCS, vol. 7186, pp. 147–160. Springer, Heidelberg (2012). https://doi.org/10.1007/978-3-642-29860-8_12
8. Bakhirkin, A., Basset, N.: Specification and efficient monitoring beyond STL. In: Vojnar, T., Zhang, L. (eds.) TACAS 2019. LNCS, vol. 11428, pp. 79–97. Springer, Cham (2019). https://doi.org/10.1007/978-3-030-17465-1_5
9. Bakhirkin, A., Basset, N., Maler, O., Requeno, J.I.: Learning pareto front from membership queries. Working paper or preprint (2019). https://hal.archives-ouvertes.fr/hal-02125140
10. Bakhirkin, A., Basset, N., Maler, O., Jarabo, J.-I.R.: ParetoLib: a python library for parameter synthesis. In: André, É., Stoelinga, M. (eds.) FORMATS 2019. LNCS, vol. 11750, pp. 114–120. Springer, Cham (2019). https://doi.org/10.1007/978-3-030-29662-9_7
11. Bakhirkin, A., Ferrére, T., Maler, O.: Efficient parametric identification for STL. In: Proceedings of the 21st International Conference on Hybrid Systems: Computation and Control, HSCC 2018, pp. 177–186. ACM, New York (2018)

12. Bombara, G., Vasile, C.I., Penedo, F., Yasuoka, H., Belta, C.: A decision tree approach to data classification using signal temporal logic. In: Proceedings of the 19th International Conference on Hybrid Systems: Computation and Control, HSCC 2016, pages 1–10. ACM, New York (2016)

13. Chen, T., Diciolla, M., Kwiatkowska, M., Mereacre, A.: A Simulink hybrid heart model for quantitative verification of cardiac pacemakers. In: Proceedings of the 16th International Conference on Hybrid Systems: Computation and Control, HSCC 2013, pp. 131–136. ACM, New York (2013)

14. Cutulenco, G., Joshi, Y., Narayan, A., Fischmeister, S.: Mining timed regular expressions from system traces. In: Proceedings of the 5th International Workshop on Software Mining, Software Mining 2016, pp. 3–10. ACM, New York (2016)

15. Dau, H.A.: et al.: The UCR time series classification archive, October 2018. https://www.cs.ucr.edu/~eamonn/time_series_data_2018/

16. Goldberger, A.L., et al.: PhysioBank, physiotoolkit, and physionet: components of a new research resource for complex physiologic signals. Circulation 101(23), e215–e220 (2000)

17. Jha, S., Tiwari, A., Seshia, S.A., Sahai, T., Shankar, N.: TeLEx: learning signal temporal logic from positive examples using tightness metric. Formal Methods Syst. Des. 54(3), 364–387 (2019). https://doi.org/10.1007/s10703-019-00332-1

18. Kolmogorov, A.N., Tikhomirov, V.M.: ε-entropy and ε-capacity of sets in function spaces. Uspekhi Matematicheskikh Nauk, 14(2(86)), 386 (1959)

19. Kong, Z., Jones, A., Ayala, A.M., Gol, E.A., Belta, C.: Temporal logic inference for classification and prediction from data. In: Proceedings of the 17th International Conference on Hybrid Systems: Computation and Control (part of CPS Week), HSCC 2014, pp. 273–282. ACM, New York (2014)

20. Kong, Z., Jones, A., Belta, C.: Temporal logics for learning and detection of anomalous behavior. IEEE Trans. Automatic Control 62(3), 1210–1222 (2017)

21. Lemieux, C., Park, D., Beschastnikh, I.: General LTL specification mining (T). In: Proceedings of the 30th IEEE/ACM International Conference on Automated Software Engineering, ASE 2015, pp. 81–92. IEEE (2015)

22. Maler, O.: Learning monotone partitions of partially-ordered domains (work in progress). Working paper or preprint (2017) https://hal.archives-ouvertes.fr/hal-01556243

23. Mohammadinejad, S., Deshmukh, J.V., Puranic, A.G.: Mining environment assumptions for cyber-physical system models. In: Proceedings of the 11th ACM/IEEE International Conference on Cyber-Physical Systems (to appear), ICCPS 2020. IEEE (2020)

24. Mohammadinejad, S., Deshmukh, J.V., Puranic, A.G., Vazquez-Chanlatte, M., Donzé, A.: Interpretable classification of time-series data using efficient enumerative techniques. In: Proceedings of the 23rd International Conference on Hybrid Systems: Computation and Control (to appear), HSCC 2020. ACM, New York (2020)

25. Moody, G.B., Mark, R.G.: The impact of the MIT-BIH arrhythmia database. IEEE Eng. Med. Biol. Mag. 20(3), 45–50 (2001)

26. Neider, D., Gavran, I.: Learning linear temporal properties. In: Proceedings of the 18th International Conference on Formal Methods in Computer Aided Design, FMCAD 2011, pp. 1–10. ACM, Austin (2018)

27. Ničković, D., Qin, X., Ferrère, T., Mateis, C., Deshmukh, J.: Shape expressions for specifying and extracting signal features. In: Finkbeiner, B., Mariani, L. (eds.) RV 2019. LNCS, vol. 11757, pp. 292–309. Springer, Cham (2019). https://doi.org/10.1007/978-3-030-32079-9_17

28. Vazquez-Chanlatte, M., Deshmukh, J.V., Jin, X., Seshia, S.A.: Logical clustering and learning for time-series data. In: Majumdar, R., Kunčak, V. (eds.) CAV 2017. LNCS, vol. 10426, pp. 305–325. Springer, Cham (2017). https://doi.org/10.1007/978-3-319-63387-9_15

29. Vazquez-Chanlatte, M., Ghosh, S., Deshmukh, J.V., Sangiovanni-Vincentelli, A., Seshia, S.A.: Time-series learning using monotonic logical properties. In: Colombo, C., Leucker, M. (eds.) RV 2018. LNCS, vol. 11237, pp. 389–405. Springer, Cham (2018). https://doi.org/10.1007/978-3-030-03769-7_22

30. von Birgelen, A., Niggemann, O.: Using self-organizing maps to learn hybrid timed automata in absence of discrete events. In: Proceedings of the 22nd IEEE International Conference on Emerging Technologies and Factory Automation, ETFA 2017, pp. 1–8. IEEE (2017)

On Subgame Perfect Equilibria
in Turn-Based Reachability Timed Games

Thomas Brihaye[1] and Aline Goeminne[1,2(✉)]

[1] Université de Mons (UMONS), Mons, Belgium
{thomas.brihaye,aline.goeminne}@umons.ac.be
[2] Université libre de Bruxelles (ULB), Brussels, Belgium

Abstract. We study multiplayer turn-based timed games with reachability objectives. In particular, we are interested in the notion of subgame perfect equilibrium (SPE). We prove that deciding the constrained existence of an SPE in this setting is EXPTIME-complete.

Keywords: Multiplayer turn-based timed games · Reachability objectives · Subgame perfect equilibria · Constrained existence problem

1 Introduction

Games. In the context of *reactive systems*, *two-player zero-sum games played on graphs* are commonly used to model the purely antagonistic interactions between a system and its environment [18]. The system and the environment are the two players of a game played on a graph whose vertices represent the configurations. Finding how the system can ensure the achievement of his objective amounts to finding, if it exists, a *winning strategy* for the system.

When modeling complex systems with several agents whose objectives are not necessarily antagonistic, the two-player zero-sum framework is too restrictive and we rather rely on *multiplayer non zero-sum games*. In this setting, the notion of winning strategy is replaced by various notions of *equilibria* including the famous concept of *Nash equilibrium* (NE) [16]. When considering games played on graphs, the notion of *subgame perfect equilibrium* (SPE) is often preferred to the classical Nash equilibrium [17]. Indeed, Nash equilibrium does not take into account the sequential structure of the game and may allow irrational behaviors in some subgames.

Timed Games. *Timed automata* [19] is now a well established model for complex systems including real time features. Timed automata have been naturally extended into two-player zero-sum *timed games* [2,4,11,14]. Multiplayer non zero-sum extensions have also been considered [5,7,15]. In these models both time and multiplayer aspects coexist. In this non zero-sum timed framework, the main focus has been on NE, and, to our knowledge, not on SPE.

This work is supported by the ARC project "Non-Zero Sum Game Graphs: Applications to Reactive Synthesis and Beyond" (Fédération Wallonie-Bruxelles).

N. Bertrand and N. Jansen (Eds.): FORMATS 2020, LNCS 12288, pp. 94–110, 2020.
https://doi.org/10.1007/978-3-030-57628-8_6

Main Contributions and Organization of the Paper. In this paper, we consider *multiplayer, non zero-sum, turn-based timed games with reachability objectives* together with the concept of SPE. We focus on the constrained existence problem (for SPE): given a timed game, we want to decide whether there exists an SPE where some players have to win and some other ones have to lose. The main result of this paper is a proof that the SPE constrained existence problem is EXPTIME-complete for reachability timed games. Let us notice that the NE constrained existence problem for reachability timed games is also EXPTIME-complete [7]. This may look surprising as often, there is a complexity jump when going from NE to SPE, for example the constrained existence problem on qualitative reachability game is NP-complete for NE [12] and PSPACE-complete for SPE [8]. Intuitively, the complexity jump is avoided because the exponential blow up due to the transition from SPE to NE is somehow absorbed by the classical exponential blow up due to the classical region graph used for the analysis of timed systems.

In order to obtain an EXPTIME algorithm, we proceed in different steps. In the first step, we prove that the game variant of the *classical region graph* is a good abstraction for the SPE constrained existence problem. In fact, we identify conditions on *bisimulations* under which the study of SPE of a given (potentially infinite game) can be reduced to the study of its quotient. This is done in Sect. 3 for (untimed) games with general objectives. In Sect. 4, we then focus on (untimed) finite reachability game and provide an EXPTIME algorithm to solve the constrained existence problem. Proving this result may look surprising, as we already know from [8] that this problem is indeed PSPACE-complete for (untimed) finite games. However the PSPACE algorithm provided in [8] did not allow us to obtain the EXPTIME algorithm for timed games. The latter EXPTIME algorithm is discussed in Sect. 5.

Related Works. There are many results on games played on graphs, we refer the reader to [10] for a survey and an extended bibliography. Here we focus on the results directly related to our contributions. The constrained existence of SPEs is studied in finite multiplayer turn-based games with different kinds of objectives, for example: (qualitative) reachability and safety objectives [8], ω-regular winning conditions [20], quantitative reachability objectives [9],... In [5], they prove that the constrained existence problem for Nash equilibria in concurrent timed games with reachability objectives is EXPTIME-complete. This same problem in the same setting is studied in [7] with others qualitative objectives.

2   Preliminaries

Transition Systems, Bisimulations and Quotients. A *transition system* is a tuple $T = (\Sigma, V, E)$ where *(i)* Σ is a finite alphabet; *(ii)* V a set of *states* (also called *vertices*) and *(iii)* $E \subseteq V \times \Sigma \times V$ a set of *transitions* (also called *edges*). To ease the notation, an edge $(v_1, a, v_2) \in E$ is sometimes denoted by $v_1 \xrightarrow{a} v_2$. Notice that V may be uncountable. We said that the transition system is *finite* if V and E are finite.

Given two transition systems on the same alphabet $T_1 = (\Sigma, V_1, E_1)$ and $T_2 = (\Sigma, V_2, E_2)$, a *simulation of T_1 by T_2* is a binary relation $\mathbf{R} \subseteq V_1 \times V_2$ which satisfies the following conditions: *(i)* $\forall v_1, v_1' \in V_1$, $\forall v_2 \in V_2$ and $\forall a \in \Sigma$: $((v_1, v_2) \in \mathbf{R}$ and $v_1 \xrightarrow{a}_1 v_1') \Rightarrow (\exists v_2' \in V_2, v_2 \xrightarrow{a}_2 v_2'$ and $(v_1', v_2') \in \mathbf{R})$ and *(ii)* for each $v_1 \in V_1$ there exists $v_2 \in V_2$ such that $(v_1, v_2) \in \mathbf{R}$. We say that T_2 *simulates* T_1. It implies that any transition $v_1 \xrightarrow{a}_1 v_1'$ in T_1 is simulated by a corresponding transition $v_2 \xrightarrow{a}_2 v_2'$ in T_2.

Given two transition systems on the same alphabet $T_1 = (\Sigma, V_1, E_1)$ and $T_2 = (\Sigma, V_2, E_2)$, a *bisimulation between T_1 and T_2* is a binary relation $\mathbf{R} \subseteq V_1 \times V_2$ such that $\mathbf{R}$ is a simulation of T_1 by T_2 and the converse relation $\mathbf{R}^{-1}$ is a simulation of T_2 by T_1 where $\mathbf{R}^{-1} = \{(v_2, v_1) \in V_2 \times V_1 \mid (v_1, v_2) \in \mathbf{R}\}$. When $\mathbf{R}$ is a bisimulation between two transition systems, we write β instead of $\mathbf{R}$. If $T = (\Sigma, V, E)$ is a transition system, a bisimulation on $V \times V$ is called a bisimulation on T.

Given a transition system $T = (\Sigma, V, E)$ and an equivalence relation $\sim$ on V, we define the *quotient of T by $\sim$*, denoted by $\tilde{T} = (\Sigma, \tilde{V}, \tilde{E})$, as follows: *(i)* $\tilde{V} = \{[v]_\sim \mid v \in V\}$ where $[v]_\sim = \{v' \in V \mid v \sim v'\}$ and *(ii)* $[v_1]_\sim \xrightarrow{a}_\sim [v_2]_\sim$ if and only if there exist $v_1' \in [v_1]_\sim$ and $v_2' \in [v_2]_\sim$ such that $v_1' \xrightarrow{a} v_2'$. When the equivalence relation is clear from the context, we write $[v]$ instead of $[v]_\sim$.

Given a transition system $T = (\Sigma, V, E)$, a bisimulation $\sim$ on T which is also an equivalence relation is called a *bisimulation equivalence*. In this context, the following result holds.

Lemma 1. *Given a transition system T and a bisimulation equivalence $\sim$, there exists a bisimulation $\sim_q$ between T and its quotient $\tilde{T}$. This bisimulation is given by the function $\sim_q : V \to \tilde{V} : v \mapsto [v]_\sim$*

Turn-Based games

Arenas, plays and histories An *arena* $\mathbf{A} = (\Sigma, V, E, \Pi, (V_i)_{i \in \Pi})$ is a tuple where *(i)* $T = (\Sigma, V, E)$ is a transition system such that for each $v \in V$, there exists $a \in \Sigma$ and $v' \in V$ such that $(v, a, v') \in E$; *(ii)* $\Pi = \{1, \dots, n\}$ is a finite set of players and *(iii)* $(V_i)_{i \in \Pi}$ is a partition of V between the players. An arena is finite if its transition system T is finite.

A *play* in $\mathbf{A}$ is an infinite path in its transition system, *i.e.*, $\rho = \rho_0 \rho_1 \dots \in V^\omega$ is a play if for each $i \in \mathbb{N}$, there exists $a \in \Sigma$ such that $(\rho_i, a, \rho_{i+1}) \in E$. A *history* h in $\mathbf{A}$ can be defined in the same way but $h = h_0 \dots h_k \in V^*$ for some $k \in \mathbb{N}$ is a finite path in the transition system. We denote the set of plays by Plays and the set of histories by Hist. When it is necessary, we use the notation $\text{Plays}_\mathbf{A}$ and $\text{Hist}_\mathbf{A}$ to recall the underlying arena $\mathbf{A}$. Moreover, the set Hist_i is the set of histories such that their last vertex v is a vertex of Player i, *i.e.*, $v \in V_i$. A play (resp. a history) in $(\mathcal{G}, v_0)$ is then a play (resp. a history) in $\mathcal{G}$ starting in v_0. The set of such plays (resp. histories) is denoted by $\text{Plays}(v_0)$ (resp. $\text{Hist}(v_0)$). We also use the notation $\text{Hist}_i(v_0)$ when these histories end in a vertex $v \in V_i$.

Given a play $\rho \in$ Plays and $k \in \mathbb{N}$, its suffix $\rho_k \rho_{k+1} \ldots$ is denoted by $\rho_{\geq k}$. We denote by $\mathrm{Succ}(v) = \{v' | (v, a, v') \in E$ for some $a \in \Sigma\}$ the set of successors of v, for $v \in V$, and by Succ^* the transitive closure of Succ. Given a play $\rho = \rho_0 \rho_1 \ldots$, the set $\mathrm{Occ}(\rho) = \{v \in V \mid \exists k, \rho_k = v\}$ is the set of vertices *visited* along ρ.

Remark 1. When we consider a play in an arena $A = (\Sigma, V, E, \Pi, (V_i)_{i \in \Pi})$, we do not care about the alphabet letter associated with each edge of the play. It is the reason why two different infinite paths in $T = (\Sigma, V, E)$ $v_0 \xrightarrow{a} v_1 \xrightarrow{a} \ldots \xrightarrow{a} v_n \xrightarrow{a} \ldots$ and $v_0 \xrightarrow{b} v_1 \xrightarrow{b} \ldots \xrightarrow{b} v_n \xrightarrow{b} \ldots$ correspond to only one play $\rho = v_0 v_1 \ldots v_n \ldots$ in A. The same phenomenon appears with finite paths and histories. We explain later why this is not a problem for our purpose.

Multiplayer Turn-Based Game. An *(initialized multiplayer Boolean turn-based) game* is a tuple $(\mathcal{G}, v_0) = (A, (g_i)_{i \in \Pi})$ such that: *(i)* $A = (\Sigma, V, E, \Pi, (V_i)_{i \in \Pi})$ is an arena; *(ii)* $v_0 \in V$ is the *initial vertex* and *(iii)* for each $i \in \Pi$, $g_i :$ Plays $\to \{0, 1\}$ is a gain function for Player i. In this setting, each player $i \in \Pi$ is equipped with a set $\Omega_i \subseteq$ Plays that we call the *objective* of Player i. Thus, for each $i \in \Pi$, for each $\rho \in$ Plays: $g_i(\rho) = 1$ if and only if $\rho \in \Omega_i$. If $g_i(\rho) = 1$ (resp. $= 0$), we say that Player i *wins* (resp. *loses*) along ρ. In the sequel of this document, we refer to the notion of initialized multiplayer Boolean turn-based game by the term "game". For each $\rho \in$ Plays, we write $g(\rho) = p$ for some $p \in \{0, 1\}^{|\Pi|}$ to depict $g_i(\rho) = p_i$ for each $i \in \Pi$.

Strategies and Outcomes. Given a game $(\mathcal{G}, v_0)$, a *strategy* of Player i is a function $\sigma_i : \mathrm{Hist}_i(v_0) \to V$ with the constraint that for each $hv \in \mathrm{Hist}_i(v_0)$, $\sigma_i(hv) \in \mathrm{Succ}(v)$. A play $\rho = \rho_0 \rho_1 \ldots$ is *consistent* with σ_i if for each ρ_k such that $\rho_k \in V_i$, $\rho_{k+1} = \sigma_i(\rho_0 \ldots \rho_k)$. A *strategy profile* $\sigma = (\sigma_i)_{i \in \Pi}$ is a tuple of strategies, one for each player. Given a game $(\mathcal{G}, v_0)$ and a strategy profile σ, there exists a unique play from v_0 consistent with each strategy σ_i. We call this play the *outcome* of σ and denote it by $\langle \sigma \rangle_{v_0}$.

Remark 2. We follow up Remark 1. The objectives we consider are of the form $\Omega \subseteq$ Plays. These objectives only depend on the sequence of visited states along a play (for example: visiting infinitely often a given state) regardless of the sequence of visited alphabet letters. This is why defining the strategy of a player with a choice of the next vertex instead of a couple of an alphabet letter and a vertex is not a problem. Actually, in all this paper one may consider that the alphabet is $\Sigma = \{a\}$. The reason why we allow alphabet letters on edges is to be able to consider *synchronous products* of (timed) automata [3,19]. In this way, we could consider wider class of objectives (see Sect. 5.4).

Subgame Perfect Equilibria. In the multiplayer game setting, the solution concepts usually studied are *equilibria* (see [13]). We here recall the concepts of Nash equilibrium and subgame perfect equilibrium.

Let $\sigma = (\sigma_i)_{i \in \Pi}$ be a strategy profile in a game $(\mathcal{G}, v_0)$. When we highlight the role of Player i, we denote σ by (σ_i, σ_{-i}) where σ_{-i} is the profile $(\sigma_j)_{j \in \Pi \setminus \{i\}}$. A strategy $\sigma_i' \neq \sigma_i$ is a *deviating* strategy of Player i, and it is a *profitable deviation* for him if $g_i(\langle \sigma \rangle_{v_0}) < g_i(\langle \sigma_i', \sigma_{-i} \rangle_{v_0})$. A strategy profile σ in a game $(\mathcal{G}, v_0)$ is a *Nash equilibrium* (NE) if no player has an incentive to deviate unilaterally from his strategy, *i.e.*, no player has a profitable deviation.

A refinement of NE is the concept of *subgame perfect equilibrium* (SPE) which is a strategy profile being an NE in each subgame. Formally, given a game $(\mathcal{G}, v_0) = (A, (g_i)_{i \in \Pi})$ and a history $hv \in \text{Hist}(v_0)$, the game $(\mathcal{G}_{\restriction h}, v)$ is called a *subgame* of $(\mathcal{G}, v_0)$ such that $\mathcal{G}_{\restriction h} = (A, (g_{i \restriction h})_{i \in \Pi})$ and $g_{i \restriction h}(\rho) = g_i(h\rho)$ for all $i \in \Pi$ and $\rho \in V^\omega$. Notice that $(\mathcal{G}, v_0)$ is subgame of itself. Moreover if σ_i is a strategy for Player i in $(\mathcal{G}, v_0)$, then $\sigma_{i \restriction h}$ denotes the strategy in $(\mathcal{G}_{\restriction h}, v)$ such that for all histories $h' \in \text{Hist}_i(v)$, $\sigma_{i \restriction h}(h') = \sigma_i(hh')$. Similarly, from a strategy profile σ in $(\mathcal{G}, v_0)$, we derive the strategy profile $\sigma_{\restriction h}$ in $(\mathcal{G}_{\restriction h}, v)$. Let $(\mathcal{G}, v_0)$ be a game, following this formalism, a strategy profile σ is a *subgame perfect equilibrium* in $(\mathcal{G}, v_0)$ if for all $hv \in \text{Hist}(v_0)$, $\sigma_{\restriction h}$ is an NE in $(\mathcal{G}_{\restriction h}, v)$.

Studied Problem. Given a game $(\mathcal{G}, v_0)$, several SPEs may coexist. It is the reason why we are interested in the *constrained existence* of an SPE in this game: some players have to win and some other ones have to lose. The related decision problem is the following one:

Definition 1 (Constrained existence problem). *Given a game $(\mathcal{G}, v_0)$ and two gain profiles $x, y \in \{0, 1\}^{|\Pi|}$, does there exist an SPE σ in $(\mathcal{G}, v_0)$ such that $x \leq g(\langle \sigma \rangle_{v_0}) \leq y$.*

3   SPE in a Game and Its Quotient

In this section, we first define the concepts of *bisimulation between games* and of *bisimulation on a game*. Then, we explain how given such bisimulations we can obtain a new game, called the *quotient game*, thanks to a quotient of the initial game. Finally, we prove that if there exists an SPE in a game with a given gain profile, there exists an SPE in its associated quotient game with the same gain profile, and vice versa.

3.1   Game Bisimulation

We extend the notion of bisimulation between transition systems (resp. on a transition system) to the one of bisimulation between games (resp. on a game). In this paper, by bisimulation between games (resp. on a game) we mean:

Definition 2 (Game bisimulation). *Given two games* $(\mathcal{G}, v_0) = (A, (g_i)_{i \in \Pi})$ *and* $(\mathcal{G}', v_0') = (A', (g_i')_{i \in \Pi})$ *with the same alphabet and the same set of players, we say that* $\sim \subseteq V \times V'$ *is a bisimulation between* $(\mathcal{G}, v_0)$ *and* $(\mathcal{G}', v_0')$ *if (i)* $\sim$ *is a bisimulation between* $T = (\Sigma, V, E)$ *and* $T' = (\Sigma, V', E')$ *and (ii)* $v_0 \sim v_0'$. *In the same way, if* $\sim \subseteq V \times V$ *we say that* $\sim$ *is a bisimulation on* $(\mathcal{G}, v_0)$ *if* $\sim$ *is a bisimulation on* $T = (\Sigma, V, E)$.

The notion of bisimulation equivalence on a transition system is extended in the same way to games. In the rest of this document, we use the following notations: *(1)* If $\sim \subseteq V \times V'$ is a bisimulation between $(\mathcal{G}, v_0) = (A, (g_i)_{i \in})$ and $(\mathcal{G}', v_0') = (A', (g_i')_{i \in})$, for each $\rho \in \text{Plays}_A$ and for all $\rho' \in \text{Plays}_{A'}$, we write $\rho \sim \rho'$ if and only if for each $n \in \mathbb{N}$: $\rho_n \sim \rho_n'$. *(2)* If $\sim \subseteq V \times V$ is a bisimulation on $(\mathcal{G}, v_0) = (A, (g_i)_{i \in})$, for each $\rho \in \text{Plays}_A$ and for all $\rho' \in \text{Plays}_A$, we write $\rho \sim \rho'$ if and only if for each $n \in \mathbb{N}$: $\rho_n \sim \rho_n'$. *(3)* Notations 1 and 2 can be naturally adapted to histories[1].

A natural property that should be satisfied by a bisimulation on a game is the respect of the vertices partition. It means that if a vertex bisimulates an other vertex, then these vertices should be owned by the same player.

Definition 3 ($\sim$ respects the partition). *Given a game* $(\mathcal{G}, v_0) = (A, (g_i)_{i \in \Pi})$ *and a bisimulation* $\sim$ *on* $(\mathcal{G}, v_0)$, *we say that* $\sim$ *respects the partition if for all* $v, v' \in V$ *such that* $v \sim v'$, *if* $v \in V_i$ *then* $v' \in V_i$.

3.2   Quotient Game

Given a game $(\mathcal{G}, v_0)$ and a bisimulation equivalence $\sim$ on it which respects the partition, one may consider its associated *quotient game* $(\tilde{\mathcal{G}}, [v_0])$ such that its transition system is defined as the quotient of the transition system of $(\mathcal{G}, v_0)$.

Definition 4 (Quotient game). *Given a game* $(\mathcal{G}, v_0) = (A, (g_i)_{i \in \pi})$ *such that* $A = (\Sigma, V, E, \Pi, (V_i)_{i \in \Pi})$, *if* $\sim$ *is a bisimulation equivalence on* $(\mathcal{G}, v_0)$ *which respects the partition, the associated* quotient game $(\tilde{\mathcal{G}}, [v_0]) = (\tilde{A}, (\tilde{g}_i)_{i \in \Pi})$ *is defined as follows: (i)* $\tilde{A} = (\Sigma, \tilde{V}, \tilde{E}, (\tilde{V}_i)_{i \in \Pi})$ *is such that* $\tilde{T} = (\Sigma, \tilde{V}, \tilde{E})$ *is the quotient of* T *and, for each* $i \in \Pi$, $[v] \in \tilde{V}_i$ *if and only if* $v \in V_i$ *and (ii) for each* $i \in \Pi$, $\tilde{g}_i : \text{Plays}_{\tilde{A}} \to \{0, 1\}$ *is the gain function of Player* i.

In order to preserve some equivalent properties between a game and its quotient game, the equivalence relation on the game should respect the gain functions in both games. It means that if we consider two bisimulated plays either both in the game itself or one in the game and the other one in its quotient game, the gain profile of these plays should be equal.

---

[1] Once again, with this convention it is possible that two plays (or histories) such that $\rho \sim \rho'$ do not preserve the sequence of alphabet letters as it should be when we classically consider bisimulated paths in two bisimulated transitions systems. Remark 2 explains why it is not a problem for us.

Definition 5 ($\sim$ respects the gain functions). *Given an initialized game* $(\mathcal{G}, v_0) = (A, (g_i)_{i \in \pi})$ *such that* $A = (\Sigma, V, E, \Pi, (V_i)_{i \in \Pi})$ *and a bisimulation equivalence* $\sim$ *on* $(\mathcal{G}, v_0)$, *we say that* $\sim$ *respects the gain functions if the following properties hold:* (i) *for each* ρ *and* ρ' *in* Plays, *if* $\rho \sim \rho'$ *then* $g(\rho) = g(\rho')$ *and* (ii) *for each* $\rho \in$ Plays$_A$ *and* $\tilde{\rho} \in$ Plays$_{\tilde{A}}$, *if* $\rho \sim_q \tilde{\rho}$ *then* $g(\rho) = \tilde{g}(\tilde{\rho})$.

3.3 SPE Existence

The aim of this section is to prove that, if there exists an SPE in a game equipped with a bisimilation equivalence which respects the partition and the gain functions, there exists an SPE in its associated quotient game with the same gain profile, and vice versa.

Theorem 1. *Let* $(\mathcal{G}, v_0) = (A, (g_i)_{i \in \pi})$ *be a game and* $(\tilde{\mathcal{G}}, [v_0]) = (\tilde{A}, (\tilde{g}_i)_{i \in \Pi})$ *its associated quotient game where* $\sim$ *is a bisimulation equivalence on* $(\mathcal{G}, v_0)$. *If* $\sim$ *respects the partition and the gain functions, we have that: there exists an SPE* σ *in* $(\mathcal{G}, v_0)$ *such that* $g(\langle \sigma \rangle_{v_0}) = p$ *if and only if there exists an SPE* τ *in* $(\tilde{\mathcal{G}}, [v_0])$ *such that* $\tilde{g}(\langle \tau \rangle_{[v_0]}) = p$.

The key idea is to prove that: if there exists an SPE in a game equipped with a bisimulation equivalence, there exists an SPE in this game which is *uniform* and with the same gain profile (see Proposition 1). If σ_i is a uniform strategy, each time we consider two histories $h \sim h'$, the choices of Player i taking into account h or h' are in the same equivalence class (see Definition 6).

Definition 6. *Let* $(\mathcal{G}, v_0)$ *be a game and* $\sim$ *a bisimulation on it, we say that the strategy* σ_i *is uniform if for all* $h, h' \in$ Hist$_i(v_0)$ *such that* $h \sim h'$, *we have that* $\sigma_i(h) \sim \sigma_i(h')$. *A strategy profile* σ *is uniform if for all* $i \in \Pi$, σ_i *is uniform.*

Proposition 1. *Let* $(\mathcal{G}, v_0) = (A, (g_i)_{i \in \pi})$ *be a game and* $\sim$ *be a bisimulation equivalence on* $(\mathcal{G}, v_0)$ *which respects the partition and such that for each* ρ *and* ρ' *in* Plays, *if* $\rho \sim \rho'$ *then* $g(\rho) = g(\rho')$, *there exists an SPE* σ *in* $(\mathcal{G}, v_0)$ *such that* $g(\langle \sigma \rangle_{v_0}) = p$ *if and only if there exists an SPE* τ *in* $(\mathcal{G}, v_0)$ *which is uniform and such that* $g(\langle \tau \rangle_{v_0}) = p$.

4 Reachability Games

In this section we focus on a particular kind of game called *reachability game*. In these games, each player has a subset of vertices that he wants to reach. First, we formally define the concepts of *reachability games* and *reachability quotient games*. Then, we provide an algorithm which solves the constrained existence problem in finite reachability games in time complexity at most exponential in the number of players and polynomial in the size of the transition system of the game.

4.1 Reachability Games and Quotient Reachability Games

Definition 7. *A* reachability game $(\mathcal{G}, v_0) = (A, (g_i)_{i \in \Pi}, (F_i)_{i \in \Pi})$ *is a game where each player* $i \in \Pi$ *is equipped with a* target set F_i *that he wants to reach. Formally, the objective of Player* i *is* $\Omega_i = \{\rho \in \text{Plays} \mid \text{Occ}(\rho) \cap F_i \neq \emptyset\}$ *where* $F_i \subseteq V$. *This is a* reachability objective.

Given a reachability game $(\mathcal{G}, v_0) = (A, (g_i)_{i \in \Pi}, (F_i)_{i \in \Pi})$ and a bisimulation equivalence $\sim$ on this game which respects the partition, one may consider its quotient game $(\tilde{\mathcal{G}}, [v_0]) = (\tilde{A}, (\tilde{g}_i)_{i \in \Pi}, (\tilde{F}_i)_{i \in \Pi})$ where for each $i \in \Pi$, $\tilde{F}_i \subseteq \tilde{V}$. In attempts to ensure the respect of the gain functions by $\sim$, we add a natural property on $\sim$ (see Definition 8) and define the sets $\tilde{F}_i$ in a proper way. In the rest of this paper, we assume that this property is satisfied and that the quotient game of a reachability game is defined as in Definition 9.

Definition 8 ($\sim$ respects the target sets). *Let* $(\mathcal{G}, v_0)$ *be a reachability game and* $\sim$ *be a bisimulation equivalence on this game, we say that* $\sim$ *respects the* target sets *if for all* $v \in V$ *and for all* $v' \in V$ *such that* $v \sim v' : v \in F_i \Leftrightarrow v' \in F_i)$.

Definition 9 (Reachability quotient game). *Given a reachability game* $(\mathcal{G}, v_0) = (A, (g_i)_{i \in \Pi}, (F_i)_{i \in \Pi})$ *and a bisimulation equivalence* $\sim$ *on this game which respects the partition and the target sets, its quotient game is the reachability game* $(\tilde{\mathcal{G}}, [v_0]) = (\tilde{A}, (\tilde{g}_i)_{i \in \Pi}, (\tilde{F}_i)_{i \in \Pi})$ *where* $\tilde{F}_i = \{[v]_\sim \mid v \in F_i\}$ *for each* $i \in \Pi$. *We call this game the* reachability quotient game.

Lemma 2. *Let* $(\mathcal{G}, v_0)$ *be a reachability game and let* $\sim$ *be a bisimulation equivalence. If* $\sim$ *respects the target sets in this game, then* $\sim$ *respects the gain functions.*

4.2 Complexity Results

It is proved that the constrained existence problem is PSPACE-complete in finite reachability games [8]. Our final purpose is to obtain an EXPTIME algorithm for the constrained existence problem on *reachability timed games* (see Sect. 5). Naively applying the PSPACE algorithm of [8] to the region games would lead to an EXPSPACE algorithm. That is why we provide here an alternative EXPTIME algorithm to solve the constrained existence problem on (untimed) finite games. This new algorithm will have the advantage to have a running time at most exponential only in the number of players (and polynomial in the size of its transition system). This feature will be crucial to obtain the EXPTIME algorithm on timed games.

Theorem 2. *Given a finite reachability game* $(\mathcal{G}, v_0)$, *the constrained existence problem can be solved by an algorithm whose time complexity is at most exponential in* $|\Pi|$ *and polynomial in the size of its transition system.*

This approach follows the proof for quantitative reachability games in [9]. This latter proof relies on two key ingredients: *(i)* the *extended game* of a reachability game and *(ii)* an *SPE outcome characterization based on a fixpoint computation of a labeling function of the states*. Those two key ingredients will be defined below. Further technical details can be found in [9] for the quantitative case.

Extended Game. Let $(\mathcal{G}, v_0)$ be a finite reachability game, its associated *extended game* $(\mathcal{X}, x_0) = (X, (g_i^X)_{i \in \Pi}, (F_i^X)_{i \in \Pi})$ is the reachability game such that the vertices are enriched with the set of players that have already visited their target sets along a history. The arena $X = (\Sigma, V^X, E^X, \Pi, (V_i^X)_{i \in \Pi})$ is defined as follows: *(i)* $V^X = V \times 2^\Pi$; *(ii)* $((v, I), a, (v', I')) \in E^X$ if and only if $(v, a, v') \in E$ and $I' = I \cup \{i \in \Pi \mid v' \in F_i\}$; *(iii)* $(v, I) \in V_i^X$ if and only if $v \in V_i$; *(iv)* $(v, I) \in F_i^X$ if and only if $i \in I$ and *(v)* $x_0 = (v_0, I_0)$ where $I_0 = \{i \in \Pi \mid v_0 \in F_i\}$.

The construction of $(\mathcal{X}, x_0)$ from $(\mathcal{G}, v_0)$ causes an exponential blow-up of the number of states. The main idea of this construction is that if you consider a play $\rho = (v_0, I_0)(v_1, I_1) \ldots (v_n, I_n) \ldots \in \text{Plays}_X(x_0)$, the set I_n means that each player $i \in I_n$ has visited his target set along $\rho_0 \ldots \rho_n$. The important points are that there is a one-to-one correspondence between plays in $\text{Plays}_A(v_0)$ and $\text{Plays}_X(x_0)$ and that the gain profiles of two corresponding plays beginning in the initial vertices are equal. From these observations, we have:

Proposition 2. *Let $(\mathcal{G}, v_0)$ be a reachability game and $(\mathcal{X}, x_0)$ be its associated extended game, let $p \in \{0, 1\}^{|\Pi|}$ be a gain profile, there exists an SPE σ in $(\mathcal{G}, v_0)$ with gain profile p if and only if there exists an SPE τ in $(\mathcal{X}, x_0)$ with gain profile p.*

In the rest of this section, we will write $v \in V^X$ (instead of (u, I)) and we depict by $I(v)$ the set I of the players who have already visited their target set.

Outcome Characterization. Once this extended game is built, we want a way to decide whether a play in this game corresponds to the outcome of an SPE or not: we want an *SPE outcome characterization*. The vertices of the extended game are labeled thanks to a *labeling function* $\lambda^* : V^X \rightarrow \{0, 1\}$. For a vertex $v \in V^X$ such that $v \in V_i^X$, the value 1 imposes that Player i should reach his target set if he follows an SPE from v and the value 0 does not impose any constraint on the gain of Player i from v.

The labeling function λ^* is obtained thanks to an iterative procedure such that each step k of the iteration provides a λ^k-labeling function. This procedure is based on the notion of λ-*consistent play*: that is a play which satisfies the constraints given by λ all along it.

Definition 10. *Let $\lambda : V^X \rightarrow \{0, 1\}$ be a labeling function and $\rho \in \text{Plays}_X$, we say that ρ is λ-consistent if for each $i \in \Pi$ and for each $n \in \mathbb{N}$ such that $\rho_n \in V_i^X : g_i^X(\rho_{\geq n}) \geq \lambda(\rho_n)$. We write $\rho \models \lambda$.*

The iterative computation of the sequence $(\lambda^k)_{k\in\mathbb{N}}$ works as follows: (i) at step 0, for each $v \in V^X$, $\lambda^0(v) = 0$, (ii) at step $k+1$, for each $v \in V^X$, by assuming that $v \in V_i^X$, $\lambda^{k+1}(v) = \max_{v'\in\text{Succ}(v)} \min\{g_i^X(\rho) \mid \rho \in \text{Plays}_X(v') \wedge \rho \models \lambda^k\}$ and (iii) we stop when we find $n \in \mathbb{N}$ such that for each $v \in V^X$, $\lambda^{n+1}(v) = \lambda^n(v)$. The least natural number k^* which satisfies (iii) is called the *fixpoint* of $(\lambda^k)_{k\in\mathbb{N}}$ and λ^* is defined as λ^{k^*}. The following lemma states that this natural number exists and so that the iterative procedure stops.

Lemma 3. *The sequence* $(\lambda^k)_{k\in\mathbb{N}}$ *reaches a fixpoint in* $k^* \in \mathbb{N}$. *Moreover,* k^* *is at most equal to* $|V| \cdot 2^{|\Pi|}$.

Proof (Proof sketch). In the initialization step, all the vertex values are equal to 0. Then at each iteration, (i) if the value of a vertex was equal to 1 in the previous step, then it stays equal to 1 all along the procedure and (ii) if the value of the vertex was equal to 0 then it either stays equal to 0 (for this iteration step) or it becomes equal to 1 (for all the next steps thanks to (i)). At each step, at least one vertex value changes and when no value changes the procedure has reached a fixpoint which corresponds to the values of λ^*. Thus, it means that λ^* is obtained in at most $|V| \times 2^{|\Pi|}$ steps.

As claimed in the following proposition, the labeling function λ^* exactly characterizes the set of SPE outcomes. The proof is quite the same as for the quantitative setting [9].

Proposition 3. *Let* $(\mathcal{X}, x_0)$ *be the extended game of a finite reachability game* $(\mathcal{G}, v_0)$ *and let* $\rho^X \in \text{Plays}_X(x_0)$ *be a play, there exists an SPE* σ *with outcome* ρ^X *in* $(\mathcal{X}, x_0)$ *if and only if* ρ^X *is* λ^*-*consistent.*

Complexity. Proposition 3 allows us to prove Theorem 2. Indeed, we only have to find a play in the extended game which is λ^*-consistent and with a gain profile which satisfies the constrained given by the decision problem.

Proof (Proof sketch of Theorem 2). Let $(\mathcal{G}, v_0) = (A, (g_i)_{i\in\Pi}, (F_i)_{i\in\Pi})$ be a reachability game and let $(\mathcal{X}, x_0) = (X, (g_i^X)_{i\in\Pi}, (F_i^X)_{i\in\Pi})$ be its associated extended game. The game $(\mathcal{X}, x_0)$ is built from $(\mathcal{G}, v_0)$ in time at most exponential in the number of players and polynomial in the size of the transition system of A.

The proof will be organized in three steps whose respective proofs will rely on the previous step(s): (i) given a gain profile $p \in \{0,1\}^{|\Pi|}$, given λ^k for some $k \in \mathbb{N}$ and given some $v \in V^X$, we show that we can decide in the required complexity the existence of a play which is λ^k-consistent, beginning in v and with gain profile p; (ii) given λ^k for some $k \in \mathbb{N}$, we show that the computation of λ^{k+1} can be performed within the required complexity; and finally (iii) given $x, y \in \{0,1\}^{|\Pi|}$, we show that the existence of a λ^*-consistent play beginning in x_0 with a gain profile p such that $x \leq p \leq y$ can be decided within the required complexity.

- **Proof of *(i)*:** Given λ^k, $v \in V^X$ and $p \in \{0,1\}^{|\Pi|}$, we want to know if there exists a play $\rho \in \text{Plays}_X(v)$ which is λ^k-consistent and with gain profile p. If a play ρ is such that $g^X(\rho) = p$, then for each $i \in \Pi$ such that $p_i = 1$, the condition of being a λ^k-consistent play is satisfied. For those such that $p_i = 0$, for each $n \in \mathbb{N}$ such that $\rho_n \in V_i^X$, $g_i^X(\rho_{\geq n}) = 0$ should be greater than $\lambda^k(\rho_n)$. This condition is satisfied if and only if for each $n \in \mathbb{N}$ such that $\rho_n \in V_i^X$, $\lambda^k(\rho_n) \neq 1$. Thus, we remove from $(\mathcal{X}, x_0)$ all vertices (and all related edges) $v \in V_i^X$ such that $\lambda^k(v) = 1$, for each player i such that $p_i = 0$. Then, we only have to check if there exists a play ρ which begins in v and with gain profile p in this modified extended reachability game. This can be done in $O(2^{|\Pi|} \cdot (|V^X| + |E^X|))$ ([8, Lemma 23]), thus this procedure runs in time at most exponential in the number of players and polynomial in the size of the transition system of A.
- **Proof of *(ii)*:** Given λ^k, we want to compute λ^{k+1}. For each $v \in V^X$, $\lambda^{k+1}(v) = \max_{v' \in \text{Succ}(v)} \min\{g_i^X(\rho) \mid \rho \in \text{Plays}_X(v') \wedge \rho \models \lambda^k\}$ (by assuming that $v \in V_i^X$). Thus for each $v' \in \text{Succ}(v)$, we have to compute $min = \min\{g_i^X(\rho) \mid \rho \in \text{Plays}_X(v') \wedge \rho \models \lambda^k\}$. But $min = 0$ if and only if there exists $\rho \in \text{Plays}_X(v')$ which is λ^k-consistent and such that $g_i^X(\rho) = 0$. Thus for each $p \in \{0,1\}^{|\Pi|}$ such that $p_i = 0$, we use point *(i)* to decide if $min = 0$. From that follows a procedure which runs in $O(|V^X| \cdot |V^X| \cdot 2^{|\Pi|} \cdot 2^{|\Pi|} \cdot (|V^X| + |E^X|))$ (running time at most exponential in the number of players and polynomial in the size of the transition system A).
- **Proof of *(iii)*:** It remains to prove that the existence of a λ^*-consistent play beginning in x_0 with a gain profile p such that $x \leq p \leq y$ can be decided within the required complexity. In order to do so, we evaluate the complexity to obtain λ^*. First, we build λ^0 such that $\lambda^0(v) = 0$ for all $v \in V^X$ in $O(|V^X|)$ time. Then, we apply point *(ii)* at most $|V| \cdot 2^{|\Pi|}$ times (by Lemma 3) to obtain λ^*. Given $x, y \in \{0,1\}^{|\Pi|}$, we consider each $p \in \{0,1\}^{|\Pi|}$ such that $x \leq p \leq y$ (at most $2^{|\Pi|}$ such ones) and we use point *(i)* to check if there exists a play which begins in x_0 with gain profile p and which is λ^*-consistent. This can be done in running time at most exponential in the number of players and polynomial in the size of the transition system of A.

We conclude the proof by applying Proposition 3.

5   Application to Timed Games

In this section, we are interested in models which are enriched with *clocks* and *clock guards* in order to consider time elapsing. *Timed automata* [19] are well known among such models. We recall some of their classical concepts, then we explain how *(turn-based) timed games* derive from timed automata.

5.1   Timed Automata and Timed Games

In this section, we use the following notations. The set $C = \{c_1, \ldots, c_k\}$ denotes a set of k *clocks*. A *clock valuation* is a function $\nu : C \to \mathbb{R}^+$. The set of clock valuations is depicted by C_V. Given a clock valuation ν, for $i \in \{1, \ldots, k\}$, we sometimes write ν_i instead of $\nu(c_i)$. Given a clock valuation ν and $d \in \mathbb{R}^+$, $\nu + d$ denote the clock valuation $\nu + d : C \to \mathbb{R}^+$ such that $(\nu + d)(c_i) = \nu(c_i) + d$ for each $c_i \in C$. A *guard* is any finite conjunctions of expressions of the form $c_i \diamond x$ where c_i is a clock, $x \in \mathbb{N}$ is a natural number and $\diamond$ is one of the symbols $\{\leq, <, =, >, \geq\}$. We denote by G the set of guards. Let g be a guard and ν be a clock valuation, notation $\nu \models g$ means that $(\nu_1, \ldots, \nu_k)$ satisfies g. A *reset* $Y \in 2^C$ indicates which clocks are reset to 0. We denote by $[Y \leftarrow 0]\nu$ the valuation ν' such that for each $c \in Y$, $\nu'(c) = 0$ and for each $c \in C \backslash Y$, $\nu'(c) = \nu(c)$.

A *timed automaton* (TA) is a tuple $(\mathcal{A}, \ell_0) = (\Sigma, L, \to, C)$ where: *(i)* Σ is a finite alphabet; *(ii)* L is a finite set of *locations*; *(iii)* C is a finite set of *clocks*; *(iv)* $\to \subseteq L \times \Sigma \times G \times 2^C \times L$ a finite set of transitions; and *(v)* $\ell_0 \in L$ an initial location. Additionnally, we may equip a timed automaton with a set of players and partition the locations between them. It results in a *players partitioned timed automaton*.

Definition 11 ((Reachability) Players partitioned timed automaton). *A* players partioned timed automaton *(PPTA)* $(\mathcal{A}, \ell_0) = (\Sigma, L, \to, C, \Pi, (L_i)_{i \in \Pi})$ *is a timed automaton equipped with: (i) Π a finite set of players and (ii) $(L_i)_{i \in \Pi}$ a partition of the locations between the players.*

If $(\mathcal{A}, \ell_0)$ is equipped with a target set $\mathrm{Goal}_i \subseteq L$ *for each player $i \in \Pi$, we call it a* reachability *PPTA.*

The semantic of a timed automaton $(\mathcal{A}, \ell_0)$ is given by its associated transition system $T_\mathcal{A} = (\Sigma, V, E)$ where: *(i)* $V = L \times C_V$ is a set of vertices of the form (ℓ, ν) where ℓ is a location and $\nu : C \to \mathbb{R}^+$ is a clock valuation; and *(ii)* $E \subseteq V \times \Sigma \times V$ is such that $((\ell, \nu), a, (\ell', \nu')) \in E$ if $(\ell, a, g, Y, \ell') \in \to$ for some $g \in G$ and some $Y \in 2^C$, and there exists $d \in \mathbb{R}^+$ such that: *(1)* for each $x \in X \backslash Y$: $\nu'(x) = \nu(x) + d$ **(time elapsing)**; *(2)* for each $x \in Y$: $\nu'(x) = 0$ **(clocks resetting)**; *(3)* $\nu + d \models g$ **(respect of the guard)**.

In the same way, the semantic of a PPTA $(\mathcal{A}, \ell_0)$ is given by its associated game $(\mathcal{G}_\mathcal{A}, v_0)$.

Definition 12 ((Reachability) Timed games $\mathcal{G}_\mathcal{A}$). *Let $(\mathcal{A}, \ell_0) = (\Sigma, L, \to, C, \Pi, (L_i)_{i \in \Pi})$ be a PPTA, its associated game $(\mathcal{G}_\mathcal{A}, v_0) = (\mathrm{A}_\mathcal{A}, (g_i)_{i \in \Pi})$, called* timed game, *is such that: (i) $\mathrm{A}_\mathcal{A} = (\Sigma, V, E, \Pi, (V_i)_{i \in \Pi})$ where $T_\mathcal{A} = (\Sigma, V, E)$ is the associated transition system of $(\mathcal{A}, \ell_0)$ and, for each $i \in \Pi$, $(\ell, \nu) \in V_i$ if and only if $\ell \in L_i$; (ii) for each $i \in \Pi$, $g_i : \mathrm{Plays}_{\mathrm{A}_\mathcal{A}} \to \{0, 1\}$ is a gain function; (iii) $v_0 = (\ell_0, \mathbf{0})$ where $\mathbf{0}$ is the clock valuation such that for all $c \in C$, $\mathbf{0}(c) = 0$.*

If $(\mathcal{A}, \ell_0)$ is a reachability PPTA, its associated timed game is a reachability game $(\mathcal{G}_\mathcal{A}, v_0) = (\mathrm{A}_\mathcal{A}, (g_i)_{i \in \Pi}, (F_i)_{i \in \Pi})$ *such that for each $i \in \Pi$, $(\ell, \nu) \in F_i$ if and only if $\ell \in \mathrm{Goal}_i$. We call this game a* reachability timed game.

Thus, in a timed game, when it is the turn of Player i to play, if the play is in location ℓ, he has to choose a delay $d \in \mathbb{R}^+$ and a next location ℓ' such that $(\ell, a, g, Y, \ell') \in \to$ for some $a \in \Sigma$, $g \in G$ and $Y \in 2^C$. If the choice of d

respects the guard g, then the choice of Player i is valid: the clock valuation evolves according to the past clock valuation, d and Y and location ℓ' is reached. Then, the play continues.

5.2   Regions and Region Games

In this section, we consider a bisimulation equivalence on $T_{\mathcal{A}}$ (the classical time-abstract bisimulation from [19]) which allows us to solve the constrained existence in the quotient of the original timed game (the region game). All along this section we use the following notations. We denote by x_i the maximum value in the guards for clock c_i. For all positive number $d \in \mathbb{R}^+$, $\lfloor d \rfloor$ is the integral part of d and $\overline{d}$ is the fractional part of d.

Definition 13 ($\approx$ and region)

- *Two clock valuations ν and ν' are equivalent (written $\nu \approx \nu'$) iff: (i) $\lfloor \nu_i \rfloor = \lfloor \nu'_i \rfloor$ or $\nu_i, \nu'_i > x_i$, for all $i \in \{1, \ldots, k\}$; (ii) $\overline{\nu_i} = 0$ iff $\overline{\nu'_i}$, for all $i \in \{1, \ldots, k\}$ with $\nu_i \leq x_i$ and (iii) $\overline{\nu_i} \leq \overline{\nu_j}$ iff $\overline{\nu'_i} \leq \overline{\nu'_j}$ for all $i \neq j \in \{1, \ldots, k\}$ with $\nu_j \leq x_j$ and $\nu_i \leq x_i$.*
- *We extend the equivalence relation to the states ($\approx \subseteq V \times V$): $(\ell, \nu) \approx (\ell', \nu')$ iff $\ell = \ell'$ and $\nu \approx \nu'$;*
- *A region r is an equivalence class for some $v \in V$: $r = [v]_{\approx}$.*

This equivalence relation on clocks and its extension to states of $T_{\mathcal{A}}$ is usual and the following result is well known [19].

Lemma 4 ([19]). *Let $(\mathcal{A}, \ell_0)$ be a TA, $\approx \subseteq V \times V$ is a bisimulation equivalence on $T_{\mathcal{A}}$.*

It means that if $(\mathcal{G}_{\mathcal{A}}, v_0)$ is a (reachability) timed game, $\approx$ is a bisimulation equivalence on it. Moreover, it respects the partition. Thus, we can consider the (reachability) quotient game of this game. We call this game the *(reachability) region game*. Notice that $\approx$ respects the target sets, so the reachability quotient game is defined as in Definition 9.

Definition 14 ((Reachability) region game). *Let $(\mathcal{G}_{\mathcal{A}}, v_0)$ be a (reachability) timed game and $\approx \subseteq V \times V$ be the bisimulation equivalence defined in Definition 13, its associated (reachability) region game is its associated (reachability) quotient game $(\tilde{\mathcal{G}}_{\mathcal{A}}, [v_0])$.*

We recall [19] that the size of $\tilde{T}_{\mathcal{A}}$, i.e., its number of states (regions) and edges, is in $O((|V| + | \to |) \cdot 2^{|\delta(\mathcal{A})|})$ where $\delta(\mathcal{A})$ is the binary encoding of the constants (guards and costs) appearing in $\mathcal{A}$. Thus $|\tilde{T}_{\mathcal{A}}|$ is in $O(2^{|\mathcal{A}|})$ where $|\mathcal{A}|$ takes into account the locations, edges and constants of $\mathcal{A}$. From this follows the following lemma.

Lemma 5. *The (reachability) region game* $(\tilde{\mathcal{G}}_{\mathcal{A}}, [v_0])$ *is a finite (reachability) game.*

Finally, in light of the construction of the reachability region game, the bisimulation equivalence $\approx$ respects the gain functions of the reachability timed game and of the reachability region game.

Lemma 6. *Given* $(\mathcal{G}_{\mathcal{A}}, v_0) = (\mathsf{A}_{\mathcal{A}}, (\mathsf{g}_i)_{i \in \Pi}, (F_i)_{i \in \Pi})$ *be a reachability timed game and* $(\tilde{\mathcal{G}}_{\mathcal{A}}, [v_0]) = (\tilde{\mathsf{A}}_{\mathcal{A}}, (\tilde{\mathsf{g}}_i)_{i \in \Pi}, (\tilde{F}_i)_{i \in \Pi})$ *its associated region game,* $\approx$ *respects the gain functions.*

Remark 3. Let $\mathcal{A} = (\Sigma, L, \rightarrow, C)$ be a timed automaton, $T_{\mathcal{A}} = (\Sigma, V, E)$ be its associated transition system and $\approx$ be the bisimulation equivalence on $T_{\mathcal{A}}$ as defined in Definition 13, we have that $((\ell, \nu), a, (\ell', \nu')) \in E$ if and only if there exist $g \in G$, $Y \in 2^C$ and $d \in \mathbb{R}^+$ such that $(\ell, a, g, Y, \ell') \in \rightarrow$, $\nu' = [Y \leftarrow 0](v+d)$ and $v + d \models g$. Thus, we abstract the notion of time elapsing in the edges of the transition system.

Then, since $\approx$ is a bisimulation equivalence on $T_{\mathcal{A}}$, for all $((\ell_1, \nu_1), a, (\ell_1', \nu_1')) \in E$ and for all $(\ell_2, \nu_2) \in V$ such that $(\ell_1, \nu_1) \approx (\ell_2, \nu_2)$, there exists $(\ell_2', \nu_2') \in V$ such that $((\ell_2, \nu_2), a, (\ell_2', \nu_2')) \in E$ and $(\ell_1', \nu_1') \approx (\ell_2', \nu_2')$. The time elapsing between ν_1 and ν_1' is not necessarily the same as between ν_2 and ν_2'. Thus, $\approx$ is a timed abstract bisimulation in the classical way [19].

5.3 Complexity Results

Theorem 3. *Given a reachability PPTA* $(\mathcal{A}, \ell_0)$ *and* $x, y \in \{0,1\}^{|\Pi|}$, *the constrained existence problem in reachability timed games is EXPTIME-complete.*

The EXPTIME-hardness is due to a reduction from *countdown games* and is inspired by the one provided in [7, Section 6.3.3]. Thus, we only prove the EXPTIME-easiness.

Proof (EXPTIME-easiness). Given a PPTA $(\mathcal{A}, \ell_0)$ with target sets $(\mathrm{Goal}_i)_{i \in \Pi}$ and given $x, y \in \{0,1\}^{|\Pi|}$. Thanks to Theorem 1, it is equivalent to solve this problem in the reachability region game. Moreover, the size of the reachability region game is exponential, because its transition system $\tilde{T}_{\mathcal{A}}$ is exponential in the size of $\mathcal{A}$, but not in the number of players. Then, since the reachability region game is a finite reachability game (Lemma 5), we can apply Theorem 2. It causes an exponential blow-up in the number of players but is polynomial in the size of transition system $\tilde{T}_{\mathcal{A}}$. Thus, this entire procedure runs in (simple) exponential time in the size of the PPTA $(\mathcal{A}, \ell_0)$.

Notice that, since there always exists an SPE in a finite reachability game [20], there always exists an SPE in the region game and so in the reachability timed game (Theorem 1).

5.4 Time-Bounded Reachability, Zenoness and Other Extensions

In this paper, we focus on (qualitative) reachability timed games, and ignore the effect of Zeno behaviors[2]. Nevertheless we believe that our approach is rather robust and can be extended to richer objectives and take into account Zeno behaviors. In the following paragraphs, we try to briefly explain how this could be achieved.

Time-Bounded Reachability. A natural extension of our framework would be to equip the objective of each player with a time-bound. Player i aims at visiting F_i within TB_i time units. We believe that this time-bound variant of our constrained problem is decidable. Indeed, for each player, his time-bound reachability objective can easily be encoded via a deterministic timed automaton (on finite timed words) $\mathcal{A}_i$. Given a timed game $\mathcal{G}_b$ equipped with a timed-bounded objective for each player (described via $\mathcal{A}_i$), we could, via standard product construction build a new reachability timed game (without time-bound) $\mathcal{G}$. Solving the constrained existence problem (with time-bound) in $\mathcal{G}_b$ is equivalent to solving the constrained existence problem (of Definition 1) in $\mathcal{G}$ (the constrained being encoded in the $\mathcal{A}_i$'s). This approach could extend to any property that can be expressed via a deterministic timed automaton.

Towards ω-regular Objectives. Let us briefly explain how our approach could be adapted to prove the decidability of the constrained existence problem for timed games with ω-regular objectives. For the sake of clarity, we here focus on parity objectives. First, let us notice that the results of Sect. 3 (including Theorem 1) apply to a general class of games, including infinite games with classical ω-regular objectives such as parity. An algorithm to decide the constrained existence problem (Definition 1) on parity on finite games can be found in [20] via translation into tree automata. Equipped with these two tools, we believe that we could adapt the definitions and results of Sect. 5 to obtain the decidability of the constrained existence problem for parity timed games. Notice that, in order to obtain our complexity results for finite reachability games, we use other simpler tools than tree automata.

About Zenoness. In the present paper, we allow a player to win (or to prevent other players to win) even if his strategy is responsible of Zeno behaviors. In [1], the authors propose an elegant approach to *blame* a player that would prevent divergence of time. The main idea is to transform the ω-regular objective of each player into another one which will make him lose if he blocks the time. We believe that this idea could be exploited in our framework in order to prevent from winning a "blocking time player".

---

[2] A run $\rho = (\ell_0, \nu_0) \xrightarrow{d_1, a_1} (\ell_1, \nu_1) \xrightarrow{d_2, a_2} \dots$ in a timed automaton is said *timed-divergent* if the sequence $(\sum_{j \leq i} d_j)_i$ diverges. A timed automaton is *non-Zeno* if any finite run can be extended into a time-divergent run [6].

References

1. de Alfaro, L., Faella, M., Henzinger, T.A., Majumdar, R., Stoelinga, M.: The element of surprise in timed games. In: Amadio, R., Lugiez, D. (eds.) CONCUR 2003. LNCS, vol. 2761, pp. 144–158. Springer, Heidelberg (2003). https://doi.org/10.1007/978-3-540-45187-7_9
2. Asarin, E., Maler, O.: As soon as possible: time optimal control for timed automata. In: Vaandrager, F.W., van Schuppen, J.H. (eds.) HSCC 1999. LNCS, vol. 1569, pp. 19–30. Springer, Heidelberg (1999). https://doi.org/10.1007/3-540-48983-5_6
3. Baier, C., Katoen, J.P.: Principles of Model Checking. The MIT Press, Cambridge (2008)
4. Behrmann, G., Cougnard, A., David, A., Fleury, E., Larsen, K.G., Lime, D.: UPPAAL-tiga: time for playing games!. In: Damm, W., Hermanns, H. (eds.) CAV 2007. LNCS, vol. 4590, pp. 121–125. Springer, Heidelberg (2007). https://doi.org/10.1007/978-3-540-73368-3_14
5. Bouyer, P., Brenguier, R., Markey, N.: Nash equilibria for reachability objectives in multi-player timed games. In: Gastin, P., Laroussinie, F. (eds.) CONCUR 2010. LNCS, vol. 6269, pp. 192–206. Springer, Heidelberg (2010). https://doi.org/10.1007/978-3-642-15375-4_14
6. Larsen, K.G., Pettersson, P., Yi, W.: Model-checking for real-time systems. In: Reichel, H. (ed.) FCT 1995. LNCS, vol. 965, pp. 62–88. Springer, Heidelberg (1995). https://doi.org/10.1007/3-540-60249-6_41
7. Brenguier, R.: Nash equilibria in concurrent games : application to timed games. Theses, École normale supérieure de Cachan - ENS Cachan, November 2012. https://tel.archives-ouvertes.fr/tel-00827027
8. Brihaye, T., Bruyère, V., Goeminne, A., Raskin, J.: Constrained existence problem for weak subgame perfect equilibria with ω-regular boolean objectives. GandALF **2018**, 16–29 (2018)
9. Brihaye, T., Bruyère, V., Goeminne, A., Raskin, J., van den Bogaard, M.: The complexity of subgame perfect equilibria in quantitative reachability games. In: CONCUR 2019, pp. 13:1–13:16 (2019)
10. Bruyère, V.: Computer aided synthesis: a game-theoretic approach. In: DLT, pp. 3–35 (2017)
11. Cassez, F., David, A., Fleury, E., Larsen, K.G., Lime, D.: Efficient on-the-fly algorithms for the analysis of timed games. In: Abadi, M., de Alfaro, L. (eds.) CONCUR 2005. LNCS, vol. 3653, pp. 66–80. Springer, Heidelberg (2005). https://doi.org/10.1007/11539452_9
12. Condurache, R., Filiot, E., Gentilini, R., Raskin, J.: The complexity of rational synthesis. In: Chatzigiannakis, I., Mitzenmacher, M., Rabani, Y., Sangiorgi, D. (eds.) ICALP 2016. LIPIcs, vol. 55, pp. 121:1–121:15. Schloss Dagstuhl - Leibniz-Zentrum für Informatik (2016)
13. Grädel, E., Ummels, M.: Solution concepts and algorithms for infinite multiplayer games. In: New Perspectives on Games and Interaction. vol. 4, pp. 151–178. Amsterdam University Press (2008)
14. Jurdziński, M., Trivedi, A.: Reachability-time games on timed automata. In: Arge, L., Cachin, C., Jurdziński, T., Tarlecki, A. (eds.) ICALP 2007. LNCS, vol. 4596, pp. 838–849. Springer, Heidelberg (2007). https://doi.org/10.1007/978-3-540-73420-8_72

15. Kwiatkowska, M., Norman, G., Parker, D.: Verification and control of turn-based probabilistic real-time games. In: The Art of Modelling Computational Systems: A Journey from Logic and Concurrency to Security and Privacy - Essays Dedicated to Catuscia Palamidessi on the Occasion of Her 60th Birthday, pp. 379–396 (2019)
16. Nash, J.F.: Equilibrium points in n-person games. In: PNAS, vol. 36, pp. 48–49. National Academy of Sciences (1950)
17. Osborne, M.: An Introduction to Game Theory. Oxford University Press, Oxford (2004)
18. Pnueli, A., Rosner, R.: On the synthesis of a reactive module. In: POPL, pp. 179–190. ACM Press (1989)
19. Alur, R., Dill, D.L.: A theory of timed automata. Theor. Comput. Sci. **126**, 183–235 (1994)
20. Ummels, M.: Rational behaviour and strategy construction in infinite multiplayer games. In: Arun-Kumar, S., Garg, N. (eds.) FSTTCS 2006. LNCS, vol. 4337, pp. 212–223. Springer, Heidelberg (2006). https://doi.org/10.1007/11944836_21

Computing Maximally-Permissive Strategies in Acyclic Timed Automata

Emily Clement[1,2]($\boxtimes$) (iD), Thierry Jéron[1]($\boxtimes$) (iD), Nicolas Markey[1]($\boxtimes$) (iD), and David Mentré[2]($\boxtimes$) (iD)

[1] IRISA, Inria & CNRS & Univ. Rennes, Rennes, France
{emily.clement,thierry.jeron,nicolas.markey}@inria.fr
[2] Mitsubishi Electric R&D Centre Europe, Rennes, France
d.mentre@fr.merce.mee.com

Abstract. Timed automata are a convenient mathematical model for modelling and reasoning about real-time systems. While they provide a powerful way of representing timing aspects of such systems, timed automata assume arbitrary precision and zero-delay actions; in particular, a state might be declared reachable in a timed automaton, but impossible to reach in the physical system it models.

In this paper, we consider *permissive* strategies as a way to overcome this problem: such strategies propose *intervals of delays* instead of single delays, and aim at reaching a target state whichever delay actually takes place. We develop an algorithm for computing the optimal permissiveness (and an associated maximally-permissive strategy) in acyclic timed automata and games.

1 Introduction

Timed automata [AD94] are a powerful formalism for modelling and reasoning about real-time computer systems: they offer a convenient way of modelling timing conditions (not relying on discretization) while allowing for efficient verification algorithms; as a consequence, they have been widely studied by the formal-verification community, and have been applied to numerous industrial case studies thanks to advanced tools such as Uppaal [BDL+06], TChecker [HPT19] or Chronos [BDM+98].

One drawback of timed automata is that they are a mathematical model, assuming infinite precision in the measure of time; this does not correspond to physical devices such as computers. As a consequence, properties that are proven to hold on the model may fail to hold on any implementation. As a very simple example, consider two (or even infinitely-many) consecutive actions that have to be performed at the exact same time: while this would be possible in a mathematical model, this would not be possible on a physical device.

Several approaches have attempted to address such problems, depending on the property to be checked. When considering safety properties, timing imprecisions may add new behaviours, which have to be taken into account in the safety

---

This work was partially funded by ANR project Ticktac (ANR-18-CE40-0015).

N. Bertrand and N. Jansen (Eds.): FORMATS 2020, LNCS 12288, pp. 111–126, 2020.
https://doi.org/10.1007/978-3-030-57628-8_7

check. In that setting, *guard enlargement* [Pur00, DDMR04] has been proposed as a way to model the fact that some timing conditions might be considered true even if they are (slightly) violated: the existence of an enlargement value for which the set of executions is safe is decidable. When dealing with reachability properties, timing imprecisions may prevent a run to be valid. A topological approach has been proposed, where a state is declared reachable only if there is a *tube of trajectories* reaching the target state [GHJ97]. Game-based approaches have also been proposed, where a state is said reachable if there is a strategy to reach this state when an opponent player is allowed to modify (up to a certain point) the values of the delays [BMS15, BFM15].

In this paper, we build on the approach of [BFM15], where the authors aim at computing *maximally-permissive* strategies for reaching a target state. While in classical timed automata, reachability is witnessed by a sequence of delays and transitions leading to a target state, here the aim is to propose *intervals* of delays, leaving it to an opponent player to decide which delay will indeed take place. Of course, the strategy has to be able to respond to any choice of the opponent, eventually reaching the target state.

We can then have several ways of measuring permissiveness of a strategy, the general idea being that larger intervals of delays are preferred. In [BFM15], each interval is associated with a penalty, which is the inverse of the length of the interval. Penalties are summed up along paths, and maximally-permissive strategies are those having minimal worst-case penalty. This favours both large intervals and short paths, but computing optimal strategies could only be achieved in the case of one-clock timed automata in [BFM15].

In the present paper, permissiveness of a strategy is defined as the size of the smallest interval proposed by that strategy. We develop an algorithm to compute the permissiveness of any (winning) configuration in acyclic timed automata and games, with any number of clocks. Consider for instance a scheduling problem, where a number of tasks have to be performed in a certain order within a given delay. Classical reachability algorithms would just say whether a given set of tasks are schedulable (in the mathematical model); this then requires launching some of the tasks at very precise dates, as the computed schedule need not be correct if delays are slightly modified. Instead, our algorithm could compute the permissiveness of the best schedule, thereby measuring the amount of imprecision that can be allowed, depending on the deadline by which all tasks have to be finished.

This paper is organized as follows: in Sect. 2, we introduce the necessary definitions, in particular of timed automata and permissiveness of strategies, and prove basic results. Sect. 3 is devoted to solving the case of *linear* timed automata, where all states have at most one outgoing transition, thereby focusing only on choices of delays. Sect. 4 extends this to acyclic timed automata and games.

By lack of space, most of the proofs could not be included in this version of the paper. They can be found in the long version [CJMM20] of this article.

2   Definitions

2.1   Piecewise-Affine Functions

A valuation for a set $\mathcal{C}$ of variables is a mapping $v \colon \mathcal{C} \to \mathbb{R}_{\geq 0}$, assigning a nonnegative real value to each variable. We write $\mathbf{0}$ for the valuation defined as $\mathbf{0}(c) = 0$ for any $c \in \mathcal{C}$. We write $(\mathbb{R}_{\geq 0})^{\mathcal{C}}$ for the set of valuations for $\mathcal{C}$, which we identify with $(\mathbb{R}_{\geq 0})^n$ when $\mathcal{C}$ has exactly n variables. We write $\overline{\mathbb{R}}$ for $\mathbb{R} \cup \{-\infty; +\infty\}$.

Definition 1. *An n-dimensional affine function is a mapping $f \colon \mathbb{R}_{\geq 0}^n \to \overline{\mathbb{R}}$ s.t.*

- *either there exists a vector $(F_k)_{0 \leq k \leq n} \in \mathbb{R}^{n+1}$ such that $f(v) = F_0 + \sum_{1 \leq i \leq n} F_i \cdot v_i$;*
- *or $f(v) = -\infty$ for all $v \in \mathbb{R}_{\geq 0}^n$; in that case we can still write $f(v) = F_0 + \sum_{1 \leq i \leq n} F_i \cdot v_i$, by setting $F_0 = -\infty$ and $F_i = 0$ for all $1 \leq i \leq n$;*
- *or $f(v) = +\infty$ for all $v \in \mathbb{R}_{\geq 0}^n$; similarly, this corresponds to setting $F_0 = +\infty$ and $F_i = 0$ for all $1 \leq i \leq n$.*

A linear function f is an affine function for which $f(\mathbf{0}) = 0$.

If $\Phi = (\varphi_k)_{1 \leq k \leq m}$ is a set of n-dimensional affine functions and $b = (b_k)_{1 \leq k \leq m}$ is a set of intervals, we write $[\![\Phi, b]\!]$ for the intersection $\bigcap_{1 \leq k \leq m} \varphi_k^{-1}(b_k)$. This defines a convex polyhedron of $\mathbb{R}_{\geq 0}^n$.

An n-dimensional piecewise-affine function is a mapping $f \colon \mathbb{R}_{\geq 0}^n \to \overline{\mathbb{R}}$ for which there exists a partition $S = (S_k)_{1 \leq k \leq m}$ of $\mathbb{R}_{\geq 0}^n$ into convex polyhedra, and a family $(f_k)_{1 \leq k \leq m}$ of affine functions such that for any $x \in \mathbb{R}_{\geq 0}^n$, writing k for the (unique) index in $[1; m]$ such that $x \in S_k$, it holds $f(x) = f^k(x)$.

2.2   Timed Automata

Given a valuation v and a nonnegative real d, we denote with $v + d$ the valuation w such that $w(c) = v(c) + d$ for all $c \in \mathcal{C}$. For any subset $I \subseteq \mathbb{R}_{\geq 0}$, we write $v + I$ for the set of valuations $\{v + d \mid d \in I\}$. Given a valuation v and a subset $r \subseteq \mathcal{C}$, we write $v[r \to 0]$ for the valuation w such that $w(c) = 0$ if $c \in r$ and $w(c) = v(c)$ if $c \notin r$.

The set of linear constraints over $\mathcal{C}$ is defined as $\mathcal{G}(\mathcal{C}) \ni g ::= c \sim n \mid g \wedge g$ where c ranges over $\mathcal{C}$, n ranges over $\mathbb{N}$, and $\sim \in \{<, \leq, =, \geq, >\}$. That a clock valuation v satisfies a clock constraint g, denoted $v \models g$ (and sometimes $v \in g$, seeing g as a convex polyhedron), is defined inductively as

$$v \models c \sim n \iff v(c) \sim n \qquad v \models g_1 \wedge g_2 \iff v \models g_1 \text{ and } v \models g_2$$

For the rest of this paper, we fix a finite alphabet Σ.

Definition 2 ([AD94]). *A timed automaton over Σ is a tuple $\mathcal{A} = (\mathcal{C}, L, T, I)$ where $\mathcal{C}$ is a finite set of clocks, L is a finite set of states (or locations), and $T \subseteq L \times \mathcal{G}(\mathcal{C}) \times \Sigma \times 2^{\mathcal{C}} \times L$ is a finite set of transitions, and $I \colon S \to \mathcal{G}(\mathcal{C})$ define the invariant constraints in locations.*

A *configuration* of a timed automaton is a pair (ℓ, v) where ℓ is a location of the automaton and v is a clock valuation such that $v \models I(\ell)$. The semantics of timed automata can be defined as an infinite-state labelled transition system whose states are the set of configurations, and whose transitions are of two kinds:

- *delay transitions* model time elapsing: no transitions of the timed automaton are taken, but the values of all clocks are augmented by the same value. For any configuration (ℓ, v) and any delay $d \in \mathbb{R}_{\geq 0}$, there is a transition $(\ell, v) \xrightarrow{d} (\ell, v + d)$, provided that $v + d \models I(\ell)$;
- *action transitions* represent the effect of taking a transition in the timed automaton. For any configuration (ℓ, v) and any transition $t = (\ell, g, a, r, \ell')$, if $v \models g$, then there is a transition $(\ell, v) \xrightarrow{a} (\ell', v[r \to 0])$, provided that $v[r \to 0] \models I(\ell')$.

We write $(\ell, v) \xrightarrow{d,a} (\ell', v')$ when there exists (ℓ'', v'') such that $(\ell, v) \xrightarrow{d} (\ell'', v'')$ and $(\ell'', v'') \xrightarrow{a} (\ell', v')$. A run of a timed automaton is a sequence of configurations $(\ell_i, v_i)_i$ such that there exists $d \in \mathbb{R}_{\geq 0}$ and $a \in \Sigma$ such that $(\ell_i, v_i) \xrightarrow{d,a} (\ell_{i+1}, v_{i+1})$ for all i. Even if it means adding a sink state and corresponding transitions, we assume that from any configuration, there always exists a transition $\xrightarrow{d,a}$ for some $d \in \mathbb{R}_{\geq 0}$ and some $a \in \Sigma$. This way, any finite run can be extended into an infinite run (in terms of its number of transitions). We also assume that, from any location ℓ and any action a, there is at most one transition from ℓ labelled with a.

One of the most basic problems concerning timed automata is that of reachability of a location: given a timed automaton $\mathcal{A}$, a source configuration (ℓ_0, v_0) (usually assuming $v_0 = \mathbf{0}$) and a target location ℓ_f, it amounts to deciding whether there exists a run from (ℓ_0, v_0) to some configuration (ℓ_f, v_f) in the infinite-state transition system defining the semantics of $\mathcal{A}$. This problem has been proven decidable (and PSPACE-complete) in the early 1990s [AD94], using *region equivalence*, which provides a finite-state automaton that is (time-abstracted) bisimilar to the original timed automaton.

2.3   Permissive Strategies in Timed Automata

Solving reachability using the algorithm above, we can obtain a sequence of delays and transitions to be taken for reaching the target location. Playing this sequence of delays and transitions however requires infinite precision in order to meet all timing constraints, which might not be possible on physical devices.

In this paper, we address this problem by building on the setting studied in [BFM15]: in that setting, the delays that are played may be slightly perturbed, and it can be required to adapt the future delays (and possibly actions) so as to make sure that the target is indeed reached.

We encode the imprecisions using a game setting: the player proposes an interval of possible delays (together with the action to be played), and its opponent selects, in the proposed interval, the exact delay that will take place.

Formally, in our setting, a *move* from some configuration (ℓ, v) is a pair (I, a), where $I \subseteq \mathbb{R}_{\geq 0}$ is a closed[1] interval, possibly right-unbounded, and $a \in \Sigma$, such that there is a transition (ℓ, g, a, r, ℓ') for which $v + I \subseteq g$ (*i.e.*, for any valuation $w \in v + I$, it holds $w \models g$). We write $\mathsf{moves}(\ell, v)$ for the set of moves from (ℓ, v).

A *permissive strategy* is a function σ mapping finite runs $(\ell_i, v_i)_{0 \leq i \leq n}$ to moves in $\mathsf{moves}(\ell_n, v_n)$. A run $\rho = (\ell_i, v_i)_i$ is *compatible* with a permissive strategy σ if, for any finite prefix $\pi = (\ell_i, v_i)_{0 \leq i \leq j}$ of ρ, $\sigma(\pi)$ is defined and, writing $\sigma(\pi) = (I, a)$, there exists $d \in I$ such that $(\ell_j, v_j) \xrightarrow{d,a} (\ell_{j+1}, v_{j+1})$. A permissive strategy σ is *winning* from a given configuration (ℓ_0, v_0) if any infinite run originating from (ℓ_0, v_0) that is compatible with σ is winning (which, in our setting, means that it visits the target location ℓ_f). Notice that classical strategies (which propose single delays instead of intervals of delays) are special cases of permissive strategies. It follows that, as soon as there is a path from some configuration (ℓ, v) to ℓ_f, there exists a winning permissive strategy from (ℓ, v) (possibly proposing punctual intervals). Such configurations are said winning, and the *winning zone* is the set of all winning configurations.

Our aim is to compute *maximally-permissive* winning strategies. In this work, we measure the permissiveness of a strategy σ in a configuration (ℓ, v), denoted $\mathsf{Perm}_\sigma(\ell, v)$, as the length of the smallest interval it may return. Formally:

Definition 3. *Let σ be a permissive strategy, and (ℓ, v) be a configuration of $\mathcal{A}$. The permissiveness of σ in (ℓ, v), denoted with $\mathsf{Perm}_\sigma(\ell, v)$, is defined as follows:*

- *if σ is not winning from (ℓ, v), the permissiveness of σ in (ℓ, v) is $-\infty$;*
- *otherwise, $\mathsf{Perm}_\sigma(\ell, v) = \inf\{|I| \mid \exists \pi.\ \sigma(\pi) = (I, a)$ for some $a\}$.*

The permissiveness of configuration (ℓ, v) is then defined as

$$\mathsf{Perm}(\ell, v) = \sup_\sigma \mathsf{Perm}_\sigma(\ell, v).$$

In this paper, we prove that Perm is a piecewise affine function, and develop an algorithm for computing that function. Intuitively, this corresponds to computing how much precision is needed in order to reach the target configuration.

Remark 4. Notice that our definition of permissiveness is similar in spirit with that of [BFM15]. However, in [BFM15], each move (I, a) was associated a penalty (namely $1/|I|$), and penalties are summed up along the execution. This tends to make the player favour shorter paths with possibly small intervals (hence demanding more accuracy when playing) over long paths with larger intervals. Our setting only aims at maximizing the size of the smallest interval to be played.

Our work can also be seen as a kind of quantitative extension of *tubes of trajectories* of [GHJ97]: permissiveness could be seen as the minimal width of such a tube. However, we are in a game-based setting, and (except in Sect. 3) the strategy could suggest to take different transitions if they allow for more permissiveness.

---

[1] We only consider closed intervals here to simplify the presentation.

Finally, and perhaps more importantly, our setting is quite close to that of [BMS15], but with a more quantitative focus: we aim at computing the optimal permissiveness for all winning configurations (with reachability objective), while only a global lower bound (of the form $1/m$ where m is doubly-exponential in the size of the input) is obtained in [BMS15]. Similar results to those of [BMS15] are obtained in [SBMR13, BGMRS19] for Büchi objectives; such extensions are part of our future work.

Remark 5. The term *permissive* strategy is sometimes used to refer to *non-deterministic*, returning the set of all moves that lead to winning configurations. In particular, Uppaal-Tiga [BCD+07] can compute maximally-permissive strategies in that sense. But this is only a local view of permissiveness, while our aim is to allow for high permissiveness all along the execution.

2.4 Iterative Computation of Permissiveness

Towards computing Perm, we define:

$$\mathcal{P}_i(\ell_f, v) = +\infty \qquad \text{for all valuations } v \text{ and all } i \geq 0;$$
$$\mathcal{P}_0(\ell, v) = -\infty \qquad \text{for all valuations } v, \text{ and for all } \ell \neq \ell_f;$$

$$\mathcal{P}_{i+1}(\ell, v) = \begin{cases} \sup\limits_{(I,a) \in \text{moves}(\ell,v)} \min(|I|, \inf\{\mathcal{P}_i(\ell', v') \mid \exists d \in I. \ (\ell, v) \xrightarrow{d,a} (\ell', v')\}) \\ \qquad\qquad\qquad\qquad\qquad\qquad\qquad\qquad \text{if moves}(\ell, v) \neq \varnothing \\ -\infty \qquad\qquad\qquad\qquad\qquad\qquad\qquad\qquad \text{otherwise} \end{cases}$$

In the rest of section, we prove some basic properties of this sequence of functions, and in particular its link with permissiveness. The next sections will be devoted to its computation on acyclic timed automata.

Our first two results are concerned with the evolution of the sequence with i. They are proved by straightforward inductions.

Lemma 6. *For any (ℓ, v), the sequence $(\mathcal{P}_i(\ell, v))_{i \in \mathbb{N}}$ is nondecreasing.*

Lemma 7. *If the longest path from ℓ to ℓ_f has at most i transitions, then for any v and any $j \geq 0$, it holds $\mathcal{P}_{i+j}(\ell, v) = \mathcal{P}_i(\ell, v)$.*

The following lemma ties the link between the sequence $(\mathcal{P}_i)$ and permissiveness:

Proposition 8. *For any $i \in \mathbb{N}$ and for any configuration (ℓ, v), it holds:*

1. *$\mathcal{P}_i(\ell, v) = -\infty$ if, and only if, there are no runs of length at most i from (ℓ, v) to ℓ_f;*
2. *for any $p \in \mathbb{R}_{\geq 0}$, and any $i \in \mathbb{N}$, it holds $\mathcal{P}_i(\ell, v) > p$ if, and only if, there is a permissive strategy with permissiveness larger than p that is winning from (ℓ, v) within i steps.*

Proof. We begin with the first equivalence, which we prove by induction on i. The result is trivial for $i = 0$. Now, assume that the result holds up to index i. There may be two reasons for having $\mathcal{P}_{i+1}(\ell, v) = -\infty$ for some (ℓ, v): either $\mathsf{moves}(\ell, v)$ is empty, or it is not empty and for any $(I, a) \in \mathsf{moves}(\ell, v)$, it holds

$$\inf\{\mathcal{P}_i(\ell', v') \mid \exists d \in I.(\ell, v) \xrightarrow{d,a} (\ell', v')\} = -\infty.$$

This is true in particular when $I = \{d\}$ is punctual: for any (d, a), the successor (ℓ', v') such that $(\ell, v) \xrightarrow{d,a} (\ell', v')$ is such that $\mathcal{P}_i(\ell', v') = -\infty$. From the induction hypothesis, there can be no path from those (ℓ', v') to ℓ_f with i steps or less. Hence there are no paths from (ℓ, v) to ℓ_f with at most $i + 1$ steps.

Conversely, if there are no paths having at most $i + 1$ steps from (ℓ, v) to ℓ_f, then either this is because $\mathsf{moves}(\ell, v) = \varnothing$, or this is because all moves lead to a configuration from which there are no paths of length at most i to ℓ_f. By induction hypothesis, all successor configurations have infinite $\mathcal{P}_i$, hence also $\mathcal{P}_{i+1}(\ell, v) = -\infty$.

We now prove the second claim, still by induction. The base case is again trivial. Now, assume that the result holds up to some index i. We fix some $p \in \mathbb{R}_{\geq 0}$, and first consider a configuration (ℓ, v) with $\mathcal{P}_{i+1}(\ell, v) > p$. This entails that $\mathsf{moves}(\ell, v)$ is non-empty, and that there is a move (I, a) with $|I| > p$ such that $\mathcal{P}_i(\ell', v') > p$ for all (ℓ', v') such that $(\ell, v) \xrightarrow{d,a} (\ell', v')$ with $d \in I$. Applying the induction hypothesis, there is an i-step winning strategy with permissiveness larger than p from each successor configuration (ℓ', v'), from which we can build an $i + 1$-step winning strategy with permissiveness larger than p from (ℓ, v).

Conversely, pick an $i+1$-step winning strategy σ_p from (ℓ, v) with permissiveness larger than p. Write $\sigma_p(\ell, v) = (I_0, a_0)$. Then for any $d \in I_0$, in the location (ℓ', v') such that $(\ell, v) \xrightarrow{d,a_0} (\ell', v')$, strategy σ_p is an i-step winning strategy with permissiveness larger than p, so that, following the induction hypothesis, $\mathcal{P}_i(\ell, v) > p$. It immediately follows that $\mathcal{P}_{i+1}(\ell, v) > p$. $\square$

Our next three results focus on properties of the functions $\mathcal{P}_i$. First, we identify zones on which $\mathcal{P}_i$ is constant. This will be useful for proving correctness of our algorithm computing $\mathcal{P}_i$ in the next section:

Lemma 9. *Let $\mathcal{A}$ be a timed automaton, with maximal constant M. Let ℓ be a location, and $i \in \mathbb{N}$. Take two valuations v and v' such that, for any clock c, we have either $v(c) = v'(c)$, or $v(c) > M$ and $v'(c) > M$. Then $\mathcal{P}_i(\ell, v) = \mathcal{P}_i(\ell, v')$.*

Next we prove that the functions $\mathcal{P}_i$ are 2-Lipschitz continuous (on the zone where they take finite values):

Proposition 10. *For any integer $i \in \mathbb{N}$ and any location ℓ, the function $\tau_\ell : v \mapsto \mathcal{P}_i(\ell, v)$ is 2-Lipschitz on the set of valuations where it takes finite values.*

Finally, the following lemma shows the (rather obvious) fact that $\mathcal{P}_i(\ell, v+t) \leq \mathcal{P}_i(\ell, v)$. A consequence of this property is that, for any non-resetting transition, the optimal choice for the opponent is the largest delay in the interval proposed by the player[2]. This corresponds to the intuition that by playing later, the opponent will force the player to react faster at the next step. As Example 1 below shows, this is not the case in general: in that example, from $(\ell_0, \langle x = 0; y = 0 \rangle)$, if the player proposes interval $[1/4; 1]$, the optimal choice for the opponent is $d = 1/4$).

Lemma 11. *Let (ℓ, v) be a configuration, $t \in \mathbb{R}_{\geq 0}$ such that $(\ell, v + t)$ is a configuration of the automaton, and $i \in \mathbb{N}$. Then $\mathcal{P}_i(\ell, v) - t \leq \mathcal{P}_i(\ell, v + t) \leq \mathcal{P}_i(\ell, v)$.*

Example 1. Consider the automaton of Fig. 1. We compute the optimal permissiveness (and corresponding strategies) for this small example. First, $\mathcal{P}_i(\ell_f, v) = +\infty$ for all i, and $\mathcal{P}_0(\ell_0, v) = \mathcal{P}_0(\ell_1, v) = -\infty$.

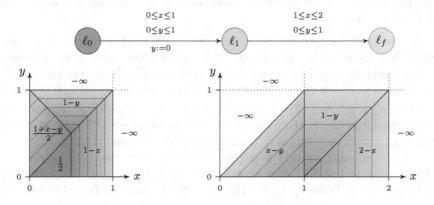

Fig. 1. A linear timed automaton and its permissiveness at ℓ_0 and ℓ_1

We first focus on ℓ_1, with some valuation v: obviously, if $v(x) > 2$ or $v(y) > 1$, the set $\mathsf{moves}(\ell_1, v)$ is empty, and $\mathcal{P}_1(\ell_1, v) = -\infty$ in that case; similarly if $v(y) > v(x)$. Since $\mathcal{P}_0(\ell_f, v)$ does not depend on v, the optimal move for the player is the largest possible interval satisfying the guard:

- if $v(x) \leq 1$ and $v(y) \leq 1$ (and $v(x) \leq v(y)$), the optimal interval of delays is $[1 - v(x); 1 - v(y)]$, whose length is $v(x) - v(y)$;
- if $v(y) \leq 1 \leq v(x) \leq 2$, the transition is immediately available, so that the lower bound of the interval will be 0. For the upper bound, there are two cases:
  - if $v(y) \geq v(x) - 1$, the optimal interval is $[0; 1 - v(y)]$;
  - if $v(y) \leq v(x) - 1$, the optimal interval is $[0; 2 - v(x)]$.

---

[2] This also holds for any transition in a one-clock timed automaton (because in case the clock is reset, the new valuation does not depend on the delay chosen by the opponent).

This defines the permissiveness for ℓ_1.

We now look at ℓ_0: first, $\mathcal{P}_1(\ell_0, v) = -\infty$ for all v, and only configurations (ℓ_0, v) where $v(x) \leq 1$ and $v(y) \leq 1$ are winning, so that $\mathcal{P}_2(\ell_0, v) = -\infty$ as soon as $v(x) > 1$ or $v(y) > 1$. Fix a valuation v for which $v(x) \leq 1$ and $v(y) \leq 1$. We have to find the interval $I = [\alpha, \beta]$ such that $v(x) + \beta \leq 1$ and $v(y) + \beta \leq 1$, and for which $\min\{\beta - \alpha, \inf_{\gamma \in [\alpha, \beta]} \mathcal{P}_1(\ell_1, (v + \gamma)[y \rightarrow 0])\}$ is maximized. Noticing that $(v + \gamma)[y \rightarrow 0]$ is the valuation $(x \mapsto v(x) + \gamma; y \mapsto 0)$, and that $\mathcal{P}_1(\ell_1, w) = w(x)$ for any w satisfying $w(x) \in [0; 1]$ and $w(y) = 0$, we have to maximize $\min\{\beta - \alpha, \inf_{\gamma \in [\alpha, \beta]} v(x) + \gamma\}$ over the domain defined by $0 \leq \alpha \leq \beta \leq \min(1 - v(x); 1 - v(y))$. Obviously, $\inf_{\gamma \in [\alpha, \beta]} v(x) + \gamma = v(x) + \alpha$, so we have to maximize $\min\{\beta - \alpha, v(x) + \alpha\}$ on the set $\{(\alpha, \beta) \mid 0 \leq \alpha \leq \beta \leq \min(1 - v(x); 1 - v(y))\}$.

We consider two cases:

- if $v(y) \leq v(x)$: clearly, it is optimal to maximize β, so we let $\beta = 1 - v(x)$. Hence we have to maximize $\min\{1 - (v(x) + \alpha), v(x) + \alpha\}$ over $0 \leq \alpha \leq 1 - v(x)$. Again, there are two cases, depending on whether $v(x)$ is larger or smaller than $1/2$; in the former case, $\min\{1 - (v(x) + \alpha), v(x) + \alpha\} = 1 - v(x) - \alpha$ when α ranges over $[0; 1 - v(x)]$; it is maximized for $\alpha = 0$, and we get $\mathcal{P}_2(\ell_0, v) = 1 - v(x)$. If $v(x) \leq 1/2$, the maximal value is reached when $\alpha = 1/2 - v(x)$, and $\mathcal{P}_2(\ell_0, v) = 1/2$.
- if $v(y) \geq v(x)$: then it is optimal to let $\beta = 1 - v(y)$. Again there are two cases for maximizing $\min\{1 - v(y) - \alpha, v(x) + \alpha\}$: if $1 - v(y) \leq v(x)$, then $\alpha = 0$ is optimal, and $\mathcal{P}_2(\ell_0, v) = 1 - v(y)$; otherwise, $\alpha = (1 - v(x) - v(y))/2$ is optimal, and $\mathcal{P}_2(\ell_0, v) = (1 - v(y) + v(x))/2$.

We end up with the diagram represented on the left of Fig. 1 (where for the sake of readability we write x and y in place of $v(x)$ and $v(y)$).

Our aim in the rest of this paper is to compute the sequence of functions $\mathcal{P}_i$, and to evaluate the complexity of this computation. Following Lemma 7, this will provide us with an algorithm for computing permissiveness in acyclic timed automata.

3   Computing Optimal Strategies in Linear Timed Automata

In this section, we consider the simpler case of linear timed automata, where each location has at most one successor.

3.1   Optimal Strategy for the Opponent

We begin with focusing on the optimal choice of the opponent: given a configuration (ℓ, v) and an interval I of delays proposed by the player (there is a single outgoing transition, so the action to be played is fixed), what is the best delay that the opponent will choose so as to minimize the permissiveness of the resulting configuration?

As we already mentioned, Lemma 11 answers this question for non-resetting transitions: for such transitions, the best option for the opponent is to choose the maximal delay in the interval proposed by the player. On the other hand, Example 1 provides a situation where the opponent prefers to play as early as possible.

It turns out that, for linear timed automata, the optimal choice of the opponent is always one of these two extremal choices. This property will be a corollary of the following lemma, stating concavity of the permissiveness function in linear timed automata:

Proposition 12. *Let $i \in \mathbb{N}$. Let ℓ be a location of a linear timed automaton, let v_1 and v_2 be two clock valuations such that $\mathcal{P}_i(\ell, v_1)$ and $\mathcal{P}_i(\ell, v_2)$ are finite. Let $\lambda \in [0; 1]$, and $v_\lambda = \lambda \cdot v_1 + (1 - \lambda) \cdot v_2$. Then*

$$\mathcal{P}_i(\ell, v_\lambda) \geq \lambda \cdot \mathcal{P}_i(\ell, v_1) + (1 - \lambda) \cdot \mathcal{P}_i(\ell, v_2).$$

The aim of the opponent being to select the valuation in $V = \{v + \delta[r \to 0] \mid 0 \leq \delta \leq d\}$ that minimizes the permissiveness. Writing $v_1 = v[r \to 0]$ and $v_2 = v + d[r \to 0]$, we have $V = \{\lambda v_1 + (1 - \lambda)v_2 \mid 0 \leq \lambda \leq 1\}$. Proposition 12 entails that the permissiveness is minimized either in v_1 or in v_2. This corresponds to our claim that the best choice for the opponent always is to select one of the bounds of the interval proposed by the player.

Corollary 13. *Let ℓ be a location of a linear timed automaton, v and v' be two clock valuations, $\lambda \in [0; 1]$, and $v_\lambda = \lambda \cdot v + (1 - \lambda) \cdot v'$. Then for all i:*

$$\mathcal{P}_i(\ell, v_\lambda) \geq \min\{\mathcal{P}_i(\ell, v), \mathcal{P}_i(\ell, v')\}.$$

In particular, for any valuation v, any bounded interval $[\alpha, \beta]$, and any transition $\ell \xrightarrow{g,a,r} \ell'$:

$$\inf\{\mathcal{P}_i(\ell', v') \mid \exists d \in [\alpha, \beta]. \ (\ell, v) \xrightarrow{d,a} (\ell', v')\} = \min\{\mathcal{P}_i(\ell', v'_\alpha), \mathcal{P}_i(\ell', v'_\beta)\}$$

where $(\ell, v) \xrightarrow{\alpha,a} (\ell', v'_\alpha)$ and $(\ell, v) \xrightarrow{\beta,a} (\ell', v'_\beta)$.

3.2   Computing the Most-Permissive Strategy

Now that we have a better understanding of the optimal strategy of the opponent, we can compute the most-permissive strategy of the player for reaching the target location ℓ_f. We prove that for all i, $\mathcal{P}_i$ is in fact a piecewise-affine function that can be computed in doubly-exponential time.

First notice that, following Lemma 7, for any location ℓ of a linear timed automaton with n locations, the sequence of functions $(\mathcal{P}_i)_i$ converges in at most n steps.

Theorem 14. *The permissiveness function for a linear timed automaton with d locations and n clocks is a piecewise-affine function. It can be computed in time $O((n+1)^{8^d})$.*

The following technical lemma will be the central tool in the computation of $\mathcal{P}_i$:

Lemma 15. *Let $m_\alpha \leq M_\alpha$ and $m_\beta \leq M_\beta$, and $D = \{(\alpha, \beta) \in \mathbb{R}_{\geq 0}^2 \mid m_\alpha \leq \alpha \leq M_\alpha,\ m_\beta \leq \beta \leq M_\beta,\ \alpha \leq \beta\}$. Let $f: \alpha \mapsto a\alpha + b$ and $g: \beta \mapsto c\beta + d$ be two 1-dimensional affine functions, and $\mu: (\alpha, \beta) \mapsto \min\{\beta - \alpha, f(\alpha), g(\beta)\}$. Then the maximal value that μ may take over D is of one of the following five forms: $M_\beta - m_\alpha$, $\lambda \cdot f(\nu)$, $\lambda \cdot g(\mu)$, $\frac{ad-bc}{a-c}$ and $\frac{ad-bc}{(a+1)(1-c)-1}$, with $\lambda \in \{1, \frac{1}{1-c}, \frac{1}{a+1}\}$ and $\nu \in \{m_\alpha, M_\alpha, m_\beta, M_\beta\}$. This value can be computed by checking inequalities between expressions of the same forms.*

The following lemma corresponds to one step of our inductive computation of $\mathcal{P}_i$:

Lemma 16. *Let $\mathcal{A}$ be a linear timed automaton with n clocks. Let (ℓ, g, a, z, ℓ') be a transition of $\mathcal{A}$, and assume that $v \mapsto \mathcal{P}_{i-1}(\ell', v)$ is piecewise affine, with m cells. Then $v \mapsto \mathcal{P}_i(\ell, v)$ is piecewise affine. It can be computed in time $O(m^4 \cdot (m+n)^4)$. It can be defined using a polyhedral partition of size $O(m^4 \cdot (m+n)^4)$, and with coefficients polynomial in those of $\mathcal{P}_{i-1}$.*

Proof. We assume that $\mathcal{P}_{i-1}(\ell', v)$ is not constantly $-\infty$ (if it were the case, then also $\mathcal{P}_i(\ell, v) = -\infty$ for all v). Similarly, we assume that $\mathsf{moves}(\ell, v)$ is non-empty for some v. Since $v \mapsto \mathcal{P}_{i-1}(\ell', v)$ is piecewise-affine: we can then fix a polyhedral partition $[\![\Phi, P]\!]$ and, for each cell h in this partition, an affine functions f_h, such that $\mathcal{P}_{i-1}(\ell', v) = f_h(v)$ for the only cell h containing v.

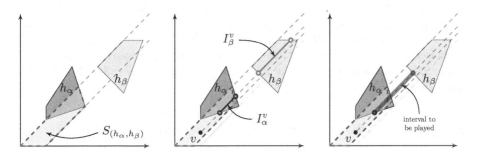

Fig. 2. Three steps of our procedure: $S_{(h_\alpha, h_\beta)}$; then compute expressions for I_α^v and I_β^v (notice that we had to refine $S_{(h_\alpha, h_\beta)}$, because the expression for I_β^v would be different for the lower part of $S_{(h_\alpha, h_\beta)}$ since it ends of a different facet of h_β); finally select best values for α and β.

Our procedure for computing $\mathcal{P}_i$ in ℓ consists in listing the possible pairs of cells defining $\mathcal{P}_{i-1}$ in ℓ' where the left- and right-bounds of the interval to be proposed lie. For each pair (h_α, h_β) of such cells, we perform the following three steps (illustrated on Fig. 2):

- characterize the set $S_{(h_\alpha, h_\beta)}$ of all valuations from which those cells can be reached by taking the transition from ℓ to ℓ'. We compute this polyhedron using quantifier elimination;
- compute the ranges for α and β that can be played in order to indeed end up respectively in h_α and h_β. These are intervals I_α and I_β, whose bounds are expressed as functions of v. Computing these bounds may require refining the polyhedron obtained at the previous step into several subpolyhedra, in order to express them as affine functions of $v \in S_{(h_\alpha, h_\beta)}$;
- for each subpolyhedron, compute the optimal values for α and β: following Corollary 13, this amounts to find values for $\alpha \in I_\alpha$ and $\beta \in I_\beta$ that maximize the following function:

$$\mu \colon (\alpha, \beta) \mapsto \min\{\beta - \alpha; \mathcal{P}_{i-1}(\ell', (v + \alpha)[z \to 0]); \mathcal{P}_{i-1}(\ell', (v + \beta)[z \to 0])\}.$$

This is performed by applying our technical Lemma 15; it may again require another refinement of the subpolyhedra, and returns an affine function for each subpolyhedron.

For each pair (h_α, h_β), we end up with a (partial) piecewise-affine function, defined on $S_{(h_\alpha, h_\beta)}$, returning the optimal permissiveness that can be obtained if playing interval $[\alpha, \beta]$ such that taking the transition to ℓ' after delay α (resp. β) leads to h_α (resp. h_β). Our final step to compute $\mathcal{P}_i$ in ℓ consists in taking the maximum of all these partial functions on their (possibly overlapping) domains; this may introduce on more refinement of our polyhedron.

Notice that all these computations are performed symbolically w.r.t v: we manipulate affine functions of v, with conditions on v for our computations to be valid. □

Assuming that $v \mapsto \mathcal{P}_{i-1}(\ell', v)$ has m cells, computing $v \mapsto \mathcal{P}_i(\ell, v)$ takes time $O(m^4 \cdot (m + n)^4)$, where n is the number of clocks, and this function has $O(m^4 \cdot (m + n)^4)$ many cells.

It follows that, for a linear timed automaton having d locations, we obtain the permissiveness function in the initial state as a piecewise-affine function in time $O((n + 1)^{8^d})$, which proves Theorem 14.

4   Extension to Acyclic Timed Automata and Games

4.1   Adding Branching

We extend the previous study to the case of acyclic timed automata (with branching). In that case, we can still apply our inductive approach, with a few changes:

at each step, we would compute the optimal move of the player for each single action, and then select the optimal action by "superimposing" the resulting permissiveness functions and selecting the action that maximizes permissiveness. This however breaks the result of Proposition 12: the maximum of two concave functions need not be concave. Example 2, derived from Example 1, displays an example where the permissiveness function is not concave.

Example 2. Consider the automaton of Fig. 3. The transition from ℓ_0 to ℓ_f has the same constraint as that from ℓ_1 to ℓ_f; hence the permissiveness offered by that action is the same as the one from ℓ_1, which we already computed. Hence the global permissiveness from ℓ_0 is the (pointwise) maximal of the two piecewise-affine functions displayed on Fig. 1, which is depicted on Fig. 3. On this diagram, the blue area corresponds to points from where it is better (or only possible) to go via ℓ_1, while the red area corresponds to valuations from where it is better (or only possible) to take the bottom transition.

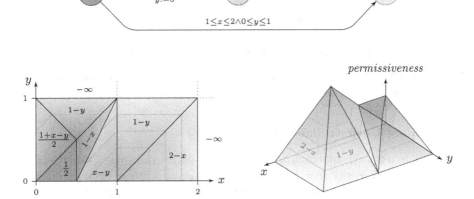

Fig. 3. A timed automaton and its (non-concave) permissiveness function in ℓ_0 (Color figure online)

We prove by induction that the permissiveness functions still are piecewise-affine in that setting. Hence all four steps of our proof of Lemma 16 still apply, with some adaptations. For each location ℓ, for each transition t from ℓ to some ℓ', the procedure now is as follows:

- for the first step, we again consider two cells h_α and h_β in the partition defining $\mathcal{P}_{i-1}(\ell')$, together with a set H of cells that will be visited between h_α and h_β. Again applying Fourier-Motzkin, we get a polyhedron $S_{(h_\alpha,h_\beta,H)}$ of valuations from which those cells can indeed be visited;
- the computation of the intervals I_α^v and I_β^v is unchanged;

- for each cell $h \in H$, we can compute the values d_h^{in} and d_h^{out} for which $(v + d_h^{\text{in}})[z \to 0]$ enters h and $(v + d_h^{\text{out}})[z \to 0]$ leaves h (notice that this may require further refinement of the polyhedron being considered). Since $\mathcal{P}_{i-1}$ is affine on cell h, it reaches its maximum on this cell either at $(v + d_h^{\text{in}})[z \to 0]$ or at $(v + d_h^{\text{out}})[z \to 0]$. The function we need to maximize now looks like

$$\mu' : (\alpha, \beta) \mapsto \min(\{\beta - \alpha, \mathcal{P}_{i-1}(\ell', (v + \alpha)[z \to 0]), \mathcal{P}_{i-1}(\ell', (v + \beta)[z \to 0])\} \cup \{\mathcal{P}_{i-1}(\ell', (v + d_h^{\text{in}})[z \to 0]), \mathcal{P}_{i-1}(\ell', (v + d_h^{\text{out}})[z \to 0]) \mid h \in H\}).$$

Now, we notice that all values in the second set are constant, not depending on α and β. We can thus still apply Lemma 15 in order to maximize $\mu(\alpha, \beta)$, and then take the above constants into account (which may again refine the polyhedra).
- the above three steps have to be performed for all outgoing transitions from the location ℓ being considered. The last step still consists in selecting the maximum of all the resulting functions.

The complexity of our procedure is much higher than that of linear automata: because we consider sets of cells already at the first step, we have $O(2^m)$ sets to consider. Assuming that $\mathcal{P}_{i-1}$ is made of m cells, we may end up with $\mathcal{P}_i$ having more than 2^m cells. Since we have to repeat this procedure up to $|T|$ times, so that the time complexity is in $O(^{|T|}2)$ (where $^n a$ is tetration). Hence our procedure is non-elementary in the worst case. In the end:

Theorem 17. *The permissiveness function for acyclic timed automata is piecewise affine. It can be computed in non-elementary time.*

4.2 Adding Uncontrollable States

We finally extend our approach to (acyclic) two-player turn-based timed games.

This setting is easily seen to preserve piecewise-affineness of the permissiveness function. Indeed, in order to compute $\mathcal{P}_i$ in a location ℓ belonging to the opponent, it suffices to first compute the functions $\mathcal{P}_i^{\ell \to \ell'}$ for all outgoing transitions from ℓ to some ℓ'; this follows the same procedure as above, and results in a piecewise-affine function, assuming (inductively) that $\mathcal{P}_{i-1}$ is piecewise affine. We then compute the (still piecewise-affine) minimum $\mathcal{M}_i(\ell, v)$ of all those functions, and finally

$$\mathcal{P}_i(\ell, v) = \min_{\substack{d \text{ s.t.} \\ v + d \models \text{Inv}(\ell)}} \mathcal{M}_i(\ell, v + d)$$

which is easily computed and remains piecewise-affine. The computation for locations that belong to the player is similar as in the case of plain timed automata. It follows:

Theorem 18. *The permissiveness function for acyclic turn-based timed games is piecewise affine, and can be computed in non-elementary time.*

5   Conclusions and Perspectives

In this paper, we addressed the problem of measuring the amount of precision needed in a timed automaton to reach a given target location. We built on the formalism of permissive strategies defined in [BFM15], and developed an algorithm for computing the optimal permissiveness in acyclic timed automata and games.

There are several directions in which we will extend this work: as a first task, we will have a closer look at the complexity of our procedure, trying to either find examples where the number of cells indeed grows exponentially (for linear timed automata) or exponentially at each step (for acyclic timed automata). A natural continuation of our work consists in tackling cycles. We were unable to prove our intuition that there is no reason for the player to iterate a cycle. Following [BGMRS19], we might first consider fixing a timed automaton made of a single cycle, study how permissiveness evolves along one run in this cycle, and compute the optimal permissiveness for being able to take a cycle forever. Exploiting 2-Lipschitz continuity of the permissiveness function, we could also develop approximating techniques, both for making our computations more efficient in the acyclic case and to handle cycles. Finally, other interesting directions include extending our approach to linear hybrid automata, or considering a stochastic opponent, thereby modelling the fact that perturbations need not always be antagonist.

References

[AD94]   Alur, R., Dill, D.L.: A theory of timed automata. Theor. Comput. Sci. **126**(2), 183–235 (1994)

[BCD+07]   Behrmann, G., Cougnard, A., David, A., Fleury, E., Larsen, K.G., Lime, D.: UPPAAL-tiga: time for playing games!. In: Damm, W., Hermanns, H. (eds.) CAV 2007. LNCS, vol. 4590, pp. 121–125. Springer, Heidelberg (2007). https://doi.org/10.1007/978-3-540-73368-3_14

[BDL+06]   Behrmann, G., et al.: UPPAAL 4.0. In: Proceedings of the 3rd International Conference on Quantitative Evaluation of Systems, QEST 2006, pp. 125–126. IEEE Computer Society Press, September 2006

[BDM+98]   Bozga, M., Daws, C., Maler, O., Olivero, A., Tripakis, S., Yovine, S.: Kronos: a model-checking tool for real-time systems. In: Hu, A.J., Vardi, M.Y. (eds.) CAV 1998. LNCS, vol. 1427, pp. 546–550. Springer, Heidelberg (1998). https://doi.org/10.1007/BFb0028779

[BFM15]   Bouyer, P., Fang, E., Markey, N.: Permissive strategies in timed automata and games. In: Grov, G., Ireland, A. (eds.) Proceedings of the 15th International Workshop on Automated Verification of Critical Systems, AVOCS 2015, volume 72 of Electronic Communications of the EASST. European Association of Software Science and Technology, September 2015

[BGMRS19]   Busatto-Gaston, D., Monmege, B., Reynier, P.-A., Sankur, O.: Robust controller synthesis in timed Büchi automata: a symbolic approach. In: Dillig, I., Tasiran, S. (eds.) CAV 2019. LNCS, vol. 11561, pp. 572–590. Springer, Cham (2019). https://doi.org/10.1007/978-3-030-25540-4_33

[BMS15] Bouyer, P., Markey, N., Sankur, O.: Robust reachability in timed automata and games: a game-based approach. Theor. Comput. Sci. **563**, 43–74 (2015)

[CJMM20] Clement, E., Jéron, T., Markey, N., Mentré, D.: Computing maximally-permissive strategies in acyclic timed automata. Technical Report. arXiv:2007.01815 (2020)

[DDMR04] De Wulf, M., Doyen, L., Markey, N., Raskin, J.-F.: Robustness and implementability of timed automata. In: Lakhnech, Y., Yovine, S. (eds.) FORMATS/FTRTFT -2004. LNCS, vol. 3253, pp. 118–133. Springer, Heidelberg (2004). https://doi.org/10.1007/978-3-540-30206-3_10

[GHJ97] Gupta, V., Henzinger, T.A., Jagadeesan, R.: Robust timed automata. In: Maler, O. (ed.) HART 1997. LNCS, vol. 1201, pp. 331–345. Springer, Heidelberg (1997). https://doi.org/10.1007/BFb0014736

[HPT19] Herbreteau, F., Point, G., Tran, T.-T.: TChecker, an open-source model-checker for timed systems (2019). https://github.com/fredher/tchecker

[Pur00] Puri, A.: Dynamical properties of timed systems. Discrete Event Dyn. Syst. **10**(1–2), 87–113 (2000). https://doi.org/10.1023/A:1008387132377

[SBMR13] Sankur, O., Bouyer, P., Markey, N., Reynier, P.-A.: Robust controller synthesis in timed automata. In: D'Argenio, P.R., Melgratti, H. (eds.) CONCUR 2013. LNCS, vol. 8052, pp. 546–560. Springer, Heidelberg (2013). https://doi.org/10.1007/978-3-642-40184-8_38

Dynamic Causes for the Violation
of Timed Reachability Properties

Martin Kölbl[(✉)], Stefan Leue[(✉)], and Robert Schmid[(✉)]

University of Konstanz, Konstanz, Germany
{Martin.Koelbl,Stefan.Leue,Robert.Schmid}@uni-konstanz.de

Abstract. When a real-time model checker detects the violation of a timed reachability property for a given Timed Automata model it returns a counterexample, here referred to as a Timed Diagnostic Trace (TDT). In this paper, we present a TDT analysis that computes actual dynamic causes in terms of delay ranges that can be considered causal for the violation of the property. The determination of actual causes can help in system analysis as well as design space exploration. The causal analysis is based on counterfactual reasoning and encoded in linear real arithmetic. We apply an implementation of the analysis in the tool CATIRA to a number of Timed Automata models taken from the literature.

1 Introduction

The analysis of causes for the violation of a desired property has various applications in the design of systems. We are particularly interested in developing notions of causality and related analyses for models describing system computations. We have defined Causality Checking in [14] as a means to compute actual causes [10] for the violation of reachability properties, relying on a counterfactual [15] notion of causality inspired by the seminal works of Halpern and Pearl [10].

The actual causes computed in this work rely on choices made during the dynamic execution of the model, for instance, a non-deterministically chosen interleaving of concurrent events during the execution of the model, and we refer to this type of a cause as *dynamic actual causes*. In other work, we have considered the syntactic repair of timed automata models based on an analysis of timed diagnostic traces obtained in real-time model checking [12]. In that work, syntactic features of the model are considered to be actual causes for the violation of timed reachability properties, and we refer to this type of causes as *static actual causes*. Both analyses are based on the counterfactual argument and compare the alternative worlds that differ in the choice of delays or features to find minimal sets of choices that lead to the effect. The analysis of both static and dynamic actual causes can help in identifying possible modifications to design-time models, establishing safety cases for those types of models, or helping in forensic system failure analysis.

© Springer Nature Switzerland AG 2020
N. Bertrand and N. Jansen (Eds.): FORMATS 2020, LNCS 12288, pp. 127–143, 2020.
https://doi.org/10.1007/978-3-030-57628-8_8

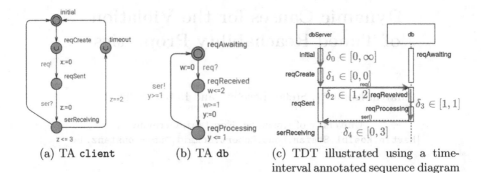

(a) TA client   (b) TA db   (c) TDT illustrated using a time-
                                          interval annotated sequence diagram

Fig. 1. Network of Timed Automata - running example

Real-time model checking [3] is a well-established design space exploration technique aiming at analyzing the real-time behavior of a system and its compliance with non-functional real-time requirements. A commonly used model of computation for real-time systems is that of Timed Automata [3]. Timed Automata (TA) describe the real-time behavior of a system in terms of states, labeled with invariant conditions referring to bounds on system clocks, and transition guards, labeled with clock constraints on the enabledness of transitions. Properties of Timed Automata are typically expressed in timed CTL [3]. In this paper, we restrict ourselves to timed reachability properties [3].

It is the objective of this paper to propose the first steps towards a framework of dynamic actual causality in the analysis of timed reachability properties of Timed Automata. We will focus on the question of whether the dynamic timing of the model during system execution can be considered an actual cause, based on a counterfactual argument, of the violation of a timed reachability property. In Timed Automata, the time that the automaton spends in a certain location can be non-deterministically chosen, as long as it complies with the timing constraints specified in the model. The question is then whether there are timing choices that can be considered causal for the violation of a desired timed reachability property.

We now illustrate the idea of our analysis on the time automata of a database request represented in Figure 1. In the model, a client sends a request req to a database db and expects to receive a response ser in the location serReceiving in less than 4 time units. A clock x is reset with sending the request and measures the time until the response is received with leaving location serReceiving. The timed model checker UPPAAL [2] finds a property violation in this model and returns a timed sequence of transitions leading to the property violation in the form of a TDT. A TDT is an alternating sequence of delay transition δ_i, which describe the time that a system remains in state i, and action transitions Θ_i. A TDT for the example in Fig. 1 is $\delta_0, \theta_0 \ldots \delta_3, \theta_3, \delta_4$ with the action transitions

$\theta_0 = ((\text{initial}, \text{reqAwaiting}), \emptyset, \tau, \emptyset, (\text{reqCreate}, \text{reqAwaiting}))$

$\theta_1 = ((\text{reqCreate}, \text{reqAwaiting}), \emptyset, \tau, \{x\}, (\text{reqSent}, \text{reqReceived}))$

$\theta_2 = ((\text{reqSent}, \text{reqReceived}), \{x \geq 1\}, \tau, \{y\}, (\text{reqSent}, \text{reqProc.}))$

$\theta_3 = ((\text{reqSent}, \text{reqProc.}), \{y \geq 1\}, \tau, \{z\}, (\text{serReceiving}, \text{reqAwait.})).$

A TDT is symbolic in that it describes a set of executions where the time delays before taking the next transition are represented by symbolic variables and constrained by symbolic constraints. The TDT of the database example and the possible time delays are depicted by the sequence diagram in Fig. 1(c). For the remainder of the paper, we use this TDT as a running example. A concrete assignment of the delay values $\delta_0 ... \delta_4$ is a realization, and represents the real-time characteristics of a concrete execution of the TDT S. A realization may, or may not, violate the considered property. An assignment in which the minimal possible values are assigned to all δ_j, in other words, the realization $\delta_0 = 0$, $\delta_1 = 0$, $\delta_2 = 1$, $\delta_3 = 1$ and $\delta_4 = 0$, leads to a trace that does not violate the considered property. Notice that the values of δ_1 and δ_3 are fixed. The values of δ_0, δ_2 and δ_4 in a concrete execution may be determined by environmental effects, or by non-deterministic internal decisions of the two involved subsystems, for instance as a result of task scheduling or memory management. If we consider an alternate execution in which $\delta_4 = 3$, while all other delay values remain as above, then this execution violates the considered property. Some assignments of values to the delays satisfy the property, while others violate the property. This indicates that the cause for the property violation is to be found in the value assignment of certain delays. We are interested in characterizing value assignments to the δ_is that inevitably lead to a property violation using linear constraints. We base the analysis on counterfactual causal reasoning [9] and call such constraints causal ranges. The causal ranges for the example TDT are $2 \leq \delta_4 \leq 3$ and $3 \leq \delta_2 + \delta_4 \leq 5$. It is the objective of this paper to present automated algorithmic ways to compute such causal ranges.

Related Work. Causal reasoning for real-time systems is considered in [7,19] and for reactive systems in [6]. In these three approaches, a system consists of several components and the analysis searches for a causal set of faulty components, whereas we are interested in constraints on a set of causal delays. There is research on system analysis based on counterfactual causal reasoning [10], for instance, in [1,8,10,13]. We are not aware of any work to compute causal time delays for a property violation in a TA.

Structure of the Paper. We exemplify our idea of timed causes in Sect. 2 and discuss in Sect. 3 the foundations of our work. In Sect. 4, we present a formal framework of dynamic trace analysis for causal delays and causal ranges, and present an algorithm to compute causal ranges in Sect. 5. We evaluate an implementation of the algorithm in the tool CATIRA in Sect. 6 by computing causal ranges for several Timed Automata models. In Sect. 7, we draw conclusions and suggest future developments.

2 A Motivating Example

We motivate our definition of a cause for delays and exemplify our proposed causal analysis. A TDT contains all information regarding possible assignments of the delay variables, in particular the constraints determining possible value ranges for these assignments. As discussed above, these value assignments in a concretization of a TDT determine whether a property is violated.

In keeping with standard practice in engineering science, we will use a counterfactual argument [15] to establish when certain assignments of delay variables constitute a cause for a property violation. This argument says that one phenomenon is a *cause* of another phenomenon, called *effect*, if and only if

I. whenever the cause applies, the effect is observed (regularity argument),
II. when the cause does not apply, the effect will not be observed either (counterfactual argument), and
III. no true subset of the cause ensures I. and II (minimality argument).

In order to establish a causal relation between an assignment of values to the delay variables and the violation of a temporal reachability property, we develop criteria for what we understand to be a cause. For a TA, a dynamic actual cause is a constraint on delay assignments where every assignment that satisfies the cause violates a given property (condition I). Our interpretation of II is that several independent causes can result in a property violation but at least one assignment exists that is not violating the property. III is a minimality argument and removes from a cause any constraint that has no influence on whether an assignment violates the property or not.

Applying this reasoning to the running example from Fig. 1, choosing either $2 \leq \delta_4 \leq 3$ or $3 \leq \delta_2 + \delta_4 \leq 5$, with arbitrary but admissible values assigned to all other δ_js, means that the desired property is violated. Also a different choice of the delay variables value not according to these two expression exists where the property violation cannot be observed. We conclude that, following the counterfactual argument, these two constraint expressions are to be considered independent causes for the property violation.

We now illustrate the computation of a cause in the form of a *causal range* for the running example. For a range expression, to be causal, the values for all δ_js in this range have to violate the considered property (I.). Furthermore, it needs to satisfy the counterfactual argument (II.) which means that there is a different assignment of values to at least one of the δ_js such that this assignment violates the range constraint and does not lead to a property violation. This means that in order to check whether II. is satisfied overall we can test II. on every δ_j in isolation. To illustrate this point, consider the realization $\delta_0 = 1$, $\delta_1 = 0$, $\delta_2 = 1.5$, $\delta_3 = 1$, and $\delta_4 = 1.5$. The realization also violates the considered property with any other value for δ_0, while a decrease of the assigned values of δ_2 or δ_4 results in a realization that satisfies the property. The assignment of δ_0 has no impact on the property since its satisfaction solely depends on the values of δ_2, δ_3 and δ_4. The values of δ_1 and δ_3 are fixed and, hence, they have no admissible alternative assignment. We conclude that only δ_2 and δ_4 have the potential to prevent the violation of the property and, hence, satisfy II. We, therefore, call them causal delay variables. Next, we determine the range in which δ_2 and δ_4 have realizations that violate the considered property.

- A realization with an assignment of δ_4 in the range $[0, 1[$ never violates the property. On the other hand, any realization with an assignment of δ_4 in the range $[2, 3]$ leads to a violation. For every of these realizations, a realization exists that is identical, except for the value of δ_4, that does not violate the property. This means that I. and II. are satisfied and we conclude that the constraint $2 \leq \delta_4 \leq 3$ is a causal range.
- For any realization with an assignment of δ_4 in the range $[1, 2[$, the violation of the property depends on the assignment of the delay variable δ_2. Hence, we analyze which values can be assigned to δ_2 so that this assignment is admissible according to the constraints in the TDT. We then detect that for any admissible assignment of δ_2 in our running example, it conversely depends on the assignment of δ_4 whether a realization violates the property. Thus, δ_2 and δ_4 need to jointly be considered when determining causal ranges. In order to specify the interdependence of δ_2 and δ_4, we consider their sum. We, hence, analyze the range of assigned values for which the sum of δ_2 and δ_4 violates the property. We see that any realization satisfying $3 \leq \delta_2 + \delta_4 \leq 5$ violates the property and a realization not in this range exists that satisfies the property. This means that I. and II. are satisfied and $3 \leq \delta_2 + \delta_4 \leq 5$ is a second causal range.

In the sequel of this paper, we will present an algorithmic way of determining the constraints describing causal ranges.

3   Preliminaries

The Timed Automaton model that we use to represent models of timed systems is adapted from [3]. Given a set of *clocks* C, we denote by $\mathcal{B}(C)$ the finite set of all *clock constraints* over C, which are conjunctions of *atomic clock constraints* of the form $c \sim n$, where $c \in C$, $\sim \in \{<, \leq, =, \geq, >\}$ and $n \in \mathbb{N}_0^+$.

A *Timed Automaton (TA)* T is a tuple $T = (L, l_0, C, \Sigma, \Theta, I)$ where L is a finite set of locations, $l_0 \in L$ is an initial location, C is a finite set of clocks, Σ is a set of action labels, $\Theta \subseteq L \times \mathcal{B}(C) \times \Sigma \times 2^C \times L$ denotes the *transition relation*, and $I : L \to \mathcal{B}(C)$ denotes a labeling of locations with clock constraints, referred to as location invariants. For $\theta \in \Theta$ with $\theta = (l, g, a, r, l')$, we refer to g as the *guard* of θ, to a as the *action label* and to r as its *clock resets*. An urgent location is a location that has to be left again without any delay in time [4]. Urgent locations are syntactic sugar of Uppaal and can be expressed as an additional clock p which is reset with entering the location and a location invariant $p = 0$.

The operational semantics of TAs [3] is given via the definition of *action* and *delay* transitions. Action transitions take the TA from a location l to a location l', execute an action from Σ, reset a subset of the clocks in C while the clock assignments comply with the clock constraints on transition guards and location invariants. Delay transitions only advance the value of all clocks in C by a non-deterministically chosen delay satisfying the invariant condition in the location in which they occur.

The type of properties that we are interested in are time bounded reachability properties, i.e., properties that state that a certain state will (or will not) be reached while a certain clock is satisfying a given bound. When a real-time model checker such as UPPAAL is noticing a violation of such a property, it produces a TDT which we represent symbolically as a *symbolic timed trace* (STT) [12]. A STT is a sequence of actions $S = \theta_0, \ldots, \theta_{n-1}$. A *realization* of S is a sequence of delay values $\delta_0, \ldots, \delta_n$ such that there exist states $s_0, \ldots, s_n, s_{n+1}$ with $s_i \xrightarrow{\delta_i} \xrightarrow{\theta_i} s_{i+1}$ for all $i \in [0, n)$ and $s_n \xrightarrow{\delta_n} s_{n+1}$.

We encode the symbolic semantics of the TDT in linear real arithmetic as a *timed diagnostic trace constraint system* (TDTCS) [12]. A TDTCS $\mathcal{T}$ encodes every transition $\theta_j = (l_j, g_j, a, r_j, l_{j+1})$ in the TDT and is a conjunction of the following constraints:

$$\mathcal{C}_0 \equiv \bigwedge_{c \in C} c_0 = 0 \qquad \text{(clock initialization)}$$

$$\mathcal{A} \equiv \bigwedge_{j \in [0,n]} \delta_j \geq 0 \qquad \text{(time advancement)}$$

$$\mathcal{R} \equiv \bigwedge_{c \in r_j,} c_{j+1} = 0 \qquad \text{(clock resets)}$$

$$\mathcal{D} \equiv \bigwedge_{c \notin r_j} c_{j+1} = c_j + \delta_j \qquad \text{(sojourn time)}$$

$$\mathcal{I} \equiv \bigwedge_{(c \sim \beta) \in I(l_j)} c \sim \beta \wedge c + \delta_j \sim \beta \qquad \text{(location invariants)}$$

$$\mathcal{G} \equiv \bigwedge_{(c \sim \beta) \in g_j} c + \delta_j \sim \beta \qquad \text{(transition guards)}$$

$$\mathcal{L} \equiv @l_n \wedge \bigwedge_{l \neq l_n} \neg @l \qquad \text{(location predicates)}$$

A model satisfies the TDTCS iff the sequence of the delay values $\delta_0, \ldots, \delta_n$ in the model is a realization of the STT [12]. We denote a realization by $\mathcal{T}[\delta_0 \ldots \delta_n]$. A TDTCS is convex since it is a conjunction of constraints [17]. The clock variables are syntactic sugar and can be removed from the TDTCS by replacing all occurrences of a clock variable c_j with $\Sigma_{j' \leq i \leq j} \delta_i$ where $j' = 0$ or the index of the last transition with a reset of clock c before c_j. A partial realization $\delta = \delta_0 \ldots \delta_j$ of $\mathcal{T}$ with $0 \leq j \leq n$ is a realization of a TDTCS $\mathcal{T}_j$, where $\mathcal{T}_j$ encodes only the first j transitions of a given TDT. A suffix blocking partial realization $\delta'_0 \ldots \delta'_j$ is a partial realization that satisfies $\mathcal{T}_j[\delta'_0 \ldots \delta'_j]$ while $\mathcal{T}[\delta'_0 \ldots \delta'_j]$ is unsatisfiable.

We also logically encode a given timed safety property Π as a property constraint system ϕ. The original property Π contains location constraints and time constraints for a clock set C. A location predicate $@l \in \mathcal{L}$ is satisfied when the Timed Automaton is in location l. Let $\phi \equiv \Pi[\mathbf{c}_{n+1}/\mathbf{c}]$ where $\Pi[\mathbf{c}_{n+1}/\mathbf{c}]$ is obtained from property Π by substituting the location constraints by location predicates and all occurrences of clocks $c \in C$ by c_{n+1}. This substitution replaces a clock c referred to in property Π by the variable referring to the clock c_{n+1} in the final location n of the TDT. The logical encoding of the property in Fig. 1 is $\neg @client.serReceiving \lor x_5 < 4$.

4 Formalizations to Compute Causal Ranges

We first introduce the notion of a *delay set*, which is a subset of the indices of the delay variables $\delta_0, \ldots, \delta_n$ occurring in the STT. For instance, the set $\{\delta_2, \delta_4\}$ is represented by the delay set $\{2, 4\}$. The aim of this section is to define a causal range as a range of values for a given delay set D where any value satisfies the regularity argument (I.), the counterfactual argument (II.) and the minimality argument (III.).

Before we define a causal range, we need to determine a delay set D. Any delay variable δ_j in D shall be causal, thus, a realization δ exists where the value assignment of δ_j matters whether δ violates or satisfies the property. In case δ exists, we call δ_j a *causal delay variable*. Whether δ satisfies or violates the property can interdepend on the value assignment of several causal delay variables as we have seen before. In this case, a realization δ exists such that a different value assignment of any δ_j in D can results in a realization that satisfies the property. We formally define the existence of δ for a delay set D in Definition 1. CV1 in Definition 1 ensures that a realization δ exists for a value v where the sum of the delay assignments with an index in D is equivalent to $v = \sum_{j \in D} \delta_j$. This δ violates a given property ϕ and this satisfies the regularity argument (I.). CV2 ensures II. by requiring the existence of an alternate assignment for every delay variable with an index in D, resulting in a realization δ' that does not violate the property. δ' can also be a suffix blocking partial realization $\delta_0 \ldots \delta_{j-1} \delta'_j$ which cannot be completed to a full realization in a way that would violate the property. For instance, consider a TDT with a guard on a transition that leads to an immediate property violation and where the guard is enabled for an assignment $\delta_j < 2$ and disabled for an assignment $\delta_j \geq 2$. Thus, assigning $\delta_j = 2$ prevents the property violation to be reachable. In conclusion, a causal value satisfies I. and II. for a realization δ, and witnesses that any δ_j in D is a causal delay variable.

Definition 1 (Causal Value). *Assume a TDTCS $\mathcal{T}$ for a TDT of length n, a delay set D of $\mathcal{T}$ and a property constraint system ϕ. A causal value is a value v in a delay set constraint $v = \sum_{j \in D} \delta_j$ where $\delta_j \in \mathbb{R}_0^+$ that satisfies:*

CV1 *There exists a realization $\delta = \delta_0 ... \delta_n$ with delay values $\delta_j \in \mathbb{R}_0^+$ for $0 \leq j \leq n$, $v = \sum_{j \in D} \delta_j$ is satisfied and ϕ is violated.*

CV2 *For every delay value δ_j with $j \in D$, a different delay value δ'_j with $\delta_j \neq \delta'_j$ exists that either $\delta_0 \ldots \delta_{j-1} \delta'_j$ is a suffix blocking partial realization or $\delta_0 \ldots \delta_{j-1} \delta'_j \delta_{j+1} \ldots \delta_n$ satisfies $\mathcal{T}$ and ϕ.*

In the TDT in the example from Fig. 1(c), a causal value of the delay set $\{4\}$ is every value in the range $[1,3]$, of the delay set $\{2\}$ every value in the range $[1,2]$ and of the delay set $\{2,4\}$ is every value in the range $[3,4]$.

Not all values from a causal range are causal values. For instance, in the TDT in Fig. 1(c), the value $v = 5$ is part of the causal range $3 \leq \delta_2 + \delta_4 \leq 5$, and has a realization with the assignments $\delta_2 = 2$ and $\delta_4 = 3$ that violates the property ϕ, thus satisfying conditions CV1 and I. CV2 requires that an alternative assignment for each of δ_2 and δ_4 exists that prevents the property violation. Such an assignment does not exist for δ_2 but for δ_4 with the assignment $\delta_4 = 0$. Thus, $v = 5$ is not a causal value since it violates CV2, even though it satisfies II. The purpose of a causal value is different from a causal range. A causal value ensures that the assignment of every delay variable in D influences for at least one realization whether the realization violates the property. In difference, a causal range is a cause and ensures that for every realization that satisfies the cause a different assignment exists that satisfies the property.

Next, we define a causal range for a delay set D in Definition 2. A causal range is a constraint of the form $l \sim \sum_{j \in D} \delta_j \sim u$ with a lower bound l and an upper bound u. Every value v in a causal range has to satisfy the causal arguments I and II. Condition CR1 in Definition 2 claims that every value v in the causal range has a realization with $v = \sum_{j \in D} \delta_j$. CR2 ensures the regularity argument I that any realization which satisfies the causal range violates the property. Also, a partial realization $\delta_0 \ldots \delta_m$ can satisfy the causal range constraints when all delays in D are assigned a value $m \geq \max(D)$ where $\max(D)$ returns the maximal value of all elements in D. In order to satisfy causal condition I, this partial realization is not allowed to be a suffix blocking partial realization that prevents the property violation. CR2 refers to all partial realizations. Notice that in particular a partial realization with $m = n$ satisfies $\mathcal{T}$ and violates the property ϕ. We conclude that any realization that satisfies the causal range constraint violates the property, and CR2 actually ensures I. Condition CR3 ensures that a causal value v_c in the range exists that is not a causal value for a true subset of D. We interpret the causal minimality argument III such that we require the number of delay variables that are part of a causal range to be minimal. When v_c is already part of a causal range r' for a true subset of the variables in D, then we conclude that r' is a more concise cause for the violation of property ϕ, thus satisfying III. The existence of v_c, as required by CR3, will be used in the proof of Theorem 1. Condition CR4 claims that the causal range r is maximal in the sense that there is no truly larger range encompassing r which satisfies CR1 to CR3. We include this constraint on the assumption that an analysis result consisting of fewer causal ranges is easier to interpret than one with more causal ranges.

Definition 2 (Causal Range). *Assume a TDTCS $\mathcal{T}$ for a TDT of length n and a property constraint system ϕ. A causal range r is a constraint for a delay set D of the form $l \sim \sum_{j \in D} \delta_j \sim u$ and $\sim \in \{<, \leq\}$, where $l, u \in \mathbb{R}_{\geq 0}$, delay values $\delta_j \in \mathbb{R}_0^+$ and the following conditions hold:*

CR1 *Every value $v \in [l, u]$ has a realization $\delta_0 \ldots \delta_n$ with $v = \sum_{j \in D} \delta_j$.*

CR2 *For every partial realization* $\delta_0 \ldots \delta_m$ *where* $max(D) \leq m \leq n$ *and the value* $v = \sum_{j \in D} \delta_j$ *is in* $[l, u]$, *there exists a realization* $\delta_0 \ldots \delta_m \ldots \delta_n$ *that violates* ϕ.

CR3 *At least one value* v_c *in the causal range is a causal value of* D, *and* v_c *is not a causal value for a true subset of* D.

CR4 *The range* r *is maximal, that means any lower bound* $l' < l$ *and any higher bound* $u' > u$ *will not satisfy CR1 to CR3.*

As an example, the constraint $2 \leq \delta_4 \leq 3$ and the constraint $3 \leq \delta_2 + \delta 4 \leq 5$ satisfy the definition of a causal range for the example in Fig. 1(c).

A causal range is only a cause when it satisfies the counterfactual argument (II.) and is ensured by Theorem 1. CR2 ensures that every realization r with value v violates a given property ϕ. The counterfactual argument is satisfied for v when for every r a different value assignment only of the delay variables in D exists such that the resulting realization satisfies ϕ.

Theorem 1. *For every value in a causal range, the counterfactual argument II. is satisfied.*

We have argued above that CR2 ensures the regularity argument I. and CR3 ensures the minimality argument III. In combination with Theorem 1, we conclude that a causal range represents a cause for the property violation according to the definition in Sect. 2.

5   Causal Range Algorithm

We present the `Causal Range Algorithm` to compute a set of causal ranges for a given TDT T and a given property ϕ. The input of the algorithm is a TDTCS $\mathcal{T}$ derived from T and a property constraint ϕ created for the considered property. The output of the algorithm is a set of causal ranges, where any causal range is characterized by a real valued lower bound, a real valued upper bound and a delay set taken from the power set of the TDT delay variables. The algorithm performs the search for causal ranges by solving three satisfiability problems. These problems

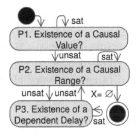

Fig. 2. Control flow diagram of Causal Range Algorithm

are depicted in the control flow diagram given in Fig. 2. By solving the problem $P1$ the algorithm starts to iteratively compute the causal delay variables for $\mathcal{T}$. For every computed causal delay variable it creates a delay set. Next, the algorithm computes for every delay set D a causal range by solving the problem $P2$. After the range computation of a delay set D, the algorithm solves problem $P3$ to check whether another causal delay variable δ_k depends on D. In case δ_k exists, the algorithm found a new delay set $D' = D \cup \{k\}$. The algorithm solves $P2$ and $P3$ for every delay set. We encode the problems $P1$ to $P3$ in linear real arithmetic as follows:

Problem P1: Existence of a Causal Value. The algorithm first checks for every delay variable δ_j in the TDT whether it is a causal delay variable. A delay variable δ_j is causal when a causal value for $D = \{\delta_j\}$ exists. We encode the conditions that CV1 and CV2 in Definition 1 specify for a causal value in the constraint $\mathcal{C}_j$ (1). The constraint ensures that a realization $\delta = \delta_0, \ldots, \delta_n$ with δ_j and value $v = \delta_j$ exists. δ is a realization when it satisfies $\mathcal{T}$, and has to violate ϕ in order to satisfy CV1 in Definition 1. The constraint $\mathcal{C}_j$ also ensures that CV2 is satisfied. It is satisfiable when an assignment δ'_j that is different from δ_j exists, such that either $\delta' = \delta_0 \ldots \delta_{j-1}\delta'_j$ is a suffix blocking partial realization, or $\delta[\delta_j/\delta'_j]$ is a realization that satisfies ϕ. When δ' is a suffix blocking partial realization, it satisfies $\mathcal{T}^*$ (2). T^* ensures that δ' satisfies the constraint $\mathcal{T}_j$ for a partial realization and no assignment of δ'_{j+1} to δ'_n exists such that $\delta_0 \ldots \delta_{j-1}\delta'_j\delta'_{j+1}, \ldots, \delta'_n$ is a realization that satisfies $\mathcal{T}$.

$$\mathcal{C}_j \equiv (\exists \delta_0, \ldots, \delta_n, \delta'_j)(\mathcal{T} \wedge \neg\phi \wedge (\mathcal{T}^*[\delta_0 \ldots \delta_{j-1}\delta'_j] \vee (\mathcal{T}[\delta_j/\delta'_j] \wedge \phi[\delta_j/\delta'_j]))) \quad (1)$$

$$\mathcal{T}^*[\delta_0 \ldots \delta_{j-1}\delta'_j] \equiv \mathcal{T}_j[\delta_0 \ldots \delta_{j-1}\delta'_j] \wedge \neg(\exists \delta'_{j+1}, \ldots \delta'_n)(\mathcal{T}[\delta_0 \ldots \delta_{j-1}\delta'_j \ldots \delta'_n]) \quad (2)$$

By iteratively determining the satisfiability of the constraint $\mathcal{C}_j$ for all delay variables δ_j occurring in $\mathcal{T}$, the algorithm checks whether these δ_js actually are causal delay variables. In the implementation of the algorithm, we combine all $\mathcal{C}_j$ into one linear constraint system $\mathcal{C}$ of the form $\bigwedge_{0 \leq j \leq n} \neg c_j \vee C_j$ in which we add a fresh Boolean variable c_j for every occurring δ_j. These c_j are defined such that if some $\mathcal{C}_j$ is unsatisfiable, then $\neg c_j$ holds. We use a MaxSMT solver in order to determine the minimum number of $c_j = $ true assertions that need to be violated in order to render $\mathcal{C}$ satisfiable. A delay variable δ_j is causal if and only if c_j is true in the solution to the MaxSMT problem. Subsequently, for every computed causal delay variable δ_j the algorithm adds a delay set $\{\delta_j\}$ to a first-in-first-out queue X. This queue stores every computed delay set and will be handed over to the algorithm addressing problem P2, which computes a causal range for every element of X. For the example in Fig. 1(c), the queue passed on to P2 is $X = \{\{4\}, \{2\}\}$.

Problem P2: Existence of a Causal Range. The algorithm solving problem P2 removes a delay set D from queue X and computes the causal ranges of D. We encode the computation of a causal range as a satisfiability problem. We formalize the conditions CR1 to CR3 in Definition 2 as individual constraints $\mathcal{R}_1$ to $\mathcal{R}_3$. The satisfiability of this conjunction yields an answer to problem P2 and computes causal ranges if they exist. CR1 claims that every value t in the causal range $[l, u]$ has a realization. If $\mathcal{R}_1^b$ is satisfiable, then there exists a realization of $\mathcal{T}$ with a value $b = \sum_{j \in D} \delta_j$. We now check whether $\mathcal{R}_1^b[b/l]$ and $\mathcal{R}_1^b[b/u]$ are satisfiable, respectively. If both are satisfiable, due to the convexity of $\mathcal{T}$ we can conclude that $\mathcal{R}_1^b[b/t]$ is satisfiable for any value $t \in [l, u]$.

$$\mathcal{R}_1^b \equiv (\exists \delta_0 \ldots \delta_n)(\mathcal{T} \wedge b = \sum_{j \in D} \delta_j) \quad (3)$$

CR2 claims that for every partial realization $\delta_0 \ldots \delta_j$ which satisfy $l \leq \sum_{j \in D} \delta_j \leq u$ there exists $\delta_0 \ldots \delta_j\delta_{j+1} \ldots \delta_n$ that violates the property ϕ. We formalize CR2 as follows:

$$\mathcal{R}_2 \equiv \bigwedge_{max(D) \leq j \leq n} (\forall \delta_0 \dots \delta_j)(\mathcal{T}_j[\delta_0 \dots \delta_j] \wedge (l \leq \sum_{j \in D} \delta_j \leq u) \tag{4}$$
$$\Rightarrow (\exists \delta_{j+1} \dots \delta_n)(\mathcal{T} \wedge \neg \phi))$$

We project a realization $\delta = \delta_0 \dots \delta_n$ to a single value v with the formula $v = \sum_{j \in D} \delta_j$. If $v \in [l, u]$ we say that δ is contained in $[l, u]$. Constraint $\mathcal{R}_3$ (5) ensures that a realization δ contained in $[l, u]$ exists and δ is not contained in any causal range $[l_i, u_i]$ of a subset D_i of D. When this δ exists, CR3 is fulfilled. Notice that the subset D_i is not necessarily a true subset of D and therefore ignores previously found causal ranges contained in D. If further causal ranges are contained in D these will also be computed by the algorithm solving P2.

$$\mathcal{R}_3 \equiv \exists \delta_0 \dots \delta_n . \mathcal{T} \wedge l \leq \sum_{j \in D} \delta_j \leq u \wedge \bigwedge_{D_i \subseteq D} (\sum_{i \in D_i} \delta_i < l_i) \vee (u_i < \sum_{i \in D_i} \delta_i) \tag{5}$$

A satisfying assignment for the conjunction of $\mathcal{R}_1^l$, $\mathcal{R}_1^u$, $\mathcal{R}_2$, and $\mathcal{R}_3$ contains a causal range $[l, u]$ which is not necessarily maximal. The algorithm takes advantage of the optimization possibilities of the SMT solver Z3 [16] to minimize l and to maximize u in the conjunction in order to ensure a maximal range (c.f. CR4). In the example of Fig. 1(c) for the delay set $D = \{4\}$, the algorithm computes the causal range $2 \leq \delta_4 \leq 3$. Since no further causal range is found, then the algorithm proceeds with extending D by solving problem P3.

Problem P3: Existence of a Dependent Delay. A delay variable δ_k is dependent on a delay set D when the delay set $D' = D \cup \{k\}$ has a causal value. The algorithm solving P3 extends a delay set D with the index of a delay variable δ_k depending on D. We encode the question whether a causal value for D' exists as the problem whether constraint $\mathcal{C}_k$ (6) is satisfiable. The satisfiability of $\mathcal{C}_k$ yields an answer to problem P3. A satisfying model then yields the dependent delays δ_k, if any exist. $\mathcal{C}_k$ ensures that there exists a realization $\delta = \delta_0 \dots \delta_n$ with value v that violates the property ϕ. For every index j in the delay set D' a realization exists that differs from δ only in the assignment of δ_j and does not violate ϕ, thus satisfying CV2 in Definition 1.

$$\mathcal{C}_k \equiv \exists \delta_0, \dots, \delta_n . \mathcal{T} \wedge \neg \phi \wedge \bigwedge_{j \in D'} \exists \delta_j' . \mathcal{T}^*[\delta_0 \dots \delta_{j-1} \delta_j'] \vee (\mathcal{T}[\delta_j / \delta_j'] \wedge \phi[\delta_j / \delta_j']) \tag{6}$$

For every causal delay variable δ_k with $k \notin D$ for which $\mathcal{C}_k$ is satisfiable, the algorithm adds $D' = D \cup \{k\}$ to the queue X. To illustrate this step, for the TDT in Fig. 1(c) and the delay set $D = \{4\}$, $\mathcal{C}_k$ is satisfiable for $k = 2$ and the queue $X = \{\{2\}\}$ is extended to $X = \{\{2\}, \{4, 2\}\}$. The algorithm proceeds with removing the next delay set from X, solving problems P2 and P3 for this delay set, and terminates when X is empty.

Correctness of the Algorithm. The theorems below show that the algorithm to compute causal ranges is correct with respect to soundness and completeness.

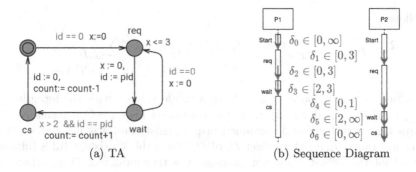

(a) TA   (b) Sequence Diagram

Fig. 3. Fischer's protocol

Theorem 2 (Soundness of Causal Range Computation). *Every causal range returned by the Causal Range Algorithm for a TDTCS $\mathcal{T}$ and a delay set D satisfies CR1 to CR4.*

Theorem 3 (Completeness of Causal Range Computation). *The Causal Range Algorithm returns every maximal causal range for any given TDT.*

6   Evaluation

We implemented the Causal Range Algorithm in a tool that we call *Causal Timed Range Analyser* (CATIRA) and evaluated the tool by computing causal ranges for several case studies taken from the literature.

Evaluation Methodology. CATIRA is intended to be used at design time to support design space exploration based on causal information regarding the dynamic timing behavior. We foresee a usage of CATIRA at an intermediate design stage when a considered preliminary model does not yet satisfy all required properties. The objective of the analysis is to point the designer to variations in the delay timings at certain locations in a TDT, which may motivate changes in, for instance, timing bounds in the model. Such preliminary design models are not available for experimentation. Therefore, it is necessary that we use published, correct models and revert them to a preliminary state by seeding syntactic code variations. We emphasize that the objective is not to locate these code variations, or even propose repairs to syntactic elements, but to illustrate to the designer what ranges of delay variations contribute to avoiding the observed property violation. The designer can then decide to perform syntactic changes to the model in order to constrain the timing of the system in such a way that property violations will be avoided.

Database Example [12]. For the running example in Fig. 1, the analysis found the causal delays δ_2 and δ_4, and the causal ranges $2 \leq \delta_4 \leq 3$ and $3 \leq \delta_2 + \delta_4 \leq 5$.

Fischer's Protocol [18]. The purpose of Fischer's protocol is to ensure mutual exclusion. The TA in Fig. 3 is a process of the protocol with a unique id *pid* and requests for the critical section *cs*. The global variable *id* controls the access to the critical section and allows a process only to enter the critical location *cs* when id = pid. In order to request access to the critical section, a process checks the transition guard $id == 0$ to check that no other process currently requests access to the critical section, and subsequently enters the location *req*. Afterwards the process enters the location *wait* within 3 time units for the critical section and overwrites *id* with its unique *pid*. The process has to wait for 2 time units to ensure that when another process also requests access to the critical section, then this process will have left the location *req*. In this model, the timing is not correct and it is possible that a process enters location *cs* and the other process is in location *req*. We reverted the model to a preliminary state by replacing the invariant $x \leq 2$ as in [18] by $x \leq 3$. We checked mutual exclusion of this model with UPPAAL and obtained a TDT depicted by the sequence diagram in Fig. 3(b).

For this TDT, the causal range analysis by CATIRA finds the causal delays δ_1 to δ_3, and the causal ranges $2 < \delta_1 \leq 3$, $0 \leq \delta_2 < 1$, $2 < \delta_3 \leq 3$, and $0 \leq \delta_1 + \delta_2 < 1$. Notice that the TDT of Fischer's protocol has no realization that satisfies the property. The causal ranges were computed because the Causal Range Algorithm also considers suffix blocking partial realization to satisfy the counterfactual argument (II.).

The causal ranges with the causal delay variables δ_1, δ_2 and δ_3 are reasonable since during these time delays the TDT is in the location *req*, labeled with the seeded constraint $x \leq 3$. During the time delay δ_4, the TDT is also in location *req*. However, δ_4 is not a causal delay variable since no different delay assignment exists for it that prevents the property violation. The interval of the causal ranges $2 < \delta_1 \leq 3$ and $2 < \delta_3 \leq 3$ is identical to the seeded faulty extension of the constraint. The choice of delay assignments that satisfies $0 \leq \delta_2 < 1$ and $0 \leq \delta_1 + \delta_2 < 1$ ensures that TA *P1* leaves location *req* early enough that the extension of the constraint comes into effect and the property violation will be reached. We see that the causal ranges actually express the choices of delay assignments that will lead to a property violation.

Camel Transporter (Adapted from [5]*)*. In this model, in every location *load1* to *load4* a worker loads a bag on a camel. The weight of a bag is between 1 and 4 units and is modeled by the time that the worker stays in a location. The camel will only arrive at the destination when the weight is not more than 7 units. The worker checks the payload of the camel with loading the third bag on the camel but is in a rush and does not check the payload after loading the fourth bag. A verification of the model with UPPAAL results in a TDT depicted in the Fig. 4(b). We manually computed the possible assignments of the delay variables and added them in red to the diagram. For this TDT, CATIRA computes the causal delays δ_0 to δ_3, and the causal ranges $7 < \delta_0 + \delta_3 \leq 8$, $7 < \delta_1 + \delta_3 \leq 8$, $7 < \delta_2 + \delta_3 \leq 8$, $7 < \delta_0 + \delta_1 + \delta_3 \leq 11$, $7 < \delta_0 + \delta_2 + \delta_3 \leq 11$, $7 < \delta_1 + \delta_2 + \delta_3 \leq 11$, and $7 < \delta_0 + \delta_1 + \delta_2 + \delta_3 \leq 11$.

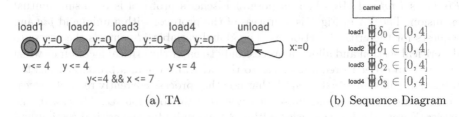

(a) TA   (b) Sequence Diagram

Fig. 4. Camel transporter (Color figure online)

All causal ranges contains the delay variable δ_3 of the location *load4*. This is reasonable since an overload of the camel is checked in location *load3*. The load limit of 7 can only be exceeded in a combination of at least two delay assignments since the maximal delay assignment is 4 for every delay variable. Also, even two variable assignments can already result in an overload of the camel, every delay assignment has an impact on whether the camel is overloaded. This becomes obvious by the realization $\delta_0 = 2$, $\delta_1 = 2$, $\delta_3 = 2$, $\delta_4 = 2$ that is contained only by the causal range $7 < \delta_0 + \delta_1 + \delta_2 + \delta_3 \leq 11$. In this realization, every delay assignment contributes to the overload of the camel but no subset of the delay assignments can overload the camel. We see that the causal ranges express the dynamic timing behavior that leads to the property violation.

The Pacemaker Model [11] that we consider originally satisfies all properties. We analyze this model since it is a realistic model and of a reasonable size. A modified version of the model, which contains a property violation, is analyzed in [12]. The violated property expresses that the time delay between two ventricular heartbeats is not too high. For the TDT illustrating the property violation, CATIRA computes the causal delays δ_0 and δ_6, and the causal range $150 < \delta_6 < 350$.

The results can be interpreted as follows. After the time delay of δ_0, the first heartbeat happens and a timer starts to measure the time delay until the next ventricular heartbeat. For some realization of the TDT that violate the property, an increase of the value assignment of δ_0 can prevent the property violation, thus, δ_0 is a causal delay variable. However, no causal range with δ_0 exists since each of these realizations is already contained by the causal range $150.0 < \delta_6 < 350.0$. Only during the time delay δ_6, the TDT is in the location in which a constraint was altered when reverting the model. The modification of the constraint corresponded to an increase of 1200 time units of a bound. However, the possible assignments in this location that lead to a property violation are in the range from $[150, 350]$. Thus, only the increase of the constraint bound by the first 200 time units has an impact on the possible execution. We see that the causal range shows the erroneous timing behavior of the TDT.

Quantitative Results. The quantitative results of every model are represented in Table 1. For every model, we indicate the time T_{UP} that UPPAAL needed to

Table 1. Quantitative experimental results.

Model	T_{UP}	Ln	#CD	#CR	T	M	#Cn	#Vr	T_{Z3}	M_{Z3}
Database [12]	0.010	4	2	2	0.420	13.2	66	19	0.020	6.7
Fischer's protocol [18]	0.010	6	3	4	0.626	26.5	78	23	0.040	6.9
Camel Transporter [5]	0.008	3	4	7	4.724	35.9	138	105	0.350	7.1
Pacemaker [11]	0.015	7	2	1	0.587	33.5	226	114	0.080	7.3

compute a TDT for the model and the length Ln of the TDT. For a given TDT, CATIRA computes a number #CD of causal delay variables and a number #CR of causal ranges. The computation of the causal ranges takes in total a time T in seconds and consumes at most an amount M of memory in megabytes. Z3 solves constraint systems with at most a count #Cn of clauses and at most a number #Vr of variables. Z3 needs at most the time T_{Z3} in seconds to solve a constraint system with a maximal memory usage of M_{Z3} in megabytes.

All experiments were performed with the SMT-solver Z3 (Version 4.8.3) on a computer with an i7-6700K CPU (4.00 GHz), 60 GB of RAM and a Linux operating system. For the considered models, we found a total of 11 causal delay variables and 14 causal ranges. The highest computation effort for a causal range computation can be observed in the camel transporter TDT with 35.9 MB memory consumption and 4.724 s computation time. In line with this, Z3 has the highest computation effort in time (0.350 s) with this model. The intrinsic complexity of this TDT seems to be high since with 138 clauses it has fewer clauses than the TDT of the Pacemaker model with 226 clauses.

The most complex model is the Pacemaker model since it takes the most time (0.015) for UPPAAL to compute the TDT. Also, its TDT is the longest with 7 transitions. With 226 the encoding of the analysis has the most clauses and with 114 the most variables. Even so, the computation effort of the causal ranges is moderate with 0.587s and 33.5 MB. In conclusion, the analyses results show that the causal range analysis requires a reasonable computation effort.

7 Conclusion

We have presented the Causal Range Algorithm and its implementation in the tool CATIRA. Based on a counterfactual causality argument, the Causal Range Algorithm performs an analysis to determine dynamic causes for timed reachability property violations in the timing behavior of a timed system as documented by TDTs. Using various case studies we have shown that the analysis is both efficient and effective. In particular, our work shows that using interpretations of counterfactual causal reasoning can lead to precise and intuitive explanations for dynamic timing behaviors.

In future work, we plan to generalize our findings to the analysis of hybrid systems. Another direction of research is to develop causal analyses that do not just rely on a single execution, as given by a TDT, but on the full structure of a Timed Automaton model.

References

1. Beer, I., Ben-David, S., Chockler, H., Orni, A., Trefler, R.J.: Explaining counterexamples using causality. Formal Methods Syst. Des. **40**(1), 20–40 (2012). https://doi.org/10.1007/s10703-011-0132-2

2. Bengtsson, J., Larsen, K., Larsson, F., Pettersson, P., Yi, W.: UPPAAL—A tool suite for automatic verification of real-time systems. In: Alur, R., Henzinger, T.A., Sontag, E.D. (eds.) HS 1995. LNCS, vol. 1066, pp. 232–243. Springer, Heidelberg (1996). https://doi.org/10.1007/BFb0020949

3. Bengtsson, J., Yi, W.: Timed automata: semantics, algorithms and tools. In: Desel, J., Reisig, W., Rozenberg, G. (eds.) ACPN 2003. LNCS, vol. 3098, pp. 87–124. Springer, Heidelberg (2004). https://doi.org/10.1007/978-3-540-27755-2_3

4. Bouyer, P., Fahrenberg, U., Larsen, K.G., Markey, N., Ouaknine, J., Worrell, J.: Model checking real-time systems. In: Clarke, E., Henzinger, T., Veith, H., Bloem, R. (eds.) Handbook of Model Checking, pp. 1001–1046. Springer, Cham (2018). https://doi.org/10.1007/978-3-319-10575-8_29

5. Chapman, A.: Camels, diamonds and counterfactuals: a model for teaching causal reasoning. In: Teaching History, pp. 46–53 (2003)

6. Dimitrova, R., Majumdar, R., Prabhu, V.S.: Causality analysis for concurrent reactive systems (extended abstract). In: CREST@ETAPS, EPTCS, vol. 286, pp. 31–33 (2018)

7. Goessler, G., Astefanoaei, L.: Blaming in component-based real-time systems. In: EMSOFT, pp. 7:1–7:10. ACM (2014)

8. Groce, A., Chaki, S., Kroening, D., Strichman, O.: Error explanation with distance metrics. STTT **8**(3), 229–247 (2006)

9. Halpern, J.Y., Pearl, J.: Causes and explanations: a structural-model approach - part II: explanations. Br. J. Philos. Sci. **56**, 889–911 (2005)

10. Halpern, J.Y., Pearl, J.: Causes and explanations: a structural-model approach. Part I: causes. Br. J. Philos. Sci. **56**, 843–887 (2005)

11. Jiang, Z., Pajic, M., Moarref, S., Alur, R., Mangharam, R.: Modeling and verification of a dual chamber implantable pacemaker. In: Flanagan, C., König, B. (eds.) TACAS 2012. LNCS, vol. 7214, pp. 188–203. Springer, Heidelberg (2012). https://doi.org/10.1007/978-3-642-28756-5_14

12. Kölbl, M., Leue, S., Wies, T.: Clock bound repair for timed systems. In: Dillig, I., Tasiran, S. (eds.) CAV 2019. LNCS, vol. 11561, pp. 79–96. Springer, Cham (2019). https://doi.org/10.1007/978-3-030-25540-4_5

13. Kumazawa, T., Tamai, T.: Counterexample-based error localization of behavior models. In: Bobaru, M., Havelund, K., Holzmann, G.J., Joshi, R. (eds.) NFM 2011. LNCS, vol. 6617, pp. 222–236. Springer, Heidelberg (2011). https://doi.org/10.1007/978-3-642-20398-5_17

14. Leitner-Fischer, F., Leue, S.: Causality checking for complex system models. In: Giacobazzi, R., Berdine, J., Mastroeni, I. (eds.) VMCAI 2013. LNCS, vol. 7737, pp. 248–267. Springer, Heidelberg (2013). https://doi.org/10.1007/978-3-642-35873-9_16

15. Lewis, D.: Counterfactuals. Wiley-Blackwell, Hoboken (2001)

16. de Moura, L., Bjørner, N.: Z3: an efficient SMT solver. In: Ramakrishnan, C.R., Rehof, J. (eds.) TACAS 2008. LNCS, vol. 4963, pp. 337–340. Springer, Heidelberg (2008). https://doi.org/10.1007/978-3-540-78800-3_24

17. Oppen, D.C.: Complexity, convexity and combinations of theories. Theor. Comput. Sci. **12**, 291–302 (1980)

18. Uppaal: Uppaal benchmarks (2017). http://www.it.uu.se/research/group/darts/uppaal/benchmarks/#benchmarks. Accessed 23 Jan 2020
19. Wang, S., Ayoub, A., Kim, B.G., Gössler, G., Sokolsky, O., Lee, I.: A causality analysis framework for component-based real-time systems. In: Legay, A., Bensalem, S. (eds.) RV 2013. LNCS, vol. 8174, pp. 285–303. Springer, Heidelberg (2013). https://doi.org/10.1007/978-3-642-40787-1_17

Active Learning of Timed Automata
with Unobservable Resets

Léo Henry$^{(\boxtimes)}$ ⓘ, Thierry Jéron ⓘ, and Nicolas Markey ⓘ

Univ Rennes, Inria, CNRS, Rennes, France
{leo.henry,thierry.jeron,nicolas.markey}@inria.fr

Abstract. Active learning of timed languages is concerned with the inference of timed automata by observing some of the timed words in their languages. The learner can query for the membership of words in the language, or propose a candidate model and ask if it is equivalent to the target. The major difficulty of this framework is the inference of *clock resets*, which are central to the dynamics of timed automata but not directly observable.

Interesting first steps have already been made by restricting to the subclass of *event-recording automata*, where clock resets are tied to observations. In order to advance towards learning of general timed automata, we generalize this method to a new class, called *reset-free* event-recording automata, where some transitions may reset no clocks.

Central to our contribution is the notion of *invalidity*, and the algorithm and data structures to deal with it, allowing on-the-fly detection and pruning of reset hypotheses that contradict observations. This notion is a key to any efficient active-learning procedure for generic timed automata.

1 Introduction

Active learning [Ang87a] is a type of learning in which a teacher assesses the learner's progress and direct the learning effort toward meaningful decisions. The learner can request information from the teacher via *membership queries*, asking about a specific observation, and *equivalence queries*, proposing to compare the current hypothesis to the correct model; in the latter case, the teacher either accepts the hypothesis or returns a counter-example exemplifying mispredictions of the learner's hypothesis.

This framework is well-studied in the setting of finite-state automata [Ang87a, Ang87b, Ang90], and allows to make sound proofs for both correctness and complexity of learning algorithms. As most real-life systems dispose of *continuous* components, attempts have been made to leverage this framework to take them into account. One of the most classic additions is *time*. An observation is then a timed word, made of actions and delays between them. One of the most recognized models for such timed languages is the timed automaton (TA),

This work was partially funded by ANR project Ticktac (ANR-18-CE40-0015).

N. Bertrand and N. Jansen (Eds.): FORMATS 2020, LNCS 12288, pp. 144–160, 2020.
https://doi.org/10.1007/978-3-030-57628-8_9

but its dynamics are complex: TAs measure time using a set of *clocks* that hold a positive real value progressing with time, can be compared with integer constants to allow or disallow transitions, and reset to zero along those transitions. For a learning algorithm, one of the main challenges is to deal with those resets, that are typically not observable, but play a central role in the system dynamics.

Some work has already been done in the active learning of subclasses of TAs, mostly deterministic TAs with only one clock [ACZ+20] and deterministic event-recording automata (DERA) [GJP06, Gri08], which have as many clocks as actions in the alphabet, and where each clock encodes exactly the time elapsed since the last corresponding action was taken. These classes of automata present the advantages of having a low-dimensional continuous behaviour (for 1-clock TAs) and to allow to derive the resets of the clocks directly from the observations (for DERA). Other approaches have been investigated for the learning of timed systems. Learning of TAs from tests has been studied using genetic algorithms [TALL19], which is a very different approach to ours to exploit a similar setting. Inference of simple TAs from positive data [VWW08, VWW12] has also been well studied. These works are more loosely related to ours, as our setting greatly differs from positive inference.

We propose in this work to generalize to a class of timed automata enjoying both several clocks and different possible resets that can not be inferred directly from observations. This allows us to design and prove algorithms that handle all the main difficulties that arise in deterministic TAs, making this contribution an important first step towards active learning for generic deterministic TAS.

To our knowledge, the closest works are Grinchtein's thesis on active learning of DERA [Gri08] and the paper proposing to learn one clock TAs [ACZ+20]. The work of Grinchtein *et al.* [GJP06] is the most related to ours, as we use some of the data structures they developed and keep the general approach based on timed decision trees. The main difference between our work and this one is that we handle the inference of resets in a class of models in which they can not be *directly* deduced from observations. The approach reported in [ACZ+20] proposes to deal with reset guessing, but makes it in a somewhat "brute force" manner, by directly applying a branch-and-bound algorithm and jumping from model to model. In order to be able to deal with larger dimensions, *e.g.* to handle TAs with a large set of clocks, we need to be more efficient by exploiting the theory built around TAs and detecting invalid models as early as possible.

For the details of the proofs and algorithms, we refer the reader to the long version [HJM20].

2 Preliminaries

2.1 Timed Automata

For the rest of this paper, we fix a finite alphabet Σ.

Let X be a finite set of variables called *clocks*. A valuation for X is a function $v \colon X \to \mathbb{R}_{\geq 0}$. We write $\mathbf{0}$ for the clock valuation associating 0 with all clocks. For any $\delta \in \mathbb{R}_{\geq 0}$ and any valuation v we write $v + d$ for the valuation such that

$(v + \delta)(x) = v(x) + \delta$ for each clock x; this corresponds to elapsing δ time units from valuation v. The future of a valuation v is the set $v^{\nearrow} = \{v + t \mid t \in \mathbb{R}_{\geq 0}\}$ of its time successors. Finally, for any $X' \subseteq X$ and any valuation v, we write $v_{[X' \leftarrow 0]}$ for the valuation such that $v_{[X' \leftarrow 0]}(x) = v(x)$ for all $x \notin X'$ and $v_{[X' \leftarrow 0]}(x) = 0$ for all $x \in X'$.

Simple clock constraints are expressions of the forms $x - x' \sim n$ and $x \sim n$, for $x, x' \in X$, $\sim \in \{<, \leq, =, \geq, >\}$ and $n \in \mathbb{N}$. We call *zone* over X any finite conjunction of such constraints, and write $\mathcal{Z}_X$ for the set of zones over X. Given a valuation v and a zone z, we write $v \models z$ when v satisfies all the constraints in z. We may identify a zone z with the set of valuations z such that $v \models z$. We call *guard* any zone not involving constraints of the form $x - x' \sim n$, and write $\mathcal{G}_X$ for the set of guards. We extend all three operations on valuations to zones elementwise.

Definition 1. *A* timed automaton *(TA) over Σ is a tuple $\mathcal{T} = (\mathcal{L}, l_0, X, E, \mathsf{Accept})$ such that: $\mathcal{L}$ is a finite set of* locations, *and $l_0 \in \mathcal{L}$ is the* initial *location; X is a finite set of* clocks; $\mathsf{Accept} \subseteq \mathcal{L}$ *is a set of* accepting locations; $E \subseteq \mathcal{L} \times \Sigma \times \mathcal{G}_X \times 2^X \times \mathcal{L}$ *is a set of* transitions. *For a transition (l, a, g, r, l'), we call g its* guard, *a its* action *and r its* reset.

We write $K_{\mathcal{T}}$ (or K when the context is clear) for the *maximal constant* appearing in $\mathcal{T}$. We say that a TA is *deterministic* when, for any two transitions (l, a, g, r, l') and (l, a, g', r', l'') where $g \wedge g'$ is satisfiable, it holds $l' = l''$ and $r = r'$. We only consider deterministic TAs in the sequel, as active-learning methods can only target this (strict) subclass of TAs.

Definition 2. *With a TA $\mathcal{T} = (\mathcal{L}, l_0, X, E, \mathsf{Accept})$, we associate the transition system $\mathcal{S}^{\mathcal{T}} = (S = \mathcal{L} \times \mathbb{R}_{\geq 0}^{|X|}, (l_0, \mathbf{0}), \Delta, \mathsf{Accept}_{\mathcal{S}^{\mathcal{T}}})$ where $\mathcal{L} \times \mathbb{R}_{\geq 0}^{|X|}$ is the set of* configurations, *$(l_0, \mathbf{0})$ is the initial configuration, $\mathsf{Accept}_{\mathcal{S}^{\mathcal{T}}} = \{(l, v) \mid l \in \mathsf{Accept}\}$ is the set of accepting configurations, and $\Delta \subset S \times (\mathbb{R}_{\geq 0} \cup E) \times S$ a set of transitions, such that for any $(l, v) \in S$: (a) for any $\delta \in \mathbb{R}_{\geq 0}$, we have $((l, v), \delta, (l, v + \delta))$ in Δ; (b) for any $e = (l, a, g, r, l') \in E$ s.t. $v \models g$, we have $((l, v), e, (l', v_{[r \leftarrow 0]}))$ in Δ.*

A path in a timed automaton $\mathcal{T}$ is a sequence of transitions in the associated transition system $\mathcal{S}^{\mathcal{T}}$. A *timed word with resets* of $\mathcal{T}$ is a path $w_{tr} = ((l_i, v_i) \xrightarrow{e_i} (l_{i+1}, v_{i+1}))_{i \in [0,n]} \in (S \times (\Delta \cup \mathbb{R}_{\geq 0}))^* \times S$ of its semantics $\mathcal{S}^{\mathcal{T}}$. A timed word with resets is *accepting* when its final configuration is in $\mathsf{Accept}_{\mathcal{S}^{\mathcal{T}}}$.

In order to obtain a finite representation of the infinite set of timed words with resets, we use an abstraction based on the following notion of K-*equivalence*.

Definition 3. *Two nonnegative reals x and y are K-equivalent, noted $x \approx_K y$, when either $x > K$ and $y > K$, or $x = y$ are integers, or x and y are non-integers and they have the same integral part. Two valuations v and v' are K-equivalent if $v(x) \approx_K v'(x)$ for all $x \in X$. We say that two configurations are K-equivalent when their valuations are, and that two timed words with reset are K-equivalent*

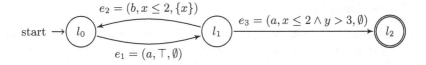

Fig. 1. A simple TA

when they have the same size and the configurations of same indices in both words are K-equivalent.

Notice that K-equivalence is coarser than the usual notion of *region equivalence* of [AD94], as it aims to encode direct indistinguishability by a guard along words, instead of indistinguishability in the future.

We call *zone-word with resets* a timed word with resets in which all valuations are replaced with zones. A timed word with resets $r = ((l_i, v_i) \xrightarrow{e_i} (l_{i+1}, v_{i+1}))_{i \in [0,n]}$ is *compatible* with a zone word with resets $zr = ((l_i, z_i) \xrightarrow{e_i} (l_{i+1}, z_{i+1}))_{i \in [0,n]}$, written $r \models zr$, when $v_i \models z_i$ for all i. We call K-*closed word* a zone word in which all zones are K-equivalence classes.

Lemma 4. *For any timed word with reset r of a (deterministic) timed automaton $\mathcal{T}$, there is a unique K-closed word zr such that $r \models zr$. For any timed word with resets r' compatible with zr, r' is accepting if, and only if, r is.*

Event recording automata (ERA) [AFH99] are a subclass of TAs in which there is one clock x_a per letter a of the alphabet, such that x_a is reset exactly along a-transitions. We slightly extend them as *reset-free ERAs* (RERAs), in which transitions may or may not reset their clock: we let $X_\Sigma = \{x_a \mid a \in \Sigma\}$, and $\mathcal{Z}_\Sigma$ and $\mathcal{G}_\Sigma$ be shortcuts for $\mathcal{Z}_{X_\Sigma}$ and $\mathcal{G}_{X_\Sigma}$ respectively.

Definition 5. *A reset-free event recording automaton (RERA) over Σ is a TA $\mathcal{T} = (\mathcal{L}, l_0, X_\Sigma, E, \text{Accept})$ such that for all transitions $(l, a, g, r, l') \in E$, it holds $r \in \{\{x_a\}, \emptyset\}$.*

Example 1. Consider the timed automaton depicted in Fig. 1. This TA is actually a RERA, by associating clock x to letter b and clock y to letter a. An accepting timed word with resets of this automaton is $(l_0, 0) \xrightarrow{1.5} (l_0, (\begin{smallmatrix}1.5\\1.5\end{smallmatrix})) \xrightarrow{a,\emptyset} (l_1, (\begin{smallmatrix}1.5\\1.5\end{smallmatrix})) \xrightarrow{b,\{x\}} (l_0, (\begin{smallmatrix}0\\1.5\end{smallmatrix})) \xrightarrow{a,\emptyset} (l_1, (\begin{smallmatrix}0\\1.5\end{smallmatrix})) \xrightarrow{2} (l_1, (\begin{smallmatrix}2\\3.5\end{smallmatrix})) \xrightarrow{a,\emptyset} (l_2, (\begin{smallmatrix}2\\3.5\end{smallmatrix}))$. The corresponding path is $l_0 \xrightarrow{e_1} l_1 \xrightarrow{e_2} l_0 \xrightarrow{e_1} l_1 \xrightarrow{e_3} l_2$.

Although closely related, ERA and RERA differ in a central way w.r.t. our learning problem: while the resets of an ERA can be directly inferred from observations, in a RERA this is not directly possible. Thus, generalizing a learning method from ERA to RERA requires dealing with the inference of resets—one of the central challenges of the learning of general deterministic TA.

2.2   Timed Languages

Automata-learning techniques are based on the identification of a candidate automaton that generalizes the *observations* obtained during the learning process. Angluin's tabular approach [Ang87a] directly identifies a set of observations (*i.e.* words) having good properties, and builds a deterministic automaton from it. Our contribution, as well as all the active-learning algorithms that we are aware of, follow a similar approach. An important issue for extending this approach to timed words is the infinite number of observations fitting even the simplest model, due to time density. We thus have to use good abstractions to represent classes of these words, and use these classes to direct the learning process. A first such extension was initiated in [GJP06].

A timed word with resets of a RERA can be seen as an element of $(\mathbb{R}_{\geq 0} \times \Sigma \times \{\top, \bot\})^*$. A timed word is the projection of a timed word with resets on $(\mathbb{R}_{\geq 0} \times \Sigma)^*$; timed words correspond to observations of timed words with resets.

In order to represent infinitely many timed words with resets in a succinct way, we define *guarded words with resets* $w_{gr} \in (\mathcal{G}_\Sigma \times \Sigma \times \{\top, \bot\})^*$, which correspond to paths in a RERA. For a timed word w_t and a guarded word with resets w_{gr} we say that w_t *satisfies* w_{gr}, noted $w_t \models w_{gr}$, if w_t is a possible observation of w_{gr}. We extend this correspondence to timed words with resets by ensuring that the resets match. The satisfiability relation between timed words and guarded words with resets will be central in the rest of the paper, as it relates an observation to the unfolding of a RERA (or of our hypothesis).

Example 2. The timed word $w_t = (1.3, a).(0.4, b)$ satisfies the guarded word with reset $w_{gr} = (x_b > 1, a, \{x_a\}).(x_a < 1, b, \emptyset)$: indeed, w_t and w_{gr} have the same untimed projection, and the timed word with resets $w_{tr} = \mathbf{0} \xrightarrow{1.3} \left(\begin{smallmatrix} 1.3 \\ 1.3 \end{smallmatrix} \right) \xrightarrow{a, \{x_a\}} \left(\begin{smallmatrix} 0 \\ 1.3 \end{smallmatrix} \right) \xrightarrow{0.4} \left(\begin{smallmatrix} 0.4 \\ 1.7 \end{smallmatrix} \right)$ satisfies the guards of w_{gr}. Notice that $w_t \not\models w'_{gr} = (x_b > 1, a, \emptyset).(x_a < 1, b, \emptyset)$, as modifying resets changes the valuations that appear in the corresponding timed word with resets.

Zone words with resets can be seen as elements w_z of $(\mathcal{Z}_\Sigma \times \Sigma \times \{\top, \bot\})^*.\mathcal{Z}_\Sigma$. From a guarded word with resets $w_{gr} = (g_i, a_i, r_i)_{i \in [0,n]}$ we can define the corresponding zone word with resets $w_z = (z_i, a_i, r_i)_{i \in [0,n]} z_{n+1}$ with $z_0 = \{0\}^\nearrow$ and $z_{i+1} = (z_i \wedge g_i)^\nearrow$ if $r_i = \bot$ and $z_{i+1} = (z_i \wedge g_i)_{[x_{a_i} \leftarrow 0]}^\nearrow$ otherwise.

In our learning process, we will manipulate linear combinations of timed words. For two timed words $w_t^1 = ((t_i^1, a_i))_{i \in [0,n]}$ and $w_t^2 = ((t_i^2, a_i))_{i \in [0,n]}$ with the same untimed projection, we define their λ-*weighted sum* $w_t^3 = \lambda.w_t^1 + (1 - \lambda)w_t^2$, as the timed word $w_t^3 = ((\lambda.t_i^1 + (1 - \lambda).t_i^2, a_i)_{i \in [0,n]})$. Such linear combinations have the following property:

Proposition 6. *For any two timed words $w_t^j = (t_i^j, a_i)_{i \in [0,n]}$ for $j \in \{1, 2\}$ with the same untimed projection, for any $\lambda \in [0, 1]$ and for any reset word $(r_i)_{i \in [0,n]}$, all the valuations $v_{i,r}^3$ reached along $w_{tr}^3 = ((\lambda.t_i^1 + (1 - \lambda).t_i^2, a_i, r_i)_{i \in [0,n]})$ are such that for all clocks $x_a \in X_\Sigma$, $v_{i,r}^3(x_a) = \lambda.v_{i,r}^1(x_a) + (1 - \lambda).v_{i,r}^2(x_a)$ for $v_{i,r}^j$ the valuations reached along $w_{tr}^j = (t_i^j, a_i, r_i)$.*

3 Observation Structure

The general principle of (untimed) active-learning is to learn a model from observations acquired by membership queries and equivalence queries. In membership queries, a timed word is provided to a teacher, who in return informs us about the membership of this world in the target language. In an equivalence query, we propose an hypothesis (model) to the teacher; she either accepts it if it is equivalent to the model we wish to learn, or otherwise provides us with a counterexample, *i.e.*, a timed word that separate the language of the model and that of our hypothesis. The set of observations is formalized as a partial function Obs mapping words to acceptance status ($+$ or $-$). To build a model, we then want to identify a prefix-closed subset U of $\mathsf{Dom}(\mathsf{Obs})$ such that for all letters a in the alphabet and words $u \in U$, $u.a \in \mathsf{Dom}(\mathsf{Obs})$ and either $u.a \in U$, or there is another word $u' \in U$ having the same observed behaviour as $u.a$. When transferring this approach to timed words, one has to deal with two difficulties: first, the uncountable number of possible delays before each discrete action; second, the fact that observations do not include clock valuations (nor clock resets), which we also have to learn.

In this section, we describe the structures used to represent and process these timed observations acquired during the learning *and* the decisions on the built structures made based on those observations. We generalize timed decision trees defined in [GJP06], so as to encode timed words *with possible resets*. We basically use a *timed decision graph*, a model close to acyclic timed automata, to encode the current knowledge inferred about the model from observations, and a *timed observation graph* (TOG) to *implement* Obs with a step of abstraction and help decisions.

Our data structure is centered around the notion of *observation structure* composed of a *timed decision graph*, which stores the current hypothesis (and will later be folded into a TA), and an *observation function*, which stores current observations.

Definition 7. *An* observation structure *is a pair* $(\mathcal{N}, \mathsf{Obs})$ *made of a timed decision graph (TDG) and a partial mapping* Obs *from timed words to* $\{+, -\}$. *The TDG is a labelled bipartite graph* $\mathcal{N} = (S, E)$ *with* $S = S_l \uplus S_d$ *where:*

- $S_l \subseteq \{s_0 = (\epsilon, \{\mathbf{0}\}^{\nearrow})\} \cup (\mathcal{G}_\Sigma \times \Sigma \times \{\top, \bot\})^+ \times \mathcal{Z}_\Sigma$ *is a set of* language states, *made of a prefix-closed finite set of guarded words with resets paired with zones;* s_0 *is the root state.*
- $S_d \subseteq S_l \times \Sigma \times \mathcal{G}_\Sigma$ *is a set of* decision states *such that for any* $s_l \in S_l$ *and* $a \in \Sigma$, *if* $I = \{g \in \mathcal{G}_\Sigma \mid (s_l, a, g) \in S_d\}$ *is non-empty, then* $\bigvee_{g \in I} g \equiv \top$ *and for all* g *and* g' *in* I, *if* $g \neq g'$ *then* $g \wedge g' \equiv \bot$;
- $E \subseteq S \times (\Sigma \times \mathcal{G}_\Sigma \cup \{\top, \bot\}) \times S$ *is defined such that transitions to a decision state* $s_d = (s_l, a, g)$ *are of the form* (s_l, a, g, s_d) *and if* $s_l = w_{gr}.z$ *transitions from* s_d *are* $(s_d, \top, (w_{gr}.(g, a, \top), (z \wedge g)_{[x_a \leftarrow 0]}^{\nearrow}))$ *and* $(s_d, \bot, (w_{gr}.(g, a, \bot), (z \wedge g)^{\nearrow}))$.

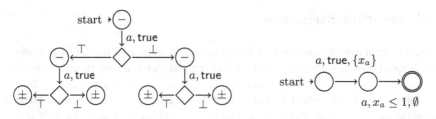

(a) A first observation structure   (b) The RERA providing observations

Fig. 2. An active-learning setting

The labelling *of an observation structure maps language states to the set of observations compatible with them:*

$$label(s_l = (w_{gr}.z)) = \{Obs(w_t) \mid w_t \in Dom(Obs) \wedge w_t \models w_{gr}\}.$$

It can be seen from this definition that TDGs are trees. For a guarded word w_{gr}, we note $s_0 \xrightarrow{w_{gr}}_{\mathcal{N}} s_l$ when there is a path in $\mathcal{N}$ from s_0 to s_l labelled with w_{gr}, and note $w_{gr} \in \mathcal{N}$ when such a path exists.

Observation structures store both the words that have been observed (in **Obs**) and the inferred guards and enforced resets (or absence thereof) (in $\mathcal{N}$). We can extend **Obs** to guarded words with resets by considering them as language states and using their labels. The labels are used to carry the observation information to the TDG.

Example 3. Figure 2a represents an observation structure storing some words observed from the RERA in Fig. 2b. Language states are depicted as circles and decision states as diamonds. Notice that in this example the leaves have labels of size 2: they model both accepting and non-accepting observations *e.g.* $((0.7, a)(0.9, a), +)$ and $((0.7, a)(1.2, a), -)$.

We define some desired properties of information structures.

Definition 8. *For an observation structure* $(\mathcal{N}, Obs)$, *a subtree* $\mathcal{N}'$ *of* $\mathcal{N}$ *rooted in* $s_l^{\mathcal{N}'} = w'_{gr}.z'$ *is said:*

- complete *when all observations in* **Obs** *are taken into account, i.e. for any* $w_t \in Dom(Obs)$ *such that* $w_t = w'_t.w''_t$ *with* $w'_t \models w'_{gr}$ *there is* $s_l^{\mathcal{N}'} \xrightarrow{w''_{gr}} s_l$ *such that* $w''_t \models w''_{gr}$ *and for all such* w''_{gr} *and* s_l, $Obs(w_t) \in label(s_l)$);
- consistent *when it separates accepting and non accepting behaviours, i.e. for any* s_l *in the subtree,* $|label(s_l)| = 1$.

We say that an observation structure is complete or consistent when $\mathcal{N}$ *is.*

Detecting and handling inconsistencies is central to our algorithms, as it characterizes the need to introduce new guards to split language nodes in the timed decision graph.

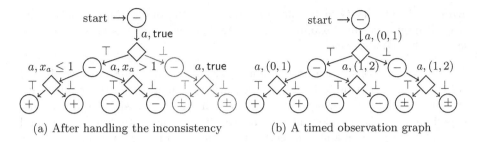

(a) After handling the inconsistency   (b) A timed observation graph

Fig. 3. Detecting an invalidity

Example 4. The leaves of the TDG in Fig. 2a are inconsistent. The inconsistency can be resolved for the left branch by splitting the transition, as made in Fig. 3a. This leaves a label of size two in the right branch, but there exists no guard that can separate the observations.

We now define *timed observation graphs*, a structure used to encode the observation function Obs efficiently and abstractly. More precisely, it represents the undistinguishable tube around each observation (*i.e.* the K-closed-words with resets), and allows to detect on-the-fly when two observations sharing the same K-closed word do not agree on acceptance and when reset combinations cannot happen.

Definition 9. *A timed observation graph (TOG) is a TDG where all guards and zones correspond to K-equivalence classes, language states are called* observation states $s_O \in S_O$ *and transitions from decision to observation states do not use the future operator, i.e. for $(s_d = (w.z), \top, s_O) \in E$, $s_O = w.(g, a, \top).g_{[x_a \leftarrow 0]}$ and same for $\bot$. We add a labelling $l: S_O \rightarrow \mathcal{P}(\{+, -\})$ for observation states and* words: $S_O \rightarrow \mathcal{P}((\mathbb{R}_{\geq 0}.\Sigma)^*)$ *a function associating to each observation state a set of observations that it represents. For two observation states s_O and s'_O, we note $s_O \xrightarrow{w_{zr}} s'_O$ if there is a path from s_O to s'_O and there exists a zone word $w.z$ such that $s_O = w.z$ and $s'_O = w.w_{zr}$.*

As for TDGs, TOGs are trees. Timed observation graphs will allow to detect impossible combinations of resets denoted by labels of observation states of cardinality larger than one. This is ensured by an encoding of Obs into the TOG, in a way defined as follows:

Definition 10. *A timed observation graph Obs_e is said to* implement *an observation function Obs when the following two conditions are fulfilled:*

Correspondence: *all observations are encoded in the TOG, i.e. for all $w_t \in Dom(Obs)$, for any w_{tr} compatible with w_t, there is a path $s_\epsilon \xrightarrow{w_{zr}} s_O = w_{zr}$ in Obs_e such that $w_{tr} \models w_{zr}$, $w_t \in words(s_O)$ and $Obs(w_t) \in l(s_O)$;*
Coverage: *all observation states are covered by $Dom(Obs)$, i.e. for any $s_O = (w_{zr}) \in S_O$, $words(s_O) \neq \emptyset$ and for any $w_t \in words(s_O)$, $w_t \in Dom(Obs)$, $w_t \models w_{zr}$ and $Obs(w_t) \in l(s_O)$.*

Example 5. The TOG in Fig. 3b corresponds to the observation structure displayed in our previous examples. Notice that it has a label of size two on the leafs of the right branch.

The pruning of the timed decision graph relies on *invalidity* of words and states, our key contribution to the active learning framework for timed automata. It allows to characterize reset combinations that are impossible for a given K-closed word. This complements inconsistency and allows to prune resets and schedule guards to be added when resets are not tied to observations.

Definition 11. *A K-closed word with reset $w_{zr} = (z_i, a_i, r_i)_{i \in [0,n]} z$ is invalid with respect to an observation graph Obs_e if one of the following conditions holds: $|l(w_{zr})| = 2$, or a prefix of w_{zr} is invalid w.r.t. Obs_e, or there exists z_{n+1}, a_{n+1} such that both $(z_i, a_i, r_i)_{i \in [0,n]} \cdot (z_{n+1}, a_{n+1}, \top) z_{n+1}{}_{[a \leftarrow 0]}$ and $(z_i, a_i, r_i)_{i \in [0,n]} \cdot (z_{n+1}, a_{n+1}, \bot) z_{n+1}$ are invalid w.r.t. Obs_e.*

A zone word with reset (or a guarded word with reset) is invalid if it models an invalid K-closed word with reset.

Invalid guarded words with resets encode behaviours that can not correspond to any model, and thus should be pruned in the TDG:

Proposition 12. *If a timed observation graph Obs_e has an invalid observation state $s_O = w_{zr}$, there is no TA model having execution w_{zr}.*

Situations may arise where a guarded word with reset is not invalid but all its successors by a given action are; an example is presented below. In such situations, two different K-closed words with resets make the successors invalid, and a guard has to be added.

Example 6. Consider the partial set of observations $\{((1.7, a)(1, a), +), ((1.7, a)(1.1, a), -), ((2.9, a)(1.1, a), -), ((2.7, a)(1.1, a), +)\}$ over the alphabet $\Sigma = \{a\}$. The corresponding partial timed observation graph Obs_e is displayed in Fig. 4[1].

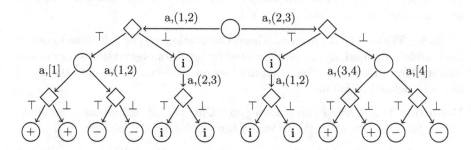

Fig. 4. A (partial) timed observation graph with some invalid nodes.

---

[1] In order to avoid overloading the explanation, we call the observation and graph partial because we do not mention some of the observations that would be necessary to have the implementation property.

We do not represent the actual K-equivalent classes on the graph so as to keep the figure as simple as possible. It can be seen that both resetting and not resetting the clock after the first action may sometimes lead to an invalidity. Hence, taking these observations into account in a timed decision graph with a $\top$ guard on this transition leads to pruning both successors of a decision tree.

This is problematic, as a decision state should always have successors. Hence it is necessary to introduce a guard to distinguish the different invalidities.

4   Updating a Timed Observation Structure

We define the algorithms used to update the previously defined data structures. The general idea is to add observations while preserving the good properties of the data structures, which requires detecting inconsistencies and invalidities on-the-fly, and resolving them by adding new guards.

The algorithms in Sect. 4.1 handle new observations while keeping most of the good properties of the structures, except for consistency. When inconsistencies arise, calls are scheduled to the algorithms proposed in Sect. 4.2. Sect. 4.3 deals with a similar but different problem arising from different invalidities meeting each others. Finally an algorithm to rebuild (parts of) the structure using the informations gathered using the previous section algorithms is described in Sect. 4.4.

4.1   Adding a New Observation

In essence, our algorithms propagate new words in the TDG $\mathcal{N}$, using satisfiability between guarded words with resets and timed words to guide the descent in the tree. When new states have to be created, membership queries are launched to get a label for them. All of this is complemented by a similar work on the TOG Obs_e, in order to take into account all the new observations. The main difference between the two algorithms is that in the TDG, labels of size 2 are detected and left for a future handling as the procedure to identify guards is potentially heavy, while in the TOG, invalidity leads to immediate pruning in order to limit the size of the structures.

We use the functions $\mathsf{FindPath}_{\mathcal{N}}$ and $\mathsf{FindPath}_{\mathsf{Obs}_e}$ to propagate new observations in the existing structures. Subsequent creation of new nodes is made with the functions $\mathsf{AddWord}_{\mathcal{N}}$ and $\mathsf{AddWord}_{\mathsf{Obs}_e}$. Membership queries and the resulting function calls are handled by the $\mathsf{Request}$ function, and the effective pruning is made in $\mathsf{SearchPrune}$.

The $\mathsf{FindPath}_{\mathcal{N}/\mathsf{Obs}_e}$ algorithms execute the descent through the existing structures, while the $\mathsf{AddWord}_{\mathcal{N}/\mathsf{Obs}_e}$ ones extend the structures, and make calls to $\mathsf{Request}$. The latter algorithm first checks if a fitting observation already exists before making a membership query if necessary. The $\mathsf{SearchPrune}$ procedure follows the lines of the definition of invalidity and finds the root of the invalid subtree before pruning it.

The following three statements express soundness of our algorithms. They ensure that the good properties of the structures are invariant by the call to the FindPath algorithms. Property 13 states that FindPath$_\mathcal{N}$ keeps the good properties of $\mathcal{N}$, except consistency, that is handled by in later. Property 14 does the same for FindPath$_{\mathsf{Obs}_e}$ and Obs_e, while Property 15 ensures that the calls made to SearchPrune during the execution of the FindPath algorithm prunes exactly the invalid words.

Proposition 13. *Starting from a complete observation structure $(\mathcal{N}, \mathsf{Obs})$ such that $|\mathsf{Obs}(w_{gr})| \geq 1$ for all $w_{gr} \in \mathcal{N}$, and a new word w_t associated with an observation o, a call to* FindPath$_\mathcal{N}(w_t, o, \epsilon, \mathbf{0}, s_0)$ *terminates and modifies the observation structure in such a way that it is complete, $w_t \in \mathsf{Dom}(\mathsf{Obs})$, $\mathsf{Obs}(w_t) = o$, and $|\mathsf{Obs}(w_{gr})| \geq 1$ for all $w_{gr} \in \mathcal{N}$.*

Proposition 14. *Starting from a timed observation graph Obs_e implementing an observation function Obs, and a new timed word w_t associated with the observation o, a call to* FindPath$_{\mathsf{Obs}_e}(w_t, o, \epsilon, \epsilon, \mathbf{0}, s_\epsilon)$ *terminates and modifies the timed observation graph in such a way that it implements the valid part of Obs extended to w_t.*

Proposition 15. *Starting from an observation structure $(\mathcal{N}, \mathsf{Obs})$ where Obs is implemented by Obs_e and no invalid states can be reached in $\mathcal{N}$, calling* FindPath$_\mathcal{N}$ *or* FindPath$_{\mathsf{Obs}_e}$ *modifies Obs_e and $\mathcal{N}$ in such a way that no invalid states can be reached in $\mathcal{N}$. Furthermore, no valid words are made unreachable.*

4.2   Dealing with Inconsistency

An inconsistency arises when a language state of the TDG contains both accepting and non-accepting observations. It means that a guard must be added somewhere in the structure in order to distinguish between these observations.

For this we search for a pair of *adjacent* words, which intuitively identify the boundary between accepting and non-accepting behaviours. We then build a finite set of *differences* between adjacent words, each of which corresponds to a possible guard. This procedure is described in the AdjPair algorithm.

We use K-equivalence to define the notion of adjacency. Intuitively adjacent words have the same projection on actions and resets, and their valuations either are K-equivalent, or they materialize a boundary between the accepted and non-accepted words.

Definition 16. *For two timed words with resets $w_{tr} = (v_i \xrightarrow{t_i, a_i, r_i} v_{i+1})_{i \in [0,n]}$ and $w'_{tr} = (v'_i \xrightarrow{t'_i, a_i, r_i} v'_{i+1})_{i \in [0,n]}$, we say that w_{tr} is adjacent to w'_{tr} when for all $i \in [0, n]$ and $x_a \in X_\Sigma$:*

– if $v_i(x_a) + t_i \in \mathbb{N}$ then $|(v_i(x_a) + t_i) - (v'_i(x_a) + t'_i)| < 1$,
– otherwise, $v_i(x_a) + t_i \approx_K v'_i(x_a) + t'_i$.

Notice that adjacency is not a symmetric relation. We will sometimes abuse the notations and say that a pair w, w' is adjacent to mean that w is adjacent to w'. We use adjacency to identify *differences* between the words as possible new guards that resolve the inconsistency.

Definition 17. *The* difference *between two words $w_{tr} = (v_i \xrightarrow{t_i, a_i, r_i} v_{i+1})_{i \in [0,n]}$ adjacent to $w'_{tr} = (v'_i \xrightarrow{t'_i, a_i, r_i} v'_{i+1})_{i \in [0,n]}$, noted diff$(w_{tr}, w'_{tr})$ is the set of quadruples defined as: if for a clock x, $v_i(x) + t_i = k \in \mathbb{N}$, then if $v'_i(x_a) + t'_i < k$, $(i, x, k, \geq) \in$ diff(w_{tr}, w'_{tr}) and if $v'_i(x_a) + t'_i > k$, $(i, x, k, \leq) \in$ diff(w_{tr}, w'_{tr}).*

Using these definitions, we can derive from two adjacent words a set of candidates to make a new guard. AdjPair makes membership queries on linear combinations of the two initial observations to perform a binary search until the clock values of the pair have less than 1 time unit of distance. Then it forces every non-K-equivalent pair of clock values to have one of its elements be an integer with more linear combinations. Finally, in order to ensure that only one of the two words have such integer distinctions, it compares them with their mean. This gives an adjacent pair.

Proposition 18. *The AdjPair algorithm constructs an adjacent pair using at most $\mathcal{O}(m|\Sigma|log(K))$ membership queries.*

Proof. We refer the reader to the proof of Theorem 5.8 in [GJP06].

4.3   Dealing with Invalidity

A label of size two in the TOG indicates an invalidity. It points to a combination of resets being impossible combined with those precise observations. Invalidity is simply dealt with by pruning the invalid parts of the TDG and TOG. But a challenge can arise, as explained in Example 6: sometimes *all* successors of a decision state of the TDG following a *valid* language state are pruned, due to invalidities. In this case, a guard must be introduced to separate the different invalidities and allow to rebuild the graph accordingly. As for inconsistencies, it is important to introduce guards that model as closely as possible the changes in behaviours of the observation.

For this purpose, we again use a binary search, but this time manipulating a pair of *sets* of words. Furthermore, as the invalidities are often detected by the precise combination of *fractional values*, the delays in the words are only modified by *integer values*. For two timed words $w^i_t = (t^i_j, a_j)_{j \in [1, n_i]}$ with $n_1 \leq n_2$, we define the operator $w^1_t \odot w^2_t = (\lfloor t^1_j \rfloor + \langle t^2_j \rangle, a_j)_{j \in [1, n_1]} . (t^2_j, a_j)_{j \in [n_1 + 1, n_2]}$ to describe the operation used in the algorithm (where $\lfloor t \rfloor$ and $\langle t \rangle$ respectively represent the integral and fractional parts of t).

Of course, it is impossible to obtain a good precision while keeping all fractional values: clock values can not be modified to become integers. For this reason our algorithm only identifies a set of integer constants separating two behaviours, but does not find which behaviour the constants belong to. This means that we have to wait for a counterexample from an equivalence query to correct the possible wrong guesses we made.

Procedure InvalidityGuard outputs a *validity guard* $(s_l, a, g, x, \sim, k)$ where $a \in \Sigma$, g is a guard, x a clock, $k \in \mathbb{N}$ and $\sim \in \{<, \leq, \top\}$. Such validity guard states that in the language state s_l, after playing a with guard g, adding $x \sim k$ to the guard separates the two causes of invalidity. We use $\top$ to denote that both strict and large inequalities could fit the current observations. The InvalidityGuard algorithm conducts a binary search between two sets of timed words, while keeping the fractional part of the clock values unchanged thanks to the $\odot$ operator, while the K-closed sets corresponding to the sets of words do not touch each other.

Proposition 19. *Algorithm* InvalidityGuard *terminates after* $\mathcal{O}(m(|W_1| + |W_2|) \cdot |\Sigma| \cdot \log(K))$ *membership queries, where m is the size of a largest word in $W_1 \cup W_2$.*

Proof. The proof uses the same arguments as the one of AdjPair.

4.4 Rebuilding the Graph

To rebuild a subtree is to introduce new guards using adjacent pairs and validity guards only when necessary, and re-propagate the informations in the new guarded words with resets they satisfy. We use Algorithm Rebuild for this. From an adjacent pair, we extract *consistency guards*, which will be used to reconstruct a decision graph that is consistent with respect to the adjacent pair.

Definition 20. *For an adjacent pair w_{tr}, w'_{tr}, clock constraint $x_a \leq k$ is a consistency guard at depth i if $(i, x_a, k, \prec) \in \text{diff}(w_{tr}, w'_{tr})$ and there is no $(j, x_a, l, \prec') \in \text{diff}(w_{tr}, w'_{tr})$ such that $j < i$ or $j = i$ and $l < k$.*

The consistency guards are taken on the first difference, so as to ensure that they can not be overwritten later (there are no guards that can separate the pair before the guard), and to avoid large constants as much as possible.

Notice that we can not always infer a unique guard from an adjacent pair, as multiple clocks can be different at the same time. Intuitively, Rebuild only introduces guards "when needed", which is formalized by the following *well-guardedness* property.

Definition 21. *A timed decision graph is said* well guarded *if, for all transitions $(s_l, a, g, s_d) \in E_\Sigma$ and all constraints $x_b \prec k$ in g, either there is w_{tr} adjacent to w'_{tr} such that both pass by s_l and $x_b \prec k$ is a consistency guard for the pair at this depth or $(s_l, a, g', x_b, \sim, k)$ is a validity guard with $g \subset g'$ and $\prec$ is either $\sim$ or $\neg \sim$.*

Rebuild constructs a complete, consistent and well-guarded subtree if it is called high enough in the tree.

Proposition 22. *Running* Rebuild *on a valid and consistent state s_l of which no successors have inconsistencies that lead to consistency guards at a depth lesser than $|s_l|$, constructs a subtree rooted in its argument that is* complete, consistent *and* well-guarded. *It furthermore does not have* invalid *states.*

This proposition tells us we can keep the timed decision graph up-to-date with respect to observations (*i.e.*, complete and consistent) while keeping the good properties that were ensured by the previous algorithms. It remains to show how a candidate timed automaton can be constructed from this structure.

5   Building a Candidate Timed Automaton

Following the active learning approach, our purpose is to identify a subset of nodes in the decision graph that will correspond to locations of the automaton, and then fold transitions according to an order on the remaining nodes. [GJP06] discusses such orders when resets are fixed. To handle RERA we first have to fix a *reset strategy* before applying the original method. This gives as many hypotheses as we have strategies.

Reset Selection. We present the general framework but do not discuss good strategies in the following. Such strategies would rely on heuristics.

Definition 23. *A reset strategy over a timed decision graph $\mathcal{N}$ is a mapping $\pi \colon S_d \to \{\top, \bot\}$, assigning a decision to each decision states.*

A reset strategy π is said *admissible* if for any state s_d, there is a language state s_l such that $(s_d, \pi(s_d), s_l) \in E$.

Proposition 24. *In a timed decision graph constructed using the* FindPath *and* Rebuild *algorithms and where every scheduled call to* Rebuild *has been done, there always exists at least one admissible reset strategy.*

An admissible reset strategy is used to prune the decision graph in such a way that only one reset combination is considered for each transition. The effect of an admissible reset strategy π on its timed decision graph $\mathcal{N}$ is the TDG $\pi(\mathcal{N})$ defined from $\mathcal{N}$ by keeping only outgoing transitions from decision states that agree with π. We call this TDG the *resulting graph* of π. It can be seen quite directly that a resulting graph always has exactly one successor to each decision state. Using this, we can notice that those resulting graphs are very close to timed decision trees of [GJP06], in which no decision states exist and the transitions from language states to language states directly hold the (only possible) reset.

Orders and Folding. Once an admissible reset strategy is fixed, it is possible to fold the resulting graph into a RERA. This is made through the use of a preorder on states: we want to find a maximal subset for this order.

We define the *height* of a language state s_l, noted *height*(s_l), as the height of the subtree it is the root of. A preorder $\sqsubseteq$ on language states is said *height-monotone* when $s_l \sqsubseteq s_l'$ implies *height*$(s_l) \leq$ *height*(s_l').

Definition 25. *Let $\mathcal{N}$ be a timed decision graph and $\sqsubseteq$ a preorder on its language states. A prefix-closed subset U of $\mathcal{N}$ is called $\sqsubseteq$-closed if $s_l \sqsubseteq U$ for all successors of U and $\sqsubseteq$-unique if for all $s_l, s_l' \in U$, $s_l \neq s_l' \Rightarrow \neg(s_l \sqsubseteq s_l')$.*

$\sqsubseteq$-closedness is used to construct a RERA by folding the successors of U into comparable states of U. $\sqsubseteq$-uniqueness is useful to bound the number of states in U and thus the size of the resulting automaton.

The following lemma (Lemma 6.2 in [GJP06]) ensures that there always exists a satisfying set of states U. For its constructive proof, we refer the reader to the original paper.

Lemma 26. *Let $\sqsubseteq$ be a height-monotone preorder on states in a resulting graph $\pi(\mathcal{N})$. Then there exists a $\sqsubseteq$-closed and $\sqsubseteq$-unique prefix-closed subset of the language states of $\pi(\mathcal{N})$.*

Using such a subset, we can fold the resulting graph into a RERA as follows:

Definition 27. *Let $(Obs, \mathcal{N})$ be a consistent observation structure, π an admissible reset strategy and $\sqsubseteq$ a preorder on language states of $\pi(\mathcal{N})$. Consider a $\sqsubseteq$-unique, $\sqsubseteq$-closed and prefix-closed subset U of $\pi(\mathcal{N})$. Then a $U_\sqsubseteq$-merging of $(Obs, \mathcal{N})$ according to π is a RERA $(U, \epsilon, X_\Sigma, E, \mathsf{Accept})$ such that $\mathsf{Accept} = \{u \in U \mid \mathsf{label}(u) = \{+\}\}$ and for any language node $u.(a, g, r)$ of $\pi(\mathcal{N})$ with $u \in U$, there is exactly one edge of the form $(u, a, g, r, u') \in E$ with $u.(a, g, r) \sqsubseteq u'$. Notice that, by the second condition, a $U_\sqsubseteq$-merging RERA is deterministic.*

Furthermore, if the observation structure is complete, a $U_\sqsubseteq$-merging generalizes the observations obtained so far.

Constructing a Candidate RERA. Using the results of the previous subsections, we can now construct a candidate RERA from our observation structure. All admissible reset strategies can be constructed by branch and bound. Then a merging is constructed for each resulting graph, and equivalence queries are launched.

For each of the RERA constructed by merging, either a counter-example will be returned by the equivalence query, or the candidate is deemed correct. In the latter case, we return this RERA; in the former case, we include the counter-example in our observation structure and repeat the process.

6   Conclusion

In this paper, we propose an active learning method for deterministic reset-free event recording automata. We add a key feature to the state of the art: invalidity, that allows to detect incorrect guesses of resets when they are not tied to observations. This required to rework all the data structures and algorithms involved to handle invalidity on the fly. Most importantly, this brings the lacking notion to scale up to the class of deterministic timed automata (DTAs).

A clear future work is to generalize this method to actually handle DTAs. This mostly requires to handles resets of sets of clocks instead of single ones.

As the complexity would be greatly increased, this calls for some optimization. An promising addition would be to use an implicit structure. Instead of storing all possible reset configurations, only storing a small set of them at the same time would decrease the memory cost. As the models are built directly from observations, and not from previous states, the computational overhead may be limited. An other interesting trail for future development is to find a way to build a timed automaton from the observation structure that exploits the different admissible reset strategies without building all of them. Works on approximate determinization of timed automata through games [BSJK11] deal with similar problems and offer interesting leads. Finally, in [GJP06], the authors propose to refine the adjacent pairs into *critical pairs*, that have a minimal set of differences. This allows to better identify the guards to be added, and thus can have a positive effect on both the size of the constructed models and the computational cost. Sadly, no precise procedure is given to construct the pairs, so creating one would be beneficial to the approach. More generally, studying the efficiency of this algorithm and of the variants proposed as future work could help better understand the applicability and bottlenecks of the approach.

References

[ACZ+20] An, J., Chen, M., Zhan, B., Zhan, N., Zhang, M.: Learning one-clock timed automata. In: Biere, A., Parker, D. (eds.) TACAS 2020. LNCS, vol. 12078, pp. 444–462. Springer, Cham (2020). https://doi.org/10.1007/978-3-030-45190-5_25

[AD94] Alur, R., Dill, D.L.: A theory of timed automata. Theor. Comput. Sci. **126**(2), 183–235 (1994)

[AFH99] Alur, R., Fix, L., Henzinger, T.A.: Event-clock automata: a determinizable class of timed automata. Theor. Comput. Sci. **211**(1–2), 253–273 (1999)

[Ang87a] Angluin, D.: Learning regular sets from queries and counterexamples. Inf. Comput. **75**(2), 87–106 (1987)

[Ang87b] Angluin, D.: Queries and concept learning. Mach. Learn. **2**(4), 319–342 (1987). https://doi.org/10.1023/A:1022821128753

[Ang90] Angluin, D.: Negative results for equivalence queries. Mach. Learn. **5**, 121–150 (1990). https://doi.org/10.1023/A:1022692615781

[BSJK11] Bertrand, N., Stainer, A., Jéron, T., Krichen, M.: A game approach to determinize timed automata. In: Hofmann, M. (ed.) FoSSaCS 2011. LNCS, vol. 6604, pp. 245–259. Springer, Heidelberg (2011). https://doi.org/10.1007/978-3-642-19805-2_17

[GJP06] Grinchtein, O., Jonsson, B., Pettersson, P.: Inference of event-recording automata using timed decision trees. In: Baier, C., Hermanns, H. (eds.) CONCUR 2006. LNCS, vol. 4137, pp. 435–449. Springer, Heidelberg (2006). https://doi.org/10.1007/11817949_29

[Gri08] Grinchtein, O.: Learning of timed systems. Ph.D. thesis, Uppsala University, Sweden (2008)

[HJM20] Henry, L., Jéron, T., Markey, N.: Active learning of timed automata with unobservable resets. Technical Report. arXiv:2007.01637, April 2020

[TALL19] Tappler, M., Aichernig, B.K., Larsen, K.G., Lorber, F.: Time to learn –
          learning timed automata from tests. In: André, É., Stoelinga, M. (eds.)
          FORMATS 2019. LNCS, vol. 11750, pp. 216–235. Springer, Cham (2019).
          https://doi.org/10.1007/978-3-030-29662-9_13
[VWW08]   Verwer, S., Weerdt, M., Witteveen, C.: Efficiently learning simple timed
          automata. In: Proceedings of the Second International Workshop on the
          Induction of Process Models at ECML PKDD, pp. 61–68 (2008)
[VWW12]   Verwer, S., Weerdt, M., Witteveen, C.: Efficiently identifying deterministic
          real-time automata from labeled data. Mach. Learn. 86, 295–333 (2012).
          https://doi.org/10.1007/s10994-011-5265-4

Computation of the Transient
in Max-Plus Linear Systems
via SMT-Solving

Alessandro Abate[1] , Alessandro Cimatti[2] , Andrea Micheli[2] ,
and Muhammad Syifa'ul Mufid[1](✉)

[1] Department Computer Science, University of Oxford, Oxford, UK
{alessandro.abate,muhammad.syifaul.mufid}@cs.ox.ac.uk
[2] Fondazione Bruno Kessler, Povo, Italy
{cimatti,amicheli}@fbk.eu

Abstract. This paper proposes a new approach, grounded in Satisfiability Modulo Theories (SMT), to study the transient of a Max-Plus Linear (MPL) system, that is the number of steps leading to its periodic regime. Differently from state-of-the-art techniques, our approach allows the analysis of periodic behaviors for subsets of initial states, as well as the characterization of sets of initial states exhibiting the same specific periodic behavior and transient. Our experiments show that the proposed technique dramatically outperforms state-of-the-art methods based on max-plus algebra computations for systems of large dimensions.

1 Introduction

Max-Plus Linear (MPL) systems are a class of discrete-event systems (DES) that are based on the max-plus algebra, an algebraic system using the two operations of maximisation and addition. MPL systems are employed to model applications with features of synchronization without concurrency, and as such are widely used for applications in transportation networks [4], manufacturing [14] and biological systems [6,10]. In MPL models, the states correspond to time instances related to discrete events.

A fundamental and well-studied property of MPL systems is related to the periodic behavior of its states: from an initial vector, the trajectories of an MPL system are eventually periodic (in max-plus algebraic sense) starting from a specific event index called the *transient*, and with a specific period called *cyclicity* [4]. As explained in [14, Section 3.1], the transient is closely related to the notion of *cycle-time* vector, which governs the asymptotic behaviour of MPL systems.

The transient is key to solve a number of fundamental problems of MPL systems, such as reachability analysis [17] and bounded model checking [18]: it plays a crucial role as the "completeness threshold" (namely, the maximum iteration that is sufficient for the termination of the algorithm) [9] for those two problems. The computation of the transient is an interesting problem, as it is in general not

© Springer Nature Switzerland AG 2020
N. Bertrand and N. Jansen (Eds.): FORMATS 2020, LNCS 12288, pp. 161–177, 2020.
https://doi.org/10.1007/978-3-030-57628-8_10

correlated to the dimension of the MPL system. Thus, it is possible for the resulting transient to be relatively large for a small-dimensional MPL system. There are several known upper bounds [8, 16, 19, 20] for the transient, which are mostly computed via the corresponding precedence graph and are, in practice, much larger than the actual values.

This paper has two specific contributions. The first is to provide a novel procedure to compute the transient by means of Satisfiability Modulo Theory (SMT) solving [5]. The main idea underpinning the new method is to transform the problem instance into a formula in difference logic, and then passing the formula into an SMT solver, which outputs the transient. More precisely, in order to check the validity of the formula, we check the unsatisfiability of its negation. If the SMT solver reports "satisfied", then the original formula admits a counterexample, from which we can refine the formula. On the other hand, if SMT solver reports "unsatisfied", then from the formula we obtain the transient and the corresponding cyclicity. The second contribution of this work is to provide a procedure to synthesize the subset of the state space of an MPL system that corresponds to a specific transient/cyclicity pair. We show that one can partition the state space into sets corresponding to different transient/cyclicity pairs.

The rest of the paper is structured as follows. Section 2 describes the basics of MPL systems, including the key notion of cycle-time vector. In Sect. 3, we provide the formal definition of transient over MPL systems and also a standard linear algebra procedure, based on matrix multiplication, to compute the transient (cf. Algorithm 1), which is later used as a benchmark. Section 4 is divided into four parts. The first part provides the background on SMT and including the underlying relevant theory. The translation of inequalities over max-plus algebra to formulae in difference logic is explained in the second part. In the third part, we provide SMT-based methods (cf. Algorithms 2 and 3) to compute the transient. The spatial synthesis problem is discussed in the last part. The comparison of the performance of the novel algorithm against the standard linear algebra procedure is presented in Sect. 5. The paper is concluded with Sect. 6. The proofs of the propositions and theorems are presented in a longer version of this paper [1]. The developed code and generated data can be found in https://es.fbk.eu/people/amicheli/resources/formats20/.

2 Preliminaries

2.1 Max-Plus Linear Systems

Max-plus algebra is a modification of linear algebra derived over the max-plus semiring $(\mathbb{R}_{\max}, \oplus, \otimes)$ where $\mathbb{R}_{\max} := \mathbb{R} \cup \{\varepsilon := -\infty\}$ and $a \oplus b := \max\{a, b\}, a \otimes b := a + b$, for all $a, b \in \mathbb{R}_{\max}$. The zero and unit elements of $\mathbb{R}_{\max}$ are ε and 0, respectively. The max-plus algebraic operations can be extended to matrices and vectors in a natural way. For $A, B \in \mathbb{R}_{\max}^{m \times n}, C \in \mathbb{R}_{\max}^{n \times p}$ and $\alpha \in \mathbb{R}_{\max}$,

$$[\alpha \otimes A](i, j) = \alpha + A(i, j),$$
$$[A \oplus B](i, j) = A(i, j) \oplus B(i, j),$$
$$[A \otimes C](i, j) = \bigoplus_{k=1}^{n} A(i, k) \otimes C(k, j).$$

Given $A \in \mathbb{R}_{\max}^{n \times n}$ and $t \in \mathbb{N}$, $A^{\otimes t}$ denotes $A \otimes \ldots \otimes A$ (t times). For $t = 0$, $A^{\otimes 0}$ is an n-dimensional max-plus identity matrix where all diagonal and non-diagonal elements are 0 and ε, respectively.

Given $V = \{v_1, \ldots, v_p\}$ as a set of vectors in $\mathbb{R}_{\max}^n$, we use the same notation to denote a matrix where all columns are in V i.e., $V(\cdot, i) = v_i$ for $1 \le i \le p$. A vector $v \in \mathbb{R}^n$ is *a max-plus linear combination* of V if $v = \alpha_1 \otimes v_1 \oplus \ldots \oplus \alpha_p \otimes v_p$ for some scalars $\alpha_1, \ldots, \alpha_p \in \mathbb{R}$ or equivalently there exists $w \in \mathbb{R}^p$ such that $V \otimes w = v$. The set of all max-plus linear combinations of V is called *max-plus cone*[1] and is denoted by $\mathsf{cone}(V)$ [7]. It is formally expressed as

$$\mathsf{cone}(V) = \{V \otimes w \mid w \in \mathbb{R}^p\}. \tag{1}$$

Furthermore, we denote as $v_1, \ldots, v_p$ the basis of $\mathsf{cone}(V)$. Notice that the max-plus cone is closed under the operations $\oplus$ and $\otimes$: if v, w are in $\mathsf{cone}(V)$, then so is $\alpha \otimes v \oplus \beta \otimes w$ for $\alpha, \beta \in \mathbb{R}$. Max-plus cones are the analogues of vector subspaces in classical linear algebra.

A dynamical system over the max-plus algebra is called a Max-Plus Linear (MPL) system and is defined as

$$\mathbf{x}(k + 1) = A \otimes \mathbf{x}(k), \quad k = 0, 1, \ldots \tag{2}$$

where $A \in \mathbb{R}_{\max}^{n \times n}$ is the system matrix, and vector $\mathbf{x}(k) = [x_1(k) \ \ldots \ x_n(k)]^\top$ encodes the state variables [4]. For example, $\mathbf{x}$ can be used to represent the time stamps associated to the discrete events, while k corresponds to the events counter. Hence, it is more convenient to consider $\mathbb{R}^n$ (instead of $\mathbb{R}_{\max}^n$) as the state space. Applications of MPL systems are significantly found on systems where the time variable is essential, such as transportation networks [14], scheduling or [3] manufacturing [15] problems, or biological systems [6,10].

Definition 1 (Precedence Graph [4]). The precedence graph of $A \in \mathbb{R}_{\max}^{n \times n}$, denoted by $\mathcal{G}(A)$, is a weighted directed graph with nodes $1, \ldots, n$ and an edge from j to i with weight $A(i, j)$ for each $A(i, j) \neq \varepsilon$. $\qquad\square$

Definition 2 (Regular Matrix [14]). A matrix $A \in \mathbb{R}_{\max}^{n \times n}$ is called *regular* if A contains at least one finite element in each row. $\qquad\square$

Definition 3 (Irreducible Matrix [4]). A matrix $A \in \mathbb{R}_{\max}^{n \times n}$ is called *irreducible* if $\mathcal{G}(A)$ is strongly connected. $\qquad\square$

---

[1] Unlike in [7,13], we require each max-plus cone to be a subset of $\mathbb{R}^n$.

Recall that a directed graph is strongly connected if, for any two different nodes i, j, there exists a path from i to j. The weight of a path $p = i_1 i_2 \ldots i_k$ is equal to the sum of the edge weights in p. A circuit, namely a path that begins and ends at the same node, is called *critical* if it has maximum average weight, which is the weight divided by the length of the path [4].

Each irreducible matrix $A \in \mathbb{R}_{\max}^{n \times n}$ admits a unique max-plus eigenvalue $\lambda \in \mathbb{R}$ and a corresponding max-plus eigenspace $E(A) = \{x \in \mathbb{R}^n \mid A \otimes x = \lambda \otimes x\}^2$. The scalar λ is equal to the average weight of critical circuits in $\mathcal{G}(A)$, and $E(A)$ can be computed from $A_\lambda^+ = \bigoplus_{k=1}^{n} ((-\lambda) \otimes A)^{\otimes k}$. More specifically, $E(A)$ is the max-plus linear combination of the ith column of A_λ^+, for i such that $A_\lambda^+(i, i) = 0$ [4]. Thus, the eigenspace $E(A)$ is a max-plus cone. A reducible matrix may have multiple eigenvalues, where the maximum one equals to the average weight of critical circuits of $\mathcal{G}(A)$.

Example 1. Consider a two-dimensional MPL system $\mathbf{x}(k+1) = A \otimes \mathbf{x}(k)$, with

$$A = \begin{bmatrix} 2 & 5 \\ 3 & 3 \end{bmatrix},$$

which represents a simple railway network between two cities [4, Sec. 0.1], as shown in Fig. 1. The dynamics w.r.t. (2) can be expressed as

$$\begin{bmatrix} x_1(k+1) \\ x_2(k+1) \end{bmatrix} = \begin{bmatrix} \max\{x_1(k) + 2, x_2(k) + 5\} \\ \max\{x_1(k) + 3, x_2(k) + 3\} \end{bmatrix}.$$

For $1 \leq i, j \leq 2$, the element $A(i, j)$ corresponds to the time taken to travel from station S_j to S_i, while $x_i(k)$ is the time of the k-th departure at station S_i.

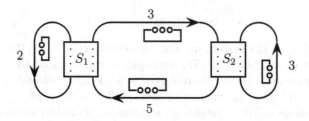

Fig. 1. A simple railway network represented by an MPL system.

From an initial vector, say $\mathbf{x}(0) = [0 \ 0]^\top$, one can compute vectors denoting the next departure times, as follows

$$\begin{bmatrix} 5 \\ 3 \end{bmatrix}, \begin{bmatrix} 8 \\ 8 \end{bmatrix}, \begin{bmatrix} 13 \\ 11 \end{bmatrix}, \begin{bmatrix} 16 \\ 16 \end{bmatrix}, \ldots$$

Leaving the details aside, the matrix A has eigenvalue $\lambda = 4$ and eigenspace $E(A) = \{\mathbf{x} \in \mathbb{R}^2 \mid x_1 - x_2 = 1\}$. □

---

^{2} Because we regard $\mathbb{R}^n$ to be the state space of the MPL system (2), we only consider eigenvectors with finite elements.

2.2   Cycle-Time Vector

This section presents the definition of cycle-time vector of MPL systems. The computation of the cycle-time vector is indeed important, as it can shed light on the asymptotic behavior of MPL systems. In this section, we show its relationship with the eigenspace and eigenvalue of the underlying state matrix. Furthermore, as it will be clear in Sect. 3, the cycle-time vector can be used to determine whether the states of an MPL system are eventually periodic.

Definition 4 (Cycle-Time Vector [14]). Consider a regular MPL system (2), and assume that for all $j \in \{1, \dots, n\}$ the quantity η_j, defined by

$$\eta_j = \lim_{k \to +\infty} (x_j(k)/k),$$

exists. Then the vector $\chi = [\eta_1 \ \dots \ \eta_n]^\top$ is called the the cycle-time vector of the given sequence $\mathbf{x}(k)$ with respect to A. $\qquad\square$

It has been shown in [14, Theorem 3.11] that if the cycle-time vector of A exists for at least one initial vector then it exists for any initial vector. Instead of computing the limit as in Definition 4, the cycle-time vector can be generated using a procedure [12, Algorithm 31].

Theorem 1 ([12]). Suppose we have a regular MPL system (2). For each $\mathbf{x}(0) \in \mathbb{R}^n$ there exist natural numbers p, q such that $\mathbf{x}(k+q) = (q \times \chi) + \mathbf{x}(k)$ for all $k \geq p$, where $\chi = [\eta_1 \ \dots \ \eta_n]^\top$ is the cycle-time vector of A and the multiplication $q \times \chi$ is defined in the classical algebra. $\qquad\square$

By Theorem 1, the trajectories of a regular MPL system (2) starting from any initial vector is governed by the corresponding cycle-time vector χ. In general, the elements of χ may be different, as shown in [12, Example 1]. However, if $E(A) \neq \emptyset$ then the elements of χ are all equal.

Proposition 1. Suppose a regular MPL system (2) has maximum eigenalue λ. The eigenspace $E(A)$ is not empty iff $\chi = [\lambda \ \dots \ \lambda]^T \in \mathbb{R}^n$. $\qquad\square$

3   Transient in Max-Plus-Linear Systems

The transient of MPL systems is related to the sequence of the powers of matrix A, namely $A^{\otimes k}$ for $k \geq 0$.

Proposition 2 (Transient [4,14]). For an irreducible matrix $A \in \mathbb{R}^{n \times n}_{\max}$ and its max-plus eigenvalue $\lambda \in \mathbb{R}$, there exist $k_0, c \in \mathbb{N}_0$, such that $A^{\otimes(k+c)} = (\lambda \times c) \otimes A^{\otimes k}$ for all $k \geq k_0$. The smallest such k_0 and c are called the *transient* and the *cyclicity* of A, respectively. $\qquad\square$

For the rest of this paper, we denote the transient and the cyclicity of A as $\text{tr}(A)$ and $\text{cyc}(A)$, respectively. While $\text{cyc}(A)$ is related to critical circuits in the precedence graph $\mathcal{G}(A)$ (see [4, Definition 3.94] for more details[3]), $\text{tr}(A)$ is unrelated to the dimension of A. Even for a small n, the transient of $A \in \mathbb{R}_{\max}^{n \times n}$ can be large. Upper bounds of the transient have been discussed in [8,16,19,20].

By Proposition 2, each *irreducible* MPL system enjoys a *periodic* behaviour with a rate λ: for each initial vector $\mathbf{x}(0) \in \mathbb{R}^n$ we have $\mathbf{x}(k + \text{cyc}(A)) = (\lambda \times \text{cyc}(A)) \otimes \mathbf{x}(k)$ for all $k \geq \text{tr}(A)$ where the vectors $\mathbf{x}(1), \mathbf{x}(2)$ are computed recursively by (2). A similar condition may be found on reducible MPL systems: we denote the corresponding transient and cyclicity as global, as per Proposition 2. The local transient and cyclicity for a specific initial vector $\mathbf{x} \in \mathbb{R}^n$ and for a set $X \subseteq \mathbb{R}^n$ is defined as follows.

Definition 5. Given $A \in \mathbb{R}_{\max}^{n \times n}$ with maximum eigenvalue λ and an initial vector $\mathbf{x} \in \mathbb{R}^n$, the local transient and cyclicity of $\mathbf{x}(0)$ w.r.t. A are respectively the smallest $k_0, c \in \mathbb{N}_0$ such that $\mathbf{x}(k + c) = \lambda c \otimes \mathbf{x}(k)$ for all $k \geq k_0$. We denote those scalars as $\text{tr}(A, \mathbf{x})$ and $\text{cyc}(A, \mathbf{x})$, respectively. Furthermore, for $X \subseteq \mathbb{R}^n$, $\text{tr}(A, X) = \max\{\text{tr}(A, \mathbf{x}(0)) \mid \mathbf{x}(0) \in X\}$ and $\text{cyc}(A, X) = \text{lcm}\{\text{cyc}(A, \mathbf{x}(0)) \mid \mathbf{x}(0) \in X\}$, where lcm stands for the "least common multiple". $\square$

By definition, we have $\text{tr}(A, \mathbb{R}^n) = \text{tr}(A)$. For a max-plus cone $X = \text{cone}(V)$, we show that the local cyclicity and transient can be computed from the corresponding bases, provided that $\text{tr}(A, v_i)$ exists for all $1 \leq i \leq p$.

Proposition 3. Given a max-plus cone $X = \text{cone}(V)$ where $V = \{v_1, \ldots, v_p\}$, we have $\text{tr}(A, X) = \text{tr}(A, V) = \max\{\text{tr}(A, v) \mid v \in V\}$, and $\text{cyc}(A, X) = \text{cyc}(A, V) = \text{lcm}\{\text{cyc}(A, v) \mid v \in V\}$. $\square$

Definition 6. Suppose we have a regular matrix $A \in \mathbb{R}_{\max}^{n \times n}$. The underlying MPL system (2) is classified into three categories as follows:

  i. *never periodic*: $\text{tr}(A, \mathbf{x}(0))$ does not exist for all $\mathbf{x}(0) \in \mathbb{R}^n$,
  ii. *boundedly periodic*: $\text{tr}(A, \mathbf{x}(0))$ exists for all $\mathbf{x}(0) \in \mathbb{R}^n$ and $\text{tr}(A)$ exists,
  iii. *unboundedly periodic*: $\text{tr}(A, \mathbf{x}(0))$ exists for all $\mathbf{x}(0) \in \mathbb{R}^n$ but $\text{tr}(A)$ does not.

We call (2) *periodic* if it is either *unboundedly periodic* or *boundedly periodic*. $\square$

We show that the periodic behavior of an MPL system is indeed related to the eigenspace and cycle-time vector of its corresponding state matrix.

Theorem 2. Suppose we have a regular matrix $A \in \mathbb{R}_{\max}^{n \times n}$ with a maximum eigenvalue λ and cycle-time vector χ. The following statements are equivalent.

  a. The underlying MPL system (2) is *periodic*.
  b. The corresponding cycle-time vector is $\chi = [\lambda \ \ldots \ \lambda]^\top \in \mathbb{R}^n$.
  c. The eigenspace $E(A)$ is not empty. $\square$

---

[3] In this reference, one can find the cyclicity for reducible and irreducible matrices using graph-theoretical approaches.

Proposition 4. Suppose we have a regular matrix $A \in \mathbb{R}_{\max}^{n \times n}$ with maximum eigenvalue λ and non-empty eigenspace $E(A)$. If there exist $i \in \{1, \ldots, n\}$ and natural numbers k_0', c' such that $A^{\otimes k + c'}(\cdot, i) = \mu c' \otimes A^{\otimes k}(\cdot, i)$ for all $k \geq k_0'$ with $\mu < \lambda$ then (2) is *unboundedly periodic*. □

We now will provide the procedure to compute the transient of MPL systems. As per Proposition 2, the common method to obtain the (global) transient of $A \in \mathbb{R}_{\max}^{n \times n}$ is by computing the power of the matrix $A^{\otimes 0}, A^{\otimes 1}, \ldots$ until we find $k_0 \geq 0$ such that $A^{\otimes (k_0 + c)} = \lambda^{\otimes c} \otimes A^{\otimes k_0}$ where λ, c is respectively the max-plus eigenvalue and cyclicity of A. Similarly, to find the transient of A w.r.t. a max-plus cone $X = \mathsf{cone}(V)$ one needs to compute $A^{\otimes 0} \otimes V, A^{\otimes 1} \otimes V, \ldots$.

Algorithm 1 illustrates the procedure to compute transient (and cyclicity) for a max-plus cone $\mathsf{cone}(V)$ w.r.t. $A \in \mathbb{R}_{\max}^{n \times n}$. While originally designed for irreducible matrices, it also can be applied to find the transient of reducible matrices (if any). For this reason, we assign a maximum bound as termination condition. It is important to note that Algorithm 1 can also be used to compute the local transient and cyclicity for a vector: that is, when V has only one column. The algorithm starts by computing the cycle-time vector χ of the state matrix. If the entries of χ are not all the same then the transient for $\mathsf{cone}(V)$ does not exist. In line 11, we perform equality checking w.r.t. a scalar between $A^{\otimes it - m} \otimes V$ and $A^{\otimes it} \otimes V$.

By Theorem 2 and Proposition 4, one can classify an MPL system (2) into a category in Definition 6. As a result, determining the existence of global transient is a decidable problem. For *boundedly periodic* MPL systems, computing the global transient is also a decidable problem. This is because they ensure the existence of a finite transient, meaning that Algorithm 1 eventually terminates. However, Algorithm 1 is sound but does not necessarily terminate (in general) for *unboundedly periodic* MPL systems.

Algorithm 1. Computation of cyclicity and transient of A w.r.t. $\mathsf{cone}(V)$

1: **function** TRANSCONE(A, V, N)
2:     $\mathbf{M} \leftarrow$ EMPTYVECTOR()   ▷ empty vector used to store
3:     $\mathbf{M}$.push_back(V) $A^0 \otimes V, A^1 \otimes V, \ldots$
4:     $it \leftarrow 0$ ▷ number of iterations
5:     $\chi \leftarrow$ CYCLETIMEVECTOR(A)   ▷ computing cycle-time vector
6:     **if** elements of χ are all equal **then**
7:         **while** ($it \leq N$) **do**
8:             $\mathbf{M}$.push_back($A \otimes \mathbf{M}[it]$)
9:             $it \leftarrow it + 1$
10:            **for** $1 \leq m < it$ **do**
11:                **if** ($\mathbf{M}[it] = (\lambda \times m) \otimes \mathbf{M}[it - m]$) **then**
12:                    **return** $\langle it - m, m \rangle$
13:        **if** ($it > N$) **then**
14:            **print** "terminated after reaching maximum bound"
15:    **else**
16:        **print** "the transient does not exist"

Remark 1. The procedure in Algorithm 1 only employs matrix operations in max-plus algebra. It can be improved by computing the cyclicity of the matrix from the corresponding precedence graph. If the resulting cyclicity is c then the range in line 10 of Algorithm 1 can be taken between 1 and c. □

Example 2. Suppose we have a regular and reducible MPL system $\mathbf{x}(k + 1) = B \otimes \mathbf{x}(k)$, where

$$B = \begin{bmatrix} 2 & 8 & \varepsilon \\ 10 & 5 & \varepsilon \\ 3 & \varepsilon & a \end{bmatrix}, \tag{3}$$

and where $a \geq 8$. The corresponding eigenvalue for B is $\lambda = 9$ if $8 \leq a \leq 9$; $\lambda = a$ otherwise. Taking the power of the matrix, we have

$$B^{\otimes 2} = \begin{bmatrix} 18 & 13 & \varepsilon \\ 15 & 18 & \varepsilon \\ a+3 & 11 & 2a \end{bmatrix}, B^{\otimes 3} = \begin{bmatrix} 23 & 26 & \varepsilon \\ 28 & 23 & \varepsilon \\ b & a+11 & 3a \end{bmatrix}, B^{\otimes 4} = \begin{bmatrix} 36 & 31 & \varepsilon \\ 33 & 36 & \varepsilon \\ a+b & 2a+11 & 4a \end{bmatrix},$$

where $b = \max\{21, 2a + 3\}$. One can check that, for $a > 9$, the matrix does not admit an eigenvector over $\mathbb{R}^3$ (but it still has eigenvector over $\mathbb{R}_{\max}^3$). As a result, B is *never periodic*.

On the other hand, for $8 \leq a \leq 9$, the corresponding $E(B)$ is not empty. Thus, B is *periodic*. Furthermore, for $k \geq 2$, we have

$$[B^{\otimes k+2}](i, \cdot) = \begin{cases} 18 \otimes [B^{\otimes k}](\cdot, i), & \text{if } i \in \{1, 2\}, \\ 2a \otimes [B^{\otimes k}](\cdot, i), & \text{if } i = 3, \end{cases}$$

which shows that B is *boundedly periodic* with global transient $\mathsf{tr}(B) = 2$ if and only if $a = 9$. Thus, when $8 \leq a < 9$ B is *unboundedly periodic*. □

4   Computation of Transient of MPL Systems with SMT

This section describes a new procedure to compute the transient of MPL systems by means of Satisfiability Modulo Theories (SMT). We first mention some basic notions on SMT.

4.1   Background on SMT

Given a first-order formula ψ in a background theory T, the Satisfiability Modulo Theory (SMT) problem consists in deciding whether there exists a model (i.e. an assignment to the free variables in ψ) that satisfies ψ [5]. For example, consider the formula $(x \leq y) \wedge (x + 3 = z) \vee (z \geq y)$ within the theory of real numbers. The formula is satisfiable and a valid model is $\{x := 5, y := 6, z := 8\}$.

SMT solvers can support different theories. A widely used theory is Linear Real Arithmetic (LRA). A formula in LRA is an arbitrary Boolean combination, or universal ($\forall$) and existential ($\exists$) quantification, of atoms in the form $\sum_i a_i x_i \bowtie c$ where $\bowtie \in \{>, <, \geq, \leq, \neq, =\}$, every x_i is a real variable, and every a_i and c are rational constants. Difference logic (RDL) is the subset of LRA in which all atoms are restricted to the form $x_i - x_j \bowtie c$. Both theories are decidable [5, Section 26.2.2.2].

4.2   From Max-Plus Algebra to Difference Logic

Before providing the main contribution, we show that the inequalities in max-plus algebra can be expressed as a formula in difference logic. For the rest of this paper, $\sim$ is either $\geq$ or $>$. We write $\neg(a \sim b)$ if it is not the case that $a \sim b$.

Proposition 5. Given $a_1, \ldots, a_p, a, b \in \mathbb{R}_{\max}$, real-valued variables $x_1, \ldots, x_p$, and $1 \leq j \leq p$, we have

$$\bigoplus_{i=1}^{p}(x_i + a_i) \sim a \equiv \bigvee_{i=1}^{p}(x_i + a_i \sim a), \tag{4}$$

$$a \sim \bigoplus_{i=1}^{p}(x_i + a_i) \equiv \bigwedge_{i=1}^{p}(a \sim x_i + a_i), \tag{5}$$

$$\bigoplus_{i=1}^{p}(x_i + a_i) \sim x_j + b \equiv \begin{cases} \text{true,} & \text{if } (a_j \sim b), \tag{6} \\ \bigvee_{\substack{i=1 \\ i \neq j}}^{p}(x_i + a_i \sim x_j + b), & \text{otherwise,} \tag{7} \end{cases}$$

$$x_j + b \sim \bigoplus_{i=1}^{p}(x_i + a_i) \equiv \begin{cases} \bigwedge_{\substack{i=1 \\ i \neq j}}^{p}(x_j + b \sim x_i + a_i), & \text{if } (b \sim a_j), \tag{8} \\ \text{false,} & \text{otherwise.} \tag{9} \end{cases}$$

Proposition 6 (Reduced Formula). Given real valued variables $x_1, \ldots, x_p$ and $a_1, \ldots, a_p, b_1, \ldots, b_p \in \mathbb{R}_{\max}$, the inequality

$$F \equiv \bigoplus_{i=1}^{p}(x_i + a_i) \sim \bigoplus_{j=1}^{p}(x_j + b_j) \tag{10}$$

is equivalent to

$$F^* \equiv \bigoplus_{i \in S_1}(x_i + a_i) \sim \bigoplus_{j \in S_2}(x_j + b_j), \tag{11}$$

where $S_1 = \{1, \ldots, p\} \setminus \{1 \leq k \leq p \mid a_k = \varepsilon \text{ or } \neg(a_k \sim b_k)\}$ and $S_2 = \{1, \ldots, p\} \setminus \{1 \leq k \leq p \mid b_k = \varepsilon \text{ or } a_k \sim b_k\}$, respectively. □

Proposition 6 ensures that any inequality expression in max-plus algebra can be reduced to a simpler one in which no a variable appears on both sides i.e., $S_1 \cap S_2 = \emptyset$. However, S_1 and S_2 cannot be both empty if there exists at least one finite scalar in both sides of (10). We call (11) as a non-trivial reduced formula if both $S_1 \neq \emptyset$ and $S_2 \neq \emptyset$.

Proposition 7. Given a non-trivial reduced formula in (11), then

$$F^* \equiv \bigwedge_{j \in S_2} \left(\bigvee_{i \in S_1} (\mathbf{x}_i - \mathbf{x}_j \sim b_j - a_i) \right) \equiv \bigvee_{i \in S_1} \left(\bigwedge_{j \in S_2} (\mathbf{x}_i - \mathbf{x}_j \sim b_j - a_i) \right). \quad (12)$$

If $S_1 = \emptyset$ then $F^* \equiv \texttt{false}$. On the other hand, if $S_2 = \emptyset$ then $F^* \equiv \texttt{true}$. $\square$

Proposition 7 shows that any non-trivial formula of (11) can be expressed as a difference logic formula in disjunctive and conjunctive normal forms.

4.3   Procedure to Compute Transient of MPL Systems with SMT

We now will discuss the procedure to compute the transient of an MPL system via SMT-solving. The idea behind the SMT-based procedure is to transform the equality checking in line 11 of Algorithm 1 into a formula in difference logic. Notice that the quantity $\mathbf{M}[it]$ in Algorithm 1 corresponds to $A^{\otimes it} \otimes V$ next, and $\mathsf{cone}(V)$ can be expressed as matrix V. Thus, it can be equivalently written as

$$(A^{\otimes it} \otimes V) \otimes \mathbf{x} = (\lambda \times m) \otimes (A^{\otimes it-m} \otimes V) \otimes \mathbf{x}, \quad \forall \mathbf{x} \in \mathbb{R}^p, \quad (13)$$

where p is the number of columns of V. By denoting $R = A^{\otimes it} \otimes V$ and $S = (\lambda \times m) \otimes A^{\otimes it-m} \otimes V$, (13) can be expressed as

$$\bigwedge_{k=1}^{n} \left(\left(\bigoplus_{i=1}^{p} (\mathbf{x}_i + r_{ki}) \geq \bigoplus_{j=1}^{p} (\mathbf{x}_j + s_{kj}) \right) \wedge \left(\bigoplus_{i=1}^{p} (\mathbf{x}_i + s_{ki}) \geq \bigoplus_{j=1}^{p} (\mathbf{x}_j + r_{kj}) \right) \right), \quad (14)$$

where r_{ki} (resp. s_{ki}) is the element of R (resp. S) at row k and column i. For simplicity, we denote (14) as $\texttt{EqFunc}(R, S)$. By Proposition 7, each disjunct in (14) can be expressed as a formula in difference logic.

Algorithm 2 summarizes the SMT-based version of Algorithm 1. If the corresponding eigenspace of the matrix is not empty, we set the value for transient and cyclicity respectively to $k_0 = 0$ and $c = 1$ (the smallest possible for both). Then, we generate the corresponding difference logic formula F w.r.t. (13) in line 10. To check the validity of F, we use an SMT solver to check the unsatisfiability of the negation. If it is not satisfiable then the original formula is valid, and then we obtain the transient and cyclicity from the current value of k_0 and c.

On the other hand, if it is satisfiable then there exists a counterexample falsifying formula F. We express the counterexample from a satisfying assignment of $\neg F$ as a real-valued vector $w \in \mathbb{R}^p$ (line 15). Vector $v = V \otimes w$ corresponds to the counterexample: its transient is greater than k_0 or its cyclicity is greater than c. The resulting transient and cyclicity of v become the updated value for (k_0, c). This process is repeated until either the SMT solver reports "unsatisfiable" in line 12 or $k_0 + c$ exceeds the maximum bound N. (which corresponds to the termination condition of Algorithm 1).

Unlike Algorithm 1, which only works on max-plus cones, Algorithm 2 can be modified (into Algorithm 3) so that it can be applied on any set of initial conditions $X \subseteq \mathbb{R}^n$. Although (14) is can be translated exclusively to RDL, we can extend X as an LRA formula. In line 9 of Algorithm 3, we generate a formula F which corresponds to the equality checking between $A^{\otimes k_0}$ and $A^{\otimes k_0 + c}$. If $X \to F$ is valid then for all $\mathbf{x}(0) \in X$ we have $\mathsf{tr}(A, \mathbf{x}(0)) \leq k_0$ and $\mathsf{cyc}(A, \mathbf{x}(0)) \leq c$. Again, to check the validity of $X \to F$, we check the unsatisfiability of its negation.

Algorithm 2. Computation of transient and cyclicity of A w.r.t. $\mathsf{cone}(V)$ via SMT-solving

---

1: **function** TRANSCONESMT(A, V, N)
2:     $\chi \leftarrow$ CYCLETIMEVECTOR(A)
3:     **if** elements of χ are all equal **then**
4:         $n \leftarrow$ NRROWS(A)
5:         $p \leftarrow$ NRCOLS(V)
6:         **for** $i \in \{1 \cdots p\}$ **do**
7:             $x[i] \leftarrow$ MAKESMTREALVAR$(\ )$ ▷ symbolic variables
8:         $k_0 \leftarrow 0, c \leftarrow 1$
9:         **while** $((k_0 + c) \leq N)$ **do**
10:             $F \leftarrow$ EqFunc$(A^{\otimes k_0 + c} \otimes V, (\lambda \times c) \otimes A^{\otimes k_0} \otimes V)$
11:             $model \leftarrow$ GETSMTMODEL$(\neg F)$
12:             **if** $model = \bot$ **then**   ▷ formula is unsatisfiable
13:                 **return** $\langle k_0, c \rangle$
14:             **else**   ▷ formula is satisfiable
15:                 $w \leftarrow \langle model(x[1]), \cdots model(x[p]) \rangle$ ▷ vector in $\mathbb{R}^p$
16:                 $v \leftarrow V \otimes w$ ▷ vector in $\mathbb{R}^n$
17:                 $\langle k'_0, c' \rangle \leftarrow$ TRANSCONE$(A, A^{\otimes k_0} \otimes v)$ ▷ computed by Algorithm 1
18:                 $k_0 \leftarrow k_0 + k'_0$
19:                 $c \leftarrow$ LCM(c, c')
20:         **if** $((k_0 + c) > N)$ **then**
21:             **print** "terminated after reaching maximum bound"
22:     **else**
23:         **print** "the transient does not exist"

Algorithm 3. Computation of transient and cyclicity of A w.r.t. a set of initial conditions X via SMT-solving

---

1: **function** TRANSSMT(A, X, N)
2:     $\chi \leftarrow$ CYCLETIMEVECTOR(A)
3:     **if** elements of χ are all equal **then**
4:         $n \leftarrow$ ROW(A) ▷ number of rows of A
5:         **for** $i \in \{1 \cdots n\}$ **do**
6:             $x[i] \leftarrow$ MAKESMTREALVAR$( )$ ▷ symbolic variables
7:         $k_0 \leftarrow 0, c \leftarrow 1$
8:         **while** $(k_0 + c) \leq 1000$ **do**
9:             $F \leftarrow$ EqFunc$(A^{\otimes k_0 + c}, (\lambda \times c) \otimes A^{\otimes k_0})$
10:             $model \leftarrow$ GETSMTMODEL$(X \wedge \neg F)$
11:             **if** $model = \bot$ **then**   ▷ formula is unsatisfiable
12:                 **return** $\langle k_0, c \rangle$
13:             **else**   ▷ formula is satisfiable
14:                 $v \leftarrow \langle model(x[1]), \cdots model(x[N]) \rangle$
15:                 $\langle k_0', c' \rangle \leftarrow$ TRANSCONE$(A, A^{\otimes k_0} \otimes v)$
16:                 $k_0 \leftarrow k_0 + k_0'$
17:                 $c \leftarrow$ LCM(c, c')
18:         **if** $((k_0 + c) > N)$ **then**
19:             **print** "terminated after reaching maximum bound"
20:     **else**
21:         **print** "the transient does not exist"

4.4   A Synthesis Problem

In addition to computing the transient and cyclicity of $A \in \mathbb{R}_{\max}^{n \times n}$ w.r.t. a set of initial conditions, we show that by means of difference logic and SMT, one can synthesise sets of states corresponding to specific transient (and cylicity) defined as follows

$$\mathcal{S}_{p,q}(A) = \{x \in \mathbb{R}^n \mid \text{tr}(A, x) = p, \text{cyc}(A, x) = q\}, \tag{15}$$

$$\mathcal{S}_p(A) = \{x \in \mathbb{R}^n \mid \text{tr}(A, x) = p\}. \tag{16}$$

On the one hand, the computation of (16) has been discussed in [2, Section 4.2] by applying backward reachability analysis. On the other hand, to the best of the authors' knowledge, there is no approach to generate (15). The following proposition shows that both (15) and (16) can be computed symbolically by expressing them as difference logic formulae: the set (15) (resp. (16)) is not empty if and only if the corresponding formula (17) (resp. (18)) is satisfiable.

Proposition 8. Given $A \in \mathbb{R}_{\max}^{n \times n}$ with global cyclicity c and maximum eigenvalue λ, we have

$$\mathcal{S}_p(A) = \begin{cases} \text{EqFunc}(A^{\otimes p + c}, \lambda c \otimes A^{\otimes p}), & \text{if } p = 0, \\ \text{EqFunc}(A^{\otimes p + c}, \lambda c \otimes A^{\otimes p}) \wedge \\ \quad \neg \text{EqFunc}(A^{\otimes p - 1 + c}, \lambda c \otimes A^{\otimes p - 1}), & \text{if } p > 0, \end{cases} \tag{17}$$

and

$$
\mathcal{S}_{p,q}(A) = \begin{cases}
\begin{aligned}
& \mathsf{EqFunc}(A^{\otimes p+q}, \lambda q \otimes A^{\otimes p}) \wedge \\
& \quad \bigwedge_{d \in \mathtt{Div}(q) - \{q\}} \neg \mathsf{EqFunc}(A^{\otimes p+d}, \lambda d \otimes A^{\otimes p}),
\end{aligned} & \text{if } p = 0, \\[2em]
\begin{aligned}
& \mathsf{EqFunc}(A^{\otimes p+q}, \lambda q \otimes A^{\otimes p}) \wedge \neg \mathsf{EqFunc}(A^{\otimes p-1+q}, \lambda q \otimes A^{\otimes p-1}) \wedge \\
& \quad \bigwedge_{d \in \mathtt{Div}(q) - \{q\}} \neg \mathsf{EqFunc}(A^{\otimes p+d}, \lambda d \otimes A^{\otimes p}),
\end{aligned} & \text{if } p > 0,
\end{cases}
\tag{18}
$$

where $\mathtt{Div}(q)$ is a set of divisors of q. $\qquad\square$

As both (15) and (16) can be expressed as formulae in difference logic, the problem of determining the emptiness of both sets is decidable. By definition, for *never periodic* MPL system, $\mathcal{S}_{p,q} = \mathcal{S}_p = \emptyset$ for all p, q. Furthermore, for irreducible MPL systems the emptiness of (15) and (16) is related to the global transient and cyclicity of A.

Proposition 9. For an irreducible matrix $A \in \mathbb{R}^{n \times n}_{\max}$ with global transient k_0 and cyclicity c we have $\mathcal{S}_0(A) = E(A^{\otimes c})$ and $\mathcal{S}_{0,1}(A) = E(A)$. Furthermore,

i. $\mathcal{S}_p(A) \neq \emptyset$ iff $p \leq k_0$,
ii. If $p > k_0$ or q is not a divisor of c then $\mathcal{S}_{p,q}(A) = \emptyset$,
iii. If $\mathcal{S}_{p,q}(A)$ is empty then so is $\mathcal{S}_{p+1,q}(A)$. $\qquad\square$

Example 3. Let us recall the 3×3 MPL system in Example 2 with $a = 8$. From the precedence graph $\mathcal{G}(B)$, the global cyclicity is $c = 2$. Leaving details aside, for $p \geq 1$, we have

$$
\mathsf{EqFunc}(B^{p+2}, 18 \otimes B^{\otimes p}) \equiv \begin{cases}
(\mathbf{x}_1 - \mathbf{x}_3 \geq 6 - p) \vee (\mathbf{x}_2 - \mathbf{x}_3 \geq 8 - p), & \text{if } p \text{ is odd}, \\
(\mathbf{x}_1 - \mathbf{x}_3 \geq 7 - p) \vee (\mathbf{x}_2 - \mathbf{x}_3 \geq 7 - p), & \text{if } p \text{ is even}.
\end{cases}
$$

Thus, by Proposition 8, for $p \geq 2$ we have

$$
\mathcal{S}_p(B) = \begin{cases}
\{\mathbf{x} \in \mathbb{R}^3 | (6 - p \leq x_1 - x_3 < 8 - p) \wedge (x_2 - x_3 < 8 - p)\}, & \text{if } p \text{ is odd}, \\
\{\mathbf{x} \in \mathbb{R}^3 | (x_1 - x_3 < 7 - p) \wedge (7 - p \leq x_2 - x_3 < 9 - p)\}, & \text{if } p \text{ is even}.
\end{cases}
$$

An illustration of the above sets is depicted in Fig. 2. From an initial vector $\mathbf{x}(0) = [4 \ 2 \ 0]^\top \in \mathcal{S}_3(B)$ one can compute $\mathbf{x}(k)$ for $k = 1, \ldots, 5$ as follows:

$$
\begin{bmatrix} 10 \\ 14 \\ 8 \end{bmatrix}, \begin{bmatrix} 22 \\ 20 \\ 16 \end{bmatrix}, \begin{bmatrix} 28 \\ 32 \\ 25 \end{bmatrix}, \begin{bmatrix} 40 \\ 38 \\ 33 \end{bmatrix}, \begin{bmatrix} 46 \\ 50 \\ 43 \end{bmatrix}.
$$

Notice that, $\mathbf{x}(5) = 18 \otimes \mathbf{x}(3)$ which confirms that the local transient for $\mathbf{x}(0)$ is $\mathrm{tr}(B, \mathbf{x}(0)) = 3$. It is straightforward to conclude that the global transient for B does not exist. $\qquad\square$

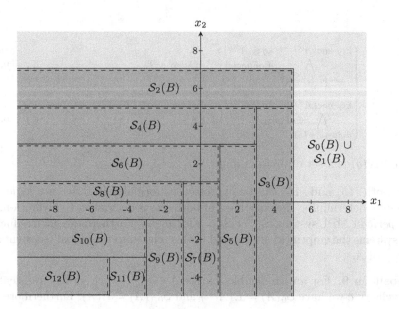

Fig. 2. Plots of the synthesized sets projected on the plane $x_3 = 0$. The solid and dashed lines represent $\geq$ and $>$, respectively.

5   Computational Benchmarks

We compare the performance of Algorithms 1 and 3, to compute the transient of MPL systems. The experiments for both procedures are implemented in Python. For the SMT solver, we use Yices 2.2 [11]. The computational benchmark has been implemented on an Intel® Xeon® CPU E5-1660 v3, 16 cores, 3.0 GHz each, and 16 GB of RAM. For the experiments, we generate 1000 irreducible matrices of dimension n, with m finite elements in each row, where the values of the finite elements are rational numbers $\frac{p}{q}$ with $1 \leq p \leq 100$ and $1 \leq q \leq 5$. The locations of the finite elements are chosen randomly. We focus on irreducible matrices to ensure the termination of the algorithms. Algorithm 1 is initialised by setting V to be a max-plus identity matrix, while for Algorithm 3 the set of initial conditions is expressed as $X \equiv \texttt{true}$. For all experiments, we choose $N = 10000$ as the maximum bound. The benchmarks are stored at https://es-static.fbk.eu/people/amicheli/resources/formats20/, where we have chosen $n \in \{4, 6, 8, 10, 20, 30, 40\}$ and three different values of m for each n.

Figure 3(a)–(c) illustrate the experiments for $n = 40$ and $m \in \{20, 30, 40\}$ (the experiments for other pairs (n, m) are presented in [1]). They show the plots of the running times of Algorithm 1 (dashed lines) and of Algorithm 3 (solid lines) against the resulting transient k_0 and cyclicity c - the scattered plots (in black) correspond to the resulting $k_0 + c$. If there are several experiments with the same value of $k_0 + c$ then we display the average running time among those experiments. It is evident that most of the experiments result in small $k_0 + c$.

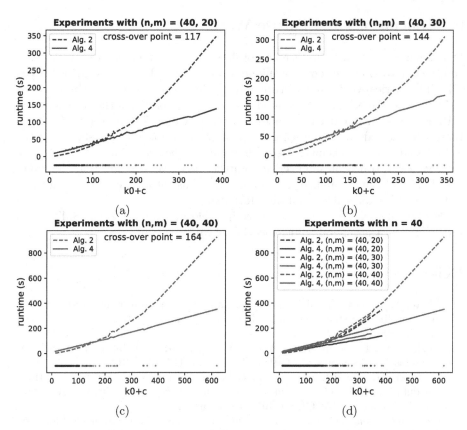

Fig. 3. The plots of running time of Algorithms 1 and 3 from 1000 experiments with $n = 40$ and $m \in \{20, 30, 40\}$. A "cross-over point" is the smallest value of $k_0 + c$ when Algorithm 3 is faster.

With regards to the running time, the matrix-multiplication algorithm is faster when the values of $k_0 + c$ are quite small. On the other hand, the larger the value of $k_0 + c$, the better the performance of the SMT-based algorithm is. We argue that this is because in Algorithm 3 there may be a large increment from the current guess of transient and cyclicity to the new ones. Whereas in Algorithm 1, the next candidate of transient and cyclicity is increased by one at each iteration.

As depicted in Fig. 3(d), the number of finite elements m clearly affects the running time of the algorithms. We recall that the running time of Algorithm 3 depends on the satisfaction checking of a difference logic formula in line 11. The more are the finite elements, the more likely the formula is complex, and therefore the slower is the associated running time. Interestingly, based on the outcomes of the benchmarks which are presented in [1], the finite elements also affect the cross-over points, which tend to increase gradually as the number of finite elements grows larger.

6 Conclusions and Future Work

In this paper, we have introduced a novel, SMT-based approach to compute the transient of MPL systems: our technique encodes the problem as a sequence of satisfiability queries over formulae in difference logic, which can be solved by standard SMT solvers. We have also presented a procedure to partition the state-space of MPL systems w.r.t. a given transient and cyclicity pair. The procedure has been thoroughly tested on computational benchmarks and the results show how the SMT-based algorithm is much faster that state-of-the-art techniques to compute large values of transient and cyclicity. Furthermore, we highlight that the SMT-based method can be applied to compute the transient for any initial condition, as long as it is expressible as an LRA formula.

For future research, we are interested in exploring and developing SMT-based procedures for the general model checking of MPL systems.

References

1. Abate, A., Cimatti, A., Micheli, A., Mufid, M.S.: Computation of the transient in max-plus linear systems via SMT-solving. arXiv e-prints, July 2020. https://arxiv.org/abs/2007.00505v2
2. Adzkiya, D., De Schutter, B., Abate, A.: Backward reachability of autonomous max-plus-linear systems. IFAC Proc. Vol. **47**(2), 117–122 (2014)
3. Alirezaei, M., van den Boom, T.J., Babuska, R.: Max-plus algebra for optimal scheduling of multiple sheets in a printer. In: Proceedings of the 31st American Control Conference (ACC), pp. 1973–1978, June 2012
4. Baccelli, F., Cohen, G., Olsder, G.J., Quadrat, J.P.: Synchronization and Linearity: An Algebra for Discrete Event Systems. Wiley, New York (1992)
5. Barrett, C.W., Sebastiani, R., Seshia, S.A., Tinelli, C.: Satisfiability modulo theories. In: Biere, A., Heule, M., van Maaren, H., Walsh, T. (eds.) Handbook of Satisfiability, Frontiers in Artificial Intelligence and Applications, vol. 185, pp. 825–885. IOS Press (2009). https://doi.org/10.3233/978-1-58603-929-5-825
6. Brackley, C.A., Broomhead, D.S., Romano, M.C., Thiel, M.: A max-plus model of ribosome dynamics during mRNA translation. J. Theor. Biol. **303**, 128–140 (2012)
7. Butkovič, P., Schneider, H., et al.: Generators, extremals and bases of max cones. Linear Algebra Appl. **421**(2–3), 394–406 (2007)
8. Charron-Bost, B., Függer, M., Nowak, T.: New transience bounds for max-plus linear systems. Discrete Appl. Math. **219**, 83–99 (2017)
9. Clarke, E., Kroening, D., Ouaknine, J., Strichman, O.: Completeness and complexity of bounded model checking. In: Steffen, B., Levi, G. (eds.) VMCAI 2004. LNCS, vol. 2937, pp. 85–96. Springer, Heidelberg (2004). https://doi.org/10.1007/978-3-540-24622-0_9
10. Comet, J.P.: Application of max-plus algebra to biological sequence comparisons. Theoret. Comput. Sci. **293**(1), 189–217 (2003)
11. Dutertre, B.: Yices 2.2. In: Biere, A., Bloem, R. (eds.) CAV 2014. LNCS, vol. 8559, pp. 737–744. Springer, Cham (2014). https://doi.org/10.1007/978-3-319-08867-9_49
12. Fahim, K., Subiono, S., van der Woude, J.: On a generalization of power algorithms over max-plus algebra. Discrete Event Dyn. Syst. **27**(1), 181–203 (2017)

13. Gaubert, S., Katz, R.D.: Minimal half-spaces and external representation of tropical polyhedra. J. Algebraic Comb. **33**(3), 325–348 (2011)
14. Heidergott, B., Olsder, G.J., Van der Woude, J.: Max Plus at Work: Modeling and Analysis of Synchronized Systems: A Course on Max-Plus Algebra and Its Applications. Princeton University Press, Princeton (2014)
15. Imaev, A., Judd, R.P.: Hierarchial modeling of manufacturing systems using max-plus algebra. In: Proceedings of the American Control Conference 2008, pp. 471–476 (2008)
16. Merlet, G., Nowak, T., Sergeev, S.: Weak CSR expansions and transience bounds in max-plus algebra. Linear Algebra Appl. **461**, 163–199 (2014)
17. Mufid, M.S., Adzkiya, D., Abate, A.: Symbolic reachability analysis of high dimensional max-plus linear systems. arXiv e-prints, July 2020. https://arxiv.org/abs/2007.04510, accepted at the International Workshop on Discrete Event Systems (WODES)
18. Syifaul Mufid, M., Adzkiya, D., Abate, A.: Bounded model checking of max-plus linear systems via predicate Abstractions. In: André, É., Stoelinga, M. (eds.) FORMATS 2019. LNCS, vol. 11750, pp. 142–159. Springer, Cham (2019). https://doi.org/10.1007/978-3-030-29662-9_9
19. Nowak, T., Charron-Bost, B.: An overview of transience bounds in max-plus algebra. Trop. Idempot. Math. Appl. **616**, 277–289 (2014)
20. Soto Y Koelemeijer, G.: On the behaviour of classes of min-max-plus systems. Ph.D. thesis, Delft University of Technology (2003)

Clairvoyant Monitoring for Signal Temporal Logic

Xin Qin$^{(\boxtimes)}$ and Jyotirmoy V. Deshmukh$^{(\boxtimes)}$

University of Southern California, Los Angeles, USA
{xinqin,jyotirmoy.deshmukh}@usc.edu

Abstract. In this paper, we consider the problem of monitoring temporal patterns expressed in Signal Temporal Logic (STL) over time-series data in a *clairvoyant* fashion. Existing offline or online monitoring algorithms can only compute the satisfaction of a given STL formula on the time-series data that is available. We use off-the-shelf statistical time-series analysis techniques to fit available data to a model and use this model to forecast future signal values. We derive the joint probability distribution of predicted signal values and use this to compute the satisfaction probability of a given signal pattern over the prediction horizon. There are numerous potential applications of such prescient detection of temporal patterns. We demonstrate practicality of our approach on case studies in automated insulin delivery, unmanned aerial vehicles, and household power consumption data.

1   Introduction

Safety-critical cyber-physical systems (CPS) such as autonomous ground vehicles, unmanned aerial vehicles and medical devices often operate in highly uncertain and noisy environments. It is often impossible to anticipate all possible exogenous inputs to such systems at design-time; and most designers typically test their applications in only a finite number of scenarios. An alternative approach is to perform runtime monitoring to ensure that such systems do not have catastrophic failures of safety. A key aspect of runtime monitoring is the ability to raise alarms when the violation of a safety property is detected.

There has been considerable amount of recent work on the use of real-time temporal logics such as Signal Temporal Logic (STL) to specify correctness properties of safety-critical CPS applications [1,4,5,15,16,18,19,22]. Essentially, STL allows specification of properties of real-valued signals defined over dense time. A basic building block of an STL formula is a signal predicate (i.e. some condition over signal values for a given time), and general STL formulas can be constructed by combining signal predicates using Boolean ($\land, \lor, \neg$) or temporal (such as always, eventually, etc.) operators. In addition to Boolean satisfaction of a formula φ by a signal trace $x(t)$, *quantitative semantics* for STL allow us to define a *robust satisfaction value* or *robustness* which can be viewed as a signed distance between the signal $x(t)$ and the set of signals satisfying (or violating) φ, where a positive (resp. negative) sign indicates that φ is satisfied (resp. violated).

© Springer Nature Switzerland AG 2020
N. Bertrand and N. Jansen (Eds.): FORMATS 2020, LNCS 12288, pp. 178–195, 2020.
https://doi.org/10.1007/978-3-030-57628-8_11

Existing algorithms for monitoring STL specifications are either *offline* or *online*, and either compute the Boolean satisfaction or the robustness value. Offline algorithms assume that the entire signal trace is available, while online algorithms can estimate satisfaction or violation when only a prefix of a given signal is available. Online algorithms potentially provide early detection of safety violations of the system; however, by their nature, online algorithms are limited in identifying violations "as they happen." In this paper, we propose a new class of algorithms for *clairvoyant monitoring* that go beyond existing online algorithms by predicting future signal values and give probabilistic bounds on the satisfaction or violation of the STL formula in the future. Our notion of clairvoyance is derived from literature on statistical techniques for forecasting signals. In this paper, we focus on *signal patterns* specified by STL formulas, i.e., instead of the traditional use of STL to express formulas that are satisfied or violated true over an entire trace, we focus on bounded horizon STL formulas that are evaluated over the given prediction horizon[1].

To understand the motivation for clairvoyant monitoring using patterns specified in STL, consider a weather forecasting system that decides the advent of winter by checking if the forecasted temperature is lower than a certain threshold for a certain number of days. A single day of forecasted low temperature can easily be an outlier, and hence we want to estimate the probability of a certain event repeating for a number of days. Such a specification can be easily expressed in STL: $\mathbf{F}_{[0,10]}\mathbf{G}_{[0,5]}(\theta < 40)$. This specification says that in the next 10 days, there is some 5 day period where the temperature is consistently lower than 40 °F.

Our clairvoyant monitoring framework consists of three main components: (1) a *predictor* that uses past values of a signal to produce n predictions of the signal value at future time-points, (2) an algorithm to *enumerate possible scenarios* in which the given STL formula may be satisfied, and, (3) a *probability estimator*, that, given a target robustness value of the STL specification, computes the probability of exceeding that value.

We demonstrate clairvoyant monitoring on three applications: (1) monitoring hypo- and hyper-glycemia conditions in an automated insulin delivery system model, (2) monitoring safety of an unmanned aerial vehicle, and (3) monitoring power consumption.

The main technical contributions of our paper are:

1. For a given STL formula, a technique to automatically enumerate each distinct conjunction of signal predicates that lead to formula satisfaction.
2. We use statistical time-series analysis techniques to forecast future signal values, and we derive the joint probability distribution across the predicted time-points. We assume that the data can be modeled as a realization of an ARMA or ARIMA process. In case these models are not a good fit, the methods in this paper are not applicable.

---

[1] We can easily extend clairvoyant monitoring of unbounded horizon STL formulas over entire traces by considering the notion of nominal robustness [10]. This would also require us to track the robustness over the signal prefix.

3. We use basic laws of probability to compute the probability of a signal satisfying or violating a given STL formula φ utilizing the above two results. We can also compute the probability of the robust satisfaction value of the predicted signal (w.r.t. φ) exceeding or falling below a given threshold.

1.1 Illustrative Example

We use scenario depicted in Fig. 1 to illustrate the clairvoyant monitoring technique presented in this paper.

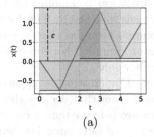 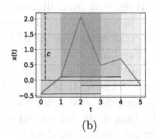

     (a)   (b)

Fig. 1. A signal behavior satisfies an STL pattern – expressed as a disjunction over conjunctions of signal predicates – as long as there exists one satisfying disjunct. Figure (1a)(1b) shows two different possible scenarios that the signal in future satisfies STL formula φ_1 in Eq. (1.1). Each green block indicates one satisfying conjunction of signal predicates, where four consecutive time steps all have signal values greater than zero. (Color figure online)

Suppose we are observing a series of data generated by a system and at time t, we want to know if the formula φ_1 in Eq. (1.1) is true over a prediction horizon of length 6.

$$\varphi_1 \equiv \mathbf{F}_{[0,2]}\mathbf{G}_{[0,3]}(x(t) \geq 0) \tag{1.1}$$

Figure 1 shows a subset of possible predicate conjunctions that make the inner formula $\mathbf{G}$ true, and in this case φ_1 also. If we know the joint probability distribution of signal values within the prediction horizon, we can use marginal distributions and inclusion-exclusion principle to calculate the probability of the STL formula to be satisfied.

In order to predict future signal values and also to compute joint probability distribution over these predictions, we rely on statistical time-series models such as auto-regressive and moving-average models.

2   Background on Signal Temporal Logic

Definition 2.1 (Univariate Signal, Time Horizon). *A time domain* $\mathbb{T}$ *is a finite set of uniform time instants* $\{t_0, t_1, \ldots, t_N\}$ *where* $t_0 = 0$, *and* $t_i \in \mathbf{R}^{\geq 0}$, *and* $t_{i+1} - t_i = \Delta$, *for some* $\Delta \in \mathbf{R}^{>0}$. *Let* $\mathcal{D}$ *be a bounded subset of* $\mathbf{R}$. *A signal* *x (also called a* trace *or* time-series *is a function*[2] *from* $\mathbb{T}$ *to* $\mathcal{D}$*. The set* $\mathcal{D}$ *is also called the* value domain*. The quantity* horizon $= \max(\mathbb{T})$ *is known as the time horizon of the signal.*

Signal Temporal Logic (STL). STL is a real-time logic, typically interpreted over a dense-time domain for signals that take values in a continuous metric space (such as $\mathbf{R}^m$). The basic primitive in STL is a *signal predicate* μ that is a formula of the form $f(x(t)) > 0$, where $x(t)$ is the value of the signal x at time t, and f is a function from the signal domain $\mathcal{D}$ to $\mathbf{R}$. STL formulas are then defined recursively using Boolean combinations of subformulas, or by applying an interval-restricted temporal operator to a subformula. The syntax of STL is formally defined as follows:

$$\varphi ::= \mu \mid \neg\varphi \mid \varphi \wedge \varphi \mid \mathbf{G}_I\varphi \mid \mathbf{F}_I\varphi \mid \varphi\mathbf{U}_I\varphi \mid \varphi\mathbf{R}_I\varphi \tag{2.1}$$

Here, I is an interval over $\mathbf{R}^{\geq 0}$. The precise Boolean semantics of STL can be defined in recursive fashion (we omit the formal semantics for brevity). The semantics of Boolean combinations of subformulas define the obvious meaning. A temporal subformula, for example, $\varphi\mathbf{U}_{[a,b]}\psi$ holds at time t if there exists a time t' in $[t+a, t+b]$ where ψ is satisfied, and for all times t'' in $[t, t')$, φ must be satisfied. For some interval I, the formula $\mathbf{F}_I\varphi$ is an abbreviation for $true\mathbf{U}_I\varphi$, and $\mathbf{G}_I\varphi$ is equivalent to $\neg\mathbf{F}_I\neg\varphi$. Next, we introduce the notion of quantitative semantics for STL:

The quantitative semantics for STL defines the notion of a degree to which a given signal satisfies an STL formula φ. This is technically done by defining a function ρ that maps the signal and φ to a real value at each time t. This is defined recursively on the formula structure of STL as follows:

Definition 2.2 (Robust Satisfaction Value or Robustness Value)

$$
\begin{aligned}
\rho(f(x) > c, x, t) &= f(x(t)) - c \\
\rho(\neg\varphi, x, t) &= -\rho(\varphi, x, t) \\
\rho(\varphi_1 \wedge \varphi_2, x, t) &= \min(\rho(\varphi_1, x, t), \rho(\varphi_2, x, t)) \\
\rho(\mathbf{G}_I\varphi, x, t) &= \inf_{t' \in t \oplus I} \rho(\varphi, x, t') \\
\rho(\mathbf{F}_I\varphi, x, t) &= \sup_{t' \in t \oplus I} \rho(\varphi, x, t') \\
\rho(\varphi_1\mathbf{U}_I\varphi_2, x, t) &= \sup_{t' \in t \oplus I} \left(\min\left(\rho(\varphi_2, x, t'), \inf_{t'' \in [t,t')} \rho(\varphi_1, x, t'') \right) \right) \\
\rho(\varphi_1\mathbf{R}_I\varphi_2, x, t'') &= \inf_{t' \in t \oplus I} \left(\max\left(\rho(\varphi_2, x, t'), \sup_{t'' \in [t,t']} \rho(\varphi_1, x, t'') \right) \right)
\end{aligned}
\tag{2.2}
$$

---

[2] When signals are evaluated w.r.t. Signal Temporal Logic formulas, we assume that the signal is defined at each time point in the interval $[0, t_N]$. We can do this using piecewise constant interpolation, i.e. $\forall i \in [0, N-1] : (t_i \leq t < t_{i+1}) \implies x(t) = x(t_i)$.

The robustness of a signal x w.r.t. a formula φ is then defined as $\rho(\varphi, x, 0)$ by convention. Note that if the robustness value is positive, the signal satisfies the STL formula, and if it is negative, it violates the STL formula. The convention is to treat the robustness value of 0 as the signal satisfying the formula.

We remark that in this paper, we focus on *signal patterns* expressed using STL. A signal pattern is essentially a bounded horizon STL formula, i.e. the scope of any temporal operator is upper bounded by some (small) finite time constant. A signal pattern is evaluated in the future of a given time t, and the robustness of signal pattern φ at time t is simply $\rho(\varphi, x, t)$. Examples of signal patterns include: $\mathbf{F}_{[0,3]}(x < 0)$, $\mathbf{F}_{[0,2]}\mathbf{G}_{[0,3]}(x > 0)$, $\mathbf{F}_{[0,1]}(x > 0 \wedge \mathbf{F}_{[0,1]}(x < -1 \wedge \mathbf{F}_{[0,1]}(x > 0)))$.

3 Background on Signal Forecasting

In this section, we give basic background on stochastic processes, and some key results that help us derive some guarantees on monitoring STL formulas in a predictive fashion in Sect. 4. Most of the definitions in this section have been adapted from the following reference: [8].

Definition 3.1 (Probability Space, Random Variables). *A probability space is a triple $(\Omega, \mathcal{F}, \mathcal{P})$, where Ω is a finite or infinite set describing possible outcomes, $\mathcal{F}$ is the σ-algebra over Ω (i.e. a collection of subsets of Ω including the empty set, that is closed under complement, countable unions and intersections), and $\mathcal{P}$ is a probability measure. Given a measurable state-space E, a random variable x is measurable function $x : \Omega \to E$.*

Definition 3.2 (Stochastic Process, Realizations, and Purely Random Process). *A stochastic process x is a finite or infinite collection of random variables ordered in (discrete or continuous) time. We denote the random variable at time t by $x(t)$ if time is continuous, and by x_t if time is discrete. A realization of a stochastic process is a signal that assigns concrete values from the signal range to each of the random variables $x(t)$. A discrete-time process consisting of a sequence of random variables z_t that are mutually independent and identically distributed is called a purely random process.*

Example 1 (Random Walk). Suppose z_t is a discrete, purely random process with mean μ and variance σ_z^2. A process x_t is said to be a random walk if $x_t = x_{t-1} + z_t$

Definition 3.3 (Stationary Processes). *A stochastic process x is called strictly stationary if the joint distribution of $x(t_1), \ldots, x(t_n)$ is the same as the joint distribution of $x(t_1+h), \ldots, x(t_n+h)$, for all $t_1, \ldots, t_n, h$. A stochastic process is called weakly stationary if its expected value is constant, and its covariance function only depends on the lag, formally,*

$$E[x(t)] = \mu \qquad Cov(x(t), x(t+h)) = \gamma(h) \tag{3.1}$$

Definition 3.4 (Autocovariance Function and Autocorrelation Function). *Let x_t be a stationary time series. The autocovariance function (ACVF) denoted $\gamma(h)$ is defined in Eq. (3.2) and autocorrelation function (ACF) $\rho(h)$ is defined as $\frac{\gamma(h)}{\gamma(0)}$.*

$$\gamma(h) = E[x(t) - \mu][(x(t+h) - \mu] = Cov[x(t), x(t+h)] \tag{3.2}$$

3.1 Linear Process and ARMA (ARIMA) Process

We first define the notion of a linear process.

Definition 3.5 (Linear Process). *A stochastic process x is called a linear process if it can be represented as: $x_t = \sum_{j=-\infty}^{\infty} \psi_j z_{t-j}$, where for all t, $\{z_t\} \sim \mathcal{N}(0, \sigma_z^2)$ and ψ_j is a constant series with $\sum_{j=-\infty}^{\infty} |\psi_j| < \infty$.*

Linear processes include all of the autoregressive (AR) processes, moving-average processes (MA), AR with MA (ARMA) processes and AR with integrated moving-average (ARIMA) models. Linear process models provide basic properties for studying ARMA, ARIMA, SARIMA and any other linear models. In what follows, it is convenient to define a new operator called the backward operator B, essentially, $Bx(t) = x(t+1)$, $B^h x(t) = x(t+h)$, etc. Using this operator, we can define an AR process with moving average.

Definition 3.6 (ARMA). *An ARMA process represents a combination of an autoregressive process (a process that can be represented as $\phi(B)x_t$), and a moving average process (a process that can be represented as $\theta(B)z_t$). Here, $\phi(B)$ and $\theta(B)$ are polynomials in the operator B, i.e. $\phi(B) = 1 - \sum_{i=1}^{p} \phi_i B^i$, and $\theta(B) = 1 + \sum_{j=1}^{q} \theta_j B^j$. An ARMA process thus has the following form:*

$$\phi(B)x_t = \theta(B)z_t \tag{3.3}$$

ARMA models are one of the most popular models used for forecasting values of a time-series. ARMA models are used for time-series data that can be viewed as a realization of a stationary stochastic process. However, ARMA models may not be adequate when the underlying process is not stationary, i.e. has trends. In such a case, an ARIMA (AR with integrated moving average) process model can be used.

Definition 3.7 (ARIMA). *An ARIMA model can be described by Eq. (3.4).*

$$\phi(B)(1 - B)^d x_t = \theta(B)z_t \tag{3.4}$$

Here, when $d = 1$, an ARIMA model is suitable to model linear trends in the data, and for higher values of d, the model can be used to handle higher order trends (quadratic, cubic, etc.).

3.2 Forecasting Procedure

Given a signal-prefix up to time t_n, a forecasting procedure predict h future values of the signal, i.e. $x(t_{n+1}), \ldots, x(t_{n+h})$. Here, h is called the *prediction horizon*. Forecasting signal values involves several steps. The first step is to assume that the signal is the realization of a particular stochastic process, and then estimate the parameters of the stochastic process model from the signal values. This usually involves estimating the autocovariance and autocorrelation of the signal, and then using these to do *model fitting*. Model fitting attempts to identify the parameters of the chosen model (say ARMA), by solving certain optimization problems. A popular technique to do model fitting is based on Yule Walker equations [8].

After fitting the model, we have to forecast a time series. Since either ARMA or ARIMA model are all linear process, the *best linear predictor* is the optimal predictor for forecasting future values for the signal [8]. We now define the best linear predictor, and explain how it is computed.

Definition 3.8 (Best linear predictor). *The best linear predictor based on observation $\{x_1, x_2, \ldots, x_n\}$ of an ARMA or ARIMA process $\{x_t\}$ is given by Eq. (3.5). Let $\overline{x_t}$ denote the predicted value of x_t.*

$$\overline{x_{n+h}} = a_0^h + \sum_{i=1}^n a_i^h x_{n+1-i}$$
$$where, \quad \arg\min_{a_0^h, a_1^h, \ldots, a_n^h} \quad E[\overline{x_{n+h}} - x_{n+h}]^2. \tag{3.5}$$

The optimized a_i is determined by two variables: since $\{x_t\}$ is a stationary process, denoting $\gamma_x(h) = Cov(x_{t+h}, x_t)$.

$$\Gamma_n = [Cov(x_{n-i+1}, x_{n-j+1})]_{i,j=1}^n = [\gamma_x(|i-j|)]_{i,j=1}^n \tag{3.6}$$

$$\gamma_n(h) = [\gamma_x(h+i-1)]_{i=1}^n \tag{3.7}$$

With these two variables we can define a_i as $(a_1, a_2, \ldots, a_n)^\top = \Gamma_n^{-1} \gamma_n(h)$ and $a_0 = \mu_x(1 - \sum_{i=1}^n a_i)$.

Now we see the prediction value for a single time step, in Sect. 4.1 we introduce how to derive a joint distribution for multiple time steps.

4 Clairvoyant Monitoring Procedure

To perform clairvoyant monitoring, we essentially need to forecast signal values using an appropriate stochastic process model, and more importantly compute the probability that a signal pattern is satisfied by the predicted signal values. To do the latter, we need to compute the joint distribution of the predicted values for the given stochastic process.

4.1   Deriving the Joint Distribution of Predictions

We first consider this computation for ARMA processes. By Definition 3.6 and Eq. (3.5), we can see the signal prediction values $\overline{x_{n+h}}$ produced by the best linear predictor are linear combinations of x_t and $\mathbf{a}$. We show that we can construct the joint distribution of multiple prediction values $\{\overline{x_{n+1}}, \ldots, \overline{x_{n+h}}\}$ by a sequence of linear transformations. First, we recall a standard result on linear combinations of normally distributed variables in Lemma 1.

Lemma 1. *If a random variable* $X \sim \mathcal{N}(\mu_x, \Sigma_x)$, *and* $Y = CX + D$ *is some linear transformation of* X *using matrices* C *and* D, *then* $Y \sim \mathcal{N}(C\mu_x + D, C\Sigma_x C^\top)$.

Theorem 1. *The joint distribution of* h *predicted values using the best linear predictor for an ARMA process* x *has a multivariate normal distribution* $\mathcal{N}(\mathbf{a}, \Sigma)$, *where* $\mathbf{a}$ *is vector* $[a_0^1, \ldots, a_0^h]^\top$, Σ *is given by the following equation:*

$$\Sigma = A\Phi^+ \Theta \, \Sigma_z \, \Theta^\top (\Phi^+)^\top A^\top. \tag{4.1}$$

Here, A, Φ *and* Θ *are matrices of coefficients used in the ARMA model Definition 3.6 and the best linear predictor (3.5). (Precise definitions of each follow in the proof).*

Proof. After using a standard technique to fit an ARMA model with order p and q [8], we obtain the set of equations in (4.2). This is simply the repeated application of Definition 3.6.

$$x_{p+1} + \phi_1 x_p + \phi_2 x_{p-1} + \cdots + \phi_{1p} x_1 = z_{p+1} + \theta_1 z_p + \theta_2 z_{p-1} + \cdots + \theta_q z_{1+p-q}$$
$$x_{p+2} + \phi_1 x_{p+1} + \phi_2 x_p + \cdots + \phi_p x_2 = z_{p+2} + \theta_1 z_{p+1} + \theta_2 z_p + \cdots + \theta_q z_{2+p-q}$$
$$\vdots$$
$$x_n + \phi_1 x_{n-1} + \phi_2 x_{n-2} + \cdots + \phi_p x_{n-p} = z_n + \theta_1 z_{n-1} + \theta_2 z_{n-2} + \cdots + \theta_q z_{n-q}$$
$$\tag{4.2}$$

We can write (4.2) as a matrix with appropriate zero padding to get:

$$\Phi \begin{pmatrix} x_1 \\ x_2 \\ \vdots \\ x_n \end{pmatrix} = \Theta \begin{pmatrix} z_{1+p-q} \\ z_{2+p-q} \\ \vdots \\ z_n \end{pmatrix} \tag{4.3}$$

Here, Θ is $(n-p) \times (n-p+q)$ matrix, and Φ is a $(n-p) \times n$ matrix. For a matrix M, let M^+ denote its Moore-Penrose inverse or its pseduo-inverse. We can multiply both sides of Eq. (4.3) Φ^+ to get Eq. (4.4).

$$\begin{pmatrix} x_1 \\ x_2 \\ \vdots \\ x_n \end{pmatrix} = \Phi^+ \Theta \begin{pmatrix} z_{1+p-q} \\ z_{2+p-q} \\ \vdots \\ z_n \end{pmatrix} \tag{4.4}$$

Recall the definition of best linear predictor in Definition 3.5:

$$\overline{x}_{n+h} = a_0^h + \sum_{i=1}^{n} a_i^h x_{n-i+1} \tag{4.5}$$

Writing this equation for each of the prediction steps from $n+1$ to $n+h$, we get Eq. (4.6).

$$\begin{cases} \overline{x}_{n+1} = a_n^1 x_1 + a_{n-1}^1 x_2 + \cdots + a_1^1 x_n + a_0^1 \\ \overline{x}_{n+2} = a_n^2 x_1 + a_{n-1}^2 x_2 + \cdots + a_1^2 x_n + a_0^2 \\ \quad \vdots \\ \overline{x}_{n+h} = a_n^h x_1 + a_{n-1}^h x_2 + \cdots + a_1^h x_n + a_0^h \end{cases} \tag{4.6}$$

This can be further written compactly as follows:

$$\begin{pmatrix} \overline{x}_{n+1} \\ \overline{x}_{n+2} \\ \vdots \\ \overline{x}_{n+h} \end{pmatrix} = A \begin{pmatrix} x_1 \\ x_2 \\ \vdots \\ x_n \end{pmatrix} + \begin{pmatrix} a_0^1 \\ a_0^2 \\ \vdots \\ a_0^h \end{pmatrix}, \tag{4.7}$$

where A denotes the following coefficient matrix.

$$A = \begin{pmatrix} a_n^1 & a_{n-1}^1 & \cdots & a_1^1 \\ a_n^2 & a_{n-1}^2 & \cdots & a_1^2 \\ \vdots & \vdots & \ddots & \vdots \\ a_n^h & a_{n-1}^h & \cdots & a_1^h \end{pmatrix}. \tag{4.8}$$

Finally, substituting vector $[x_1, x_2, \ldots, x_n]^\top$ from Eq. (4.4), we achieved in rewriting the vector of predicted values into a linear transformation of white noise:

$$\begin{pmatrix} \overline{x}_{n+1} \\ \overline{x}_{n+2} \\ \vdots \\ \overline{x}_{n+h} \end{pmatrix} = A\varPhi^+\varTheta \begin{pmatrix} z_{1+p-q} \\ z_{2+p-q} \\ \vdots \\ z_n \end{pmatrix} + \begin{pmatrix} a_0^1 \\ a_0^2 \\ \vdots \\ a_0^h \end{pmatrix} \tag{4.9}$$

As white noise is normally distributed, from Lemma 1 we have the joint probability distribution of predictions of h steps for an ARMA process. ∎

Theorem 2. *The normalized prediction value in an ARIMA process x_h has a multivariate normal distribution $\mathcal{N}(0, \Sigma)$, where Σ is given by the following equation:*

$$\Sigma = T_2 T_1 \Sigma_z T_1^\top T_2^\top. \tag{4.10}$$

Here, T_2, T_1 are matrices representing terms appearing in the best linear predictor expression (3.5) across h predictions and the ARIMA model Definition (3.4).

Proof. (Sketch) We omit the proof due to lack of space, but it follows a very similar recipe as the proof for the ARMA model. See [21] for details.

4.2 Enumerating Distinct Conjunctions of Signal Predicates

This is essentially a combinatorial problem. First, we assume that the formula is in Negation Normal Form (NNF), i.e. all negations are pushed to the signal predicates. This can always be done, cf. [14]. Further, note that we can replace negated atomic predicates by new atomic predicates, e.g. $\neg(x > 0) \equiv (x \leq 0)$. The basic idea of the algorithm is to expand the evaluation of the satisfaction probability of the STL formula (over the prediction horizon) into a disjunctive formula, where each disjunct is a conjunction of atomic predicates. This is an expensive step because of the complexity of a CNF to DNF conversion, but for small prediction horizons, this does not become prohibitive. The exact procedure to do this is through Algorithm 1, which essentially computes an expanded DNF representation for an STL formula. The above algorithm is invoked with the value $i = n + 1$. Each value of i is a time instant for predictions, so i ranges over $[n + 1, n + h]$. It essentially recursively travels the STL formula building the desired expression. We omit the case for the release operator for brevity, but the expansion follows the definition of the release operator. The following lemma can be easily proved using properties of Boolean operators $\vee$ and $\wedge$.

Algorithm 1: $\text{Expand}_h(\varphi, i)$

---

1 **switch** φ **do**
2   **case** $f(\overline{x}(t_i)) > c$
3          $\lfloor$ **return** $f(\overline{x}(t_i)) > c$

4   **case** $\varphi_1 \wedge \varphi_2$
5          $A \leftarrow \text{Expand}_h(\varphi, i)$
6          $B \leftarrow \text{Expand}_h(\varphi, i)$
7          $Res \leftarrow \{\ \};$
8   **foreach** $C \in A$ **do**
9   **foreach** $D \in B$ **do**
10                 $\lfloor$ $Res \leftarrow Res \cup \{C \wedge D\}$

11   **case** $\varphi_1 \mathbf{U}_{[a,b]} \varphi_2$
12         $Res \leftarrow \{\}$
13   **foreach** $j \in [i, h - \text{horizon}(\varphi_2)]$ **do**
14             $Res_j \leftarrow \{\}$
15             $A_j \leftarrow \text{Expand}_h(\varphi_1, j)$
16   **foreach** $k \in [i, j]$ **do**
17                 $\lfloor$ $B_k \leftarrow \text{Expand}_h(\varphi_2, k)$
18             $Res_j \leftarrow \text{Expand}_h(A_j \wedge \bigwedge_k B_k, j)$
19         $Res \leftarrow \text{Expand}_h(\bigwedge_j Res_j, i)$

Lemma 2. *The result of calling $\text{Expand}_h(\varphi, n+1)$ on an STL formula results in a disjunction over terms, where each term is a conjunction of atomic predicates at some times in $[n + 1, n + h]$.*

4.3   Calculating Probabilistic Guarantees for Monitoring

Now we have the joint distribution (across multiple time steps) for predicted signal values using Theorem 1 (for ARMA) and Theorem 2 (for ARIMA), and the disjunction over conjunctions of signal predicates corresponding to the STL-based signal pattern. The next step is to accumulate probabilities of these conjunctions of signal predicates. Direct addition will result in parts of joint distribution be integrated more than once. We use the inclusion-exclusion principle for computing probability of unions shown in (4.11) to solve the problem of calculating $P(\cup_{i=1}^{n} A_i)$.

$$\sum_{i=1}^{n} P(A_i) - \sum_{i<j} P(A_i \cap A_j) + \sum_{i<j<k} P(A_i \cap A_j \cap A_k) - \cdots + (-1)^{n-1} P(\cap_{i=1}^{n} A_i)$$

(4.11)

Probabilities of each conjunctions of atomic predicates in (4.11) can easily be done by marginalizing all other variables. Formally, let K indicate the set of times over which we want to compute the joint PDF. Then, we can compute the marginal probability using Eq. (4.12).

$$P(\bigwedge_{k \in K} A_k) = \int \cdots \int P(A_1; \ldots; A_h) dA_{j_1} \ldots dA_{j_\ell}$$

(4.12)

Here, $\{j_1, \ldots, j_\ell\} = \{1, \ldots, h\} \setminus K$.

4.4   Complexity of the Algorithm

The complexity of our clairvoyant monitoring procedure depends on the exact form of STL formula involved. In this section, we list the upper bound of complexity for some formula forms. Assume that querying the marginal probability from the joint distribution is of complexity $O(1)$.

Consider the signal pattern $\mathbf{F}_{I_1} \mathbf{G}_{I_2}$. For this pattern, the complexity of computing the probability bounds is $O(2^{\lceil \frac{|I_1|}{4} \rceil})$, as there are $|I_1|$ disjunctive marginal probability terms, and applying Eq. (4.11) will cost $O(2^n)$, where n equals to $\lceil \frac{|I_1|}{4} \rceil$. Similarly, for a formula of the form $\mathbf{G}_{I_1} \mathbf{F}_{I_2}$, the complexity will be $O(2^{\lceil \frac{|I_2|}{4} \rceil \lceil \frac{|I_1|}{4} \rceil})$. For a general signal pattern, the worst-case complexity will depend on the number of conjunctions that will be enumerated.

5   Experimental Evaluation

In this section we experimentally demonstrate the power of predictive monitoring on interesting examples from the cyber-physical systems domain.

Table 1. The probability of predicted traces satisfying the specified STL pattern and runtime for computing the probabilities for the case studies on blood glucose prediction in insulin delivery and velocity prediction for a UAV.

Case Study	ψ	φ_1	φ_2	φ_3	φ_4
I	$P(BG(t) \models \psi)$ $(\sigma_1 = 50, \sigma_2 = \infty)$	1	1	1	1
	Time (s)	0.1068	0.1107	0.0944	2.9037
	$P(BG(t) \models \psi)$ $(\sigma_1 = 50, \sigma_2 = 150)$	0.3836	0.3838	0.3846	0.8462
	Time (s)	0.1067	0.3551	0.0705	26.9337
II	$P(v(t) \models \psi)(\sigma_1 = -0.5, \sigma_2 = 0.5)$	0.1452	0.3446	0.4160	0.2723
	Time (s)	0.0615	0.0792	0.0634	2.3367

Case Study I: Automated Insulin Delivery. Monitoring blood glucose levels is a crucial task for diabetes patients. In certain kinds of severe diabetes (e.g., type I diabetes), patients use automated insulin delivery systems (such as infusion pumps) to give a basal dose of insulin, and to optionally provide a *bolus* if the patient thinks that they are exceeding their usual intake of food (e.g. rich in carbohydrates). The tricky aspect of such devices is that while the response of the blood glucose to insulin is very slow, the response to carbohydrates is relatively fast. Thus, a patient upon seeing a high blood glucose level may exceed their required insulin dose. This can lead to a life-threatening condition called hypoglycemia. Thus, it is crucially important to monitor the blood glucose level in a *predictive fashion*. Similarly, if the blood glucose remains too high for a prolonged period of time (also known as prolonged hyperglycemia), then the patient can suffer long term consequences that can also eventually lead to death.

We have developed a simple linear Simulink® model representing the blood-glucose dynamics in a patient. For this experiment, we obtained the blood glucose (BG) signal by simulating the model with a fixed eating pattern by the patient. We simulated the patient behavior for one week, where BG was monitored at 15 min intervals. We fit an ARIMA process with order $p = 5, d = 2, q = 1$ to the BG signal, and used that for prediction. We checked various requirements (Eqs. (5.1)-(5.4)) on the blood glucose signal. For brevity, we write the formulas in a way that 1 time unit in the formula refers to 15 min of time.

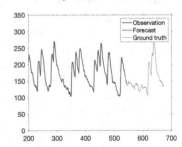

Fig. 2. BG signal with 5 prediction steps (Color figure online)

$$\varphi_1 \equiv \mathbf{G}(\mathbf{F}_{[0,1]}\mathbf{G}_{[0,2]}(\sigma_1 < x(t) < \sigma_2)) \tag{5.1}$$

$$\varphi_2 \equiv \mathbf{G}(x(t) \leq \sigma_1 \implies \mathbf{F}_{[0,1]}\mathbf{G}_{[0,2]}(\sigma_1 < x(t) < \sigma_2)) \tag{5.2}$$

$$\varphi_3 \equiv \mathbf{G}(x(t) \leq \sigma_1 \implies \mathbf{F}_{[0,2]}(\sigma_1 < x(t) < \sigma_2)) \tag{5.3}$$

$$\varphi_4 \equiv \mathbf{G}(\mathbf{F}_{[0,1]}(\sigma_1 < x(t) < \sigma_2)) \tag{5.4}$$

In formulas (5.1)–(5.4), we assume that x is BG. Formula (5.1) is an artificial requirement that says that any time, within the next 15 min the BG signal should remain within the given bounds for 30 min. Formula (5.2) says that if the BG signal is ever lower than the safe threshold, it should return to the safe threshold within 15 min, and stay in the threshold for 30 min. Formula (5.3) is a weaker requirement demanding the BG signal to simply return to the safe region. Finally, formula (5.4) says that eventually always within 15 min the BG signal should return to the safe region. We picked these formulas more to highlight that our algorithm works with different STL formulas with different temporal operator alternations. Some of these formulas are similar to the ones found in [9]. We picked a prediction horizon of 5 time steps (i.e. 75 min). In Fig. 2, we show the predicted blood glucose traces. We conducted two experiments, one where we picked σ_2 to be ∞ and the other where σ_2 was 150 mg/dL. σ_1 was fixed to 50 mg/dL. The results are shown in Table 1.

The first row of Table 1 shows that the patient can never become hypoglycemic, with very high probability[3]. From the third row, we can see that the controller that we implemented for automated insulin delivery does not do a good job with the hyperglycemia requirements (except for the last formula). From Fig. 2, we can see that for a small prediction horizon, the decreasing value of the BG signal (shown in red) gives enough confidence that in the next 15 min, the patient will not be hyperglycemic.

Case Study II: UAV Vertical Velocity. Now we look into the case of Unmanned Aerial Vehicle (UAV). We apply our technique to monitor vertical velocity, which is a crucial component affecting how vehicle control system adjust its rudder angle.

Monitoring Vertical Velocity. Vertical velocity is hard to directly observe, we obtain it through the observed acceleration signal given by gyroscope. The vertical velocity is vital for UAVs, as if the vertical velocity exceeds some threshold it will cause the vehicle to be damaged. We observed the autocorrelation function for the velocity trajectories, and used that to set the parameters $p = 12, d = 4, q = 8$ for the ARIMA model then do a 5 step look-ahead prediction. Conducting 5 steps look-ahead prediction in our data is equivalent to predicting 1 s ahead.

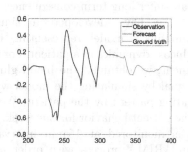

Fig. 3. UAV vertical velocity signal and predictions

The transverse velocity of UAV can achieve over 130 m/s, which makes behaviors that may happen in future 5 steps meaningful. The prediction results are

---

[3] Our implementation was done in Matlab, and Matlab has a certain precision when computing probabilities, and the number 1 is actually $1 - \delta$, where δ is smaller than the machine precision. This indicates that the probability is so high that it is practically 1.

shown in Fig. 3, and the probability guarantees of the predicted trace satisfy the STL requirement are shown in Table 1.

Case Study III: Monitoring Power Consumption Patterns. Household power consumption is an important factor that allows utility companies to estimate the overall power demand. In this case study, we study various STL formulas representing typical queries a utility company may find valuable. To perform this study, we use data from the UCI Machine Learning Repository [11]. The dataset is a multivariate time series dataset that describes the power consumption for a single household over four years. Each time step represents the average power consumption over a day. We fit an ARIMA model to this data with the model parameters $p = 5, d = 2, q = 1$. We are interested in computing the probabilistic guarantees on the STL formulas depicted in Eq. (5.5). In these formulas, $p(t)$ represents the power consumption at time t in KW, and c represents a threshold value.

$$\varphi_1 = \mathbf{G}_{[0,n]}(p(t) > c) \qquad \varphi_2 = \mathbf{G}_{[0,n]}(p(t) < c)$$
$$\varphi_3 = \mathbf{F}_{[0,n]}(p(t) > c) \qquad \varphi_4 = \mathbf{F}_{[0,2]}\mathbf{G}_{[0,5]}(p(t) > c) \qquad (5.5)$$

The formula φ_1 seeks to answer if there are n consecutive future days where the power consumption exceeds the threshold c. The formula φ_2 is true if the expected power consumption over the next n consecutive days is always below c. The formula φ_3 checks if it is always true if there is some day within the next two week period where the power consumption exceeds a threshold. Finally, φ_4 checks if there is some future time within two time steps where it is true that starting from that point, the power consumption always exceeds some threshold c. For each experiment, we assumed that the prediction horizon was 15. Our tool reads the first 139 samples to fit the ARIMA model, and then does its predictions on the next 15 time steps. We summarize the results in Fig. 4b.

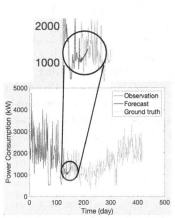

Formula	Parameters		Probability
	n	c	
φ_1	3	500	1
φ_1	3	1010	0.4139
φ_1	3	1120	0
φ_2	10	500	0
φ_2	10	1120	0.0531
φ_2	10	1200	0.3633
φ_2	10	1400	0.9976
φ_3	14	500	1
φ_3	14	1120	0.5468
φ_3	14	1500	0
φ_4	–	500	1
φ_4	–	1100	0.2968
φ_4	–	1500	0

(a) Power consumption signal and predictions

(b) The probability guarantee of power consumption

Fig. 4. Power consumption case study

While the results generally agree with the ground truth data shown in Fig. 4a, in case of the formula φ_2, the experiments indicate that there is over 99% chance of never exceeding 1400 KW of power consumption. Clearly, the ground truth data shows otherwise. The problem here is that the ARIMA model has an effect of smoothing the data and focussing on the trends. If we were to fit the ARIMA model to data over a smaller granularity, it is possible that the model would track sharp local variations more faithfully. In general, if the time-step of the model is too coarse to capture all meaningful trends, the predictive monitoring algorithm can give misleading answers. For this case study, the runtime for fitting the ARIMA model and computing the probabilities was less than 3 s on a standard laptop machine with a 2.6 GHz processor.

6   Related Work and Conclusion

Related Work. Monitoring techniques for specifications in real-time temporal logics such as STL, Timed Propositional Temporal Logic (TPTL) and Metric Temporal Logic (MTL) have received considerable attention recently. See [6] for a recent survey. In [27], the authors define predictive semantics for LTL: these are similar to the three-valued semantics for LTL on incomplete traces and use a system model and model checking over trace suffixes to compute one of the three values (true, false or unknown). However, this approach does not compute violation probabilities. In [2,3], the authors define an interesting predictive monitoring approach. The key idea is to construct an Hidden Markov Model abstraction of a system and use that to predict satisfaction of a given temporal property. This is an alternate way of modeling probabilities in the system, and represents a different take on the same problem. In future work, we will consider extending our signal predictors to those based on Markovian assumptions on the underlying process. We note that these papers focus on LTL with Boolean predicates rather than STL (which has signal predicates).

Also of relevance is the work in the R2U2 monitoring framework [13,20,23,24]. The R2U2 framework uses efficient temporal observers for LTL coupled with dynamic Bayesian networks to probabilistically estimate the state and health of system components. The work proposed in [7,17,26] also addresses a similar problem. In many ways, these are also monitoring problems that are predictive in nature, but the prediction here is regarding hidden system states, rather than predictions in time. Seminal work on *monitorability* of various kinds of stochastic dynamical models (typically with Markovian assumptions) refers to this problem as internal monitoring [25], and we distinguish our work in its clairvoyant abilities.

7   Conclusion

In this paper, we present monitoring framework for signal patterns expressed using Signal Temporal Logic (STL). The main contribution of this paper is an algorithm for clairvoyant monitoring that computes the probability of a signal pattern being satisfied/violated by a set of future/unseen signal values. To achieve clairvoyance, the algorithm utilizes using statistical time-series modeling techniques, assuming that observed data is the realization of a linear stochastic process (such as ARMA or ARIMA). The key technical result is a technique to compute the joint probability distribution of the predicted values and use it to compute the satisfaction probability of the given temporal pattern. In future work, we will consider techniques that help calibrate the prediction result, give expected value for robustness and also explore techniques based on reachability, such as those in [12], to compute forward reachable sets to estimate satisfaction probabilities of STL formulas.

Acknowledgments. We thank the anonymous reviewers for their careful reading of the paper and the constructive feedback. We gratefully acknowledge the support by the National Science Foundation under grant no. CCF/SHF-1910088, and a grant from Toyota Motors R&D North America. We thank Yue Wu and Weixin Cai for fruitful discussions that helped shape the proofs for Theorem 1.

References

1. Annpureddy, Y., Liu, C., Fainekos, G., Sankaranarayanan, S.: S-TaLiRo: a tool for temporal logic falsification for hybrid systems. In: Abdulla, P.A., Leino, K.R.M. (eds.) TACAS 2011. LNCS, vol. 6605, pp. 254–257. Springer, Heidelberg (2011). https://doi.org/10.1007/978-3-642-19835-9_21
2. Babaee, R., Gurfinkel, A., Fischmeister, S.: Predictive run-time verification of discrete-time reachability properties in black-box systems using trace-level abstraction and statistical learning. In: Colombo, C., Leucker, M. (eds.) RV 2018. LNCS, vol. 11237, pp. 187–204. Springer, Cham (2018). https://doi.org/10.1007/978-3-030-03769-7_11
3. Babaee, R., Gurfinkel, A., Fischmeister, S.: *Prevent*: a predictive run-time verification framework using statistical learning. In: Johnsen, E.B., Schaefer, I. (eds.) SEFM 2018. LNCS, vol. 10886, pp. 205–220. Springer, Cham (2018). https://doi.org/10.1007/978-3-319-92970-5_13
4. Bartocci, E., Bortolussi, L., Sanguinetti, G.: Learning temporal logical properties discriminating ECG models of cardiac arrhytmias. arXiv preprint arXiv:1312.7523 (2013)
5. Bartocci, E., Bortolussi, L., Sanguinetti, G.: Data-driven statistical learning of temporal logic properties. In: Legay, A., Bozga, M. (eds.) FORMATS 2014. LNCS, vol. 8711, pp. 23–37. Springer, Cham (2014). https://doi.org/10.1007/978-3-319-10512-3_3
6. Bartocci, E., et al.: Specification-based monitoring of cyber-physical systems: a survey on theory, tools and applications. In: Bartocci, E., Falcone, Y. (eds.) Lectures on Runtime Verification. LNCS, vol. 10457, pp. 135–175. Springer, Cham (2018). https://doi.org/10.1007/978-3-319-75632-5_5
7. Bartocci, E., et al.: Adaptive runtime verification. In: Qadeer, S., Tasiran, S. (eds.) RV 2012. LNCS, vol. 7687, pp. 168–182. Springer, Heidelberg (2013). https://doi.org/10.1007/978-3-642-35632-2_18
8. Brockwell, P.J., Davis, R.A., Calder, M.V.: Introduction to Time Series and Forecasting, vol. 2. Springer, Heidelberg (2002). https://doi.org/10.1007/b97391

9. Cameron, F., Fainekos, G., Maahs, D.M., Sankaranarayanan, S.: Towards a verified artificial pancreas: challenges and solutions for runtime verification. In: Bartocci, E., Majumdar, R. (eds.) RV 2015. LNCS, vol. 9333, pp. 3–17. Springer, Cham (2015). https://doi.org/10.1007/978-3-319-23820-3_1

10. Deshmukh, J.V., Donzé, A., Ghosh, S., Jin, X., Juniwal, G., Seshia, S.A.: Robust online monitoring of signal temporal logic. Formal Meth. Syst. Des. **51**(1), 5–30 (2017). https://doi.org/10.1007/s10703-017-0286-7

11. Dua, D., Graff, C.: UCI machine learning repository (2017). http://archive.ics.uci.edu/ml

12. Duggirala, P.S., Mitra, S., Viswanathan, M., Potok, M.: C2E2: a verification tool for stateflow models. In: Baier, C., Tinelli, C. (eds.) TACAS 2015. LNCS, vol. 9035, pp. 68–82. Springer, Heidelberg (2015). https://doi.org/10.1007/978-3-662-46681-0_5

13. Geist, J., Rozier, K.Y., Schumann, J.: Runtime observer pairs and Bayesian network reasoners on-board FPGAs: flight-certifiable system health management for embedded systems. In: Bonakdarpour, B., Smolka, S.A. (eds.) RV 2014. LNCS, vol. 8734, pp. 215–230. Springer, Cham (2014). https://doi.org/10.1007/978-3-319-11164-3_18

14. Ho, H.-M., Ouaknine, J., Worrell, J.: Online monitoring of metric temporal logic. In: Bonakdarpour, B., Smolka, S.A. (eds.) RV 2014. LNCS, vol. 8734, pp. 178–192. Springer, Cham (2014). https://doi.org/10.1007/978-3-319-11164-3_15

15. Hoxha, B., Abbas, H., Fainekos, G.: Benchmarks for temporal logic requirements for automotive systems. In: Frehse, G., Althoff, M. (eds.) ARCH14-15. 1st and 2nd International Workshop on Applied veRification for Continuous and Hybrid Systems. EPiC Series in Computing, vol. 34, pp. 25–30. EasyChair (2015)

16. Jin, X., Deshmukh, J.V., Kapinski, J., Ueda, K., Butts, K.: Powertrain control verification benchmark. In: Proceedings of the 17th International Conference on Hybrid Systems: Computation and Control, pp. 253–262. ACM (2014)

17. Kalajdzic, K., Bartocci, E., Smolka, S.A., Stoller, S.D., Grosu, R.: Runtime verification with particle filtering. In: Legay, A., Bensalem, S. (eds.) RV 2013. LNCS, vol. 8174, pp. 149–166. Springer, Heidelberg (2013). https://doi.org/10.1007/978-3-642-40787-1_9

18. Kapinski, J., et al.: ST-Lib: a library for specifying and classifying model behaviors. In: SAE Technical Paper. SAE (2016)

19. Kong, Z., Jones, A., Medina Ayala, A., Aydin Gol, E., Belta, C.: Temporal logic inference for classification and prediction from data. In: Proceedings of HSCC, pp. 273–282 (2014)

20. Moosbrugger, P., Rozier, K.Y., Schumann, J.: R2U2: monitoring and diagnosis of security threats for unmanned aerial systems. Formal Methods Syst. Des. **51**(1), 31–61 (2017). https://doi.org/10.1007/s10703-017-0275-x

21. Qin, X., Deshmukh, J.V.: Joint probability distribution of prediction errors of ARIMA. CoRR abs/1811.04685 (2018), http://arxiv.org/abs/1811.04685

22. Roehm, H., Gmehlich, R., Heinz, T., Oehlerking, J., Woehrle, M.: Industrial examples of formal specifications for test case generation. In: Workshop on Applied veRification for Continuous and Hybrid Systems, ARCH. pp. 80–88 (2015)

23. Schumann, J., Moosbrugger, P., Rozier, K.Y.: R2U2: monitoring and diagnosis of security threats for unmanned aerial systems. In: Bartocci, E., Majumdar, R. (eds.) RV 2015. LNCS, vol. 9333, pp. 233–249. Springer, Cham (2015). https://doi.org/10.1007/978-3-319-23820-3_15

24. Schumann, J., Moosbrugger, P., Rozier, K.Y.: Runtime analysis with R2U2: a tool exhibition report. In: Falcone, Y., Sánchez, C. (eds.) RV 2016. LNCS, vol. 10012, pp. 504–509. Springer, Cham (2016). https://doi.org/10.1007/978-3-319-46982-9_35
25. Sistla, A.P., Žefran, M., Feng, Y.: Monitorability of stochastic dynamical systems. In: Gopalakrishnan, G., Qadeer, S. (eds.) CAV 2011. LNCS, vol. 6806, pp. 720–736. Springer, Heidelberg (2011). https://doi.org/10.1007/978-3-642-22110-1_58
26. Stoller, S.D., et al.: Runtime verification with state estimation. In: Khurshid, S., Sen, K. (eds.) RV 2011. LNCS, vol. 7186, pp. 193–207. Springer, Heidelberg (2012). https://doi.org/10.1007/978-3-642-29860-8_15
27. Zhang, X., Leucker, M., Dong, W.: Runtime verification with predictive semantics. In: Goodloe, A.E., Person, S. (eds.) NFM 2012. LNCS, vol. 7226, pp. 418–432. Springer, Heidelberg (2012). https://doi.org/10.1007/978-3-642-28891-3_37

Embedding Online Runtime Verification for Fault Disambiguation on Robonaut2

Brian Kempa[✉][iD], Pei Zhang[iD], Phillip H. Jones[iD], Joseph Zambreno[iD], and Kristin Yvonne Rozier[iD]

Iowa State University, Ames, IA 50010, USA
{bckempa,peizhang,phjones,zambreno,kyrozier}@iastate.edu
http://temporallogic.org/research/R2U2/

Abstract. Robonaut2 (R2) is a humanoid robot onboard the International Space Station (ISS), performing specialized tasks in collaboration with astronauts. After deployment, R2 developed an unexpected emergent behavior. R2's inability to distinguish between knee-joint faults (e.g., due to sensor drift versus violated environmental assumptions) began triggering safety-preserving freezes-in-place in the confined space of the ISS, preventing further motion until a ground-control operator determines the root-cause and initiates proper corrective action. Runtime verification (RV) algorithms can efficiently disambiguate the temporal signatures of different faults in real-time. However, no previous RV engine can operate within the limited available resources and specialized platform constraints of R2's hardware architecture. An attempt to deploy the only runtime verification engine designed for embedded flight systems, R2U2, failed due to resource constraints. We present a significant redesign of the core R2U2 algorithms to adapt to severe resource and certification constraints and prove their correctness. We further define an optimization enabled by our new algorithms and implement the new version of R2U2. We encode specifications describing real-life faults occurring onboard Robonaut2 using Mission-time Linear Temporal Logic (MLTL) and detail our process of specification debugging, validation, and refinement. We deployed this new version of R2U2 on Robonaut2, demonstrating successful real-time fault disambiguation and mitigation triggering of R2's knee-joint faults without false positives.

Keywords: Online runtime verification · Temporal logic specification · Steam-based runtime verification · MLTL · R2U2

1 Introduction

Safe integration of autonomous robotic systems necessitates embedding runtime checks into specialized, domain-specific platforms designed for utility and efficiency. Robonaut2 (R2) [8] is a humanoid robot capable of performing complex

Supported by NASA ECF NNX16AR57G and NSF CAREER Award CNS-1552934.

N. Bertrand and N. Jansen (Eds.): FORMATS 2020, LNCS 12288, pp. 196–214, 2020.
https://doi.org/10.1007/978-3-030-57628-8_12

tasks on-board the International Space Station (ISS) while interacting safely with humans [12]. Even carefully-designed, formally-verified cyber-physical systems experience unanticipated emergent behaviors when deployed to complex, dynamic environments like the ISS. In R2's case, position sensors within rotational joints can return faulty position data indistinguishable from high-torque data to the control system. Disambiguating between sensing errors and high-torque states would enable autonomous operation, rather than freezing for safety reasons and contacting Houston ground-control for help; choosing the incorrect mitigation action can have disastrous consequences. Autonomous operation demands the real-time reasoning and safety guarantees provided by runtime verification, on increasingly domain-specific hardware, including post-deployment.

This fault-disambiguation problem poses several challenges that previously prevented an effective solution. Runtime Verification (RV) could detect the faults, but R2 is already deployed on the ISS; no new resources will be launched to run an RV engine. Low-level joint control resides on a heavily-optimized Field Programmable Gate Array (FPGA) adjacent to the knee with limited remaining space. Consequently, the only available resources in which to implement a solution are tightly-constrained. RV needs to run in hardware in the remaining space on that critical FPGA with provable non-interference with the existing joint controller. The RV engine must be real-time, online, and stream-based to continuously evaluate faults throughout R2's operation. RV on R2 must be a remotely-configurable process; we cannot bring R2 back to Earth or requisition astronaut time to change the runtime observer specification. Given that systems on the ISS are frequently repurposed and operate in a continuously-changing environment, we need to be able to change RV observers without re-synthesizing hardware, and quickly adapt to updated conditions and requirements.

Most RV tools are implemented in software, require significant resources and overhead, or have incompatible expression languages. R2 is running the Robot Operating System (ROS) [20] and some formal verification tools for ROS exist; however, none of these fit the requirements of the R2 project. Others have developed a generic approach to formally verify real-time properties of ROS-based applications [10], at design time, using timed automata and a model checker in an approach that cannot be scaled to R2's resource constraints. Similarly, ROSCoq extends the Coq theorem prover to enable reasoning about the cyber-physical behavior for developing certified ROS systems [7]. ROSRV [11] and Declarative Robot Safety (DeRoS) [1] integrate RV into ROS by generating ROS nodes that monitor properties during execution. But, they are software-based, limited to data published on the ROS message bus, and incur significant runtime overhead. EgMon eagerly checks for violations of specifications in a future-bounded, propositional metric temporal logic that avoids instrumentation of already-certified components [13]. But, EgMon is a software implementation that would not work in R2's architecture: it reads previously-logged inputs, adds significant overhead, and allows a high level of false positives that would be unacceptable. Formal verification of autonomous robot systems is a burgeoning research area; see [16] for a survey.

R2 requires a hardware-based solution with consideration for resource constraints; Table 1 summarizes four options. IoTA considers some resource constraints in implementing RV, but for software [5]. RVS is the only other modern hardware RV implementation; its limited expression language only monitors the internal behavior of a real-time operating system and RVS requires resynthesis to change monitored properties [27]. The Realizable Responsive Unobtrusive Unit [22] (R2U2) is the only RV tool that starts an encoding with the resource constraints and then optimizes the verification configuration to reliably detect as many faults as possible, rather than, e.g., starting with runtime monitors and creating resource-consuming implementations. R2U2's online, stream-based, hardware (FPGA) implementation, provable unobtrusiveness, and ability to change monitors without resynthesis fit the R2 project. R2U2's compositional, hierarchical design and more flexible specification language made it most likely to fit in the space left over on R2's knee joint's FPGA; these features proved useful in other case studies on real aerospace systems [9,24–26]. However, an initial trial proved that even R2U2's most optimized configuration would not fit; *no currently existing RV tools were capable of on-board, real-time fault detection for R2's knee joint.* We would have to build a custom tool to bridge that gap.

Table 1. Comparison of hardware monitor tools.

Tool	P2V[15]	BusMOP[18]	HW-CBMC [17]	R2U2 [21]
Method	Automata synthesis			Formula decomposition
Type	Hard-coded			Programmable
Target	Software	COTS Peripheral	HW-SW Co-design	Sensor
Spec logic	Past time only			Future/past time
Last update	2007	2008	2017	2019

Using R2U2 as a base, we designed and proved correct new observer-encoding algorithms suitable for R2 and developed an optimization until we were able to deploy RV on the real Robonaut2 knee joint successfully. A previously unnoticed fault syndrome prevented the simple original specification from operating correctly. Our revised specification set provided the required accuracy but utilized significantly more resources. The new specifications only fit on the FPGA because of the optimization enabled by our new encoding, resulting in successful fault disambiguation.

This paper contributes: (1) a significant revision of all asynchronous future-time MLTL monitor encodings of [21] with new proofs of correctness; (2) an optimization to online RV for operation under resource constraints using these encodings; (3) an implementation of these monitors with an empirical evaluation showing improvement in resource consumption; (4) specification design, debugging, validation, refinement techniques, and lessons learned from the deployment of RV on an autonomous robot; (5) a case study embedding online, stream-based, hardware RV on Robonaut2 hardware on loan from NASA, demonstrating successful real-time fault disambiguation in this resource-constrained environment. Section 2 overviews the logic MLTL and notation used. Sect. 3 gives the new monitoring encodings with correctness proofs, then implementions with optimization appear in Sect. 4, along with experimental performance characterizations. Section 5 covers embedding of these observers on Robonaut2 and development of specifications for fault disambiguation. Finally, lessons learned and opportunities for future work appear in Sect. 6.

2   Preliminaries

R2U2 uses Mission-time LTL (MLTL) for future-time temporal specification [14, 21]. MLTL is a bounded variant of MTL [2] with closed natural number interval bounds on each temporal operator.

Definition 1 *(MLTL Syntax). The syntax of an MLTL formula φ over a set of atomic propositions $\mathcal{AP}$ is recursively defined as:*

$$\varphi ::= \text{true} \mid \text{false} \mid p \mid \neg\varphi \mid \varphi_1 \wedge \varphi_2 \mid \varphi_1 \vee \varphi_2 \mid \Box_I\varphi \mid \Diamond_I\varphi \mid \varphi_1\mathcal{U}_I\varphi_2 \mid \varphi_1\mathcal{R}_I\varphi_2$$

where $p \in \mathcal{AP}$ is an atom, φ_1 and φ_2 are MLTL formulas. I is an interval $[lb, ub]$, $lb \leq ub$ and $lb, ub \in \mathbb{N}$, or simply $[ub]$ if $lb = 0$. Given two MLTL formulas φ_1, φ_2, we denote $\varphi_1 \equiv \varphi_2$ if they are semantically equivalent. In MLTL semantics, we define $\text{false} \equiv \neg\text{true}$, $\varphi_1 \vee \varphi_2 \equiv \neg(\neg\varphi_1 \wedge \neg\varphi_2)$, $\neg(\varphi_1\mathcal{U}_I\varphi_2) \equiv (\neg\varphi_1\mathcal{R}_I\neg\varphi_2)$ and $\neg\Diamond_I\varphi \equiv \Box_I\neg\varphi$. MLTL keeps the standard operator equivalences from LTL, including $\Diamond_I\varphi \equiv (\text{true}\ \mathcal{U}_I\varphi)$, $(\Box_I\varphi) \equiv (\text{false}\ \mathcal{R}_I\varphi)$. Notably, MLTL discards the next ($\mathcal{X}$) operator, which is essential in LTL, since $\mathcal{X}\varphi$ is semantically equivalent to $\Box_{[1,1]}\varphi$ (see [14]). Let π be a finite computation and let $|\pi|$ represent the length of π (where $|\pi| < +\infty$). Every position $\pi[i]$ (where $i \geq 0$) is an assignment over $2^{\mathcal{AP}}$; let π_i represent the suffix of π starting from position i (including i).

Definition 2 *(MLTL Semantics). The satisfaction of an MLTL formula φ, over a set of propositions $\mathcal{AP}$, by a computation/trace π starting from position i (denoted as $\pi, i \models \varphi$) is recursively defined as:*

- $\pi, i \models p \in \mathcal{AP}$ *iff* $p \in \pi[0]$,   • $\pi, i \models \neg\varphi$ *iff* $\pi, i \not\models \varphi$,
- $\pi, i \models \varphi_1 \wedge \varphi_2$ *iff* $\pi, i \models \varphi_1$ *and* $\pi, i \models \varphi_2$,
- $\pi, i \models \varphi_1\mathcal{U}_{[lb,ub]}\varphi_2$ *iff* $|\pi| \geq i + lb$ *and there exists* $j \in [i + lb, i + ub]$ *such that* $\pi, j \models \varphi_2$ *and for every* $k < j$, $k \in [i + lb, i + ub]$, $\pi, k \models \varphi_1$.

2.1   Abstract Syntax Tree and Execution Sequence

As a reconfigurable monitor, R2U2 uses external specification data. This allows changes to the specification without recompilation or resynthesis of the R2U2 engine. R2U2 executes runtime reconfigurable specifications by constructing an *Abstract Syntax Tree* (AST) of logical observers wherein each node produces an *execution sequence* as output that can be used by other nodes in the tree.

Definition 3 *(Execution Sequence) (adapted from [21]). An* **execution sequence** *for an MLTL formula φ, denoted by $\langle T_\varphi \rangle$, over computation π is a sequence of verdict tuples $T_\varphi = (v, \tau)$ where $\tau \in \mathbb{N}_0$ is a time stamp and $v \in \{true, false\}$ is a verdict. We use a superscript integer to access a particular element in $\langle T_\varphi \rangle$, e.g., T_φ^0 is the first element in execution sequence $\langle T_\varphi \rangle$. We write $T_\varphi.\tau$ to access τ and $T_\varphi.v$ to access v of element T_φ. We say T_φ holds if $T_\varphi.v$ is true and T_φ does not hold if $T_\varphi.v$ is false. For a given execution sequence $\langle T_\varphi \rangle = T_\varphi^0, T_\varphi^1, T_\varphi^2, T_\varphi^3, \ldots$, the tuple accessed by T_φ^n represents a non-empty set of verdicts: for all time stamps $i \in [T_\varphi^{n-1}.\tau + 1, T_\varphi^n.\tau]$, $\pi, i \models \varphi$ in case $T_\varphi^n.v$ is true and $\pi, i \not\models \varphi$ in case $T_\varphi^n.v$ is false. Intuitively, if $T_\varphi^0 = (\mathsf{false}, 0)$ and $T_\varphi^1 = (\mathsf{true}, 5)$ then T_φ^1 represents that φ holds from $\tau = 0$ through $\tau = 1$.*

2.2 Propagation Delay

Each temporal operator in MLTL is accompanied by a closed natural integer bound, $I = [lb, ub]$. A node of the AST is decidable at a given time when sufficient information is known to determine the verdict at that time. As these observers chain together, the decidability of a given node becomes a function of its bound and the bounds of its inputs.

Definition 4 *(Propagation Delay). The propagation delay of an MLTL formula φ is the time between when a set of propositions $\pi[i]$ (i.e., input) arrives at φ, and when it is possible to know if $\pi, i \models \varphi$ (i.e., output). A node's worst propagation delay* **(wpd)** *is the maximum propagation delay it can experience, and the minimum value is the* best propagation delay **(bpd)**.

Definition 5 *(Propagation Delay Semantics). Let φ be an MLTL formula where $\varphi.bpd$ is the best-case propagation delay of formula φ and $\varphi.wpd$ is its worst-case propagation delay. If φ is a unary operator, then let its direct subformula be ψ; else, if φ is a binary operator, then let ψ_1, ψ_2 be its direct subformulas. Let Propagation Delay of formula φ be defined as follows:*

$$if\ \varphi \in \mathcal{AP} : \begin{cases} \varphi.wpd &= 0 \\ \varphi.bpd &= 0 \end{cases} \qquad if\ \varphi = \neg\psi : \begin{cases} \varphi.wpd &= \psi.wpd \\ \varphi.bpd &= \psi.bpd \end{cases}$$

$$if\ \varphi = \Box_{[\varphi.lb, \varphi.ub]}\psi\ or\ \varphi = \Diamond_{[\varphi.lb, \varphi.ub]}\psi : \begin{cases} \varphi.wpd &= \psi.wpd + \varphi.ub \\ \varphi.bpd &= \psi.bpd + \varphi.lb \end{cases}$$

$$if\ \varphi = \psi_1 \vee \psi_2\ or\ \varphi = \psi_1 \wedge \psi_2 : \begin{cases} \varphi.wpd &= max(\psi_1.wpd, \psi_2.wpd) \\ \varphi.bpd &= min(\psi_1.bpd, \psi_2.bpd) \end{cases}$$

$$if\ \varphi = \psi_1 \mathcal{U}_{[\varphi.lb, \varphi.ub]}\psi_2\ or\ \varphi = \psi_1 \mathcal{R}_{[\varphi.lb, \varphi.ub]}\psi_2 : \begin{cases} \varphi.wpd &= max(\psi_1.wpd, \psi_2.wpd) + \varphi.ub \\ \varphi.bpd &= min(\psi_1.bpd, \psi_2.bpd) + \varphi.lb \end{cases}$$

3 New Future-Time Algorithms for R2U2

To improve real-time performance and reduce resource usage, we contribute new encodings of asynchronous, future time MLTL operators. Single-writer, many-reader, ring buffers called *shared connection queues* (SCQs) replace the single-writer, single-reader buffers of the original operators [21]. The SCQ-backed operators enable a further implementation optimization, discussed in Sect. 4. While developed to reduce real-time resource requirements, we found SCQ-backed operators necessary for other advancements like model-predictive runtime verification [29].

3.1 Shared Connection Queues

A SCQ is a circular buffer of verdict tuples with one write pointer and one or more read pointers that buffers verdicts from a child subformula to be read by multiple parent expressions. These supplant the synchronization queues utilized in [21]. Shared Ring Buffers, which are similar structures from multi-threading software (e.g., [28]), inspired the SCQ. Figure 1 shows how SCQs are embedded in an MLTL AST, with read pointers for each parent and a write pointer for the child.

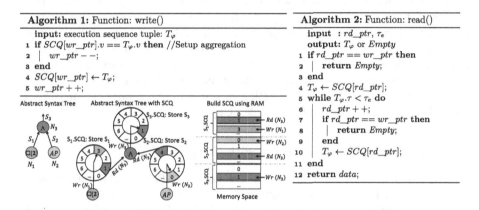

Algorithm 1: Function: write()

input: execution sequence tuple: T_φ
1 if $SCQ[wr\_ptr].v == T_\varphi.v$ then //Setup aggregation
2 | wr_ptr--;
3 end
4 $SCQ[wr\_ptr] \leftarrow T_\varphi$;
5 wr_ptr++;

Algorithm 2: Function: read()

input : rd_ptr, τ_e
output: T_φ or $Empty$
1 if $rd\_ptr == wr\_ptr$ then
2 | return $Empty$;
3 end
4 $T_\varphi \leftarrow SCQ[rd\_ptr]$;
5 while $T_\varphi.\tau < \tau_e$ do
6 | rd_ptr++;
7 | if $rd\_ptr == wr\_ptr$ then
8 | | return $Empty$;
9 | end
10 | $T_\varphi \leftarrow SCQ[rd\_ptr]$;
11 end
12 return $data$;

Fig. 1. Representative AST fragment showing a $\wedge$ operation (N_3) and it's children/inputs. The output of all three nodes are buffered with SCQs where N_3 holds read pointers to S_1 and S_2. The SCQs are arranged linearly in memory as shown.

Reading and Writing. Algorithms 1 and 2 show SCQ read and write operations. Each SCQ manages a write pointer while observers maintain read pointers for each child queue. SCQs store verdict intervals using *aggregation* [21], wherein the latest tuple's timestamp is overwritten by subsequent timestamp values if their truth values (and therefore verdicts) are equal. For example, if the SCQ contains $\{(\mathsf{true}, 10), (\mathsf{false}, 15)\}$, then during the timestamp interval $[11, 15]$ the verdicts are all false. If the next input is $(\mathsf{false}, 16)$, the content becomes $\{(\mathsf{true}, 10), (\mathsf{false}, 16)\}$.

Reading from a non-empty SCQ returns verdicts with monotonically increasing time steps. This prevents reprocessing verdicts a reader has already observed. To enforce monotonic reads, the last timestamp seen by each reader is tracked in the variable τ_e. When reading, the first verdict found after the read pointer with a timestamp greater or equal to τ_e is returned; else, it returns empty. The circular structure of the SCQ is omitted from the algorithms for clarity. In practice, the pointer increments and decrements by the size of a verdict tuple, modulo the size of the queue.

Queue Sizing. The required buffer size for each observer is computed a priori by recursively sizing the SCQs in its MLTL AST based on the best and worst-case delays of their subexpressions. We call the maximum number of verdicts a SCQ can hold the depth, and the individual positions we call slots. We compute the size of the output queue for a node g with sibling nodes $\mathbb{S}_g$ that share a common parent with:

$$size(g.Queue) = max(max\{\forall s \in \mathbb{S}_g s.wpd\} - g.bpd, 0) + 1.$$

The minimum queue size is one because even with no delay the verdict must be passed between nodes. Sizing queues based on the worst-case delay guarantees that verdicts are consumed by the parent nodes before the write pointer recirculates, overwriting old data. This safely bounds the memory required to evaluate each node in the worst case. Software RV monitors can use these precomputed bounds to avoid dynamic allocation when desired. In hardware RV, we build SCQs using Block RAMs (BRAMs), an FPGA memory resource. Each BRAM can be partitioned into multiple SCQs.

3.2   MLTL Operator Observers with SCQs

Algorithms 3–6 in Fig. 2 demonstrate our new encodings of the four required future-time MLTL asynchronous observers using SCQs. Whereas [21] used one of two observers for $\Box_{[lb,ub]}$ depending on the bounds, this encoding only uses one observer. Negation (algorithm 3) returns all input verdicts after inverting their truth values. Until (algorithm 4) tracks the falling edges of ψ and the latest seen timestamp of φ. If ψ is true or φ is false, then the output is trivially true or false, respectively. Additionally, failure by elapsed time is detected from the time since the falling edge of ψ. And (algorithm 5) considers 4 cases to eagerly evaluate false verdicts. If both inputs are true, the output is true up to the smaller input timestamp. If both inputs are false, the output is false up to the largest observed timestamp; this is classic Boolean "short-circuiting" behavior. Otherwise, the verdict is false up to the timestamp of the false input. The Globally operator (algorithm 6) counts time stamps since the last rising edge. It outputs *true* when the length of the *true* signal meets or exceeds the duration of the interval. Operators with non-zero lower bounds can be treated as zero-bounded operators of equivalent duration by offsetting the returned timestamps. This shift equivalence (a separate operator in [21]) is directly embedded in our new encoding.

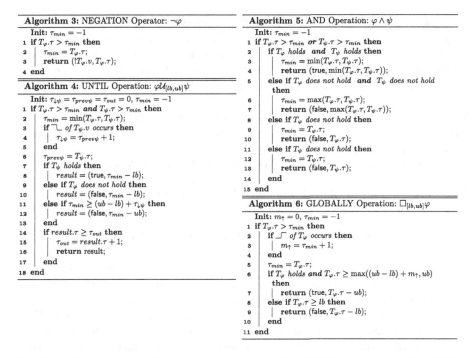

Fig. 2. Implementations of asynchronous, future-time MLTL observers using SCQs. For each algorithm: $\mathcal{N}$ is the current node, $\mathcal{N}.SCQ$ is the output SCQ of $\mathcal{N}$, and $\mathcal{N}.iSCQ$ is input SCQ being read. In binary operators, there are two input queues: $\mathcal{N}.iSCQ\_0$ and $\mathcal{N}.iSCQ\_1$

3.3 Correctness of New MLTL Observers

Correctness of algorithm 3 follows immediately from the SCQ read and write operations.

Theorem 1 (Correctness of the $\square$-operator). *Let execution sequence $\langle T_\varphi \rangle$ be the output of Algorithm 6 with interval $[lb, ub]$ over computation π. Algorithm 6 correctly implements $\square_{[lb,ub]}\varphi$, that is $\forall i \; T_\varphi = (i, \mathsf{true}) \Leftrightarrow \pi, i \models \square_{[lb,ub]}\varphi$.*

Proof (Proof of Theorem 1). In [21] the following equivalence with the globally operator is developed: $\forall i : (i - lb \in [\tau, \tau + ub - lb] \rightarrow \pi, i \models \varphi) \Leftrightarrow \pi, \tau \models \square_{[lb,ub]}\varphi$

Since $(ub - lb) \not< 0$, $\square_{lb,ub}\varphi$ holds at τ iff $\pi, i \models \varphi$ where $(i - ub) \leq \tau \leq (i - lb)$. From these conditions, we see that $\square_{[lb,ub]}\varphi$ is equivalent to the verdicts $\square_{[0,ub-lb]}\varphi$ shifted back by lb, i.e., φ must hold for $ub - lb$ or longer.

$\Leftarrow$: In Algorithm 6, a rising edge of φ is detected by line 2–5 which account for aggregation. If φ has held for at least $ub - lb$, then line 7 returns a true verdict, shifted by ub. Otherwise, a false verdict is returned (line 9) which eagerly fails all time steps unable to meet the condition $\pi, i \models \varphi$ for $(i - lb) \geq \tau$. The check on line 8 prevents premature output of false verdicts on initialization.

$\Rightarrow$: True verdicts are only returned from line 7, which requires φ to have held for at least $ub - lb$ per the check in line 6. False verdicts are only returned from line 9, which requires φ has not sufficiently held (line 9) but sufficient information is available (line 8).

Verdicts are returned iff they satisfy the original equivalence.   □

Due to size, proofs for Algorithm 4 and Algorithm 5 are available online.[1]

4   Optimization and Experimental Performance Analysis

In a set of MLTL formulas, repeated sub-expressions can generate redundant observer instructions, needlessly increasing required queue space and execution time. Compilers use *common subexpression elimination* (CSE) [6] to share the output of repeated expressions. Figure 3 demonstrates the application of CSE to MLTL ASTs. CSE is not possible with single-reader buffers and requires SCQs with multiple readers. Algorithm 7 removes duplicate branches of a formula's AST. Sub-expressions are eliminated both within and between formulas.

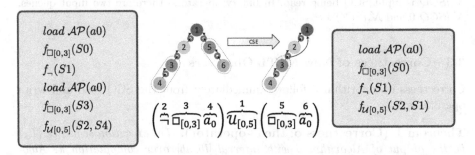

Fig. 3. Example of CSE on an MLTL formula where nodes 3 and 5 have identical children. On the left is the AST and resulting R2U2 institution representing the above formula. The AST and instructions on the right are produced by applying CSE. Sharing the output of node 3 removes one repetition of this sequence, saving two queues and two instructions.

Experimental Demonstration of Improved Average Performance. To measure the impact of CSE with SCQs, we tested the 10,000 random MLTL benchmark formulas used in [14] by converting them to observer trees and queue configurations with and without CSE enabled. The benchmark set formulas vary in length, number of variables, and probability of choosing the $\mathcal{U}$-operator.

The R2U2 configuration compiler is a single-threaded Python application and was run in parallel (12 instances at a time) on a

---

Algorithm 7: $\mathrm{CSE}(T, S)$

Input : AST Tree: T, Set: $S = \{(label, node)\}$
Output: optimized AST: T

1 // Recuse through T in post-order
2 Let $N = \mathrm{root}(T)$
3 if leftChild$(N) \neq \emptyset$ then CSE(leftChild$(N), S)$
4 if rightChild$(N) \neq \emptyset$ then
   CSE(rightChild$(N), S)$
5 // Build expression label
6 N.label $= ['(']$
7 if leftChild(N) then
   N.label $+=$ leftChild(N).*label*
8 N.label $+= N$.name
9 if rightChild(N) then
   N.label $+=$ rightChild(N).*label*
10 N.label $+= [')']$
11 // Trim common subexpressions
12 if $(N$.label, $\bullet) \notin S$ then
13 | // Unique subtree, store reference
14 | $S = S \cup (N$.label, $N)$
15 else
16 | // Common subtree, link existing
17 | Let $M \in T$ such that $(N$.label, $M) \in S$
18 | $T = T \cup ($parent$(N), M)$
19 | $T = T - ($parent$(N), N)$
20 end

2019 MacBook Pro with a i9-9880H Intel CPU and 32 GB system RAM. The duration of each process was measured using the Python 3.7.7 standard time library process_time function which counts system and user CPU (but not sleep) time with the most precise clock available. In total, the 10,000 runs across 12 parallel processes completed in under 15 s wall clock time.

Over the whole set, the number of R2U2 observer nodes dropped 27.06% from 788,095 to 574,822 and the total queue slots required decreased 4.28% from 42,300,361 to 40,491,507. Adding CSE to the R2U2 configuration compiler increased the configuration time 10.25% from 57.66 to 63.57 total seconds of CPU time. Figure 4 shows histograms of AST and SCQ reduction respectively. Only 30 of the 10,000 saw no improvement.

The reduction in AST nodes is significant and translates proportionally to execution time. The 24% AST node reduction over random formulas gives hope for similar or greater reductions in encoding real specifications due to the greater repetition in human-written specifications. The queue space reduction saved a median of 100 slots per formula, which is important as BRAMs are less plentiful on FPGAs. The benchmark formulas use large operator intervals, which limit

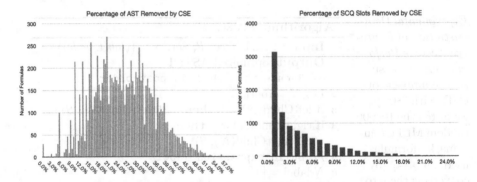

Fig. 4. Reduction in AST nodes (left) and SCQ slots (right) as percentage of unoptimized size. The y-axis indicates the number of formulas from MLTL benchmark set [14].

our SCQ reductions by requiring sufficient space for their worst-case propagation delays. We expect to see increased queue space savings on formulas with shorter intervals; we will explore this in future work.

5   Theory into Practice: Robonaut2

Robonaut2's legs are comprised of series-elastic actuators with torsional springs, causing external force to register on the internal position sensors [19]. Precise measurements of the spring displacement cap applied force, affording near-human dexterity while remaining safe in confined spaces with astronauts [3]. After deployment, NASA observed that the *Absolute Position Sensors* (APSs) sporadically initialize incorrectly by ≈ 2.1 rad (120°). In this fault condition, safety checks fail due to a perceived high torque loading. This is well beyond the physical hard-stop of the joint, but R2 cannot distinguish it from sensor drift. To increase availability and resilience, Robonaut2 must be able to automatically trigger corrective action without compromising existing safety guarantees.

Constraints. The Robonaut2 team requested fault disambiguation directly on the joint controller FPGA. This provides increased observability, minimizes additional messages on the control bus, and does not invalidate the flight code certification of the paired microcontroller. However, the left-over space on the FPGA is limited and additional runtime verification logic must not impact the response time of the existing controller. Additionally, the system's remote deployment limits available debug information. We derived our initial specification from a plain-language description of the fault mechanics by subject-matter experts while awaiting a real trace.

Solution Architecture. Figure 5 shows the desired architecture. During development, a serial debug port loads specifications and returns verdicts. In flight, Robonaut2's configuration system will handle specification loading. R2U2 is realizable, responsive, and unobtrusive [22]; it embeds observers for Robonaut2's symptoms in hardware, returns observer verdicts at the system clock rate, and is adaptable to the highly-constrained operational environment without affecting existing joint control, respectively. We

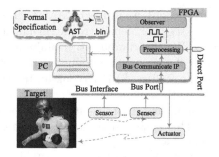

Fig. 5. R2U2 observers, encoded on the FPGA, monitor internal sensor values passed over the R2 control bus.

apply two of R2U2's reasoning layers: signal processing (which processes incoming signals into Boolean atomics) and temporal observation (which evaluates MLTL specifications). Our use-case requires early-as-possible identification of failure, necessitating using R2U2's asynchronous mode. The existing flight configuration routes all sensors, actuator control, and communications through the FPGA while a microcontroller runs high-rate model-based control algorithms [4]. Since the FPGA is the nexus of the actuator's sensors, all required data can be accessed on-chip.

5.1 Embedding Runtime Verification

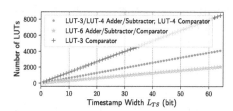

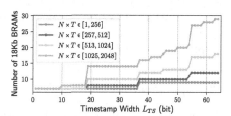

Fig. 6. LUT resource usage for timestamp length L_{TS}. Growth is linear, but the rate is dependent on FPGA process type.

Fig. 7. BRAM resource usage for timestamp length L_{TS} where $N \times T$ is the number of binary operators N, times $T = \max n.wcd \ \forall n \in N$ i.e. total queue space.

R2U2 allows runtime configuration of the observer specifications, while the size and duration limits of these specifications are design-time parameters. For R2U2 to dynamically reconfigure specifications at runtime (without resynthesis or recertification), we utilize BRAMs for instruction memory, variable memory, and queues; see [22]. Memory requirements are driven by queue depth and timestamp length. We can compute the minimum required resources of a given specification, or the maximum parameters that fit within a given design. Figures 6 and 7 show the scaling of FPGA look-up-tables (LUTs) and BRAM required as timestamp width is increased, respectively. We selected a max queue depth of 20 and timestamp length of 16-bits from expert and system operator's recommendations. This increased the LUT utilization of the FPGA from 51.2% to 79.81% and increased the number of BRAMs used from 2 to 27 out of 32. A video demo[2] shows R2U2 running live on the R2 platform, reasoning over the joint state, evaluating temporal observers, and dynamically configuring specifications without stopping the robot.

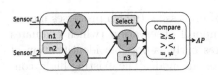

Fig. 8. R2U2 atomic checker. Orange blocks are configurable online. (Color figure online)

Boolean Checker Construction. R2U2's runtime-configurable Atomic Checkers, shown in Fig. 8, convert the native sensor format to Boolean variables used in specification. For example, the *EncPos* sensors value indicates the rotation degree of the motor. Robonaut2's native encoder format is a 19-bit integer, where the highest bit is an error flag and the lower 18 bits represent the encoder count. This presents two challenges: (1) the *EncPos* is reset to 0 at initialization regardless of the actual position; (2) to compare with the APS values, this count must be scaled and offset. Taken together, R2U2 must reconfigure the offset before using encoder values. For *EncPos*, we let **sensor_1** take the raw value as input while **sensor_2** always returns 1. In this configuration, **n1** is the scale factor, and **n2** is the configurable offset. The final *AP* output is the Boolean result of comparison with the **n3** reference value.

5.2   Specification

Design. Our specifications need to disambiguate between three modes (APS1 faulty, APS2 faulty, or no fault) without false positives. We initially encode Robonaut2's team's fault description: *If the differences between APSs are larger than 1 rad, then the APS that disagrees with the encoder by more than 0.01 rad is at fault.* We assume: (1) agreement with the encoder value implies correct APS position, (2) agreement between any two position sources implies the minority opinion is incorrect, i.e., sensor voting. To prevent false positives due to sensor outliers, we ensure states hold for at least three timesteps before reporting a fault. Robonaut2's existing logic sets an "encoder fault position" signal when the encoder and APS1 disagree. Our MLTL specifications reason over the APS1 position, APS2 position, encoder position, and encoder fault position sensor inputs;

---

see Table 2. The corresponding R2U2 configuration for this set of specifications requires 17 instructions, 14 SCQs, and 29 queue slots with a max depth of 4 without CSE. Applying CSE reduces that to 14 instructions, 11 SCQs, and 26 queue slots with a max depth of 4.

Table 2. Fault disambiguation specification – revision 1

R2U2 Configuration	
Bus Values	Temporal Formulas
APS1: Position [rad]	$\varphi_1 = \Box_{[0,3]}(V_{\text{threshold}})$
APS2: Position [rad]	$\varphi_2 = \text{FaultEncPos} \wedge \Box_{[0,3]}(Agree_{\text{Enc,APS2}}) \to \text{APS1}_{\text{Wrong}}$
EncPos: Position [rad]	$\varphi_3 = \varphi_1 \vee !\text{FaultEncPos} \to \text{APS2}_{\text{Wrong}}$
EncFaultPos: Encoder Fault [bool]	Observer Tree
Signal Processing	$\varphi_1 \longleftarrow \varphi_3 \quad \varphi_2$
$V_{\text{threshold}} = \|\text{APS1} - \text{APS2}\| > 1 \text{ rad}$	$V_{\text{threshold}} \quad Agree_{\text{Enc,APS2}}$
$Agree_{\text{Enc,APS2}} = \|\text{APS2} - \text{EncPos}\| < 0.01 \text{ rad}$	$APS1 \quad APS2 \quad EncPos \quad EncFaultPos$

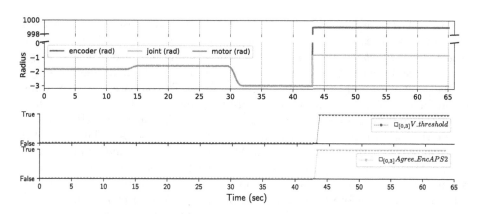

Fig. 9. Ground R2: APS fault (Color figure online)

Validation. After initial specification development, a terrestrial Robonaut2 developed the fault of interest. To validate our specifications, we ran R2U2 over the recorded traces. In Fig. 9 and 10 the top timeline shows the encoder (red), APS1 (blue, labeled motor), and APS2 (yellow, labeled joint) positions in radians. The lower timeline shows the R2U2 verdicts of the fault-case specifications. In Fig. 9 the APS fault occurs at 43 s. The expected > 2.1 rad shift in APS position is flagged by $V_{\text{threshold}}$ correctly. Notice that the encoder jumps to an

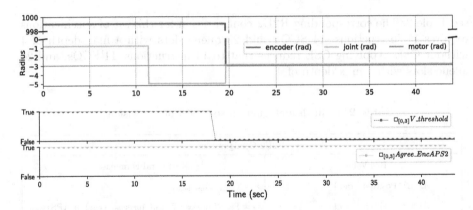

Fig. 10. Ground R2: unsuccessful recovery (Color figure online)

implausible 998 rad, violating the sensor voting assumption. Figure 10 records an attempted recovery. While appearing successful, the difference between the three sensors after time 19 is still too wide to unlock the emergency stop. Additionally, the Boolean $V_{threshold}$ correctly detects that we are not in the failure mode of interest after time 19. This data reveals an implicit assumption that encoder values freeze during a fault.

Revision. With our new insight on the fault behavior, we revise the specification strategy: *If there is a sudden, large jump in the encoder and an APS's position report, the APS that jumped is at fault.* The assumptions of our new strategy are: (1) a sufficiently large discontinuity in the data is the fault signature, (2) in the fault case, only the faulty APS "moves." To compare the APS value before and after a fault, we must identify the timestep of the fault – which is when the encoder goes out-of-range. To determine the "moving" APS, we can divide the joint range into sections and use the signal processing layer to get a Boolean a_n indicating the signal from APS1 is in region n (and similarly with b_n and APS2). Now the temporal observers can check if each APS is in the same region before and after the encoder jump. The size of n dictates the maximum rotation distance before triggering a region change. We select n such that the maximum rotation is about half the fault discontinuity: ≈ 1 rad. The range of the APS is $[-\pi, \pi]$, requiring 6 regions, $(a_1, a_2, \ldots, a_6)$ and $(b_1, b_2, \ldots, b_6)$ to meet the target region size. The fault only occurs when arming a parked actuator so we are not concerned with rotation during a fault. Also, encoder range errors do not register in the *EncPos* signal stream when an actuator experiences nominal joint rotation across a boundary, further preventing false positives. Table 3 lists the MLTL and signal layer specification. The final R2U2 configuration requires 154 instructions, 140 SCQs, and 196 SCQ slots with a max depth of 3 without CSE. CSE reduces this to 100 instructions, 86 SCQs, and 142 SCQ slots with a max depth of 3. The 33% reduction in instructions shows the impact of CSE optimization on human-written specifications that necessarily contain repeated references to important subsystems. While CSE results in a 38% reduction in SCQ quantity, the significance of this reduction is that the number of SCQs in the unoptimized R2U2 configuration crosses a power-of-two boundary, requiring 8 bits to encode but the same specification requires only 7 bits with CSE enabled. When embedding hardware monitors, bus size increases account for multiplicative jumps in resource requirements (as in Fig. 7). Our RV specification would not fit in Robonaut2's knee's available FPGA space without SCQ-based encodings reduced by CSE.

Table 3. Fault disambiguation specification – revision 2

R2U2 Configuration	
Bus Values	Temporal Formulas
APS1: Position [rad]	$\varphi_n = (a_n \land \neg e) \land \diamond_{[1,2]}(\neg a_n \land e) \to \text{APS1}_{\text{Fault}} \quad \forall n \in [0,5]$
APS2: Position [rad]	$\varphi_{m+6} = (b_m \land \neg e) \land \diamond_{[1,2]}(\neg a_m \land e) \to \text{APS2}_{\text{Fault}} \quad \forall m \in [0,5]$
EncPos: Position [rad]	Observer Tree
Signal Processing	$\varphi_{[0,5]} \quad \varphi_{[6,11]}$
$e = \text{EncPos} > 100$	
$a_n = \pi(\frac{n}{6} - 1) < \text{APS1} < \pi(\frac{n+1}{6} - 1) \forall n \in [0,5]$	$a_{[0,5]} \quad b_{[6,11]} \quad\quad e$
$b_n = \pi(\frac{n}{6} - 1) < \text{APS2} < \pi(\frac{n+1}{6} - 1) \forall n \in [0,5]$	$\downarrow \quad\quad \downarrow \quad\quad \downarrow$
	$APS1 \quad APS2 \quad EncPos$

Verification. Following the best-practices for specification debugging established in [23], we checked each specification, its negation, and the conjunction of all specifications for satisfiability. We utilized the MLTL SMT solver from [14] to prove the specifications were both satisfiable and falsifiable. Finally, we played back all available recorded traces of both faulty and nominal operation through the real hardware, with our final R2U2 configuration running, to check that we successfully catch the fault with no false positives during nominal operation.

6   Conclusion

We have successfully embedded R2U2 to provide trusted fault-disambiguation for automatic mitigation. Our new encodings enabled CSE optimization, a crucial step in meeting the resource limitation challenges of the R2 platform. Importantly, the techniques presented in Sects. 3 and 4 are not exclusive to this application or to R2U2, but could be ported to other RV algorithms, tools, and application domains.

Working with FPGA limitations provided important lessons on the relation between specification complexity and hardware resources. In Fig. 6 LUT requirements scale linearly with timestamp length; however, transistor count (and therefore chip space and power) scales exponential with LUT size. Also, the discontinuities in Fig. 7 are due to BRAM width alignment. Since both LUT type and BRAM width are properties of the FPGA, the target hardware can drastically change the maximum size of a specification's encoding, even with the same amount of LUTs and BRAM free. For a hardware R2U2 deployment, BRAM will probably be the limiting resource. This may not be true for other RV engines, but it's the price of reconfigurability, which allows RV to be embedded, certified, and deployed flexibly, and which was a requirement of the R2 team.

Future Work. In the current implementation, we utilize the equivalence relations in Sect. 2 to represent full MLTL semantics; next we plan to implement direct encodings, e.g., for the $\mathcal{R}$ operator. Encoding every operator directly would reduce the number of negations in the AST and therefore, the amount of SCQ space required. We will then investigate additional design-time optimizations to the AST.

On the application side, we are working toward distributing specifications across RV monitors on multiple FPGAs. This extension has the potential to increase the number of specifications we can monitor on a given platform, both by utilizing more of the leftover fabric on the platform, and by allowing observers to reason over proprieties that cannot by observed from a single location.

References

1. Adam, S., Larsen, M., Jensen, K., Schultz, U.P.: Towards rule-based dynamic safety monitoring for mobile robots. In: Brugali, D., Broenink, J.F., Kroeger, T., MacDonald, B.A. (eds.) SIMPAR 2014. LNCS (LNAI), vol. 8810, pp. 207–218. Springer, Cham (2014). https://doi.org/10.1007/978-3-319-11900-7_18
2. Alur, R., Henzinger, T.A.: Real-time logics: complexity and expressiveness. Inf. Comput. **104**(1), 35–77 (1993)
3. Badger, J., Hulse, A., Taylor, R., Curtis, A., Gooding, D., Thackston, A.: Model-based robotic dynamic motion control for the Robonaut 2 humanoid robot. In: 2013 13th IEEE-RAS International Conference on Humanoid Robots (Humanoids), pp. 62–67, October 2013. https://doi.org/10.1109/HUMANOIDS.2013.7029956
4. Badger, J., Gooding, D., Ensley, K., Hambuchen, K., Thackston, A.: ROS in space: a case study on Robonaut 2. In: Koubaa, A. (ed.) Robot Operating System (ROS). SCI, vol. 625, pp. 343–373. Springer, Cham (2016). https://doi.org/10.1007/978-3-319-26054-9_13
5. Clemens, J., Pal, R., Sherrell, B.: Runtime state verification on resource-constrained platforms. In: MILCOM 2018–2018 IEEE Military Communications Conference (MILCOM), pp. 1–6. IEEE (2018)
6. Cooper, K., Eckhardt, J., Kennedy, K.: Redundancy elimination revisited. In: Proceedings of the 17th International Conference on Parallel Architectures and Compilation Techniques, pp. 12–21. ACM (2008)
7. Cowley, A., Taylor, C.J.: Towards language-based verification of robot behaviors. In: 2011 IEEE/RSJ International Conference on Intelligent Robots and Systems, pp. 4776–4782. IEEE (2011)
8. Diftler, M.A., et al.: Robonaut 2 - the first humanoid robot in space. In: 2011 IEEE International Conference on Robotics and Automation, pp. 2178–2183, May 2011. https://doi.org/10.1109/ICRA.2011.5979830

9. Geist, J., Rozier, K.Y., Schumann, J.: Runtime observer pairs and Bayesian network reasoners on-board FPGAs: flight-certifiable system health management for embedded systems. In: Bonakdarpour, B., Smolka, S.A. (eds.) RV 2014. LNCS, vol. 8734, pp. 215–230. Springer, Cham (2014). https://doi.org/10.1007/978-3-319-11164-3_18

10. Halder, R., Proença, J., Macedo, N., Santos, A.: Formal verification of ROS-based robotic applications using timed-automata. In: 2017 IEEE/ACM 5th International FME Workshop on Formal Methods in Software Engineering (FormaliSE), pp. 44–50. IEEE (2017)

11. Huang, J., et al.: ROSRV: runtime verification for robots. In: Bonakdarpour, B., Smolka, S.A. (eds.) RV 2014. LNCS, vol. 8734, pp. 247–254. Springer, Cham (2014). https://doi.org/10.1007/978-3-319-11164-3_20

12. Badger, J.M., Hulse, A.M., Thackston, A.: Advancing safe human-robot interactions with Robonaut 2. In: Proceedings of the 12th International Symposium on Artificial Intelligence, Robotics and Automation in Space (2014)

13. Kane, A., Chowdhury, O., Datta, A., Koopman, P.: A case study on runtime monitoring of an autonomous research vehicle (ARV) system. In: Bartocci, E., Majumdar, R. (eds.) RV 2015. LNCS, vol. 9333, pp. 102–117. Springer, Cham (2015). https://doi.org/10.1007/978-3-319-23820-3_7

14. Li, J., Vardi, M.Y., Rozier, K.Y.: Satisfiability checking for mission-time LTL. In: Dillig, I., Tasiran, S. (eds.) CAV 2019. LNCS, vol. 11562, pp. 3–22. Springer, Cham (2019). https://doi.org/10.1007/978-3-030-25543-5_1

15. Lu, H., Forin, A.: The design and implementation of p2v, an architecture for zero-overhead online verification of software programs. Technical report MSR-TR-2007-99, Microsoft Research, August 2007

16. Luckcuck, M., Farrell, M., Dennis, L., Dixon, C., Fisher, M.: Formal specification and verification of autonomous robotic systems: a survey. arXiv preprint arXiv:1807.00048 (2018)

17. Mukherjee, R., Purandare, M., Polig, R., Kroening, D.: Formal techniques for effective co-verification of hardware/software co-designs. In: Proceedings of the 54th Annual Design Automation Conference 2017, p. 35. ACM (2017)

18. Pellizzoni, R., Meredith, P., Caccamo, M., Rosu, G.: Hardware runtime monitoring for dependable cots-based real-time embedded systems. In: 2008 Real-Time Systems Symposium, pp. 481–491, November 2008

19. Pratt, G.A., Williamson, M.M.: Series elastic actuators. In: Proceedings 1995 IEEE/RSJ International Conference on Intelligent Robots and Systems. Human Robot Interaction and Cooperative Robots, vol. 1, pp. 399–406, August 1995. https://doi.org/10.1109/IROS.1995.525827

20. Quigley, M., et al.: ROS: an open-source robot operating system. In: ICRA Workshop on Open Source Software, vol. 3, p. 5. Kobe, Japan (2009)

21. Reinbacher, T., Rozier, K.Y., Schumann, J.: Temporal-logic based runtime observer pairs for system health management of real-time systems. In: Ábrahám, E., Havelund, K. (eds.) TACAS 2014. LNCS, vol. 8413, pp. 357–372. Springer, Heidelberg (2014). https://doi.org/10.1007/978-3-642-54862-8_24

22. Rozier, K.Y., Schumann, J.: R2U2: tool overview. In: Proceedings of International Workshop on Competitions, Usability, Benchmarks, Evaluation, and Standardisation for Runtime Verification Tools (RV-CUBES), vol. 3, pp. 138–156. Kalpa Publications, Seattle, September 2017. TBD, https://easychair.org/publications/paper/Vncw

23. Rozier, K., Vardi, M.: LTL satisfiability checking. Int. J. Software Tools Technol. Transfer (STTT) **12**(2), 123–137 (2010). https://doi.org/10.1007/s10009-010-0140-3

24. Schumann, J., Moosbrugger, P., Rozier, K.Y.: R2U2: monitoring and diagnosis of security threats for unmanned aerial systems. In: Bartocci, E., Majumdar, R. (eds.) RV 2015. LNCS, vol. 9333, pp. 233–249. Springer, Cham (2015). https://doi.org/10.1007/978-3-319-23820-3_15

25. Schumann, J., Moosbrugger, P., Rozier, K.Y.: Runtime analysis with R2U2: a tool exhibition report. In: Falcone, Y., Sánchez, C. (eds.) RV 2016. LNCS, vol. 10012, pp. 504–509. Springer, Cham (2016). https://doi.org/10.1007/978-3-319-46982-9_35

26. Schumann, J., Rozier, K.Y., Reinbacher, T., Mengshoel, O.J., Mbaya, T., Ippolito, C.: Towards real-time, on-board, hardware-supported sensor and software health management for unmanned aerial systems. Int. J. Prognost. Health Manage. (IJPHM) **6**(1), 1–27 (2015)

27. Solet, D., Béchennec, J.L., Briday, M., Faucou, S., Pillement, S.: Hardware runtime verification of a RTOS kernel: Evaluation using fault injection. In: 2018 14th European Dependable Computing Conference (EDCC), pp. 25–32. IEEE (2018)

28. Wong, L., Arora, N.S., Gao, L., Hoang, T., Wu, J.: Oracle streams: a high performance implementation for near real time asynchronous replication. In: 2009 IEEE 25th International Conference on Data Engineering, pp. 1363–1374. IEEE (2009)

29. Zhang, P., Zambreno, J., Jones, P.H., Rozier, K.: Model predictive runtime verification for embedded platforms with real-time deadlines (2020, Under submission)

Guarded Autonomous Transitions Increase Conciseness and Expressiveness of Timed Automata

Susanna Donatelli[1]($^{(\boxtimes)}$) and Serge Haddad[2]

[1] Dipartimento di Informatica, Università di Torino, Turin, Italy
donatelli@di.unito.it
[2] LSV, ENS Paris-Saclay, CNRS, Inria, Université Paris-Saclay, Cachan, France
haddad@lsv.fr

Abstract. Timed Automata (TA) are an appropriate model for specifying timed requirements for Continuous Time Markov Chains (CTMC). However in order to keep tractable the model checking of a TA over a CTMC, temporal logics based on TA, like CSL^{TA}, restrict TA to have a single clock and to be deterministic (DTA). Different variants of DTAs have been proposed to address the issue of their expressiveness and conciseness. Here we study the effect of two possible features: (1) autonomous transitions which are triggered by time elapsing in addition to synchronized transitions and (2) transitions guarded by propositional formulas instead of propositional formulas guarding locations. We first show that autonomous guarded transitions increase the expressiveness of DTAs (as already shown for guarded locations). Then we identify a hierarchy of DTAs subclasses all equivalent to DTAs without guarded autonomous transitions and we analyze their respective conciseness. In particular we show that eliminating resets in autonomous transitions implies an exponential blow-up, while eliminating autonomous transitions without reset can be performed in polynomial time if decision diagrams are used. Finally we compare TA with guarded transitions to TA with guarded locations showing that the former model is exponentially more concise than the latter one.

1 Introduction

Model Checking CTMC. Defining a temporal logic for specifying properties of a CTMC is a natural goal, since a CTMC can be represented as a (probabilistic) transition system. In fact the first temporal logic that has been proposed, CSL [3], is a variant of CTL where (1) the 'for all paths' and 'there exists a path' operators have been replaced by the operator expressing 'the probability that a random path is greater (or smaller) than some threshold' and (2) the 'until' operator is equipped with a time interval. The core of the associated model checking

© Springer Nature Switzerland AG 2020
N. Bertrand and N. Jansen (Eds.): FORMATS 2020, LNCS 12288, pp. 215–230, 2020.
https://doi.org/10.1007/978-3-030-57628-8_13

procedure consists in building some (formula-dependent) CTMCs and to analyze their transient behavior. CSL has been extended in several directions [4,5] and tailored for dealing with CTMCs generated by generalized stochastic Petri nets [11].

Another approach consists in specifying the formula by a timed automaton (or even an hybrid automaton) as in [2,7,12]. However without restrictions, the model checking procedure can (1) either be based on simulation which only provides an estimation of the probability to be computed or (2) solve numerically multiple integrals, which do not scale at all. When the Timed Automaton is restricted to have a single clock and to be Deterministic (DTA), there is an efficient model checking procedure that exploits Markov regenerative process. In addition, the logic CSL^{TA} [10] which follows such an approach has be proven [10] to extend CSL and most of its variants.

Classes of DTAs. The basic family of DTAs only includes *synchronized transitions*: transition with a clock constraint and a set of synchronizing actions. The joint evolution (synchronized product) of the CTMC and the DTA *is driven by the CTMC*: it evolves when a transition of the CTMC can be matched by a transition of a DTA (i.e. the clock constraint is satisfied and the action labelling the transition of the CTMC is included in the set of synchronizing actions of the DTA transition). In order to increase the expressive power of the basic family, *autonomous transitions* can be added: these are transitions with a clock time threshold, and when the clock reaches this threshold, in the synchronized product *the DTA evolves autonomously*. When the CTMC states are labelled with atomic propositions, it is possible to further restricts the possible joint evolutions, with different semantics depending on whether the DTA has atomic propositional formulas associated to locations (DTA class denoted as A_s) or associated to transitions (DTA class denoted as A_t). In A_s the joint evolution is possible only when the formula associated to the location is satisfied by the atomic proposition of the CTMC state, in A_t each DTA arc has a pair of propositional formulas and the evolution is possible only when the formulas are satisfied, respectively, by the source state and the target state of the CTMC transition.

Expressiveness and Conciseness. In order to compare the *expressiveness* of families of DTAs, the usual qualitative notion is related to their timed languages: a family A is at least as expressive as a family A' if for any DTA in A there is a DTA in A' with the same language. Since the DTAs we study are used for defining the acceptance probability of a CTMC, we also introduce a quantitative notion: a family A is at least as expressive as a family A' if for any DTA in A there is a DTA in A' such that for any CTMC their acceptance probabilities are equal. When a family A is at least as expressive as a family A', it raises other issues: (1) *effectiveness*, does there exist an algorithm for producing an equivalent DTA? (2) *cost*, what is the complexity of this algorithm? and (3) *conciseness*, what is the size of the equivalent DTA w.r.t. the size of the original one?

Our Contributions. We first show that in $\mathbb{A}_t$ autonomous transitions strictly increase expressiveness even w.r.t. the quantitative notion (as already proved for $\mathbb{A}_s$ in [8]). Then we characterize a large subclass of $\mathbb{A}_t$, denoted $\mathbb{A}_t^{rc}$ for which autonomous transitions do not increase expressiveness even w.r.t. the qualitative notion. This class $\mathbb{A}_t^{rc}$ includes the class of DTAs with no clock reset on autonomous transitions, denoted $\mathbb{A}_t^{nra}$, but we prove that $\mathbb{A}_t^{rc}$ is exponentially more concise than $\mathbb{A}_t^{nra}$. Furthermore, we establish that one can transform a DTA in $\mathbb{A}_t^{nra}$ into an equivalent DTA with no autonomous transition in polynomial time. This reduction requires to encode propositional formulas by decision diagrams. Finally we compare $\mathbb{A}_t$ and $\mathbb{A}_s$ showing that the former family is exponentially more concise than the latter one.

Organization. Section 2 introduces the syntax and semantics of DTAs with autonomous and guarded transitions and defines qualitative and quantitative notions of expressiveness. Section 3 presents a hierarchy of subclasses of DTAs with autonomous and guarded transitions and establish a full classification w.r.t. expressiveness and conciseness. Section 4 establishes that using guarded transitions yields an exponentially more concise model than the one with guarded locations. Some perspectives for this work are given in Sect. 5.

2   Preliminaries

A DTA can be used to specify requirements on timed paths of a CTMC, so that we can refer to CTMC paths accepted or rejected by a DTA. The CTMCs we consider are CTMCs with actions from a set *Act* and a valuation of a set of propositions *AP* associated to the CTMC states.

Definition 1 (CTMC). *A continuous time Markov chain $\mathcal{M}$ with state and action labels is represented by the tuple $\mathcal{M} = \langle S, s_0, Act, AP, lab, \boldsymbol{R} \rangle$, where S is a finite set of states, $s_0 \in S$ the initial state, Act is a finite set of action names, AP is a finite set of atomic propositions, $lab : S \to \{\top, \bot\}^{AP}$ is a state-labeling function that assigns to each state s a valuation of the atomic propositions, $\boldsymbol{R} : S \times Act \times S \to \mathbb{R}_{\geqslant 0}$ is a rate function. If $\boldsymbol{R}(s, a, s') > 0$, we write $s \xrightarrow{a, \boldsymbol{R}(s,a,s')} s'$.*

We assume that each state has at least one successor (possibly the state itself): for all $s \in S$, there exists $a \in Act$, $s' \in S$ such that $\boldsymbol{R}(s, a, s') > 0$. CTMC executions lead to timed paths, and a CTMC is a generator of a random path.

Definition 2 (Timed Path). *Given a set AP of atomic propositions and a set Act of actions, a timed (infinite) path is a sequence $(v_0, \delta_0) \xrightarrow{a_0} (v_1, \delta_1) \xrightarrow{a_1} \cdots (v_i, \delta_i) \xrightarrow{a_i} \cdots$ such that for all $i \in \mathbb{N} : v_i \in \{\top, \bot\}^{AP}, a_i \in Act, \delta_i \in \mathbb{R}_{\geqslant 0}$.*

where v_i, the $(i + 1)$-th state of the timed path, is a boolean evaluation of the atomic propositions, δ_i is the delay before action a_i, or equivalently the sojourn time in state i. A timed path leaves state v_i with action a_i after a sojourn time in the state equal to δ_i. If τ_i indicates the time elapsed until exiting state i, then: $\tau_i = \delta_i + \tau_{i-1}$, with $\tau_{-1} = 0$.

*Example 1 (**Timed path**).* In writing timed paths we indicate v_i as the set of elements in AP that evaluate to $\top$. Given $AP = \{p, q\}$ and $Act = \{a, b\}$ the timed path $(\{p, q\}, 0.3) \xrightarrow{a} (\{p\}, 0.2) \xrightarrow{b} (\{q\}, 1) \xrightarrow{a} \cdots$, is interpreted as (1) the system staying in a state fulfilling $p \wedge q$ in the time interval $[0, 0.3]$, where at time 0.3 action a takes place, (2) the system moves to a state fulfilling $p \wedge \neg q$, stays there for 0.2 time units and then action b takes place, and (3) the system moves to a state fulfilling $\neg p \wedge q$, stays there for 1 time units and then action a takes place (at the elapsed time $\tau = 1.5$).

The definition of a DTA includes a clock x and two types of clock constraints associated with transitions: boundary ones, $\mathsf{BoundC} = \{x = \alpha, \alpha \in \mathbb{N}\}$ and inner ones, $\mathsf{InC} = \{\alpha \bowtie x \bowtie' \beta\}$, with $\bowtie, \bowtie' \in \{<, \leqslant, \}, \alpha \in \mathbb{N}$, and $\beta \in \mathbb{N} \cup \{\infty\}$. In the sequel, C is the largest time constant occurring in a DTA. Transitions also have an input and an output guard on atomic propositions (indicated with φ^- and φ^+ respectively).

Before formally defining the syntax and semantic of a DTA (Definitions 3, 4 and 5), let us introduce its main ingredients. During the execution of a stochastic discrete event system (e.g. a CTMC), represented by a timed path, the current location of the DTA, say ℓ, is matched with the current state of the system, say $s = (v_i, \delta_i)$. This matching evolves in three ways depending on the delay $d \leqslant \delta_i$ (initially equals to δ_0), elapsed until the next transition $(v_i, \delta_i) \xrightarrow{a_i} (v_{i+1}, \delta_{i+1})$.

- Either after some delay $\delta \leqslant d$, there is an outgoing *autonomous transition* from ℓ which is *enabled*, meaning that (1) its boundary condition (say $x = \alpha$) is satisfied and (2) v_i fulfills φ^-. Then after delay δ, ℓ' is matched with s and d is decreased by δ.
- Else if there is a *synchronizing transition* outgoing from ℓ after time d has elapsed is *enabled* meaning that (1) v_i satisfies φ^-, (2) its inner condition (say $\alpha \bowtie x \bowtie' \beta$) is satisfied, (3) the action a belongs to the subset of actions associated with the synchronizing transition, and (4) v_{i+1} satisfies φ^+. Then after delay δ_i, ℓ' is matched with $s' = (v_{i+1}, \delta_{i+1})$ and d is set to δ_{i+1}.
- Otherwise there is no possible matching and the timed path is rejected by the DTA.

When a transition of the DTA is fired, clock x may keep its current value or may be reset. In the first two cases above, when $\ell' = \ell_f$ (ℓ_f being the *final location* of the DTA), the timed path is accepted by the DTA whatever its future. This is ensured by the existence of the unique (looping) synchronizing transition from ℓ_f with no boolean guards, no timing and no action conditions. Observe that the synchronization may go on forever without visiting ℓ_f: in this case the timed path is rejected.

Furthermore the synchronization of the stochastic system with the DTA should not introduce non-determinism. So (1) synchronizing transitions outgoing from the same location are never simultaneously enabled, (2) autonomous transitions outgoing from the same location are never simultaneously enabled, and (3) autonomous transitions have priority over synchronizing transitions.

Definition 3 (DTA). *A DTA is defined by a tuple* $\mathcal{A} = \langle L, \ell_0, \ell_f, AP, Synch,$
$Aut \rangle$ *where* L *is a finite set of* locations, $\ell_0 \in L$ *is the* initial location, $\ell_f \in L$ *is*
the final location, $Synch \subseteq L \times \mathcal{B}_{AP} \times \mathsf{InC} \times 2^{Act} \times \{\varnothing, \downarrow\} \times \mathcal{B}_{AP} \times L$ *is the set*
of synchronizing transitions, *and* $Aut \subseteq L \times \mathcal{B}_{AP} \times \mathsf{BoundC} \times \{\sharp\} \times \{\varnothing, \downarrow\} \times L$
is the set of autonomous transitions.
Furthermore $\mathcal{A}$ *fulfills the following conditions, where we indicate with*
$\ell \xrightarrow{\varphi^-, \gamma, B, r, \varphi^+} \ell'$ *the synchronized transition* $(\ell, \varphi^-, \gamma, B, r, \varphi^+, \ell')$, *and with*
$\ell \xrightarrow{\varphi^-, \gamma, \sharp, r(,\varphi^-)} \ell'$ *the autonomous transition* $(\ell, \varphi^-, \gamma, \sharp, r, \ell')$ *(repeating some-*
times the φ^- *formula for unifying the notation).*

- **Determinism on actions.** $\forall B, B' \subseteq Act\ s.t.\ B \cap B' \neq \varnothing, \forall \ell, \ell', \ell'' \in L,$
  if $\ell \xrightarrow{\varphi^-, \gamma, B, r, \varphi^+} \ell' \wedge \ell \xrightarrow{\varphi'^-, \gamma', B', r', \varphi'^+} \ell''$ *then*
  $\varphi^- \wedge \varphi'^- \Leftrightarrow \bot\ or\ \varphi^+ \wedge \varphi'^+ \Leftrightarrow \bot\ or\ \gamma \wedge \gamma' \Leftrightarrow \bot.$
- **Determinism on autonomous transitions.** $\forall \ell, \ell', \ell'' \in L,$
  if $\ell \xrightarrow{\varphi^-, x=\alpha, \sharp, r} \ell'$ *and* $\ell \xrightarrow{\varphi'^-, x=\alpha', \sharp, r'} \ell''$ *then* $\varphi^- \wedge \varphi'^- \Leftrightarrow \bot\ or\ \alpha \neq \alpha'.$
- **Condition on the final location.** $\ell_f \xrightarrow{\top, \top, Act, \varnothing, \top} \ell_f \in Synch.$

$\mathbb{A}_t$ denotes the family of automata identified by Definition 3. We informally write
"a transition with reset" or "a transition without reset" to indicate the condition
$r = \downarrow$ and $r = \varnothing$ respectively.

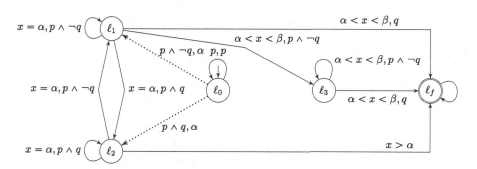

Fig. 1. A DTA specification of $pU^{]\alpha,\beta[}q$ with $\alpha > 0$.

*Example 2 (**DTA example**).* Figure 1 shows a DTA with locations ℓ_0, ℓ_1, ℓ_2,
ℓ_3 and ℓ_f. The initial location is ℓ_0. Autonomous transitions are depicted as
dotted arcs, while synchronizing are depicted as solid arcs. For readability and
conciseness we omit in the figures: 1) the symbol $\sharp$ on autonomous transitions;
2) the reset indication when there is no reset; 3) Act if a transition accepts all
actions; 4) trivially true clock guards (like $x \geqslant 0$) and input or output guards; 5)
the name x of the clock in $x = \alpha$ guards of autonomous transitions. As a result
an autonomous transition is depicted as either $l \xrightarrow{\varphi^-, \alpha} l'$, or as $l \xrightarrow{\varphi^-, \alpha, \downarrow} l'$, if

there is a clock reset. The two dotted arcs out of ℓ_0 correspond to autonomous transitions, mutually exclusive due to their guards. Note that the self loop on ℓ_0 represents a synchronizing transitions, so it is mutually exclusive with the other two transitions out of ℓ_0 because of priority. Note that guards of the form $x = \alpha$, typically associated with autonomous transitions, can also be associated to synchronizing transitions. Figure 1 illustrates how to specify the CSL formula $p\mathbf{U}]^{\alpha,\beta}[q$ with a DTA $\mathcal{A} \in \mathbb{A}_t$. Since the clock is used to count the time elapsed, no reset occurs. Observe that in the interval $[0, \alpha[$, the current location can only be ℓ_0 with the additional requirement that if an action occurs then p has to be fullfilled inside the whole interval. At time α, the current location can only be ℓ_1 or ℓ_2 depending on the truth value of q and with the guarantee that p holds in the interval $[0, \alpha]$. Considering the first action that occurs after α, there are three possible cases: (1) $p \wedge q$ was satisfied and the formula is satisfied (by taking transition from ℓ_2 to ℓ_f), (2) $p \wedge \neg q$ was satisfied, q is now satisfied and the action occurs before β and so the formula is satisfied (by taking transition from ℓ_1 to ℓ_f) (3) or $p \wedge \neg q$ was satisfied and it is still satisfied and the action occurs before β, and so (by taking transition from ℓ_1 to ℓ_3) there is the same possibility to satisfy the formula represented by location ℓ_3.

Definition 4 (Run of a DTA).

A run of $\mathcal{A} \in \mathbb{A}_t$ is a sequence: $\rho = (\ell_0, v_0, \bar{x}_0, \delta_0) \xrightarrow{\varphi_0^-, \gamma_0, B_0, r_0, \varphi_0^+} (\ell_1, v_1, \bar{x}_1, \delta_1)$
$\xrightarrow{\varphi_1^-, \gamma_1, B_1, r_1, \varphi_1^+} \cdots (\ell_i, v_i, \bar{x}_i, \delta_i) \xrightarrow{\varphi_i^-, \gamma_i, B_i, r_i, \varphi_i^+} \cdots$ *such that for all $i \in \mathbb{N}$, $\ell_i \in L$,*
$v_i \in \{\bot, \top\}^{AP}$, $\delta_i \in \mathbb{R}_{\geqslant 0}$, $\ell_i \xrightarrow{\varphi_i^-, \gamma_i, B_i, r_i, \varphi_i^+} \ell_{i+1} \in E = Synch \cup Aut$, $v_i \models \varphi_i^-$,
$v_{i+1} \models \varphi_i^+$, $\bar{x}_i + \delta_i \models \gamma_i$, $\bar{x}_{i+1} = \begin{cases} 0 & \text{if } r_i = \downarrow \\ \bar{x}_i + \delta_i & \text{otherwise} \end{cases}$

Let $\bar{x}_\sharp = min\{\alpha \mid \exists \ell_i \xrightarrow{\varphi, x=\alpha, \sharp, r} \ell' \in E \wedge \bar{x}_i \leqslant \alpha \wedge v_i \models \varphi\}$.
If $B_i = \sharp$ then $\bar{x}_i + \delta_i = \bar{x}_\sharp$ and $v_{i+1} = v_i$ else $\bar{x}_i + \delta_i < x_\sharp$.

*Example 3 (**DTA run**).* In the run we, again, describe v in terms of the subset of AP that evaluate to $\top$. Let us describe a possible run of the DTA of Fig. 1, assuming $\alpha = 1$ and $\beta = 4$. The run starts with $v_0 = \{p\}$; at time 0.4, it goes from ℓ_0 to ℓ_0 by performing the synchronizing transition of the self-loop over ℓ_0. Then at time 1.0, it autonomously goes to location ℓ_2. If the next action happens at time 6.0 then it goes to ℓ_f. Note that this is a case in which the formula is satisfied already at time β, since $\beta = 4$, but the run reaches the final location only at time $5.0 > \beta$, when the first synchronizing transition takes place, and stays in the final location forever. The run described above corresponds, in more formal terms, to:

$(\ell_0, \{p\}, \bar{x}_0 = 0.0, \delta_0 = 0.4) \xrightarrow{p, x \geqslant 0, Act, \varnothing, p} (\ell_0, \{p, q\}, 0.4, 0.6) \xrightarrow{p \wedge q, x=1, \sharp, \varnothing}$
$(\ell_f, \{p, q\}, 1.0, 5.0) \xrightarrow{\top, x>1, Act, \varnothing, \top} (\ell_f, \{p\}, 6.0, 2.4) \xrightarrow{\top, x \geqslant 0, Act, \varnothing, \top} (\ell_f, \varnothing, 8.4,$
$0.7) \cdots$

A timed path σ is recognized by a run ρ of $\mathcal{A}$ such that the occurrences of the actions in σ are matched by the synchronizing transitions in ρ. This requires to define a mapping to "couple" the points in the paths in which synchronizing transitions take place. This can be done by identifying a strictly increasing mapping for the indices of the timed path σ to the subset of the indices of the run ρ that correspond to a synchronizing transition.

Definition 5. *Let* $\sigma = (v_0, \delta_0) \xrightarrow{a_0} (v_1, \delta_1) \xrightarrow{a_1} \cdots (v_i, \delta_i) \xrightarrow{a_i} \cdots$ *be a timed path and* $\rho = (\ell_0, v_0', \bar{x}_0, \delta_0') \xrightarrow{\varphi_0^-, \gamma_0, B_0, r_0, \varphi_0^+} \cdots (\ell_i, v_i', \bar{x}_i, \delta_i') \xrightarrow{\varphi_i^-, \gamma_i, B_i, r_i, \varphi_i^+} \cdots$ *be a run of a DTA* $\mathcal{A}$*. Then* σ *is recognized by* ρ *if there is a strictly increasing mapping* $\kappa : \mathbb{N} \to \mathbb{N}$ *(extended to* $\kappa(-1) = -1$*), such that for all* $i \in \mathbb{N}$*:*

- $a_i \in B_{\kappa(i)}$ *and* $\delta_i = \sum_{\kappa(i-1) < h \leqslant \kappa(i)} \delta_h'$*;*
- $\forall h,\ \kappa(i-1) < h \leqslant \kappa(i) \Rightarrow v_h' = v_i$ *and* $h \notin \kappa(\mathbb{N}) \Rightarrow B_h = \natural$*.*

A timed path σ *is accepted by* $\mathcal{A}$ *if* σ *is recognized by a run* ρ *that visits* ℓ_f*. The language* $\mathcal{L}(\mathcal{A})$ *of* $\mathcal{A}$ *is the set of the timed paths accepted by* $\mathcal{A}$*.*

Note that, due to determinism, if such a run exists, it is unique. We define by $\mathbf{Pr}_{\mathcal{M}}(\mathcal{A})$ the probability that the random path of $\mathcal{M}$ is accepted by $\mathcal{A}$ (probability measure of all paths accepted by $\mathcal{A}$ as defined in [6]).

*Example 4 (**Timed path recognized by a DTA run**).* The timed path $\sigma = (\{p\}, 0.4) \xrightarrow{a} (\{p, q\}, 5.6) \xrightarrow{b} (\{p\}, 2.4) \xrightarrow{c} (\varnothing, 0.7) \cdots$ is accepted by the DTA of Fig. 1 using the run of Example 3, with the mapping κ. where $\kappa(0) = 0$ and for all $i > 0\ \kappa(i) = i + 1$.
The (Zeno) timed path $\sigma = (\{p\}, 0) \xrightarrow{a} (\{p\}, 0) \xrightarrow{a} (\{p\}, 0) \cdots$ is recognized (but not accepted) by the DTA of Fig. 1 using the run $(\ell_0, \{p\}, 0, 0) \xrightarrow{p, x \geqslant 0, Act, \varnothing, p} (\ell_0, \{p\}, 0, 0) \xrightarrow{p, x \geqslant 0, Act, \varnothing, p} (\ell_0, \{p\}, 0, 0) \cdots$, with mapping κ being the identity.

Our objective is to compare different classes of DTAs in qualitative terms (i.e., w.r.t. timed path languages) and in probabilistic terms (i.e., w.r.t. accepting probabilities of the accepted path in a CTMC). These notions are independent of the type of DTAs, and they have been already defined in [8].

Definition 6. *Let* $\mathbb{A}_1$ *and* $\mathbb{A}_2$ *be families of DTAs. Then:*

- $\mathbb{A}_2$ *is at least as expressive as* $\mathbb{A}_1$ *w.r.t. language, denoted* $\mathbb{A}_1 <_{\mathcal{L}} \mathbb{A}_2$*, if for all* $\mathcal{A}_1 \in \mathbb{A}_1$ *there exists* $\mathcal{A}_2 \in \mathbb{A}_2$ *such that* $\mathcal{L}(\mathcal{A}_2) = \mathcal{L}(\mathcal{A}_1)$*;*
- $\mathbb{A}_2$ *is at least as expressive as* $\mathbb{A}_1$ *w.r.t. CTMCs, denoted* $\mathbb{A}_1 <_{\mathcal{M}} \mathbb{A}_2$*, if for all* $\mathcal{A}_1 \in \mathbb{A}_1$ *there exists* $\mathcal{A}_2 \in \mathbb{A}_2$ *such that for all CTMC* $\mathcal{M}$*,* $\mathbf{Pr}_{\mathcal{M}}(\mathcal{A}_2) = \mathbf{Pr}_{\mathcal{M}}(\mathcal{A}_1)$*.*

Derived relations are defined as usual and we write $\sim_{\mathcal{L}}$ and $\sim_{\mathcal{M}}$ for *equally expressive* and $\lessgtr_{\mathcal{L}}$ and $\lessgtr_{\mathcal{M}}$ for *strictly more expressive*. Observe that by definition $\mathbb{A}_1 <_{\mathcal{L}} \mathbb{A}_2$ implies $\mathbb{A}_1 <_{\mathcal{M}} \mathbb{A}_2$.

3   Eliminating Autonomous Transitions in $\mathbb{A}_t$

This section studies the role of autonomous transitions in $\mathbb{A}_t$. The role of autonomous transitions for DTAs in which conditions are associated with locations (as in [10]) has been investigated in [8], where it was shown that there are indeed certain subclasses of DTAs for which autonomous transitions can be removed, but that in general this is not the case. The work in [8] also provides a construction to eliminate such autonomous transitions, when possible, together with an analysis of its time and memory cost. In this section we investigate when, and at which cost, it is possible to eliminate autonomous transitions from DTAs of the $\mathbb{A}_t$ class. We propose the following hierarchy of subclasses $\mathbb{A}_t^{na} \subseteq \mathbb{A}_t^{nc} \subseteq \mathbb{A}_t^{nra} \subseteq \mathbb{A}_t^{rc} \subseteq \mathbb{A}_t$ where:

Restricted cycles. $\mathbb{A}_t^{rc}$ is the subclass of DTAs $\mathcal{A} \in \mathbb{A}_t$ in which all cycles of $\mathcal{A}$ including an autonomous transition with a reset also include a synchronizing transition $(\ell, \varphi^-, \gamma, B, r, \varphi^+, \ell')$ with either $r = \downarrow$ or $\gamma = (x > C)$.

No reset on autonomous transitions. $\mathbb{A}_t^{nra}$ is the subclass of DTAs $\mathcal{A} \in \mathbb{A}_t^{rc}$ in which there is no autonomous transition that resets the clock: $\mathbb{A}_t^{nra} = \{\mathcal{A} \in \mathbb{A}_t \mid (\ell, \varphi, \gamma, \sharp, r, \ell') \in Aut(\mathcal{A}) \Rightarrow r = \varnothing\}$.

No reset and no cycle of autonomous transitions. $\mathbb{A}_t^{nc}$ is the subclass of DTAs $\mathcal{A} \in \mathbb{A}_t^{nra}$ in which there is no cycle of autonomous transitions.

No autonomous transitions. $\mathbb{A}_t^{na}$ the subclass of DTAs $\mathcal{A} \in \mathbb{A}_t^{nc}$ with no autonomous transitions.

The DTA of Fig. 1 belongs to $\mathbb{A}_t^{nc} \setminus \mathbb{A}_t^{na}$ and the DTA in Fig. 2 to $\mathbb{A}_t \setminus \mathbb{A}_t^{rc}$.

Let us explain why we introduce the intermediate subclasses between $\mathbb{A}_t$ and $\mathbb{A}_t^{na}$. $\mathbb{A}_t^{rc}$ points out which syntactical restrictions must be satisfied by automata in $\mathbb{A}_t$ in order not to extend the expressive power of $\mathbb{A}_t^{na}$. $\mathbb{A}_t^{nra}$ which forbids the clock reset by autonomous transitions disables the capacity to combine time constants depending on the execution. $\mathbb{A}_t^{nc}$ which in addition forbids loops of autonomous transitions is mainly introduced for simplifying the translations as we will show that it is equivalent to $\mathbb{A}_t^{nra}$ w.r.t. conciseness.

Our results are summarized in the frame below. Let us emphasize the main result: the elimination of autonomous transitions without reset can be performed in polynomial time. This is particularly interesting considering that the same elimination for DTAs with guarded locations, according to [8], requires exponential time. When referring to the size of a DTA$_t$ we consider the number of locations and transitions and the size of the formulas associated with transitions.

$$\mathbb{A}_t^{na} \sim_{\mathcal{L}} \mathbb{A}_t^{nc} \sim_{\mathcal{L}} \mathbb{A}_t^{nra} \sim_{\mathcal{L}} \mathbb{A}_t^{rc} \lesssim_{\mathcal{M}} \mathbb{A}_t$$
with $\mathbb{A}_t^{rc}$ exponentially more concise than $\mathbb{A}_t^{nra}$ and a quadratic translation from $\mathbb{A}_t^{nra}$ to $\mathbb{A}_t^{nc}$ and a polynomial translation from $\mathbb{A}_t^{nc}$ to $\mathbb{A}_t^{na}$.

In the framework of DTAs with guarded locations, the main result (Theorem 1 in [8]) is that autonomous transitions strictly increase the expressiveness w.r.t. $<_{\mathcal{M}}$, and therefore also w.r.t. $<_{\mathcal{L}}$. The adaptation to $\mathbb{A}_t$ is immediate, since the automaton $\mathcal{A}^*$ of Fig. 2 that is used as a counterexample in [8], does not include any boolean expression over atomic propositions. It then immediately follows that:

Proposition 1. *There exists $\mathcal{A}^* \in \mathbb{A}_t$ such that for all $\mathcal{A} \in \mathbb{A}_t^{na}$ there exists a CTMC $\mathcal{M}$ with $\mathbf{Pr}_{\mathcal{M}}(\mathcal{A}) \neq \mathbf{Pr}_{\mathcal{M}}(\mathcal{A}^*)$. Therefore $\mathbb{A}_t^{na} \precsim_{\mathcal{M}} \mathbb{A}_t$.*

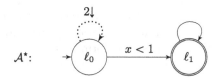

Fig. 2. The DTA $\mathcal{A}^*$, counterexample for Proposition 1.

From $\mathbb{A}_t^{rc}$ to $\mathbb{A}_t^{nra}$. Observe that due to the loop around location ℓ_0, $\mathcal{A}^*$ does not belong to $\mathbb{A}_t^{rc}$. The remaining results of the section simultaneously establish that: (1) $\mathbb{A}_t^{rc}$ characterize the DTAs for which autonomous transitions can be eliminated and (2) characterize the cost of this elimination in terms of time complexity and size of produced automata. First we establish that eliminating autonomous transitions with reset induces an unavoidable exponential blow-up.

Proposition 2. *There exists an algorithm operating in exponential time that takes as input $\mathcal{A} \in \mathbb{A}_t^{rc}$ and outputs $\mathcal{A}' \in \mathbb{A}_t^{nra}$ with $\mathcal{L}(\mathcal{A}') = \mathcal{L}(\mathcal{A})$.*
There exists a family $\{\mathcal{A}_n\}_{n \in \mathbb{N}}$ in $\mathbb{A}_t^{rc}$ such that the size of $\mathcal{A}_n$ belongs to $O(n^2)$ and for all $\mathcal{A} \in \mathbb{A}_t^{nra}$ with $\mathcal{L}(\mathcal{A}) = \mathcal{L}(\mathcal{A}_n)$, $(|Aut(\mathcal{A})| + 1) \cdot |Synch(\mathcal{A})| \geqslant 2^n$.

Proof. The proof is given in [9]. Here we exhibit the family $\{\mathcal{A}_n\}_{n \in \mathbb{N}}$ emphasizing that depending on the initial valuation there are 2^n different delays before a sequence of autonomous transitions reaches the final location.

From $\mathbb{A}_t^{nra}$ to $\mathbb{A}_t^{nc}$. Observe that when autonomous transitions do not reset the clock, if a run visits twice the same autonomous transition without visiting synchronized transitions, then no time has elapsed and it will diverge infinitely repeating a cycle of autonomous transitions. The idea of the transformation corresponding to the next proposition consists in duplicating locations by associating a counter to them. This counter represents the number of autonomous transitions visited since the last visit to a synchronized transition (or the beginning of the run). When the counter exceeds the number of autonomous transitions of the DTA, then a cycle has been detected and the run ends up in a deadlock location. The proof of this proposition can be found in [9].

Proposition 3. *There exists an algorithm operating in quadratic time that takes as input $\mathcal{A} \in \mathbb{A}_t^{nra}$ and outputs $\mathcal{A}' \in \mathbb{A}_t^{nc}$ with $\mathcal{L}(\mathcal{A}') = \mathcal{L}(\mathcal{A})$.*

From $\mathbb{A}_t^{nc}$ to $\mathbb{A}_t^{na}$. An interesting feature of specifying propositional formulas on transitions is that the final transformation can be performed in polynomial time. To this aim we introduce a particular case of decision diagram (DD) for representing formulas as follows. Let DG be a directed acyclic graph rooted in u_0 including a final vertex u_f such that all vertices are reachable from u_0 and can reach u_f as depicted in Fig. 3. Every transition is labelled by a formula and the formulas labeling outgoing transitions from a vertex are mutually exclusive (for each variable valuation at most one formula is true). Given a valuation v, $v \models DG$ if there is a path from u_0 to u_f such that $v \models \varphi$ for all φ labeling the transitions of the path. Observe that there is at most one such path. Thus deciding whether $v \models DG$ can be performed in linear time (assuming that the satisfaction of a formula labeling a transition by a valuation can be performed in linear time which is the case for standard representation of formulas).

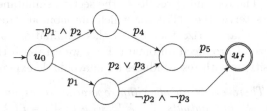

Fig. 3. A DD for formula $(\neg p_1 \wedge p_2 \wedge p_4 \wedge p_5) \vee (p_1 \wedge (p_2 \vee p_3) \wedge p_5) \vee (p_1 \wedge \neg p_2 \wedge \neg p_3)$.

The following proposition eliminates autonomous transitions when they do not reset the clock and there is no cycle made only of autonomous transitions. The associated transformation which is polynomial makes use of DDs for the formulas of the transitions.

Proposition 4. *There exists an algorithm operating in polynomial time that takes as input $\mathcal{A} \in \mathbb{A}_t^{nc}$ and outputs $\mathcal{A}' \in \mathbb{A}_t^{na}$ with $\mathcal{L}(\mathcal{A}') = \mathcal{L}(\mathcal{A})$.*

Proof. The transformation proceeds in three stages

- The first stage consists in duplicating the locations w.r.t. *time regions*. Let $0 = \alpha_0 < \ldots < \alpha_m = C$ be the time constants occurring in $\mathcal{A}$ (adding 0 if necessary). The set of time regions is $\{\alpha_0\},]\alpha_0, \alpha_1[, \{\alpha_1\}, \ldots, \{\alpha_m\},]\alpha_m, \infty[$. For all location ℓ and all region rg, one creates a location $\langle \ell, rg \rangle$. The initial location is $\langle \ell_0, \{\alpha_0\} \rangle$ with ℓ_0 the initial location of $\mathcal{A}$.

  For all synchronized transition $\ell \xrightarrow{\varphi^-, \gamma, B, r, \varphi^+} \ell'$ and all regions rg and rg' one creates a transition $\langle \ell, rg \rangle \xrightarrow{\varphi^-, \gamma \wedge x \in rg', B, r, \varphi^+} \langle \ell', rg' \rangle$. For all autonomous transition $\ell \xrightarrow{\varphi, x=i, \sharp, \varnothing} \ell'$ and all region rg, one creates a transition $\langle \ell, rg \rangle \xrightarrow{\varphi, x=i, \sharp, \varnothing} \langle \ell', \{i\} \rangle$. This step is polynomial.

- Let $\mathcal{A}_1$ be the DTA produced by the first stage, the second stage produces a DTA $\mathcal{A}_2$ where the priority of the autonomous transitions is made explicit by restricting the temporal formulas of outgoing transitions. Let $\langle \ell, rg \rangle$ be a location and $\{t_k = \langle \ell, rg \rangle \xrightarrow{\varphi_k, x = \alpha_k, \sharp, \varnothing} \langle \ell_k, \{\alpha_k\}\rangle\}_{k \leqslant K}$ be the autonomous transitions outgoing from $\langle \ell, rg \rangle$ with $rg \leqslant \alpha_1 \leqslant \cdots \leqslant \alpha_K$ (the other autonomous transitions are useless and are assumed to be deleted).

  For all k, one creates an autonomous transition $\langle \ell, rg \rangle \xrightarrow{\varphi_k \wedge \bigwedge_{k' < k} \neg \varphi_{k'}, x = \alpha_k, \sharp, \varnothing} \langle \ell_k, \{\alpha_k\}\rangle$.

  For all synchronized transition $\langle \ell, rg \rangle \xrightarrow{\varphi^-, \gamma, B, r, \varphi^+} \langle \ell', rg' \rangle$, one creates a transition

  $$\langle \ell, rg \rangle \xrightarrow{\varphi^- \wedge \bigwedge_{\alpha_k \leqslant rg'} \neg \varphi_k, \gamma, B, r, \varphi^+} \langle \ell', rg' \rangle$$

  Also this step is polynomial.

- Since in $\mathcal{A}_2$ the priority of autonomous transitions becomes irrelevant, $\mathcal{A}_2$ can be treated as a DTA with no priority for autonomous transitions, so the final stage consists in removing autonomous transitions by aggregating in a single synchronized transition a path of autonomous transitions followed by a synchronized one. The resulting DTA $\mathcal{A}'$ is therefore produced from $\mathcal{A}_2$ by deleting the autonomous transitions and adding new synchronized transitions as follows. For all $\langle \ell, rg \rangle$ and $\langle \ell', \{i\}\rangle$ such that there is a path of autonomous transitions from $\langle \ell, rg \rangle$ to $\langle \ell', \{i\}\rangle$, and a synchronized transition out of $\langle \ell', \{i\}\rangle$, one specifies the formula $\varphi_{\ell, rg}^{\ell', i}$ by a DD whose vertices are locations both reachable from $\langle \ell, rg \rangle$ by autonomous transitions and can reach $\langle \ell', \{i\}\rangle$ by autonomous transitions. The edges of the DD are the autonomous transitions between such vertices, and the edges are labeled by the formulas of the autonomous transitions (remember that autonomous transitions only have input guards).The DD is directly obtained from the subgraph of $\mathcal{A}_2$ that includes all paths of autonomous transitions from $\langle \ell, rg \rangle$ to $\langle \ell', \{i\}\rangle$, and the DD size is the size of such subgraph. Then for all synchronized transition $\langle \ell', \{i\}\rangle \xrightarrow{\varphi^-, \gamma, B, r, \varphi^+} \langle \ell'', rg'' \rangle$, one creates a transition

  $$\langle \ell, rg \rangle \xrightarrow{\varphi_{\ell, rg}^{\ell', i} \wedge \varphi^-, x \geqslant i \wedge \gamma, B, r, \varphi^+} \langle \ell'', rg'' \rangle.$$

A new final location ℓ'_f (with its loop) is added to $\mathcal{A}'$, and, for all $\langle \ell_f, rg \rangle$ the transition $\langle \ell_f, rg \rangle \xrightarrow{true, x \geqslant o, Act, \varnothing, true} \ell'_f.$ is added to $\mathcal{A}'$.

Illustration of Proposition 4. Figure 1 illustrates how to specify the temporal formula $p\mathbf{U}^{]\alpha, \beta[}q$ with a DTA $\mathcal{A} \in \mathbb{A}_t^{nra}$ (and therefore also $\in \mathbb{A}_t^{nc}$) Observe that in the interval $[0, \alpha[$, the current location can only be ℓ_0 with the additional requirement that if an action occurs then p has to be fullfilled inside the whole interval. At time α, the current location can only be ℓ_1 or ℓ_2 depending on the truth value of q and with the guarantee that p holds in the interval $[0, \alpha]$. Considering the first action that occurs after α, there are three possible cases: (1) $p \wedge q$ was satisfied and the formula is satisfied, (2) $p \wedge \neg q$ was satisfied, q is now satisfied and the action occurs before β and so the formula is satisfied (3)

$p \wedge \neg q$ was satisfied and it is still satisfied and the action occurs before β and so there is the same possibility to satisfy the formula represented by location ℓ_3.

Figure 4 depicts the DTA $\mathcal{A}' \in \mathbb{A}_t^{na}$ obtained by applying the transformation of Proposition 4 to the DTA $\mathcal{A} \in \mathbb{A}_t^{nc}$ depicted in Fig. 1. W.r.t. the defined transformation, we have done some simplifications. Since ℓ_1 and ℓ_2 can only be entered at time α there is no need to duplicate them. Since ℓ_3 can only be entered in interval $]\alpha, \beta[$ there is no need to duplicate it. In addition we have merged $\langle \ell_0, 0 \rangle$ and $\langle \ell_0,]0, \alpha[\rangle$ since their outgoing transitions are identical (up to the merging). We have also omitted locations that cannot reach the final location. Finally, no DD is necessary since there are no path of two autonomous transitions in the original DTA.

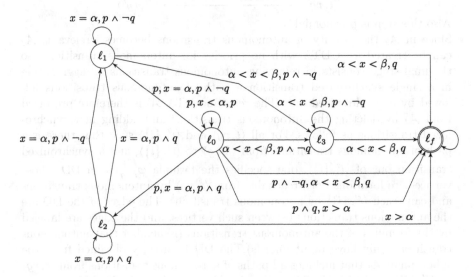

Fig. 4. Another DTA specification of $p \mathrm{U}^{]\alpha, \beta[} q$ with $\alpha > 0$.

4   DTA$_t$ Versus DTA$_s$

This section compares the conciseness of guarded transitions versus guarded locations, i.e. comparing $\mathbb{A}_t$ with $\mathbb{A}_s$. We show that a DTA in $\mathbb{A}_s$ can be converted into a DTA in $\mathbb{A}_t$ in a quadratic time, while it takes an exponential time to convert a DTA in $\mathbb{A}_t$ into a DTA in $\mathbb{A}_s$, due to an (unavoidable) exponential growth of locations. A DTA in $\mathbb{A}_s$ has conditions associated only with locations. A transition $(v_i, \delta_i) \xrightarrow{a_i} (v_{i+1}, \delta_{i+1})$ of a timed path is recognized by a transition from location ℓ to ℓ' of a such a DTA only if, given that all the time and action requirements are satisfied (as for $\mathbb{A}_t$) only if $v_{i+1} \models \Lambda(\ell')$, where $\Lambda(\ell')$ is the boolean condition associated with location ℓ'. We briefly recall here the definition of a DTA in $\mathbb{A}_s$, its runs, acceptance of timed path by a run. More explanations and examples can be found in [8].

Definition 7 (DTA). $\mathcal{A} \in \mathbb{A}_s$ *is defined by a tuple* $\mathcal{A} = \langle L, \Lambda, L_0, \ell_f, AP,$
Synch, Aut$\rangle$ *where L is a finite set of* locations, $L_0 \subseteq L$ *is the set of* initial
locations, $\ell_f \in L$ *is the* final location, $\Lambda : L \to \mathcal{B}_{AP}$ *is a function that assigns
to each location a boolean expression over the set of propositions AP, Synch $\subseteq$
$L \times \mathsf{InC} \times 2^{Act} \times \{\varnothing, \downarrow\} \times L$ is the set of synchronizing transitions, and Aut $\subseteq$
$L \times \mathsf{BoundC} \times \sharp \times \{\varnothing, \downarrow\} \times L$ is the set of* autonomous transitions, *with $E =$
Synch $\cup$ Aut. $\ell \xrightarrow{\gamma, B, r} \ell'$ denotes the transition $(\ell, \gamma, B, r, \ell')$.
Furthermore $\mathcal{A}$ fulfills the following conditions.*

- **Initial determinism.** $\forall \ell, \ell' \in L_0, \Lambda(l) \wedge \Lambda(l') \Leftrightarrow \bot$.
- **Determinism on actions.** $\forall B, B' \subseteq Act$ *s.t.* $B \cap B' \neq \varnothing, \forall \ell, \ell', \ell'' \in L$,
  if $\ell \xrightarrow{\gamma, B, r} \ell'$ *and* $\ell \xrightarrow{\gamma', B', r'} \ell''$ *then* $\Lambda(\ell') \wedge \Lambda(\ell'') \Leftrightarrow \bot$ *or* $\gamma \wedge \gamma' \Leftrightarrow \bot$.
- **Determinism on autonomous transitions.** $\forall \ell, \ell', \ell'' \in L$,
  if $\ell \xrightarrow{x = \alpha, \sharp, r} \ell'$ *and* $\ell \xrightarrow{x = \alpha', \sharp, r'} \ell''$ *then* $\Lambda(\ell') \wedge \Lambda(\ell'') \Leftrightarrow \bot$ *or* $\alpha \neq \alpha'$.
- **Conditions on the final location** ℓ_f. $\Lambda(\ell_f) = \top$ *and* $(\ell_f, \top, Act, \varnothing, \ell_f) \in$
  Synch.

Definition 8 (Run of $\mathcal{A}$). *A   run   of $\mathcal{A}$ $\in$ $\mathbb{A}_s$ is   a   sequence:*
$(\ell_0, v_0, \bar{x}_0, \delta_0) \xrightarrow{\gamma_0, B_0, r_0} (\ell_1, v_1, \bar{x}_1, \delta_1) \cdots (\ell_i, v_i, \bar{x}_i, \delta_i) \xrightarrow{\gamma_i, B_i, r_i} \cdots$ *such that for
all* $i \in \mathbb{N}$: $\ell_i \in L, l_0 \in L_0, v_i \in \{\top, \bot\}^{AP}, \delta_i \in \mathbb{R}_{\geqslant 0}$:

$$\ell_i \xrightarrow{\gamma_i, B_i, r_i} \ell_{i+1} \in E \;,\; v_i \models \Lambda(\ell_i) \;,\; \bar{x}_i + \delta_i \models \gamma_i \;,\; \bar{x}_{i+1} = \begin{cases} 0 & \text{if } r = \downarrow \\ \bar{x}_i + \delta_i & \text{otherwise} \end{cases}$$

To enforce priority of autonomous transitions,
let $\bar{x}_\sharp = min\{\alpha \mid \exists \ell_i \xrightarrow{x = \alpha, \sharp, r} \ell \in E \wedge \bar{x}_i \leqslant \alpha \wedge v_i \models \Lambda(\ell)\}$ *(min($\varnothing$) $= \infty$)*
If $B_i = \sharp$ *then* $\bar{x}_i + \delta_i = \bar{x}_\sharp$ *and* $v_{i+1} = v_i$ *else* $\bar{x}_i + \delta_i < x_\sharp$.

Definition 9 (Path recognized by $\mathcal{A}$ and $\mathcal{L}(\mathcal{A})$). *Let* $\sigma = (v_0, \delta_0) \xrightarrow{a_0}$
$(v_1, \delta_1) \xrightarrow{a_1} \cdots (v_i, \delta_i) \xrightarrow{a_i} \cdots$ *be a timed path and* $\rho = (\ell_0, v_0', \bar{x}_0, \delta_0') \xrightarrow{\gamma_0, B_0, r_0}$
$\cdots (\ell_i, v_i', \bar{x}_i, \delta_i') \xrightarrow{\gamma_i, B_i, r_i} \cdots$ *be a run of a DTA$_s$ $\mathcal{A}$, according to Definition 8.
Then σ is recognized by ρ if there is a strictly increasing mapping* $\kappa : \mathbb{N} \to \mathbb{N}$
(extended to $\kappa(-1) = -1$), such that for all $i \in \mathbb{N}$

- $a_i \in B_{\kappa(i)}$ *and* $\delta_i = \sum_{\kappa(i-1) < h \leqslant \kappa(i)} \delta_h'$
- $\forall h, \kappa(i-1) < h \leqslant \kappa(i) \Rightarrow v_h' = v_i$ *and* $h \notin \kappa(\mathbb{N}) \Rightarrow B_h = \sharp$

*A timed path σ is accepted by $\mathcal{A}$ if σ is recognized by a run ρ and ρ visits ℓ_f.
The language $\mathcal{L}(\mathcal{A})$ of $\mathcal{A}$ is the set of the timed paths σ accepted by $\mathcal{A}$.*

We first consider the translation from $\mathbb{A}_s$ to $\mathbb{A}_t$, which mainly consists in
shifting the formula of a location to its incoming transitions with a particular
handling of the initial locations.

Proposition 5. *There exists an algorithm operating in quadratic time that takes
as input $\mathcal{A}_s \in \mathbb{A}_s$ and outputs $\mathcal{A}_t \in \mathbb{A}_t$ with $\mathcal{L}(\mathcal{A}_s) = \mathcal{L}(\mathcal{A}_t)$.*

Proof. $\mathcal{A}_t$ has the same structure as $\mathcal{A}_s$ except that it has an additional location ℓ_0 which is taken as the initial one.

For all synchronized transition $\ell \xrightarrow{\gamma,B,r} \ell'$ in $\mathcal{A}_s$, $\mathcal{A}_t$ includes the synchronized transition $\ell \xrightarrow{\top,\gamma,B,r,\Lambda(\ell')} \ell'$ and if $\ell \in L_0$ then $\mathcal{A}_t$ includes the synchronized transition $\ell_0 \xrightarrow{\Lambda(\ell),\gamma,B,r,\Lambda(\ell')} \ell'$.

For all autonomous transition $\ell \xrightarrow{x=\alpha,\sharp,r} \ell'$ in $\mathcal{A}_s$, $\mathcal{A}_t$ includes the autonomous transition $\ell \xrightarrow{\Lambda(\ell'),x=\alpha,\sharp,r} \ell'$ and if $\ell \in L_0$ then $\mathcal{A}_t$ includes the autonomous transition: $\ell_0 \xrightarrow{\Lambda(\ell) \wedge \Lambda(\ell'),x=\alpha,\sharp,r} \ell'$.

The quadratic factor is due to the substitution of the $|L|$ formulas of $\mathcal{A}_s$ by at least $|E|$ formulas in $\mathcal{A}_t$.

The reverse translation is more costly and consists in duplicating a location w.r.t. the guards of the incoming and outgoing transitions.

Proposition 6. *There exists an algorithm operating in exponential time that takes as input $\mathcal{A}_t \in \mathbb{A}_t$ and outputs $\mathcal{A}_s \in \mathbb{A}_s$ with $\mathcal{L}(\mathcal{A}_t) = \mathcal{L}(\mathcal{A}_s)$.*

Proof. Given $\ell \in L$, let $\varphi_1^\ell, \ldots \varphi_{n_\ell}^\ell$ be the formulas of entering guards of transitions incoming ℓ and exiting guards of transitions outgoing ℓ. Then $L_s = \{\langle \ell, I \rangle \mid \ell \in L \wedge I \subseteq \{1, \ldots, n_\ell\}\} \cup \{\ell_f^*\}$ where ℓ_f^* is the final state (fulfilling the requirements of a DTA in $\mathbb{A}_s$) and for all $\langle \ell, I \rangle$, .

For all synchronized transition $\ell \xrightarrow{\varphi_i^\ell,\gamma,B,r,\varphi_{i'}^{\ell'}} \ell'$ in $\mathcal{A}_t$ and all I, I' such that $i \in I$ and $i' \in I'$, $\mathcal{A}_s$ includes the synchronized transition: $\langle \ell, I \rangle \xrightarrow{\gamma,B,r} \langle \ell', I' \rangle$.

For all autonomous transition $\ell \xrightarrow{\varphi_i^\ell,x=\alpha,\sharp,r} \ell'$ in $\mathcal{A}_t$ and all I, I' such that $i \in I$ and $i' \in I'$ with $\varphi_i^\ell = \varphi_{i'}^{\ell'}$, $\mathcal{A}_s$ includes the autonomous transition: $\langle \ell, I \rangle \xrightarrow{x=\alpha,\sharp,r} \langle \ell', I' \rangle$.

For all $\langle \ell_f, I \rangle$, there is a transition $\langle \ell_f, I \rangle \xrightarrow{\top,Act,\varnothing} \ell_f^*$.

Proposition 5 and 6 above can be trivially extended to sub-classes of $\mathbb{A}_s$ and $\mathbb{A}_t$, because the proofs are general and do not involve creation of autonomous transitions.

The exponential blow-up due to the duplication of locations is unavoidable even without timing considerations, as shown by the next proposition.

Proposition 7. *There exists a family of automata $\{\mathcal{A}_t^k\}_{k \in \mathbb{N}}$ in $\mathbb{A}_t^{na}$ such that the size of $\mathcal{A}_t^k$ belongs to $O(k \log(k))$ and for all $\mathcal{A}_s \in \mathbb{A}_s$ with $\mathcal{L}(\mathcal{A}_s) = \mathcal{L}(\mathcal{A}_t^k)$ the number of its locations is at least $2^k - 1$.*

Proof. Consider the automaton $\mathcal{A}_t^k$ described below.

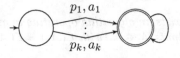

This automaton accepts timed paths whose first action may be a_i only if the initial state fullfills p_i. Consider in $\mathcal{A}_s$ the locations reached at time 0 by the runs before the first action is performed. At least $2^k - 1$ initial valuations must reach such a location. Assume that $\mathcal{A}_s$ has less than $2^k - 1$ locations. Then two initial valuations reach the same location. Let p_i be some proposition on which they differ. Thus there exists a initial valuation v with $v(p_i) = \bot$ such that a timed path starting with a_i is accepted which yields a contradiction.

5   Conclusions and Future Work

The results of this paper, together with those of a companion paper [8] allows to build a better understanding of DTAs and of the various CSL^{TA} definitions.

We have established that DTAs with autonomous transitions are more expressive that DTAs without autonomous transitions when there are cycles made only of autonomous transitions on which there is at least a reset, irrespectively of whether guards are associated to locations or to transitions.

Secondly, even when autonomous transitions do not enhance expressiveness, they improve conciseness: if feasible, removing autonomous transitions may lead to an exponential blow-up of the DTA.

Finally, removing autonomous transitions from a DTA in $\mathbb{A}_t$ is less expensive than doing it for a DTA in $\mathbb{A}_t$. In particular to remove autonomous transitions from a DTA with no reset on autonomous transitions (i.e. belonging to $\mathbb{A}_t^{nra}$) is polynomial if decision diagrams are used to represent propositional formulas, while the analogous operations for a DTA belonging to $\mathbb{A}_t^{nra}$ is exponential. This result has motivated a throughout comparison of DTA$_s$ and DTA$_t$, that has shown that guards on transitions may lead to more concise DTAs: indeed the translation from $\mathbb{A}_t$ to $\mathbb{A}_s$ is exponential, while the opposite translation is quadratic.

Various types of DTAs have been used for the definition of the stochastic logic CSL^{TA}. We can now assert that CSL^{TA} definitions that include autonomous transitions are more expressive than CSL^{TA} that do not. The counter-example of the proof of Proposition 1 has a clear interpretation in terms of periodic behaviour, showing that CSL^{TA} without autonomous transitions are not adequate to express certain periodicity properties. We can also state that CSL^{TA} specifications that include guarded transitions can be more concise than CSL^{TA} that considers guarded locations.

Future work includes the model-checking algorithms and the presence of multiple clocks. Since the number of locations may significantly affect the complexity of model-checking CSL^{TA}, we plan to investigate how the component-based model-checking of CSL^{TA} [1] can take advantage of the results of this paper to lower the cost of CSL^{TA} model-checking.

DTAs with multiple clocks have also been used for CTMC model-checking, at the cost of a significant increase of the complexity of the model-checking procedure. The classes of DTAs used do not include autonomous transitions: it is our plan to investigate which are the classes of DTAs with multiple clocks for which the introduction of autonomous transitions increases the expressiveness.

References

1. Amparore, E.G., Donatelli, S.: Efficient model checking of the stochastic logic CSL^{TA}. Performance Eval. **123–124**, 1–34 (2018)
2. Amparore, E.G., Ballarini, P., Beccuti, M., Donatelli, S., Franceschinis, G.: Expressing and computing passage time measures of GSPN models with HASL. In: Colom, J.-M., Desel, J. (eds.) PETRI NETS 2013. LNCS, vol. 7927, pp. 110–129. Springer, Heidelberg (2013). https://doi.org/10.1007/978-3-642-38697-8_7
3. Aziz, A., Sanwal, K., Singhal, V., Brayton, R.: Model-checking continuous-time Markov chains. ACM Trans. Comput. Logic **1**(1), 162–170 (2000)
4. Baier, C., Cloth, L., Haverkort, B.R., Kuntz, M., Siegle, M.: Model checking Markov chains with actions and state labels. IEEE TSE **33**, 209–224 (2007)
5. Baier, C., Haverkort, B., Hermanns, H., Katoen, J.-P.: On the logical characterisation of performability properties. In: Montanari, U., Rolim, J.D.P., Welzl, E. (eds.) ICALP 2000. LNCS, vol. 1853, pp. 780–792. Springer, Heidelberg (2000). https://doi.org/10.1007/3-540-45022-X_65
6. Baier, C., Haverkort, B., Hermanns, H., Katoen, J.-P.: Model-checking algorithms for continuous-time Markov chains. IEEE TSE **29**(6), 524–541 (2003)
7. Chen, T., Han, T., Katoen, J.-P., Mereacre, A.: Model checking of continuous-time Markov chains against timed automata specifications. Logical Methods Comp. Sci. **7**(1), 56 (2011)
8. Donatelli, S., Haddad, S.: Expressiveness and conciseness of timed automata for the verification of stochastic models. In: Leporati, A., Martín-Vide, C., Shapira, D., Zandron, C. (eds.) LATA 2020. LNCS, vol. 12038, pp. 170–183. Springer, Cham (2020). https://doi.org/10.1007/978-3-030-40608-0_11
9. Donatelli, S., Haddad, S.: Guarded autonomous transitions increase conciseness and expressiveness of timed automata. Research report, Inria Saclay Ile de France; LSV, ENS Cachan, CNRS, INRIA, Université Paris-Saclay, Cachan (France); Universita degli Studi di Torino, July 2020. to be released
10. Donatelli, S., Haddad, S., Sproston, J.: Model checking timed and stochastic properties with CSL^{TA}. IEEE TSE **35**(2), 224–240 (2009)
11. Kuntz, M., Haverkort, B.R.: GCSRL-a logic for stochastic reward models with timed and untimed behaviour. In: 8th PMCCS, pp. 50–56 (2007)
12. Obal II, W.D., Sanders, W.: State-space support for path-based reward variables. Performance Evaluation, **35**, 233–251 (1999)

Probabilistic Guarantees for Safe Deep Reinforcement Learning

Edoardo Bacci[(✉)] and David Parker

University of Birmingham, Birmingham, UK
exb461@bham.ac.uk, d.a.parker@cs.bham.ac.uk

Abstract. Deep reinforcement learning has been successfully applied to many control tasks, but the application of such controllers in safety-critical scenarios has been limited due to safety concerns. Rigorous testing of these controllers is challenging, particularly when they operate in probabilistic environments due to, for example, hardware faults or noisy sensors. We propose MOSAIC, an algorithm for measuring the safety of deep reinforcement learning controllers in stochastic settings. Our approach is based on the iterative construction of a formal abstraction of a controller's execution in an environment, and leverages probabilistic model checking of Markov decision processes to produce probabilistic guarantees on safe behaviour over a finite time horizon. It produces bounds on the probability of safe operation of the controller for different initial configurations and identifies regions where correct behaviour can be guaranteed. We implement and evaluate our approach on controllers trained for several benchmark control problems.

1 Introduction

Deep reinforcement learning is the application of deep neural networks to solve reinforcement learning tasks. This technique has been shown to solve many complex control tasks successfully [5,28,31]. However, real-world applications of these methods, especially in safety-critical scenarios such as autonomous driving, is limited because it is difficult to establish guarantees on their safety.

Formal verification is a rigorous approach to checking the correctness of computerised systems. It is particularly appealing for systems that are based on neural networks, because the training process often yields models that are large, complex and opaque. Furthermore, the input space is typically too large to allow exhaustive testing, and there now exist a variety of approaches to construct adversarial attacks, i.e., small and imperceptible perturbations to the inputs of the neural network that cause it to produce erroneous outputs.

In recent years, there has been growing interest in verification techniques for neural networks [15,18,21], with a particular focus on the domain of image classification. These aim to prove the absence of particular classes of adversarial attack, typically those that are "close" to inputs for which the correct output is known. Methods proposed include mapping the verification to an SMT (satisfiability modulo theories) problem and the use of abstract interpretation.

© Springer Nature Switzerland AG 2020
N. Bertrand and N. Jansen (Eds.): FORMATS 2020, LNCS 12288, pp. 231–248, 2020.
https://doi.org/10.1007/978-3-030-57628-8_14

There are also various approaches to tackling safety in reinforcement learning. For example, safe reinforcement learning [14] factors in safety objectives into the learning process. Using formal specifications of the objectives has also been proposed, such as maximising the probability of satisfying a temporal logic objective [6,13,17] or restricting learning to a set of verified policies [19]. More recently, formal verification of deep reinforcement learning systems has been considered [22], by leveraging existing neural network verification methods.

A further challenge for verifying the safe operation of controllers synthesised using deep reinforcement learning is the fact they are often developed to function in uncertain or unpredictable environments. This necessitates the use of stochastic models to train, and to reason about, the controllers. One source of probabilistic behaviour is dynamically changing environments and/or unreliable or noisy sensing. Another source, and the one we focus on here, is the occurrence of faults, e.g., in the hardware for actuators in the controller.

In this paper, we propose novel techniques to establish *probabilistic* guarantees on the safe behaviour of deep reinforcement learning systems which can be subject to faulty behaviour at runtime. Our approach, which we call MOSAIC (MOdel SAfe Intelligent Control) uses a combination of abstract interpretation and probabilistic verification to synthesise the guarantees.

Formally, we model the runtime execution of a deep reinforcement learning based controller as a continuous-space discrete-time Markov processes (DTMP). This is built from: (i) the neural network specifying the controller; (ii) a controller fault model characterising the probability with which faults occur when attempting to execute particular control actions; and (iii) a deterministic, continuous-space model of the physical environment, which we assume to be known.

We concern ourselves with finite-horizon safety specifications and consider the probability with which a failure state is reached within a specified number of time steps. More precisely, our main aim is to identify "safe" regions of the possible initial configurations of the controller, for which this failure probability is guaranteed to be below some specified threshold.

One key challenge to overcome, due to the continuous-space model, is that the number of initial configurations is infinite. We construct a finite-state abstraction as a Markov decision process (MDP), comprising abstract states (based on intervals) that represent regions of the state space of the concrete controller model. We then use standard probabilistic model checking techniques on the MDP abstraction, and show that this yields upper bounds on the step-bounded failure probabilities for different initial regions of the controller model.

A second challenge is that constructing the abstraction requires extraction of the controller policy from its neural network representation. We perform a symbolic analysis of the neural network, for which we design a branch-and-bound algorithm, and an abstraction process that explores the reachable abstract states of the environment. We also iteratively refine the abstraction to yield more accurate bounds on the failure probabilities. We evaluate our approach by applying it to deep reinforcement learning controllers for two benchmark control problems: a cartpole and a pendulum.

Related Work. As discussed above, various verification techniques for neural networks exist, including those based on abstract interpretation. Some use abstractions based on intervals [1,29,33], as we do; others use more sophisticated representations such as polyhedra and zonotopes [15]. Recently, correctness for Bayesian neural networks has been considered, using probabilistic notions of robustness, e.g., [9]. Mostly, these approaches focus on supervised learning, often for image classification, but they have also been built upon for verified deep reinforcement learning [22], where (non-probabilistic) safety and liveness properties are checked. Other, non-neural network based, reinforcement learning has also been verified, e.g., by extracting and analysing decision trees [3].

In the context of probabilistic verification, neural networks have been used to find POMDP policies with guarantees [10,11], but with recurrent neural networks and for discrete, not continuous, state models. Also related are techniques to verify continuous space probabilistic models, e.g., [25,32] which build finite-state abstractions as Markov chains or interval Markov chains. Finally, there is a large body of work on abstraction for probabilistic verification; ours is perhaps closest in spirit to the game-based abstraction approach for MDPs from [20].

2 Preliminaries

We will use $Dist(X)$ to denote the set of discrete probability distributions over the set X, i.e., functions $\mu : X \to [0,1]$ where $\sum_{x \in X} \mu(x) = 1$. The support of μ, denoted $Supp(\mu)$, is defined as $Supp(\mu) = \{x \in X \mid \mu(x) > 0\}$. In some cases, we will use distributions where the set X is uncountable but where the support is finite. We also write $\mathcal{P}(X)$ to denote the powerset of X.

We use two probabilistic models: *discrete-time Markov processes* (DTMPs) to model controllers, and *Markov decision processes* (MDPs) for abstractions.

Definition 1 (Discrete-time Markov process). *A (finite-branching) discrete-time Markov process is a tuple $(S, S_0, \mathbf{P}, AP, L)$, where: S is a (possibly uncountably infinite) set of states; $S_0 \subseteq S$ is a set of initial states; $\mathbf{P} : S \times S \to [0,1]$ is a transition probability matrix, where $\sum_{s' \in Supp(\mathbf{P}(s,\cdot))} \mathbf{P}(s,s') = 1$ for all $s \in S$; AP is a set of atomic propositions; and $L : S \to AP$ is a labelling function.*

The process starts in some initial state $s_0 \in S_0$ and then evolves from state to state in discrete time steps. When in state s, the probability of making a transition to state s' is given by $\mathbf{P}(s,s')$. We assume that the process is finite-branching, i.e., the number of possible successors of each state is finite, despite the continuous state space. This simplifies the representation and suffices for the probabilistic behaviour that we model in this paper.

A *path* is an infinite sequence of states $s_0 s_1 s_2 \ldots$ through the model, i.e., such that $\mathbf{P}(s_i, s_{i+1}) > 0$ for all i. We write $Path(s)$ for the set of all paths starting in a state s. In standard fashion [23], we can define a probability space Pr_s over $Path(s)$. Atomic propositions from the set AP will be used to specify properties for verification; we write $s \models b$ for $b \in AP$ if $b \in L(s)$.

Definition 2 (Markov decision process). *A Markov decision process is a tuple* $(S, S_0, \mathbf{P}, AP, L)$, *where:* S *is a finite set of states;* $S_0 \subseteq S$ *are initial states;* $\mathbf{P} : S \times \mathbb{N} \times S \rightarrow [0,1]$ *is a transition probability function, where* $\sum_{s' \in S} \mathbf{P}(s, j, s') \in \{0, 1\}$ *for all* $s \in S, j \in \mathbb{N}$; *AP is a set of atomic propositions; and* $L : S \rightarrow AP$ *is a labelling function.*

Unlike discrete-time Markov processes above, we assume a finite state space. A transition in a state s of an MDP first requires a choice between (finitely-many) possible probabilistic outcomes in that state. Unusually, we do not use action labels to distinguish these choices, but just integer indices. Primarily, this is to avoid confusion with the use of actions taken by controllers, which do not correspond directly to these choices. The probability of moving to successor state s' when taking choice j in state s is given by $\mathbf{P}(s, j, s')$.

As above, a path is an execution through the model, i.e., an infinite sequence of states and indices $s_0 j_0 s_1 j_1 \ldots$ such that $\mathbf{P}(s_i, j_i, s_{i+1}) > 0$ for all i. A *policy* of the MDP selects the choice to take in each state, based on the history of its execution so far. For a policy σ, we have a probability space Pr_s^σ over the set of paths starting in state s. If ψ is an event of interest defined by a measurable set of paths (e.g., those reaching a set of target states), we are usually interested in the minimum or maximum probability of the event over all policies:

$$Pr_s^{\min}(\psi) = \inf_\sigma Pr_s^\sigma(\psi) \quad \text{and} \quad Pr_s^{\max}(\psi) = \sup_\sigma Pr_s^\sigma(\psi)$$

3 Controller Modelling and Abstraction

In this section, we formalise the problem of modelling and verifying deep reinforcement learning controllers, and then describe the MDP abstraction that underlies our MOSAIC approach to performing the verification.

3.1 Controller Execution Model

We consider controllers acting over continuous state spaces systems with a discrete action space. We assume a set of n real-valued state space variables and denote the state space by $S = \mathbb{R}^n$. There is a finite set $A = \{a_1, \ldots, a_m\}$ of m actions that can be taken by the controller. For simplicity, we assume that all actions are available in every state.

To describe the execution of a controller, we require three things: (i) a *controller policy*; (ii) an *environment model*; and (iii) a *controller fault model*. Each is described in more detail below.

Definition 3 (Controller policy). *A controller policy is a function* $\pi : S \rightarrow A$, *which selects an action* $\pi(s)$ *for the controller to take in each state* $s \in S$.

We restrict our attention to policies that are memoryless (choosing the same action in each state s) and deterministic (selecting a fixed single action, with no randomisation). In this work, policies are represented by neural networks, and generated through deep reinforcement learning. However, for the purposes of this section, we treat the policy simply as a function from states to actions.

Definition 4 (Environment model). *An environment model is a function* $E : S \times A \rightarrow S$ *that describes the state* $E(s,a)$ *of the system after one time step if controller action* a *is (successfully) taken in state* s.

The environment represents the effect that each action executed by a controller has on the system. We assume a deterministic model of the environment; probabilistic behaviour due to failures is introduced separately (see below).

We also extend E to define the change in system state when a *sequence* of zero or more actions are executed, still within a single time step. This will be used below to describe the outcome of controller execution faults. Re-using the same notation, for state $s \in S$ and action sequence $w \in A^*$, we write $E(s,w)$ to denote the outcome of taking actions w in s. This can be defined recursively: for the empty action sequence ϵ, we have $E(s,\epsilon) = s$; and, for a sequence of k actions $a_1 \ldots a_k$, we have $E(s, a_1 \ldots a_k) = E(E(s, a_1 \ldots a_{k-1}), a_k)$.

Definition 5 (Controller fault model). *A controller fault model is a function* $f : A \rightarrow Dist(A^*)$ *that gives, for each possible controller action, the sequences of actions that may actually result and their probabilities.*

This lets us model a range of controller faults. A simple example is the case of an action a failing to execute with some probability p: we have $f(a)(\epsilon) = p$, $f(a)(a) = 1-p$ and $f(a)(w) = 0$ for all other action sequences w. Another example, is a "sticky" action [26] a which executes twice with probability p, i.e., $f(a)(aa) = p$, $f(a)(a) = 1-p$ and $f(a)(w) = 0$ for any other w.

Now, given a controller policy π, an environment model E and a controller fault model f, we can formally define the behaviour of the execution of the controller within the environment. We add two further ingredients: a set $S_0 \subseteq S$ of possible *initial states*; and a set $S_{fail} \subseteq S$ of *failure states*, i.e., states of the system where we consider it to have failed. We refer to the tuple $(\pi, E, f, S_0, S_{fail})$ as a *controller execution*. Its *controller execution model* is a (continuous-space, finite-branching) discrete-time Markov process defined as follows.

Definition 6 (Controller execution model). *Given a controller execution* $(\pi, E, f, S_0, S_{fail})$, *the corresponding* controller execution model *describing its runtime behaviour is the DTMP* $(S, S_0, \mathbf{P}, AP, L)$ *where* $AP = \{fail\}$, *for any* $s \in S$, $fail \in L(s)$ *iff* $s \in S_{fail}$ *and, for states* $s, s' \in S$:

$$\mathbf{P}(s, s') = \sum \{f(\pi(s))(w) \mid w \in A^* \; s.t. \; E(s,w) = s'\}.$$

For each state s, the action chosen by the controller policy is $\pi(s)$ and the action sequences that may result are given by the support of the controller fault model distribution $f(\pi(s))$. For each action sequence w, the resulting state is $E(s,w)$. In the above, to define $\mathbf{P}(s,s')$ we have combined the probability of all such sequences w that lead to s' since there may be more than one that does so.

Recall the example controller fault models described above. For an action a that fails to be executed with probability p, the above yields $\mathbf{P}(s,s) = p$ and $\mathbf{P}(s, E(s,a)) = 1-p$. For a "sticky" action a (with probability p of sticking), it yields $\mathbf{P}(s, E(E(s,a),a)) = p$ and $\mathbf{P}(s, E(s,a)) = 1-p$.

3.2   Controller Verification

Using the model defined above of a controller operating in a given environment, our aim is to verify that it executes safely. More precisely, we are interested in the probability of reaching *failure* states within a particular time horizon. We write $Pr_s(\lozenge^{\leqslant k} fail)$ for the probability of reaching a failure state within k time steps when starting in state s, which can be defined as:

$$Pr_s(\lozenge^{\leqslant k} fail) = Pr_s(\{s_0 s_1 s_2 \cdots \in Path(s) \mid s_i \models fail \text{ for some } 0 \leqslant i \leqslant k\})$$

Since we work with discrete-time, finite-branching models, we can compute finite-horizon reachability probabilities recursively as follows:

$$Pr_s(\lozenge^{\leqslant k} fail) = \begin{cases} 1 & \text{if } s \models fail \\ 0 & \text{if } s \not\models fail \wedge k=0 \\ \sum_{s' \in Supp(\mathbf{P}(s,\cdot))} \mathbf{P}(s,s') \cdot Pr_{s'}(\lozenge^{\leqslant k-1} fail) & \text{otherwise.} \end{cases}$$

For our controller execution models, we are interested in two closely related verification problems. First, for a specified probability threshold p_{safe}, we would like to determine the subset $S_0^{safe} \subseteq S_0$ of "safe" initial states from which the error probability is below the threshold:

$$S_0^{safe} = \{s \in S_0 \mid Pr_s(\lozenge^{\leqslant k} fail) < p_{safe}\}$$

Alternatively, for some set of states S', typically the initial state set S_0, or some subset of it, we wish to know the maximum (worst-case) error probability:

$$p_{S'}^+ = \sup\{Pr_s(\lozenge^{\leqslant k} fail) \mid s \in S'\}$$

This can be seen as a *probabilistic guarantee* over the executions that start in those states. In this paper, we tackle approximate versions of these problems, namely under-approximating S_0^{safe} or over-approximating $p_{S'}^+$.

3.3   Controller Execution Abstraction

A key challenge in tackling the controller verification problem outlined above is the fact that it is over a continuous-state model. In fact, since the model is finite-branching and we target finite-horizon safety properties, for a specific initial state, the k-step probability of a failure could be computed by solving a finite-state Markov chain. However, we verify the controller for a *set* of initial states, giving infinitely many possible probabilistic executions.

Our approach is to construct and solve an *abstraction* of the model of controller execution. The abstraction is a finite-state MDP whose states are *abstract states* $\hat{s} \subseteq S$, each representing some subset of the states of the original concrete model. We denote the set of all possible abstract states as $\hat{S} \subseteq \mathcal{P}(S)$. In our approach, we use intervals (i.e., the "Box" domain; see Sect. 4).

In order to construct the abstraction of the controller's execution, we build on an abstraction $\hat{E}$ of the environment $E : S \times A \rightarrow S$. This abstraction is a function $\hat{E} : \hat{S} \times A \rightarrow \hat{S}$ which soundly over-approximates the (concrete) environment, i.e., it satisfies the following definition.

Definition 7 (Environment abstraction). *For environment model $E : S \times A \rightarrow S$ and set of abstract states $\hat{S} \subseteq \mathcal{P}(S)$, an* environment abstraction *is a function $\hat{E} : \hat{S} \times A \rightarrow \hat{S}$ such that: for any abstract state $\hat{s} \in \hat{S}$, concrete state $s \in \hat{s}$ and action $a \in A$, we have $E(s, a) \in \hat{E}(\hat{s}, a)$.*

Using interval arithmetic, we can construct $\hat{E}$ for a wide range of functions E. As for E, the environment abstraction $\hat{E}$ extends naturally to action sequences, where $\hat{E}(\hat{s}, w)$ gives the result of taking a sequence w of actions in abstract state $\hat{s}$. It follows from Definition 7 that, for any abstract state $\hat{s} \in \hat{S}$, concrete state $s \in \hat{s}$ and action sequence $w \in A^*$, we have $E(s, w) \in \hat{E}(\hat{s}, w)$.

Our abstraction is an MDP whose states are abstract states from the set $\hat{S} \subseteq \mathcal{P}(S)$. This represents an over-approximation of the possible behaviour of the controller, and computing the maximum probabilities of reaching failure states in the MDP will give upper bounds on the actual probabilities in the concrete model. The choices that are available in each abstract state $\hat{s}$ of the MDP are based on a partition of $\hat{s}$ into subsets $\{\hat{s}_1, \ldots, \hat{s}_m\}$. Intuitively, each choice represents the behaviour for states in the different subsets $\hat{s}_j$.

Definition 8 (Controller execution abstraction). *For a controller execution $(\pi, E, f, S_0, S_{fail})$, a set $\hat{S} \subseteq \mathcal{P}(S)$ of abstract states and a corresponding environment abstraction $\hat{E}$, the* controller execution abstraction *is defined as an MDP $(\hat{S}, \hat{S}_0, \hat{\mathbf{P}}, AP, \hat{L})$ satisfying the following:*

- *for all $s \in S_0$, $s \in \hat{s}$ for some $\hat{s} \in \hat{S}_0$;*
- *for each $\hat{s} \in \hat{S}$, there is a partition $\{\hat{s}_1, \ldots, \hat{s}_m\}$ of $\hat{s}$ that is consistent with the controller policy π (i.e., $\pi(s) = \pi(s')$ for any $s, s' \in \hat{s}_j$ for each j) and, for each $j \in \{1, \ldots, m\}$ we have:*

$$\hat{\mathbf{P}}(\hat{s}, j, \hat{s}') = \sum \left\{ f(\pi(\hat{s}_j))(w) \mid w \in A^* \text{ such that } \hat{E}(\hat{s}_j, w) = \hat{s}' \right\}$$

where $\pi(\hat{s}_j)$ is the action that π chooses for all states $s \in \hat{s}_j$;
- *$AP = \{fail\}$ and $fail \in \hat{L}(\hat{s})$ iff $fail \in L(s)$ for some $s \in \hat{s}$.*

The idea is that each $\hat{s}_j$ within abstract state $\hat{s}$ represents a set of concrete states that have the same behaviour at this level of abstraction. This is modelled by the jth choice from $\hat{s}$, which we construct by finding the controller action $\pi(\hat{s}_j)$ taken in those states, the possible action sequences w that may arise when taking $\pi(\hat{s}_j)$ due to the controller fault model f, and the abstract states $\hat{s}'$ that result when applying w in $\hat{s}_j$ according to the abstract model $\hat{E}$ of the environment.

The above describes the general structure of the abstraction; in practice, it suffices to construct a fragment of at most depth k from the initial states. Once constructed, computing maximum probabilities for the MDP yields upper bounds on the probability of the controller exhibiting a failure. In particular, we have the following result (see [2] for a proof):

Theorem 1. *Given a state $s \in S$ of a controller model DTMP, and an abstract state $\hat{s} \in \hat{S}$ of the corresponding controller abstraction MDP for which $s \in \hat{s}$, we have $Pr_s(\lozenge^{\leqslant k} \textit{fail}) \leqslant Pr_{\hat{s}}^{\max}(\lozenge^{\leqslant k} \textit{fail})$.*

This also provides a way to determine sound approximations for the two verification problems discussed in Sect. 3.2, namely finding the set S_0^{safe} of states considered "safe" for a particular probability threshold p_{safe}:

$$S_0^{safe} \supseteq \{s \in \hat{s} \mid \hat{s} \in \hat{S}_0 \text{ and } Pr_{\hat{s}}^{\max}(\lozenge^{\leqslant k} \textit{fail}) < p_{safe}\}$$

and the worst-case probability $p_{S'}^+$ for a set of states S':

$$p_{S'}^+ \leqslant \max\{Pr_{\hat{s}}^{\max}(\lozenge^{\leqslant k} \textit{fail}) \mid \hat{s} \in \hat{S} \text{ such that } \hat{s} \cap S' \neq \varnothing\}$$

4   Policy Extraction and Abstraction Generation

Building upon the ideas in the previous section, we now describe the key parts of the MOSAIC algorithm to implement this. We explain the abstract domain used, how to extract a controller policy over abstract states from a neural network representation, and then how to build this into a controller abstraction. We also discuss data structures for efficient manipulation of abstract states.

Abstract Domain. The abstraction described in Sect. 3.3 assumes an arbitrary set of abstract states $\hat{S} \subseteq \mathcal{P}(S)$. In practice, our approach assumes $S \subseteq \mathbb{R}^n$ and uses the "Box" abstract domain, where abstract states are conjunctions of intervals (or hyperrectangles), i.e., abstract states are of the form $[l_1, u_1] \times \cdots \times [l_n, u_n]$, where $l_j, u_i \in \mathbb{R}$ are lower and upper bounds for $1 \leqslant i \leqslant n$.

4.1   Neural Network Policy Extraction

Controller policies are functions $\pi : S \to A$, represented as neural networks. To construct an abstraction (see Definition 8), we need to divide abstract states into subregions which are *consistent* with π, i.e., those where $\pi(s)$ is the same for each state s in the subregion. Our overall approach is as follows. For each action a, we first modify the neural network, adding an *action layer* to help indicate the states (network inputs) where a is chosen. Then, we adapt a branch-and-bound style optimisation algorithm to identify these states, which builds upon methods to approximate neural network outputs by propagating intervals through it.

Branch and Bound. Branch and bound (BaB) is an optimisation algorithm which aims to minimise (or maximise) a given objective function. It works iteratively, starting from the full domain of possible inputs. BaB estimates a maximum and minimum value for the domain using estimator functions, which are

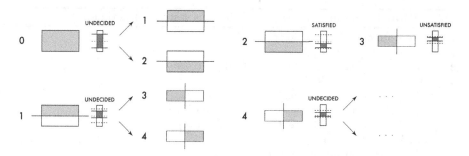

Fig. 1. Illustrating branch-and-bound to identify actions. Each box represents an abstract state and the bar on the right represents upper and lower bounds on the output of the network. 0) The upper and lower bounds of the domain do not give a definite answer, the domain is split into two subregions; 1) The boundaries are tighter than in the previous iteration but the subregion is still undecided; 2) The upper bound is < 0, the property "action taken is a" is always true in this subregion; 3) The lower bound is > 0, the property "action taken is a" is always false in this subregion; 4) The interval between upper and lower bound still contains 0, the action taken in this interval is still unknown so we continue to branch. (Color figure online)

quick to compute and approximate the real objective function by providing an *upper bound* (UB) and a *lower bound* (LB) between which the real function lies. The chosen bounding functions must be admissible, meaning we can guarantee that the real function will always lie within those boundaries.

At each iteration of BaB, the domain is split (or "branched") into multiple parts. In the absence of any additional assumptions about the objective function, the domain is split halfway across the largest dimension. For each part, the upper and lower bounds are calculated and regions whose lower bounds are higher than the current global minimum upper bound (the minimum amongst all regions' upper bounds) are discarded because, thanks to the admissibility property of the approximate functions, they cannot ever have a value lower than the global minimum upper bound.

The algorithm proceeds by alternating the branching phase and the bounding phase until the two boundaries converge or the difference between the bounds is less than an acceptable error value. After that, the current region is returned as a solution to the optimisation problem, and the algorithm terminates.

Finding Consistent Regions. In order to frame the problem of identifying areas of the domain that choose an action a as an optimisation problem, we construct an additional layer that we call an "action layer", and append it on top of the neural network architecture. This is built in such a way that the output is strictly negative if the output is a, and strictly positive value if not. We adopt the construction from [8], which uses a layer to encode a correctness property to be verified on the output of the network.

Algorithm 1: Finding subregions of abstract state $\hat{s}$ for action a

---

```
1  function find_action_subregions(net, a, ŝ):
2  │   queue = {ŝ}, sat = { }, unsat = { }
3  │   mod_net = add_action_layer (net, a)
4  │   while queue ≠ ∅ do
5  │   │   curr_domain = queue.pop()
6  │   │   UB = compute_UB (mod_net, curr_domain)
7  │   │   LB = compute_LB (mod_net, curr_domain)
8  │   │   if UB < 0 then
9  │   │   │   sat.append(curr_domain)
10 │   │   else if LB > 0 then
11 │   │   │   unsat.append(curr_domain)
12 │   │   else
13 │   │   │   dom₁, dom₂ = split (curr_domain)
14 │   │   │   queue.append(dom₁)
15 │   │   │   queue.append(dom₂)
16 │   return sat,unsat
```

The techniques of [8] also adapt branch-and-bound algorithms, using optimisation to check if a correctness property is true. But our goal is different: identifying areas within abstract states where action a is chosen, so we need a different approach. Rather than minimising the modified output of the neural network, we continue splitting domains until we find areas that consistently either do or do not choose action a or we reach a given precision. We do not keep track of the global upper or lower bound since we only need to consider the local ones to determine which actions are taken in each subregion. In the modified branch-and-bound algorithm, after calculating upper and lower bounds for an interval, we have 3 cases:

- $UB > LB > 0$: the controller will never choose action a for the interval;
- $0 > UB > LB$: the controller will always choose action a;
- $UB > 0 > LB$: the outcome of the network is still undecided, so we split the interval and repeat for each sub-interval.

At the end of the computation, we will have a list of intervals which satisfy the property "the controller always take action a" and intervals which always violate it. From these two lists we can summarise the behaviour of the controller within the current region of the state space.

Algorithm 1 shows pseudocode for the overall procedure of splitting an abstract state $\hat{s}$ into a set of subregions where an action a is always taken, and a set where it is not. Figure 1 illustrates the algorithm executing for a 2-dimensional input domain. The blue subregions are the ones currently being considered; the orange bar indicates the range between computed lower and upper bounds for the output of the network, and the red dashed line denotes the zero line.

Approximating Neural Network Output. The branch-and-bound algorithm requires computation of upper and lower bounds on the neural network's output for a specific domain (`compute_UB` and `compute_LB` in Algorithm 1). To approximate the output of the neural network, we use the *Planet* approach from [12]. The problem of approximating the output of the neural network lies in determining the output of the non-linear layers, which in this case are composed of ReLU units. ReLU units can be seen as having 2 phases: one where the output is a constant value if the input is less than 0 and the other where the unit acts as the identity function. The algorithm tries to infer the phase of the ReLU function (whether $x < 0$ or $x \geqslant 0$) by constraining the range of values from the input of the previous layers. In the case of the algorithm not being able to determine the phase of the activation function, some linear over-approximation boundaries are used to constrain the output of each ReLU within the section. The constraints used are $y > 0$, $y > x$ and $y \leqslant (u \cdot (x-l))/(u-l)$ where u and l are the upper and lower bounds inferred from the boundaries of the input domain by considering the maximum and minimum values of each input variable.

4.2   Building the Abstraction

Section 3.3 describes our approach to defining an abstract model of controller execution, as an MDP, and Definition 8 explains the structure required of this MDP such that it can be solved to produce probabilistic guarantees, i.e., upper bounds on the probability of a failure occurring within some time horizon k. Here, we provide more details on the construction of the abstraction.

Algorithm 2 shows pseudo code for the overall procedure. We start from the initial abstract states $\hat{S}_0$, which are the initial states of the MDP, and then repeatedly explore the "frontier" states, whose transitions have yet to be constructed, stopping exploration when either depth k (the required time horizon) or an abstract state containing a failure state is reached. For each abstract state $\hat{s}$ to be explored, we use the techniques from the previous section to split $\hat{s}$ into subregions of states for which the controller policy selects the same action.

Determining successor abstract states in the MDP uses the environment abstraction $\hat{E}$ (see Definition 7). Since we use the "Box" abstract domain, this means using interval arithmetic, i.e., computing the successors of the corner points enclosing the intervals while the remaining points contained within them are guaranteed to be contained within the enclosing successors. The definitions of our concrete environments are therefore restricted to functions that are extensible to interval arithmetic.

4.3   Refining the Abstraction

Although the MDP constructed as described above yields upper bounds on the finite-horizon probability of failure, we can improve the results by *refining* the abstraction, i.e., further splitting some of the abstract states. The refinement step aims to improve the precision of states which are considered unsafe (assuming some specified probability threshold p_{safe}), by reducing the upper bound closer to the real probability of encountering a failure state.

Algorithm 2: Build MDP

---

1   **function** build_mdp(net, $\hat{S}_0$):

2    $\hat{S}_{frontier} = \hat{S}_0$, $t = 0$

3   **while** $t < k$ **do**

4   **foreach** $\hat{s} \in \hat{S}_{frontier}$ **do**

5   **foreach** $a \in A$ **do**

6          $\hat{S}_a, \hat{S}_{\overline{a}} =$ find_action_subregions $(net, a, \hat{s})$

7   **foreach** $\hat{s}_j \in \hat{S}_a$ and $p_i{:}w_i$ in $f(a)$ **do**

8            $\hat{s}' = \hat{E}(\hat{s}_j, w_i)$

9   store $(\hat{s}, p_i, \hat{s}')$ in MDP

10   add $\hat{s}'$ to $\hat{S}_{frontier}$ unless $\hat{s}' \cap fail \neq \varnothing$

11      $t = t + 1$

Regions of initial abstract states that are considered unsafe are split into smaller subregions and we then recreate the branches of the MDP abstraction from these new subregions in the same way as described in Algorithm 2. This portion of the MDP is then resolved, to produce a more accurate prediction of their upper bound probability of encountering a failure state, potentially discovering new safe subregions in the initial abstract state. The refinement process is executed until either there are no more unsafe regions in the initial state or the maximum size of the intervals are less than a specified precision ϵ.

4.4 Storing and Manipulating Abstract States

Very often abstract states have a topological relationship with other abstract states encountered previously. One abstract state could completely encapsulate or overlap with another, but simply comparing all the possible pairs of states would be infeasible. For this reason we need a data structure capable of reducing the number of comparisons to just the directly neighbouring states. A tree-like structure is the most appropriate and significant progress has been made on tree structures capable of holding intervals. However, most of them do not scale well for n-dimensional intervals with $n > 3$.

R-tree [16] is a data-structure that is able to deal with n-dimensional intervals, used to handle GIS coordinates in the context of map loading where only a specific area needs to be loaded at a time. This data structure allows us to perform "window queries" which involve searching for n-dimensional intervals that intersect with the interval we are querying in $O(\log_n(m))$ time, where m is the number of intervals stored. R-tree organises intervals and coordinates in nested "subdirectories" so that only areas relevant to the queried area are considered when computing an answer.

Here, we use an improved version of R-tree called R*-tree [4] which reduces the overlapping between subdirectories at the cost of higher computational cost of $O(n \log(m))$. This modification reduces the number of iterations required during the queries effectively speeding up the calculation of the results. When an abstract domain is queried for the actions the controller would choose, only the areas which were not previously visited get computed.

5   Experimental Results

We have implemented our MOSAIC algorithm, described in Sects. 3 and 4, and evaluated it on deep reinforcement learning controllers trained on two different benchmark environments from OpenAI Gym [7], a pendulum and a cartpole, modified to include controller faults. For space reasons, we consider only "sticky" actions [26]: each action is erroneously executed twice with probability $p = 0.2$.

Implementation. Our implementation uses a combination of Python and Java. The neural network architecture is handled through the Pytorch library [38], interval arithmetic with `pyinterval` [37] and graph analysis with `networkX` [35]. Abstract domain operations are performed with `Rtree` [39], building on the library `libspatialindex` [34]. Constructing and solving MDPs is done using PRISM [24], through its Java API, built into a Python wrapper using `py4j` [36].

5.1   Benchmarks and Policy Learning

Pendulum. The pendulum environment consists of a pole pivoting around a point at one of its ends. The controller can apply a rotational force to the left or to the right with the aim of balancing the pole in its upright position. The pole is underactuated which means that the controller can only recover to its upright position when the pole is within a certain angle. For this reason, if the pole goes beyond a threshold from which it cannot recover, the episode terminates and the controller is given a large negative reward. Each state is composed of 2 variables: the angular position and velocity of the pole.

Cartpole. The cartpole environment features a pole being balanced on top of a cart that can either move left or right. The cartpole can only move within fixed bounds and the pole on top of it cannot recover its upright state after its angle exceeds a given threshold. In this problem the size of each state is 4 variables: the position of the cart on the x-axis, the speed of the cart, the angle of the pole and the angular velocity of the pole.

Policy Construction. We train our own controller policies for the benchmarks, in order to take into account the controller failures added. For the policy neural networks, we use 3 fully connected layers of size 64, followed by an output layer whose size equals the number of controller actions in the benchmark. The training is performed by using the Deep Q-network algorithm [27] with prioritised experience replay [30], which tries to predict the action value in each state and choosing the most valuable one. For both environments, we train the controller for 6000 episodes, limiting the maximum number of timesteps for each episode to 1000. We linearly decay the epsilon in the first 20% of the total episodes up to a minimum of 0.01 which we keep constant for the rest of the training. The remaining hyperparameters remain the same as suggested in [27] and [30].

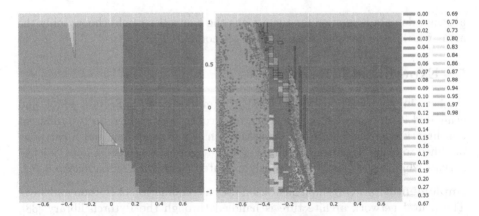

Fig. 2. Heatmaps of failure probability upper bounds for subregions of initial states for the pendulum benchmark (x/y-axis: pole angle/angular velocity). Left: the initial abstraction; Right: the abstraction after 50 refinement steps. (Color figure online)

5.2 Results

We have run the MOSAIC algorithm on the benchmark controller policies described above. We build and solve the MDP abstraction to determine upper bounds on failure probabilities for different parts of the state space. Figure 2 (left) shows a heatmap of the probabilities for various subregions of the initial states of the pendulum benchmark, within a time horizon of 7 steps. Figure 2 (right) shows the heatmap for a more precise abstraction, obtained after 50 steps of refinement. We do not fix a specific probability threshold p_{safe} here, but the right-hand part (in blue) has upper bound zero, so is "safe" for any $p_{safe} > 0$. The refined abstraction discovers new areas which are safe due to improved (i.e., lower) upper bounds in many regions.

Results for the cartpole example are harder to visualise since the state space has 4 dimensions. Figure 4 shows a scatterplot of failure probability bounds within 7 time steps for the subregions of the initial state space; the intervals have been projected to two dimensions using principal component analysis, the size of the bubble representing the volume occupied by the interval. We also plot, in Fig. 3, a histogram showing how the probabilities are distributed across the volume of the subregions of the initial states. For a given value p_{safe} on the x-axis, our analysis yields a probabilistic guarantee of safety for the sum of all volumes shown to the left of this point.

Scalability and Efficiency. Lastly, we briefly discuss the scalabilty and efficiency of our prototype implementation of MOSAIC. Our experiments were run on a 4-core 4.2 GHz PC with 64 GB RAM running Ubuntu 18.04. We successfully built and solved abstractions up to time horizons of 7 time-steps on both benchmark environments. For the pendulum problem, the size of the MDP built ranged up to approximately 160,000 states after building the initial abstraction, reaching approximately 225,000 states after 50 steps of refinement. For the

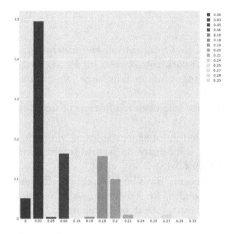

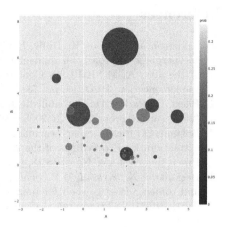

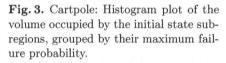

Fig. 3. Cartpole: Histogram plot of the volume occupied by the initial state subregions, grouped by their maximum failure probability.

Fig. 4. Cartpole: probability bounds for initial state subregions (projection using principal component analysis; size denotes the volume occupied by the interval). We can see that large sections of the state space have max probability close to 0.

cartpole problem, the number of states after 7 time-steps ranged up to approximately 75,000 states. The time required was roughly 50 min and 30 min for the two benchmarks, respectively.

6   Conclusions

We have presented a novel approach called MOSAIC for verifying deep reinforcement learning systems operating in environments where probabilistic controller faults may occur. We formalised the verification problem as a finite-horizon analysis of a continuous-space discrete-time Markov process and showed how to use a combination of abstract interpretation and probabilistic model checking to compute upper bounds on failure probabilities. We implemented our techniques and successfully applied them to two benchmark control problems.

Future work will include more sophisticated refinement and abstraction approaches, including the use of lower bounds to better measure the precision of abstractions and to guide their improvement using refinement. We also aim to improve scalability to larger time horizons and more complex environments, for example by investigating more efficient abstract domains.

Acknowledgements. This project has received funding from the European Research Council (ERC) under the European Union's Horizon 2020 research and innovation programme (grant agreement No. 834115, FUN2MODEL).

References

1. Anderson, G., Pailoor, S., Dillig, I., Chaudhuri, S.: Optimization and abstraction: a synergistic approach for analyzing neural network robustness. In: Proceedings of the 40th ACM SIGPLAN Conference on Programming Language Design and Implementation, PLDI'19, pp. 731–744 (2019)
2. Bacci, E., Parker, D.: Probabilistic guarantees for safe deep reinforcement learning (2020). arXiv preprint arXiv:2005.07073
3. Bastani, O., Pu, Y., Solar-Lezama, A.: Verifiable reinforcement learning via policy extraction. In: Proceedings of the 2018 Annual Conference on Neural Information Processing Systems, NeurIPS'18, pp. 2499–2509 (2018)
4. Beckmann, N., Kriegel, H.P., Schneider, R., Seeger, B.: The R*-tree: an efficient and robust access method for points and rectangles. In: Proceedings of the 1990 ACM SIGMOD International Conference on Management of Data, pp. 322–331 (1990)
5. Bougiouklis, A., Korkofigkas, A., Stamou, G.: Improving fuel economy with LSTM networks and reinforcement learning. In: Proceedings of the International Conference on Artificial Neural Networks, ICANN'18, pp. 230–239 (2018)
6. Brázdil, T., et al.: Verification of Markov decision processes using learning algorithms. In: Cassez, F., Raskin, J.-F. (eds.) ATVA 2014. LNCS, vol. 8837, pp. 98–114. Springer, Cham (2014). https://doi.org/10.1007/978-3-319-11936-6_8
7. Brockman, G., et al.: OpenAI gym (2016). arXiv preprint arXiv:1606.01540
8. Bunel, R., Turkaslan, I., Torr, P., Kohli, P., Kumar, P.: A unified view of piece-wise linear neural network verification. In: Proceedings of the 32nd International Conference on Neural Information Processing Systems, NIPS'18, pp. 4795–4804 (2018)
9. Cardelli, L., Kwiatkowska, M., Laurenti, L., Paoletti, N., Patane, A., Wicker, M.: Statistical guarantees for the robustness of Bayesian neural networks. In: Proceedings of the International Joint Conference on Artificial Intelligence, IJCAI-19 (2019)
10. Carr, S., Jansen, N., Topcu, U.: Verifiable RNN-based policies for POMDPs under temporal logic constraints. In: Proceedings of the IJCAI'20 (2020, to appear)
11. Carr, S., Jansen, N., Wimmer, R., Serban, A.C., Becker, B., Topcu, U.: Counterexample-guided strategy improvement for POMDPs using recurrent neural networks. In: Proceedings of the IJCAI'19, pp. 5532–5539 (2020)
12. Ehlers, R.: Formal verification of piece-wise linear feed-forward neural networks. In: D'Souza, D., Narayan Kumar, K. (eds.) ATVA 2017. LNCS, vol. 10482, pp. 269–286. Springer, Cham (2017). https://doi.org/10.1007/978-3-319-68167-2_19
13. Fu, J., Topcu, U.: Probably approximately correct MDP learning and control with temporal logic constraints. In: Proceedings of Robotics: Science and Systems (2014)
14. Garcia, J., Fernandez, F.: A comprehensive survey on safe reinforcement learning. J. Mach. Learn. Res. **16**, 1437–1480 (2015)
15. Gehr, T., Mirman, M., Drachsler-Cohen, D., Tsankov, P., Chaudhuri, S., Vechev, M.T.: AI2: safety and robustness certification of neural networks with abstract interpretation. In: Proceedings of the 2018 IEEE Symposium on Security and Privacy (S&P), pp. 3–18. IEEE Computer Society (2018)
16. Guttman, A.: R-trees: a dynamic index structure for spatial searching. In: Proceedings of the 1984 ACM SIGMOD International Conference on Management of Data, SIGMOD '84, pp. 47–57. ACM (1984)

17. Hahn, E.M., Perez, M., Schewe, S., Somenzi, F., Trivedi, A., Wojtczak, D.: Omega-regular objectives in model-free reinforcement learning. In: Vojnar, T., Zhang, L. (eds.) TACAS 2019. LNCS, vol. 11427, pp. 395–412. Springer, Cham (2019). https://doi.org/10.1007/978-3-030-17462-0_27

18. Huang, X., Kwiatkowska, M., Wang, S., Wu, M.: Safety verification of deep neural networks. In: Majumdar, R., Kunčak, V. (eds.) CAV 2017. LNCS, vol. 10426, pp. 3–29. Springer, Cham (2017). https://doi.org/10.1007/978-3-319-63387-9_1

19. Junges, S., Jansen, N., Dehnert, C., Topcu, U., Katoen, J.-P.: Safety-constrained reinforcement learning for MDPs. In: Chechik, M., Raskin, J.-F. (eds.) TACAS 2016. LNCS, vol. 9636, pp. 130–146. Springer, Heidelberg (2016). https://doi.org/10.1007/978-3-662-49674-9_8

20. Kattenbelt, M., Kwiatkowska, M., Norman, G., Parker, D.: A game-based abstraction-refinement framework for Markov decision processes. Form. Meth. Syst. Des. **36**(3), 246–280 (2010)

21. Katz, G., Barrett, C., Dill, D.L., Julian, K., Kochenderfer, M.J.: Reluplex: an efficient SMT solver for verifying deep neural networks. In: Majumdar, R., Kunčak, V. (eds.) CAV 2017. LNCS, vol. 10426, pp. 97–117. Springer, Cham (2017). https://doi.org/10.1007/978-3-319-63387-9_5

22. Kazak, Y., Barrett, C.W., Katz, G., Schapira, M.: Verifying deep-RL-driven systems. In: Proceedings of the 2019 Workshop on Network Meets AI & ML, NetAI@SIGCOMM'19, pp. 83–89. ACM (2019)

23. Kemeny, J., Snell, J., Knapp, A.: Denumerable Markov Chains, 2nd edn. Springer, New York (1976)

24. Kwiatkowska, M., Norman, G., Parker, D.: PRISM 4.0: verification of probabilistic real-time systems. In: Gopalakrishnan, G., Qadeer, S. (eds.) CAV 2011. LNCS, vol. 6806, pp. 585–591. Springer, Heidelberg (2011). https://doi.org/10.1007/978-3-642-22110-1_47

25. Lahijania, M., Andersson, S.B., Belta, C.: Formal verification and synthesis for discrete-time stochastic systems. IEEE Trans. Autom. Control **60**(8), 2031–2045 (2015)

26. Machado, M.C., Bellemare, M.G., Talvitie, E., Veness, J., Hausknecht, M., Bowling, M.: Revisiting the arcade learning environment: evaluation protocols and open problems for general agents. J. Artif. Intell. Res. **61**, 523–562 (2018)

27. Mnih, V., et al.: Human-level control through deep reinforcement learning. Nature **518**(7540), 529–533 (2015)

28. Ohn-Bar, E., Trivedi, M.M.: Looking at humans in the age of self-driving and highly automated vehicles. IEEE Trans. Intell. Veh. **1**(1), 90–104 (2016)

29. Ruan, W., Huang, X., Kwiatkowska, M.: Reachability analysis of deep neural networks with provable guarantees. In: Proceedings of the 27th International Joint Conference on Artificial Intelligence, IJCAI'18 (2018)

30. Schaul, T., Quan, J., Antonoglou, I., Silver, D.: Prioritized experience replay (2015). arXiv preprint arXiv:1511.05952

31. Shalev-Shwartz, S., Shammah, S., Shashua, A.: Safe, Multi-Agent, Reinforcement Learning for Autonomous Driving (2016). arXiv preprint arXiv:1610.03295

32. Soudjani, S.E.Z., Gevaerts, C., Abate, A.: FAUST^2: Formal Abstractions of Uncountable-STate STochastic Processes. In: Baier, C., Tinelli, C. (eds.) TACAS 2015. LNCS, vol. 9035, pp. 272–286. Springer, Heidelberg (2015). https://doi.org/10.1007/978-3-662-46681-0_23

33. Wang, S., Pei, K., Whitehouse, J., Yang, J., Jana, S.: Formal security analysis of neural networks using symbolic intervals. In: Proceedings of the 27th USENIX Security Symposium, pp. 1599–1614 (2018)

34. libspatialindex. https://libspatialindex.org/. Accessed 7 May 2020
35. Networkx - network analysis in Python. https://networkx.github.io/. Accessed 7 May 2020
36. Py4j - a bridge between Python and Java. https://www.py4j.org/. Accessed 7 May 2020
37. Pyinterval - interval arithmetic in Python. https://pyinterval.readthedocs.io/en/latest/. Accessed 7 May 2020
38. Pytorch. https://pytorch.org/. Accessed 7 May 2020
39. Rtree: Spatial indexing for Python. https://rtree.readthedocs.io/en/latest/. Accessed 7 May 2020

Incremental Methods for Checking Real-Time Consistency

Thierry Jéron[1]([✉])[iD], Nicolas Markey[1][iD], David Mentré[2][iD], Reiya Noguchi[2], and Ocan Sankur[1][iD]

[1] Univ Rennes, INRIA, CNRS, Rennes, France
{thierry.jeron,nicolas.markey,ocan.sankur}@inria.fr
[2] Mitsubishi Electrics R&D Centre Europe, Rennes, France
{d.mentre,r.noguchi}@fr.merce.mee.com

Abstract. Requirements engineering is a key phase in the development process. Ensuring that requirements are consistent is essential so that they do not conflict and admit implementations. We consider the formal verification of *rt-consistency*, which imposes that the inevitability of definitive errors of a requirement should be anticipated, and that of *partial consistency*, which was recently introduced as a more effective check. We generalize and formalize both notions for discrete-time timed automata, develop three incremental algorithms, and present experimental results.

1 Introduction

In the process of developing computer systems, requirement engineering consists in defining, documenting and maintaining the requirements. Requirements can be of different nature, but since we are interested in timed systems, i.e. systems where time constraints are of importance, we will focus here on timed functional ones. Requirements are the primary phase of the development process, and are used to partly drive the testing campaign in order to check that they are indeed satisfied by the implementation. In a formal approach, it is thus important to design formal requirements that are consistent, *i.e.* that are not contradictory and admit implementations that conform to them.

In this paper, we study two prominent consistency notions studied in the literature for real-time system requirements, called *rt-consistency* [PHP11a] and *partial consistency* [Bec19]. Partial consistency concentrates the notion of consistency on Simplified Universal Patterns (SUP) [BTES16] which are simple real-time temporal patterns used to define real-time requirements, essentially comprising an assumption (named *trigger*), a guarantee (named *action*), together with timed constraints on delays of these and between them. The advantage of SUPs is that they define a specification language that is expressive enough yet

This work was partially funded by ANR project Ticktac (ANR-18-CE40-0015), and by a MERCE/Inria collaboration.

N. Bertrand and N. Jansen (Eds.): FORMATS 2020, LNCS 12288, pp. 249–264, 2020.
https://doi.org/10.1007/978-3-030-57628-8_15

easy to understand, even by non experts. The counterpart is that the notion of partial consistency is specific to them and tricky.

Rt-consistency requires that all finite executions that do not violate the requirements, have infinite extensions that satisfy all of requirements. Put differently, this means that if an implementation produces a finite execution whose all continuations necessarily lead to the violation of some requirement, then there must be a requirement that is already violated by the finite execution. In simple words, inevitability of errors should be anticipated by the set of requirements. Thus, rt-consistency ensures that the set of requirements is well designed and sane. This is interesting in that it may reveal conflicts between requirements and catch subtle problems, but it is rather expensive to check. Several directions can be investigated to mitigate this complexity: restrict to sub-classes of requirements, in particular SUPs, restrict to subsets of requirements, examine alternative and cheaper notions of consistency. However these lead in general to false positives and false negatives, and avoiding them requires additional conditions or checks.

Partial consistency is one of these alternative notions of consistency that only considers pairs of SUP requirements. It checks that if there are possibly different executions that trigger both requirements and satisfy one of them, then there should be a common execution in which both requirements are triggered and satisfied. This check is perhaps better understood as a necessary condition for the rt-consistency of *subsets* of requirements (but this does not imply the rt-consistency of the whole set). We formalize this link in this paper. The general motivation is to gain in efficiency, both by restricting to pairs of requirements, but also by focusing on particular situations where inconsistencies may arise. Nevertheless partial consistency can still be costly to check.

Contributions. We address the efficiency issue mentioned above by considering an incremental approach to checking consistency and finding inconsistencies in real-time requirements. In fact, rt-consistency and (bounded) partial consistency are rather expensive to check already on small examples, and because of the state-space explosion problem (which is a classical problem when composing several systems or properties), there is no hope that the approaches would scale to large sets of requirements. Our algorithms improve the scalability of this approach by allowing one to check larger sets of requirements. We also define a new notion of incremental consistency, and allow to get different degrees of confidence about consistency (up to full rt-consistency).

We show that checking rt-consistency can be reduced to CTL model checking for discrete-time systems, providing an alternative approach to duration calculus and timed automata model checking of [PHP11a]. Then, we develop incremental algorithms for checking rt-consistency and a variant of partial consistency generalized for automata. Inconsistencies are searched by starting with small batches of requirements. Whenever we find a counterexample to consistency, we either confirm it (by checking that it fulfills the other requirements) or start the analysis again with more precision by adding a new requirement in the batch. This helps us to scale our analysis to larger sets of requirements. This idea is applied separately for both consistency notions. Moreover, we formalize the relation between the two notions, showing how to obtain counterexamples to rt-inconsistency from counterexamples to partial consistency. Due to space constraints, all proofs are given in the appendix of the full paper [JMM+20].

Related works. Consistency notions appear naturally in the contract-based design of systems [BCN+18]. In this setting, consistency is defined as the existence of an implementation of a contract, which relates environment and system behaviors via assumptions and guarantees. The related notion of *existential consistency* is studied in [ESH14], where consistency consists in the existence of an execution satisfying the requirements.

Simplified Universal Patterns were introduced in [BTES16] to simplify the writing of requirements by non-experts. The patterns are in the form of an assumption and guarantee. In this paper, the notion of consistency ensures the existence of an execution which realizes one requirement (both the assumption and the guarantee) without violating any other one. In [BTES16], the authors also use coverage notions to measure sets of consistent executions to give a quantitative measure of consistency. The notion considered there is thus related to *non-vacuity* (see e.g. [PHP11b]).

More reactive notions were studied as in [AHL+17] where consistency requires that the system should react to uncontrollable inputs along the execution so as to satisfy all requirements. The notion is thus formalized as a game between the system and the environment, and an SMT-based algorithm is given to check consistency within a given bound. This notion thus relies on alternation of quantifiers at each step. Rt-consistency and partial consistency, which we consider in this paper, lie between the two extreme approaches (that is simply existential *versus* game semantics). In fact, a single quantifier alternation is needed to define rt-consistency (see Sect. 2.4). The rt-consistency checking algorithm of [PHP11a] considers systems in a continuous-time setting, and uses duration calculus and timed automata model checking. We consider discrete-time systems (with unit delays rather than arbitrary real-valued delays).

2 Definitions

2.1 Computation Tree Logic

We use CTL to characterize certain kinds of inconsistencies. CTL formulas are defined as $\text{CTL} \ni \phi ::= p \mid \neg\phi \mid \phi \vee \phi \mid \mathbf{AX}\phi \mid \mathbf{EG}\phi \mid \mathbf{E}\phi\mathbf{U}\phi$, where p ranges over AP. CTL formulas are evaluated at the root of computation trees. We thus consider computation trees labeled by valuations of atomic propositions: a tree t is a set of finite non-empty traces, i.e. words over 2^{AP}, closed under prefix, hence containing exactly one trace of size 1 (called its root, and denoted with $r(t)$). We denote $\prec_p$ the prefix ordering on traces. Given a node in the tree represented by a trace $\sigma \in t$, we write t_σ for the subtree of t rooted at σ (i.e., the set of all traces σ' such that $\sigma \cdot \sigma' \in t$). We write $\sigma[i]$ for the prefix of length i of σ. That a tree t satisfies a formula $\phi \in \text{CTL}$ is defined as follows:

$$\begin{aligned}
t &\models p & \iff & \quad p \in r(t)(p) \\
t &\models \neg\phi & \iff & \quad t \not\models \phi \\
t &\models \phi \vee \phi' & \iff & \quad t \models \phi \text{ or } t \models \phi' \\
t &\models \mathbf{AX}\phi & \iff & \quad \forall \sigma \in t.\ (t_{\sigma[1]} \models \phi) \\
t &\models \mathbf{E}\phi\mathbf{U}\phi' & \iff & \quad \exists \sigma \in t.\ (t_\sigma \models \phi' \text{ and } \forall \sigma'.\ (r(t) \prec_p \sigma' \prec_p \sigma) \Rightarrow t_{\sigma'} \models \phi) \\
t &\models \mathbf{EG}\phi & \iff & \quad \exists \sigma \in t.\ (\forall i.\ t_{\sigma[i]} \models \phi)
\end{aligned}$$

Using $\mathbf{AX}$, we can define $\mathbf{EX}$ by $\mathbf{EX}\phi \equiv \neg\mathbf{AX}\neg\phi$. Similarly, $\mathbf{AF}\phi \equiv \neg\mathbf{EG}\neg\phi$ means that ϕ holds along any infinite branch of the tree, and finally $\mathbf{A}\phi\mathbf{U}\phi' \equiv \mathbf{AF}\phi' \wedge \neg\mathbf{E}(\neg\phi')\mathbf{U}(\neg\phi \wedge \neg\phi')$ means that along all infinite branch, ϕ' eventually holds and ϕ holds at all intermediary nodes.

2.2 Timed Automata

We consider requirements expressible by a class of *timed automata* (TA) [AD90]. These extend finite-state automata with variables, called *clocks*, that can be used to measure (and impose constraints on) delays between various events along executions. More precisely, given a set $X = \{c_i \mid 1 \leq i \leq k\}$ of clocks, the set of *clock constraints* is defined by the grammar: $g ::= c \sim n \mid g \wedge g$, where $c \in X$, $n \in \mathbb{N}$, and $\sim \in \{<, \leq, =, \geq, >\}$. Let $C(X)$ denote the set of all clock constraints.

We consider integer-valued clocks whose semantics of constraints is defined in the expected way: given a clock valuation $v: X \to \mathbb{N}$, a constraint $g \in C(X)$ is true at v, denoted $v \models g$, if the formula obtained by replacing each occurrence of c by $v(c)$ holds. For a valuation $v: X \to \mathbb{N}$, an integer $d \in \mathbb{N}$, and a subset $R \subseteq X$, we define $v + d$ as the valuation $(v + d)(c) = v(c) + d$ for all $c \in X$, and $v[R \leftarrow 0]$ as $v[R \leftarrow 0](c) = 0$ if $c \in R$, and $v[R \leftarrow 0](c) = v(c)$ otherwise. Let $\mathbf{0}$ be the valuation mapping all variables to 0.

We consider timed automata as monitors of the evolution of the system through the observation of values of Boolean variables. We thus consider a set $\mathsf{AP} = \{b_i \mid 1 \leq i \leq n\}$ of atomic propositions, and define the set of Boolean constraints $\mathcal{B}(\mathsf{AP})$ as the set of all propositional formulas built on AP.

Definition 1. *A timed automaton is a tuple* $\mathcal{T} = \langle S, S_0, AP, X, T, F \rangle$ *where* S *is a finite set of states,* $S_0 \subseteq S$ *is a set of initial states,* AP *is a finite set of atomic propositions,* X *is a finite set of clocks,* $T \subseteq S \times \mathcal{B}(AP) \times C(X) \times 2^X \times S$ *is a finite set of transitions, and* $F \subseteq S$ *is the set of accepting states.*

We distinguish the following classes of timed automata. A *safety* timed automaton is such that there are no transitions from $S \backslash F$ to F. Conversely a *co-safety* timed automaton is such that there are no transitions from F to $S \backslash F$.

For a transition $t = (s, c, g, r, s') \in T$ of a timed automaton, we define $\mathsf{src}(t) = s$, $\mathsf{tgt}(t) = s'$, $\mathsf{bool}(t) = c$, $\mathsf{guard}(t) = g$, and $\mathsf{reset}(t) = r$. Note that guards are pairs of Boolean and timed guards that can be interpreted (and will be noted) as conjunctions since the two types of guards do not interfere.

With a timed automaton $\mathcal{T}$, we associate the infinite-state automaton $S(\mathcal{T}) = \langle Q, Q_0, \Sigma, D, Q_F \rangle$ that defines its semantics, where

- the set of states Q contains all *configurations* $(s, v) \in S \times \mathbb{N}^X$;
- the initial states are obtained by adjoining the null valuation (all clocks are mapped to zero) to initial states S_0, i.e. $Q_0 = S_0 \times \mathbf{0}$;
- $\Sigma = 2^{AP}$ is the alphabet of actions, i.e. valuations of all Boolean variables;
- transitions in D are combinations of a transition of the TA and a one-time-unit delay. Formally, given a letter $\sigma \in \Sigma$ and two configurations (s, v) and (s', v'), there is a transition $((s, v), \sigma, (s', v'))$ in D if, and only if, there is a transition (s, c, g, r, s') in T such that $\sigma \models c$ and $v \models g$, and $v' = (v[r \leftarrow 0]) + 1$.
- $Q_F = F \times \mathbb{N}^X$ is the set of accepting configurations.

Our semantics thus makes it compulsory to alternate between taking a transition of the TA (possibly a self-loop) and taking a one-time-unit delay. Self-loops can be used to emulate invariants in states.

The transition system $\mathcal{S}(\mathcal{T})$ is infinite because we impose no bound on the values of the clocks during executions. However, as in the setting of TA [AD90], the exact value of a clock is irrelevant as soon as it exceeds the largest integer constant with which it is compared. We could thus easily modify the definition of $\mathcal{S}(\mathcal{T})$ in such a way that it only contains finitely many states.

A *run* of $\mathcal{T}$ is a run of its associated infinite-state automaton $\mathcal{S}(\mathcal{T})$. It can be represented as a sequence along which configurations and actions alternate: $(s_0, v_0) \cdot \sigma_1 \cdot (s_1, v1) \cdot \sigma_2 \cdots (s_n, v_n) \cdots$. A finite run is accepted if it ends in Q_F.

A *trace* of a run is its projection on the set of actions. In other terms, it is a finite or infinite sequence $\sigma = (\sigma_i)_{0 \leq i < l}$ of actions where $l \in \mathbb{N} \cup \{+\infty\}$ is the length of σ, denoted by $|\sigma|$. Finite traces belong to Σ^* and infinite ones to Σ^ω. A finite trace is accepted by $\mathcal{T}$ if a run on that trace is accepted. We note $\mathrm{Tr}(\mathcal{T})$ the set of accepted traces. For $P \subseteq Q$ we will also note $\mathrm{Tr}_P(\mathcal{T})$ the set of traces of runs ending in P.

Consider the following sets, where F is an atomic proposition denoting Q_F:

- **Success**$_\mathcal{T} = F \wedge \mathbf{AG}F$: accepting configurations from which non-accepting configurations are unreachable are called *success*; notice that it is impossible to escape from **Success**$_\mathcal{T}$ since **Success**$_\mathcal{T} \implies \mathbf{AG}\ \textbf{Success}_\mathcal{T}$;
- **Error**$_\mathcal{T} = \neg F \wedge \mathbf{AG}\neg F$: non-accepting configurations from which accepting configurations are unreachable are called *error*; notice also that it is impossible to escape from **Error**$_\mathcal{T}$ since **Error**$_\mathcal{T} \implies \mathbf{AG}\ \textbf{Error}_\mathcal{T}$;

Note that in safety TAs, $\neg F \implies \mathbf{AG}\neg F$ since it is impossible to escape from the set of non-accepting configurations, thus **Error**$_\mathcal{T} = \neg F$; symmetrically in co-safety TAs, $F \implies \mathbf{AG}\ F$ since it is impossible to escape from the set of accepting configurations, thus **Success**$_\mathcal{T} = F$.

We require that our TAs are *complete*, meaning that from any (reachable) configuration (s, v), and for any subset b of AP, there is $t = (s, c, g, r, s') \in T$ such that $b \models c$ and $v \models g$. This is no loss of generality since missing transitions can be directed to a trap state, and self-loops can be added to allow time elapse.

The TAs that we consider are also *deterministic*: for any two transitions (s, c_1, g_1, r_1, s_1) and (s, c_2, g_2, r_2, s_2) issued from a same source s, if both $c_1 \wedge c_2$

and $g_1 \wedge g_2$ are satisfiable, then $s_1 = s_2$ and $r_1 = r_2$. Examples of complete, deterministic TAs expressing requirements are depicted on Fig. 2, in Example 1.

We consider the product of timed automata, as follows:

Definition 2. *Given two TAs* $\mathcal{T}_1 = \langle S_1, S_{1,0}, AP_1, \mathcal{X}_1, T_1, F_1 \rangle$ *and* $\mathcal{T}_2 = \langle S_2, S_{2,0}, AP_2, \mathcal{X}_2, T_2, F_2 \rangle$ *with disjoint clock sets (i.e.,* $\mathcal{X}_1 \cap \mathcal{X}_2 = \emptyset$), *their product* $\mathcal{T}_1 \otimes \mathcal{T}_2$ *is a TA* $\mathcal{T} = \langle S, S_0, AP, \mathcal{X}, T, F \rangle$ *where* $S = S_1 \times S_2$, $S_0 = S_{1,0} \times S_{2,0}$, $AP = AP_1 \cup AP_2$, $\mathcal{X} = \mathcal{X}_1 \cup \mathcal{X}_2$, $F = F_1 \times F_2$ *and the set of transitions is defined as follows: there is a transition* $((s_1, s_2), c, g, r, (s'_1, s'_2))$ *in* T *if there are transitions* $(s_1, c_1, g_1, r_1, s'_1)$ *in* T_1 *and* $(s_2, c_2, g_2, r_2, s'_2)$ *in* T_2 *with* $c = c_1 \wedge c_2$, $g = g_1 \wedge g_2$, *and* $r = r_1 \cup r_2$.

Note that completeness and determinism are preserved by product. The product of TAs can be generalized to an arbitrary number of TAs: for a set $\mathcal{R} = \{R_i\}_{i \in I}$ of requirements, each specified by a TA $\mathcal{T}_i(R_i)$, we note $\otimes \mathcal{R}$ the requirement specified by the TA $\otimes_{i \in I} \mathcal{T}_i(R_i)$.

Note that in this definition, clocks of factor automata are disjoint, while atomic propositions are not, which may cause conflicts in guards of the product, and possibly inconsistencies as will be seen later. Also note that the product of two automata visits its accepting states if both automata do ($F = F_1 \wedge F_2$), while by complementation it visits non-accepting states if one of the automata does ($\neg F = \neg F_1 \vee \neg F_2$). For the product automaton, we directly define (without relying on F) **Success**$_\mathcal{T}$ = **Success**$_{\mathcal{T}_1}$ $\wedge$ **Success**$_{\mathcal{T}_2}$ and **Error**$_\mathcal{T}$ = **Error**$_{\mathcal{T}_1}$ $\vee$ **Error**$_{\mathcal{T}_2}$, and both are trap sets. The definitions of **Error** and **Success** thus depend on the context: these are defined by the formulas $\neg F_i \wedge \mathbf{AG} \neg F_i$ and $F_i \wedge \mathbf{AGF}_i$ for the TAs $\mathcal{T}_i$ representing the given requirements; for the *products* of these automata, **Error**$_\mathcal{T}$ (resp. **Success**$_\mathcal{T}$) is the disjunction (resp. conjunction) of **Error**$_{\mathcal{T}_i}$ (resp. **Success**$_{\mathcal{T}_i}$) of their operands. Notice that we have **Success**$_\mathcal{T}$ = $F \wedge \mathbf{AGF}$, but only **Error**$_\mathcal{T}$ $\subseteq \neg F \wedge \mathbf{AG} \neg F$. The inclusion is in general strict, but becomes an equality when both $\mathcal{T}_1$ and $\mathcal{T}_2$ are safety TAs.

For the rest of this document, we consider complete deterministic timed automata (CDTAs for short) with accepting states F.

2.3 Timed Automata as Requirements

We use complete deterministic TAs to encode requirements and identify the requirements with the CDTAs that define them. Remember that **Error** (resp. **Success**) are sets of configurations from which one cannot escape. Intuitively, entering an **Error** (resp. **Success**) configuration of a CDTA corresponds to violating (resp. satisfying) the corresponding requirement definitively:

Definition 3. *For any requirement* R *defined by a complete deterministic timed automaton and any finite or infinite trace* σ, *we write* σ **fails** R *if running* σ *in* R *enters* **Error**$_R$, *and write* σ **succeeds** R *if it enters* **Success**$_R$.

Note that for a finite trace σ, it could be the case that it does not hit **Error**$_R$ (resp. **Success**$_R$) but all infinite continuations inevitably do. We are particularly interested in such cases; we thus define the following notations for finite traces:

Definition 4. *For a finite trace σ, and a requirement R defined by a CDTA, we write σ* **I-fails** R *if for all infinite traces σ', $\sigma \cdot \sigma'$ fails R. Similarly σ* **I-succeeds** R *if for all infinite traces σ', $\sigma \cdot \sigma'$ succeeds R.*

Clearly, for finite traces, **fails** (resp. **succeeds**) is stronger than **I-fails** (resp. **I-succeeds**). Indeed σ **fails** R (σ **succeeds** R) means reaching a configuration in **Error**$_R$ (resp. **Success**$_R$), while σ **I-fails** R (σ **I-succeeds** R) means reaching a configuration in **AF Error**$_R$ (resp. **AF Success**$_R$). And **Error**$_R$ implies **AG Error**$_R$, which implies **AF Error**$_R$ (and similarly for **Success**$_R$).

For a given trace σ, and *set* of timed automata $\mathcal{R} = \{\mathcal{T}_i\}_{i \in I}$, we write σ **fails** $\mathcal{R}$ (resp σ **succeeds** $\mathcal{R}$) to mean that σ **fails** $\otimes \mathcal{R}$ (resp. σ **succeeds** $\otimes \mathcal{R}$). Note the following simple facts: given $\mathcal{R}' \subseteq \mathcal{R}$, for any finite trace σ, if σ **fails** $\mathcal{R}'$ then σ **fails** $\mathcal{R}$, and if σ **I-fails** $\mathcal{R}'$ then σ **I-fails** $\mathcal{R}$, while conversely, if σ **succeeds** $\mathcal{R}$ then σ **succeeds** $\mathcal{R}'$, and if σ **I-succeeds** $\mathcal{R}$ then σ **I-succeeds** $\mathcal{R}'$.

Simplified Universal Patterns (SUP). TAs can be used to express the semantics of Simplified Universal Pattern (SUP) [TBH16,Bec19], a pattern language that is used to define requirements. Compared to TAs, SUPs offer a more intuitive but less expressive way of writing requirements. Since partial consistency was introduced for SUP, we briefly introduce them. An SUP has the following form:

$$(\text{TSE}, \text{TC}, \text{TEE})[\text{Tmin}, \text{Tmax}] \xrightarrow{[\text{Lmin},\text{Lmax}]} (\text{ASE}, \text{AC}, \text{AEE})[\text{Amin}, \text{Amax}],$$

where TSE, TC, TEE, ASE, AC, AEE, are Boolean formulas on a set AP of atomic propositions, Tmin, Tmax, Lmin, Lmax, Amin, Amax are integers.

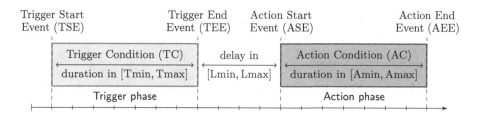

Fig. 1. Intuitive semantics of SUP

Figure 1 illustrates the intuitive semantics of SUP. A *trigger phase* (left) is realized, if TSE is confirmed within a duration in [Tmin; Tmax], that is, if TC holds until TEE occurs; otherwise the trigger is *aborted*. For the SUP instance to be satisfied, following each realized trigger phase, an *action phase* must be realized: an action phase starts with ASE within [Lmin; Lmax] time units after the end of the trigger phase, and then AC must hold until AEE occurs within [Amin, Amax] time units. Otherwise, the SUP is *violated*. Following [Bec19], one can translate SUP instances (and repetitions of them) into complete deterministic timed automata. In fact all SUPs can be written as safety or co-safety CDTAs.

Example 1. Consider the following two SUPs: R_1 : request $\xrightarrow{[3;4]}$ response, and R_2 : repair $\xrightarrow{[5;5]}$ ¬response[3; 3], where an SUP of the form $(p, p, p)[0; 0] \xrightarrow{[0;1]}$ $(q, q, q)[0; 0]$ is written $p \xrightarrow{[0;1]} q$.

The first requirement models a system that has to respond to any request within 3 to 4 time units. The second requirement states that if the system enters a maintenance phase, then it will be off (and cannot respond) after 5 time units, and for a duration of 3 time units. Figure 2 displays the (safety) automata encoding these two SUPs where E_i states are non-accepting trap states and all other ones are accepting.

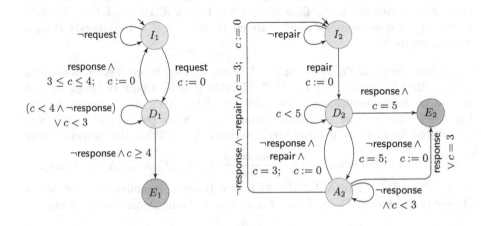

Fig. 2. Timed automata encoding R_1 and R_2

2.4   Consistency Notions

RT-consistency. We reformulate the original rt-consistency notion, introduced in [PHP11a].

Definition 5. *Let $\mathcal{R}$ be a set of requirements. Then $\mathcal{R}$ is rt-consistent if, and only if, for all finite traces σ, if σ I-fails $\mathcal{R}$ then σ fails $\mathcal{R}$.*

Thus the set $\mathcal{R}$ is rt-consistent if any finite trace that inevitably fails, immediately fails. This is indeed equivalent to the formulation in [PHP11a], which says that all finite traces not violating any requirement can be extended to an infinite trace not violating any of them (i.e. ¬(σ **fails** $\mathcal{R}$) implies ¬(σ **I-fails** $\mathcal{R}$)). Notice that rt-consistency (w.r.t. **Error**$_\mathcal{R}$) could be generalized to rt-consistency w.r.t **Success**$_\mathcal{R}$: if σ **I-succeeds** $\mathcal{R}$ then σ **succeeds** $\mathcal{R}$; and all following results easily generalize to rt-consistency w.r.t. **Success**$_R$ with similar treatment.

Observe that even when all individual requirements are rt-consistent (i.e., for all $R \in \mathcal{R}$ and all traces σ, it holds σ **I-fails** $R \implies \sigma$ **fails** R) their conjunction (i.e. the product $\otimes\mathcal{R}$) may not be rt-consistent; for instance, taken individually, both requirements R_1 and R_2 of Example 1 are rt-consistent, but their product is not, as explained in Example 2). Rt-consistency requires that **fails** and **I-fails** be equivalent for all traces in the product automaton.

Rather than using duration calculus as in [PHP11a], we show that CTL model checking can be used in a discrete-time setting to check rt-consistency. In CTL, rt-consistency of $\mathcal{R}$ can be expressed by requiring **AF Error**$_\mathcal{R}$ $\Leftrightarrow$ **Error**$_\mathcal{R}$ at all reachable states. Since **Error**$_\mathcal{R}$ is absorbing, a trace ending in a configuration in $\neg$**Error**$_\mathcal{R}$ $\wedge$ **AF Error**$_\mathcal{R}$ is a *witness to rt-inconsistency*. Moreover, only configurations in $\neg$**Error**$_\mathcal{R}$ need to be traversed to reach such configurations; and such a configuration exists if, and only if, configurations exist in $\neg$**Error**$_\mathcal{R}$ with all immediate successors in **Error**$_\mathcal{R}$, i.e., **AX Error** is true. In fact, we obtain the following property.

Lemma 1. *A given set of requirements $\mathcal{R}$ has a witness to rt-inconsistency if, and only if, $\mathcal{R} \models \mathbf{E}(\neg\mathbf{Error}_\mathcal{R}\ U\ (\neg\mathbf{Error}_\mathcal{R} \wedge \mathbf{AX}\ \mathbf{Error}_\mathcal{R}))$.*

Example 2. The requirements in Example 1 are not rt-consistent: consider a finite trace σ where the repairsignal is received, followed 3 time units later with a request. Then $\neg(\sigma\ \mathbf{fails}\ R_1 \wedge R_2)$; the joint run of the automata are as follows:

$$(I_1, I_2, \begin{smallmatrix} c_1=0 \\ c_2=0 \end{smallmatrix}) \xrightarrow[(+\text{delay})]{\text{repair}} (I_1, D_2, \begin{smallmatrix} c_1=1 \\ c_2=1 \end{smallmatrix}) \xrightarrow[(+\text{delay})]{\star} (I_1, D_2, \begin{smallmatrix} c_1=2 \\ c_2=2 \end{smallmatrix})$$

$$\xrightarrow[(+\text{delay})]{\star} (I_1, D_2, \begin{smallmatrix} c_1=3 \\ c_2=3 \end{smallmatrix}) \xrightarrow[(+\text{delay})]{\text{request}} (D_1, D_2, \begin{smallmatrix} c_1=1 \\ c_2=4 \end{smallmatrix}).$$

From this last configuration, it can be checked that no continuations of this trace will avoid reaching E_1 or E_2: indeed, both automata will first loop in their current states D_1 and D_2, reaching configuration $(D_1, D_2), c_1 = 2, c_2 = 5$. In order to avoid visiting E_2, the next two steps must satisfy $\neg$response, thereby reaching $(D_1, A_2), c_1 = 4, c_2 = 2$. From there, we have a conflict: if response is true at the next step, R_2 reaches E_2, while if response is false, R_1 reaches E_1.

Now, assume we add the following requirement, which expresses that no request can be received during maintenance: R_3 : repair $\rightarrow \neg$request$[5; 5]$. This rules out the above trace, and it can be checked that the resulting set of requirements is now rt-consistent.

Partial Consistency. *Partial consistency* was introduced in [Bec19] as an alternative, more efficient check to detect inconsistencies in SUP requirements. We here generalize this notion to CDTAs. The name *partial consistency* might be misleading since it does not directly compare with rt-consistency: partial inconsistency identifies risky situations for pairs of requirements that could cause rt-inconsistency of the whole set. In this paper, we formalize this link, and show how to lift witnesses of partial inconsistencies to witnesses of rt-inconsistencies.

In a requirement R_i, let us call *action* configurations those configurations allowing to enter immediately **Error**$_{R_i}$ (i.e. satisfying **EX Error**$_{R_i}$).[1]

---

[1] For SUPs, such configurations correspond to *action* phases, hence the name.

Then, action configurations that have an infinite continuation that avoids $\mathbf{Error}_{R_i}$ are characterized by $\mathbf{EX}\ \mathbf{Error}_{R_i} \wedge \neg \mathbf{AF}\ \mathbf{Error}_{R_i}$. Now, $\mathbf{EX}\ \mathbf{Error}_{R_1} \wedge \mathbf{EX}\ \mathbf{Error}_{R_2}$ means we are simultaneously at action configurations of both R_1 and R_2. In this case, even though there are separate continuations that avoid $\mathbf{Error}_{R_1}$ and $\mathbf{Error}_{R_2}$, there may not be a common one. In our generalization of partial consistency, we focus our attention to checking that a common continuation exists for this type of configurations which are seen as "risky" since they are in the proximity of error.

Let $\mathbf{reach}_k(\mathcal{R})$ denote the set of configurations of $\mathcal{R}$ reachable within k steps.

Definition 6. *Consider requirements R_1, R_2 and a set $\mathcal{R}'$ of requirements. We say that R_1 and R_2 are* partially consistent *w.r.t. $\mathcal{R}'$ if for all $k \in \mathbb{N}$,*

$$if, for\ all\ i \in \{1,2\},$$
$$\exists s_i \in \mathbf{reach}_k(\mathcal{R}_1 \times \mathcal{R}_2 \times \mathcal{R}'). \ s_i \models \mathbf{EX}\ \mathbf{Error}_{R_1} \wedge \mathbf{EX}\ \mathbf{Error}_{R_2} \wedge$$
$$\neg \mathbf{AF}(\mathbf{Error}_{\mathcal{R}'} \vee \mathbf{Error}_{R_i})$$
$$then$$
$$\exists s \in \mathbf{reach}_k(\mathcal{R}_1 \times \mathcal{R}_2 \times \mathcal{R}'). \ s \models \mathbf{EX}\ \mathbf{Error}_{R_1} \wedge \mathbf{EX}\ \mathbf{Error}_{R_2} \wedge$$
$$\neg \mathbf{AF}(\mathbf{Error}_{\mathcal{R}'} \vee \mathbf{Error}_{R_1} \vee \mathbf{Error}_{R_2}). \quad (1)$$

Partial consistency requires that for all depths k, if infinite traces for both requirements can be found leading to an action configuration within k steps, and neither violate the requirement itself nor $\mathcal{R}'$, then a single infinite trace must exist that reaches action configurations of both requirements within k steps, and does not violate any of them, nor $\mathcal{R}'$. Therefore, a witness of partial inconsistency is a number $k \geq 0$ and two infinite sequences σ_1 and σ_2 such that, σ_i reaches actions phases of both requirements within k steps, and never fails R_i or $\mathcal{R}'$, such that there are no infinite traces that do so without violating one of the requirements R_1, R_2 or $\mathcal{R}'$.

We establish that partial consistency is a necessary condition for the rt-consistency of the *subset* $\mathcal{R}' \cup \{R_1, R_2\}$, since counterexamples for the former provide counterexamples for the latter:

Lemma 2. *If R_1 and R_2 are partially inconsistent w.r.t. $\mathcal{R}'$, then $\mathcal{R}' \cup \{R_1, R_2\}$ is rt-inconsistent.*

To efficiently find counterexamples to partial consistency, we consider the following approximation, which is similar to that of [Bec19] but generalized to CDTAs. Given bounds $\alpha, \beta > 0$, requirements R_1, R_2 are (α, β)-*bounded partially consistent* if for all $k \leq \alpha$,

$$if,\ for\ all\ i \in \{1,2\},$$
$$\exists s_i \in \mathbf{reach}_k(\mathcal{R}_1 \times \mathcal{R}_2 \times \mathcal{R}'). \ s_i \models \mathbf{EX}\ \mathbf{Error}_{R_1} \wedge \mathbf{EX}\ \mathbf{Error}_{R_2} \wedge$$
$$\neg \mathbf{AF}_{\alpha-k}(\mathbf{Error}_{\mathcal{R}'} \vee \mathbf{Error}_{R_i})$$
$$then$$
$$\exists s \in \mathbf{reach}_k(\mathcal{R}_1 \times \mathcal{R}_2 \times \mathcal{R}'). \ s \models \mathbf{EX}\ \mathbf{Error}_{R_1} \wedge \mathbf{EX}\ \mathbf{Error}_{R_2} \wedge$$
$$\neg \mathbf{AF}_{\alpha+\beta-k}(\mathbf{Error}_{\mathcal{R}'} \vee \mathbf{Error}_{R_1} \vee \mathbf{Error}_{R_2}). \quad (2)$$

where $\mathbf{AF}_l\phi$ means the inevitability of ϕ within l steps, which can be expressed in CTL as the disjunction of all formulas of the form $\mathbf{AX}(\phi\vee\mathbf{AX}(\cdots\phi\vee\mathbf{AX}\phi))$ with l repetitions of $\mathbf{AX}$. Thus the approximation consists in looking for witnesses of bounded length for the satisfaction of the Eq. 1). But notice that witnesses of failure of Eq. 2 are not witnesses of failure of Eq. 1 which require infinite traces (see below).

Example 3. We consider again the requirements of Example 1. Requirements R_1 and R_2 are not partially consistent under empty $\mathcal{R}'$: as soon as a trace reaches action configurations of both requirements, error states of any of them can be avoided, but not both of them. Under requirement R_3, requirements R_1 and R_2 cannot reach their action phases simultaneously, so that with $\mathcal{R}' = \{R_3\}$, those two requirements are partially consistent.

There are a few differences with the original definition of partial consistency of [Bec19]. First, partial consistency of [Bec19] only checks the very first trigger of the traces. Moreover, it focuses on situations where, after respective triggers, no timing allows requirements to avoid being simultaneously in action phases. In our case, $\mathbf{EX\ Error}_{R_1} \wedge \mathbf{EX\ Error}_{R_2}$ does not restrict simultaneous action phases to such particular ones. Thus we can detect more subtle inconsistencies.

The second difference is that the bounded approximation in [Bec19] checks for the existence of a lasso-shaped execution in the automata that recognize the SUP requirements. The advantage of this is that such a lasso describes an infinite execution, so if partial consistency holds, so does the bounded approximation; while the converse is not true. In other terms, a witness for bounded partial inconsistency is a witness for partial inconsistency. In our case, we do not look for a lasso in the premise of (2), so this implication does not hold. We do prove, on the other hand, that rt-consistency implies (2); see Lemma 5.

Third, in [Bec19], $\mathcal{R}'$ contains only a specific type of requirements called invariants. In our case, $\mathcal{R}'$ is an arbitrary subset of the requirement set.

3   Incremental Algorithms

We provide three incremental methods to check rt-consistency of a given set of requirements $\mathcal{R}$. The first one provides strong guarantees and can assess the rt-consistency of the whole set $\mathcal{R}$, or that of its subsets, and uses CTL model checking. The second one uses SAT/SMT solving and scales to larger sets. It can *detect* rt-inconsistencies of $\mathcal{R}$, but cannot *prove* rt-consistency; it can only ensure partial consistency. The third one can quickly find rt-inconsistencies.

In all algorithms we consider a set $\mathcal{R} = \{R_i\}_{i\in I}$ of requirements, each given as a CDTA, and their product $\otimes\mathcal{R}$.

3.1   Incremental Rt-consistency Checking

In this section, we present our incremental algorithm for rt-consistency checking. Unlike the previous work of [Hoe06], which uses duration calculus [ZHR91],

Input: A set $\mathcal{R}$ of requirements given as CDTAs, $2 \leq n \leq |\mathcal{R}|$
$\phi(\mathcal{R}) \leftarrow \mathbf{E}[\neg\mathbf{Error}_{\mathcal{R}} \mathbf{U}(\neg\mathbf{Error}_{\mathcal{R}} \wedge \mathbf{AX}\ \mathbf{Error}_{\mathcal{R}})]$
for all *pairs* $\{R_1, R_2\} \subseteq \mathcal{R}$ **do**
$\quad$ $\mathcal{R}' \leftarrow \{R_1, R_2\}$
$\quad$ **while** $|\mathcal{R}'| \leq n$ *and* $\mathcal{R}' \models \phi(\mathcal{R}')$ **do**
$\quad\quad$ $\sigma \leftarrow$ witness of $\phi(\mathcal{R}')$ // σ witnesses rt-inconsistency of $\mathcal{R}'$
$\quad\quad$ **if** $\exists R \in \mathcal{R} \setminus \mathcal{R}'$ *s.t.* σ **fails** R **then**
$\quad\quad\quad$ $\mathcal{R}' \leftarrow \mathcal{R}' \cup \{R\}$
$\quad\quad$ **else**
$\quad\quad\quad$ **return** σ // σ witnesses rt-inconsistency of $\mathcal{R}$
return $\emptyset$ // no witness for the rt-inconsistency of $\mathcal{R}$ is found

Algorithm 1: Incremental rt-consistency checking algorithm. In order to avoid checking the same subsets of $\mathcal{R}'$ several times, one can store the subsets seen so far and break the while loop when $\mathcal{R}'$ has already been treated.

our algorithm is based on *computation tree logic* (CTL) model checking. Rt-inconsistency of $\mathcal{R}$ reduces to checking whether a finite trace exists along which $\mathbf{Error}_{\mathcal{R}}$ remains false such that, from the last configuration, $\mathbf{Error}_{\mathcal{R}}$ is inevitable. Such a finite trace σ is called a *witness* for the rt-inconsistency of $\mathcal{R}$. Remember that, by Lemma 1, this can be written in CTL as $\mathbf{E}[\neg\mathbf{Error}_{\mathcal{R}} \mathbf{U} (\neg\mathbf{Error}_{\mathcal{R}} \wedge \mathbf{AX}\ \mathbf{Error}_{\mathcal{R}})]$ to be checked in $\otimes\mathcal{R}$.

When the size of $\mathcal{R}$ is too large for model-checking tools to handle, we consider subsets $\mathcal{R}'$ of $\mathcal{R}$. Such incomplete checks alone do not provide any guarantee; indeed if $\mathcal{R}' \subseteq \mathcal{R}$, consistency of $\mathcal{R}$ does not imply consistency of $\mathcal{R}'$, nor the opposite. Nevertheless, they can be used to detect rt-inconsistencies with an additional check:

Lemma 3. *Let $\sigma \in \Sigma^*$ be a witness for the rt-inconsistency of $\mathcal{R}' \subseteq \mathcal{R}$. If $\neg(\sigma$ fails $\mathcal{R})$, then σ is also a witness for the rt-inconsistency of $\mathcal{R}$.*

Let us now describe our procedure summarized in Algorithm 1. Given $\mathcal{R}$ and a bound $n \leq |\mathcal{R}|$, we consider subsets of $\mathcal{R}$ of size up to n, starting with subsets of size 2. Assume a subset $\mathcal{R}' \subseteq \mathcal{R}$ is found to be rt-inconsistent with a witness trace σ. We check whether σ **fails** $\mathcal{R} \backslash \mathcal{R}'$. If this is the case, we select $R \in \mathcal{R} \backslash \mathcal{R}'$ such that σ **fails** R, and restart the analysis with $\mathcal{R}' \cup \{R\}$. Notice that if $\mathcal{R}' \cup \{R\}$ is inconsistent, then σ cannot be a witness trace since it violates R. This ensures that a new requirement will be added to the set at each iteration. Otherwise, by Lemma 3, we conclude that $\mathcal{R}$ is rt-inconsistent and σ is a witness. If no confirmed witnesses are found, then we stop and report that no rt-inconsistency is found. If $n \geq |\mathcal{R}|$, then one can conclude that $\mathcal{R}$ is rt-consistent; otherwise the check is incomplete.

To increase the precision (to have a better chance to detect rt-inconsistencies), one can increase the bound n. In order to reduce the number of cases to check, thus giving up on completeness, one might restrict only to some subsets, for instance making sure that each requirement is covered by at least one subset.

Input: A set $\mathcal{R}$ of requirements given as CDTAs, parameters $\alpha, \beta > 0$
for all *pairs* $\{R_1, R_2\} \subseteq \mathcal{R}$ **do**
   | $\mathcal{R}' \leftarrow \emptyset$
   | **while** *Equation* (2) *fails* **do**
   | | $(\sigma_1, \sigma_2) \leftarrow$ witness traces for the premise of (2) for some $k \leq \alpha$
   | | **if** $\exists i \in \{1, 2\}, \neg(\sigma_i$ **fails** $\mathcal{R})$ **then**
   | | | **return** σ_i // witness of rt-inconsistency of $\mathcal{R}$
   | | **else**
   | | | **if** $\mathcal{R} = \mathcal{R}' \cup \{R_1, R_2\}$ **then**
   | | | | **break** // No witness is found for this pair
   | | | **else**
   | | | | Choose $R \in \mathcal{R}$ such that σ_i **fails** R for some $i \in \{1, 2\}$
   | | | | $\mathcal{R}' \leftarrow \mathcal{R}' \cup \{R\}$
return $\emptyset$ // no counterexample is found

Algorithm 2: Incremental partial consistency checking algorithm.

3.2 Incremental Partial Consistency Checking

We now present an incremental algorithm for checking partial consistency via the *bounded* partial consistency checking in the same vein as the previous section.

Ideally, we would like to check Eq. (2) for all pairs $\{R_1, R_2\}$ of requirements with respect to $\mathcal{R}' = \mathcal{R} \backslash \{R_1, R_2\}$; in fact, considering the whole set $\mathcal{R}'$ makes sure that counterexample traces do not trivially violate requirements. This is costly in general, so we will start with an empty $\mathcal{R}'$ and let it grow incrementally by adding requirements as needed. The following lemma exhibits when such counterexamples can be lifted to witnesses of rt-inconsistency:

Lemma 4. *Let σ_1, σ_2 and k be witnesses of bounded partial inconsistency for $R_1, R_2 \in \mathcal{R}$ and $\mathcal{R}' \subseteq \mathcal{R}$, i.e. counterexamples of Eq. 2. If, for some i, $\neg(\sigma_i$ fails $\mathcal{R})$, then σ_i is also a witness for the rt-inconsistency of $\mathcal{R}$.*

The procedure is summarized in Algorithm 2. Given pair (R_1, R_2) and set $\mathcal{R}' \subseteq \mathcal{R} \backslash \{R_1, R_2\}$, integer parameters $\alpha, \beta > 0$, checking the (α, β)-bounded partial-consistency consists in verifying Eq. (2). A negative check is witnessed by some $k \leq \alpha$ and a pair of traces σ_1, σ_2. If $\neg(\sigma_i$ **fails** $\mathcal{R})$ holds for some $i \in \{1, 2\}$, the trace is returned as a counterexample by Lemma 4. Otherwise, a requirement $R \in \mathcal{R}$ such that σ_i **fails** R is added to the set $\mathcal{R}'$ and the procedure is repeated. Thus, subsequent iterations will discard σ_i and look for other traces. The following lemma shows that all counterexamples returned by Algorithm 2 are witnesses to rt-inconsistency:

Lemma 5. *Let $\mathcal{R}$ be a set of requirements, and σ be a finite trace returned by Algorithm 2. Then σ is a witness for rt-inconsistency for $\mathcal{R}$.*

3.3 Incremental Partial Rt-consistency Checking

We now propose an algorithm for rt-consistency checking, that combines an incremental approach targeting subsets of requirements (hence the name partial),

Input: A set $\mathcal{R}$ of requirements, parameters $\alpha > 0$, $n \in [1, |\mathcal{R}|]$
for all *subsets* $S \subseteq \mathcal{R}$ *such that* $|S| \leq n$ **do**
  $\mathcal{R}' \leftarrow \emptyset$
  while $S \times \mathcal{R}' \models \phi_{p,\alpha}$ **do**
    $\sigma \leftarrow$ witness trace for $\phi_{p,\alpha}$
    if $\neg(\sigma$ **fails** $\mathcal{R})$ **then**
      $\mid$ **return** σ // Counterexample for $\mathcal{R}$
    else
      if $\mathcal{R} = \mathcal{R}' \cup S$ **then**
        $\mid$ **break** // No counterexample is found for this subset
      else
        Choose $R \in \mathcal{R}$ such that σ **fails** R
        $\mathcal{R}' \leftarrow \mathcal{R}' \cup \{R\}$
return $\emptyset$ // no counterexample is found

Algorithm 3: Incremental partial rt-consistency checking algorithm.

and a bounded search, providing an alternative to Algorithm 1 amenable to using SMT solvers. Intuitively, we check for the existence of configurations where all requirements in a subset S of $\mathcal{R}$ *immediately conflict* i.e. **AX Error$_S$**, meaning that at the next step they inevitably violate at least one requirement of S.

Let S be a subset of requirements of $\mathcal{R}$. We say that S is *partially rt-consistent* with respect to $\mathcal{R}'$ if for all configurations s,

$$s \models \neg\mathbf{Error}_{S \cup \mathcal{R}'} \implies \neg\mathbf{AX\ Error}_S. \tag{3}$$

This clearly implies that S is rt-consistent, but also that no immediate conflict affects the subset S in any configuration. A witness of partial rt-inconsistency is a trace σ that reaches a configuration s satisfying $\neg\mathbf{Error}_{S \cup \mathcal{R}'} \wedge \mathbf{AX\ Error}_S$. Since $\mathbf{AX\ Error}_S$ implies $\mathbf{AX\ Error}_{\mathcal{R}}$ (because $\mathbf{Error}_S$ implies $\mathbf{Error}_{\mathcal{R}}$), if additionally $\neg(\sigma$ **fails** $\mathcal{R})$ it is also a witness of rt-inconsistency by Lemma 3. Similarly to Lemma 1, the existence of a witness of partial inconsistency reduces to checking the formula $\phi_p = \mathbf{E}(\neg\mathbf{Error}_{S \cup \mathcal{R}'} \mathbf{U}\ (\neg\mathbf{Error}_{S \cup \mathcal{R}'} \wedge \mathbf{AX\ Error}_S))$.

Partial rt-consistency can be further restricted by bounding the size of S and restricting the exploration depth. For integers n and α, we say that $\mathcal{R}$ is α-*bounded* n-*partially rt-consistent* if Formula 3 holds for any subset S of size $|S| \leq n$, and configurations $s \in \mathbf{reach}_\alpha(\mathcal{R})$. Checking α-*bounded* n-*partial rt-inconsistency* can be done by replacing $\mathbf{U}$ by $\mathbf{U}_\alpha$ in ϕ_p thus checking $\phi_{p,\alpha} = \mathbf{E}(\neg\mathbf{Error}_{S \cup \mathcal{R}'} \mathbf{U}_\alpha (\neg\mathbf{Error}_{S \cup \mathcal{R}'} \wedge \mathbf{AX\ Error}_S))$.

We summarize the procedure in Algorithm 3, where, similarly to Algorithm 2, the set $\mathcal{R}'$ is augmented by requirements failed by tentative counterexamples. We easily get the following lemma since a witness of α-bounded n-partial rt-inconsistency that does not fail $\mathcal{R}$ is also a witness of rt-inconsistency.

Lemma 6. *Let $\mathcal{R}$ be a set of requirements, and σ be a finite trace returned by Algorithm 3. Then σ is a witness for rt-inconsistency.*

Table 1. Experiments on our case study. The size shows the number of timed requirements + the number of (non-timed) Boolean requirements of the instance. The parameters were chosen as $\alpha = 40$ and $n = 2$. The sign ✓ means that no inconsistencies were found. The experiments were run on a 1.9 Ghz processor with a timeout of 3 h.

Set	Size	rt-consistency Algorithm 1	Partial consistency Algorithm 2	Partial rt-consistency Algorithm 3
#1	6 + 9	5 inconsist. (24 s)	4 inconsist. (36 s)	5 inconsist. (39 s)
#2	8 + 10	1 inconsist. (21 s)	✓ (55 s)	1 inconsist. (101 s)
#3	8 + 10	✓ (24 s)	✓ (61 s)	✓ (115 s)
#4	10 + 16	✓ (359 s)	✓ (85 s)	✓ (141 s)
#5	12 + 16	✓ (1143 s)	✓ (133 s)	✓ (227 s)
#6	13 + 16	✓ (5311 s)	✓ (138 s)	✓ (232 s)

4   Preliminary Experiments

We experimented the different algorithms on a factory automation use case. In this system, a carriage and an arm cooperate to convey material: objects are pushed onto the carriage, which brings them to a position where a pushing arm places them on a conveyor belt. The correctness of this system relies on several timed requirements between different elements of the system.

Table 1 shows the inconsistencies found with our algorithms on sets of requirements of varying sizes. The largest set we considered contained 29 requirements of which 13 are timed and the other 16 are purely Boolean. We compare the incremental partial consistency and partial rt-consistency algorithms (implemented using the SMT solver Z3 [Z3]), with the incremental rt-consistency algorithm (implementing CTL model-checking using NuSMV [NuS]). Inconsistencies were detected in the first two sets, but partial consistency failed in detecting any in set #2.

These preliminary experiments show that the incremental method can help detect inconsistencies quickly. However, since the methods are not complete, we encourage using several algorithms in parallel.

5   Conclusion

In this paper, we studied the notions of rt-consistency and partial consistency. We showed how to reduce the problem to CTL model checking on timed automata models, and presented algorithms that can detect rt-inconsistencies. Our preliminary experiments show encouraging results. As future work, we will extensively evaluate the ability of these algorithms to capture inconsistencies, and their performances on large realistic use cases. One might investigate other variants of the (partial) consistency notions, with the goal of detecting more inconsistencies more efficiently. There is a trade-off to find for such partial consistency algorithms. In fact, they might allow one to examine more potential counterexample witnesses, which means that one might detect more inconsistencies, but one might also have to deal with more false positives. Another interesting question is how to correct rt-inconsistencies e.g. by adding new requirements.

References

[AD90] Alur, R., Dill, D.: Automata for modeling real-time systems. In: Paterson, M.S. (ed.) ICALP 1990. LNCS, vol. 443, pp. 322–335. Springer, Heidelberg (1990). https://doi.org/10.1007/BFb0032042

[AHL+17] Aichernig, B.K., Hörmaier, K., Lorber, F., Ničković, D., Tiran, S.: Require, test, and trace it. Int. J. Softw. Tools Technol. Transfer **19**(4), 409–426 (2017)

[BCN+18] Benveniste, A., et al.: Contracts for system design. Found. Trends Electron. Des. Autom. **12**(2–3), 124–400 (2018)

[Bec19] Becker, J.S.: Analyzing consistency of formal requirements. Electron. Commun. EASST (AVOCS 2018) **76** (2019)

[BTES16] Bienmüller, T., Teige, T., Eggers, A., Stasch, M.: Modeling requirements for quantitative consistency analysis and automatic test case generation. In: Workshop on Formal and Model-Driven Techniques for Developing Trustworthy Systems at 18th International Conference on Formal Engineering Methods (2016)

[ESH14] Ellen, C., Sieverding, S., Hungar, H.: Detecting consistencies and inconsistencies of pattern-based functional requirements. In: Lang, F., Flammini, F. (eds.) FMICS 2014. LNCS, vol. 8718, pp. 155–169. Springer, Cham (2014). https://doi.org/10.1007/978-3-319-10702-8_11

[Hoe06] Hoenicke, J.: Combination of Processes, Data, and Time. Ph.D. thesis, University of Oldenburg(2006)

[JMM+20] Jéron, T., Markey, N., Mentré, D., Noguchi, R., Sankur, O.: Incremental methods for checking real-time consistency. Technical report 2007.01014, arXiv (2020)

[NuS] NuSMV: a new symbolic model checker. http://nusmv.fbk.eu/

[PHP11a] Post A., Hoenicke J., Podelski A.: rt-Inconsistency: a new property for real-time requirements. In: Giannakopoulou D., Orejas F. (eds.) FASE 2011. LNCS, vol 6603, pp.34–49. Springer, Heidelberg (2011). https://doi.org/10.1007/978-3-642-19811-3_4

[PHP11b] Post, A., Hoenicke, J., Podelski, A.: Vacuous real-time requirements. In: IEEE 19th International Requirements Engineering Conference, pp. 153–162 (August 2011)

[TBH16] Teige, T., Bienmüller, T., Holberg, H.J.: Universal pattern: formalization, testing, coverage, verification, and test case generation for safety-critical requirements. In: Wimmer, R. (ed.) 19th GI/ITG/GMM Workshop Methoden und Beschreibungssprachen zur Modellierung und Verifikation von Schaltungen und Systemen, MBMV'16, pp. 6–9. Albert-Ludwigs-Universität Freiburg (2016)

[Z3] The Z3 theorem prover. https://github.com/Z3Prover/z3

[ZHR91] Zhou, C., Hoare, C.A.R., Ravn, A.P.: A calculus of durations. Inf. Process. Lett. (IPL) **40**(5), 269–276 (1991)

Reachability Analysis of Nonlinear Systems Using Hybridization and Dynamics Scaling

Dongxu Li[1], Stanley Bak[3], and Sergiy Bogomolov[1,2(✉)]

[1] Australian National University, Canberra, Australia
dongxu.li@anu.edu.au
[2] Newcastle University, Newcastle upon Tyne, UK
sergiy.bogomolov@newcastle.ac.uk
[3] Stony Brook University, Stony Brook, NY, USA
stanleybak@gmail.com

Abstract. Reachability analysis techniques aim to compute which states a dynamical system can enter. The analysis of systems described by nonlinear differential equations is known to be particularly challenging. Hybridization methods tackle this problem by abstracting nonlinear dynamics with piecewise linear dynamics around the reachable states, with additional inputs to ensure overapproximation. This reduces the analysis of a system with nonlinear dynamics to the one with piecewise affine dynamics, which have powerful analysis methods. In this paper, we present improvements to the hybridization approach based on a *dynamics scaling* model transformation. The transformation aims to reduce the sizes of the linearization domains, and therefore reduces overapproximation error. We showcase the efficiency of our approach on a number of nonlinear benchmark instances, and compare our approach with Flow*.

1 Introduction

A hybrid automaton [26] is a widely used model for dynamical systems that exhibit complex mixed discrete-continuous behavior. *Reachability analysis* [12,22,30] computes an envelope on the set of the states the hybrid automaton can visit within a given time frame. While efficient approaches and tools exist for hybrid automata with affine dynamics [3,10,11,13,23,24,32], reachability analysis of nonlinear systems remains a challenging problem. The current approaches to analyze nonlinear systems can be roughly categorized as follows:

- *Hybridization based approaches* [1,4–7,9,25–27] reduce the analysis of nonlinear systems to the analysis of affine systems with uncertain inputs and thus leverage the power of reachability algorithms for simpler classes of dynamics.
- *Taylor model based approaches* [15,16] approximate nonlinear dynamics using a Taylor expansion, i.e. a combination of polynomials and an interval remainder. The computation of Taylor models is done by iteratively applying Picard operator.

© Springer Nature Switzerland AG 2020
N. Bertrand and N. Jansen (Eds.): FORMATS 2020, LNCS 12288, pp. 265–282, 2020.
https://doi.org/10.1007/978-3-030-57628-8_16

- *Constraint solving based approaches* [21, 29] encode the reachability problem as a satisfiability modulo theory (SMT) problem. Note that such approaches normally do not provide an explicit representation of the reachable set.
- *Simulation based approaches* compute the reachable set by simulating a hybrid automaton multiple times and then enclosing these simulations into reachability tubes. For example, the tool C2E2 [20] uses annotations to computes reachability tubes. Similarly, the tool Breach [19] employs sensitivity analysis for the same purpose.

In the rest of the paper, we focus on hybridization based approaches for purely continuous nonlinear dynamical systems. We note that the existing hybridization approaches can be mainly classified into *static* and *dynamic* approaches. Static approaches [5, 7, 9, 26, 27] partition the continuous state space and *abstract* nonlinear dynamics with its linear approximation in each of the partitions. The resulting model is then forwarded for further analysis to a reachability analysis tool which supports affine dynamics. Such approaches suffer from the following two limitations. First, as the partition and thus all the *abstraction domains* are fixed prior to the reachability analysis, the analysis cannot make use of any information about the system behavior. Therefore, the partition strategy can be ineffective and inaccurate. Second, state space partitioning usually leads to an exponential number of discrete modes in the resulting hybrid automaton, which might make the reachability analysis computationally infeasible for large dynamical systems. In contrast, in dynamic approaches [1, 4, 6, 25], the construction of abstraction domains is performed on-the-fly and namely is interleaved with the reachability analysis. In particular, a dynamic approach ensures that, for each time moment, the abstraction domain encloses the *currently-tracked set of states*, i.e. the set of states the system is currently at. As a larger domain normally results in a larger linearization error, the effectiveness of dynamic hybridization approaches crucially depends on the choice of the abstraction domains.

Due to system nonlinearity, individual system states can evolve in quite different ways. As a result, the currently-tracked set of states, can *stretch* in course of the analysis. Thus, the abstraction domain can quickly grow as well, which might lead to the drastic increase of the noise to be added to ensure conservativeness of the linearized dynamics. In order to mitigate this issue, in our approach, we combine a hybridization scheme with a model transformation technique named *dynamics scaling*, which works by manipulating the dynamics of the original system and aggregating reachable states over a time segment. We have implemented the proposed techniques and benchmarked them against Flow* [15], a state-of-art reachability analysis tool for nonlinear hybrid automata, on a number of challenging benchmarks. We observe that on the majority of the benchmarks our techniques show superior precision and runtime (of 1–2 orders of magnitude). As a consequence, our tool succeeds in verifying more safety properties within a given time limit.

The main contributions of the paper are as follows:

1. We present a novel dynamic hybridization approach to perform reachability analysis of nonlinear continuous dynamical systems, which relies on support-function set representation. As part of our approach, we employ an enhanced

error model for linear time-invariant systems which uses the input set decomposition.

2. We embed into our workflow a dynamic scaling technique, which helps to flatten the reachable sets, and in this way leads to reduction of the hybridization errors. We propose a scaling function that is particularly suitable in the hybridization context. In addition, we automate the process of dynamics scaling using a heuristic.

3. We implement the proposed techniques and evaluate their effectiveness in comparison to `Flow*` on a number of challenging benchmarks with 2–30 state variables.

The rest of the paper is organized as follows. Section 2 presents the necessary mathematical background to introduce our approach. Section 3 describes the hybridization reachability algorithm and the improved error model based on support functions. We present the enhancement of hybridization using dynamics scaling transformation in Sect. 4. In Sect. 5, we report the evaluation results. We conclude the paper in Sect. 6.

2   Preliminaries

In order to describe our method, we first review hybrid automata (Sect. 2.1) and reachability analysis of affine systems using support functions (Sect. 2.2).

2.1   Hybrid Automaton

Definition 1 (Hybrid automaton). *A hybrid automaton $\mathcal{H}$ is defined as a tuple, $\mathcal{H} = (\mathcal{M}, \mathcal{X}, Inv, Init, Flow, Trans)$, where $\mathcal{M} = \{m_1, ..., m_k\}$ is a finite set of modes; $\mathcal{X}$ is a finite set of n-dimensional real-valued variables; Inv is a mapping $\mathcal{M} \rightarrow 2^{\mathbb{R}^n}$, and $Inv(m_i)$ defines the invariant condition for the mode $m_i \in \mathcal{M}$; Init $\subseteq \mathcal{M} \times \mathbb{R}^n$ defines the initial condition for variables and the initial mode; Flow is a mapping of the locations to differential equations in the form of $\dot{x} = f(x)$, which defines how variables within a location evolve; Trans is a finite set of discrete transitions $t = (m, g, reset, m')$ that may change the mode of $\mathcal{H}$ from m to m' and update the variables according to reset when the guard condition g is satisfied. A state of $\mathcal{H}$ is a tuple $s \in \mathcal{M} \times \mathbb{R}^n$.*

The behaviors of a hybrid automaton are formally described as *runs*, which are alternating sequences of time elapse, during which $\mathcal{X}$ evolves according to *Flow*, and discrete transitions *Trans*, which updates $\mathcal{X}$ on *reset*. A state s is *reachable* if there exists a run that starts from $s_0 \in Init$ and ends at s.

2.2   Reachability Analysis Using Support Functions

We consider bounded-time reachability analysis problem, which aims at computing an over-approximation of the set of reachable states upon time T originating from a set of initial states $\mathcal{X}_0$, denoted as $\mathcal{R}_{[0,T]}(\mathcal{X}_0)$. Efficient reachability analysis algorithms using *support functions* [22,30,32] were proposed for hybrid systems with *Flow* of the affine form $\dot{x} = Ax(t) + u(t)$, $u(t) \in \mathcal{U}$, where $\mathcal{U}$ is the uncertain input to the system. These algorithms establish the basis of our work on nonlinear systems.

Support Functions. The support function [14] of a compact continuous set $\mathcal{S} \subset \mathbb{R}^n$ given a direction vector $\ell \in \mathbb{R}^n$ is defined as

$$\rho(\ell, \mathcal{S}) = \max_{x \in \mathcal{S}} \ell \cdot x$$

and a set $\mathcal{S}$ is uniquely defined by its support functions on all the directions: $\mathcal{S} = \bigcap_{\ell \in \mathbb{R}^n} \{x \mid \ell \cdot x \leq \rho(\ell, \mathcal{S})\}$. In the case where $\mathcal{S}$ is defined as the intersection of hyperplanes, its support function can be computed by calling linear programmes (LP). Support functions enable efficient implementation of the majority of set operations used in reachability analysis:

- *linear map*: For a linear map $A \in \mathbb{R}^n \times \mathbb{R}^n$, $\rho(\ell, A\mathcal{S}) = \rho(A^T \ell, \mathcal{S})$

- *Minkowski sum*: For sets $\mathcal{S}$, $\mathcal{S}'$, denote their Minkowski sum as $\mathcal{S} \oplus \mathcal{S}'$, then $\rho(\ell, \mathcal{S} \oplus \mathcal{S}') = \rho(\ell, \mathcal{S}) + \rho(\ell, \mathcal{S}')$

- *convex hull*: For sets $\mathcal{S}$, $\mathcal{S}'$, denote their convex hull as $\mathrm{CH}(\mathcal{S}, \mathcal{S}')$, then $\rho(\ell, \mathrm{CH}(\mathcal{S}, \mathcal{S}')) = \max(\rho(\ell, \mathcal{S}), \rho(\ell, \mathcal{S}'))$

Checking emptiness of the intersection between a convex set with a halfspace using support functions is straightforward [31]. Given a set $\mathcal{S}$ and a halfspace $\mathcal{G} = \{x \in \mathbb{R}^n \mid a \cdot x \leq d\}$, where $a \in \mathbb{R}^n$ and $d \in \mathbb{R}$, $\mathcal{S} \cap \mathcal{G} \neq \emptyset$ if and only if $d \geq -\rho(-a, \mathcal{S})$.

Affine Reachability Algorithms. The reachability algorithm for affine dynamics adopts the time discretization scheme with a fixed time step. Given a time step δ, the algorithm overapproximates the reachable states with the union of convex sets $\Omega_0, \ldots, \Omega_{N-1}$, called a *flowpipe*, where $\lceil N = T/\delta \rceil$. The approximation relies on the *error model* operating on $\mathcal{X}_0$, $\mathcal{U}$ and δ, which mainly constitutes two operators $\Psi_{[0,\delta]}(\cdot)$ and $\Psi_\delta(\cdot)$:

- $\Psi_{[0,\delta]}(\cdot)$ overapproximates the reachable states originating from $\mathcal{X}_0$ over the time *interval* $[0, \delta]$, i.e. $\mathcal{R}_{[0,\delta]}(\mathcal{X}_0) \subseteq \Psi_{[0,\delta]}(\mathcal{X}_0, \mathcal{U})$,
- $\Psi_\delta(\cdot)$ overapproximates the disturbance of the system due to the uncertain input, i.e. $\mathcal{R}_{[\delta,\delta]}(\{0\}) \subseteq \Psi_\delta(\mathcal{U})$.

Each convex set of the flowpipe is computed as follows:

$$\Omega_0 = \Psi_{[0,\delta]}(\mathcal{X}_0, \mathcal{U}) \tag{1}$$

$$\Omega_{i+1} = e^{A\delta} \Omega_i \oplus \Psi_\delta(\mathcal{U}) \tag{2}$$

The instantiation of $\Psi_{[0,\delta]}(\cdot)$ and $\Psi_\delta(\cdot)$ differs among different error models.

3   Hybridization with Support Functions

In this section, we describe the hybridization process, and improve one of the essential steps that causes overapproximation error during hybridization.

A nonlinear continuous system can be modeled as a single-mode hybrid automaton with nonlinear dynamics:

$$\dot{x} = f(x), \ x \in \mathcal{X} \tag{3}$$

where $f(\cdot)$ is a locally Lipschitz continuous vector function. For a single-mode hybrid automaton, we mainly refer to its continuous component of its state. Given an initial set of states $\mathcal{X}_0$ defined by a *hyperbox*, i.e. Cartesian product of intervals, and a time horizon T, we aim at computing the set of reachable states of $f(\cdot)$ originating from $\mathcal{X}_0$ over time interval $[0, T]$.

3.1   Overview of Hybridization Scheme

To compute an overapproximation of the time-bounded set of reachable states of a nonlinear system in Eq. 3, the hybridization approach first overapproximates the nonlinear dynamics with affine dynamics, and then performs reachability analysis on the resultant affine system. The overapproximation is performed multiple times, each time restricted to a portion of the state space, which in our case is a hyperbox. The process uses two concepts: (i) *abstraction domain* and (ii) *linearization function*.

Definition 2 (Abstraction domains and linearization functions). *An abstraction domain $\mathcal{D} \subset \mathbb{R}^n$ is a hyperbox enclosing the reachable sets. We denote the center of $\mathcal{D}$ as c. Given an abstraction domain $\mathcal{D}$ and nonlinear dynamics $f(\cdot)$, a linearization function $\mathcal{L}(\cdot)$ applies Jacobian linearization on $f(\cdot)$ with an additive input set:*

$$\mathcal{L}(f(\cdot)) = \begin{cases} \dot{x}(t) = Ax(t) + u(t) \\ u(t) \in \mathcal{U} \end{cases} \tag{4}$$

where A is the evaluation of Jacobian matrix at the domain center c, i.e. $J_f(c)$. $\mathcal{U}$ is the set of conservative inputs such that $\forall x(t) \in \mathcal{D}, f(x(t)) - Ax(t) \in \mathcal{U}$.

One can show that $\mathcal{L}(f(\cdot))$ simulates $f(\cdot)$ in $\mathcal{D}$ and therefore proves the soundness of the hybridization approach.

In addition to Definition 2, our algorithm uses two procedures `next_discrete` and `next_dense`. The procedure `next_discrete` takes a sequence of linearized dynamics and computes an overapproximation of $\mathcal{R}_{[t,t]}(\mathcal{X}_0)$, i.e. the set of reachable states at t time instance. The procedure `next_dense` takes a sequence of linearized dynamics and a reachable set $\mathcal{X}_i$ at discrete time t and computes an overapproximation of $\mathcal{R}_{[0,\delta]}(\mathcal{X}_i)$, i.e. the set of reachable states over the *time interval* $[t, t + \delta]$. The details of these procedures are described in Sect. 3.2.

The general hybridization algorithm is shown in Algorithm 1. At each step, we first compute a minimal enclosing box of the reachable sets (line 11) and enlarge it by pushing the boundaries outwards for μ distance (line 12). We then take the enlarged enclosing box as the abstraction domain $\mathcal{D}$ and compute linearized dynamics within the domain (line 13). After we have the linearized dynamics, we attempt to compute the dense-time reachable set at step $i + 1$ (line 15). Importantly, we need to ensure that the abstraction domain always contains the reachable sets to maintain the conservativeness (line 16). If $\Omega' \subseteq \mathcal{D}$ holds, we compute an overapproximation of $\mathcal{R}_{[(i+1)\delta,(i+1)\delta]}(\mathcal{X}_0)$, which is required by next_dense for further computations (line 18). At the end of the step, we reset μ and advance time (line 19, 20). In case the containment check fails, we increase μ (line 22) and compute a new abstraction domain by creating a box containing both Ω_i and Ω' (line 11) and redo the computation for Ω'. Note that for a readability reason we have omitted checking whether Ω_0 stays within $\mathcal{D}$ in Algorithm 1, although we have implemented this containment checking practically. Correctness of the algorithm follows from the following two observations: (i) $\mathcal{R}_{[i\delta,i\delta]}(\mathcal{X}_0) \subseteq$ next_discrete$(\mathcal{X}_0, \Theta)$, where Θ is the sequence of $\langle A_j, \mathcal{U}_j \rangle$, $0 \leq j < i$ and (ii) $\mathcal{R}_{[i\delta,(i+1)\delta]}(\mathcal{X}_0) \subseteq$ next_dense$(\mathcal{X}_i, \Theta) = \Omega_i$. Therefore, $\mathcal{R}_{[0,T]}(\mathcal{X}_0) = \cup_{i=0}^{N-1} \mathcal{R}_{[i,(i+1)\delta]}(\mathcal{X}_0) \subseteq \cup_{i=0}^{N-1} \Omega_i$.

Algorithm 1 differs from [17,35] mainly in two aspects. Firstly, we construct a new abstraction domain at each time step. In principle, it might be beneficial to avoid doing so as long as the reachable set does not leave the current domain, in order to reduce the runtime cost in computing new linearized dynamics. However, since the domain is constructed by enclosing the reachable sets and enlarged by a small amount, the domain is rarely large enough for multiple steps in practice. Moreover, constructing domains tightly confining reachable sets helps to reduce the linearization errors and consequently improves the precision. Secondly, when there happens a switch in the linearized dynamics, existing approaches [17,35] take the set of reachable states over a time interval (Ω_i in our notation) as the new initial set for the sebsequent computation, which is, however, not necessary since the switch always happens on a time instance. In contrary, at the $(i + 1)^{th}$ step, instead of taking Ω_i as the initial set of states, we compute $\mathcal{X}_i$ which overapproximates the reachable set at the time instance $i\delta$. Therefore, the approximation error in the computation of Ω_i does not propagate. Additionally, as we will see later in Sect. 3.2, because support functions provide an exact representations for $\mathcal{X}_i$, we do not introduce wrapping effects when switching the abstraction domain.

3.2 Support Functions Computations

Since the hybridization approach uses affine reachability operators, the approximation quality is dependent on the accuracy of the error model. In this section, we present the error model we use for affine reachability analysis and describe the extension to the hybridization context through a recurrent formulation.

Improved Affine Reachability Error Model. We use the same error model to compute the dense-time reachable sets (next_dense) as [32] and present an improved error model over [22] to compute the discrete-time reachable (next_discrete) sets by better approximating the input sets.

Algorithm 1: Hybridization Reachability Algorithm

Input: Initial state: $\mathcal{X}_0$, dynamics: $f(\cdot)$, total steps: N, time step: δ
Output: Sequence of reachable sets: $\{\Omega_0, \ldots, \Omega_{N-1}\}$

1 $i \leftarrow 0$;
2 $\mu_0 \leftarrow 10^{-9}$;
3 $\mu \leftarrow \mu_0$;
4 $\mathcal{D} \leftarrow$ enclosing_box($\{\mathcal{X}_0\}$);
5 $\langle A_0, U_0 \rangle \leftarrow \mathcal{L}(f(\cdot), \mathcal{D})$;
6 $\Theta \leftarrow$ List($\langle A_0, U_0 \rangle$);
7 $\Omega_0 \leftarrow$ next_dense($\mathcal{X}_0, \Theta$);
8 $\Omega' \leftarrow \Omega_0$;
9 $\mathcal{X}_1 \leftarrow$ next_discrete($\mathcal{X}_0, \Theta$);
10 **while** $i < N$ **do**
11 $\quad$ $\mathcal{D} \leftarrow$ enclosing_box($\{\Omega_i, \Omega'\}$);
12 $\quad$ $\mathcal{D} \leftarrow$ bloat($\mathcal{D}, \mu$);
13 $\quad$ $\langle A_i, \mathcal{U}_i \rangle \leftarrow \mathcal{L}(f(\cdot), \mathcal{D})$;
14 $\quad$ Θ.append($\langle A_i, \mathcal{U}_i \rangle$);
15 $\quad$ $\Omega' \leftarrow$ next_dense($\mathcal{X}_{i+1}, \Theta$);
16 $\quad$ **if** $\Omega' \subseteq \mathcal{D}$ **then**
17 $\quad\quad$ $\Omega_{i+1} \leftarrow \Omega'$;
18 $\quad\quad$ $\mathcal{X}_{i+1} \leftarrow$ next_discrete($\mathcal{X}_0, \Theta$);
19 $\quad\quad$ $i \leftarrow i + 1$;
20 $\quad\quad$ $\mu \leftarrow \mu_0$;
21 $\quad$ **else**
22 $\quad\quad$ $\mu \leftarrow 2\mu$;
23 $\quad\quad$ Θ.remove($\langle A_i, \mathcal{U}_i \rangle$);

Lemma 1 *(adapted from [32]). Assuming $\mathcal{X}_i$ overapproximates the reachable set at time $i\delta$, A is the a linear map of the linearized dynamics during the time interval $[i\delta, (i+1)\delta]$, let Ω_i be the convex set defined by:*

$$\Omega_i = \mathrm{CH}(\mathcal{X}_i, e^{A\delta}\mathcal{X}_i \oplus \delta\mathcal{U} \oplus \alpha_\delta B) \tag{5}$$

where $\alpha_\delta = (e^{\|A\|\delta} - 1 - \delta\|A\|)(R_{\mathcal{X}_i} + \frac{R_{\mathcal{U}}}{\|A\|})$, B denotes the unit ball for the considered norm, $R_{\mathcal{X}_i} = \max_{x \in \mathcal{X}_i} \|x\|$ and $R_{\mathcal{U}} = \max_{u \in \mathcal{U}} \|u\|$. Then

$$\mathcal{R}_{[i\delta, (i+1)\delta]}(\mathcal{X}_i) \subseteq \Omega_i \tag{6}$$

We refer readers to [32] for the proof. Lemma 1 can be roughly understood as follows. $e^{A\delta}\mathcal{X}_i \oplus \delta\mathcal{U}$ is an overapproximation of the reachable set at time $(i+1)\delta$; the bloating operation and the convex hull operation give the overapproximation of the reachable set over the time interval $[i\delta, (i + 1)\delta]$. The bloating factor α_δ is computed such as to ensure the overapproximation.

The support function of Ω_i on ℓ is computed as follows:

$$\rho(\ell, \Omega_i) = \max(\rho(\ell, \mathcal{X}_i), \rho((e^{A\delta})^T \ell, \mathcal{X}_i) + \delta\rho(\ell, \mathcal{U}) + \alpha_\delta\rho(\ell, B) \quad (7)$$

Before we present the improved error model on the computation of discrete-time reachable sets, we introduce the following notations: $\square(\mathcal{S})$, which denotes the symmetric interval hull of a set $\mathcal{S} \subset \mathbb{R}^n$, is defined as $[-\overline{|x_1|}; \overline{|x_1|}] \times \ldots \times [-\overline{|x_n|}; \overline{|x_n|}]$ where $\forall i : 1 \leq i \leq n, \overline{|x_i|} = \max\{|x_i| \mid x \in \mathcal{S}\}$. $|\cdot|$ is the element-wise absolute operation over a matrix or vector. The model relies on the following matrices:

$$\Phi_1(A, \delta) = \sum_{i=0}^{\infty} \frac{\delta^{i+1}}{(i+1)!} A^i, \qquad \Phi_2(A, \delta) = \sum_{i=0}^{\infty} \frac{\delta^{i+2}}{(i+2)!} A^i \quad (8)$$

If A is invertible, Φ_1 and Φ_2 can be computed as $\Phi_1(A, \delta) = A^{-1}(e^{A\delta} - I)$, $\Phi_2(A, \delta) = A^{-2}(e^{A\delta} - I - A\delta)$. Otherwise they can be computed as sub-matrices of a block matrix exponential [22].

The rationale behind the improvement is as follows. Since the error model on the input relies on $\square(A\mathcal{U})$, the symmetric interval hull operation can be too coarse if the input set is not centered around the origin. From this observation, we decompose $\mathcal{U}$ into $\{u_c\} \oplus \mathcal{W}$, where u_c is the geometric center of $\mathcal{U}$ and $\mathcal{W}$ is a set that centers around the origin. This way, we reduce the overapproximation introduced during the symmetric hull operation. The improved error model is formalised by the following lemma:

Lemma 2. *Assuming A is the linear map of the linearized dynamics during the time interval $[i\delta, (i + 1)\delta]$, $\mathcal{X}_i$ overapproximates the reachable set at time $i\delta$, let $\mathcal{X}_{i+1}$ be the set defined by*

$$\mathcal{X}_{i+1} = e^{A\delta}\mathcal{X}_i \oplus \Psi_\delta(\mathcal{U}) \quad (9)$$

$$\Psi_\delta(\mathcal{U}) = \delta\mathcal{W} \oplus \varepsilon_\mathcal{W} \oplus \Phi_1(A, \delta) \cdot u_c \quad (10)$$

$$\varepsilon_\mathcal{W} = \square(\Phi_2(|A|, \delta) \square (A\mathcal{W})) \quad (11)$$

Then $\mathcal{R}_{[(i+1)\delta, (i+1)\delta]} \subseteq \mathcal{X}_{i+1}$.

Proof. See a technical report [34].

Lemma 2 provides a way to compute the discrete-time reachable set of the next time instance given that of the current time instance and the linearized dynamics. As opposed to [22], our model improves the accuracy of the approximation by better handling the uncertainty in the input set. The support function of $\mathcal{X}_{i+1}$ on ℓ is computed as follows:

$$\rho(\ell, \mathcal{X}_{i+1}) = \rho(\ell, (e^{A\delta})^T \mathcal{X}_i) + \rho(\ell, \Psi_\delta(\mathcal{U})) \quad (12)$$

$$\rho(\ell, \Psi_\delta(\mathcal{U})) = \delta\rho(\ell, \mathcal{W}) + \rho(\ell, \varepsilon_\mathcal{W}) + \ell \cdot \Phi_1(A, \delta) \cdot u_c \quad (13)$$

Support Function Computations for Nonlinear Systems. As described in Procedure 1, the reachability analysis of a nonlinear system is reduced to analyzing a sequence of linearized systems with uncertain inputs. Since we create a hybridization domain for each step, after k steps we have k pairs of $\langle A_i, \mathcal{U}_i \rangle$, using which we can extend the error model for the discrete reachable sets to the nonlinear systems.

Lemma 3. *Given the initial states $\mathcal{X}_0$ and a sequence of linearized dynamics $\Theta = \{\langle A_k, \mathcal{U}_k \rangle\}$ $(0 \leq k < i)$, let $\mathcal{X}_{i+1}$ be the set defined by:*

$$\mathcal{X}_{i+1} = \Big(\prod_{r=0}^{i} e^{A_{i-r}\delta} \Big) \mathcal{X}_0 \oplus \bigoplus_{r=1}^{i} \Big(\prod_{m=0}^{i-r} e^{A_{i-m}\delta} \Big) \Psi_\delta(\mathcal{U}_{r-1}) \oplus \Psi_\delta(\mathcal{U}_i) \qquad (14)$$

Then it follows that $\mathcal{R}_{[(i+1)\delta, (i+1)\delta]} \subseteq \mathcal{X}_{i+1}$.

Proof. See a technical report [34].

The support function of $\mathcal{X}_{i+1}$ on the direction ℓ is as follows:

$$\rho(\ell, \mathcal{X}_{i+1}) = \rho\Big(\prod_{r=0}^{i} (e^{A_r \delta})^T \ell, \mathcal{X}_0 \Big)$$

$$+ \sum_{r=1}^{i} \rho\Big(\prod_{m=r}^{i} (e^{A_m \delta})^T \ell, \Psi_\delta(\mathcal{U}_{r-1}) \Big) + \rho(\ell, \Psi_\delta(\mathcal{U}_i)) \qquad (15)$$

The support function of $\Psi_\delta(\mathcal{U}_{p-1})$ and $\Psi_\delta(\mathcal{U}_i)$ can be computed according to Eq. 13. In Eq. 15, the number of linear programs to solve grows linearly in the number of steps i. As a result, the total number of linear programs to solve is quadratic in relation to the number of steps $\lceil T/\delta \rceil$, which can be several thousands in typical cases. Although the result from the computation perspective is polynomial, the number of calls needed to an LP solver is a source of significant slowdown. Nevertheless, by restricting $\mathcal{X}_0$ to be the Cartesian product of intervals of an n−dimensional space, all the convex sets involved in Eq. 15 are hyperboxes. And the following well-known property of hyperboxes allows us to compute $\rho(\ell, \mathcal{X}_{i+1})$ without calling an LP solver.

Proposition 1 (Support function of a hyperbox). *Given a hyperbox $\mathcal{B} = [a_1, b_1] \times \ldots \times [a_n, b_n]$, the support function of $\mathcal{B}$ on the direction $\ell = (\ell_1, \ldots, \ell_n)$ is given by:*

$$\rho(\ell, \mathcal{B}) = \sum_{i=1}^{n} \ell_i \cdot h_i, \text{ where } h_i = \begin{cases} a_i, & \text{if } l_i \leq 0 \\ b_i, & \text{otherwise} \end{cases} \qquad (16)$$

Proposition 1 enables the computation of support functions for a set of hyperboxes in a batch by properly vectorizing the matrix multiplication operations, which leads to some performance gains in practice.

4 Dynamics Scaling for Hybridization

The main source of overapproximation error in hybridization methods comes from the overapproximation of the nonlinear dynamics within the abstraction domains. Instead of hyperboxes, some methods have used simplices [18] or other polyhedra [3] as abstraction domains. However, since individual trajectories may evolve quite differently and end up with reaching different states given a specific time instance, domains may need to stretch out irrespective of the domain shape, in order to contain all the reachable states within one step. In this section, we propose a dynamics scaling technique applied to the hybridization context, which helps to reduce the error in the reachable sets by properly manipulating the dynamics of the system. The dynamics scaling technique was first proposed in [8] to reduce the error during the conversion of guard conditions for *affine* systems. The main idea behind dynamics scaling is to create an additional mode in the automaton that multiplies the original dynamics by a scaling function. It is also shown in [8] that if the scaling function always outputs a nonnegative number for any states considered, the set of reachable states computed for time-bounded reachability does not change.

We employ the dynamics scaling technique for *nonlinear* system analysis and extend it in two aspects. Firstly, we propose a new scaling function so that the trajectories lagged behind is sped up while others in front are slowed down, therefore, the reachable set is flattened (Fig. 1). As a consequence, the size of abstraction domains is reduced, which eventually leads to less approximation errors and better reachability precision. Secondly, we propose a heuristic approach to select the dwelling time in the scaling mode. To our best knowledge, this is the first attempt to exploit and automate dynamics scaling for reachability analysis of nonlinear systems.

Dynamics Scaling Function. Given nonlinear dynamics $f(\cdot)$ and the currently tracked set of states Ω, the scaled dynamics $h(\cdot)$ is detailed as below:

$$h(x) = m \cdot d(x) \cdot f(x) \tag{17}$$

$$d(x) = \frac{1}{\|a\|}(-ax + b) \tag{18}$$

$h(\cdot)$ scales the original nonlinear dynamics by the scaled distance function $d(\cdot)$, which measures the signed distance from the point x to the hyperplane defined by $ax \geq b$. Note that $d(\cdot)$ is nonnegative for any x that satisfies $ax \leq b$. The signed distance is scaled by a constant multiplier m, as we will explain later. We call $m \cdot d(x)$ the *dynamics scaling function*.

Now we describe how we choose the hyperplane $ax \geq b$. At each scaling step, we first evaluate the gradient of $f(\cdot)$ at the center of Ω, denoted as $l' = \frac{df(x)}{dx}|_{x=c_\Omega}$, c_Ω is the geometric center of Ω. Then we use the complementary halfspace of the supporting hyperplane of Ω in the direction l', i.e. $l' \cdot x \geq \rho(l', \Omega)$, as the hyperplane. By scaling dynamics using a signed distance function, the speed of trajectories that are far from the hyperplane is increased while the speed of those near the hyperplane is decreased. As a result, the size of abstraction domains is reduced which in turn leads to smaller linearization errors.

Different from affine systems, the linear map A in our approach is the evaluation of the Jacobian matrix of $f(\cdot)$ at the center of the abstraction domain. The addition of the dynamics scaling function modifies the system dynamics and consequently its Jacobian matrix. Since the error model relies on $\|A\|$, such linearization brings two possible downsides: i) as $e^{\|A\|\delta}$ grows exponentially in $\|A\|$, a linear map A of a large norm may result in a prohibitively large α_δ and leads the flowpipe to diverge; ii) a linear map A of a small norm slows down the progression of the trajectories and takes more steps to achieve the scaling effect. Therefore, we propose to add a multiplier $m = \frac{\|A_f\|}{\|A_h\|}$ which equates the norm of the scaled and unscaled linearized dynamics, where A_f is the linear map of linearized dynamics of $f(\cdot)$ and A_h is the linear map of the linearized dynamics of $d(\cdot) \cdot f(\cdot)$. We observed in practice that i) the addition of m helps maintaining the magnitude of bloating factors in a reasonable order and ii) a moderate amount of steps in the scaling mode leads to a decent scaling effect.

Heuristics for Dynamics Scaling. We apply dynamics scaling periodically during the reachability analysis. To this end, we introduce a parameter *scaling period* $p \in (0, 1)$ to indicate that we perform dynamics scaling after each $\lceil p \cdot T \rceil$ time segment. A smaller period enables dynamics scaling more often and provides a stronger scaling effect. On the other hand, because dynamics scaling introduces more nonlinearity by adding a polynomial term, the time cost of computing the linearization errors could arise. Therefore, p balances the trade-off between a stronger scaling effect and additional nonlinearity and computation runtime.

In order to decide when to enter into a scaling mode and to revert to the original dynamics, we introduce a heuristic to measure the effect of dynamics scaling. The heuristic relies on the following operation: $\square(\mathcal{S})$ denotes the *interval hull* of a set $\mathcal{S} \subset \mathbb{R}^n$, defined as $[\underline{|x_1|}; \overline{|x_1|}] \times \ldots \times [\underline{|x_n|}; \overline{|x_n|}]$. For a reachable set Ω, we approximate the volume of $\mathcal{S}$ by the volume of its interval hull: $\sigma(\Omega) \sim \sigma(\square(\Omega)) = \prod_{i=1}^{n}(\overline{|x_i|} - \underline{|x_i|})$. When $\lceil p \cdot T \rceil$ time segments passes, we enable dynamics scaling and check whether the volume of the Ω would decrease. The system then alters to the scaling mode if the check succeeds, otherwise, it remains in the original mode for the next $\lceil p \cdot T \rceil$ segments. Similarly, when dynamics scaling does not help to decrease the volume of the reachable set, the system exits the scaling mode and reverts to the normal, i.e. unscaled, dynamics.

5   Evaluation

We implemented our techniques in a prototypical tool in Python. We employ NumPy [39] to perform matrix operations. Linearization errors are computed using Kodiak library [38], which provides rigorous bounds for nonlinear global optimization problems using interval arithmetic and Bernstein enclosure. All the experiments were run on a laptop running Ubuntu 16.04 equipped with Intel i7-7600U CPU (2.80 GHz, 4 cores) and 16 GB RAM.

5.1   Benchmark Evaluation

We evaluate our tool on a number of nonlinear benchmark instances featuring from 2 to 30 dimensions with the aim to assess efficiency and precision of our approach. We compare our tool with the recent version of Flow* that participated in the ARCH competition [2].

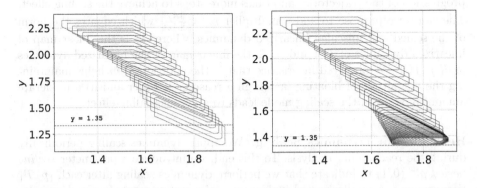

Fig. 1. Effect of dynamics scaling. For the illustration purpose, we apply dynamics scaling towards a hyperplane at $y = 1.35$. In the normal mode (left), the flowpipe passes the hyperplane while the reachable set stretches over y axis. In the dynamics scaling mode (right), the flowpipe contracts to the hyperplane (red). As a result, the size of the abstraction domain reduces. (Color figure online)

Experimental Setting. Our goal is to verify safety properties of considered benchmark instances. For each benchmark, we first considered a weak safety condition, for which the system can be proven safe easily upon finishing the reachability analysis over the time horizon. In case the condition is too weak to show the difference in precision, we either strengthened the safety condition or increased the time horizon until one or both tools failed to verify the safety. We tuned the parameters of both tools and reported the configurations with the minimal runtime on success, otherwise, the best possible configuration with which the flowpipe still contract. The timeout is set to 900 s.

Benchmarks. We use the following benchmarks in our evaluation:

Brusselator. The Brusselator is a theoretical model for a class of autocatalytic reaction [36]. The dynamics are given by $\dot{x} = 1 + x^2 \cdot y - 0.5x$, $\dot{y} = 1.5x - x^2 y$. We use the same initial set as [15], i.e. $(x, y) \in [0.8, 1] \times [0, 0.2]$.

Lotka-Volterra. The Lotka-Volterra describes the dynamics of population changes of two species that interact in a predator-prey relation. The dynamics are given by $\dot{x} = x(1.5 - y)$, and $\dot{y} = -y(3 - x)$. We use the same initial set as [15], i.e. $(x, y) \in [4.8, 5.2] \times [1.8, 2.2]$.

Biological Models. Biology I, Biology II are benchmarks presented in [15] modeling biological systems from [28]. The dynamics of Biology I (7 dimensions) are given by $\dot{x}_0 = -0.4x_0 + 5x_2x_3$, $\dot{x}_1 = 0.4x_0 - x_1$, $\dot{x}_2 = x_1 - 5x_2x_3$, $\dot{x}_3 = 5x_4x_5 - 5x_2x_3$, $\dot{x}_4 = -5x_4x_5 + 5x_2x_3$, $\dot{x}_5 = 0.5x_6 - 5x_4x_5$, $\dot{x}_6 = -0.5x_6 + 5x_4x_5$. We consider the initial set[1] $x_i \in [0.99, 1.01]$. The dynamics of Biology II (9 dimensions) are given by $\dot{x}_0 = 3x_2 - x_0x_5$, $\dot{x}_1 = x_3 - x_1x_5$, $\dot{x}_2 = x_0x_5 - 3x_2$, $\dot{x}_3 = x_1x_5 - x_3$, $\dot{x}_4 = 3x_2 + 5x_0 - x_4$, $\dot{x}_5 = 5x_4 + 3x_2 + x_3 - x_5(x_0 + x_1 + 2x_7 + 1)$, $\dot{x}_6 = 5x_3 + x_1 - 0.5x_6$, $\dot{x}_7 = 5x_6 - 2x_5x_7 + x_8 - 0.2x_7$, $\dot{x}_8 = 2x_5x7 - x_8$. We consider the same initial set as [15], i.e. $x_i \in [0.99, 1.01]$.

(Coupled) Van der Pol Oscillator. The model of a two-dimensional Van der Pol oscillator arises in the study of circuits containing vacuum tubes and is known to exhibit a limit cycle. The dynamics are given by $\dot{x} = y$, $\dot{y} = (1 - x^2) \cdot y - x$. We scaled up the benchmark up by coupling more oscillators in the way similar to the two-coupled Van der Pol oscillators (4 dimensions) [37]. The dynamics of N-coupled Van der Pol Oscillators ($N \geq 2$) are given as $\dot{x}_i = y_i$, $\dot{y}_0 = (1 - x_0^2)y_0 - x_0 + (x_1 - x_0)$, $\dot{y}_i = (1 - x_i^2)y_i - x_i + (x_{i-1} - x_i) + (x_{i+1} - x_i)$ ($1 < i < N - 1$), $\dot{y}_{N-1} = (1 - x_{N-1}^2)y_{N-1} - x_{N-1} + (x_{N-2} - x_{N-1})$. We use the same initial set as [15] and extends it to the high-dimensional instances, i.e. $x_i, y_i \in [1.25, 1.55] \times [2.25, 2.35]$.

(Coupled) Oscillator. We considered the model used in [16] to measure the scalability of the reachability analysis approaches. The model was adapted from [33] that describes the dynamics of synchronization among genetic oscillators. The model consists of N oscillators, each of which is described by five continuous variables. The dynamics are given by $\dot{x}_i = 0.1u_i - 3x_i + \frac{10}{N}\sum_{j=0}^{N-1} v_j$, $\dot{y}_i = 10x_i - 2.2y_i$, $\dot{z}_i = 10y_i - 1.5z_i$, $\dot{v}_i = 2x_i - 20v_i$, $\dot{u}_i = -5u_i^2z_i^4(10y_i - 1.5z_i)$. We use the same initial set as [16], i.e. $x_i \in [-0.003 + 0.002i, -0.001 + 0.002i]$, $y_i \in [0.197 + 0.002i, 0.199 + 0.002i]$, $z_i \in [0.997 + 0.002i, 0.999 + 0.002i]$, $v_i \in [-0.003 + 0.002i, -0.001 + 0.002i]$, $u_i \in [0.497 + 0.002i, 0.499 + 0.002i]$.

Tuning of the Tools. We tuned parameters of both tools to minimize the runtime. For our tool, we fixed the dynamics scaling period as 0.1 for all benchmarks except for (coupled) oscillators. We disabled dynamics scaling on (coupled) oscillators due to two observations: i) without dynamics scaling, the precision is sufficient to verify the safety; ii) the benefit of applying dynamics scaling did not always payoff the loss in the runtime on this particular benchmark. For each benchmark, we searched for a minimal time step until i) it is sufficiently small to verify the safety, then we increased it until the safety is violated and reported the largest safe time step; ii) it is so small that the tool timed out, we then

---

[1] https://ths.rwth-aachen.de/research/projects/hypro/biological-model-i/.

reported TO. We used `hypy` [9] to script a grid-search strategy to identify the optimal tuning parameters for `Flow*` . `Hypy` is a Python library that is able to automatically run `Flow*` with a given configuration and parse the result. We first specified a minimal time step, an increment for time step and a subset of Taylor model orders such that `Flow*` could complete the analysis. Our script then exhaustively tried various combinations of Taylor model orders and time step. The time step was increased until safety is violated. We reported the setting that proved the safety with a minimal runtime if one existed. The cut-off threshold in `Flow*` was fixed as 10^{-9} in all the experiments.

Table 1. Comparison results on benchmarks. Dim.: Dimension of benchmarks; Horizon: time horizon. Safe: safety property; TM: Taylor model order; δ: time step; t: runtime, TO: The tool/approach timed out after 900 s.

Benchmarks	Dim.	Horizon	Safe	Flow*			Ours	
				TM	δ	t	δ	t
Brusselator	2	10	$y \leq 2$	6	0.04	6.49	0.02	**5.35**
Brusselator	2	25	$y \leq 2$	9	0.001	TO	0.01	**22.46**
Lotka-Volterra	2	3	$y \leq 6$	5	0.01	**2.34**	0.01	5.14
Lotka-Volterra	2	3	$y \leq 5.6$	5	0.01	**2.32**	0.0001	TO
Biology I	7	2	$x_3 \geq 0.9$	4	0.02	28.26	0.005	**9.30**
Biology I	7	2	$x_3 \geq 0.92$	4	0.01	49.99	0.002	**16.38**
Biology II	9	2	$x_6 \geq 10$	7	0.02	TO	0.001	**236.79**
Vanderpol	2	7	$y \leq 3$	5	0.02	**2.42**	0.04	2.83
Vanderpol	2	7	$y \leq 2.7$	12	0.001	TO	0.02	**4.17**
2-coupled Vanderpol	4	7	$y_0 \leq 3$	6	0.02	100.41	0.02	**5.25**
2-coupled Vanderpol	4	7	$y_0 \leq 2.75$	7	0.015	227.76	0.01	**11.48**
3-coupled Vanderpol	6	7	$y_0 \leq 3$	5	0.01	TO	0.005	**72.31**
4-coupled Vanderpol	8	7	$y_0 \leq 3$	5	0.025	TO	0.005	**158.51**
Oscillator	5	3	$y_1 \geq 0.08$	4	0.02	**4.17**	0.005	5.99
Oscillator	5	3	$y_1 \geq 0.085$	4	0.02	**3.98**	0.0015	31.86
2-coupled oscillator	10	3	$y_1 \geq 0.08$	4	0.02	32.26	0.005	**12.30**
2-coupled oscillator	10	3	$y_1 \geq 0.085$	4	0.02	**31.63**	0.0015	63.97
3-coupled oscillator	15	3	$y_1 \geq 0.08$	4	0.02	140.39	0.005	**22.04**
3-coupled oscillator	15	3	$y_1 \geq 0.085$	4	0.02	**136.99**	0.0015	146.91
4-coupled oscillator	20	3	$y_1 \geq 0.08$	4	0.015	291.88	0.005	**32.46**
4-coupled oscillator	20	3	$y_1 \geq 0.085$	4	0.005	TO	0.0015	**284.61**
5-coupled oscillator	25	3	$y_1 \geq 0.08$	4	0.01	603.98	0.005	**50.03**
5-coupled oscillator	25	3	$y_1 \geq 0.085$	4	0.005	TO	0.0015	**398.5**
6-coupled oscillator	30	3	$y_1 \geq 0.08$	4	0.025	TO	0.005	**73.98**

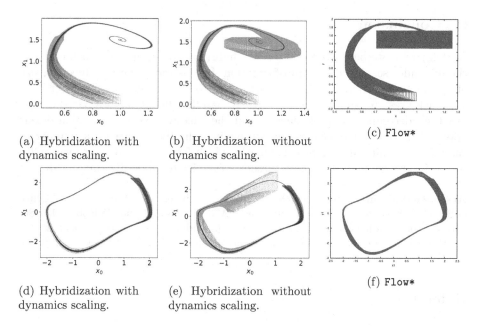

(a) Hybridization with dynamics scaling.

(b) Hybridization without dynamics scaling.

(c) Flow*

(d) Hybridization with dynamics scaling.

(e) Hybridization without dynamics scaling.

(f) Flow*

Fig. 2. Flowpipes using different approaches/tools on brusselator (above) and 2-coupled Van der Pol oscillators (below) benchmarks. (Color figure online)

Results. We show results in Table 1, which leads to the following observations: i) On Brusselator, Biology I, II, (coupled) Van der Pol oscillators benchmarks, our approach was superior in both runtime and precision. In particular, on (coupled) Van der Pol oscillators benchmark, our approach was 10–20 times faster than Flow* (2-coupled Vanderpol) and on high dimensional cases (3-coupled Vanderpol, 4-coupled Vanderpol), Flow* cannot finish within the time limit. Further investigations showed that these benchmarks are also the ones where the effect of dynamics scaling was significantly beneficial. The projections of the flowpipe (red) and the numerical simulations (dark blue) of Brusselators (horizon = 25 s) and 2-coupled Van der Pol oscillators are shown in Fig. 2. We showed the best result Flow* produced without exceeding the time limit. ii) On (coupled) oscillators, our tool usually proved the weak safety property faster and scaled better than Flow*. By using smaller time steps, our approach can prove the strengthened safety properties using a runtime that is comparable (within 1 order) to Flow* on instances with 2 or 3 oscillators. Flow* again failed on high dimensional cases while our approach succeeded in a reasonable amount of time; iii) Flow* showed better precision and speed on Lotka-Volterra model while our approach failed to prove the strengthened property. A possible explanation is that the imprecision due to nonlinearity introduced by applying the dynamics scaling outweighs the benefits of the flattening. This raises the question of how to best use dynamics scaling to improve the precision of flowpipe computation, which we will investigate in the future.

6   Conclusion

In this paper, we have proposed a novel hybridization approach which employs the dynamics scaling model transformation. In this way, we can reduce the size of abstraction domains, which in turn leads to better analysis precision. Our approach uses an enhanced error model to handle affine dynamics based on the input set decomposition. We have shown the effectiveness and precision of our approach by a comparative evaluation against the tool `Flow*` on a number of challenging nonlinear system benchmarks which feature 2 to 30 state variables. In the future, we plan to explore further strategies to guide dynamics scaling.

Acknowledgments. This research was supported in part by the Air Force Office of Scientific Research under award numbers FA2386-17-1-4065 and FA9550-19-1-0288. Any opinions, findings, and conclusions or recommendations expressed in this material are those of the authors and do not necessarily reflect the views of the United States Air Force.

References

1. Althoff, M.: Reachability analysis of nonlinear systems using conservative polynomialization and non-convex sets. In: Proceedings of the 16th International Conference on Hybrid Systems: Computation and Control, pp. 173–182. ACM (2013)
2. Althoff, M., et al.: Arch-comp18 category report: continuous and hybrid systems with linear continuous dynamics. In: Proceedings of the 5th International Workshop on Applied Verification for Continuous and Hybrid Systems, pp. 23–52 (2018)
3. Althoff, M., Le Guernic, C., Krogh, B.H.: Reachable set computation for uncertain time-varying linear systems. In: Proceedings of the 14th International Conference on Hybrid Systems: Computation and Control, pp. 93–102. ACM (2011)
4. Althoff, M., Stursberg, O., Buss, M.: Reachability analysis of nonlinear systems with uncertain parameters using conservative linearization. In: Proceedings of the 47th IEEE Conference on Decision and Control (2008)
5. Asarin, E., Dang, T., Girard, A.: Reachability analysis of nonlinear systems using conservative approximation. In: Maler, O., Pnueli, A. (eds.) HSCC 2003. LNCS, vol. 2623, pp. 20–35. Springer, Heidelberg (2003). https://doi.org/10.1007/3-540-36580-X_5
6. Asarin, E., Dang, T., Girard, A.: Hybridization methods for the analysis of nonlinear systems. Acta Informatica **43**(7), 451–476 (2007)
7. Azuma, S., Imura, J., Sugie, T.: Lebesgue piecewise affine approximation of nonlinear systems. Nonlinear Anal. Hybrid Syst. **4**(1), 92–102 (2010)
8. Bak, S., Bogomolov, S., Althoff, M.: Time-triggered conversion of guards for reachability analysis of hybrid automata. In: Abate, A., Geeraerts, G. (eds.) FORMATS 2017. LNCS, vol. 10419, pp. 133–150. Springer, Cham (2017). https://doi.org/10.1007/978-3-319-65765-3_8
9. Bak, S., Bogomolov, S., Schilling, C.: High-level hybrid systems analysis with Hypy. In: ARCH@ CPSWeek, pp. 80–90 (2016)
10. Bak, S., Duggirala, P.S.: Hylaa: a tool for computing simulation-equivalent reachability for linear systems. In: Proceedings of the 20th International Conference on Hybrid Systems: Computation and Control, pp. 173–178. ACM (2017)

11. Bak, S., Tran, H.D., Johnson, T.T.: Numerical verification of affine systems with up to a billion dimensions (2018). arXiv preprint arXiv:1804.01583

12. Bogomolov, S., Forets, M., Frehse, G., Podelski, A., Schilling, C., Viry, F.: Reach set approximation through decomposition with low-dimensional sets and high-dimensional matrices. In: 21th International Conference on Hybrid Systems: Computation and Control, HSCC 2018, pp. 41–50. ACM (2018)

13. Bogomolov, S., Forets, M., Frehse, G., Potomkin, K., Schilling, C.: JuliaReach: a toolbox for set-based reachability. In: 22nd ACM International Conference on Hybrid Systems: Computation and Control, HSCC 2019, pp. 39–44. ACM (2019)

14. Borwein, J., Lewis, A.S.: Convex Analysis and Nonlinear Optimization Theory and Examples. Springer, New York (2010). https://doi.org/10.1007/978-0-387-31256-9

15. Chen, X., Ábrahám, E., Sankaranarayanan, S.: Flow*: an analyzer for non-linear hybrid systems. In: Sharygina, N., Veith, H. (eds.) CAV 2013. LNCS, vol. 8044, pp. 258–263. Springer, Heidelberg (2013). https://doi.org/10.1007/978-3-642-39799-8_18

16. Chen, X., Sankaranarayanan, S.: Decomposed reachability analysis for nonlinear systems. In: 2016 IEEE Real-Time Systems Symposium (RTSS), pp. 13–24. IEEE (2016)

17. Dang, T., Le Guernic, C., Maler, O.: Computing reachable states for nonlinear biological models. In: Degano, P., Gorrieri, R. (eds.) CMSB 2009. LNCS, vol. 5688, pp. 126–141. Springer, Heidelberg (2009). https://doi.org/10.1007/978-3-642-03845-7_9

18. Dang, T., Maler, O., Testylier, R.: Accurate hybridization of nonlinear systems. In: Proceedings of the 13th ACM International Conference on Hybrid Systems: Computation and Control, pp. 11–20. ACM (2010)

19. Donzé, A.: Breach, a toolbox for verification and parameter synthesis of hybrid systems. In: Touili, T., Cook, B., Jackson, P. (eds.) CAV 2010. LNCS, vol. 6174, pp. 167–170. Springer, Heidelberg (2010). https://doi.org/10.1007/978-3-642-14295-6_17

20. Duggirala, P.S., Mitra, S., Viswanathan, M., Potok, M.: C2E2: a verification tool for stateflow models. In: Baier, C., Tinelli, C. (eds.) TACAS 2015. LNCS, vol. 9035, pp. 68–82. Springer, Heidelberg (2015). https://doi.org/10.1007/978-3-662-46681-0_5

21. Franzle, M., Herde, C., Teige, T., Ratschan, S., Schubert, T.: Efficient solving of large non-linear arithmetic constraint systems with complex boolean structure. J. Satisfiability Boolean Model. Comput. 1, 209–236 (2007)

22. Frehse, G., et al.: SpaceEx: scalable verification of hybrid systems. In: Gopalakrishnan, G., Qadeer, S. (eds.) CAV 2011. LNCS, vol. 6806, pp. 379–395. Springer, Heidelberg (2011). https://doi.org/10.1007/978-3-642-22110-1_30

23. Girard, A.: Reachability of uncertain linear systems using zonotopes. In: Morari, M., Thiele, L. (eds.) HSCC 2005. LNCS, vol. 3414, pp. 291–305. Springer, Heidelberg (2005). https://doi.org/10.1007/978-3-540-31954-2_19

24. Gurung, A., Deka, A.K., Bartocci, E., Bogomolov, S., Grosu, R., Ray, R.: Parallel reachability analysis for hybrid systems. In: 14th ACM-IEEE International Conference on Formal Methods and Models for System Design, MEMOCODE 2016, pp. 12–22. ACM-IEEE (2016)

25. Han, Z., Krogh, B.H.: Reachability analysis of nonlinear systems using trajectory piecewise linearized models. In: 2006 American Control Conference, p. 6. IEEE (2006)

26. Henzinger, T.A., Ho, P.H., Wong-Toi, H.: Algorithmic analysis of nonlinear hybrid systems. IEEE Trans. Autom. Control **43**(4), 540–554 (1998)

27. Johnson, T.T., Green, J., Mitra, S., Dudley, R., Erwin, R.S.: Satellite rendezvous and conjunction avoidance: case studies in verification of nonlinear hybrid systems. In: Giannakopoulou, D., Méry, D. (eds.) FM 2012. LNCS, vol. 7436, pp. 252–266. Springer, Heidelberg (2012). https://doi.org/10.1007/978-3-642-32759-9_22

28. Klipp, E., Herwig, R., Kowald, A., Wierling, C., Lehrach, H.: Systems Biology in Practice: Concepts, Implementation and Application. Wiley, Hoboken (2008)

29. Kong, S., Gao, S., Chen, W., Clarke, E.: dReach: δ-reachability analysis for hybrid systems. In: Baier, C., Tinelli, C. (eds.) TACAS 2015. LNCS, vol. 9035, pp. 200–205. Springer, Heidelberg (2015). https://doi.org/10.1007/978-3-662-46681-0_15

30. Le Guernic, C.: Reachability analysis of hybrid systems with linear continuous dynamics. Ph.D. thesis, Université Joseph-Fourier-Grenoble I (2009)

31. Le Guernic, C., Girard, A.: Reachability analysis of hybrid systems using support functions. In: Bouajjani, A., Maler, O. (eds.) CAV 2009. LNCS, vol. 5643, pp. 540–554. Springer, Heidelberg (2009). https://doi.org/10.1007/978-3-642-02658-4_40

32. Le Guernic, C., Girard, A.: Reachability analysis of linear systems using support functions. Nonlinear Anal. Hybrid Syst. **4**(2), 250–262 (2010)

33. Li, C., Chen, L., Aihara, K.: Synchronization of coupled nonidentical genetic oscillators. Phys. Biol. **3**(1), 37 (2006)

34. Li, D., Bak, S., Bogomolov, S.: Reachability analysis of nonlinear systems using hybridization and dynamics scaling: Proofs. Technical report CS-TR-1534, Newcastle University (2020)

35. Matthias, A., Ahmed, E.G., Bastian, S., Goran, F.: Report on reachability analysis of nonlinear systems and compositional verification. https://cps-vo.org/node/24199

36. Prigogine, I., Balescu, R.: Phénomènes cycliques dans la thermodynamique des processus irréversibles. Bull. Cl. Sci. Acad. R. Belg **42**, 256–265 (1956)

37. Rand, R., Holmes, P.: Bifurcation of periodic motions in two weakly coupled van der pol oscillators. Int. J. Non-Linear Mech. **15**(4–5), 387–399 (1980)

38. Smith, A.P., Muñoz, C.A., Narkawicz, A.J., Markevicius, M.: Kodiak: an implementation framework for branch and bound algorithms (2015)

39. van der Walt, S., Colbert, S.C., Varoquaux, G.: The NumPY array: a structure for efficient numerical computation. Comput. Sci. Eng. **13**(2), 22–30 (2011)

Weakness Monitors for Fail-Aware Systems

Wolfgang Granig[2] , Stefan Jakšić[1] , Horst Lewitschnig[2] ,
Cristinel Mateis[1] , and Dejan Ničković[1(✉)]

[1] AIT Austrian Institute of Technology, Vienna, Austria
dejan.nickovic@ait.ac.at
[2] Infineon Technologies Austria AG, Villach, Austria

Abstract. Fail-awareness is the ability of a system to detect an upcoming failure before it actually happens. In this paper, we propose a *weakness monitoring* approach for observing a complex system during its operation, identifying possible degradation of its behavior, and finally raising an alarm in case of an estimated upcoming failure before the system actually goes out of its specification. Our procedure uses online linear regression to monitor trends over time – it is used to optimize the system service. We evaluate our approach on three case studies from the automotive and avionics domains.

1 Introduction

Cyber-physical systems (CPS) combine heterogeneous physical, mechanical and computational elements that continuously interact with their environment via sensors and actuators. CPS applications are often *safety-critical* where malfunctions can result in catastrophes involving important material damage or even loss of human lives. A failure of a single component can propagate and cause the entire system to fail. As a result, system *reliability* is an important goal in the development of safety-critical CPS, where components are typically designed to achieve very long operation lifetime.

In spite of tremendous advances in reliable design, components do sometimes fail. Many safety-critical systems are used in rough environments that can result in slow but continuous degradation of components. In addition, every component has a certain (possibly low, but strictly positive) probability of having a small defect that can deteriorate over time. Reliable operation of safety-critical CPS is typically ensured with redundancy of software and hardware components. The redundancy-based approach achieves high reliability, though at high costs, also when sudden failures occur.

Fail-aware concept is a complementary approach for further improving safety and reliability of CPS in presence of components that can degrade over time. The fail-aware concept can minimize costs through a well-tuned on-demand (instead of regularly scheduled) maintenance process. More specifically, the fail-aware

© Springer Nature Switzerland AG 2020
N. Bertrand and N. Jansen (Eds.): FORMATS 2020, LNCS 12288, pp. 283–299, 2020.
https://doi.org/10.1007/978-3-030-57628-8_17

concept allows one to detect an upcoming failure of a component or a sub-system before it actually happens. The main ingredient in the fail-aware concept is a *weakness monitor*, a program that continuously observes different system parameters over time, detects gradual deviations from the expected behavior and identifies negative trends that can result in an imminent failure (see Fig. 1). That is, the fail-aware concept can (1) avoid expensive hardware and software redundancy mechanisms when sudden failures are not critical or unlikely to occur, and (2) replace periodic service with preventive maintenance triggered by detected weaknesses.

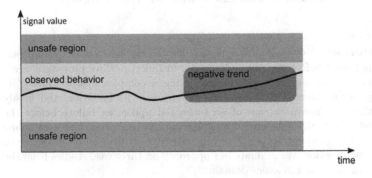

Fig. 1. Monitoring trends over time.

We propose in this paper a weakness monitoring solution that uses *online linear regression* to estimate the health status of the system and analyze trends over time. The proposed approach assumes that the weakness model is linear. We show that this is a reasonable assumption for many systems of interest. This simple, yet powerful approach can be effectively instantiated along several axes: (1) at a component, sub-system or system level, (2) during design and operation, and (3) in presence or absence of formal specification describing the intended behavior. We demonstrate the versatility of our approach on three case studies from the automotive and avionics domains: (1) a rotor position sensor, (2) the motor of a powertrain sub-system and (3) an aircraft elevator control model.

2 Related Work

In classical sense, fail-awareness is a systematic method which aims to allow asynchronous distributed system to notify the affected clients in case of perfor-mance failures [10]. However, in our work we focus on enabling an independent system to predict an upcoming failure before it happens. Such related work can be roughly classified in several groups: physics-based model, data-driven prog-nostics and hybrid approaches [12]. System health monitors can be constructed based on a physical model of the device using the physics-of-failure (PoF) app-roach [14,16,17]. The reasoning behind this method is that the initial cause for the failures originates from physical characteristics of component materials [8]. By knowing physics-of-failure and by identifying a failure precursor event [5] it is possible to estimate device remaining lifetime. In our work, we do not explicitly model physics of a system but rather use declarative specifications or learn the model from observations.

Periodic loading of material with stress such as voltage or current amplitude cycles weakens the device. Efficient counting of these load cycles is achieved with rainflow algorithm [26]. Thermal cycle counting for evaluating remaining lifetime of power converter systems was reported in [19]. Since our stress tests apply permanent load, we are interested in identifying value trends over a longer time interval rather than counting occurrences of value cycling.

In the spectrum of data-driven approaches, Kalman filters (KF) are used to estimate the state of a system and predict the future state [4,7,24,25]. The KF algorithm is based on a recursive relation for an optimal state estimate which runs in real-time. On the other hand, KF estimates only a single state of a system, and it is still necessary to use the system model to provide predictions [7]. Predicting Remaining Useful Life (RUL), a complementary topic to trend monitoring, was demonstrated using particle filtering and kernel smoothing in [18]. Celaya et al. have used Gaussian Process Regression (GPR) [4,5] to predict future fault degradation based on measurement data. Kalajdzic et al. propose another approach of using particle filtering to estimate the system's state from its partial observations [20]. However GPR and particle filtering are less favorable in our real-time monitoring setting due to high computational cost.

Model predictive control (MPC) [11] implements an iterative, finite-horizon optimization of a plant model and its input in order to satisfy a given constraint. The models used in MPC are typically used to represent the behavior of complex dynamical systems and predict their behavior over a typically short time horizon. Specifications can be used to encode the MPC constraints [15,23,29]. In our approach, we compare the observed behavior of the systems against the specification or the learned model to detect trends over long periods of time.

One of the latest approaches by Bortolussi et al. demonstrates runtime predictive monitoring for Hybrid Automata, based on deep neural networks [3]. By measuring prediction uncertainty and augmenting the training set with uncertain predictions, this method is able to significantly reduce prediction errors. Another recently developed framework, based on Hidden Markov Models, provides probabilities that the certain behavior prefix will satisfy the requirement [2]. Monitors which evaluate the probability of keeping a system in a safe state regardless of the influence from the environment, so-called *viability monitors*, are defined in [30] and evaluated on an Unmanned Aerial Vehicle (UAV) case study.

3   Weakness Monitoring

In this section, we present our approach for monitoring weaknesses in fail-aware systems. We first introduce definitions that we use to develop our procedure. A *signal* $w : \mathbb{T} \to \mathbb{R}$ is a mapping from time instants t in some time domain $\mathbb{T}$ to values $w(t)$ in $\mathbb{R}$. We call the signals with time domain $\mathbb{T} = \mathbb{R}_+$ *analog* and signals with time domain $\mathbb{T} = \mathbb{N}$ *digital*. We abuse the notation and allow a(n analog or digital) signal w to take negative time indices as argument, with $w(t) = 0$ for all $t < 0$. Given a *sampling period* Δ, the digital signal w_Δ is obtained from the analog signal w, by *periodically sampling* it such that $w_\Delta(i) = w(i\Delta)$. In this paper, we consider digital signals that are obtained by sensing and observing physical quantities at periodic rates.[1]

The procedure wmon, shown in Algorithm 1 takes as input: (1) the input signal w, (2) the safety margin λ that would be considered sufficiently close to a failure, (3) the size of the sliding window T, and (4) the sampling period Δ of w. The method wmon monitors trends in w over (long) time periods defined by the size of the sliding window T. The procedure continuously observes the digital signal w_Δ, obtained by sampling the analog signal w with period Δ. The algorithm waits for the new sample i of w_Δ to become available (line 3), computes the linear regression linreg over the window $[i - T, i]$ of w_Δ, estimating the slope a and the offset b of that signal segment. It then checks whether the weakness condition cond over the estimated signal parameters and safety margin is met (line 6), and if it is the case, an alert is raised (line 7).

Algorithm 1: Weakness monitor wmon

Input : w - input signal, λ - safety margin, T - sliding window size, Δ - sampling period

1 $i \leftarrow 0$
2 **while** *true* **do**
3 | wait $w_\Delta(i)$
4 | $u \leftarrow w_\Delta[i - T, i]$
5 | $(a, b) \leftarrow \mathsf{linreg}(u)$
6 | **if** *cond*$(a, b, \lambda, i\Delta)$ **then**
7 | | raise alert
8 | **end**
9 | $i \leftarrow i + 1$
10 **end**

The functionality of this simple monitoring procedure depends to a large extent on the exact definition of cond.

We can see that for each new sample i of w_Δ, we need to compute the linear regression over the $[i - T, i]$ segment of the signal, an operation that has *linear* time complexity in the size of the window. This computational cost is not acceptable in a real-time implementation of a weakness monitor, especially in the case of large T/Δ. To address this issue, we propose an efficient implementation of wmon that has a time complexity that is *constant* in the size of the window.

---

[1] Perfectly periodic sampling is not required for our approach, but we use it to simplify the presentation of the procedure.

The efficient variant of wmon uses Welford's *online* linear regression algorithm [28] to reduce the time complexity of the procedure. The main idea is based on the following observation – the linear regression over the segment $[i - T + 1, i + 1]$ of w_Δ can reuse the computations done for the linear regression over $[i - T, i]$.

We now shortly describe the online regression procedure. Let $\mathbf{x} = x_1, x_2, \ldots$ be an infinite sequence of real values and $\mathbf{x}_{k,T} = x_k, \ldots, x_{k+T}$ its restriction to the values indexed in the range $[k, k + T]$. In linear regression, the model inferred from a sequence of observations $y_{k,T}$ is of the form $y_i = ax_i + b + \epsilon_i$, where $i \in [k, k + T]$ and ϵ_i is the discrepancy between the estimated and the observed value. The process of calculating linear regression parameters consists in finding the values of the parameters a and b that minimize the discrepancy over all ϵ_i. We denote by $a_{k,T}$ and $b_{k,T}$ the estimates of the slope and offset over $y_{k,T}$, respectively. We recall that the slope $a_{k,T}$ can be expressed in terms of *variance* and *covariance*:

$$a_{k,T} = \frac{Cov(x,y)_{k,T}}{Var(x)_{k,T}} = \frac{\sum_{i=k}^{k+T}(x_i - \overline{x}_{k,T})(y_i - \overline{y}_{k,T})}{\sum_{i=k}^{k+T}(x_i - \overline{x}_{k,T})^2}$$

where $\overline{x}_{k,T} = \frac{1}{T+1}\Sigma_{i=k}^{k+T}x_i$ is the *mean* of $\mathbf{x}_{k,T}$.

Mean, variance and covariance all admit an incremental form, also enabling incremental computation of the slope and the offset:

$$\overline{x}_{k+1,T} = \overline{x}_{k,T} + \frac{x_{k+1+T} - x_k}{T+1}$$
$$Var(x)_{k+1,T} = Var(x)_{k,T} - \frac{(x_{k+T+1} - x_k)^2}{(T+1)^2} + \frac{(x_{k+T+1} - \overline{x}_{k,T})^2 - (x_k - \overline{x}_{k,T})^2}{T+1}$$
$$Cov(x,y)_{k+1,T} = Cov(x,y)_{k,T} - \frac{(x_{k+T+1} - x_k)(y_{k+T+1} - y_k)}{(T+1)^2} +$$
$$\frac{(x_{k+T+1} - \overline{x}_{k,T})(y_{k+T+1} - \overline{y}_{k,T}) - (x_k - \overline{x}_{k,T})(y_k - \overline{y}_{k,T})}{T+1}$$
$$a_{k+1,T} = \frac{Cov(x,y)_{k+1,T}}{Var(x)_{k+1,T}}$$
$$b_{k+1,T} = y_{k+1} - a_{k+1,T}x_{k+1}$$

Example 1. We illustrate our approach with two examples shown in Fig. 2. Each example depicts a behavior that deteriorates over time and ultimately leads to a property violation. In Fig. 2 (a), the linear regression model is used to detect a negative trend directly on the signal. This may not always be sufficient to identify a weakness. The behavior in Fig. 2 (b) has a constant slope close to zero and increasing oscillations. To detect this negative trend, we can use Algorithm 1 to monitor the evolution of the Mean Absolute Error (MAE) over time and detect the deterioration of the signal.

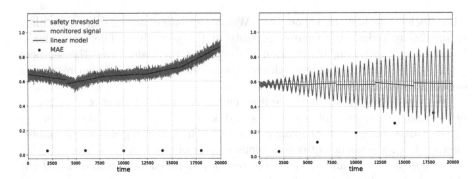

Fig. 2. Two types of weak behaviors, their linear models and normalized MAE.

4   Instantiation and Application of Weakness Monitors

In this section we instantiate and demonstrate our weakness monitoring on three use-cases from automotive and avionics industries. We first consider monitoring weaknesses of a motor angle sensor component. This use case allows us to instantiate our monitors in a setting with clearly defined safety margins. Second, we analyse a motor control circuit with measurements from a test bench and without any specification of its intended behavior. We use this second use case to show how to instantiate our approach in a pure data-driven setting. Finally, we demonstrate the monitoring approach on an aircraft elevator control system for which the functional requirements are formalized in a rich temporal specification language.

4.1   Magnetic Angle Sensor

In this section, we apply our approach to the signal traces obtained from a *simulation model* of Infineon® Giant Magneto Resistance (GMR) angle sensor which is typically used in automotive applications [13]. This sensor can be used to measure the rotor position for electric motor commutation or to sense the steering angle. The angle value is encoded using two orthogonal components $V_x = A_x \cdot sin(\varphi + \varphi_x) + O_x$ and $V_y = A_y \cdot cos(\varphi + \varphi_y) + O_y$, and is obtained using the following relation: $\varphi = \arctan(V_y/V_x)$ [1].

Due to the long expected operating lifetime of these sensors, they must be tested for reliability. Testing teams subject physical devices to different kinds of stress, according to the common electrical component qualification requirements defined in the AEC-Q100 specification [6]. By exposing a set of devices to extreme conditions stress tests accelerate the aging process and allow the manufacturers to efficiently estimate device's potential degradation.

GMR angle sensors are extremely reliable and fully compliant to requirements specified in AEC-Q100 document [6]. In order to evaluate our weakness monitoring approach, we used an artificial degradation model to generate traces, which in normal operation would never be observed. Hence, all the traces in this

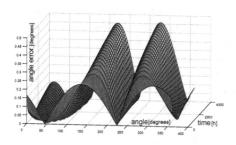
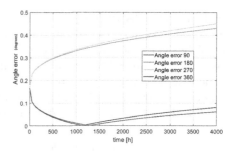

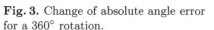

Fig. 3. Change of absolute angle error for a 360° rotation.

Fig. 4. Absolute angle error.

section were obtained solely by simulating the degradation model, and do not reflect the real measurement data.

In Fig. 3 we can observe the data collected from the degradation model in order to understand how the angle error evolves over time. The experiment consists in evaluating sensor angle error, based on a full 360° rotation. We can observe that the angle error is not equally distributed across the angles and the model deviates more for certain angle values. In Fig. 4 we observe the behavior of the absolute angle error for specific angle inputs: 90°, 180°, 270° and 360°. In our simulations, we will use similar sensitive angle value intervals to maximize the angle error produced by the model.

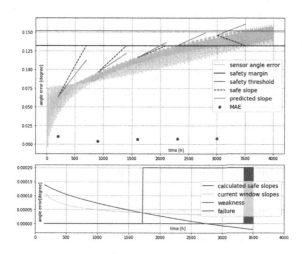

Fig. 5. Weakness monitoring of a degradation model.

We use the weakness monitoring procedure wmon as follows to detect weaknesses in the sensor degradation model. The inputs to the monitoring procedure are: the input signal w that represents the absolute difference between the input angle and the observed angle, the safety margin λ obtained as a percentage of the specification[2] $\tau = 0.15$ (in this case $\lambda = 0.85\tau$), the sliding window size $T = 500h$ (corresponding roughly to 3 weeks of observation time), the sampling period $\Delta = 6$ min and the condition cond. The condition cond is defined as follows – the weakness alert is triggered at time t if the linear regression model over the window $[t - 500h, t]$ of observed values predicts that within the next $[t, t + 500h]$ window the safety margin λ will be reached. Formally, we have

$$\mathsf{cond}(a, b, \lambda, t) = \frac{\lambda - b}{a} \le t + 500h.$$

We run our tests to cover the time interval of a lab stress test as specified in the AEC-Q100 document [6]. The monitor starts by filling the data window with data samples and then continues to calculate the linear model in an incremental fashion, using the recurrence relations from Sect. 3. The monitor continuously checks whether the condition cond evaluates to true. A weakness alert would allow the user to get a warning when the device shows serious signs of degradation but (an estimated three weeks' time) before it actually fails, thus enabling taking an action and preventing the failure. The monitor can in addition calculate MAE in order to estimate the reliability of the verdict.

In Fig. 5 we see that between time units 1500 and 2000 the monitor reports a weakness. The safe slopes are plotted and compared to slopes that would reach the angle error predicted by the linear model. Although in the beginning the behavior shows a strong increasing trend, it is still far away from the safety threshold. The magnetic field strength was set to 100 mT and the input angle was periodically varied and linearly increased, starting from $[45°, 75°]$ to $[65°, 95°]$. In our simulation, the monitor provides a warning that in three weeks time the system is likely to fail, which does occur at around approximately $t = 3300$. The criteria for detecting a weakness is based on the safety margin λ which allows enough time to react before safety threshold is crossed.

We finally note that in this experiment, we analyzed the sensor simulation model. It allowed us to directly compare the input angle to the output measurement. In reality, the input angle is not accessible. However, there are typically two GMR sensors on the same chip. Hence, the weakness monitoring problem of the sensor chip would consist in continuously comparing the measured angles between the two chips, and their evolution over time.

4.2   Motor Weakness Monitoring

In this section we instantiate our approach to a purely data-driven setting to detect weaknesses from measurements of a motor control circuit performed on a test bench. We emphasize that although the weakness monitoring concept is demonstrated here on the special case of the motor data, the same monitor

---

[2] The specification of the sensor defines the safety threshold to be equal to 2.2° or 3° depending on the model of the sensor. We set this tolerance to a much lower limit for the purpose of evaluation.

concept can be generalized to other systems monitored through sensors of various types with high sampling rates.

In contrast to the magnetic angle sensor, the motor control circuit does not have explicit specifications with a safety threshold that could be used to assess the correctness of the observed measurement data. Instead, we follow a machine learning approach in which we first collect signal data that we know behaves as expected and we use semi-supervised learning to infer a predictive model of the nominal system behaviour and to trigger an alarm when the trend of the predictions continuously deviates in time from the observations. This approach is to large extent inspired by [27] and adapted to our weakness monitoring procedure presented in Algorithm 1. In the remainder of the section, we present the details of the approach.

Data Exploration and Preprocessing. The motor control circuit consists of 3 sub-systems (denoted by abc1, abc2 and abc3) with 3 phases each (suffixed with A, B and C). Measurements corresponding to the sin/cos values of an angle sensor (PHI_COS and PHI_SIN) as well as the computed rotor position (phi) and velocity (omega) are also collected. This results into a total of 15 time series which represent the properties of the system.

The analyzed data is obtained from an experiment where a constant motor rotation speed is maintained for 60 s and measurements are sampled at 10 kHz. Figure 6a depicts just one of the 15 time series in the time domain. To identify relevant signal components, we translate the signals to frequency domain with Discrete Fourier Transform (DFT) (Fig. 6b).

Although frequency domain analysis provides useful insights, (e.g. around the frequencies 2 kHz and 4 kHz), we still need the time component to be able to monitor the signals over time. Thus we conduct our analysis in the time/frequency domain by applying the Short-Time Fourier Transform (STFT). The initial time series consisting of 600,000 data points in the time domain will result into a sequence of 958 data points. In the frequency domain, the frequency step will be ranging from 0 Hz to 5 kHz in the positive values range, yielding 12,800 positive frequencies. We collapse the number of components of a signal in the frequency dimension by binning the frequencies into 100 Hz-wide bands, spanning the range from 0 to 4.5 kHz, and by averaging the spectral amplitude over each frequency band at each time step; all frequencies above 4.5 kHz are grouped into an additional (wider) band.

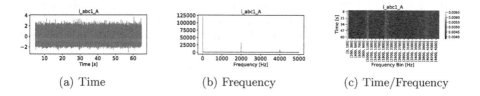

(a) Time   (b) Frequency   (c) Time/Frequency

Fig. 6. Illustration of the time series i_abc1_A in various domains

Each of the 15 original signals yields 46 time series, one for each frequency band which makes 690 time series in total. Each of these time series contains 958 data points on the time axis. These are the time series that represent inputs for our weakness monitors. Figure 6c illustrates exemplarily in form of a spectrogram the 46 time series obtained from the transformation of the time series i_abc1_A by following the STFT-based technique explained above.

Approach. For each time series (frequency band) we train an auto-regressive model on a time window using history samples. The length of the time window, i.e. the number of lags, is optimized e.g. with help of (partial) autocorrelation diagrams, by adopting the one which maximizes the model performance measured with the selected metric, e.g. coefficient of determination, on a test set. Once the model is trained, we compute the mean and standard deviation statistics of the absolute values of the residuals on the training data. In this example, we set the time window parameter equal to 10. We then learn the distribution of the residuals on the training data. We assume that prediction errors on the training data to be normally distributed (a fair assumption for non-biased models).

During the monitoring phase, the signal w that is the input to our weakness monitor wmon is not the measured signal itself, but a multidimensional signal that represents the residual error of the measured data compared to the nominal behavior per frequency band predicted by the auto-regressive models learned from the nominal history data. We expect that a healthy system will have its mean behavior similar to the predicted one with the same normal distribution of the residuals. The weakness monitor follows the evolution of the residual errors over time and detects if it has a trend of deviating from the mean and the residual distribution learned from the training data. This is achieved by setting cond to raise an alarm if the slope of the residuals grows above some threshold a_{max}.

Experimental Results with Anomaly Injection. Since the available motor data sets do not seem to contain anomalies, we inject an anomaly to evaluate the weakness monitoring approach. We define an anomaly as a sinusoidal function $y(t) = \rho + A\,sin(2\pi f t + \phi)$, where the offset ρ, the amplitude A, the frequency f and the phase ϕ are all linear functions of time with some additive Gaussian noise. For instance, the offset ρ could be specified as $\rho(t) = \rho_0 + \alpha_\rho t + \epsilon$, $\epsilon \sim \mathcal{N}(0, \sigma_\rho^2)$, meaning that the value $\rho(t)$ at any time t is drawn from the parameterized normal distribution $\mathcal{N}(\rho_0 + \alpha_\rho t, \sigma_\rho^2)$, where ρ_0, α_ρ and σ_ρ are given by the user.

A signal $s(t)$ injected with an anomaly $y(t)$ is given by $s_a(t) = s(t) + y(t)$. We select the signal i_abc1_A from the motor dataset to be injected with an anomaly of the form $y(t) = A\,sin(2\pi f t)$ starting from second 40 until the end of the experiment time window.[3] The anomaly amplitude A is drawn from the normal distribution $\mathcal{N}(\mu_A, \sigma_A^2)$ where we set (i) μ_A to linearly increase over $[0, 0.5 \times max(i\_abc1\_A)]$, yielding $\mu_A(t) = 0.076 \times t$, and (ii) $\sigma_A = 0.3 \times \mu_A$. The anomaly frequency f is set to linearly increase over $[450, 800]$ Hz with no additive Gaussian noise.

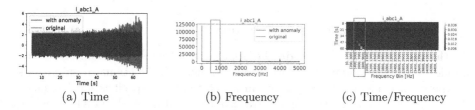

| (a) Time | (b) Frequency | (c) Time/Frequency |

Fig. 7. Signal i_abc1_A with injected anomaly

Figure 7 illustrates the signal i_abc1_A with the injected anomaly in the time, frequency and time/frequency domains, respectively. In the simulated scenario the motor behaves properly in the first 40 s, so we use the data from this time window to train the weakness monitor. We then run the learned weakness monitor on the remaining ca. 20 s of data which actually contains the simulated anomaly. Strictly speaking, we learn one weakness monitor for each averaged STFT time series, resulting into an ensemble of 690 monitors in total, defined as a multidimensional monitor above, which can be combined in various ways to fire an alarm (e.g. if at least one monitor fires, only if all monitors fire, etc.), depending on the use case; here, we consider the monitors individually, i.e. each one fires an alarm on its own.

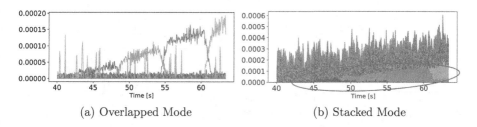

| (a) Overlapped Mode | (b) Stacked Mode |

Fig. 8. Evolution in time of residual errors per frequency bin.

Figure 8a shows an overlap of residual errors evolving in time per frequency bin. Figure 8b shows the same information that is accumulated over all bins.

---

[3] The parameters of the injected anomaly $y(t)$ have been selected in order to fit it to the short period of time in which the data have been collected. In practice, the anomaly might evolve at a different time scale but the handling approach remains the same.

We can see that while individual residual errors can vary quite a lot, there is a visible linear trend for the cumulated residual error to increase over time. This increase is shifting from one frequency bin to another over time. The continuous increase in the cumulated residual error gives a good indication that the observed behavior deteriorates over time and deviates more and more from the learned nominal behavior.

4.3   Aircraft Elevator Control System

In the last case study, we study the application of weakness monitors in the Model Based Development (MDB) process, where the functional requirements of the studied model are formalized in a rich temporal specification language. We study the Aircraft Elevator Control System (AECS), a MATLAB Simulink model of a redundant actuator control system (see Fig. 9). It has two elevators, one on the left side and one on the right side, each equipped with two hydraulic actuators. The actuators can position the elevator, but only one shall be active at any point in time. There are 3 hydraulic systems that drive the 4 actuators. In Fig. 9 we can observe the architecture of the aircraft elevator control system , with different actuators: left outer actuator (LIO), right outer actuator (RIO), left inner actuator (LDL) and right inner actuator (RDL), organized in 2 Primary Flight Control Units (PFCU).

The system uses state machines to coordinate the redundancy and make sure that it remains fail-operational at all times. To evaluate our approach, we injected a weakness into one of the sensors in the form of a linear deterioration of the measurement error.

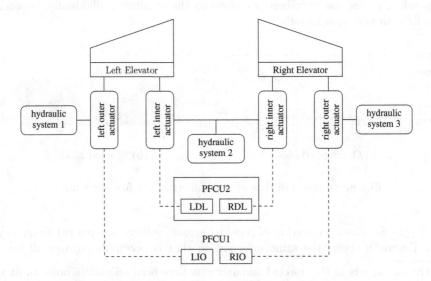

Fig. 9. Architecture of the aircraft elevator control system.

AECS has one input, the Pilot Command, and two observable outputs, the position of left and right actuators (as measured by the sensors). The intended position of the aircraft required by the pilot must be achieved within a predetermined time limit and with a certain accuracy. This can be captured with several requirements. One of them says that whenever Pilot Command (PC) goes above a threshold m, the left and the right actuator position (LEP and REP) measured by the sensor must stabilize (become at most n units away from the command signal) within $T + t$ time units.

We express this type of requirements in Signal Temporal Logic (STL) [21,22]. STL is a formal specification language for describing dynamic properties of CPS.[4] The following sentence in STL describes the bounded stabilization requirement relating the pilot command and the left elevator position (the specification relating the pilot command and the right elevator position is symmetric):

```
always ( rise (PC >= m)  implies  ( eventually [0:t] always [0:T]
    ( abs (PC - LEP) <= n )))
```

Given a behavior of the model and an STL formula, we can use *quantitative* semantics of the logic [9] to measure how *robust* is the behavior with respect to its requirement, i.e. how far it is from satisfying or violating the specification. The robustness degree is evaluated at every point in time t and takes a value in $\mathbb{R} \cup \{\infty, -\infty\}$ – the positive (negative) robustness degree indicates that the observed behavior satisfies (violates) the specification. In this scenario, weakness monitoring consists in observing the evolution of robustness over time and raising an alert when the observed behavior still satisfies the specification, but comes close to the violation.

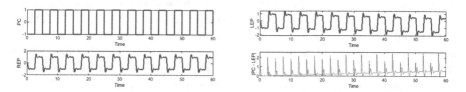

Fig. 10. Monitoring weaknesses in AECS: (top-left) Pilot Command (PC), (bottom-left) Right Elevator Position (REP), (top-right) Left Elevator Position (LEP), (bottom-right) | LEP - PC |.

Figure 10 shows the simulation results of the model with degradation of the left sensor. We can see that in contrast to the right sensor, the measurements from the left sensor deviate more and more from the expected reading, providing inaccurate position to the control system. As a consequence, the absolute difference between the command and the actual position grows linearly in time, gradually approaching the violation of the bounded stabilization specification.

---

[4] We refer to the cited papers for the definition of STL syntax and semantics.

5 Discussion

In this section, we discuss several important aspects of the proposed approach.

Assumptions: the major assumption that we have in our work is that the degradation of the observed system grows reasonably slowly and approximately linearly over time. That is, the weakness monitoring approach cannot anticipate sudden failures which are not caused by some other gradual degradations; such failures are better handled by e.g. the redundancy-based approach. However, there could be situations where we could detect anomalies such as vibrations that do not grow over time, but that can cause gradual deterioration of another system that we cannot directly observe. In that case, we would need to adapt the data-driven approach and to simply detect deviations (in a statistical sense) from the learned nominal behavior, instead of monitoring the trend.

Applicability: Algorithm 1 is a simple procedure that exposes the gradual deteriorations in the observed behaviors. The instantiation of this procedure can be nonetheless sophisticated. It is often the case that deterioration is not directly visible in the observed signals, and that raw signals need to be pre-processed and transformed to a suitable domain where the negative trends can be detected. While for some applications the intended behavior is defined by a clearly specified safety margin, in other applications there is no formal specification of the expected behavior. In these cases, our weakness monitoring approach must be combined with the inference of the reference (nominal) model by using for instance machine learning methods. We illustrate the applicability of Algorithm 1 by instantiating it to several automotive case studies. Since our method is based on online linear regression of a sliding window, the selection of a proper window size is crucial to obtain a valid result. A small window will render the method prone to outliers and sensitive to local behavior trends. A very large window size increases the influence of non-weak behavior on the overall evaluation, which then introduces a delay in identifying a weakness (an alarm may be raised too late). Choosing the right size of the time window can be part of the engineer's domain knowledge, but it can also be derived using statistical methods in the data-driven approach.

Properties of Online Linear Regression: While the online linear regression algorithm is attractive in terms of computational complexity, it has the potential issue of numerical instability when (1) the number of data points on which the regression is computed is large, and (2) the time values are high. The second aspect can be especially problematic in our applications, where the monitor is expected to work over very large time scales. However, this problem can be overcome by resetting the time origin to 0 and recomputing a full linear regression from time to time, when the time values get too large. After each time origin resetting and the corresponding full linear regression computation, the online linear regression proceeds as usual, benefiting from re-scaled time values.

6 Conclusion

In this paper we proposed a methodology for detecting weaknesses based on a simple linear model of degradation. Our approach, based on online linear regression, is resource-efficient and can be applied to real-time systems. The procedure treats the system as a black-box and is therefore independent of its level of the complexity. The proposed monitoring approach can play the central role in developing a fail-aware concept. We demonstrate the applicability of our approach on three case studies from automotive and avionics domains, showing how it can be used both at design time and during operation of the system, both in presence and absence of specifications.

Acknowledgements. We would like to thank Brno University of Technology for their comments and the measured data used in the motor weakness monitoring use case. The data were measured on a testbench located in the premises of Brno University of Technology, Central European Institute of Technology, with the motor which was developed during ENIAC-JU project MotorBrain (nr. 270693).

We would like to thank also the anonymous reviewers for their comments on the earlier drafts of the paper.

We acknowledge the support of ECSEL project Autodrive (nr. 7953297) and FFG national project IoT4CPS.

References

1. Infineon Technologies, A.G.: TLE 5009 angle sensor: GMR-based angular sensor. Rev. 1.1, 2012–04 (2012)
2. Babaee, R., Gurfinkel, A., Fischmeister, S.: *Prevent*: a predictive run-time verification framework using statistical learning. In: Johnsen, E.B., Schaefer, I. (eds.) SEFM 2018. LNCS, vol. 10886, pp. 205–220. Springer, Cham (2018). https://doi.org/10.1007/978-3-319-92970-5_13
3. Bortolussi, L., Cairoli, F., Paoletti, N., Smolka, S.A., Stoller, S.D.: Neural predictive monitoring. In: Finkbeiner, B., Mariani, L. (eds.) RV 2019. LNCS, vol. 11757, pp. 129–147. Springer, Cham (2019). https://doi.org/10.1007/978-3-030-32079-9_8
4. Celaya, J., Saxena, A., Saha, S., Goebel, K.F.: Prognostics of power MOSFETs under thermal stress accelerated aging using data-driven and model-based methodologies (2011)
5. Celaya, J.R., Saxena, A., Saha, S., Vashchenko, V., Goebel, K.: Prognostics of power MOSFET. In: 2011 IEEE 23rd International Symposium on Power Semiconductor Devices and ICs, pp. 160–163. IEEE (2011)
6. Automotive Electronics Councel: AEC-Q100 rev. h, failure mechanism based stress test qualification for integrated circuits (2014)
7. Daigle, M., Kulkarni, C.S.: A battery health monitoring framework for planetary rovers. In: 2014 IEEE Aerospace Conference, pp. 1–9. IEEE (2014)
8. Degrenne, N., Ewanchuk, J., David, E., Boldyrjew, R., Mollov, S.: A review of prognics and health management for power semiconductor modules. In: Annual Conference of the Prognostics and Health Management Society 2015, vol. 6, pp. 1–9 (2015)

9. Donzé, A., Ferrère, T., Maler, O.: Efficient robust monitoring for STL. In: Computer Aided Verification (CAV), pp. 264–279 (2013)
10. Fetzer, C., Cristian, F.: Fail-awareness in timed asynchronous systems. In: Proceedings of the Fifteenth Annual ACM Symposium on Principles of Distributed Computing, pp. 314–321 (1996)
11. Garcia, C.E., Prett, D.M., Morari, M.: Model predictive control: theory and practice - a survey. Automatica 25(3), 335–348 (1989)
12. Gouriveau, R., Medjaher, K., Zerhouni, N.: From Prognostics and Health Systems Management to Predictive Maintenance 1: Monitoring and Prognostics. Wiley, Hoboken (2016)
13. Granig, W., Weinberger, M., Reidl, C., Bresch, M., Strasser, M., Pircher, G.: Integrated gmr angle sensor for electrical commutated motors including features for safety critical applications. Procedia Eng. 5, 1384–1387 (2010)
14. Gu, J., Vichare, N., Tracy, T., Pecht, M.: Prognostics implementation methods for electronics. In: 2007 Annual Reliability and Maintainability Symposium, pp. 101–106. IEEE (2007)
15. Haghighi, I., Mehdipour, N., Bartocci, E., Belta, C.: Control from signal temporal logic specifications with smooth cumulative quantitative semantics. In: 58th IEEE Conference on Decision and Control, CDC 2019, Nice, France, 11–13 December 2019, pp. 4361–4366 (2019)
16. Hess, A., Calvello, G., Frith, P., Engel, S.J., Hoitsma, D.: Challenges, issues, and lessons learned chasing the "big p": real predictive prognostics part 2. In: 2006 IEEE Aerospace Conference, pp. 1–19. IEEE (2006)
17. Hong, S., Zhou, Z., Lv, C.: Storage lifetime prognosis of an intermediate frequency (if) amplifier based on physics of failure method. Chem. Eng. Trans. 33, 1117–1122 (2013)
18. Yang, H., Baraldi, P., Di Maio, F., Zio, E.: A particle filtering and kernel smoothing-based approach for new design component prognostics. Reliability Eng. Syst. Saf. 134, 19–31 (2015)
19. James, P.A.: Health monitoring of IGBTs in automotive power converter systems. Ph.D. thesis, University of Manchester (2013)
20. Kalajdzic, K., Bartocci, E., Smolka, S.A., Stoller, S.D., Grosu, R.: Runtime verification with particle filtering. In: Legay, A., Bensalem, S. (eds.) RV 2013. LNCS, vol. 8174, pp. 149–166. Springer, Heidelberg (2013). https://doi.org/10.1007/978-3-642-40787-1_9
21. Maler, O., Nickovic, D.: Monitoring temporal properties of continuous signals. In: Lakhnech, Y., Yovine, S. (eds.) FORMATS/FTRTFT -2004. LNCS, vol. 3253, pp. 152–166. Springer, Heidelberg (2004). https://doi.org/10.1007/978-3-540-30206-3_12
22. Maler, O., Ničković, D.: Monitoring properties of analog and mixed-signal circuits. STTT 15(3), 247–268 (2013)
23. Raman, V., Donzé, A., Maasoumy, M., Murray, R.M., Sangiovanni-Vincentelli, A.L., Seshia, S.A.: Model predictive control with signal temporal logic specifications. In: 53rd IEEE Conference on Decision and Control, CDC 2014, Los Angeles, CA, USA, 15–17 December 2014, pp. 81–87 (2014)
24. Rezvanizaniani, S.M., Liu, Z., Chen, Y., Lee, J.: Review and recent advances in battery health monitoring and prognostics technologies for electric vehicle (ev) safety and mobility. J. Power Sources 256, 110–124 (2014)

25. Roemer, M.J., Nwadiogbu, E.O., Bloor, G.: Development of diagnostic and prognostic technologies for aerospace health management applications. In: 2001 IEEE Aerospace Conference Proceedings (Cat. No. 01TH8542), vol. 6, pp. 3139–3147. IEEE (2001)
26. Rychlik, I.: A new definition of the rainflow cycle counting method. Int. J. Fatigue **9**(2), 119–121 (1987)
27. Silipo, R., Ada, I., Winters, P.: Anomaly detection in predictive maintenance. White Paper, KNIME (2018)
28. Welford, B.P.: Note on a method for calculating corrected sums of squares and products. Technometrics **4**(3), 419–420 (1962)
29. Wongpiromsarn, T., Topcu, U., Murray, R.M.: Receding horizon temporal logic planning. IEEE Trans. Automat. Contr. **57**(11), 2817–2830 (2012)
30. Yoon, H., Chou, Y., Chen, X., Frew, E., Sankaranarayanan, S.: Predictive runtime monitoring for linear stochastic systems and applications to geofence enforcement for UAVs. In: Finkbeiner, B., Mariani, L. (eds.) RV 2019. LNCS, vol. 11757, pp. 349–367. Springer, Cham (2019). https://doi.org/10.1007/978-3-030-32079-9_20

Author Index

Printed in the United States
by Baker & Taylor Publisher Services